THE GEOGRAPHY OF BRITISH INDIA

THE STUDENT'S GEOGRAPHY OF INDIA

THE GEOGRAPHY OF BRITISH INDIA

POLITICAL & PHYSICAL

By

GEORGE SMITH, LL.D., F.R.G.S.

WITH MAPS

GYAN

Published by

Gyan Publishing House
5, Ansari Road
Daryaganj, New Delhi-110002
Phone: 011-47034999, 9811692060
E-mail: books@gyanbooks.com

Distribution Network
gyanbooks.com
India, USA, Canada, UK, Australia, France

ISBN : 978-81-212-6334-4 (PB)
First Published, 1882

2nd Impression 2022

Printed at: Gyan Press, Delhi.

THE GEOGRAPHY OF BRITISH INDIA
Author: GEORGE SMITH

India.	Square miles.	Population.	Population.	Square miles.	Europe.
Prov. of Bengal . .	203,437	69,133,619	37,672,000	204,177	France.
„ Assam . .	55,384	4,908,276	25,968,286	58,320	England and Wales.
„ British Burma .	87,220	3,736,771	29,702,656	89,005	Great Britain.
„ Andaman Islands	3,285	30,000	150,000	4,200	Cyprus.
N.W. Province with Oudh	111,086	44,852,736	28,437,091	114,296	Italy.
Prov. of Panjab . .	221,749	22,703,947	37,839,427	240,942	Austria-Hungary.
„ Bombay . .	191,847	23,273,786	20,974,411	219,260	Spain and Portugal.
„ Ajmer . .	2,710	460,722	936,340	2,866	Hesse.
*Baroda State . .	4,399	2,154,469	1,506,531	5,851	Baden.
*Rajpootana States	130,934	11,005,512	27,278,911	137,066	Prussia.
*Central India States .	89,098	9,200 881	29,702,656	89,005	Great Britain.
Central Province . .	113,042	11,505,149	28,437,091	114,296	Italy.
Berar Province . .	17,728	2,672,673	2,846,102	15,992	Switzerland.
*Haidarabad State .	80,000	9,200,881	29,702,656	89,005	Great Britain.
Prov. of Madras . .	150,248	33,840,617	16,625,860	182,750	Spain.
„ Coorg . .	1,583	178,302	349,367	1,526	Brunswick.
*Mysore State . .	30,500	4,186,399	3,734,370	30,685	Scotland.

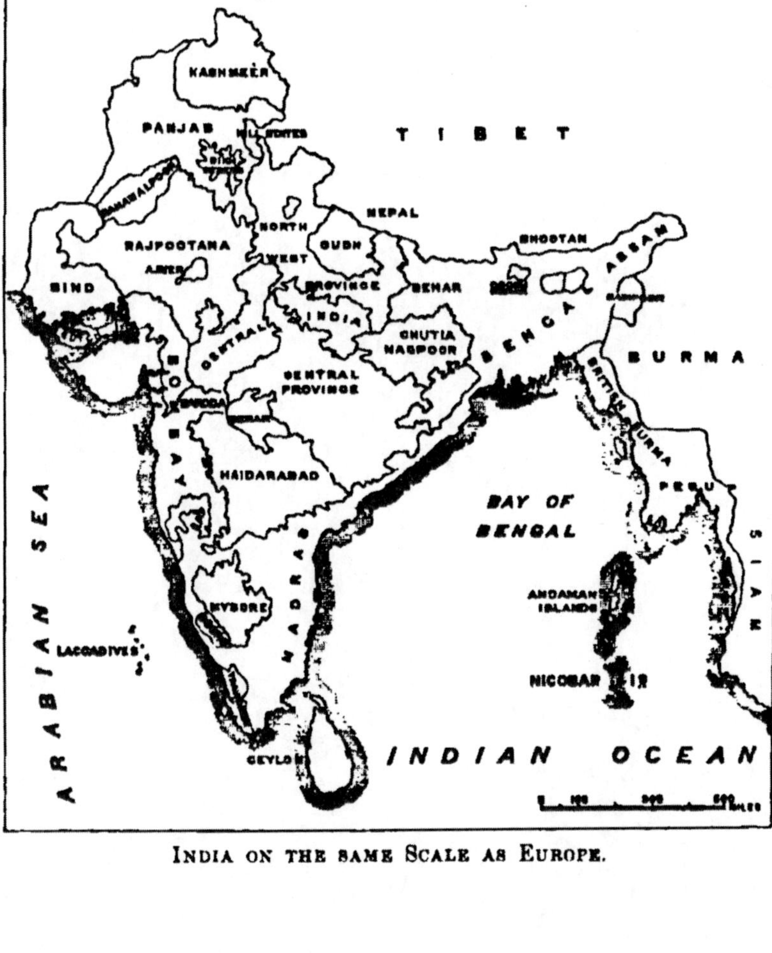

INDIA ON THE SAME SCALE AS EUROPE.

EUROPE ON THE SAME SCALE AS INDIA.

The Student's Geography of India

THE

GEOGRAPHY

OF

BRITISH INDIA

POLITICAL & PHYSICAL

By GEORGE SMITH, LL.D., F.R.G.S.

WITH MAPS

1882

PREFACE.

THIS volume is the result of twenty years of preparation. It would have been more easy and pleasant to have given adequate literary expression to the extensive and comparatively new materials in two or three volumes. But Mr. Murray's request that the facts and descriptions should be included in a work of five hundred pages, to form one of the admirable series of his Student's Manuals, involved an almost excessive degree of condensation in the writing, whilé it promised wider usefulness for the result. Though the book is thus primarily intended for the Student, from the upper-classes of schools all through the stages of College, University, Military, and Civil Service studies and examinations in England, Scotland, Ireland, and India alike, it is much more. Its generalisations as well as details will enable the ordinary reader, probably for the first time, to form a just idea of the magnitude of the British Indian Empire; of the variety of its races, and all that concerns peoples more numerous than those of Europe; of the course of the history of every Province and even District when under native rulers; of the splendid and widespread archæological and architectural remains of these rulers; and of the success of the British Government, thus far, in making the Empire a unity for the first time in history; so that, by detailed administration, education, and free religious suasion, its two hundred and fifty-three millions may be trained to govern themselves. The volume may, practically, be found by the traveller to be a Guide-book in the best form. The Index, and Maps of Provinces, in districts, should make it the most handy Gazetteer, as well as a full and an accurate work of reference for all classes.

In the year 1862 I submitted to the late Earl of Elgin, soon after he had taken his seat as Viceroy and Governor-General, a detailed statistical system for the uniform preparation of the annual *Administration Reports* ordered by Parliament in 1853, with a view to the taking of a Census of all India in 1871, and the compilation of an Imperial Gazetteer. Mr. Samuel Laing, who was at that time Indian Finance Minister, warmly supported the scheme. The Calcutta Statistical Committee was accordingly appointed; and my system, adapted from that of the International Statistical Congress, was carried into effect after three years of official discussion in India, and in the India Office when Sir Stafford Northcote was Secretary of State. Each of the Twelve Provinces of India, and many of the larger of the Hundred and Fifty-three Ruling Native States, now render an account of their stewardship to the Governor-General in Council, and to the Secretary of State, for Parliament, according to this uniform scheme.

The population of the Provinces of India were for the first time numbered about the end of 1871 and beginning of 1872, but not simultaneously. It was not till February 1881 that India was ready for a synchronous Census of all its peoples alike in the 239 Districts and in the 153 Ruling States. The preliminary total results are embodied in this volume, and are published in England for the first time. The detailed figures, in districts and towns, are given in the case of nearly all the Provinces and States. It was not thought desirable to delay the appearance of the book for another year, when the *details* of the North-Western and Madras Provinces, and of Mysore and some of the Native States, may be expected.

The first to undertake the preparation of a Scientific

Gazetteer, under the new Statistical Scheme, was Sir Richard Temple in the Central Province. In 1867 Mr. Charles Grant, Secretary to the Chief Commissioner, produced a model volume. I had meanwhile, privately and in the *Friend of India*, urged the Government of India to appoint an able member of the Civil Service to compile one Gazetteer of all India on similar lines. Mr. W. W. Hunter was recommended to the late Lord Lawrence as specially fitted for the task. The Viceroy and the Secretary of State united in ordering the preparation of the work by him; and the last of the nine volumes of *The Imperial Gazetteer of India* appeared in July 1881, based, however, on the Census statistics of 1872.

Since that time, the Census of 1881; the completion of the century's Trigonometrical Survey of India; the publication of General Walker's finished Maps of India and of Toorkestan and the countries between the British and the Russian dominions in Asia, on the scale of 32 miles to the inch; and the publication of many more volumes of the able Provincial Gazetteers, and of the noble quarto of Messrs. Fergusson and Burgess on *The Cave Temples of India*, have rendered it possible and desirable for me to write the Political Geography, which forms the bulk of this volume. The closing section on Physiography, too, could not have been compiled till Messrs. H. B. Medlicott, W. T. Blanford and Ball, had issued their official Map and *Manual of the Geology of India*, in four volumes, and Mr. Henry F. Blanford, F.R.S., had followed up his authoritative *Indian Meteorologist's Vade Mecum*, by further Memoirs and Reports. I desire specially to acknowledge the assistance of all these experts; of Colonel Yule, C.B., without whose aid, always generously rendered, no work on the geography of Asia can be satisfactorily produced; of the Honourable C. Bernard, Chief Commissioner of British Burma; and of the Honourable A. Mackenzie, his successor as Home Secretary to the Government of India.

The Governments of Lord Lytton and Lord Ripon have most promptly supplied me with recent Records. I have used some printed documents which are "confidential" only in such a way as to enrich the information now published for the first time, without touching the views of the writers. This will be found chiefly in Kashmeer, Baloochistan, the Panjab frontier, and Haidarabad State.

The plan of the Manual is this—Book I., or four-fifths of the whole volume, deals with the Political Geography of British India in detail, and with that of the colonies and countries within its political system more briefly: Book II. summarises the latest results of the Geological and Meteorological Surveys; the diamond, gold, and coal treasures are carefully described. Till the publication of the Census Reports, some time hence, the latest data for the Ethnology will be wanting. An Appendix gives the Bibliography of the subject, or a list of the best authorities, ancient, mediæval, and modern, which have been consulted or should be referred to by the reader who seeks fuller information. A detailed Index gives the names of all the places, some 5200 in number.

The first chapter states briefly what every intelligent reader ought to know of the British Indian Empire, its name, extent, and magnitude compared with Europe; its growth since 1600 and especially 1765, and present administrative system; statistics of its 12 Provinces and of the 153 Ruling States grouped together; its imperial surveys and land tenures, taxation, debt, and new municipal organisation. The second chapter pictures India as a Whole, its great mountains, rivers, waterfalls, lakes, canals, forests, and railways, and the coast of Asia from Suez to Singapore, with the harbours and lighthouses. Each of the Twelve Provinces is then described, its position, natural features, resources, tenures, and people generally; and then every District with the principal towns, places of historical and archæological interest, shrines, and mission-stations. The smaller Native States, which are under provincial control, are treated like the Districts. The larger, which are under the direct political influence of the Viceroy and Governor-General in Council, are described separately under *Baroda, *Rajpootana and *Central India, *Haidarabad and *Mysore. In every case, the *Ruling* Native State, which enjoys the Viceroy's Sannad or Patent of Adoption, first granted by Lord Canning on the 17th March 1862, is marked by an asterisk, as well as the small Portuguese and French settlements, and the protected frontier kingdoms. The political and geographical unity of the Empire is thus seen, while the difference of the two administrative systems is noted, according as that is directly British among 198½ millions who pay taxes to the Governor-General, or Native under British influence among 54½ millions of the people whose taxation goes entirely to their own Tributary Sovereigns.

The unit of the Indian Empire is the District or State corresponding to the much smaller County of English geography. For the first time it has been possible thus to treat, District by District and State by State, the vast extent and details of Indian geography, beginning with Bengal and the metropolis of Calcutta; exhausting the East in Assam, Burma, and the Andaman and Nicobar Islands; then going over the North-West with Oudh; the Panjab with Kashmeer and Baloochistan; passing West to Bombay, with Sind and Aden, Ajmer and the Baroda, the Rajpootana, and the Central India States; treating the Central Province, Berar, and the Haidarabad State; and closing with the oldest, most peaceful, and, in respect of Christianity, most progressive part of the Empire, in the South, or Madras, Coorg, and Mysore, the last recently transformed into a Native State.

As to the still vexed question of transliterating proper names from languages, so many and so opposite in some respects as those of India and Burma, Aryan, Dravidian, and even Semitic, I would have followed slavishly the frequently inconsistent system imposed on officials by a late Government of India, contenting myself with a protest. But that system has sacrificed the English pronunciation of the names to such an extent that even scholars begin to repent its adoption in books for purely English readers. If that spelling is continued, without modification at least, the time will be indefinitely postponed when we may expect an educated Englishman to be as ashamed of mispronouncing the most ordinary names and terms of the Empire entrusted to our rule, as he is in the case of European and American places and persons. I have ventured therefore to adopt such slight phonetic changes in the official spelling as will enable the English reader to pronounce the words correctly, and that without accents or other marks save to denote the quantity. The official i = ee and the u = oo—that is all. But it will go far to remove the reproach of a well-known Anglo-Indian writer, that "by the official system of spelling, we are degrading the pronunciation."

In all the Provinces specimens are given of the derivation of the names of principal places. Students in India will find it useful to add others for themselves. In every case, where possible, the information of other kinds has been brought down to the present date.

SERAMPOOR HOUSE, MERCHISTON,
EDINBURGH, *November* 1882.

TABLE OF CONTENTS.

BOOK I.—POLITICAL GEOGRAPHY.

BOOK II.—PHYSIOGRAPHY.

APPENDIX.

MAPS AND DIAGRAMS.

PAGE

Maps and Diagrams—*Continued.*

BOOK I.

POLITICAL GEOGRAPHY.

CHAPTER I.

THE BRITISH INDIAN EMPIRE.

§ 1. Name. § 2. Extent. § 3. Comparative Size. § 4. Position. § 5. Growth. § 6. Administration. § 7. Provinces and States. § 8. Imperial Surveys. § 9. Land Tenures, Taxation and Debt.

§ 1. NAME.—The whole Sanskritic race call their country (1) **Bhārata**, or Bharata-varsha, "the country of King Bharata" ("a supporter"), the chief of the lunar dynasty, who from Hastinapoor, north of Meerut, extended his sway over the land between the Himalaya and the Vindhya, and the great war between whose descendants is sung in the Epic, *Maha-bharatam.* To the same central region Manu applied the name (2) **Arya-varta**, "the abode of the Aryans." Poets and Boodhist writers use the name (3) **Jambu-dvipa**, properly the Earth as one of the seven continents circling around Meru, the mountain of the gods, and containing nine varshas (countries), of which Bharata, south of the Himavat range, is one, but restricted by such writers to India, as the most important part of the earth. From the river of Bharata's kingdom, the modern Indus, flowing through the Panjab and Sind, comes the term India, through the Persian, Hebrew, and Greek. The main stream in Sind, the five rivers and the Saraswati in the Panjab, formed the seven rivers or (4) Sapta **Sindhavah**, which in Zand or old Persian of the *Vendidad*, appear as the Hapta **Hindu**. In the Hebrew of the book of Esther (i. 1, viii. 9), the country is mentioned as one of the 127 provinces of the son of Darius Hystaspes, under the name of Hoddu, an abbreviation of

Hondu, to which correspond the Syriac Hendu and Arabic Hind. The invasion and conquest of the Panjab by Darius, B.C. 508, were preceded by the expedition of his admiral, Scylax, a Greek of Caryanda in Caria, whose report, whether he wrote the Periplus or supplied materials of which that was an abridgment, is the beginning of the Western knowledge of India under that name, as the conquest of Darius first places us on firm historical ground regarding India. The name of the river, in its modern form of **Indos**, first occurs in a fragment of Hecatæus of Miletus, the accurate Greek annalist and geographer (born B.C. 550) who preceded Herodotus. The Sanskrit Sindhu ("flowing water"), which had become the Persian "Hindu" and the Hebrew Hondu, appeared as the Greek Indos, and reappears in the later Latin as Sindus. In the Chinese of the second century B.C. India is Shin-tu or Sindhu. The word Hindustan, or "abode of the Hindus," is the late Persian and present Musalman name for the great plain between the Satlej and Benares or Patna, inhabited by the Hindee-speaking people of the modern West Bengal or Behar, the North-Western Province, and the East Panjab. But it is sometimes applied to the whole peninsula bounded by the ocean, as by the Emperor Baber.

§ 2. EXTENT.—The **British Indian Empire** consists of the southern slopes of (1) the **Himalaya** and allied mountain systems of Southern Asia on the immediate east and west; (2) of the great alluvial **Indo-Gangetic Plain** stretching from the Bay of Bengal west to the Arabian Sea and north to the Persian Gulf; and (3) of the **Peninsula** formed by the Vindhya and Western and Eastern Ghats, which terminate in the Agastya peak above the triangular apex of Cape Comorin. All other immigrants into or invaders of India, early Turanians, elder Aryans, Persians, Greeks, Arabs, Mughuls, and Afghans, have entered it from the north, except the English. Following the Portuguese, who now hold only 1086 square miles on the west coast administered from Goa; and side by side for a time with the French, who still possess but 178 on the east coast governed from Pondicheri; the British have, in less than three centuries from Queen Elizabeth to the Queen-Empress Victoria, become sole responsible rulers of the continent, by advancing or being providentially driven on from both seas to the crest of the main range of the Himalaya, to the base of the Sulaiman on the west, and the ridge of the Tenasserim mountains on the east. After working throughout this century from Cape Comorin to Toung-ngoo, Sadiya, Sikkim, Peshawar, and Karachi, the

Survey (trigonometrical, topographical, revenue, and in some cases cadastral) shows an area of 1,500,000 square miles. The population, as numbered by the second general census, taken simultaneously on the 17th February 1881, the largest ever attempted, was above 253,000,000. This reveals an increase at the rate of 6·2 per cent in ten years, notwithstanding drought and famine, under what has been called the Pax Britannica, the universal peace which since 1858 the British Government has given to the peoples of India for the first time in all the ages. At an analogous epoch, the death of Augustus, when the silent revolution was begun by Christianity, and the Roman Peace prevailed, the Breviarium drawn up for that emperor by the chief surveyor, Balbus, leads the historian to estimate the population of the Roman Empire at 85 millions in the Asiatic and European Provinces, from the fortified posts on the Euphrates to the Red Sea, the Atlas and the Ocean. Gibbon's estimate does not raise the number to more than 120 millions when Imperial Rome was at its height. In modern times the Russian Empire, European and Asiatic, has a population of 88 millions.

§ 3. COMPARATIVE SIZE OF EMPIRE AND PROVINCES.—The following figures, condensed and brought down to date from Behm and De Stein's statistics, show the British Indian and British Empires relatively to others :—

	Square Miles.	Square Kilometres.	Population.
BRITISH EMPIRE . .	8,036,007	20,090,019	303,512,568
of which,			
BRITISH INDIAN EMPIRE .	1,494,310	3,845,186	253,140,886
CHINESE EMPIRE . .	1,609,876	4,024,690	280,000,000 (estimate)
besides			
TIBET and E. TOORKESTAN	4,725,500	11,813,750	29,800,000
RUSSIAN EMPIRE . .	8,281,200	21,703,002	88,018,530
TURKISH EMPIRE . .	2,494,520	6,236,300	23,119,800
UNITED STATES, N. A. .	3,708,976	9,272,448	50,438,960
NETHERLANDS with N. INDIA	679,378	1,985,183	27,320,469
PERSIA	658,828	1,647,070	4,400,400

The British Indian Empire covers an area as great as that of the Continent of Europe proper without Russia, and has more than the population of the European States. It is twelve and a third times the size of Great Britain and Ireland, and has nearly the same ratio of population to the square mile. From the Himalaya to Cape Comorin is the same distance as from Iceland to Spain. From Calcutta to Bombay the railway distance is the same as from London to Naples. There are in India almost as many varieties of race, speech, beliefs, and customs, as in Europe.

The great Provinces and States of India are thus contrasted with the Empires, Kingdoms, and Republics of Europe :—

INDIA.	Square Miles.	Population.	Population.	Square Miles.	EUROPE.
Bengal . .	208,437	69,133,619	37,672,000	204,177	France.
Assam . .	55,384	4,908,276	25,968,286	58,320	England and Wales.
British Burma .	87,220	3,736,771	29,702,656	89,005	Great Britain.
Andaman Islands	3,285	30,000	150,000	4,200	Cyprus.
N.W. Province with Oudh .	111,086	44,851,542	28,437,091	114,296	Italy.
Panjab . .	221,749	22,712,120	37,839,427	240,942	Austria-Hungary.
Bombay . .	191,847	23,396,045	20,974,411	219,260	Spain and Portugal.
Ajmer. . .	2,710	460,722	936,340.	2,866	Hesse.
*Baroda . .	4,399	2,154,469	1,506,531	5,851	Baden.
*Rajpootana .	130,994	11,005,512	27,278,911	137,066	Prussia.
*Central India .	89,098	9,200,881	29,702,656	89,005	Great Britain.
Central Province	113,042	11,505,149	28,437,091	114,296	Italy.
Berar . . .	17,728	2,672,673	2,846,102	15,992	Switzerland.
*Haidarabad .	80,000	9,167,789	29,702 656	89,005	Great Britain.
Madras . .	150,248	33,840,617	16,625,860	182,750	Spain.
Coorg . . .	1,583	178,302	349,367	1,526	Brunswick.
*Mysore . .	30,500	4,186,399	3,734,370	30,685	Scotland.

Of the British Indian Empire (excluding protected Baloochistan, Nepal, and Bhootan) the area is, in round numbers, 1,500,000 square miles, and the population is 253,000,000, or 170 to the mile all over. Of Europe (excluding Russia and Turkey proper) the area is 1,545,000, and the population is 235,000,000, or 152 to the mile. The population of the British Indian Empire is nearly one-fifth of the human race. As to creed, roughly, 200 millions are Hindoos, Boodhists, Jains, Parsees, and aboriginal demonolaters ; 50 millions are Muhammadans, or more than in Turkey or under any Muhammadan power, and nearly 2 millions are Christians (Protestant, Syrian, and Roman Catholic) and Jews. The British army in India is 63,000 strong, and the number of Europeans and Americans besides is about 77,000, or 140,000 in all. In Asia, Great Britain rules a population five times greater than that under the other five Powers of Europe together, and independently of the number whom she indirectly influences. Russia rules 15 millions in Asia; the Netherlands, 23½ millions; Spain, 4½ millions; Portugal, 1 million; and France, 2 millions.

§ 4. POSITION.—From **Point Victoria** at the south extremity of the Tenasserim Division of British Burma in north lat. 9° 59′ and east long. 98° 32′ to **Cape Monze** at the mouth of the Hab estuary of Sind in north lat. 24° 50′ and east long. 66° 38′, the northern frontier of British India runs along the crest of successive lofty ranges and watersheds, forming an *inland line* of 4680 miles. (1) From Point Victoria, north, the Tenasserim Roma range parts the thin strip of the lowest division of British Burma from Siam. (2) Thence, a jungle-line, marked by no natural features, stretches west to the Pegu Roma range, and north along the Arakan Roma, separating the Pegu and Arakan divisions of British Burma from Upper Burma, which is farther north divided from Assam by the Barail-Patkai range. (3) Then, in lat. 28° and long. 97°, the Himalayan system begins, curving west along the north of Assam, which it separates from Tibet, to Bhootan and Nepal with Sikkim State between, when turning north, the loftiest range in the world shuts off from Tibet the North-Western Province, Panjab, and Kashmeer, till its west terminal portion, under several names, of which the Karakoram has lately become best known, sweeps round into the Hindu Koosh. (4) The Safed Koh to Bannoo and the Sulaiman Mountains take up the ring-fence and run nearly due south, dividing the Panjab from Afghanistan. Several ranges, of which the Khirthar is the chief, form the frontier between Sind and Baloochistan, from the cessation of the Sulaiman at Kashmor to Cape Monze. For a short time, under the Gandamak Treaty of 1879, the British boundary crossed the Safed Koh and the Sulaiman to the Afghan side. The *external* or *coast-line* runs for 6580 miles: (1) along the whole of the Bay of Bengal from the Crown colony of the Straits Settlements (under India till recently) to the Crown colony of Ceylon; (2) turning north from Cape Comorin it is washed by the Indian Ocean and the Arabian Sea. In length and breadth British India without Burma lies on a square of 1900 miles from east to west in the parallel of 28°, and from north to south in the meridian of 77°. Besides India proper and British Burma (with the **Nicobar**, **Andaman**, and **Mergui Archipelago** of **Islands** on the east, and the **Laccadive Islands** off the south-west coast), the military outpost of **Aden** in South-West Arabia, with **Perim Island**, commands the Red Sea highway. **Sokotra** and the rest of the coast of South-West Asia and East Africa, from the

Persian Gulf to Zanzibar and the colonies of Natal and the Cape of Good Hope, are under the political influence, by treaties and commerce, of the British Indian Empire, whose native subjects are there as capitalists, traders, and labourers. Along the whole coast of Africa, Asia, and Australia, from Delagoa Bay north to Zanzibar and Aden, Basrah and Bagdad, Karachi and Calcutta, Burma and Singapore, Batavia and Brisbane, the British, the Queensland, and the Netherlands India Steam Navigation Companies maintain regular coasting lines of steamers linked on to London through the Suez Canal.

§ 5. GROWTH.—The East India Company was incorporated on the last day of 1600, under the name of "The Governor and Company of Merchants of London, trading into the East Indies," by charter granted by Queen Elizabeth. The charter of William III. in 1698 was the foundation of the privileges of the United East India Company, until its extinction as a trading and governing body in August 1858. Under an imperial *firman* granted by Jahangeer on 11th January 1613, Surat became the first English settlement in India, trading but not territorial. Two of the Company's factors visited Patna in 1620, and Shah Jahan granted the Company a *firman* for the establishment of a factory in Bengal in 1634. But it was in 1636 that the effective privilege of planting settlements there was obtained by Mr. Boughton, a ship's surgeon, who saved the life of that emperor's daughter. Mr. Boughton first visited the port of Pipli, but the first factories were opened at Balasor, Kasimbazar, and Hoogli. (1) The Presidency of **Madras** was constituted in 1653, but there had been factories on the east coast at Masulipatam and Armegaon. The Island of Bombay was acquired by the English Crown in 1662, and (2) the **Bombay** Presidency was formed in 1668. In that year the Company sent out to China its first order for the purchase of 100 lbs. of tea; the yearly consumption of which, in Great Britain, has now risen to 160 millions of lbs., of which more than 40 millions is supplied by India, chiefly by the one province of Assam. (3) In 1715, on a *firman* from the Emperor Farokseer,—obtained under the influence of another surgeon, Mr. Hamilton,—Calcutta, granted in 1699, became the centre of the **Bengal** Presidency, which was constituted in 1682. These small territorial acquisitions were little more than trading factories till Clive's victory at Plassey in 1757, followed by three grants from Shah Alum of the Dewani, or virtual sovereignty of Bengal proper, the Karnatic and the Dekhan—the last never used—on the 12th August 1765. The Company of merchants, for some time forced by circumstances to be a fighting power, now legally became a Government, and was gradually compelled to distance all rivals, European and Native, in the chaos which had succeeded the death of Aurangzeb, and thus to give peace and prosperity to the whole Empire. In 1773, the regulating Act of Parliament made the Governor of the Bengal Presidency—then Warren Hastings—Governor-General of India, with certain powers, chiefly political and financial, over the other two. In 1784, the Board of Control was constituted by Parliament, under the title of "The Board of Commissioners for the Affairs of India." In spite of all declarations and frequent attempts in a contrary direction, the Empire of British India advanced from the two seas to its natural boundary of the Himalaya and Sulaiman mountains. Under the Marquis of Dalhousie, who conquered Pegu in 1852, the frontier reached that boundary; it has rested there, save during the second Afghan War and the treaty of Gandamak, on every side except Burma.

§ 6. ADMINISTRATION.—In 1858, after the Mutiny and Sepoy War, the East India Company gave place to the direct government of the Crown and Parliament, through the Viceroy and Governor-General with executive Council or Cabinet of six, controlled by a Secretary of State with a consultative Council of fifteen, who have only financial powers rarely exercised. In 1861 the Indian Councils Act was passed, under which Parliament directly governs India. From this time the term "Presidency" ceased to have any but a historical meaning, and "Province" took its place. In 1835 the upper valley of the Ganges and the Jumna had been created the Lieutenant-Governorship of the North-Western Province. The lower valley of the Ganges and the Brahmapootra had, in 1855, become the Lieutenant-Governorship of Bengal. The Mutiny had resulted in erecting the country from Delhi north-west of the Jumna into the Lieutenant-Governorship of the Panjab. In order to bring more backward districts up to the same administrative level, the Chief-Commissionerships of the Central Province, British Burma, and Assam were successively formed. Ajmer, Coorg, the Andaman and Nicobar Islands, are smaller Provinces of the same kind, and Berar is similarly administered subject to the payment of its surplus revenues to the State of Haidarabad. All are, however, more directly under the supervision of the Governor-General in Council than the old Presidencies of Madras and Bombay. The governors of these, for historical or conservative reasons, are directly appointed by the Crown, are better paid, and have the aid of an executive

Council of three, one of whom is the provincial Commander-in-Chief or Lieutenant-General of the Army. The Bengal Army is under the Commander-in-Chief of all India, who is one of the six members of the Governor-General's Council. Madras, Bombay, and Bengal have each a Legislative Council and a High Court of Justice. These Councils, as well as the Legislative Council of the Governor-General, consist of the executive members, of two representatives of the English mercantile community, and of two or three representatives of the Natives as extraordinary members. The North-Western Province has a High Court, and the Panjab a Chief Court. The Governor-General's Council for making laws legislates for all India in general and for the Provinces which have no legislatures of their own in detail, some of the Provinces being represented by officials. The Governor-General must sanction every Act of the three subordinate Councils before it can become law, and the Secretary of State for India may advise Her Majesty to veto any Act of the Governor-General's Legislative Council.

The administration of all the Provinces is now nearly uniform. Into some of the more backward portions of each all the laws have not been introduced, and even in the older Provinces there are still districts where a speedier judicial procedure is observed. Such districts are still sometimes termed "Non-regulation," though that term has lost its original meaning. Each Province is divided into Zillahs, or Districts, or large Counties, under Collector-Magistrates, or Deputy-Commissioners with Joint and Deputy Magistrates, or Assistant and Extra-Assistant Commissioners. These Districts are in most Provinces grouped into Divisions, each under a Commissioner supervised by a Revenue Board or Financial Commissioner. English counties average 1000 square miles in extent. In India they are much larger. In Bombay, for instance, Collectorates average about 6000 square miles, and Khandesh is about 15,000 square miles. Each District has a treasury and a jail. In Bengal, and recently elsewhere, Districts are broken up into Subdivisions under Joint, Assistant, or Deputy-Magistrates. Under the constabulary system, introduced by Act V. of 1861, each District has a Superintendent of Police, and the Districts are grouped for police purposes into circles under Deputy Inspectors-General, while the whole police force of each Province is under an Inspector-General. The constabulary, except on the North-Eastern and Trans-Indus frontiers, is a purely civil force organised on the Irish system, and subject in all respects, except internal discipline, to the civil authorities, that is, to

Commissioners of Divisions and Deputy-Commissioners or Collector-Magistrates of Districts.

The Provinces are administered by a covenanted civil service of 848 members, to which a few natives receive local appointments, while all British-born subjects may compete in England; by an uncovenanted civil service and by military officers of the three Staff Corps. Each Province has a Director of Public Instruction and Inspectors of Schools through whom grants-in-aid are administered, and provincial schools and colleges are taught. Under the Despatch of 1854, the three Universities of Calcutta, Madras, and Bombay were created on the model of the London University. The Panjab University has recently received a charter by which it may grant certain degrees after examinations conducted in the classical and vernacular languages of India. Since the extinction of the local European army in 1860, India has been garrisoned by the Queen's army, generally 63,000 strong, of whom 4400 are officers. The three sepoy armies of Bengal, Madras, and Bombay are 125,000 strong (only 900 Artillery), with 1600 officers on the irregular system. The native army, all military staff, and many political and civil appointments, are filled from the three Staff Corps, formed of the officers of the Company's regiments after the Mutiny, and continually supplied since by young Queen's officers who have undergone examination and a year's probation with a native corps.

§ 7. Provinces and Native States.—While two-thirds of India is thus administered chiefly by English officials, civil and military, in twelve Provinces, the other third is immediately ruled, subject to the Viceroy, by its own Hindoo and Musalman sovereigns and chiefs. Of such States there are 153 whose feudatory princes have Lord Canning's *sannad* or patent of 1860, which guarantees to each loyal tributary the right of adoption on the failure of natural heirs, that is, practically, non-annexation. From that third of India the revenues derive no benefit; but, on the contrary, the rest of India is charged with the excess expenditure on political establishments not met by tribute, and with the military defence. So carefully do the British officers, who reside in the principal States as the Governor-General's political agents, aid the chiefs by their counsel, and so frequently does it happen that the chiefs receive a good English education during their minority, while the principality is under temporary British management, that the Native States are coming more and more to be regarded, administratively, like

[*Continued on page* 12.

AREA AND POPULATION OF THE 12 PROVINCES, EXCLUSIVE OF THE 153 NATIVE STATES.

Provinces under the direct Administration of	Area in Square Miles.	Divisions.	Districts or Counties.	Inhabited Houses, 1871.	Population, 1871.	Population on Feb. 17, 1881.	Density of Population to Square Mile. Census of 1871.	Density of Population to Square Mile. Census of 1881.
The Governor-General—								
Ajmer	2,710	—	2	93,464	396,889	453,075	146	167
Berar	17,728	—	6	491,349	2,227,654	2,670,982	125	151
Coorg	1,583	—	1	22,900	168,312	178,283	107	114
Two Governors—								
Madras	140,430	—	22	5,892,179	31,385,820	30,839,181	224	220
Bombay (with Sind and Aden)	126,453	4	25	3,254,371	16,349,206	16,454,414	129	129
Three Lieutenant-Governors—								
Bengal	155,997	9	52	10,461,113	60,733,078	66,530,127	389	427
North-Western Province }	81,748	7	37	6,316,452	30,781,204	32,699,436	376	400
Oudh }	24,213	4	12	2,413,710	11,223,150	11,407,625	463	471
Panjab	107,010	10	32	4,015,476	17,611,498	18,850,437	164	175
Four Chief Commissioners—								
Central Provinces	84,208	3	18	1,674,291	8,173,824	9,805,149	97	118
British Burma	87,220	3	19	629,256	3,154,470	3,707,646	36	42
Andaman and Nicobar Islands	3,285	—	2	—	25,945	30,000	8	9
Assam	55,384	1	11	712,934	4,124,972	4,815,157	91	106
Total of Provinces	887,969	—	239	35,977,459	186,356,022	198,441,512	210	223½

AREA AND POPULATION OF INDIA, BRITISH PROVINCES AND STATES, AND FOREIGN POSSESSIONS.

Provinces and States.	Provinces.			Native States.			Total.		
	Sq. Miles.	Population.		Sq. Miles.	Population.		Sq. Miles.	Population.	
		Census of 1871.	Census of 1881.		Census of 1871.	Census of 1881.		Census of 1871.	Census of 1881.
Govmt. of India—									
Ajmer	2,710	396,889	453,075	—	—	—	2,710	396,889	460,722
Berar	17,728	2,227,654	2,670,982	—	—	—	17,728	2,227,654	2,672,673
Coorg	1,583	168,312	178,283	—	—	—	1,583	168,312	178,302
*Mysore	—	—	—	30,500	5,055,412	4,186,399	30,500	5,055,412	4,186,399
*Central India	—	—	—	89,098	8,360,571	9,200,881	89,098	8,360,571	9,200,881
*Rajpootana	—	—	—	130,994	10,192,871	11,005,512	130,994	10,192,871	11,005,512
*Haidarabad	—	—	—	80,000	9,000,000	9,167,789	80,000	9,000,000	9,167,789
*Baroda	—	—	—	4,399	2,000,225	2,154,469	4,399	2,000,225	2,154,469
Andaman Islands	3,285	25,945	30,000	—	—	—	3,285	25,945	30,000
Bengal	155,997	60,733,078	66,530,127	47,440	2,328,440	2,603,492	203,437	63,061,518	69,133,619
Assam	55,384	4,124,972	4,815,157	—	—	—	55,384	4,124,972	4,908,276
British Burma	87,220	3,154,470	3,707,646	—	—	—	87,220	3,154,470	3,736,771
{ N.W. Province	81,748	30,781,204	32,699,436	5,125	636,548	744,424	86,873	31,417,747	33,443,917
{ Oudh	24,213	11,223,150	11,407,625	—	—	—	24,213	11,223,150	11,407,625
Panjab	107,010	17,611,498	18,850,437	114,742	5,370,096	3,861,683	221,749	22,981,594	22,712,120
Central Province	84,208	8,173,824	9,805,149	29,112	1,049,710	1,700,000	113,042	9,223,534	11,505,149
Bombay	126,453	16,349,206	16,454,414	66,408	6,784,482	6,941,631	191,847	23,133,688	23,396,045
Madras	140,430	31,385,820	30,839,181	9,318	3,247,689	3,001,436	150,248	34,633,509	33,840,617
British India	887,969	186,356,022	198,441,512	607,636	54,026,039	54,567,716	1,494,310	240,382,061	253,140,886
French Possessions							178	285,022	280,381
Portuguese Possessions							1,086	444,617	444,987
Total of all India							1,495,574	241,111,700	253,866,254

non-regulation portions of the adjoining Provinces, while their tributary independence is jealously respected by the Suzerain. Hence, geographically, these States are hereafter described in detail either along with the Provinces of which they form a territorial part, or in such great groups as Baroda, Rajpootana, Central India, Haidarabad, and Mysore. All Native States are marked with an asterisk (*) to distinguish them at once.

Thus, by British legislation and government on the one side, and Native administration aided by British advice on the other, the vast and varied mosaic of the British Indian Empire, in itself the greatest miracle of history, is becoming a living unity, in which the respect shown to all rights and the steady increase of the natives in responsibilities and honours, seem to reduce as far as possible the inevitable drawbacks of the rule of 250,000,000 of non-Christians and 2,000,000 of Christians by any power but themselves.

§ 8. The IMPERIAL SURVEY consisted of three independent departments known as the Great Trigonometrical, Topographical, and Revenue, until 1878, when these were amalgamated under General Walker, R.E. (1) The **Great Trigonometrical Survey** was begun in 1802 by Colonel Lambton. The principal triangulation has been completed after eighty years' work. Colonel Lambton carried out the triangulation along the east coast from Madras to Cape Comorin, and measured the great Meridional Arc from Punnæ, 8 miles north-east of that Cape, in lat. 8° 9′ 38″·28 to Daumergidda in lat. 18° 3′ 23″·53. Thence his successor, Colonel Everest, extended the Arc to Kalianpoor in lat. 24° 7′ 6″·05, whereby the whole measured Arc amounted to 15° 57′ 41″·027, as described in the *Account of the Measurement of the Arc of the Meridian*, published by that great surveyor in 1830. In the midst of all the wars and disturbances of the century the principal triangulation has been carried on successfully till it is connected with Russian territory in Central Asia, and includes the Crown colony of Ceylon. In 1878-80, during the British occupation of Afghanistan, an area of 39,500 square miles there was surveyed by British officers and 7000 square miles explored by native agency, linking on Kabul to India. The Sikaram peak of the Safed Koh range, one of the most strongly fixed of all the Great Trigonometrical trans-frontier peaks, is the point of connection between the two series. In March 1881, when two expeditionary columns were sent into Wazeeristan on the eastern confines of Afghanistan and close to the British districts of Bannoo and Dera Ismail Khan, an area of 1200 square miles was surveyed in detail. Several mountains on the western frontier were ascended, including the celebrated peaks of Peerghal and Shindar (11,000 feet), which command a view of the region to the east almost up to the road from Quetta to Ghazni. Besides the principal triangulation, the eastern frontier series deals with the region outside of India proper, in Burma. That triangulation also has recently been brought to a close on a base line of verification in the Mergui township; it has been extended over Siam to the capital of Bangkok, from the Amya pass on the Tavoy frontier, known to the Siamese as Kow Den ("boundary hill"). (2) The **Topographical Survey** is carried out, chiefly in Native States and sparsely-peopled territory, on the standard scale of one inch to the mile, and on the enlarged scale of two inches to the mile. This survey, begun in 1836, was for purposes of administration, civil and military; and to obtain geographical information on a reliable basis, for the sheets of the Great Indian Atlas, of vast tracts of country to complete which, under any more expensive and elaborate system, would take upwards of a century. The system of survey is most effective and rapid. It is based on a network of secondary triangulation conducted with the larger class of Vernier Theodolites, closely connected with, and verified by, the Great Triangulation of India. The detail work, or topography, is filled in by means of the plane table, checked by routes, or traversing between the stations fixed by triangulation wherever the nature of the ground will admit of such test, or is examined by a competent officer in the field, by intersections to surrounding objects from the points of triangulation. (3) The **Revenue Survey**, in greater detail, is practically the most important of all, as the basis of the whole landed system and taxation of India. It is Mouzawar, or village, on a 4-inch scale, and Cadastral, or field by field, on the scale of 32 inches and 16 inches to the mile. The Revenue Survey began in 1822 and slowly progressed till 1830, at a rate which would have required 500 years for its completion over all India. It was revived after the first Panjab War in 1846. In fifteen years from that time it surveyed 237,028 square miles, at a cost of Rs. 22·9 per mile. The whole of the vast area of India has now been surveyed in one form or another. But owing to the progress of science and the destruction of records and landmarks in the Mutiny, many portions are being re-surveyed.

The Indian Survey is far more extensive than that of any European State, but it has been executed on a system which facilitates the final reduction of the observations. Chains of triangles are carried along the principal meridians and the course of the eastern and western frontier, and these are connected together by other chains, the northernmost of which follows the Himalayan frontier line, while the others are carried along certain parallels of latitude, at convenient intervals. Colonel Everest's Meridional Arc is, from its central position and its intrinsic value, the axis of the system. Base-lines are measured at the extremities of the longitudinal chains, and at the points where the chains cross Colonel Everest's Arc. Thus the triangulation is divisible into large quadrilateral figures, with a base-line at each corner, and somewhat resembling gridirons, with their outer framework and intermediate bars. This arrangement offers certain advantages in the reduction of the observations which are not met with in a network of triangulation, as the points of junction between the several sections of the operations are reduced to a minimum. At each junction there are necessarily two or more values of the lengths, azimuths, and co-ordinates of the sides common to two or more chains of triangles, in consequence of the errors generated in the course of the operations. The problem to be solved is to harmonise these values by the application of certain corrections to every measured angle and base-line, having due regard to the respective weights of the observations and to certain essential theoretical considerations, as well as to the imperative necessity of restricting the calculations within manageable limits. With every assistance that could be derived from the published accounts of the best geodetic operations in Europe, and from the Astronomer-Royal, it has been a matter of no small difficulty to elaborate a system of reduction which will satisfy modern theoretical requirements, and yet be susceptible of practical manipulation, when applied to the very extensive operations of the Indian triangulation. This has at last been accomplished. The great quadrilateral figure which connects Dehra Doon, the headquarters of the Survey, with Karachi, and comprises 4 base-lines and about 2500 angles appertaining to 8 chains of triangles, covers an area of nearly 300,000 square miles. On the completion of the last of the arcs of longitude between trigonometrical stations in India, the differences of longitude between Bombay, Aden, and Suez were determined. Suez had already been connected with the Royal Observatory at Greenwich; thus the electro-telegraphic connection between Greenwich and India was completed.

The **Madras Observatory** was erected in 1792, but the Madras series of astronomical observations had begun in 1787. Its longitude, as that of the secondary meridian or substitute for the prime meridian of Greenwich Observatory, is the fixed point of departure of the Trigonometrical Survey. The Observatory gives Madras or uniform time to all India for railway and other non-local purposes. The astronomer, Mr. Pogson, unites with those of the other southern Observatories at the Cape of Good Hope and Melbourne in the great survey of the southern heavens. Of the five zones into which these are divided, from the Equator south to the Pole, the Madras astronomer takes the two from the Equator to 40° S. Since 1856 the **Geological Survey** has been at work on the basis of the Revenue and Topographical Surveys, under Dr. Oldham and M. H. B. Medlicott, with valuable results detailed under Physiography, Book II. In 1867, after frequent cyclones and famines, M. H. F. Blanford of that Survey became **Meteorological Reporter** to Government; there are upwards of 125 stations of observation. Tidal registers are kept and surveys made by the **Marine Survey.** Since 1861 the **Archæological Survey** of India has been conducted by General Cunningham, and in Bombay and Madras more recently by Dr. Burgess. Following Mr. James Fergusson, LL.D., these reporters have made many rich discoveries and verifications duly noted in each District and State.

§ 9. Land Tenures and Taxation.—The Survey is the necessary preliminary of the settlement of rights in the land and assessment of the land-tax, whether it be considered rent or revenue, between the people and the State. Where a hereditary system similar to the feudalism of the Indo-Germanic peoples existed among the Hindoos, as it still does in Rajpootana, it was almost entirely obliterated by the centralised government of the Muhammadans. In India, as over nearly all Asia, the State is the proprietor of the soil, and raises the greater portion of its revenue from the landed classes, whether directly from the cultivating ryot ("protected one," as distinguished from *raees* = "noble"), or from brotherhoods and village communities of ryots, or from the zameendar ("land-holder") or talookdar, who holds large estates as middleman, or direct owner subject to the land-tax. Private property in land, in the English sense, has no existence in India, save in the few instances in sparsely-peopled districts where tea, coffee, and cinchona estates have been sold in fee-simple under waste land rules chiefly to Europeans. The right is that of holding land subject to the payment of customary rents, a right developed by the settlements made under the British rule, and made valuable by the British peace and improvements, so that it is saleable and has an increasing value according to the lightness or severity of the periodical assessment.

The British Indian land-settlements have oscillated from the principle of **Permanence** (zameendaree), as in Lower Bengal, under Lord Cornwallis in 1793, to that of **Annual Leases** (ryotwaree) under Sir Thomas Munro in Madras in 1820, and that of **Thirty Years' Leases** in the North-Western Province in 1833 under Robert Mertins Bird, followed by Thomason there, by John Lawrence in the Panjab, and in 1836 in Bombay by Sir George Wingate. The north-west famine of 1860-1, following the revelations made by the Mutiny of 1857, led Lord Canning, on Colonel Baird Smith's report, to revert to the principle of permanence of assessment for a time, which he had carried out in a modified form in the new districts of Oudh. But the apparent and immediate financial advantage of giving the State a large share in the increment of the land-rent, especially when the depreciation of silver came to be marked, again overshadowed the political and more abiding benefits of guaranteeing the people an absolute right of private property in the soil which they cultivate subject to a fixed quit-rent. Even the proposal to remove the financial objection by corn-rents, under which the State should share the increase proportionally without the expense and harassing investigations of periodical settlements, did not secure the adoption of the principle of a permanent peasant-proprietor settlement, free from the mistakes and wrongs of the permanent zameendaree or middleman settlement of Bengal, North Madras, and Benares, and from the talookdaree settlement of Oudh. Except in these districts all India is held ryotwar, on leases varying from thirty to ten years, and even annual, at the expiry of which the State landlord institutes a new, detailed, and often expensive investigation into soils, holdings, and rents, and alters generally by increasing the land-tax accordingly. The principal tenures will be found described under each Province and great State.

The net land-revenue has risen in the ten years beginning 1870-71, from £20,335,678 or nearly half the total net revenue of £42,780,417, by about two millions sterling, to £22,125,807, with a total net revenue of £49,801,664. The gross revenue of the latter year, 1879-80, was £68,484,666, the difference being derived from sources other than taxation, such as the opium monopoly. The revenue of 1880-81 was £72,920,000, and the gross expenditure £71,259,000. Including the land-revenue as land-tax, the 200 millions in the 12 Provinces of British India pay about 4s. a head of imperial taxation, besides municipal or local and provincial cesses, which purchase such local advantages as roads, schools, police, and sanitary appliances. This incidence of taxation varies from 5s. 6d. per head of the land-owning classes to 3s. 3d. for traders, 2s. for artisans, and 1s. 6d. for agricultural labourers. The fiscal policy of the Government has of late been to reduce the burden of the salt monopoly which is a poll-tax, and to abolish import duties. The 54½ millions in the Native States pay only to their own chiefs who enjoy a net annual revenue of 14 millions sterling, and pay £700,000 as tribute, or less than the cost of the military and political establishments maintained on their account. The public debt and liabilities of India, besides the capital invested in railways, amount to £157,000,000, involving interest £6,000,000, at an average rate which has gradually fallen to 3·8 per cent. Of the debt, 94 millions is ordinary, 45 is for productive public works, 10⅛ is for the East Indian Railway, and 8⅛ is for local loans and advances. To this has been added 2½ millions sterling, raised at 4 per cent for the Indian expenses in the campaign of 1882 in Egypt.

There are 880 municipalities in India which have an income of 1⅓ millions sterling chiefly from taxation. A great advance in district self-government is being made by the creation of partially elected Municipal and Local or Rural Boards. The provincial rates amount to 3 millions sterling, also from taxation. Since 1871-72 the Provinces have had assigned to them by the Central Government, for the non-imperial services involving expenditure, annual sums now amounting to 14½ millions, and making, with the above, 17½ millions out of the gross revenue. This decentralisation of finance works well in promoting public thrift, but may be abused as an excuse for increasing taxation.

CHAPTER II.

INDIA AS A WHOLE.

Great Mountains.—§ 1. The Himalaya. § 2. The Safed Koh, Sulaiman, and Khirthar Ranges. § 3. The three Roma and Patkai Ranges. § 4. The Western and Eastern Ghats. § 5. The Aravali, Vindhya, and Satpoora Ranges.

Great Rivers.—§ 6. The East Himalaya Rivers—the Ganges. § 7. The Brahmapootra. § 8. The Irawadi. § 9. The Tsit-toung and Salween. § 10. The Indus. § 11. The West Peninsular Rivers—the Narbada and the Tapti. § 12. The East Peninsular Rivers—the Mahanadi, Godavari, Kistna, and Kavari with Coleroon.

Waterfalls, Lakes, Canals, Forests, and Railways.—§ 13. Waterfalls. § 14. Lakes. § 15. Canals. § 16. Forests. § 17. Trees of India. § 18. Railways.

The Coast from Suez Canal to Singapore.—§ 19. Harbours and Roadsteads. § 20. Tides. § 21. Lighthouses and Light Vessels.

§ 1. THE HIMĀLĂYA ("snow-abode") or Himāchāl ("snow-mountain"), a word converted by the Greeks into Imaos and Emodos, and generally but incorrectly pronounced as if *y* in the last syllable were a consonant, is applied (1) to the snow-covered zone of North India, between the Brahmapootra River on the east and the Indus on the west; and (2) to the series of mountain chains forming the southern scarp of the plateau of Tibet (15,000 feet), the **Kuenlun** which overlooks the lower plains of East Toorkestan and the Gobi Desert being the northern scarp.

(1) The **Himalaya Proper** extend for 1500 miles from the gorge of the Brahmapootra in east longitude 95° 30′ to the gorge of the Indus in east longitude 72°. This unbroken watershed of above 18,000 feet bounds on the north the great plain of North India, which has an area of 500,000 square miles, gradually rising to an elevation of 1000 feet. At a point 20 or 25 miles from the outer hills the jungly morass of the **Tarai** begins and stretches from 10 or 15 miles north into the sand and boulder beds of the **Bhabar**, beneath which the

drainage of the hills passes into the Tarai. (*a*) The **Sub-Himalaya** or **Siwalik Ranges** of the Tertiary period then rise abruptly to 3000 or 4000 feet, and slope inwards to the main system, forming **Doons** (called Mari in Nepal), or valleys of 2000 to 2500 feet, such as the Dwars of Bhootan, and the fertile tea-tracts of Dehra below Mussooree-Landhaur, and Kangra below Dharmsala. West of the Jhelam, the Sub-Himalaya end in the **Salt Range**, a small plateau to the north of the line of elevation extending to the Indus. (*b*) The **Outer Himalaya Range** rises rapidly from these Doons to a height of 7000 to 9000 feet and has a breadth of 60 to 70 miles, on which the European sanitary stations from Darjeeling west by Naini Tal, Mussooree, Simla, Dharmsala, Dalhousie, and Marree, have been planted. (*c*) The **Main Himalaya** or **Snowy Range** is reached by passes which lead to the regions of the loftiest peaks in the world yet surveyed—**Mount Everest** in Nepal (29,002 feet); **Kinchinjinga** in Sikkim (28,156 feet); **Chumalhari** (23,929 feet); **Dhawalagiri** in Nepal (26,826 feet); and **Nanda-devi** in Kumaun (25,700 feet). These and others not named, such as two in the extreme west (28,278 feet), or not reached by the surveyor's eye and instruments, are grouped in masses on the first ranges within the line of perpetual snow from 20 to 30 miles south of the Indian watershed. On a line of 150 miles long between the 78th and 81st meridians in Kumaun and Garhwal, General R. Strachey notes six great snowy groups with five great rivers passing between them. He expects the number of peaks between 25,000 and 30,000 to be found greatly increased as knowledge advances, and even that points may be discovered exceeding 30,000 feet in altitude. The average elevation of the crest of the Indian watershed between the Brahmapootra and the Indus exceeds 18,000 feet; the passes leading to it from the south, used by men and animals for the scanty trade which the Government of India has done much to foster, are frequently higher than that, with the exception of that which leads from Kashmeer to Dras in Tibet (11,300 feet). The larger rivers roll down from the snowy watershed at from 800 to 1250 feet per mile through profound ravines. The large and level valleys of Kathmandoo in Nepal and Kashmeer are exceptional. Looked at in their length from south to west the Indian Himalaya are occupied from the 92d meridian to the 89th by the State of Bhootan, locally termed Lhopato; then by British and Native Sikkim, or Demojong, up to the 88th; then by the protected State of

Nepal nearly to the 80th. From that point west and north-west to the Indus, the whole southern slope from the snowy crest of the watershed to the plains consists of British Districts like Kumaun, Garhwal, and Simla, or States like Kashmeer.

(2) The **Tibeto-Himalaya** extend north from the great plain of India to the heights of the loftiest mountains, the **Indian Watershed** (Himalaya proper), the Tibetan table-land, the **Toorkish Watershed** (Kuenlun), and finally the northern slope which ends in the plains of Central Asia. On a line drawn through Simla the breadth of this mighty mountain-system is at least 400 miles. The Alps have a breadth of 75 miles from the Lake of Thun to the Lombardy plains. It is no exaggeration to say, that "along the entire range of the Himalaya there are valleys into which the whole Alps might be cast without producing any result that would be discernible at a distance of 10 or 15 miles." From this great Tibetan plateau are thrown off to south and north the rivers of India and Afghanistan; to the west the Oxus (Aksu) or Amu, and Jaxartes or Sir; to the east the rivers of China, Siam, and Burma. The plateau is not so much a tableland lying between the two chains of the Himalaya and Kuenlun, as "the summit (15,000 feet) of a great protuberance above the general level of the earth's surface, of which these alleged chains are nothing more than the south and north borders, while the other ranges which traverse it are but corrugations of the mass more or less strongly marked and locally developed." The whole mountain area extends from east to west about 2000 miles, and its average breadth, including the sloping faces, exceeds 500 miles. The Tibetan valleys differ from those of the Himalaya, like Kashmeer, being long, flat, and open, but narrow. **Gugé plateau** (15,500 feet), to the north of Kumaun, on the upper Satlej, is the largest, being 120 miles long and from 15 to 60 miles broad, with the Lakes of Rakas-tal and Manasaraur.

On the west are two watershed lines at right angles to the whole mountain-system—the **Hindu Koosh** of Afghanistan, which is the southern, and the **Terek-tagh** of North Toorkestan, which is the northern.

§ 2. The SAFED KOH ("white mountains"), continuing the north-western boundary from the Himalaya, stretch east and north. Beginning between Kabul and Ghazni, east of the Allah-Koh, the range runs into two main ridges: one north-east to the Khaibar and the Kabul rivers; the other due east to the junction of the Kabul with the Indus. It begins a few miles west of the **Shutargardan Pass**, between Kooram and Logar. Of the northern spurs, those most familiar from the Afghan wars are that which ends at Bhutkhak, the Haft Kotal, and the Gandamak, which gave its name to the suspended treaty. Of the southern spurs the Peiwar ridge is best known. **Seetaram Mountain** (15,662 feet) is the highest point of the range. The **Sulaiman Hills** continue the boundary north and south, from Bannoo in the Panjab to Sind, along the whole Derajat. Thrown off from the same Allah-Koh ridge at which the Safed Koh begins, the range forms the mountain system of East Afghanistan and Baloochistan. The eastern slopes drain into the Indus, the western into the Helmand, or the desert between Persia and Baloochistan; the southern into the Arabian Sea. On the Indian or eastern side an offshoot divides the drainage of the Kooram from the Khost valley. A spur divides Khost from Dawar, ending in Bannoo district. The Wazeeri hills and the Sarkh-Koh are also offshoots. The **Takht-i-Sulaiman** ("Solomon's Throne") is the highest point (11,295 feet), nearly due west of the town of Dera Ismail Khan. It is a niche in a rock about 10 feet below the summit, looking as if it had been cut out by hand; in front is a small ledge, below which the mountain falls precipitously. The legend is that King Solomon used to cause himself to be transported by genii to this place, and sit there to enjoy the cool air. Many pilgrims ascend the difficult path to visit the shrine on the summit. From the parallel lines of the outer Sulaiman the main range slopes down to the valley of Kandahar. The **Khirthar Range** (7000 feet), erroneously called Hala, completes the north-western border of Upper Sind to the sea. From the 26th parallel of latitude it merges in the **Pabb Hills**, which run for 90 miles to Cape Monze or Ras Muari. The range is in three parallel ridges; two sanitaria have been tried at Dhar Yaro (6000 feet), and the Dauna Towers in Mehar (4500 feet), but the access is very difficult. From the eastern ridge the arid **Lakki Hills** (2000 feet) strike for 50 miles into Karachi district.

§ 3. The ROMA MOUNTAINS (or Yoma) ("spinal ridge"), in three lines, and the **Patkai**, are the four principal ranges which, running north and south, flank the Himalaya system on the east, as the Safed Koh, Sulaiman, and Khirthar hills do on the west. (1) The **Arakan Roma** start south from the great multiple mass of mountains in Assam which, after enclosing the plain of Manipoor State and Tipura, contract into a defined chain at Chittagong, and disappear in the Bay of Bengal at Cape Negrais, 700 miles south. The line is continued in the Andaman, Sumatra, and Javanese islands. Its most prominent point is the Blue Mountain (above 8000 feet), in 21° north and 93° east, whence it throws off the watershed between the Naf and Myoo rivers west to the coast at Angoo Maw. The highest peaks are the Kyee-doung ("ever visible") on the Pegu frontier, and the double Shwe-doung Moung Hnitma ("golden brother and sister hill"). (2) The **Pegu Roma** rise from the Re-me-theng plains north of British Burma, forming the watershed between the Irawadi and the Tsit-toung; the main ridge gradually rises to 2000 feet, when it passes south by west into British territory; at Rangoon it has been levelled into the platform of the Shwe Dagon pagoda; after falling into the low wooded hills on which stands the Syriam pagoda, the range sinks into the Bay of Bengal at the rocks which impede the navigation of the Hmaw-won below Kyouk-tan. (3) The **Assam** and **Patkai Ranges** rise suddenly from the Bengal plain 220 miles north of Calcutta; stretch east under the names of the Garo, Kasi, and Naga tribes which inhabit the jungles; sweep north-east in an increasing mass, often traversed by the Burmese in their frequent invasions of Assam; and, when 14,000 feet high, meet the lofty prolongation of the southern chain of the Himalaya known as the Langtang, which sends down the Irawadi from the snows of its southern face. Thence from north-west the course turns south-east between the Irawadi and Salween; a spur approaches the Bay of Bengal near Martaban, dividing the Salween from the Tsit-toung (Sittang); 15 miles south of the latter river it throws off the Poung-loung range; 50 miles east the main range rises to an altitude of 9000 feet in Kareng-nee, after which it gradually slopes south and east towards the junction of the Bheng-laing and Salween. The principal British peak is Nat-toung ("spirit hill"), 8000 feet, south-east of Toung-ngoo. (4) The **Tenasserim Roma**, the water-parting between the Bay of Bengal and Gulf of Siam, from a point east of the Salween extends south, skirts British territory, and forms the boundary between the Tenasserim division and Siam from the gorge through which the Thoung-yeng passes, where is the immense mass of the Moo-lai-yit (5500 feet), to the Pak-chan River in the south.

§ 4. THE SAHYÁDRI OR WESTERN GHATS form the most important range in the peninsula of India proper. Running for 1000 miles along the west coast from the Tapti River to Cape Comorin, at a high elevation, this wall of "stairs" or passes from the sea tilts the whole plateau towards the Eastern Ghats and sends the great rivers into the Bay of Bengal. From north of the Tapti valley the range runs south for 800 miles to the Palghat gap of Coimbatore, through the districts of Khandesh, Nasik, Thana, Satara, Ratnagiri, and Kanara, and from that gap for 200 miles farther to the Agastya Peak above Cape Comorin, through Malabar and the Cochin and Travankor States. Their average altitude is 3000 feet, rising to 4717 in Mahableshwar, and to 7000 in Coorg, where, in the **Neelgiris**, they are joined by the Eastern Ghats. The range sends out spurs with separate local names; in the south its more isolated groups are known as the **Anamalai**, **Palnai**, **Shivarai**, and **Travankor Hills**, fast being opened up by coffee and cinchona plantations, by gold companies and as sanitaria. The **Eastern Ghats**, starting from south of the Mahanadi River, in Orissa, pass into Ganjam and Vizagapatam districts, where the higher peaks rise to 5000 feet; run south-west at a distance from the Bay of Bengal of from 50 to 150 miles; are continued in the low hills which mark the coast-line of Chengalpat and Tinnevelli; but, in their main elevation, pass from the Nellore district south-west into the plateaux and ridges of Mysore and the Neelgiris, where they are lost in the Western Ghats. This eastern chain is not continuous like the western, hence some geologists deny it a separate existence. It is composed—to the south, of the eastern scarp of the Mysore plateau; to the north, of the south-eastern scarp of the Bastar-Jaipoor plateau; and, between these, of short isolated ridges of metamorphic rocks.

§ 5. The ARAVALI ("line of peaks") run for 300 miles from north-east to south-west through Rajpootana; in Ajmer Province the separate hills and plateaux unite into a chain to Mount Aboo (5650 feet), which forms the main watershed, and, like a coast of high cliffs, protects the country to the south-east from the sand of the Rajpootana Thar or Desert. From this watershed the rivers flow south-east and south-west to the two seas. The range throws off spurs north-east to Delhi, where the Mutiny siege of 1857 has made the ridge from which the British took the city for ever famous.

The **Vindhya** ("hunter"), of old applied to the hills, including the Satpooras, which separate the great plain of Hindustan—the "middle land" of the Aryan Hindoos—from the plateau of the Dekhan, is now confined to the hills north of the Narbada. The range forms a great rock basin running east from Neemach for 600 miles to Sasseram, and north to south for 300 miles from Agra to Hoshangabad. It connects the plains of Goojarat with those of the Ganges at Rajmahal, and is still the central home of the Non-Aryan aborigines of all varieties. The eastern continuation of the Vindhya is the **Kaimoor Range**, north of the southern valley. Both ranges form the southern scarps of the Vindhya plateau occupied by the great Native States of Indore, Bhopal, Boondelkhand, and Baghelkhand.

The **Satpoora Range** ("seven towns") runs south of the Narbada valley—which it divides from the Tapti—parallel with the Vindhya from Amarkantak through the Central Province west to the Arabian Sea. The **Plateaux of Hazaribagh** and **Chutia Nagpoor**, which appear to continue this range to the east, are separate elevations formed of different rocks. The Satpoora run for 600 miles with a depth of 100 miles from north to south. Beginning at Amarkantak they form a triangular system, of which the base runs south-west to the Saletekri Hills in Bhandara, and the two sides proceeding west, shrink from a broad tableland into the two ridges which bound the Tapti valley, and end in the famous fortress of Aseergarh. The **Maikal Hills**, running south-west from the Amarkantak plateau, wall in the granary of Chateesgarh; the Central Satpoora comprise the **Pachmarhi** or **Mahadeva Hills** from Narsingpoor to Aseergarh. The range ends on the west in the **Rajpeepla Hills**.

The **Indhyadri** is a minor range between the Tapti and the Godavari.

§ 6. The East Himalayan Rivers.—Between the 77th and 88th meridians the waters of the Himalaya system fall into the Ganges; those east of the 88th into the Brahmapootra; those east of the 97th into the Irawadi and Salween. The waters to the west of the 77th meridian form the Indus. The **Ganges** is personified in Ganga ("the river"), eldest daughter of Himavat, the lord of snow. The stream was induced by the austerities of Bhagiratha (whence its most sacred name), great-grandson of Sagara (the ocean), to descend from heaven, and it fell first on Shiva. The Ganges, and its main tributary the **Jumna**, rise in a region of snowy peaks of the first magnitude from mighty glaciers, the former above the temple at Gangotri (13,800 feet), the latter to the west above the temple of Jumnotri. The Ganges is formed of the more sacred Bhagirathi from Gangotri, on the south of which is the Shiva temple of Kedarnath, and the larger Alaknanda, fed from a glacier at the Vishnu temple of Badarinath, in Garhwal, where the valleys lead into Tibet. Forty-seven miles south of the Deo Prayag, or junction, the somewhat broad stream leaves the Sub-Himalaya at Hardwar, whence it gives off the head waters of the great Ganges Canal. Thence it flows, with a tortuous and shallow but broadening course, south-east through the North-Western Province to the next sacred Prayag at Allahabad, 668 miles from its source. There it receives the sister Jumna, which, having left the hills in the 95th mile of its course, has been joined by the Chambal from the Vindhya at Malwa, has sent off several canals, and has drained 118,000 square miles. The great Ganges then rolls east by south-east through the North-Western Province for 140 miles to Benares, with its temples and cremation ghats ; receives the Goomti and Gogra from the north, and the Son from the south ; enters the Bengal Province, where it is joined by the Gandak and Kosi from the north, and at 240 miles from the Bay of Bengal begins to form the vast delta along with the Brahmapootra from the north-east at Goalunda. Under the local name of the **Megna** estuary the main volume enters the Bay of Bengal near Noakhali. That is the most easterly, as the **Hoogli** is the most westerly, and commercially most important of the many channels through which, in the network of the Soondarban, the Ganges reaches the ocean (Sagar). The Hoogli is formed by the spilling over of the Ganges during the rainy season into the three principal channels of the Bhagirathi, Jalangi, and Matabhanga, and by several rivers from the south, all described hereafter. The Ganges flows in main stream to the Megna mouth for 1557 miles, and to the Hoogli mouth 1507 miles; with its longest affluent its course is 1680 miles. It is 20 miles broad at the entrance, and from 1 to 2¼ miles in the dry season in the average channel, while its depth is 30 feet. The flood discharge of the river at Rajmahal, before the delta begins, is 1,800,000 cubic feet per second, and the ordinary discharge 207,000. The catchment basin encloses 319,100 square miles. From its glacier source, 13,800 feet above the sea, the Ganges falls to 10,319 feet in 10 miles at Gangotri; at Hardwar it is 1024, and at Cawnpoor 379 feet.

§ 7. The BRAHMAPOOTRA ("son of Brahma"), or Tsangpo, from the southern portion of the Tibetan tableland, on the same central line of 82° east longitude from which the Indus flows north-west, rises near Manasaraur Lake, proceeds south-east to 95°, where it turns south through a gorge of the Himalaya, like that of the Satlej, and as the Dihong after the confluence of the Dibong it reaches Assam, where, receiving the Lohit ("blood-red"), called by some the true Brahmapootra, from Brahmakoond, it flows south-west, forming the great valley of Assam, and, near Dhoobri, turns south to the Padma or main

Ganges at Goalunda, in union with which it reaches the head of the Bay of Bengal as the Megna. Its course is estimated at 1800 miles; it drains a basin of 361,200 square miles. All explorations, from those of Wilcox in 1828 to the native surveyors—Goorkha, Bhootea, and Burman—sent out by the Indian Survey, entitle us to believe that the Assam Lohit or Brahmapootra of the Hindoos receives the waters of the Tibetan Tachok-tsangpo ("horse-river"), or Tsangpo ("great river," like *Ganga*). Since 1865 the trained natives have traced and mapped the river from Shigatzé as far east as Chetang, and thence downwards for 120 miles, where it was found to be 250 paces wide, with slight current and very deep, on to Gyala Sindong, 287 miles from Chetang, and only 100 miles from the Dihong, as we know that to enter the Assam valley. Just below Chetang the ordinary discharge of the Brahmapootra is 15,000 cubic feet per second, and its maximum flood discharge is 250,000 cubic feet. On the right bank, in Assam, the Brahmapootra receives these main tributaries, the Subansiri; Bhoroli, Manas, Gadadhar or Sankos, Dharla, and Teesta; and on the left, the Noa Dihing, Buri Dihing, Disang, Dhansiri, and Kapili, all navigable by large boat, and some by steamer in the rainy season. The Brahmapootra itself is navigable by steamer 800 miles from the sea up to Dibroogarh. In volume, utility to agriculture, and commercial facilities, this is the third river of India, being next to the Ganges and Indus. Details regarding its course, local names, and marts, will be found under each district which it traverses in Assam and Bengal Provinces.

§ 8. The IRAWADI rises in a snowy range among the Kachins in Khamti, about latitude 28°, as seen in 1826 by Wilcox, who crossed over from Assam to north of Burma *via* the Noa Dihing, and as recently confirmed by a Burman explorer of the Indian Survey. The Irawadi, like the Ganges, has two sources, separated by one day's journey, the Eastern or smaller (Myit-ngay), and the Western or larger (Myit-gyee), which unite at 26° north. The main river, flowing southwards, receives the Mogoung from the west in 24° 50′, where at Hnote-choyone, or 800 miles from the sea, it is over a mile broad. It enters the first gorge 14 miles south, is contracted to a great depth at a spot 50 yards wide, and emerges expanding into its old breadth, while it casts up sandy shoals and encircles peopled islands. It receives the Taping from the east; enters Burma at the frontier to north of Maingna; straggles among sands in front of Bamō, where the British Political Agent resided and the trade route to

China starts; passes Koung-toung-myo, where in 1769 the last Chinese invaders were defeated; rushes through the second defile, and below Tsampanago through the third defile, after which the valley of Ava begins. The river enters British Burma three-quarters of a mile broad, is contracted between the Pegu and Arakan Roma, traverses the fourth and last defile before passing Prome, and opens out into the delta below the Akouk-toung spur of the Arakan Roma. Before reaching Henzăda it sends off the Bassein River westwards, which falls into the Bay of Bengal by two mouths, east of Hmaw-deng. At Gnyoung-doon, farther south, where the main Irawadi is 1¼ mile broad, the Pan-hlaing creek starts eastwards, and unites with the Hlaing to form the Rangoon river just north of the capital. The main river throws off another branch westwards past Pan-ta-naro, which turns southwards, and falls into the Bay of Bengal through the Pya-ma-law and Pyeng-tha-loo mouths; another eastwards, which reaches the coast as the To or China Ba-keer, and still another eastwards which debouches as the Pya-poon. The great Irawadi itself, continuing southwards, pours its waters into the sea by two mouths, the east of which is Kyoon-toon, and the west retains the name Irawadi. In British Burma the chief tributaries are the Ma-htoon or Meng-doon, Ma-dé, and Thai-lai-dan on the right, and the Kye-ni, Bhuotlay, and Na-weng on the left bank. The catchment basin is estimated at 158,000 square miles. The great flood discharge, which has led a few geographers to hold that the Tsangpo thus reaches the sea, is due to the melting snows and tremendous rainfall of Khamti. Colonel Yule calculates the basin of the Irawadi above the Mogoung to be the same as that of the Rhine at Cologne.

§ 9. The TSIT-TOUNG (Sittang), the second of the great rivers of Burma, flows like a wounded snake from its source in the hills of Upper Burma, 130 miles above the British frontier-town of Toung-ngoo, for 350 miles south to the Gulf of Martaban, draining 22,000 square miles between the Pegu Roma and Poung-loung ranges. After passing the town of the same name in the Shwe-gyeen district the river broadens to 7 or 8 miles, and then contracts rapidly into the shape of a funnel before it reaches the sea. Hence the extraordinary "bore." The great tidal wave of the Indian Ocean, joined by the tide from the south-east along the Tenasserim coast, sweeps up the narrow opening, with a foaming crest 20 feet high, and carries all before it. A heavy chop sea of sand and water following is as dangerous to boats as the curling wave. The bore is broken by a large curve below Weng-ba-daw creek, through which there is boat communication with Maulmein during the rainy season. The chief feeders are—on the west the Tshwa, Khyoung-tsouk, Kha-boung, Hpyoo, and Kwon; on the east the Kwe-thai, Thit-nau-tha, Kan-nee, Thouk-regat, Rouk-thwa-wa, Kyouk-gyee, Shwe-gyeng, and Moot-ta-ma.

The **Salween** (Nu or Lu Chiang) rises in a higher latitude than the Irawadi to its west. It traverses the Shan and Kareng-nee States south of the Yunan Province of China, as a rocky and rapid stream in a narrow valley. It is 300 yards broad at a point 200 miles from the sea, where it crosses the British frontier. Thence south to the Thoung-yeng tributary it is a navigable swift stream, between high and densely-wooded mountains, where it contracts to 30 yards, and 10 miles lower down is precipitated in great rapids over a ridge of rocks which forbids navigation. Ten miles lower are less dangerous rapids, and at the Kyo-dan it flows a clear and swift stream, in which teak timber rafts are formed. Farther south it receives the Ruon-za-leng from the west, then the Bheng-laing, Gyaing, and Attaran, after which it sends off the Dara-bouk or **Martaban River**, navigable to the sea, and flows past Maulmein for 30 miles to the Bay of Bengal at Amherst.

§ 10. The INDUS, the Sindhu, or Abba Sin ("father of rivers"), or Atak of the Hindoos, and Sintaw of the Chinese, issues from the Sin-ka-bab, or lion's mouth, on the northern slope of the peak of Kailas, the snowy mountain north of Manasaraur Lake, which, to the Hindoos, is at once the centre of the world and the abode of the gods (22,000 feet); and from the south of which the Satlej tributary also rises. The Indus has a course to the Arabian Sea of 1802 miles, and drains a basin estimated at 372,700 square miles. From Kailas to Atak in the Panjab is 860 miles, and thence to the sea through Sind is 942 miles. After flowing 160 miles from its source it receives the Ghar River on the right; enters Kashmeer, where it is crossed by the Karakoram trade-route; passes Leh north-west at a level of 11,728 feet, its source being 16,000 feet, and Skardoh in Little Tibet, where at 14,000 feet in depth it sweeps through a famous gorge; suddenly turns southwards, receiving the Gilgeet; rolls for 120 miles through the wilds of Kohistan to the Panjab border near Derbend, at the base of the Mahaban Mountain; and after receiving the Kabul River from the north, reaches Atak, which gives it a name. Here, at 13 miles an hour in the hot season, it flies past the gloomy slate rocks, Jelalia and Kemalia, in a narrow bed crossed by every invader, then opens out into a blue lake like that at Bagh Nilab, and skirts the Sulaiman, falling 20 feet per mile above Atak, 20 inches in the 110 miles from Atak to Kalabagh, and 8 inches in the 350 miles thence to Mithankot. Just above that place it receives the **Panjnad** ("five rivers"), containing the accumulated waters of the **Jhelam, Chenab, Ravi, Beas,** and **Satlej,** which give the Panjab its name. These are described under that Province. The completed Indus, below the Panjnad junction, has a breadth of from 2000 yards to several miles, according to the season. Hence from Kashmor to the sea it has formed Sind, as the Nile has produced Lower Egypt. For 580 miles it pursues a south-westerly course through Sind, and empties itself into the Arabian Sea by many changing mouths over a line of coast 120 miles in extent. The Kori or most southerly mouth separates Sind from Kach; the Hajamrao mouth is now the largest and most navigable, having gradually superseded the Khedewari.

§ 11. THE WEST PENINSULAR RIVERS.—The **Narbada** (Narmada), separating Hindustan proper from the Dekhan, flows between the Vindhya on the north and the Satpoora on the south for 801 miles, from Amarkantak Hill (3400 feet) in Rewah, the sacred name of the river, to the Gulf of Kambay, 30 miles below the city of Broach. It drains a basin of 36,400 square miles, and its maximum flood discharge is 2½ millions of cubic feet per second. Three miles from its source the river tumbles 70 feet over a basaltic cliff in the Kapila-dhara Falls, and again in the Dood-dhara ("milk stream") Fall. Winding westwards through the Mandla district of the Central Province it forms reaches or pools, termed "dohs," the finest of which is between the ruined palace of Ramnagar and Mandla town. Below this, nine miles south of Jabalpoor, the river has a fall of 30 feet, known as the Dhooan-dhara ("misty shoot") into the deep-cut channel, where it rolls between walls of marble rising from 50 to 80 feet, famous as the Marble Rocks. After passing through cotton plains, and the forest jungles of Nimar, surrounding the sacred island of Omkar Mandhata and leaving the shrines of Maheshwar and the ruins of Mandu behind, the river glides off the tableland where the Vindhya and Satpoora ranges almost meet and drops towards the rich plains of Goojarat, round Turan Mal Hill with its fine lake and through the gorge of the Haran Pal ("deer's leap"). After this the main barrier occurs, with the Makrai whirlpool, before the river enters on the plain of Broach, where it becomes a broad muddy stream like the Hoogli. The Narbada, more sacred in some Hindoo eyes than the Ganges, the merit of which is to be transferred to it in 1895, is frequented by pilgrims, who spend from one to two years in walking from the sea up one bank to the source and returning by the other bank. The drainage of the Vindhya plateau being to the north, to the Ganges valley, the Narbada is fed chiefly from the south. Its chief affluents on the left bank are the Makrar, Chakrar, Kharmer, Burhner, Banjar opposite Mandla, Teemar, Sonér between Jabalpoor and Narsingpoor, Sher Shakar, Doodhi, Korami, Machna, Tawa, Ganjal, Ajnal, Deeb, and Gohi. On the right bank the principal affluents are the Balai, Hingna, Gaur east of Jabalpoor, Hiran, Jamner, Karan, Hatni, and Aurim in Rewa Kantha. The Narbada drains but neither irrigates nor is navigable above the plains of Broach, where it widens out to two miles in breadth, and is spanned by the Bombay and Baroda Railway. The **Tapti** flows west from Multai in the Bétool district of the Central Province for 460 miles to the Arabian Sea beyond Surat, at the once famous port of Suwali. It drains 30,000 square miles, and its hourly discharge varies from 120,000,000 cubic yards in flood to 25,000 in the driest season. On its banks are 108 shrines (tirths), of which Bodhan, 15 miles east of Surat, is most frequented. On leaving the open tract of Bétool the river plunges into a gorge of the Satpoora, formed by the Chikulda and the Kalibheet spurs. Just above Boorhanpoor the valley opens out into the plateau of Khandesh, whence it begins to descend to the plain of Goojarat, and passes through the Dang forests into the rich level of Surat, where it becomes a tidal river for 32 miles. In Khandesh it receives, on the left bank, the Poorna, Waghar, Gorna, Bori, Panjhra, and Siva; on the right bank, the smaller Suki, Aver, Arunawati, Gomai, and Walha. In Surat it receives the Wareli from the western spurs of the Rajpeepla hills. Forty miles from its mouth are the Waghecha rapids, where the trap rock forms several islands. The river is not used for irrigation, nor for navigation above tidal limits.

§ 12. THE EAST PENINSULAR RIVERS.—The **Mahanadi** ("great river") rises 25 miles south of Raipoor, where the hills divide the southern plateau of Chateesgarh from Bastar State, and flows for 520 miles northwards through the Central Province, and eastwards through the Eastern Ghats and Orissa to the Bay of Bengal at False Point. With a drainage basin of 43,800 square miles, this river has the enormous discharge of 1,800,000 cubic feet per second in flood, when its depth is increased by 32 feet; in the hot season its discharge falls to 1125 feet. The canal system by which the water is utilised is described under Orissa. On reaching Seorinarain, the stream—being fed by the Seonath, Jouk, and Hasdu—becomes a river, and from Malhar, where it turns eastwards, is navigable by boats. It is joined by the Mand and Kelu during the next 60 miles, when, at Padmapoor, it turns southwards, receives the Ib from the north-east, struggles past Sambalpoor through masses of rocks, is joined by the Tel at Sonpoor, thence proceeds eastwards through rocks to Dholpoor, and rolls along unrestrained to the Eastern Ghats, which it pierces by a gorge 40 miles long, equal in beauty to that of the Godavari. It finally pours down on the Orissa delta, which it forms, through the narrow gorge of Naraj, 7 miles west of Cuttak town. From the southern bank it throws off the Katjoori, which divides into branches, and the Paika; from its northern bank it sends off the Borapat and the Chitartala, while the main river reaches the Bengal coast at False Point.

The **Godavari** (Goda = the deity) crosses nearly the whole peninsula in a length of 898 miles south-east from Trimbak in Nasik, which is only 50 miles from the Indian Ocean. It has a catchment basin of 112,200 square miles. On leaving Nasik district this noble river forms the boundary between Ahmednagar district and Haidarabad State, receives the Pranheeta near Sironcha, where it enters the Central Province, which it divides from Haidarabad; while it is fed on the left by the Indravati, Tal, and Savari. At the confluence with the last, the passage through the Eastern Ghats gives it the scenery which has caused it to be compared to the Rhine. Imprisoned for 20 miles between hills, the water flows in a deep and narrow channel, with a current occasionally of boiling whirlpools. On emerging from the hills it passes Rajamahendri a placid but mighty stream; reaches the head of the delta at Dowlaisharam, where a great current throws off numerous irrigation channels, and falls into the Bay of Bengal by the three principal mouths of Gautami Godavari at Point Koringa near Coconada port, Vainateyan Godavari, and Vashishta Godavari, the most southern, which debouches at Point Narsapoor. Three-quarters of a million sterling has been vainly spent to open the upper navigation by removing or making canals round the three great barriers of rock at Doomagoodiem, 115 miles above Rajamahendri; 68 miles higher up, below the confluence of the Pranheeta; and on the Wardha, 75 miles above that. The **Kistna** or Krishna, from Mahableshwar, 40 miles east of the Arabian Sea, crosses the peninsula eastwards for 800 miles to the Bay of Bengal. Including its great tributaries, the Bheema and Toonga-bhadra, it drains an area of 94,500 square miles. From its source (4500 feet) it rapidly flows southwards and then eastwards, receiving the Yerla, Warna, Idgarga, Ghatprabha, and Malprabha, when it enters Haidarabad State, is joined by the Bheema from Ahmednagar and Poona, and the Toonga-bhadra from Mysore, Bellary, and Karnool; forms the boundary between Haidarabad and Madras, and from the Eastern Ghats at Bezwara turns southwards for 80 miles through the Kistna district, which it has formed and irrigates, and reaches the Bay of Bengal by two mouths, Masulipatam being the chief port. The **Kavari** (Cauvery), rising farther south in Coorg, crosses the peninsula eastwards for 475 miles, draining an area of 28,000 square miles, and reaches the Bay of Bengal by two mouths in Tanjore district. From Coorg it enters Mysore State by a narrow gorge, where it is tapped by twelve canals, forms the islands of Seringapatam and Shivasamoodram with famous falls, passes into Madras between Coimbatore and Salem, sweeps past Trichinopoly rock and at the island of Srirangam breaks into streams which enclose the fertile delta of Tanjore—the Coleroon on the north and the main river on the south. Negapatam and the French Karikal are roadsteads off the delta. From Srirangam, where the flood discharge is 472,000 cubic feet a second, a Hindoo dam made in the 4th century A.D. irrigated the country. Sir A. Cotton made a similar weir across the Coleroon, so that the two rivers irrigate 835,000 acres.

§ 13. WATERFALLS.—The great rivers of India are remarkable for falls of grandeur and beauty, either as they issue from the mountain ranges in which they rise, or are precipitated from the edge of the plateaux on the plains below. The most gigantic are the gorges of the Indus and the Satlej in the Himalaya; the most beautiful, those of the Mahanadi and Godavari as they pierce the Eastern Ghats. Of waterfalls, popularly so called, the most remarkable is the *Jog* or Four Falls of **Gersoppa**, formed by the **Sharávati River** ("arrow born"), as it hurls itself down the western face of the Mysore plateau, a sheer descent of 960 feet, on its way to the Arabian Sea at Honavar in North Kanara district, 30 miles distant. Next in interest are the **Shivasamoodram Falls of the Kavari** ("sea of Shiva"), by which the river descends 300 feet, passing from Mysore State to Coimbatore district. The **Gokak Falls** of the **Ghatprabha River**, as it hurries through a picturesque gorge from its source in the Gokak flank of the Western Ghats in Belgaum district on to the plateau of the Dekhan to join the Kistna, present the spectacle of 100,000 cubic feet of water (in July) precipitated 178 feet into the fissure below, with a thundering sound heard several miles off. The **Paikára** river falls over the edge of the Neelgiri hills. The **Falls of the Yena**, familiar to visitors of the Mahableshwar sanitarium in the Western Ghats, descend 500 feet over a steep cliff, forming a scene of great beauty. The **Mawsmai**, at Cherrapoonjee, has a sheer fall of 1800 feet. The **S. Tons** falls 200 feet near Chacbai in Boondelkhand. As the mountainous districts and upper waters of the rivers of India come to be opened up, almost every elevated district will be found to reveal scenery worthy of permanent description.

§ 14. LAKES (*Tal*) are few in India proper, even in the Indian Himalaya, in comparison with the area. But they are numerous and large in the Tibeto-Himalaya, and in Tibet, north of the 30th parallel of latitude and between the 82d and 92d meridians east, where the tableland between the Indian and Toorkish Watersheds has no escape, yet known, for its waters. **Manasaraur** (15,000 feet), the source of the Satlej, and **Rakhas Tal** (Ravana-hrada) lie near the Kailas peak, from which the Indus and the Brahmapootra drain the waters of the Northern Himalaya into the Arabian Sea and the Bay of Bengal respectively. On the Pamir Steppe, or "roof of the world," is the great Pamir Lake, named **Victoria** (13,900 feet) by Captain Wood, who in 1838 found it 14 miles long and 1 broad, and more accurately described by Captain Trotter in 1874. The Oxus issues from its western end, there draining the whole Pamir; the Aksu, from the **Little Pamir Lake**, receives the eastern drainage. **Pangkong** (13,936 feet), south-east of the Karakoram division of the Himalaya, is a series of saline lakes extending for 100 miles; the lowest is 40 miles long. Sixty miles east of Manasaraur, from the Mariam-la or pass, where the comparatively low saddle which separates the valley of the Satlej from that of the Brahmapootra connects the Northern and Central Himalaya, native explorers sent by the Imperial Survey have recently visited and partially described the following:—**Palti**, in the east of the central range first visited by Manning in 1811, the remarkable ring-lake nearly encircling a great central island, separated from the upper Brahmapootra valley by the Khamba-la spur; **Chonito-dong**, farther west and north of the Arun river basin, a lake about 20 miles long and 16 broad (14,700 feet altitude); **Dalgu-chu** (15,000 feet), seen but not visited by the native surveyors, the source of the Dingri River; **Tengri-nor**, near Lhasa, reached by the native surveyor in 1872 by crossing the Khamba-la Pass, 60 miles long by from 16 to 25 broad, with large islands, and at

15,200 feet level; farther north is **Bul-cho**, 6 miles long by 5 broad, where borax is found; also **Koko-nor** ("blue sea").

In the Southern Himalaya, the lakes best known are those of Kashmeer, especially **Sreenagar**, **Manasbal**, the most beautiful, and **Woolar**, the largest; the **Konsa Nag** on the top of the Peer Panjal range; **Naini Tal**, the chief sanitarium of the North-Western Province; and the **Six Lakes of Sikkim** on the top of a range (from 12,000 to 15,000 feet), with Chumalhari's snowy cone behind. Almost every district in well-watered Provinces like Bengal has its lake-swamps or *jheels*, and those in more hilly tracts, their artificial lakes (*talao*) and vast tanks or reservoirs made by embanking a ravine. Many of these are of exquisite beauty, and all are the sources of irrigation and preservation against drought. Of salt lakes the most remarkable are **Sambhar** in Rajpootana and **Lonar** in Berar. On Mount Aboo sanitarium is the **Nakhi Talao**, or gem lake; at the deserted capital of the same name is the little **Amber Lake**. In **Ahmedabad** the **Nal** covers 49 square miles with brackish water. In Bombay the **Rann of Kach** is an inland lake of 8000 square miles in the dry season, and an arm of the sea during the rainy season, when it unites the Gulfs of Kach and Kambay. Near Sehwan, on the right bank of the Indus, is the **Manchar Lake**, which covers 160 square miles in the season of inundation. In British Burma are four lakes or lagoons—**Kandangyee** ("royal lake") near Rangoon, **Moo** in Henzada district, **Lahgyin**, and **Bassein**. Besides these, **Backwaters**, or salt lakes formed by sand-spits, run along large portions of the two coasts. On the east are the **Chilka**, **Kolar**, and **Pulikat Lakes**; on the west, running up from Cape Comorin, are the Travankor, Cochin, and Malabar backwaters. Many of these are connected by canals, and form valuable lines of communication, while their harbours are the centres of a prosperous fishing population.

§ 15. CANALS.—Since 1823, and especially since the great north-west famine of 1833, the Government of India has spent upwards of twenty millions sterling on canals, chiefly for irrigation, and partly for navigation, which are officially estimated to yield now about 5½ per cent a year on the outlay, in the proportion of £900,000 from "productive" works for which the capital was borrowed, and £200,000 on former works constructed from ordinary revenue. In Bengal and Bombay Provinces the irrigation works, especially the Orissa and Son Canals, cause a heavy loss. In the North-Western, Panjab, and Madras Provinces, the canals are estimated to yield an annual surplus of £150,000 above 4½ per cent. The most profitable works are those in Madras and the North-West, first constructed by the old native rulers, and opened out and improved by British engineers. The Government's first enterprise was in 1823, when it restored the **Firoz** and **Delhi** canals, and afterwards developed the **Western** and **Eastern Jumna Canals**. In 1836, the greatest of all irrigation works, the **Great Ganges Canal**, was surveyed, in 1848 was begun, and in 1854 was opened by Lord Dalhousie, from Hardwar at the foot of the Siwaliks to Cawnpoor. Since that time it has been largely improved and extended, so that it has protected an extensive area from successive dearths like that of 1861, and has sent food to other tracts stricken with drought. All the principal irrigation channels and reservoirs will be found described under their respective Provinces, from the **Son** and **Mahanadi** in the Behar and Orissa divisions of Bengal; from the **Satlej** at Roopar, the **Ravi** or **Bari Doab** at Madhoopoor, and the **Sirhind Canal** just opened, with a navigable length of 178 miles, and 533 with branches, in the Panjab; from the **Indus** in Sind; from the **Narbada** and **Tapti** in Bombay; from the **Lower Godavari**, **Kistna**, **Pennar**, **Kavari**, and **Coleroon** in Madras; from the **Toongha-bhadra** and **Upper Tapti** and **Kistna** in the Dekhan plateau. The Irrigation Department maintains many thousand miles of embankments, especially along the lower course of the Bengal and Burma rivers, to protect the densely-peopled and cultivated tracts from inundation. The total canal mileage of India is not under 13,000, besides a vast network of distributing channels. Of 200 millions of acres usually under cultivation in India, 30 millions are protected by irrigation—8 millions from canals and reservoirs, 12 millions from wells, and the residue from less permanent sources.

§ 16. FORESTS.—In 1846 the first attempt at forest conservancy was made in Bombay, to secure supplies of Malabar teak for the dockyard. In 1856 Dr. Cleghorn organised forest administration in Madras, and Dr. Brandis in the recently-conquered Pegu. In 1864 the success of their efforts led to the formation by the Government of India of a Forest Department under an Inspector-General. A series of Forest Acts, Regulations and Rules, from 1865 to 1878, has given India as perfect a system of forestry as any in Europe, by which 16,000 (to rise to 20,000) square miles—area of Switzerland—excluding the Native States, and Madras and Bombay, are strictly reserved and demarcated, at an annual cost to the State of nearly half a million sterling, but yielding a net surplus revenue of above a quarter of a million. **Bombay** has 7771 miles of reserved forests, and **Madras** has 806. In the Provinces, as well as in the States, there is, besides, a very large extent of private forest. Of **Assam** only 6750 square miles are under cultivation; there are 8000 square miles of State forests, of which 2015 have been reserved and another 1000 will yet be demarcated. But in the one district of **Goalpara** the large native landholders own 520 square miles of forests, while in the chief tea-producing districts of **Cachar, Seebsagar,** and **Lakhimpoor,** the European tea-planters hold 550 square miles of forest land. In **British Burma** only 5500 are cultivated out of 87,220 square miles. The rest is largely forest and grass land, of which 1600 has been demarcated, and 2000 more will be reserved. In the other Provinces the forest area is less, but there is great variety in their conditions. The area of reserved forests in **Bengal Province** is above 3000 square miles; in the **North-Western Province** with **Oudh,** 3300; in the **Panjab,** above 800; in the **Central Province,** 2600; in **Coorg,** 230; in **Ajmer,** 101; in **Berar,** 1400; and in **Mysore State,** 454. In India the aim and the results of forest conservancy are not only climatic and commercial, but to mitigate the disastrous effects of seasons of drought and famine. Roads and railways facilitate the removal of grain, but cattle-fodder cannot be so distributed to the same extent; it must either be produced on the spot, or the cattle must be driven where it is available. To meet the want of grass, and the consequent mortality among cattle which attends all famines, is a chief object of the Forest Department in planting 100 square miles of the bare hills of Ajmer-Merwara, *e.g.*, with the result of improving the water-supply in tanks and wells. Village grass-preserves are an old Hindoo institution, especially in **Rajpootana States,** like Bhartpoor, Kishengarh, and Mewar, where the cattle were saved in the famine of 1867-8, while those of Ajmer died. The department consists of 93 (to rise to 100) conservators, and 97 native rangers (to rise to 600), trained in the Forest School at Dehra Doon.

§ 17. Trees of India.—There are about 2000 species of indigenous trees in India; there are 40 in Great Britain. Those are most important which are found in large quantities, and the timber of which is most durable in a tropical climate. Of these Dr. Brandis, the first Inspector-General, names the following:—

(*a*) The Deodar (*Cedrus deodara*), found on the North-West Himalaya, between 6000 and 9500 feet, mixed with other pines and several species of oaks (*b*) The Sissoo (*Dalbergia sissoo*), a gregarious tree, found along the rivers which issue from the Himalaya, fringing their banks and extending far up into the hills to 3000 feet, and forming large forests along the rivers outside the hills. It is one of the best woods in India, of a rich brown colour, strong, durable, useful for furniture, carriage-building, and other purposes.

(*c*) The Khair (*Acacia catechu*), a gregarious and most useful tree, of very wide distribution, common in Northern India, often associated with sissoo in the valleys of the rivers which issue from the Himalaya, and also found in the drier districts of British Burma, both on low ground and on the hills. The red heart-wood is extremely durable, and is used for house-posts and building generally. The heart-wood is also used on a very large scale for the manufacture of Cutch or Catechu, a most valuable tanning material, which is an extract made by simmering chips of the wood in water, and by boiling down the dark-coloured fluid into a hard shining black mass, the Catechu of commerce.

(*d*) The Sal (*Shorea robusta*), a remarkably gregarious tree, in leaf nearly throughout the year, with great powers of reproduction. The heart-wood is hard, heavy, and durable; it is used extensively for building and for railway-sleepers throughout Northern and a great part of Central India. The sal forms extensive forests, almost pure, both at the foot of the Himalaya and on the hills of Central India, stretching from the Ganges in Bengal to the sandstone hills of Pachmarhi in the Central Province.

(*e*) The Teak (*Tectona grandis*), a deciduous tree, with large rough leaves, attaining a great size. This, the most important of the Indian timber trees, is found in mixed forests, associated with bamboos and a great variety of other trees, over the whole of Southern India and in Burma, extending in Central India and in the interior of the Trans-Gangetic Peninsula to north latitude 26°. The timber of teak is prized more in India than that of any other trees, and forms an important article of export to Europe and America from the Burma ports.

(*f*) The Blackwood (*Dalbergia latifolia*), an evergreen tree, with handsome dark-coloured heart-wood, much prized for furniture, is found in mixed forests all along the Western Ghats, where it attains a large size. The tree is also found in other parts of India, but does not there attain any large size. The blackwood or rosewood belongs to the same genus as the sissoo of Northern India, but its wood is darker coloured and more heavy.

(*g*) The Babool or Kikar (*Acacia Arabica*), a gregarious tree, with a hard and heavy heart-wood, which forms extensive forests along the Indus in Sind, where the life of the tree is maintained in an arid climate by the annual overflow of the river. It also forms extensive forests along the rivers and on stretches of low land in the dry region of the Dekhan, and is extensively cultivated in many districts of India, extending north to the foot of the Himalaya in the Panjab.

(*h*) The Toon (*Cedrela Toona*), a fast-growing tree, with bushy foliage and light red-coloured wood, somewhat resembling mahogany, nowhere gregarious, but found scattered on rich moist soil in the outer valleys of the North-West Himalaya and in Burma.

(*i*) The India-Rubber (*Ficus elastica*), a huge evergreen tree of the fig tribe, with thick leathery shining leaves, which sends numerous aërial roots down to the ground from its branches. The rubber or caoutchouc is a white milk which exudes from cuts made in the stem and roots. The tree is indigenous in the moist forests of Assam and Eastern Bengal, but does not extend south further than 24° north latitude.

(*k*) The Sandal (*Santalum album*), a small evergreen tree, with elegant hanging branches and small black berries, valuable on account of the exceedingly fragrant heart-wood, which is used for carving and incense, and is largely exported to China. The tree grows in the drier regions of Southern India, generally in open forests or on waste lands, and commonly in hedge-rows and on fields. Its chief *habitat* is Mysore State and the adjoining Madras districts, where it is held to be a royal tree, which may be cut only by permission of Government.

Teak is planted on a large scale in Burma, where a plan has been followed with great success, known under the name of *toungya* teak plantations. The Karengs and other tribes practise a shifting kind of cultivation, by cutting and burning the forest, and raising one or two crops in the ashes. On the clearances thus made, and together with the rice which is the chief crop raised, the teak seed is sown, and the result is a complete crop of that valuable tree, provided the bamboos, the coppice-shoots of other trees, grass, and herbs are cleared sufficiently. For this is the great difficulty in all sowing and planting operations in the moister and tropical parts of India, that the growth of bamboos and other trees is so luxuriant that the teak or other kinds planted get choked. On the system of these *toungya* plantations, a total area of 2515 acres had been planted up to the 1st April 1880, at a cost, on an average, of Rs. 9·14, or about 18 shillings an acre; and the plantations on this system are now being extended annually on a large scale in the forests of British Burma. Extensive plantations of india-rubber have been made in Assam. Broad lines are cleared through the forest, and the seedlings are planted out on raised mounds of earth. This plan has succeeded admirably.

Foreign trees.—Some trees of Southern Europe, such as the sweet chestnut, the Spanish olive and the Carob (*Ceratonia siliqua*), have been introduced in Northern India; and of these, the sweet chestnut has succeeded remarkably well in certain situations in the North-West Himalaya. From South America the *Pithecolobium Saman* has lately been introduced, with great success, in the tropical provinces of India, and particularly in the moister districts, its extreme rapidity of growth being its chief recommendation. The mahogany has been brought from the West Indies, and is cultivated in the Bengal and Burma forests, where it thrives well. The mahogany grown near Calcutta yields timber equal to that of the American tree. Several of the South American caoutchouc trees are also cultivated by way of experiment in Malabar and the southern districts of Burma, where the climate is favourable. Of the different species of cinchona extensive plantations have been made on the Neelgiris and in Sikkim. Of fruit trees a large number have come from America, such as the guava and custard apple. From Africa the Baobab (*Adamsonia digitata*) is an old introduction, and large specimens of this remarkable tree are found here and there near villages and Muhammadan shrines. The Tamarind tree (*Tamarindus Indica*), which is commonly cultivated on account of its fruit, is also probably from Africa. Of forest trees, the most important introductions have been made from Australia. Forests raised by planting, within the last thirty years, of the *Eucalyptus globulus* or Blue Gum, cover large areas on the Neelgiris, and several species of *Acacia* also have been extensively planted. Other species of *Eucalyptus* have been found to thrive in the plains of Northern India and in the North-West Himalaya. Some of the more important articles produced are these:—*Caoutchouc*, from the *Ficus elastica; Shell-lac* and *Lac-dye*, made by the lac insect, which lives on a great variety of trees, and which is propagated artificially on a large scale in certain districts of the Central Province; *Sandalwood; Cutch*, the extract made from the heart-wood of *Acacia catechu;* and *Myrobalans*, the dried fruit of several species of *Terminalia*, particularly of *Terminalia chebula*, a most valuable article for tanning, large quantities of which are exported to Europe and America.

§ 18. RAILWAYS.—In thirty years, since the first sod of an Indian railway was cut, the total mileage has risen to about 10,000, and other 2000 miles are under survey or construction. Lord Dalhousie planned the trunk system of strategic and commercial lines to connect Calcutta with Bombay and Lahore, Bombay with Madras, and Madras with the Malabar coast by means of companies to whom 5 per cent interest was guaranteed. On the approaching completion of these main lines, which are on the 5½ feet gauge, the Government itself entered on the construction of feeders and extensions on the narrow (metre) gauge, and exercised its right of purchasing the guaranteed East Indian line, which has been most profitably worked as a State Railway since 1880. Of the projected lines the most important is one of 366 miles to connect the East Indian line at Seetarampoor coal-fields, and pass through Chutia Nagpoor by Sambalpoor and the Mahanadi valley to the Chateesgarh line, so as to give Calcutta the shortest and most direct communication possible with Bombay by Nagpoor. This line may also be continued east to the Madras port of Bimlipatam, down the Eastern Ghats. The capital outlay to the beginning of 1882-83 was £134,200,581. In 1881 the net revenue amounted to £6,952,714, or £5 : 3s. per cent, although many of the lines were immature. The effect is seen on the foreign trade, which has risen from an average of £11,000,000 imports before 1854 to £52,000,000, and from £19,000,000 exports to £70,000,000. Since 1868 the weight of goods has increased from 3,000,000 tons to 13,211,082, and the number of passengers, chiefly third class, from 16,000,000 to 52,271,133 in 1881. Estimating the cost of transport by rail at one-fourth of that by cart, it is calculated that India saves £45,000,000 a year. The military value of the lines may be imagined, now that Peshawar is connected with Calcutta, and Sibi (for Quetta and Kandahar) with Karachi and the whole Sind and Panjab base. The progress of railway construction is thus seen :—

1871.	1st Jan. 1882.	Railways.	Total Mileage sanctioned
Miles.	Miles.	**Guaranteed.**	Miles.
1,503¼	—	East Indian	—
157	158¾	Eastern Bengal . . .	158¾
42	546¾	Oudh and Rohilkand . . .	686½
553¾ 113	553¾ 109¾	Sind, Panjab and Delhi . .	663
804¼	860⅛	Madras	860⅛
167 18¾	653½	South Indian	653½
1,273½	1,288	Great Indian Peninsula . .	1,288
934¼	421½	Bombay, Baroda and Central India .	421½
5,008¾	4,592¼	Total Guaranteed Railways .	4,833½
		State and Assisted.	
—	1,504¼	East Indian	1,510⅛
28	28	Calcutta and South-Eastern . .	56⅛
27¼	27¼	Nalhati	27¼
—	266½	Northern Bengal	300
—	48¾	Darjeeling—Himalaya . .	48¾
—	85	Tirhoot	249
—	57	Patna—Gaya	147
—	354¾	Panjab Northern . . .	425⅛
—	653	Indus Valley and Kandahar . .	654⅛
—	53	Muttra—Hathras—Achnera . .	53
—	86	Cawnpoor and Farukhabad . .	196
—	12	Dildarnargar—Ghazipoor . .	12
—	1,115¾	Rajpootana—Mālwa . . .	1,221¼
—	74¾	Sindia	74¾
—	192½	Bhaunagar—Gondal . . .	192½
—	22½	Patri	22½
—	60¼	Gaekwar of Baroda's . . .	60¼
8	8	Khamgaon	8
6	6	Amraoti	6
—	46½	Wardha Coal	46½
—	121	Nizam's	121
—	145¾	Dhond—Mammad . . .	145¾
—	98	Nagpoor and Chateesghar . .	263¾
—	161	Rangoon and Irawadi Valley . .	208
—	—	Rangoon and Tsit-toung Valley .	163½
—	58	Mysore	85¾
—	—	Bhopal	62
—	—	Amritsar—Pathankot . . .	65
—	—	Assam, Bengal Central, Baidyanath—Deogarh, Bareilly—Ranibagh, and Neelgiri	294
69¼	5,283	Total State Railways . .	7,067¾
5,077½	9,875¼	Total Guaranteed and State Railways	11,901¼

§ 19. HARBOURS.—The coast of India proper extends from **Ras Muari** or **Cape Monze**, between Baloochistan and Sind, to **Point Victoria** south of Tenasserim, 9185 miles, including the coast-line of islands. But for all commercial and political purposes the coast of Western and Southern Asia, influenced by India, extends from Port Said on the Mediterranean to Singapore. Historically, Egypt was within the limits of the East India Company on the north-west, as Cape Town was on the south-west, places to which its troops were sent, and at which its officials enjoyed Indian pay and allowances. The construction and the political history of the Suez Canal following the Mutiny of 1857, and succeeded by the War of September 1882, have strengthened the connection. We proceed to give in order all the harbours and roadsteads from Port Said to Singapore touched at by regular steamers along the west and south coasts of Asia.

No.	Harbours.	Miles.
	Port Said to—	
1.	Suez	88
2.	Jeddah	470
3.	Hodeida	230
4.	Aden	280
5.	Makulla	1200
6.	Karachi	636
7.	Muscat	450
8.	Bunder Abbas	250
9.	Linga	105
10.	Bushire	315
11.	Basrah	205
12.	Baghdad	500
	Coast of India and Ceylon.	
	Karachi to—	
13.	Bombay	500
14.	Ratnagiri	123
15.	Vingorla	76
16.	Goa	28
17.	Karwar	48
18.	Mangalore	132
19.	Cannanore	77
20.	Telicheri	13
21.	Waddagiri	13
22.	Calicut	26
23.	Beypoor	11
24.	Narakal	80
25.	Cochin	10
26.	Alleppi	34
27.	Colachel (*Cape Comorin*)	98
28.	Tuticorin	106
29.	Colombo	149
30.	Galle	69
31.	Negapatam	440
32.	Cuddalore	58
33.	Pondicheri	17
34.	Madras	79
35.	Yperpollium	194
36.	Masulipatam	80
37.	Coconada	100
38.	Vizagapatam	74
39.	Bimlipatam	17
40.	Gopalpoor (also Barwa)	112
41.	Ganjam	15
42.	Pooree	51
43.	False Point (also Chandbali)	80
44.	Calcutta	216
	Total, Bombay to Calcutta	2626
	Calcutta to—	
45.	Chittagong	376
46.	Akyab	190
47.	Kyouk Phyoo	76
48.	Sandoway	119
49.	Bassein	247
50.	Rangoon	252
51.	Maulmein	147
52.	Tavoy	207
53.	Mergui	90
54.	*Pakchan*	274
55.	Kopah	85
56.	Junkseylon	161
57.	Penang	200
58.	Malacca	265
59.	Singapore	130

From London to Calcutta, by Gibraltar, Malta, and the Canal, is 8059 miles; from London to Karachi is 6283 miles, to Bombay, 6274; from London to Brisbane, the capital of Queensland, by Batavia, is 12,811 miles. From Port Said, which is 3215 miles from London, the distance to Calcutta, touching at Suez (*Arab.* Siwaz = Sebaste), Aden, and Colombo only, is 4879 miles; to Singapore, 5123.

§ 20. TIDES.—Since 1876 the Imperial Survey of India has made a systematic record of tidal phenomena on the Indian coasts by means of self-registering tide-gauges, aneroid barometers, and anemometers, at Aden, Karachi, Bombay, Karwar, Beypoor, Paumban, Madras, Vizagapatam, False Point, Rangoon, Elephant Point, Amherst, Maulmein, and Port Blair; at Bhaunagar and Negapatam; and at Kidderpoor, Diamond Harbour, and Dublat on Sagar Island in the Hoogli River. The India Office tide-predicting machine, from the designs of Sir William Thomson, is employed in determining predictions of future tides from the constants calculated from the registration of past tides extending over twenty-five years. By spirit-levelling operations over a line of 730 miles in length, connecting the tidal stations at Madras and Bombay, the mean sea-level has been determined. The officially published tide tables of 1882 embrace fifteen ports. The tidal wave strikes Western India from the west at right angles to the mean direction of the shore line, so that there is very little difference in the times of high water along the whole length of coast except at such indentations as the Gulfs of Kambay and Kach.

§ 21. LIGHTHOUSES.—The Marine Survey, since the abolition of the Indian Navy, has charge of the lighthouses and light-vessels of British India. Including those on the Red Sea and coast of Arabia, there are more than a hundred from Suez to Singapore.

[TABLES.

RED SEA.

No.	Name of light.	Location.	Lat. N.	Long. E.
1	Suez . . .	North shore of Suez Bay, N.N.W. ¼ W., 1¾ mile from south dock head, Port Ibrahim.	29° 57′ 35″	32° 32′ 10″
1a	Suez . . .	Light-vessel off Newport Rock.	29 53 0	32 32 45
2	Zafarana . .	On the Point . .	29 6 29	32 39 40
3	Ras Gharib .	On the Cape . .	28 20 52	33 6 30
4	Ashrafi . .	N.E. part of Ashrafi Reef, Jubal Strait.	27 47 21	33 42 27
5	The Brothers .	On North Island .	26 18 50	34 50 30
6	Dædalus Shoal .	On Shoal, 200 yards within S.E. extreme.	24 55 30	35 51 30
7	Perim Island .	Half a mile S.W. of Obstruction Point.	12 38 59	43 25 6

SOUTH COAST OF ARABIA, AND GULF OF ADEN.

No.	Name of light.	Location.	Lat. N.	Long. E.
8	Aden . .	Ras Marshigh, S.E. part of Cape.	12 44 50	45 2 35
9	Aden . .	Light-vessel, south side of channel, inner harbour, moored in 18 feet.	12 46 50	44 57 45
9a	Berbereh . .	South shore of port near high-water mark.	10 25 0	44 59 30

INDIA, WEST COAST—BOMBAY PROVINCE.

No.	Name of light.	Location.	Lat. N.	Long. E.
10	Karachi (Indus River)	Adjoining S.W. bastion of Manora Fort; W. side of entrance.	24 47 21	66 58 15
	Gulf of Kach—			
11	Mandvee .	S.W. bastion of Fort	22 49 41	69 20 19
11a	Toona . .	At the edge of the mangrove swamp, south of Tekra Island.	22 55 30	70 7 5
11b	Roji . .	On Roji temple, N.E. part of Roji Island, at mouth of Nowanaga Creek.	22 32 50	70 1 30
12	Beyt . .	The highest, and nearly the central, part of Sainia Island.	22 29 0	69 4 30

INDIA, WEST COAST—BOMBAY PROVINCE (*continued*).

No.	Name of light.	Location.	Lat. N.	Long. E.
13	Dwarka . .	On the cliffs of the mainland, west of the town, and 350 feet within the high-water line.	22° 14′ 0″	68° 57′ 0″
14	Porebandar .	On a tower at the water gate of the town wall.	21 37 10	69 35 0
15	Mangarol . .	On the highest square house, 400 yards from landing place.	21 6 0	70 6 30
16	Verawal . .	On pier head, west side of harbour.	20 53 30	70 22 0
	Gulf of Kambay—			
17	Jafrabad .	Mouth of creek, south side.	20 51 30	71 23 30
18	Mowa . .	On the terrace roofing of the light-keeper's residence, situated on a prominent cliff near the entrance of Mowa Creek.	21 2 21	71 49 30
18a	Goapnath .	On a hillock 240 yards inshore of Goapnath Point.	21 11 35	72 6 0
19	Perim . .	On the ruins of an old bastion on the island.	21 35 54	72 20 37
20	Gogo or Gogah	On the beach near the Custom House.	21 40 30	72 16 0
21	Bhawanagar .	On the south shore of the creek.	21 46 40	72 12 15
22	Khunbandar .	4½ miles S. by E. of the entrance to Dholera Creek, and westward of the *Bore Rocks*.	22 10 7	72 19 10
23	Deojugan or Tankari	North shore, mouth of Dhadhar River.	21 55 0	72 30 30
24	Bhagwadandi.	On the low point of Dandi Creek entrance.	21 19 42	72 35 0
25	Tapti . .	Near Vaux's tomb, on north shore, indicating entrance to the Surat River.	21 5 20	72 37 30
26	Bulsar . .	Mouth of the Bulsar or Oranga River.	20 37 30	72 53 0

INDIA, WEST COAST—BOMBAY PROVINCE (*continued*).

No.	Name of light.	Location.	Lat. N.	Long. E.
	Bombay—			
27	Outer light-vessel	In 6 fathoms 4½ miles S.S.W. from Kolaba Point.	18° 49′ 20″	72° 46′ 50″
28	Inner light-vessel	A quarter of a mile S.E. ½ E. from Sunk Rock.	18 53 12	72 49 40
29	Prongs . .	On S.W. portion of reef extending southward from Kolaba.	18 52 40	72 47 30
30	Dolphin .	On the rock . .	18 54 46	72 49 40
31	Tourbah .	Custom House Pier .	19 1 45	72 56 20
32	Kennery or Kinhari	On the highest part of the island.	18 42 8	72 48 17
33	Ratnagiri . .	On the south bastion and highest of the Fort.	16 59 10	73 15 50
34	Rajapur or Jaitapur	On the edge of the cliff at the south point of Rájapur Bay.	16 36 10	73 18 30
34a	Malwan .	Melundi Harbour. On the beach, 230 yards north of a white stone cross.	16 2 55	73 27 25
34b	Malwan .	Light-boat, to south-east of rock at entrance to the harbour.	...	...
35	Vingorla Rocks or Burnt Islands	On the summit of the outer or western-most rock.	15 53 16	73 26 45
36	Vingorla . .	On Vingorla Point, 1 mile west of the town.	15 51 14	73 36 22
37	Goa (Portuguese)	Aguada Fort, on hill above landing place, about a mile from outer port.	15 29 26	73 45 55
38	Oyster Rock or Carwar (Sedashigar Bay)	On the summit of the Oyster Rock.	14 49 25	74 2 50
39	Konay, near Beitkul Cove (Karwar Bay)	Exhibited from the Port Office.	14 48 20	74 6 40
40	Coompta . .	Conical Hill at mouth of creek, about 1½ mile from the town.	14 25 10	74 22 55

India, West Coast—Madras Province.

No.	Name of light.	Location.	Lat. N.	Long. E.
41	Mangalore . .	On a hill above the town, and near some high trees.	12° 52′ 17″	74° 50′ 8″
42	Cannanore . .	In the old fort, on red ground.	11 51 10	75 21 45
43	Telicheri . .	On the fort wall, near the beach.	11 44 50	75 28 30
44	Calicut . .	On the sandy beach.	11 15 5	75 45 35
45	Cochin . .	On a small mound which formed a bastion of the old fort, to the south of the harbour.	9 57 47	76 13 45
46	Alleppi . .	On the sandy beach, about one cable inland, close to the flagstaff.	9 30 0	76 19 0
47	Muttum (Cadiapatam)	Upon high red-coloured land, 300 yards from sea, here fringed with steep gray cliffs.	8 7 30	77 18 10
48	Cape Comorin .	On the Cape . .	8 4 0	77 32 39

Island of Ceylon.

No.	Name of light.	Location.	Lat. N.	Long. E.
49	Colombo . .	Clock-tower, centre of fort.	6 55 40	79 50 40
50	Point de Galle .	On S.W. bastion of fort. West side of harbour.	6 1 25	80 12 32
51	Great Bassas .	On the N.E. rock .	6 10 10	81 28 0
52	Little Bassas .	On reef . . .	6 22 55	81 43 12
52a	Batticaloa . .	On the flagstaff, near the mouth of Batticaloa Lake.	7 43 50	81 41 20
53	Trinkomalee .	On Foul Point extreme.	8 32 10	81 18 30
54	Trinkomalee .	On the summit of Round Island.	8 31 40	81 13 15

INDIA, EAST COAST—MADRAS PROVINCE.

No.	Name of light.	Location.	Lat. N.	Long. E.
55	Tuticorin . .	North extreme of Hare Island or Paundiantivo, 2½ miles east of Tuticorin.	8° 47′ 10″	78° 11′ 20″
56	Paumban Pass .	On a sand-hill; about one mile east of Northern Channel.	9 17 14	79 12 38
57	Calimere . .	On the point . .	10 17 55	79 51 30
58	Negapatam .	On bastion . . .	10 45 30	79 50 20
59	Karikal (French)	At the mouth of the River Arselaar.	10 55 0	79 50 35
60	Coleroon (Porto Novo)	......	...	...
61	Pondicheri (French)	In square, near the beach.	11 55 25	79 49 35
62	Madras . .	On esplanade, north of the fort.	13 5 11	80 16 51
63	Pulikat . .	Near the beach . .	13 25 15	80 19 6
64	Armegaon . .	Mainland, village of Moona or Moonapolium.	13 53 8	80 11 47
65	Divi . . .	2 miles N.W. of Point.	15 58 55	81 9 25
66	Masulipatam .	In the fort . .	16 9 15	81 9 25
67	Coringa or Hope island	On southern part of Hope Island distant about 2½ miles from sea.	16 49 5	82 16 58
68	Cocanada (Vakalapudi)	4¾ miles north of Cocanada river, 500 yards from the shore.	17 0 40	82 16 30
69	Vizagapatam .	On the headland named Dolphin's Nose.	17 41 0	83 17 15
70	Santipilli . .	On Santipilli Hill, three-quarters of a mile inland.	18 4 56	83 37 35
71	Calingapatam .	On the Point . .	18 19 0	84 7 30
72	Gopalpoor .	On mainland, 60 yards from low-water mark.	19 13 0	84 52 0

INDIA, EAST COAST—BENGAL PROVINCE.

No.	Name of light.	Location.	Lat. N.	Long. E.
72a	Pooree . .	270 yards N.E. ½ E. of Pooree Flagstaff.	19° 48′ 10″	85° 49′ 10″
73	False Point .	At entrance to the Mahanadi, about 1½ mile west from Mahanadi Point, and 1¼ mile from the sea.	20 20 20	86 44 0
74	Pilot's Ridge (light-vessel)	On Pilot's Ridge, during the S.W. Monsoon only, in 22 fathoms water.	20 50 20	87 40 0
75	River Hoogli—Eastern Channel (light-vessel)	Entrance to Eastern Channel, in 10½ fathoms water.	21 1 19	88 13 0
75a	Intermediate (light-vessel)	Entrance to Channel, in 6¼ fathoms, between the Eastern Channel and Lower Gaspar light-vessels. Lower Gaspar light-vessel bearing N. by W. ½ W. 12 miles.	21 14 30	88 11 0
76	Lower Gaspar (light-vessel)	Lower Gaspar Channel, in 25 feet water.	21 26 15	88 6 38
77	Upper Gaspar (light-vessel)	Gaspar Channel, in 21 feet water.	21 31 0	88 2 53
78	Sagar . .	Middleton Pt. S.W. end of Saugar Island, about 200 yards from low water mark.	21 38 43	88 2 0
79	Cowcolly . .	Two miles S.W. of Kedgeree Point.	21 50 13	87 56 9
80	Mutlah (light-vessel)	Entrance to River, in 11 fathoms.	21 4 0	88 46 30
81	Chittagong .	1½ mile south of Norman Pt., southern shore, entrance to Kurnafoolee River.	22 10 50	91 48 29
82	Kutubdea . .	West part of the island.	21 52 30	91 49 58

BRITISH BURMA, etc.

No.	Name of light.	Location.	Lat. N.	Long. E.
83	Oyster Reef .	South edge of Reef, in 4 fathoms at low-water spring tides.	20° 5′ 0″	92° 39′ 0″
84	Savage Island .	On Island, entrance to Akyab harbour.	20 5 7	92 53 37
85	Terribles . .	On South Terrible .	19 23 10	93 16 15
86	Alguada . .	On Alguada Reef; the lighthouse lies S.S.W. 10¾ miles from Diamond Island Flagstaff.	15 42 14	94 11 35
87	Krishna (light-vessel)	In 4¾ fathoms, eastern side of Krishna Shoal.	15 36 15	95 34 30
88	Great Coco Group, Andaman Islands	On S.W. end of Table Island, 2 miles from Great Coco Island.	14 12 30	93 22 15
89	China Ba-Keer .	In 2 fathoms at low water spring tides. On edge of flats off entrance to the China Ba-Keer or Ton-Kwa River.	16 16 33	96 11 9
90	Eastern Grove (Rangoon River)	Close to high water mark on Grove Point, east side of entrance to river.	16 30 1	96 22 47
91	Double Island .	On the Island . .	15 52 30	97 34 36
92	Acheen (Sumatra)	N.E. point of Pulo Brasse, near Acheen Head.	5 44 55	95 4 15
		Auxiliary light to the above.	5 44 55	95 4 15

STRAITS OF MALACCA TO SINGAPORE.

No.	Name of light.	Location.	Lat. N.	Long. E.
93	Malacca Strait .	On the "One fathom bank," in 18 feet low water spring-tides.	2 52 10	100 58 40
93a	Klang Strait .	S.W. end of Pulo Lumaut.	2 52 25	101 14 28

STRAITS OF MALACCA TO SINGAPORE (*continued*).

No.	Name of light.	Location.	Lat. N.	Long. E.
94	Cape Rachada .	On the high bluff, called by the Malays "Tanjong Tuan."	2 24 8	101 51 2
95	Malacca .	On the old Portuguese Monastery, situated on St. Paul's Hill.	2 11 37	102 15 30
96	Malacca .	Outer end of the jetty	—	—
96a	Pulo Pisang .	S.E. by E., 74 miles from the town of Malacca.	1 27 30	103 15 0
97	Raffles . .	On Coney Islet, at west entrance of Singapore Strait.	1 9 50	103 44 50
98	Singapore . .	Fort Canning. Government Hill.	1 17 33	103 51 0
99	Horsburgh or Pedra Branca	On the summit of the rock.	1 19 57	104 24 30

CHAPTER III.

THE PROVINCE OF BENGAL—GENERAL.

§ 1. Name, Size, and Position. § 2. Mountains, Rivers, and Railways. § 3. Mineral and Agricultural Products. § 4. Land Tenures. § 5. Public Rent Roll. § 6. The People in Districts and States.

§ 1. Bengal Province (Banga, one of the five Aryan divisions of India named from sons of Anu, son of King Yayati; Bangálah, first in A.D. 1323) is the largest in population, resources, and net revenue, of the twelve Provinces of British India. The total area, 203,437 sq. m., of which 187,126 has been surveyed in detail, is almost that of France and just below that of Germany. The population, 69,133,619, is nearly twice that of France, and comes near to that of all Russia. The sea-borne, or foreign and coasting trade, stood at £69,222,805 in value in 1880-81, while the network of water communications, the roads, and railways, are the agencies of an inland traffic of vast dimensions for so dense a population. In the same year the Province yielded a gross imperial revenue of £15,088,911, of which at least £12,000,000 is surplus. When in 1765 the East India Company obtained the *dewani* or virtual sovereignty of Bengal proper, it became receiver of a clear yearly revenue of £1,700,000. From that time till the present the increasing surplus derived from a loyal and prosperous population has enabled the Government of India to conduct the successive campaigns, and raise to the same administrative level the other Provinces and States since conquered or annexed. Bengal, forming one-third of the whole Empire of British India, is bounded E. by Burma, with the Arakan Roma range between, and by the Assam districts of Sylhet, Garo Hills, and Goalpara, with the Brahmapootra between; N. by Bhootan and Nepal, with the Himalaya and the submontane tracts known as Tarai and Morang between; W. by the North-Western Province districts of Gorakhpoor, Ghazipoor, Benares, and Mirzapoor, by Rewah State and the Central Province States and district of Sambalpoor; and S. by the Ganjam district of Madras, the Bay of Bengal, and the Arakan district of British Burma, with the Naf River between. This territory lies between 19° 28′ and 27° 30′ N. latitude, and 92° 46′ and 81° 35′ E. longitude. Since 1854 the whole has been subject to the administration of a Lieutenant-Governor, except 3½ sq. m. belonging to the French, at Chandernagar on the Hoogli and a field near Balasor. From 1766—when, after the battle of Buxar and the Emperor of Delhi's grant of the civil authority to the East India Company, Lord Clive opened the *pooneah* or ceremonial of commencing the annual collection of revenue, at Motee Jheel, Moorshidabad—to 1854 the Lower Province of Bengal, Behar, and Orissa was directly administered by the Governor-General.

§ 2. MOUNTAINS, RIVERS, CANALS, AND RAILWAYS.—At Darjeeling and Sikkim, due N. of Calcutta, the jurisdiction of the Lieutenant-Governor embraces a small portion of the **Himalaya** chain rising from 7000 ft. in the chief sanitarium of the Province, to 28,156 ft. in mighty Kinchinjinga. On the S.W. the ranges which cross Central India descend into the deltas of the Ganges and Mahanadi after forming the uplands of Behar and Santalia, the **Rajmahal** hills round which the Ganges sweeps, and the hilly plateaux of Chutia Nagpoor to the Orissa States. On the S.E. the slope and outlying spurs of the **Roma** range drain through the Tipura and Chittagong rivers into the Bay of Bengal. In the area within these three mountain systems, or N. and S.W. and S.E., the Ganges, the Brahmapootra, the Mahanadi, and their almost innumerable tributaries, form and fertilize the deltas of Bengal and Orissa. The **Ganges**, entering Bengal from the North-Western Province at Chausa, between Buxar and Ghazipoor, receives the Gogra N., the Son S., the Gandak N., and the Kosi below Bhagalpoor, where from an easterly it follows a southerly course till it sends off the Bhagirathi, to form the Hoogli, its most westerly mouth; the main stream continues S.E. to Goalunda, where the principal confluent of the **Brahmapootra** under the name of the Jamoona or Konai amalgamates with it. The united volume, following countless channels through the Soondarban forest-swamps, reaches the Bay of Bengal. The **Mahanadi** enters Orissa from the Central Province below Sonpoor, struggles through gorges in the Orissa States to Dholpoor, whence it rolls through the Naraj gorge into the plains 7 m. W. of Cuttak, but partly escapes to the sea by the Chilka Lake on the N. border of Madras. Canals utilise, for irrigation and navigation, the water of the Mahanadi in the isolated tracts of Orissa, and that of the Son in the parched uplands of Behar. The Grand Trunk Road, leaving Calcutta on the N. or left bank, crosses the Hoogli at Palta ferry above Barrackpoor, and runs direct to Benares and Peshawar, leaving Bengal at the Karamnasa river. The **East Indian Railway** follows a more northerly route, sending off a loop-line to the Ganges at Rajmahal and opening up Behar. The **Eastern Bengal Railway** connects Calcutta with the junction of the Ganges and Brahmapootra at Goalunda, 172 m.; and from that line the **Northern State Railway**, 266½ m., continued by the **Darjeeling and Himalayan Railway**, reaches Darjeeling and Dhoobri. Other extensions are in progress to open up the Assam and Cachar valleys; from Dacca to Maimansingh; in Central Bengal from Ranaghat to Jessor and Khoolna, and from Bongong to Calcutta; from Baidyanath on the East Indian Railway to Deogarh, with branch to Rohini; from the **Tirhoot State Railway** to Pipra Ghat, Bettiah, and Hajipoor; from the **Calcutta and South-Eastern Railway** to Mugra Ghat and Diamond Harbour. The length of the **Patna and Gaya Railway** is 57 m.; the **Nalhati**, 27. From the Goalunda terminus of the Eastern Bengal Railway it is intended to run ferry steamers to Daudkhandi, where the Goomti joins the Megna, and thence to lay a line of railway by Comillah to Chittagong so as to bring that rising port within a few hours of Calcutta.

§ 3. PRODUCTS.—Coal, iron, and copper are the chief **Mineral** products of Bengal; gold-washing is pursued by the poorer natives in some of the hill streams; diamonds were found, in the days of Ptolemy and the Mughul Empire, in Chutia Nagpoor, near the Koel and Sunk rivers, in Palamau. Now coal only is worked with commercial results. Of 37 separate coal-fields reported on by the Geological Survey, 25 are in Bengal; of these, 15 are in the N. and W. of the Damodar valley, 9 are in the Son and Mahanadi valleys, and 1 is in Sikkim. Of 5 fields in all India worked with regularity, 3 are in Bengal, at Raneeganj, Karharbari, and Daltonganj. Steamers, railways, and factories in India consume more than 1½ million of tons, of which 1 million at least is supplied chiefly from Bengal. The manufacture of salt by evaporation has been almost extinguished in Bengal by the import from Liverpool. Of **Food Grains**, rice or padi (*dhan*) is first, being exported and consumed all over the Gangetic and Orissa deltas, while maize, millet, and some wheat are also used in the Behar uplands. The two great crops of each year are the *Aoos* ("early"), sown on high level lands with the first showers of spring, and gathered in July and September; and the more common *Amun* ("winter"), sown broadcast in April, or transplanted in August and reaped in November-January. Murwa and Kodo are millets cheaper than rice; barley (*jao*) is cheapest of all. Dal is the most common of the pulses, and the brinjal, or egg-plant, of the vegetables; the use of the potato is increasing. The almost vegetarian Hindoos use fish and many nitrogenous condiments, of which turmeric, ginger, coriander, cinnamon, aniseed, and chillies are the chief; also the *pan-soopari*, or leaf and nut of the betel creeper, cultivated exclusively by the Barool caste in covered gardens and gathered in November. Of the fruits, the plantain (banana), mango, and jack are most largely produced, and chiefly in the hot season. **Jute, indigo, tea,** and **cinchona** are the great commercial staples introduced by foreigners; the first in the E. and N.E. districts, the second in Nadiya and Tirhoot chiefly, and the tea (China) plant in Darjeeling, Hazaribagh, and Chittagong. **Opium** is cultivated as a State monopoly in Behar, and is manufactured at Patna. **Silk**, a somewhat declining industry, is still largely produced for export under European superintendence. The date-tree is extensively grown for sugar in Jessor district, and is driving out the cane culture. Tobacco is grown on the homestead, and is used by almost every Bengalee, young and old; at Poosa a tobacco factory flourishes. Shellac and lac-dye are exported through Calcutta from Beerbhoom, Hazaribagh, and Cossipoor, and safflower from the Dacca region.

§ 4. LAND TENURES.—The Decennial Settlement of Bengal, Behar, and Orissa—by which last term was meant at that period only the tract of country lying between the Roopnarain and Subarnarekha rivers, and now included in the district of Midnapoor—was commenced in the year 1789 and completed in 1790-91. In the latter year the total assessment amounted to sicca Rs. 2,68,00,989 (Co.'s Rs. 2,85,87,722), or £2,858,772. This was, with slight variation, declared to be permanent in 1793. The settlement embraced the tracts now comprised in the divisions of Bardwan, the Presidency, Rajshahi, Dacca, Chittagong, Patna, and Bhagalpoor. It also comprised parts of the Hazaribagh and Manbhoom districts in the Chutia Nagpoor division, as well as Jalpaigori, Goalpara, and Kooch Behar, which then formed part of Rangpoor. The total assessment of the same divisions amounts now to Rs. 3,55,00,000.

The zameendars, with whom the settlement was originally made, were for the most part powerful men, whose authority extended over wide tracts of country, police and other powers being entrusted to them. Of these tracts they were, by the settlement, constituted the proprietors ; but, under the influence of debt and mismanagement, these large zameendaries were speedily broken up. The Government demand was then one which left a small margin of profit compared with that of zameendars now. The rights of the ryots to hold at customary rates were also secured by law, and the power of the landlords over them was limited. Within the 10 years that immediately followed the Permanent Settlement, a complete revolution took place in the constitution and ownership of the estates. In 1799 the new zameendars were vested with greatly increased influence over the ryots, and again in 1812 further authority was given them, so that for 50 years of the present century they exercised a power over the ryots greater than that contemplated by the original settlement of 1793. Some additions were made to the revenue demand when the landlords were relieved of police charges, and in 1824-25 it had risen to Co.'s Rs. 2,98,62,021. After that period the revenue expanded as resumptions of invalid revenue-free tenures proceeded. Omitting Assam, Cuttak, and part of Chutia Nagpoor, the number of estates on the Government revenue roll has been enormously augmented since the Permanent Settlement—(1) by the admission to the roll of talookdars who succeeded in the claims preferred by them to hold their talooks independently of the zameendars through whom they had previously paid their revenue ; and (2) by partitions of estates. Of the increase of the land revenue of Bengal since the decennial settlement, two thirds is from Behar. In Bengal proper a quarter of a million sterling has thus been added in the century. Orissa is under a **Thirty Years' Settlement**, which was renewed in 1867 ; there are fifty large estates on which the Marathas had imposed a quit-rent before their recovery by the East India Company in 1803.

§ 5. THE GOVERNMENT RENT ROLL.—In the whole Lieutenant-Governorship of Bengal the number of estates on the revenue roll in 1880-81 was 150,420, of which 140,007 were permanently settled, 7670 were temporarily settled, 2720 were under Government, and 23 were ryotwari tracts. The land-tax on all these was Rs. 3,75,41,188, or, including arrears, almost 4 millions sterling. By Act X. of 1859 the first detailed attempt was made to apply the provisions of the Permanent Settlement for the protection of the tenants from illegal cesses.

and in their tenant right of beneficial occupancy. **Fee Simple** grants in the tea districts were made for a time after 1861. **Waste Land Rules** grant leases in the unpeopled tracts of the Soondarban, and the districts along the base of the eastern and northern hills from Chittagong to Darjeeling. In a few petty holdings the redemption of land revenue is encouraged; there are 16,500 such cases. Of the 150,420 estates on the public books there are some 500 each with an area of 20,000 acres and upwards, and 15,000 with from 500 to 20,000. The rest, or about 89 per cent of the whole number, though comparatively large in *total* area, are under 500 acres each.

§ 6. THE PEOPLE IN DISTRICTS AND STATES.—In the 50 Districts and groups of States which constitute Bengal Province, as described in detail in the next Chapter, there is a population, in round numbers, of 70 millions, including the tribes of the hill frontier and Hill Tipura. These Districts and States are grouped in nine divisions, each under a Commissioner for administrative purposes. The census taken on 17th February 1881 shows that the population has increased 10 per cent in nine years, or from 62,727,471 to 69,133,619. The percentage of increase for Bengal proper is 6, for Behar 15, and for Orissa 20. In the Bardwan division alone, along the south bank of the Hoogli, there has been a decrease, due to mortality from a long-continued epidemic of fever in the low lands above which that river is annually raising its channel. Notwithstanding this, the districts of that division opposite and to the south-west of Calcutta, still show the densest rural population in the world, or at the rate of 1335 in Howrah and 823 in Hoogli district to the square mile. Of the whole population 34,361,705 are males and 34,771,914 females, the latter exceeding the former by 1·2 per cent.

As to language, about 42 millions speak Bengalee, 22 millions speak Hindee, and 5 millions speak Ooriya.

[TABLES.

BENGAL

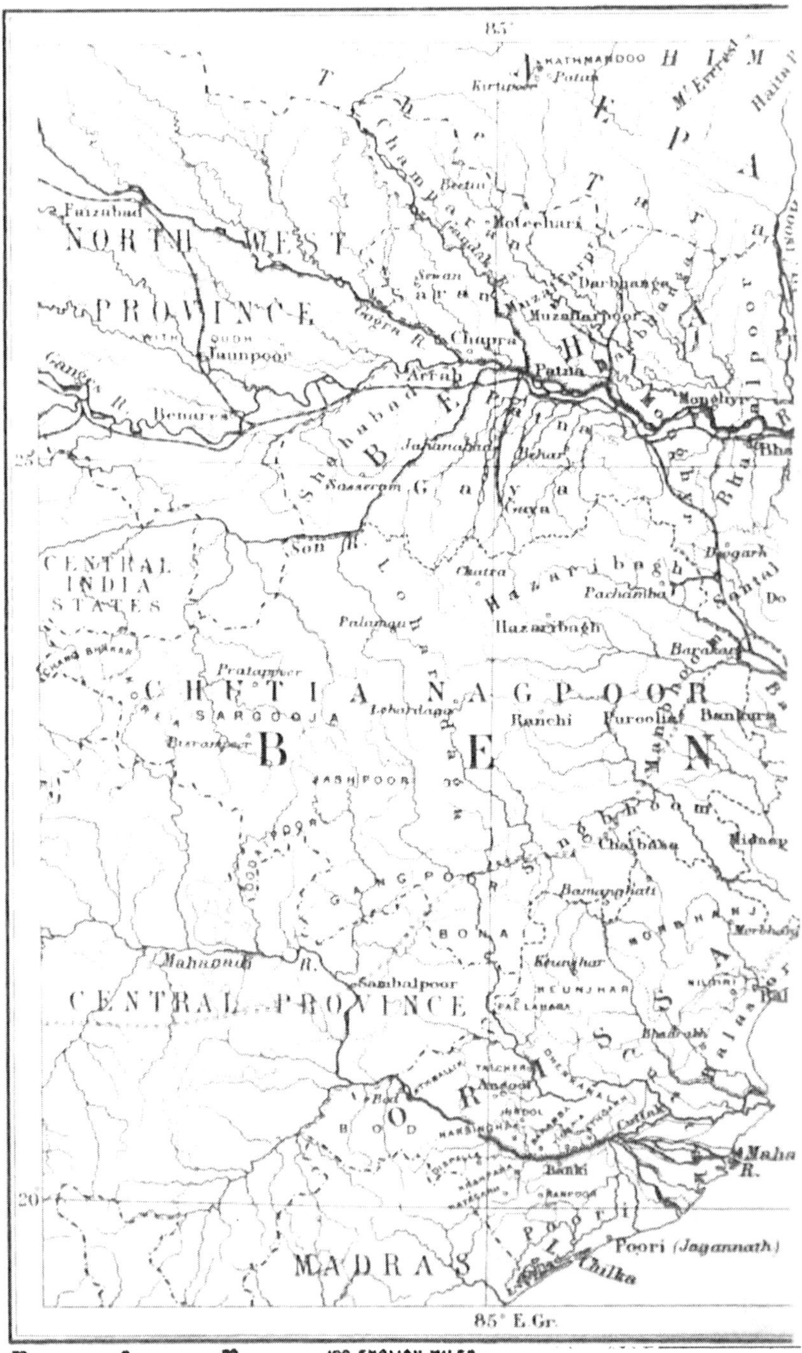
85°
KATHMANDOO
Patan
Kirtipoor
Mt. Everest
Faizabad
NORTH WEST
PROVINCE
OUDH
Jaunpoor
Ganges R.
Benares
Champaran
Bettia
Motechari
Sewan
Saran
Gogra R.
Chapra
Darbhanga
Muzaffarpoor
Patna
Arrah
Shahabad
Jahanabad
Behar
Sasseram
Gaya
Son R.
Chatra
Hazaribagh
Pachamba
Palamau
Deogarh
Sontal
CENTRAL
INDIA
STATES
Pratappoor
CHUTIA NAGPOOR
SARGOOJA
Lohardaga
Ranchi
Purooliah
Bankura
BENGAL
Chaibasa
Bamanghati
GANGPOOR
BONAI
Mahanadi R.
Sambalpoor
Keunjhar
KEUNJHAR
CENTRAL PROVINCE
Angool
Bhadrakh
BOOD
Cuttack
Banki
Maha R.
Poori
Poori (Jagannath)
Chilka
MADRAS
ORISSA
20°
25°
85° E. Gr.
50
0
50
100 ENGLISH MILES

PROVINCE.

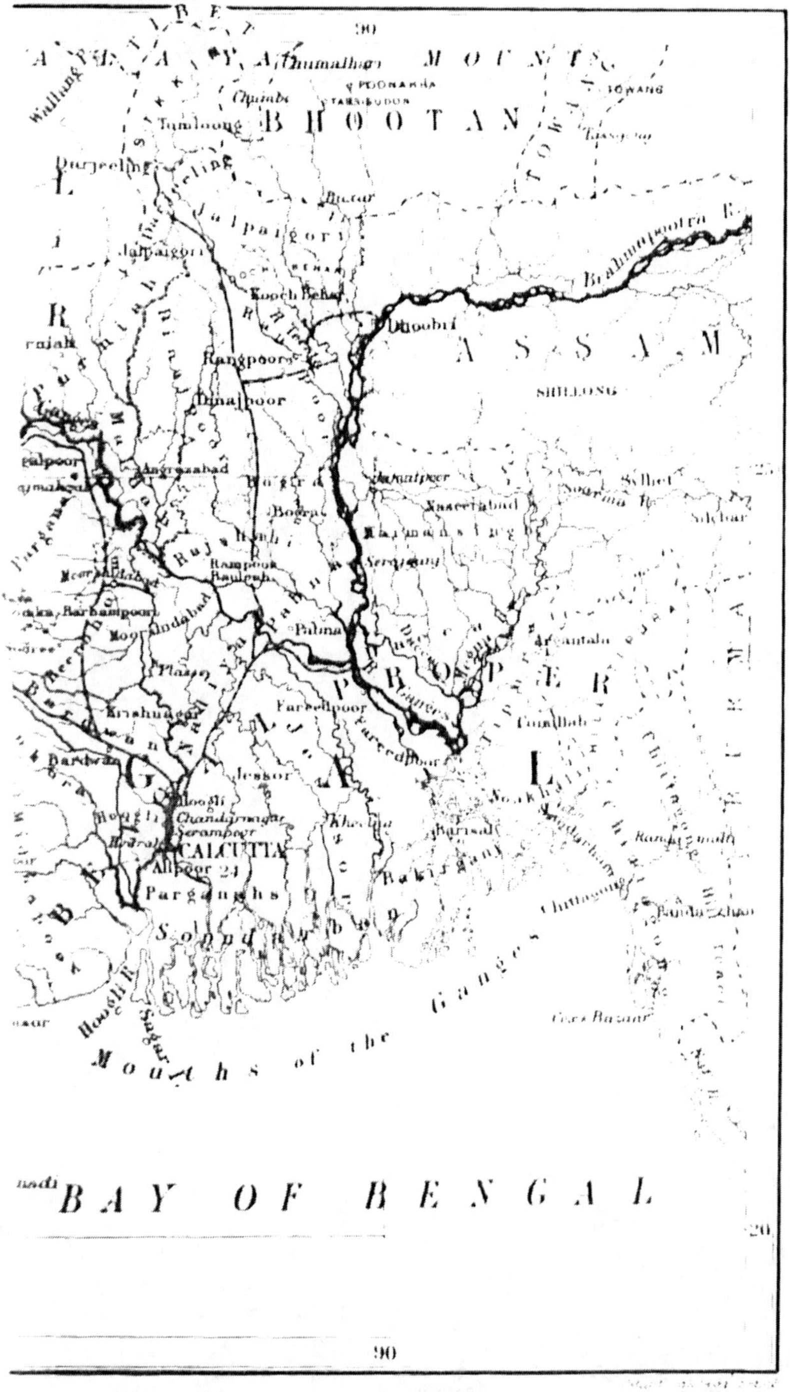
BHOOTAN
ASSAM
SHILLONG
Darjeeling
Jalpaigori
Kooch Behar
Rangpoor
Dinajpoor
Dhoobri
Brahmaputra R.
Sylhet
Silchar
Nasceeabad
Bogra
Serajgunj
Rampoor Bauleah
Barhampoor
Moorshedabad
Pubna
Plassey
Krishnagar
Bardwan
Fareedpoor
Jessor
Hoogli
Chandernagar
Serampoor
CALCUTTA
Alipoor 24
Parganahs
Khoolna
Barisal
Bakirganj
Comillah
Agartala
Noakhali
Chittagong
Cox's Bazaar
Mouths of the Ganges
BAY OF BENGAL
90

CENSUS OF BENGAL PROVINCE, 1881.

Area and Population, showing the results of the preliminary addition.

DISTRICTS.	Area in square miles.	Number of towns and villages.	Total population of both sexes.	Total Males.	Total Females.	Number of persons per square mile.	Number of towns and villages per square mile.
Presidency Division.							
Calcutta . . .	8	1	433,219	288,817	144,402	54,152·3	·1
Suburbs . . .	23	2	251,439	147,205	104,234	10,932	·08
24-Parganahs . .	2,765	6,443	1,994,199	1,015,571	978,628	721·2	2·3
Nadiya . . .	3,421	4,021	2,022,545	983,719	1,038,826	591·2	1·1
Jessor and Khoolna	3,658	5,838	2,210,898	1,126,065	1,084,833	604·4	1·5
Moorshidabad . .	2,141	8,619	1,200,825	582,033	618,792	560·8	1·6
Total . .	12,016	19,924	8,113,125	4,143,410	3,969,715	675	1·6
Rajshahi and Kooch Behar Division.							
Dinajpoor . .	4,117	7,333	1,529,906	790,270	739,636	371·6	1·7
Rajshahi . . .	2,359	5,177	1,333,237	658,313	674,924	565·1	2·2
Rangpoor . . .	3,488	9,117	2,169,699	1,100,327	1,069,372	622	2·6
Bogra . . .	1,497	4,195	733,546	371,855	361,691	490	2·8
Pabna . . .	1,847	3,962	1,312,977	650,315	662,662	710·9	2·1
Darjeeling . .	1,234	1,200	157,038	89,510	67,528	127·2	·9
Jalpaigori . .	2,911	4,000	570,210	299,068	271,142	195·8	1·3
Kooch Behar . .	1,307	1,172	600,946	310,790	290,156	459·7	·9
Total . .	18,760	36,156	8,407,559	4,270,448	4,137,111	453·5	1·9
Bardwan Division.							
Bardwan . . .	2,693	8,658	1,391,736	668,258	723,478	516·7	1·3
Bankura . . .	2,621	5,256	1,044,195	508,048	536,147	398·3	2
Beerbhoom . .	1,756	3,295	792,411	380,966	411,445	451·2	1·8
Midnapoor . .	5,082	14,918	2,514,672	1,242,606	1,272,066	494·8	2·9
Hoogli . . .	1,225	2,685	1,007,445	485,723	521,722	823	2·1
Howrah . . .	476	1,535	635,381	316,479	318,902	1,334·8	3·2
Total . .	13,853	31,342	7,385,840	3,602,080	3,783,760	533·1	2·2
Dacca Division.							
Dacca . . .	2,796	6,550	2,196,641	1,073,598	1,123,043	785·6	2·3
Fareedpoor . .	2,267	4,501	1,614,083	798,282	815,801	711·9	1·9
Bakirganj . . .	3,648	4,436	1,885,183	963,154	922,029	517	1·2
Maimansingh . .	6,287	12,883	2,950,105	1,494,105	1,456,000	469·2	2
Total . .	14,998	28,370	8,646,012	4,329,139	4,316,873	576·5	1·8
Chittagong Division.							
Chittagong . .	2,567	2,000	1,220,973	570,489	650,484	475·6	·8
Noakhali . . .	1,641	1,938	822,328	415,358	406,970	501·1	1·1
Tipura . . .	2,491	6,576	1,491,762	756,206	735,556	598·8	2·6
Hill Tipura . .	3,867	..	95,637	51,458	44,179	..	..
Chittagong hill tracts	5,419	2,000	101,467	56,491	44,976	18·7	·2
Total . .	15,985	12,514	3,732,167	1,850,002	1,882,165	*300·1	*1

* Exclusive of Hill Tipura.

CENSUS OF BENGAL PROVINCE, 1881.

Area and Population, showing the results of the preliminary addition.

DISTRICTS.	Area in square miles.	Number of towns and villages.	Total population of both sexes.	Total Males.	Total Females.	Number of persons per square mile.	Number of towns and villages per square mile.
Patna Division.							
Patna . . .	2,078	5,496	1,796,649	875,941	920,708	864·6	2·6
Gaya . . .	4,712	8,731	2,057,980	1,007,315	1,050,665	436·7	1·8
Shahabad . .	4,366	4,816	1,964,909	950,250	1,014,659	450	1·1
Muzaffarpoor . .	3,004	4,000	2,589,524	1,266,852	1,322,672	862	1·3
Darbhanga . .	3,335	3,500	2,578,090	1,266,377	1,311,718	773	1
Saran . . .	2,625	4,000	2,280,382	1,083,565	1,196,817	868·7	1·5
Champaran . .	3,531	7,899	1,708,417	862,719	845,698	483·8	2·2
Total . .	23,651	38,442	14,975,951	7,313,019	7,662,932	633	1·6
Bhagalpoor Division.							
Monghyr . . .	3,922	6,480	1,955,920	962,784	993,136	498·8	1·6
Bhagalpoor . .	4,268	6,500	1,923,276	957,354	965,922	450·6	1·5
Purniah . . .	4,957	6,664	1,823,717	920,575	903,142	367·9	1·3
Maldah . . .	1,859	3,326	710,310	347,055	363,255	382	1·8
Santal Parganahs .	5,483	10,000	1,561,385	760,000	801,385	281·1	1·8
Total . .	20,489	32,970	7,974,608	3,947,768	4,026,840	389	1·6
Chutia Nagpoor Division.							
Hazaribagh . .	7,021	7,835	1,072,486	524,260	548,226	151·7	1·1
Lohardaga . .	12,044	13,275	1,607,038	795,486	811,552	133·4	1·1
Singbhoom . .	3,897	3,937	551,348	257,999	275,349	141·4	1
Manbhoom . .	4,147	7,000	1,042,117	516,028	526,089	251·2	1·6
Tributary Mahals .	16,025	3,001	441,302	223,581	217,721	27·5	·1
Total . .	43,134	35,048	4,714,291	2,335,354	2,378,937	10 ·3	·8
Orissa Division.							
Cuttak . . .	3,516	13,087	1,731,548	844,893	886,656	592·4	3·7
Pooree . . .	2,472	5,208	885,794	444,030	441,764	358·1	2·1
Balasor . . .	2,068	6,393	942,414	461,110	481,304	456·1	3
Angool . . .	881	460	102,090	51,910	50,180	115·8	·5
Banki . . .	116	177	56,613	28,104	28,509	480	1·5
Tributary Mahals .	15,187	11,180	1,465,607	740,439	725,168	96·5	7
Total . .	24,240	36,505	5,184,066	2,570,485	2,613,581	213·3	1·5
GRAND TOTAL .	187,126	271,271	69,133,619	34,361,705	34,771,914	*376·7	*1·4

* Exclusive of Hill Tipura.

Births are registered in first class municipalities, and in such towns as in 1879 gave returns of 25 per thousand and upwards. The general rate was 23·44 per mille in 1880, and the proportion of male births to female births was as high as 116 per cent. The number of deaths registered was 26·86 per thousand of the population in urban circles, and 14·93 per thousand in rural circles. In Calcutta the recorded birth-rate was 17·5 per thousand, a rate far below European standards, but not altogether incredible having regard to the great excess of the male over the female population, and the large proportion of unmarried women and widows. The death-rate was 27·1 per thousand as compared with 30·3 per thousand in the previous year, and 28·6 per thousand the mean mortality of the previous ten years.

The following shows the mortality of 1880 in Calcutta, compared with that of 1879, the figures for the different races and sexes being separately entered :—

Race.	Ratio of Deaths per Thousand of Population.					
	Males.		Females.		Total.	
	1879.	1880.	1879.	1880.	1879.	1880.
Non-Asiatics . .	25·5	23·7	14·2	11·4	22·1	20
Mixed Races . .	49·6	40·7	49·0	42·6	49·3	41·6
Hindoos . . .	27·4	24·5	35·5	32·9	30·3	27·5
Muhammadans .	25·3	21·3	43·3	39·8	30·4	26·5

The mortality under each head of race and for each sex was lower than in 1879. Among Europeans there were altogether 187 deaths in 1880, 155 of those who died being males and 32 females. Fifty-nine of the deaths were among officers, sailors, and others who fell sick on board ship; 19 were among residents of Fort William, and the remaining 109 among the European residents of Calcutta. There were only 65 deaths among 14,774 sailors, against 73 among 14,951 in the previous year. Deaths from cholera numbered 14 against 25.

The mortality in cantonments from all causes was 17·32 per mille, against 22·95 in 1879. The death-rate from fevers decreased from 12·48 to 9·74, but that from cholera was higher than in 1879, the ratios being ·94 against ·56. Of all the military stations, Fort William exhibited the lowest mortality, or 3·89 per mille, and Segauli the highest, or 27·79.

CHAPTER IV.

THE PROVINCE OF BENGAL—DISTRICTS AND STATES.

I.—BENGAL PROPER.

Central Districts.—§ 1. Calcutta. § 2. Twenty-four Parganahs. § 3. Khoolna, including the Soondarban. § 4. Jessor. § 5. Nadiya. § 6. Moorshidabad. § 7. Pabna. § 8. Rajshahi. § 9. Bogra. § 10. Dinajpoor. § 11. Rangpoor. § 12. Darjeeling. § 13. *Sikkim. § 14. Jalpaigori. § 15. Kooch Behar.

Western Districts.—§ 16. Midnapoor. § 17. Hoogli and Howrah. § 18. Bardwan. § 19. Bankura. § 20. Beerbhoom.

Eastern Districts.—§ 21. Dacca. § 22. Bakirganj. § 23. Fareedpoor. § 24. Maimansingh. § 25. Tipura. § 26. Hill Tipura. § 27. Chittagong. § 28. Chittagong Hill Tracts. § 29. Noakhali.

II.—BEHAR.

§ 30. Patna. § 31. Gaya. § 32. Shahabad. § 33. Saran. § 34. Champaran. § 35. Muzaffarpoor. § 36. Darbhanga. § 37. Monghyr. § 38. Bhagalpoor. § 39. Purniah. § 40. Maldah. § 41. Santalia.

III.—CHUTIA NAGPOOR.

§ 42. Hazaribagh. § 43. Manbhoom. § 44. Singbhoom. § 45. Lohardaga. § 46. *Chutia Nagpoor States.

IV.—ORISSA.

§ 47. Cuttak. § 48. Balasor. § 49. Pooree. § 50. *Orissa States.

V.—PROTECTED STATES.

§ 51. *Bhootan and Towang. § 52. *Nepal.

I.—BENGAL PROPER.

Central Districts.

§ 1. **Calcutta** (*Kalkatta*, as in "Ain i Akbari;" possibly from Kalighat, old temple of Kali in S.), the capital of India since

1773, of the old Presidency of Bengal from 1707 to that year, and subordinate to Madras before that from its foundation in 1682. The city stands on the left or east bank of the Hoogli, the most westerly branch of the Ganges, 86 miles from the sea at Sagar anchoring buoy, in lat. N. 22° 33′, and long. E. 88° 23′, and 20 feet above sea-level. The city and four suburban municipalities cover an area of 31 square miles, with a fixed population of 684,658, or including Howrah, of 790,233. In Calcutta city there are 107 souls to the acre, and in the suburbs 17, or 33 in both, as against 50½ in London. The 128,671 families live in 23,751 brick and 55,648 mat or mud houses. In the city there are 5·2 souls to a family; in the suburbs, 4·8. In the city there are 11·6 souls to an inhabited house; in the suburbs, 6·6. Of the whole population, omitting Howrah suburb, 4·4 per cent are Christians (30,470), 32·2 per cent are Muhammadans (221,013), and 61·6 per cent are Hindoos (428,692); there are 487 Brahmos, 1848 Boodhists and Jains, 986 Jews, 142 Parsees, 284 Sikhs, and 728 "others," chiefly of aboriginal cults. Females form only 36·3 per cent of the whole population. Of the 30,478 Christians 6945 were born in Europe (United Kingdom, 5924), 22,535 in India, 382 in Asia outside India, 106 in Africa, 304 in America, 64 in Australia, and 60 at sea. In 1810 we know that the whole number of Europeans in Bengal, including Calcutta, was about 2000. Of 327,243 males with stated occupations, more than half are engaged in commerce, and the rest minister to their wants. The trade is that of exchanging products, and not largely of manufactures. Howrah, on the opposite bank, with which Calcutta is connected by a pontoon bridge, is as much a part of the capital as "the Surrey side" is of London. Calcutta is, in area and inhabitants, as large as London at the beginning of the nineteenth century, and rather less than one-fourth of London now.

Approaching the metropolis from the sea, we may divide it into these quarters in order:—(1) Garden Reach, a favourite suburb of European officials and merchants till it became the residence of the ex-king of Oudh, and depot of the mail-steamers; (2) Kidderpoor and Hastings, where are the Government and other dockyards, factories and pensioners' barracks; (3) Fort William, begun by Clive and built on the Vauban system, at a cost of £2,000,000 sterling, after the sack of the settlement in 1757, from which time the modern city dates; (4) Chowringhee, the principal quarter of the Europeans, around the Maidān, or Plain of the Fort, which led Lord Cornwallis first to call Calcutta the "City of Palaces;" beginning with St. Paul's Cathedral, built by Bishop Daniel Wilson, and containing the Imperial Museum, the line of massive houses in gardens runs parallel with the river for some distance, and then sweeps down to it at Dharmtola Market; Government House, erected by Lord Wellesley; the Town Hall and High Court of Justice; the Bank of Bengal, Metcalfe Hall, Dalhousie Institute, and new Post Office—the last on the site of the old fort and Black Hole; (5) the City quarter running along the embanked river from the Customs-house to the Mint, and back to "the ditch" at Circular Road, made as a defence against the Marathas; here the Eurasian, or mixed population, chiefly reside; (6) the Native Town, threaded by Chitpoor and Cornwallis Streets parallel with the river, and opened up by several fine cross-roads at right angles to these; here, especially around the grassy squares frequented by the natives after the heat of the day, are the principal colleges of the Government and the Missionaries, and the University. A circular canal bounds the city to the E. and N., but a continuous succession of suburbs, such as Cossipoor with gun factory, and Dum-Dum, seems to continue it for 16 miles up the Hoogli to Barrackpoor, the Viceroy's country seat, and Palta, whence the city draws a daily supply of 8 millions of gallons of pure water filtered from the fine river silt. Calcutta is drained on a perfect system from the higher level of the river bank eastward into the salt-water lake. A body of municipal commissioners, partly elected and partly nominated by Government which appoints an able civil servant as their head, and working through a smaller Town Council, have gradually made Calcutta the healthiest city in the tropics, giving it gas, water, drainage, and many amenities, at a cost of annual taxation amounting to £300,000, one-third of which is paid as interest on loan for such improvements. Till 1854 the city was under the direct jurisdiction of the Governor-General as Governor of Bengal and the Supreme Court. Since that time its administration only, but not law, has been immediately under the Lieutenant-Governor of Bengal, whose official residence is at Alipoor, in the suburbs.

The port, including ten miles of bank and channel, has since 1870 been controlled and improved by a body of nine European commissioners. As the focus of all the sea-borne and most of the inland trade of the Ganges and Brahmapootra, and the centre of the northern and eastern railway systems, half the commerce of India flows through Calcutta. From £10,000,000 sterling in value, at the first break of the East India Company's monopoly by the charter of 1813, the sea-borne trade has risen to £70,000,000, of which two-thirds are in exports, and one-third in imports. Outside of the United States of America no city presents such a history of rapid growth, especially in the century and a quarter since Clive began to raise it. Calcutta, as the most pushing English city of the East, has few buildings architecturally worthy of mention. It is remarkable for such colleges and hospitals as the Madrissa, founded by Warren Hastings for the education of the Muhammadans; the Presidency College, founded by the Hindoos themselves, but managed by Government; two missionary colleges established by Alexander Duff for the Established and Free Churches of Scotland; the Medical College and hospitals attached, the most extensive in the world; the colleges of the London and Church Missionary Societies; and the Doveton College, Martinière, Jesuits' College, and Free School for Eurasians chiefly. Since Clive invited Kiernander, its first Protestant missionary, to settle in the city in 1758, and Duff opened his first college in 1830, the progress of English education and Christian profession among the natives has been remarkable. There are 21 Protestant Mission centres in the city, and 17 in the suburbs. The Calcutta University, an examining body with a constitution like that of London, consists of more than 80 affiliated colleges, from which thousands of students annually go up for its examinations and degrees. The Viceroy spends the cool or winter months in Calcutta and Barrackpoor, and makes Simla, in the Outer Himalaya, his summer seat.

§ 2. TWENTY-FOUR PARGANAHS DISTRICT, bounded E. by Kabadak river, separating it from Jessor; S. by Bay of Bengal; W. by Hoogli river; N. by Nadiya and Jessor. Total area, 2765 sq. m. Excluding the forest swamp known as the Soondarban, the area of about 882 sq. m., forming the metropolitan district of British India, was ceded to the East India Company by Meer Jafar, Nawab Nazim of Bengal, in 1757, six months after the battle of Plassey. The Parganahs are twenty-four fiscal divisions then within the revenue circle of Hoogli. The grant was soon after conferred in full proprietary right by the Mughul emperor, subject to a first assignment of the revenue to Lord Clive, or Rs. 2,22,958 a year. This seaboard district is part of the great deltaic expanse of alluvial plain, rivers, creeks, and watercourses, through which and forming which the Ganges and Brahmapootra find their way to the Bay of Bengal. Of thirteen rivers in the district the seven principal are the Hoogli, Bidyadhari or Mutla, Piali, Kalindi, Eechamati or Jamoona, Kholpetua, and Kabadak. Five of these form arms of the sea, or the Malancha, Raimangal, Mutla, Jameera, and Hoogli, in order from the east. Originally containing 444 estates, the district has now above 1900. The population is dense in proportion to the cultivable area, or 1,994,199 exclusive of Calcutta, chiefly peasants and boatmen. The district has eight administrative subdivisions. Of the towns containing more than 5000 inhabitants these are the chief. On the Hoogli, above Calcutta, **Agarpara**, where early experiments in the education of Hindoo girls were made by Mrs. Wilson. **Barrackpoor** cantonment, 15 miles from Calcutta, called by the natives Chanak because Job Charnock settled there in 1689, where a sepoy mutiny took place in 1824, where the 47th Bengal Infantry refused to march for service in the first Burmese war, and the great Mutiny began on 27th February 1857; here is the country seat of the Viceroy in a noble English-like park, containing the tomb of Lady Canning. Near is Nawabgunj, with the Palta waterworks for Calcutta. In the southern suburbs of Calcutta is **Alipoor**, civil headquarters of the district, with Belvedere House, the residence of the Lieutenant-Governor of Bengal, near which Warren Hastings and Francis fought a duel; a native cantonment, and with a great jail; the temple of Kalighat, three centuries old, is near. **Dum-Dum**, 4 m. N.E. of Calcutta, long the headquarters of the Bengal Artillery. **Barasat**, Basoorhat, Satkhira, and Barooipoor, like the previous towns, are headquarters of fiscal subdivisions. **Diamond Harbour**, on the Hoogli below Calcutta, long the anchorage ground above which the East Indiamen did not ascend, a customs and telegraph and soon to be a railway station. **Port Canning**, on the Mutla river, where, in 1864, an attempt was made to create a great port to relieve the trade of Calcutta, with which it is connected by railway. Naihati is an important station of the Eastern Bengal Railway, on the Hoogli, opposite the old town of that name. At Narikelbaria, a hamlet in Basoorhat subdivision, Teetoo Miyan, a Wahabee fanatic, was defeated in 1831. At Takee, in the same subdivision, Dr. Duff opened the first Christian school in the district.

Sagar Island, or Gunga Sagar, as the last visible deposit of the Ganges, is the scene of a great but lessening gathering of pilgrims in the winter solstice, at which mothers used to sacrifice their firstborn in payment of a vow. Frequent attempts at cultivation and salt manufacture have ceased, and the island is now the abode of the tiger, and of a scanty population exposed to inundation. At Dublat the tide is registered. The lighthouse, built in 1808, and a temple, subject of the legend of Bhagirath and the sage Kapilmoonee, are the only permanent structures.

§ 3. KHOOLNA, including the SOONDARBAN which forms the sea face of the three districts of the 24-Parganahs, Jessor, and Bakirganj. The tract covers an area of 5570 sq. m., half the size of Belgium, of swamps and forests of Soondari ("red"), trees of red wood used as fuel. It stretches for 165 miles along the head of the Bay of Bengal, from the Hoogli to the Megna, with an extreme breadth inland of 81 miles. The western division, from the Hoogli to the Jamoona, is marked by embankments, securing a raised and dry cultivation on which the peasants live. The centre portion, from the Jamoona to the Baleswar, is lower, and the cultivators of the "sweet" fields, protected from the salt water, reside at a distance. The eastern or Bakirganj division, from the Baleswar to the Megna, is the most advanced in soil and water and the condition of the resident agriculturists, owing to the greater volume of river water, and the formation of a line of sand hills along the shore. The official surveyors, however, report a slow subsidence of the whole delta, the fine silt of which, 120 feet thick, rests on a semi-fluid mud 40 feet farther down. Periodically the vast tract is swept by the cyclone and the tidal wave, but a growing population and many immigrants continue the fight with nature notwithstanding. Between the Raimangal and Malancha outlets to the Bay of Bengal is the fathomless depression known as the Swatch of No-Ground, ascribed to the action of two circular tides in the funnel-shaped estuary Along the two great boat routes to Calcutta, the outer passage used in the cold season and the inner at other times, are many marts. Of these the principal are Basantpoor, at the confluence of the Kalindi and Jamoona, where the inner and outer passages converge; and Basra, on the Bidyadhari, a timber depot, —both on the border of the 24-Parganahs; Chandkali, on the Kabadak, founded in 1782 by Henckell, who first sought to reclaim the Soondarban; Morrellgunj, a port on the Pangoochi, created by Mr. Morrell, a rice-planter. **Khoolna** is the chief mart of the Soondarban, and was long the headquarters of the East India Company's salt manufacture.

§ 4. JESSOR DISTRICT, bounded E. by Fareedpoor district, S. by the Soondarban, and W. and N. by Nadiya district. Area, exclusive of Soondarban portion, 3658 sq. m.; population, including Khoolna, 2,210,898. The district is threaded by lines of tidal river drainage from north to south, with a network of interlacing streams, forming the three systems of the Kabadak,

Bhairab, and Madhumati, and reaching the Bay of Bengal through three great arms, the Kabadak, Passār, and Haringhata. The Kabadak ("dove's eye") flows from north to south along the western boundary. The Bhairab ("terrible"), the central stream, becomes tidal near Jessor station. The Madhumati ("honey-flowing") leaves the Ganges higher up, under the name of the Garai, and carries a vast volume of the waters of the great Ganges to the sea, along the eastern boundary of Jessor.

Jessor, or Kasba, station ("fame-depriving" or "very glorious") is the only town with more than 5000 inhabitants, on the Bhairab. **Chaugacha**, 16 m. N.W. from Jessor, on the Kabadak, centre of the trade in sugar and indigo seed. **Kesalpoor**, 18 m. S. of Jessor, on the Harihar, with sugar refineries and brass works. **Kotchandpoor**, 25 m. N.W. of Jessor, another sugar mart on the Kabadak; Muhammadpoor, on the right bank of the Madhumati, once capital of a Muhammadan district, now a market village with ruins of fort, tanks, and temples. Bagerhat, in the extreme S.E., with tomb of Khan Jahan, the Muhammadan who, about 1450, reclaimed much of the forest swamps. The subdivisions of this district, made after the indigo disturbances of 1860, are Jessor, Jhanidah, Magura, Naral, and Bagerhat. W. M. Thackeray's father was Collector of Jessor in 1805. Here is a Baptist Mission.

§ 5. NADIYA DISTRICT, bounded E. by Jessor and Pabna; S. by 24-Parganahs; W. by Hoogli, Bardwan, and Beerbhoom; N. by Moorshidabad and Rajshahi. Area, 3421 sq. m.; population, 2,022,545. The Padma, or main stream of the Ganges, forms the northern boundary, and spills over into what are known as the Nadiya Rivers. These are (1) the Jalangi, which joins (2) the Bhagirathi, thrown off higher up the Ganges and forming the junction known as the Hoogli, and (3) the Matabhanga, which falls into the Hoogli lower down by two branches. The three Nadiya rivers are kept open by Government for the enormous local traffic, which pays tolls yielding an average net revenue of £15,000 a year. **Krishnagar** (27,000), on the Jalangi, chief town, centre of Church Missionary Society's agency, and of a Roman Catholic Mission, seat of a Government college, known for its coloured clay figures made by the potter caste. **Santipoor** (28,000), on the Hoogli, with cloth manufactures since it was a centre of East India Company's factories. **Kooshtia** (10,000), railway station on the Padma, chief seat of river trade; here Bishop Cotton was drowned. **Ranaghat**, railway station on the Choorni. **Nadiya**, or Nabadwipa (9000), at junction of the Jalangi and

Bhagirathi, capital of last Hindoo king of Bengal, who moved here from Gaur; still, with Benares and Poona, one of the centres of Brahmanical Pandits, whose Tols or leafy colleges are aided by the State; birthplace of Chaitanya, the Vaishnaiva reformer. Mihrpoor (6000), on the Bhairab, headquarters of subdivision of same name; Kumarkhali (5500), or Commercolly, on the Garai, a railway station.

Nadiya district consists of six subdivisions—Krishnagar, Mihrpoor, Kooshtia, Chooadanga, Bangaon, and Ranaghat. It has 4021 villages, with an average population of 591 souls; and 2768 estates paying £101,755 land revenue, or £36 : 15s. on an average. Dr. Leyden was Collector at one time, and Sir William Jones, Prof. H. H. Wilson, Prof. Cowell, and other Oriental scholars have frequently visited the district. **Plassey** (Palas = a red flower) field, where Clive defeated Saraj-ood-daula in 1757, lies on the Bhagirathi, which has since swept away all Clive's grove of 3000 mango trees, save one venerated by the Muhammadans as marking the spot where one of their leaders fell.

§ 6. MOORSHIDABAD DISTRICT (from Moorshid Kooli Khan, the Brahman apostate to Islam, who transferred the Muhammadan capital from Dacca, and became second founder of Moorshidabad city), is bounded E. and N. by Rajshahi and Maldah, S. by Nadiya and Bardwan, W. by Beerbhoom and Santalia. Area, 2141 sq. m.; population, 1,200,825. The district, which is the head of the great delta of Bengal, is divided by the Bhagirathi, to E. of which is the silt delta, and to W. a nodular limestone formation. The Ganges, forming the N. and E. boundary, throws off the Bhagirathi at Chapghati, the Bhairab and Sialman lower down, and the Jalangi, which separates Moorshidabad from Nadiya district. From the west uplands the Banslai, the Dwarka, the Brahmani, and the Mor fall into the Bhagirathi. **Barhampoor** (27,000) has been the chief civil and military station, on the left bank of the Bhagirathi, since the battle of Plassey. Before 1757, Kasimbazar, the ruins of which are near that station, was the commercial capital of Bengal, where Warren Hastings at first resided. At Barhampoor the first large outbreak of the Mutiny of 1857 took place by the 19th Native Infantry. Seat of a Government college, and mission of London Missionary Society. **Moorshidabad** City (Maksoodavad = old name) (46,000), 5 m. above Barhampoor, was described by Clive as wealthier than London, and quite as populous in his time. Seat of the Muhammadan administration of Bengal, and of the British, till 1793; the Nawab Nazim's title became extinct in 1880. The Nawab of Moorshidabad's palace is in the city; the Motee Jheel, or "pearl lake," 2 m. south, the old palace, and Kuttara with tomb of Moorshid Kooli Khan, are remarkable. **Kandi** (12,000), 16 m. S.W. of Barhampoor, seat of the Rajas of Paikpara. **Jangipoor** (7000), on the Bhagirathi near the Ganges, long the centre of the silk trade. Azeemganj is the terminus of the branch railway from Nalhati on the East Indian Railway to a point three m. above Moorshidabad, and opposite Jeeaganj, a trade-centre. Dhoobran, Bogwangola, and Murari railway stations, are also large marts. Gheria, near where the Bhagirathi leaves the Ganges, was the scene of the battle in 1740 in which Moorshid's house was extinguished by Ali Vardi Khan, and of the victory of Major Adams over Meer Kasim's troops under the renegade Sumroo in 1763. Moorshidabad has 4 subdivisions—Barhampoor, Moorshidabad, Jangipoor, and Kandi.

§ 7. PABNA DISTRICT is bounded E. by Maimansingh and Dacca, S. by Nadiya and Fareedpoor, W. by Nadiya and Rajshahi, and N. by Rajshahi, Bogra, and Maimansingh. Area, 1847 sq. m. Population, 1,312,977. The district consists of the angle formed by the confluence of the Ganges and Brahmapootra, here called Jamoona. The former sends off the Eechamati, which joins the Harasagar, the principal branch of the Jamoona in the district. **Pabna** (16,000), chief town, on the Eechamati. **Serajganj** (19,000), on the Jamoona, centre of the jute trade of Eastern Bengal, with a landing-place changed according to the varying course of the river. **Belkoochi** (5500) mart, 10 m. lower down. Agrarian disturbances, due to rackrenting by new landlords, have frequently affected this district, especially in 1873.

§ 8. RAJSHAHI DISTRICT is bounded E. by Bogra and Pabna, N. by Bogra and Dinajpoor, S. by Nadiya, and W. by Moorshidabad and Maldah. Area, 2359 sq. m. Population, 1,333,237. The Ganges washes the district on the S.W. and S., and throws off the Baral. The Mahananda, which rises in the Himalaya, touches the western boundary for a few miles before it falls into the Ganges. The Atrai, a channel of the Teesta, flows through the district for 70 m. from N.W. to S.E., receiving the Jamoona from Dinajpoor. The Baranai flows through the heart of the district E. into the Atrai. Chalan Bheel or lake covers 150 sq. m. during the rainy season, near Singa on the Nattor and Bogra road. **Rampoor Bauleah** (23,000), chief town, on N. bank of Ganges, formerly seat of Dutch and East India Company's factories, and still a centre of silk and indigo trade. Seat of English Presbyterian Mission. **Nattor** (10,000), 30

m. E. of above, and Hindoo capital of district. Each town is head of a subdivision of the same name.

§ 9. BOGRA DISTRICT is bounded E. by Maimansingh, N. by Rangpoor and Dinajpoor, S. by Pabna and Rajshahi, W. by Rajshahi and Dinajpoor. Area, 150 sq. m. Population, 733,546. The Brahmapootra bounds the district to the E., and it is threaded by the Phuljhur, Karatoya, Nagar, and Jamoona, which pass into the Atrai tributary of the Brahmapootra. **Bogra** (8000), the chief town, on W. bank of Karatoya. **Sherpoor** (4500), once a Muhammadan frontier-post, and still centre of the principal native landholders. Mahastban Garh, a mound of ruins, first capital of a Hindoo dynasty, and now a centre of Muhammadan pilgrimage, is 7 m. N. of Bogra.

§ 10. DINAJPOOR DISTRICT is bounded E. by Jalpaigori and Rangpoor, W. by Purniah, and S. by Maldah, Rajshahi, and Bogra. Area, 4117 sq. m. Population, 1,529,906. The principal rivers, navigable only during the rainy season, are the Mahananda and Nagar on its W. boundary; the Kulik or chief tributary of the Nagar, and the Tangan of the Mahananda; the Chiramati, Purnababha, and Dhapa, which rise in marshes; the Atrai and Jamoona, channels of the Teesta, and the Karatoya on the E. boundary. **Dinajpoor** (13,000), only town, on E. bank of Purnababha, below the junction of the Dhapa. Grain marts abound along the rivers of this purely agricultural district, such as Chooraman on the E. bank of Mahananda, and Raiganj on the Kulik. Several annual fairs and gatherings are held at the tombs of Muhammadan saints and at Hindoo shrines, of which the greatest is the Nekmard fair, held in Bhawanpoor on the first day of the Bengalee year in April, 1 m. W. of the Kulik. Seat of Baptist Mission.

§ 11. RANGPOOR DISTRICT ("place of pleasure") is bounded E. by Goalpara and Maimansingh, N. by Jalpaigori and Kooch Behar, W. by Dinajpoor and Jalpaigori, and S. by Bogra. Area, 3488 sq. m. Population, 2,169,699. The Brahmapootra river forms the E. boundary, flowing south for 80 m.; it steadily encroaches on the right or W. bank. The Teesta, which falls into the above at Chilmari, crosses the district from N.W. to S.E. for 110 m. In the historic floods of 1787 this river changed its course from S. to the Ganges to S.E. to the Brahmapootra, sweeping all before it as it reverted to its old channel. The Ghaghat, Manas, and Gagaria are its branches. The Dharla, Sankos, and Doodhkumar are tributaries of the Brahmapootra. The Karatoya, or Old Teesta, is the principal river in the W. of the district. In the times described in the *Mahabharat* epic, it formed the boundary between the Hindoo kingdom of Kamroop and Matsya or Bengal. Kamroop, including all modern Bengal and Assam to the E., was ruled over by three successive dynasties, of which legends and ruins still give traces, before its conquest under Raja Nilambhar by Husain Shah, Afghan King of Bengal, at the end of the 15th century. **Rangpoor** (15,000), only town, on N. bank of Ghaghat; on branch railway to Dhoobri, Assam; Wesleyan Mission.

§ 12. DARJEELING DISTRICT ("the holy" or "bright spot") (British Sikkim), in the lower Himalaya, between 26° 30′ and 27° 31′ N. lat., and between 88° 2′ and 88° 56′ E. long., is bounded E. by Jalpaigori and Bhootan, N. by Sikkim State, W. by Nepal, and S. by Jalpaigori. Area, 1234 sq. m. Population, 157,038. The district consists of (1) the tarai or submontane forest and marsh between plain and hill, and (2) the valleys and ridges of the hills rising to 10,000 ft. covered with forest, from which the spur, 60 m. long, of the Singaleela range separating Sikkim from E. Nepal, runs up into Kinchinjinga. The principal hills in the district itself are on this range: Phalalum or Phalut (12,042 ft.), Subargum (10,430 ft.), and Tanglu (10,084 ft.); Situng, conical peak, S.E. of Darjeeling town. Sinchal Pahar (hill), a long range, on the top of a spur of which, stretching down to the Teesta, is the military sanitarium of Jallapahar (8067 ft.); the peaks of the latter hill are locally known as Durbin, Bara (big), and Chota (little). Darjeeling station is at a height of 7167 ft. The Teesta river reaches the district from Sikkim State, flows between the two till it receives the Great Rangeet, and then runs south to the plains through the Sivak Gola Pass, with a width of 800 yards. On its right bank it receives the Great Rangeet, the Rangjo, the Rayeng, and the Sivak; on the left, the Rang-chu and the Roli. The Mahananda rises near Mahaldiram hill, and flows between the tarai and Jalpaigori; it receives the New Balasun, Mechi, and Chenga lower down. The Great Rangeet receives on its right bank the Rang-chu, Little Rangeet, and Ramman before it falls into the Teesta. The Jaldhaka flows between Darjeeling and Bhootan and Jalpaigori, receiving on its right bank the Paralang-chu, the Rang-chu, and the Ma-chu. There are two small lakes, one 6 m. S.W. of Hope Town, and the Ramtal E. of the Teesta, ascribed to a landslip. **Darjeeling** town (4000 resident pop.), centre of municipality covering 138 sq. m. (23,000), originally ceded by Sikkim Raja, on a narrow ridge, dividing into two spurs descending 6000 ft.

to the Great Rangeet. Connected by steam tramway with plains at Siligori, 48¾ m., and by railway with Calcutta. 367 m. S. Summer quarters of Bengal Government; acquired in 1835, and enlarged after outrage on Sir J. Hooker and Dr. Campbell in 1850. Seat of Established Church of Scotland's Mission, chiefly among the aboriginal Lepchas. A centre of China tea cultivation since 1856, also at neighbouring settlement of **Hope Town.** Mungpoo and Sittong are the chief cinchona plantations since 1862 in the valley, and Rangarun, botanical garden, is near Darjeeling. **Karseang**, 20 m. S. of Darjeeling. There are 2 subdivisions—Darjeeling and Tarai. Coal, lime, and copper abound; the district is an entrepot of trade with Sikkim and Bengal.

§ 13. *SIKKIM STATE (Tibetan = Demo-jong), Boodhist Lepcha principality under a Raja protected by the British Government since the first Goorkha war in 1817, and subject to it in foreign and military affairs under treaty of 1861, while paying tribute to China through Lhasa. The State has now an area estimated at 2600 sq. m., with a population of 3000 Lepchas, 2000 Bhooteas, and 2000 Limboos. It is bounded N. and N.E. by Tibet, S.E. by Bhootan, S. by Darjeeling, and W. by Nepal. The northern passes into Tibet are of great height. Jelep-la (pass), the most southerly, rises to 13,000 ft.; Guiatu-la and Yah-la, next to it, are 14,000 ft., leading into the Chumbi valley of Tibet. The Cho-la (15,000 ft.), farther north, is on the direct road to Chumbi. The Tankra-la (16,083) is the most snowy in Sikkim. The State is drained by the Teesta and its affluents, and by the Am-machu, rising at the foot of Chumalhari peak (23,929 ft.), flowing through the Chumbi valley, and passing into Jalpaigori under the name of Torsha. **Tumloong** is the capital, at which the Raja is bound to reside nine months in the year; the other three he spends in the cooler **Chumbi** Valley. **Gantak** is the other principal village. The chief Lama monasteries are **Labrong**, near Tumloong, Pemiongchi, and Tassiding. The rapid rivers are crossed by cane bridges, as at Rangpo-tang on the Teesta, and by raft-ferries. **Rangeet** is a station where trade is registered.

§ 14. JALPAIGORI DISTRICT, the W. Bhootan Dwars conquered from Bhootan in the war of 1865, is bounded E. by Goalpara, N. by Bhootan and Darjeeling, S. by Kooch Behar and Rangpoor, and W. by Purniah, Dinajpoor, and Darjeeling. Area, 2911 sq. m. Population, 570,210. The Sinchoola range, Renigango peak 6222 ft., is the western boundary between Bhootan and British territory, below which is **Buxa** cantonment, 6 m. from frontier and 32 m. from Kooch Behar town, on a ridge from 1659 to 2457 feet, at the pass leading to Marichan in Bhootan. The principal rivers from W. to E. are the Mahananda, Karatoya, Teesta, Jaldhaka, Doodooya, Mujnai, Torsha, Kaljani, Raidhak, and Sankos, all of which are navigable by large boats in the plains, except the Karatoya which rises in the district. At the foot of the hills many of the streams disappear for a time in the porous soil. **Jalpaigori** town (6000), on right bank of Teesta, a railway station, with cantonment to the south across the Kharla stream. Titalya is a camping ground on the Mahananda. The ruins of the city of Prithu Raja, of the earliest Kamroop dynasty, were seen at the end of last century, by Dr. Buchanan-Hamilton, on the Talma, a small stream E. of the Karatoya river, in the Sanyasikata subdivision.

§ 15. KOOCH BEHAR STATE ("Koch Monastery") is bounded E. by Goalpara, N. and W. by Jalpaigori, S. by Rangpoor. Area, 1307 sq. m. Population, 600,946. These six rivers flow through it from north to south to join the Brahmapootra—the Teesta, Singimari, Torsha, Kaljani, Raidhak, and Gadadhar. On the destruction of the Hindoo Kingdom of Kamroop by the Afghan kings of Bengal at the end of the 15th century, the Kochs and other aboriginal tribes from the east founded the present State, which became powerful for a time, but had to be helped by Warren Hastings against the Bhooteas in 1773, when the State became externally subject to the British by treaty. The Raja is well educated, and has visited England. **Kooch Behar** town (10,000), on the Torsha, on northern road to Buxa and Bhootan, contains the Raja's palace. Kamatapoor, on W. bank of Dharla, has ruins of the capital of one of the Kamroop dynasties. The native administration is carried on through 3 subdivisions, somewhat after British fashion.

Western Districts.

§ 16. MIDNAPOOR DISTRICT, the most southerly, on the right bank of the Hoogli, is bounded E. by Hoogli with Howrah and River Hoogli, S. by Bay of Bengal and Balasor, W. by Morbhanj State and Puroolia, and N. by Bankura and Bardwan. Area, 5082 sq. m. Population, 2,514,672. The Roopnarayan, Haldi, and Rasoolpoor rivers, with their tributaries, flow through the district eastward to the Hoogli. The Subarnarekha passes through its western jungle tract into the Bay of Bengal. The Midnapoor High-Level Canal runs for 53 m. east and west from the district town to Ooloobareea on the Hoogli, 16 m. below Calcutta. The sea and river face of the district are protected by 37 lines of embankments for a length of 601½ m., maintained at a cost of nearly a million sterling in the past 40 years. **Midnapoor** (28,000), chief town and centre of American Baptist Mission, of brass, indigo, and silk manufactures, on the high road from Calcutta to Orissa. **Chandrakona** (22,000), to the north, long a weaving factory of the East India Company. **Ghatal** (16,000), on the Silai affluent of the Roopnarayan, a trading centre. **Tamlook** (6000), near mouth of the Roopnarayan, ancient port and capital of a Boodhist kingdom, visited by the Chinese travellers Fa Hian and Hwen T'hsang, in the 5th and 7th centuries A.D., but now 60 m. distant from the sea. Dread of Kali, the destroying goddess to whom Tamlook (Tamas + lipta = stained with darkness) is sacred, caused the Marathas to respect the place. Birkool and Chandpoor are cool spots on the southern sea-coast sometimes frequented as watering-places. **Contai**, also, was thus visited by Warren Hastings. **Kedjeree** is the outmost telegraph station for ships, in the same neighbourhood. Midnapoor has 4 subdivisions—Midnapoor, Tamlook, Contai, and Garbheta.

§ 17. HOOGLI AND HOWRAH (HABRA) DISTRICT, the most densely populated portion of the British Empire, is bounded E. by the Hoogli river, S. and W. by the Roopnarayan and Bardwan, and N. by Bardwan. Area, 1701 sq. m. Population, of Hoogli, 1,007,445; of Howrah, 635,381. Besides the Hoogli, which separates the district by a breadth of about half a mile from the 24-Parganahs and Nadiya, and the Roopnarayan, which divides it from Midnapoor on the south, the principal river is the Damodar. All three are connected by drainage and tidal channels. The Damodar, flowing from north to south, falls into the Hoogli just above the mouth of the Roopnarayan, so that the two form the James and Mary sand (jalmari = deadly waters), dreaded by ships which draw 26 ft. in the Calcutta trade. The Saraswati, now a creek, was once the main channel of the Ganges, on which was the royal port of Satgaon, a great city in the 16th century, now a village. **Hoogli** and **Chinsurah** (Chichirah) (35,000), on right bank 25 m. N. of Calcutta-Howrah, form one municipal town. The former was founded by the Portuguese in 1537 on the decay of the old capital Satgaon, the latter by the Dutch, who ceded it to Great Britain in 1825. The English settled at Hoogli in 1641, under a grant made by Shah Jahan to Dr. Boughton, who had cured his daughter. A quarrel with the Nawab of Bengal in 1685 forced Job Charnock to flee to the village which grew into Calcutta. Hoogli-Chinsurah is the seat of an Arabic and English college and Sheeah Imambara endowed by Muhammad Moshin, and of a Free Church Missionary Institution and church. Here too was the first press set up, in 1778. In the northern suburb is Bandel, with a Portuguese Priory and Church, the first (1599) built in Bengal. **Serampoor** (25,000) ("city of the worshipful Rama"), on the Hoogli opposite Barrackpoor, a Danish settlement till 1845 under the name of Frederiksnagar, which gave shelter to Carey, Marshman, and Ward, who here founded their famous Baptist Mission in 1799, and whose tombs are here. Their college with noble library; press at which thirty translations of the Scriptures, and the first Bengalee newspaper, the *Friend of India*, and much pure literature were published; paper-mill, type-foundry, botanic garden, church and Christian village, have made this clean and pretty town much visited by travellers. A Scottish jute factory now occupies the garden and press. **Howrah** (105,575), opposite Calcutta, of which it practically forms a part, and connected with it by a bridge, is the great terminus of the East Indian system of railways, till the central station be built in Calcutta. Howrah forms a magisterial district, but is part of Hoogli in other respects. Dockyards, mills, factories, a civil engineering college in what was Bishop's College, and the Botanical Garden, make this ever-growing town the most important out of Calcutta proper, or what Jersey City is to New York.

Two high strips of land, formed by the river silt, from Howrah along the Hoogli N. to Tribeni, and along the Saraswati or old Ganges parallel to this, are covered by a succession of populous towns and villages inhabited by the well-to-do Hindoo families, some of whom hold office or trade in the capital, while others attend to the land. Between the two ridges the country has been more than once devastated by fever. Still the population increases on the higher ground till it stands at between 1080 and 3000 the sq. m. Here, too, is much educational and social activity.

Chandarnagar ("city of sandal-wood"), on the Hoogli between Chinsurah and Serampoor, is still a French settlement subject administratively to Pondicheri in Madras, covers 3 sq. m., and has a population of 23,000. Founded in 1673, the settlement was made a considerable port by Dupleix, was captured by Admiral Watson in 1757 and held for six years, was a second time held by the British from 1794 to 1816.

Hoogli District has 5 subdivisions—Hoogli, Serampoor, Howrah, Mahishrakha, and Jahanabad.

§ 18. BARDWAN DISTRICT, bounded E. by Nadiya, S. by Hoogli and Midnapoor, W. by Bankura and Manbhoom, and N. by the Santal country, Beerbhoom, and Moorshidabad. When, in 1760, Meer Kasim Khan made over Bardwan to the British, it included the present district, Bankura, Hoogli, and a third of Beerbhoom. Area, 2693 sq. m. Population, 1,391,730. This is the coal region of Bengal. Besides the Bhagirathi or Hoogli on the east, the Roopnarayan on the south, and the Damodar on the north-west, the principal rivers are the Ajai and Khari. After forming the northern boundary the Ajai enters the district at Bhedia, and flows east through Katwa subdivision to the Bhagirathi. The Khari rises in a rice field near the western town of Boodbood and winds eastward to the Bhagirathi. **Bardwan** (33,000), chief station, a municipal town on the Banka tributary of the Khari, consisting of 73 villages around the palace and gardens of the Maharaja of Bardwan. Here the Church Missionary Society works. **Kalna** (28,000), port of the district, and Free Church Mission station, on the Bhagirathi; **Syambazar** (20,000), an old town south of the Ajai; **Raneeganj** (20,000), centre of the coal mining on the north bank of the Damodar; **Jahanabad** (14,000), on E. bank of Roopnarayan; **Katwa** (8000), old town at the confluence of the Ajai and Bhagirathi, where Ali Vardi Khan defeated the Marathas; **Dainhat** (8000), mart on the Bhagirathi.

The Raneeganj coal-field covers an area of 500 sq. m., between 120 and 160 m. N.W. of Calcutta, and is traversed by two lines of the East Indian Railway from Kanoo junction. Some 50 coal mines put out about half a million tons of non-coking bituminous coal every year, used for ordinary steam purposes, the very best only touching the average of English coal. There is much iron ore, but flux is scarce. From **Seetarampoor** station the direct main railway to Bombay, by Sambalpoor and Nagpoor, is likely to run. Bardwan District has 5 subdivisions—Bardwan, Katwa, Kalna, Boodbood, and Raneeganj.

§ 19. BANKURA DISTRICT, bounded E. and N. by Bardwan, S. by Midnapoor, W. by Manbhoom. Area, 2621 sq. m. Population, 1,044,195. Its uplands rise into hills, the principal of which is Susoonia (1442 ft.) The Damodar and Roopnarayan are its rivers, but neither is here navigable. **Bankura** (17,000), chief station on N. bank of Roopnarayan. **Bishnupoor** (18,000), ancient capital of Hindoo dynasty of same name, a few miles S. of Roopnarayan. There are 2 subdivisions—Bankura and Bishnupoor.

§ 20. BEERBHOOM DISTRICT ("hero" or "jungle-land") is bounded E. by Moorshidabad and Bardwan, N. by Moorshidabad and Santal country, W. by Santal country, and S. by Bardwan. Area, 1344 sq. m. Population, 792,411. Besides the Ajai, which forms the southern boundary, the only river is the Mor, which, rising in the Santal country, flows through the district from west to east, and is rarely navigable save by descending boats. The iron ore was long worked by the natives. **Sooree** (2100), chief town, 3 m. south of the Mor. **Nagar** or Rajnagar, ancient capital of the Hindoo princes of Beerbhoom; the hot springs of Tantipara are a few m. to the south. **Ganootia**, on N. bank of Mor, centre of silk industry for a century. Soorool, 5 m. N. of the Ajai, long the great commercial residence of the East India Company under Mr. Cheap, now an obscure place. Kendooli village on N. bank of Ajai, birthplace of the Vaishnaivite poet, Jaideva. There are 2 subdivisions—Sooree and Rampore Hat.

Eastern Districts.

§ 21. DACCA DISTRICT ("Dhak" tree) is bounded E. by Tipura, N. by Maimansingh, S. and W. by Bakirganj and Fareedpoor. Area, 2796 sq. m. Population, 2,196,641. The district is the centre of the three river systems of Lower Bengal, the Megna which receives the north-eastern streams from Cachar, the Brahmapootra from the north, and the Ganges from the north-west. These are interlaced by a network of streams, of which ten are navigable by large native boats. The Megna, the eastern boundary, is never fordable, is affected by the tide only in the cold and hot seasons, forms many alluvial banks or chars, and has a considerable bore at its mouth. Its principal tributaries are the Dhaleswari, from the N.W. and the old Brahmapootra. The Ganges, or Padma, which bounds the district W. and S.W., joins the Megna (1) by the four-mile channel of the Kirtinasa N. of Kartikpoor, and (2) by Naya Bagna, in Bakirganj, leaving its original channel almost dry. It throws off the Hilsamari to the Dhaleswari and the Arralkhan. The Lakhmia, a beautiful river with high wooded banks, leaves the Brahmapootra at Tok and falls into the Dhaleswari 4 m. above the confluence of that river with the Megna. The Buriganga is a loop of the Dhaleswari, from which it separates itself for 26 m. Artificial watercourses facilitate navigation and trade. In 1517 the Portuguese first visited this and the estuaries at the head of the Bay of Bengal, where they lived by piracy and trade. The English settled in Dacca about 1660. As Firinghis or Franks the Portuguese descendants have become mixed with the Bengalees, but retain their faith.

Dacca city (70,000), chief town on the Buriganga 8 m. above its reunion with the Dhaleswari. The eastern capital of the Mughuls after 1608, the site of an East India Company's factory after 1660, from which time till 1817 its fine muslins were imported into England. After decaying for a time, the jute trade which began about 1860 restored some of its prosperity. It is the seat of a Government College and Baptist Mission. Greeks and Armenians long traded here; the number of Europeans and Eurasians in the district is still about 6000. **Naraingani** (11,000), great mart extending 3 m. along W. bank of Lakhmia, where it joins the Dhaleswari. **Manikganj** (11,500), mart covering 2 sq. m. on W. bank of Dhaleswari. Bikrampoor, the Hindoo capital before the Muhammadan invasion, is now Rampal, where a mound marks Ballal Sen's palace. Sonargaon, the first Muhammadan capital, is now Painam.

Dacca District has 3 subdivisions—Dacca, Moonsheeganj, and Manikganj. It contains 8739 estates, held by 16,688 owners paying £52,700 land-tax.

§ 22. BAKIRGANJ DISTRICT is bounded E. by the Megna and Bay of Bengal, N. by Dacca and Fareedpoor, W. by Fareedpoor and Jessor, and S. by Bay of Bengal. Area, 3648 sq. m. Population, 1,885,183. The Megna, the Arial Khan offshoot of the Ganges and the Baleswar, known as the Madhumati and Garai higher up, are the principal rivers. The Barisal river flows from the Arial Khan to the sea. Other large navigable rivers, ever changing their local names, form a network through which the delta is drained into the Bay or inundated by the sea, and create islands like Dakshin Shahbazpoor. The spring tides cause a strong bore in the Megna estuary. Canals and watercourses take the place of roads, and fishing alternates with agriculture. **Barisal** (8000), a chief town on W. bank of river of same name, seat of prosperous Baptist and other Christian Missions. Nalchiti municipality on river of same name. Jhalakati, great timber mart at junction of Nalchiti and Jhalakati streams. Daulat Khan, in island of Dakshin Shahbazpoor. The district has 5 subdivisions—Barisal, Dakshin Shahbazpoor, Madaripoor, Firozpoor, and Patwakhali.

§ 23. FAREEDPOOR DISTRICT is bounded E. by Dacca, N. by Pabna, W. by Jessor, S. by Bakirganj. Area, 2267 sq. m. Population, 1,614,083. Besides the Ganges on the E. and N., the Arial Khan, and Madhumati, the principal rivers are the Chandna, with its tributary the Kumar, which leaves the Ganges and flows to the Garai and Madhumati. The Kumar flows from the Chandna near Fareedpoor station S.E. to Bakirganj swamps, swollen into lakes in the rainy season, encircling mounds artificially raised by the Chandal caste of Hindoos, many of whom are becoming Christians. **Fareedpoor** (7000), chief town on W. bank of small Mara Padma, with the Dhol Samoodra lake to the south. **Sayyidpoor** (6500), municipality and mart on the Barasia. **Goalunda** (1000), great entrepot at the junction of the main streams of the Ganges and Brahmapootra, terminus of the Eastern Bengal Railway and river port for Dacca and Assam steamers. Daulatpoor, obscure village, where the Faraizi sect of the Musalman Soonnees took their rise, and under Dudoo Miyan caused political trouble in 1857. The 2 subdivisions are Fareedpoor and Goalunda.

§ 24. MAIMANSINGH DISTRICT is bounded E. by Sylhet and Tipura, N. by Garo hills, S. by Dacca, and W. by Pabna, Bogra, and Rangpoor. Area, 6287 sq. m. Population, 2,950,105. The Susang hills form the N.W. border. The Jamoona, or main channel of the Brahmapootra, flows for 94 m. along the western boundary, with a breadth in some places of 6 m. The (old) Brahmapootra flows through the centre of the district to Tok, where it enters Dacca, a fordable stream rarely more than ¼ m. broad. It throws off the Jhinai to the Jamoona. The Kangsa is a deep stream between Maimansingh and Sylhet. **Naseerabad** or Maimansingh (10,000), chief town, on the W. bank of the Brahmapootra. **Jamalpoor** (15,000), also on W. bank of the Brahmapootra, once a military station. **Kisoriganj**, 13 m. E. of the Brahmapootra. **Sherpoor** (8000), 9 m. N. of Jamalpoor. Dhanikola (7000), on the Satua. These are the principal places in the 4 subdivisions of the same name, omitting the last.

§ 25. TIPURA DISTRICT (**Tripura** = sun-god or ruler of three worlds) is bounded E. by Hill Tipura; S. by Noakhali; W. by Megna, separating it from Maimansingh, Dacca, and Bakirganj; and N. by Maimansingh and Sylhet. Area, 2491 sq. m. Population, 1,491,762. The Lalmai range, 5 m. W. of Comillah, low wooded hills, rise into the Maynamati hill (100 ft.), a retreat for the European residents. The Megna receives the Ganges and Brahmapootra opposite Chandpoor, 60 m. farther south than in Major Rennell's time or a century ago. The Goomti, rising in the Tipura hills, divides the district and falls into the Megna at Daudkhandi. The Dakatia traverses the south part of the district for 150 m., and falls into the Megna. The Titas similarly waters the northern portion of the district. **Comillah** (Kumilla) (13,000), chief town on S. bank of Goomti, on Dacca and Chittagong road. **Brahmanbaria** (12,500), on N. bank of Titas. There are 2 subdivisions, of which these towns are the headquarters.

§ 26. HILL TIPURA, Native State bounded E. by Chittagong Hill Tracts and Looshai country, N. by Sylhet, W. by Tipura District and Noakhali, S. by Noakhali and Chittagong. Area, 3867 sq. m. Population, 95,637. Five or six terraced and parallel ranges of hills, at an average distance of 12 m. from each other, raise the country from W. to E. to Betling Seeb (3200 ft.), the highest peak in the Jampooi range. The Goomti and Pheni, the Haora, Khozai, Dulac, and Manu rivers are navigable during the rainy season. **Agartala** (1500), the capital, is a village on the N. bank of the river Haora 30 m. from Comillah. Kailashar and Oodaipoor are subdivisional stations. The Raja, according to the Bengalee verse chronicle "Rajmala," is of the lunar race; he early adopted the Shiva form of Hindooism with its practice of human sacrifice. As holder of an estate covering 589 sq. m. in Tipura District, the Raja's title is decided by the Civil Courts. The magistrate of Tipura is Political Agent of Hill Tipura, with a native assistant at Agartala. The Raja is a British subject as to his estate, and a feudatory paying a succession duty for Hill Tipura.

§ 27. CHITTAGONG DISTRICT (Saptagram = seven villages of the seven sages) is bounded E. by Hill Tracts of Chittagong and Arakan; S. by the Naf, separating it from Arakan; W. by Bay of Bengal; N. by Tipura and Noakhali. Area, 2567 sq. m. Population, 1,220,973. There are 5 ranges of low hills covered with jungle, and rising to Seetakoond in the N., as the highest point (1155 ft.). Of the three navigable rivers the largest is the Karnaphooli, which rises in the N.E. of the Hill Tracts and winds W. and S.W. to the Bay of Bengal, after receiving the Halda from the N. The Sangoo, rising in the N. Arakan Hill Tracts, winds W. and S.W. through Chittagong into the Bay 10 m. S. of the Karnaphooli mouth. The Pheni forms the boundary between Chittagong and Noakhali on the north. The coast consists of a network of creeks, swamps, and forests of the Soondarban type on the other side of the Bay. Canal cuttings connect the creeks along the coast for navigation. Small embankments keep out the salt water.

Chittagong (21,000), a port and chief town 12 m. up the

Karnaphooli, with 20 feet anchorage. The Portuguese, who settled here before Satgaon and Hoogli, named it Porto Grando. In 1665 it was taken by the Mughuls, who called it Islamabad. In 1857 the 34th Native Infantry mutinied here. Long unhealthy and decaying, the port is again rising and is next to Calcutta of the Bengal ports. There is a Roman Catholic establishment for 800 Firinghi descendants of the Portuguese, who, in all but that faith, have become identified with the natives. **Cox's Bazaar** (5000) in the south, or the Baghkali creek, inhabited chiefly by Mughs, or Boodhists of Arakan, whose fathers helped the Portuguese in their piratical attacks on the Muhammadans, and in 1638 made Chittagong over to their Government of Bengal. The Mugh immigration from Arakan to Chittagong led to the first Burmese war. Tea cultivation began in the district in 1840, and export in 1868.

§ 28. CHITTAGONG HILL TRACTS DISTRICT is bounded E. by a line which follows the Tooilenpooi or Sajjook and Tooi Chang and Thega branches of the Karnaphooli to the Arakan frontier beyond the S. hill-station of Keokradrong, S. by Akyab, W. by Chittagong, and N. by Hill Tipura. Area, 5419 sq. m. Population, 101,467. Ten ranges of hills (*tang* or *toung*), accessible only to the wild elephant, reach a maximum height of 2789 ft. in the Rang-rang-dang peak of the Tyambang range (lat. 21° 41′, long. 92° 29′). The rivers Pheni, Karnaphooli, Sangoo, and Matamoori divide the tracts into four valleys. Ramakri lake, on E. side of hill of same name, 6 m. S.E. of Politai, is of great beauty. **Rangamati**, on the Karnaphooli below Kasalarg, the limit of its navigation, administrative centre and mart for hill produce; here Goorkha veterans are settled. **Bandarban**, chief town in Sangoo or south portion, of which **Ruma**, 16 m. S.E., is seat of Assistant Commissioner. The tribes are divided into the fifteen clans of Boodhist Khyoungtha, or children of the river, and the more savage aboriginal or mixed Toungtha, or children of the hills. The former are managed through the Chakma, Bohmoug, and Mong chiefs. The Toungtha tribes are the Tipuras, Mrungs, Koomis, Miros, and Khyengs, British subjects; Bangos and Pankhos, under British influence; and Looshais or Kookees, and Shendoos, virtually independent.

§ 29. NOAKHALI DISTRICT is bounded E. by Hill Tipura and Chittagong, S. by Bay of Bengal, W. by Megna, and N. by Tipura. Area, 1641 sq. m. Population, 822,328. The Megna river here reaches the sea through the Shahbazpoor, Hatia, Bamni and Sandweep mouths, and Dakatia and Bara

Pheni (big Fenny) tributaries. The creeks and navigable watercourses are numerous. The Megna forms the islands of Sandweep and Natia on the sea face of Noakhali, besides many large *chars*, which rapidly advance the mainland seawards. Here the tidal wave is highest (40 ft.), especially at the Pheni mouth: during cyclones it submerges the islands and rolls far inland. The canals open up 41 miles of navigation.

Soodharam or Noakhali (5000), chief town on the right bank of Noakhali watercourse; once on the sea, but now 10 miles inland. Sandweep island was the centre of the Portuguese, Mugh, and Muhammadan conflicts in the seventeenth century. Bhulna in the W. was an outpost of the Mughul Empire, and scene of a battle with the Portuguese in 1610. At Jugdia, mouth of the Pheni, and other places, the ruins of the East India Company's factories, established in 1756, are seen. Three-fourths of the population are Muhammadan.

II.—BEHAR.

§ 30. PATNA DISTRICT, administrative centre of Behar or the Patna Division of the Bengal Lieutenant-Governorship, and ancient metropolitan district of the Boodhist kingdom of Maghada, lies for 93 miles along the south bank of the Ganges, between 24° 28′ and 25° 42′ N. lat. and 84° 44′ and 86° 05′ E. long. It is bounded E. by Monghyr, S. by Gaya, W. by Shahabad, and N. by Tirhoot and Saran. Area, 2078 sq. m. Population, 1,796,619. The two ridges of the Rajagriha hills divide the district in the S.E. for 50 m. from Gaya, rising to 1000 ft. with hot springs in the quartz and other igneous rocks, and clothed with jungle. The Ganges receives the Son, after it has flowed along the W. boundary of the district for 41 m., at a point which has varied several miles since 1772, when it was at Maner. If the Son is the Erranoboas (Hiranyabaha) of Megasthenes, then the confluence has gradually moved westward, for Palibothra (Patali-putra) has now been identified with the modern Patna city. The main Ganges, flowing E. from the junction, is joined by the Patna canal from the higher waters of the Son, at Deegha, receives the Gandak from the N. at Bankipoor, and the Poonpoon from the S. at Fatwa. The Ganges, raising its channel, frequently floods the district by driving back the streams from the south upon the lower lands.

Patna City ("*the* town;" Azimabad = Muhammadan name), on right bank of Ganges; sixth city of India in population (160,000), and, in Bengal, next to Calcutta commercially. The capital of Sandracottus (Chandragoopta), visited by Megasthenes, envoy from Seleukos Nikator 300 B.C., said by Diodorus to have been founded by Herakles, but, by the *Vaya Purana*, by the grandson of Ajata Satru, contemporary of Gautama, 500-543 B.C., who predicted that the village of Patali would become a great city. Megasthenes describes the circumference of the city as 25¼ m. Visited by Hwen T'hsang in 637 A.D., when the old city, then deserted, had a circumference of 11⅔ m. Capital of insurgent Sher Shah, reduced by Akbar, and ruled by Aurangzeb's grandson, Azim, whence its Muhammadan name. Scene of Meer Kasim's massacre of sixty Englishmen in 1763. The Government opium factory, *Gola* or granary built in 1786 "for the perpetual prevention of famine," college, market on ground where the Wahabee rebels plotted, and Har-Mandu temple of the Sikhs, where Govind Singh, their last teacher, was born, are the principal places of interest. Near the junction of the Son, Gandak, and Ganges, Patna is the entrepot of the river trade from the N.W. Province, Nepal, and Bengal, sending away rice, oil-seeds, and vegetables, and importing English piece-goods and salt. The Ganges is 2 m. broad at Patna.

Bankipoor, civil station of district and western suburb of Patna city, occupied chiefly by European officials. **Dinapòor** (28,000), military station, still further west, and forming, with Bankipoor and Patna, a city straggling for 14 miles along the Ganges. Local centre of the Mutiny of 1857; the non-disarming of three sepoy corps here delayed the advance of the British troops towards Cawnpoor and Lucknow, and spread revolt over South Behar. **Maner** (5500), a few miles E. of junction of Son and Ganges, which now unite near Sherpoor. **Barh** (11,500), East Indian railway town opposite Tirhoot Railway terminus of Bazetpoor on left bank of Ganges. Muhammadpoor (6000) is a suburb of Barh. **Fatwa** (10,000) at junction of Poonpoon with Ganges, and Baikathpoor (6000) 5 m. E., both frequented by Hindoo pilgrims. **Mukama** (12,000), on the Ganges, a growing railway town. **Behar** town (45,000), on the Panchana, 54 m. from Patna, ancient capital of Magadha and then of the Muhammadan viceroys, sacked by the Marathas, and further depopulated by the great famine of 1770. Here is a large *sarai* or inn for pilgrims, with a museum of Boodhist antiquities. **Rajagriha** ("royal residence"), farther south, or Rajgir, a former capital of Magadha, and residence of Boodha, described by Hwen T'hsang and Fa Hian, in the Pali annals: Rajgir, the present town, is a mile N. There are hot springs near, on the Sarsooti stream, and at Tapo'ban, much frequented by both Hindoos and Muhammadans. Giriyak, on the border of Gaya, is a village on a hill of antiquarian interest. Patna District is in 4 subdivisions—Bankipoor, Barh, Dinapoor, and Behar.

§ 31. GAYA DISTRICT is bounded E. by Monghyr, N. by Patna, W. by Shahabad, and S. and S.E. by Lohardaga and Hazaribagh. Area, 4712 sq. m. Population, 2,057,980. Isolated hills, a rainfall diminishing to 40 inches, and the dry hot winds, mark the transition from Lower Bengal to the tableland of Central India. Maher, 12 m. S.E. of Gaya Town, and the Barabar hills in south of Jahanabad subdivision, are the principal elevations, besides the Rajagriha ridges on the Patna border. The Son river, the W. boundary, cuts the Grand Trunk Road at Baroon village, below the head of the Son Canal. The river's golden sands (Hiranyabaha) originated its Greek name Erranoboas, described by Arrian as inferior only to the Indus and Ganges. Its channel is still almost equal to the Ganges. The Poonpoon rises in S. of district, and flows parallel to the Son till it joins the Ganges. The Phalgoo, formed of two hill-torrents as it enters Gaya, intersects the district N. and S., and falls by two branches into the Poonpoon ; it is dry in the hot season. The E. Main Canal and Patna Canal leave the Son in this district. **Gaya** city (67,000), including Sahibganj and railway station, on the Phalgoo, on an eminence; great place of Hindoo pilgrimage during the past six centuries. The *Vaya Purana* tells how Brahma induced the monster Gaya to remain still by the promise that the gods would dwell on the spot, and pilgrimage to which would deliver the departed from the Hindoo purgatory. The fourteen sets of dissolute Gayawals or Brahmans are very wealthy , the inferior priests or Pretiyas, said to have been brought up to fight Gaya, are at Pretseela (ghost-city), 4 m. from Gaya, one of the forty-five sacred spots. **Tikari** (8000), on the Murhar, 15 m. N.W. of Gaya, with fort of Rajas of Tikari (rental £47,000). **Sherghati** (7000), where Grand Trunk Road crosses the Murhar, decaying since railway was opened. **Boodh Gaya**, 6 m. S. of Gaya, ruins of the Vihar or monastery where the founder of Boodhism dwelt, with *pipal* tree (*Ficus religiosa*) under which he is said to have meditated. **Jahanabad** (21,500), 31 m. N. of Gaya, once centre of East India and Dutch Companies' cloth trade. **Daudnagar** (11,000), on Son, 40 m. N.E. of Gaya, once with cloth and opium factories, and still the second trading centre of the district. There are 4 subdivisions—Gaya, Nawada, Aurangabad, and Jahanabad.

§ 32. SHAHABAD DISTRICT is bounded E. by Patna and Gaya, N. by Saran and Ghazipoor (North-Western Province), W. by Ghazipoor, Mirzapoor, and Benares, and S. by Lohardaga. Area, 4366 sq. m. Population, 1,964,900. Some 800 m. of the area is occupied by the Kaimoor hills of the Vindhya range, rising to 1500 ft., with bold escarpments surmounted by forts, and fine gorges and waterfalls. The Son and Ganges form the district on E. and N. Streams from the Kaimoor hills pass through it to the Ganges. The principal of these is the Karamnassa, of evil repute among Hindoos, which flows N.W. from the Eastern Kaimoor ridge, separating Bengal from the North-Western Province before it falls into the Ganges. The Dhoba or Kao, entering the plains from the plateau at the Tarrachandi pass 2 m. S.E. of Sasseram, sends off the Koocha to the Karamnassa, and flows north to the Ganges. The Darganti flows from the plateau into the same river. The Sura, from the same hills, falls into the Darganti after a course of 25 m. The Son Canals, designed by Colonel Dickens, begin at Dehri on the Trunk Road, whence from the main western canal they are led to Arrah, Buxar, and Chausa, with branches, protecting the district from famine and increasing navigation and trade.

Arrah (40,000), chief town and railway station, 14 m. S. of Ganges, 8 m. W. of Son, and 191 m. from Calcutta. Scene of Draupadi's marriage in *Mahabharat* epic; famous for heroic defence during Mutiny of 1857, when twelve Englishmen and fifty Sikhs held Boyle's two houses against the Behar rebels under Kooar Singh till relieved by Vincent Eyre. **Buxar**, changing station of East India Railway, and formerly stud depôt. Here, in 1714, Sir Hector Munro defeated Meer Kasim in the battle which completed the British conquest of Bengal. **Sasseram** ("one thousand toys") (21,000), on trunk road, 60 m. S. of Arrah, with mausoleum of Sher Shah, the Afghan Emperor of Delhi, who defeated Hoomayoon. **Doomraon** (18,000), a railway station and municipality. **Jagdispoor** (10,000), centre of the rebel Kooar Singh's estates, granted to Mr. Burrows of Bihiya, who cleared them of jungle for military operations. **Nasriganj** (6000), centre of another escheated estate, near the Son, and place of trade and paper manufacture. **Rhotas**, fort on Kaimoor hills (1490 ft.), the ruins having a circumference of 28 m.—named after the Hindoo king whose image was destroyed by Aurangzeb, and the stronghold of Akbar's viceroy, Man Singh. Shergarh, 20 m. S.W. of Sasseram, stronghold of Sher Shah, resembling Durham Castle; 7 m. off is the sacred cave of Gooptasar, half a mile long. Chausa, village 4 m. W. of Buxar, where Sher Shah defeated the Emperor Hoomayoon in 1539, who escaped across the Ganges on a water-skin, the owner of which was rewarded with a seat on the throne, and absolute power for half a day. Shahabad is in 4 subdivisions—Arrah, Buxar, Sasseram, and Bhabwa.

§ 33. SARAN DISTRICT, the alluvial tract enclosed by the Gandak, Gogra, and Ganges, bounded on the N.W. by the North-Western Province district of Gorakhpoor, E. by Tirhoot and Champaran, and S. by Shahabad and Patna. Many drainage channels, *nadis* and *nalas*, intersect the district between the three rivers. Area, 2625 sq. m. Population, 2,280,382. **Chapra** (47,000), chief town, on left bank of Ganges, which is deserting it; long a centre of the saltpetre trade, and seat of English, Portuguese, Dutch, and French factories. **Revelganj** (14,000), the largest mart, a mile above the junction of the Gogra and Ganges, where boats tranship their cargoes between Bengal and Nepal and the North-Western Province. The tomb of the founder, Mr. Revell, in 1788, is regarded as a shrine. Here resided Gautama, founder of the Nyaya or Hindoo logic. **Sewan** (11,000), on the E. bank of Daha, 40 m. N.W. of Chapra, famous for pottery and brass-work. **Sonpoor**, at junction of Gandak and Ganges, an ancient and very sacred place of Hindoo pilgrimage, and centre of the largest social gathering of Europeans in rural Bengal for horse races. Indigo and opium are largely grown and manufactured on the rich alluvium of Saran. It has 2 subdivisions —Chapra and Sewan. The Hatwa Raja has a rent-roll of £65,000 from villages in the N.W. of Saran district. There is a German Protestant Mission (Gossner's) in Chapra.

§ 34. CHAMPARAN DISTRICT is bounded E. by Muzaffarpoor, N. by Nepal, W. by Nepal and Gorakhpoor, and S. by Saran and Muzaffarpoor. Ditches and masonry pillars mark off the N. frontier from Nepal, where there are no streams, to Aheera Siswa at the Ramnagar forest, whence the boundary runs straight to Thori, top of the Sumeswar range, and on to the source of the Pachnad, which joins the Gandak at Tribeni. Area, 3531 sq. m. Population, 1,708,417. The Doon range for 20 m., and the Sumeswar range to the N. of it for 46 m., occupy 364 m. of the area chiefly with forest. Through the pass of the Sumeswar made by the Koodi stream the British marched in the Goorkha War of 1814-15 to Deoghat in Nepal; the other passes are the Sumeswar, up the bed of the Joori stream to a beautiful spot fitted for a sanitarium, overlooking the Mauri valley of Nepal, with a view of the lofty Dhawalagiri and Everest mountains; the Kapan and Harlan Harha passes. Three of the rivers in the district are navigable by large boats. The Gandak, from the S. boundary of Central Tibet, reaches the plains at Tribeni Ghat, and thence, in tortuous course, forms the W. boundary of the district, which it often inundates. The Little Gandak flows through the centre of the district from the Sumeswar range at the Harha pass; it bears many local names. The Baghmati is a rapid stream, often flooded, which forms the E. boundary for 35 m. A chain of 43 lakes covers 139 sq. m. in the centre of the district, marking a deserted river bed. Amua, Lalsarya, Sheogaon, Motihari, Seraha, and Tataria, are the largest. The aboriginal Tharoos collect gold dust in the rivers, washed down from the Doon hills. The Raja of Ramnagar's forest covers 427 sq. m., much denuded for railway construction and by fire. **Moteehari** (8500), chief civil station on lake of same name. **Sagauli**, 15 m. from Moteehari on Bettia Road, native cavalry station, where most of the troopers mutinied and cut down the Europeans; one faithful detachment did good service in Oudh. **Bettia** (14,000), on the Harha, the largest town, a trading centre, with palace of Maharaja whose rent-roll is £115,000 from 1,167,617 acres, of which a third is let in farms. Here is a Roman Catholic Mission. Simraun, through the ruins of which the present frontier runs, was seat of a Hindoo dynasty up to the Muhammadan invasion in 1322. At Kesariya in the south, and Araraj and Lauria (pillar) Marandgarh, N. of Bettia, are Boodhist ruins, and pillars with Asoka's edicts. There are 2 subdivisions—Moteehari and Bettia.

§ 35. MUZAFFARPOOR DISTRICT was formed with Darbhanga out of the large and rich alluvial district of Tirhoot after the famine of 1874. Area, 3004 sq. m. Population, 2,589,524. Muzaffarpoor district is bounded E. by Darbhanga, N. by Nepal, W. by Champaran and Saran, and S. by Patna. The principal rivers are the Ganges, Gandak which joins it at Hajipoor, Baya which from the Gandak crosses Tirhoot to the Ganges, the Little Gandak, and the Baghmati.

Muzaffarpoor ("victorious city") (39,000), chief town on S. bank of Little Gandak, with good official and educational buildings, a seat of Gossner's mission, and the centre of the indigo culture; at Sarai factory, 18 m. S.W., is an Asoka pillar. **Seetamarhi** ("field of Seeta") (7500), on W. bank of Lakhandai in the N., mart for Nepal produce, with large export of rice and sacred thread (*janao*) of Brahmans; birthplace of Seeta, Rama's wife. **Hajipoor** (22,500), on N. bank of

Gandak, at its junction with Ganges, with *sarai* or inn, temple, and mosque, and ruins of fort in Akbar's time, worth notice; once a great city, and still an important mart. **Lalganj** (12,500), 12 m. up Gandak; near it is Singhiya, now an indigo but long a saltpetre factory of the Dutch East India Company. This district is in 3 subdivisions—Muzaffarpoor, Hajipoor, and Seetamarhi; in the last is the new mart, for Nepal, of Bairgania on the frontier.

§ 36. DARBHANGA DISTRICT is bounded E. by Bhagalpoor, N. by Nepal, S. by Monghyr, and W. by Muzaffarpoor. Besides the Tirhoot rivers which pass through it from Muzaffarpoor, there is the Tiljooga, which rises in Nepal, skirts the E. boundary of Darbhanga, receives the Bhagmati's waters through the Garai and the Khamla, and falls into the Ganges at Colgong after leaving the district. The Baraila Lake covers 20 sq. m. in the S.W. corner of the district. Area, 3335 sq. m. Population, 2,578,090. **Darbhanga** (48,000), on left bank of Little Baghmati, chief town, with palaces, old and new, of Maharaja who has a rent-roll of £202,419, and pays land-tax of £42,821. The town is connected by railway (44 m.) with Bazetpoor on the Ganges, and by steam ferry with Barh on the East Indian line, since the famines of 1866 and 1874. **Roosera** (9500), mart on Little Gandak. **Poosa**, higher up, long State stud depot, and now model farm with successful tobacco culture and manufacture. **Madhubani**, in the north, on the road to Nepal. There are 3 subdivisions—Darbhanga, Madhubani, and Tajpoor.

§ 37. MONGHYR DISTRICT is bounded E. by Bhagalpoor, N. by Bhagalpoor and Darbhanga, W. by Patna and Gaya, and S. by Hazaribagh and Santalia. Area, 3922 sq. m. Population, 1,955,920. In the south the low Kharakpoor Hills run N. and S. The Ganges cuts the districts in two, receiving the little Gandak and Tiljooga from N., and the Keul from S. North of the Ganges are many marshes, chief of which is the Kabar Lake. **Monghyr** (60,000), large town picturesquely situated on S. bank of Ganges, with fort, jail once palace of Akbar's son, and tomb of "Ashraf," Musalman poet and teacher of Aurangzeb's famous daughter, Zebunnisa Begam. In the neighbourhood are many hot springs. Here many Europeans and Eurasians reside, and there is a Baptist mission. **Jamalpoor**, township (11,000), railway junction for Monghyr town, with largest iron workshops (of East Indian Railway) in India. **Jamooi** (6000), railway station and mart on the Keul, near **Gidhaur**, seat of the old Rajpoot Maharajas. There are 3 subdivisions—Monghyr, Begoo Sarai, and Jamooi.

§ 38. BHAGALPOOR DISTRICT is bounded E. by Santalia and Purniah, N. by Nepal, W. by Tirhoot and Monghyr, S. by Santalia. Area, 4268 sq. m. Population, 1,923,276. The Ganges cuts the district in two for 60 m., receiving from the south a few hill streams, of which the Chandan, the largest, rises near Deogarh, in Santalia. The Tiljooga and other rivers from the south fall into the Googri, which flows parallel to the Ganges into Purniah, where it joins the Koosi. **Bhagalpoor** (70,000), on S. bank of Ganges, chief town, with monument erected by landholders and Government to Augustus Cleveland, who died at 29, after civilising the Dravidian Paharias (hill-men) of Rajmahal. Here the Church Missionary Society has a mission. **Colgong** (5239), now deserted by the Ganges, but long a great mart. Here died Mahmood Shah in 1539, last independent King of Bengal. **Sultanganj** (4500), on the Ganges, with two granite rocks topped by a popular Hindoo shrine and a mosque. At Singheswartan, near Nepal frontier, a large elephant fair is held every January. Mandargiri, 30 m. S. of Bhagalpoor town, a granite hill (700 ft.), famous in mythology as that piled by Vishnoo as Madhoosoodan on the giant, and used in churning the ocean; also a centre of many curiosities. There are 4 subdivisions — Bhagalpoor, Banka, Madahpoora, and Soopool.

§ 39. PURNIAH DISTRICT (Puraniya = extreme E. of the Aryans); is bounded E. by Maldah, Dinajpoor, and Jalpaigori; N. by Darjeeling and Nepal; W. by Bhagalpoor; and S. by Bhagalpoor and Santalia. Area, 4957 sq. m. Population, 1,823,717. The Koosi river, rising from 3 hill torrents in Nepal, is a mile wide where it crosses the British frontier, and flows south to the Ganges through the W. of the district. The Panar, formed by hill streams from Nepal, near the frontier, flows south to the Ganges. The Mahananda, rising in Sikkim Hills S.E. of Darjeeling, enters Purniah near Titalya, and skirts its E. border, receiving several streams. **Purniah** (16,000), on S. bank of Saura tributary of the Kala Koosi, chief town and centre of indigo and jute culture. **Karagola**, on the Ganges, terminus of East Indian Railway ferry from Sahibganj, and site of largest fair in Lower Bengal. Purniah is in 3 subdivisions—Purniah, Arariya, and Krishnaganj. It is still one of the best tiger-hunting fields in Bengal.

§ 40. MALDAH DISTRICT is bounded E. by Dinajpoor and Rajshahi; N. by Dinajpoor and Purniah; W. by Purniah, Santalia, and Moorshidabad; S. by Moorshidabad and Rajshahi. Area, 1859 sq. m. Population, 710,310. The Ganges and Mahananda form the river system, the former at the head of its delta just before it sends off the Bhagirathi to form the Hoogli. The Mahananda receives on its right at Maldah town the Kalindri, an offshoot of the Koosi, and on its left the Tangan and Purnababhha from Dinajpoor. Maldah is a great tiger-hunting district, owing to its jungles and rivers. **English Bazar** or **Angrazabad** (13,000), on right bank of Mahananda, the civil headquarters, was the site of an English silk factory before 1686. **Maldah**, or Old Maldah (5500), at the junction of the Kalindri and Mahananda, was the port of the Muhammadan capital of Pandooah, and centre of French and Dutch factories. **Haiatpoor** and Garganha form principal river mart at junction of Ganges and Kalindri. **Gaur**, once on the Ganges, now between the Mahananda and the Ganges, the first capital of Bengal under Hindoo kings, also named Laksmanati or Laknauti. The ruins, spreading over 20 sq. m., are covered with jungle. From its conquest, 1204 A.D., Gaur was the capital of the Muhammadans till, in 1575, malaria forced them to desert it for Pandooah, 20 m. N.E. Pandooah contains the Adenah mosque, the most perfect specimen of Afghan architecture, and is the most popular place of Muhammadan pilgrimage. In Maldah Mr. Charles Grant was long the East India Company's Resident. Under his protection, and that of Mr. G. Udny, his successor, Carey began his missionary career in 1794 at the out-factory of Madnabati, 32 m. N.E. within the border of Dinajpoor.

§41. SANTAL PARGANAHS DISTRICT is bounded E. by Maldah, Moorshidabad, and Beerbhoom; N. by Bhagalpoor and Purniah; W. by Bhagalpoor and Hazaribagh; and S. by Manbhoom and Bardwan. This upland tract, popularly called also Santalia, with an area of 5483 sq. m., and population of 1,561,385, was the subject of the earliest and most successful experiments in governing the aboriginal or non-Aryan races, the Dravidian Paharias or Malairs, and the Kolarian Santals. In 1780-84, under Warren Hastings and following Captain Brown, the young civilian Augustus Cleveland, above mentioned, introduced a non-regulation system of administration among the 47 Paharia chiefs, previously untamed, in the Rajmahal hills. An inner hilly tract of 1366 sq. m. was in 1832 marked off by masonry pillars as the Daman-i-koh ("skirts of the hills"), and kept under the direct management of Government for the hill people against the encroachments of the Bhagalpoor landholders. On this tract the Santals from Hazaribagh and Beerbhoom gradually settled, and here they revolted against the extortion of the Hindoo usurers in 1854-5, with the result that Sir George Yule did for them what Cleveland had done for the Paharias 70 years before. The Santal race, about a million in all districts, here number more than a third of the population, and are being gradually christianised by the Church of England, Free Church of Scotland, and Baptist Missionaries, some of the last being Americans and Swedes.

The Rajmahal Hills, an isolated group of recent basaltic trap, quite detached from the Vindhyas, and forming the turning-point of the Ganges, cover an area of 1366 sq. m., rising no higher than 2000 feet. In the N. they contain a central valley for 24 m., overlooked by such hills as the Mori and Sendgarsa peaks. Other low ranges are the Mahuasarhi, to the S.; the Ramgarh, S. of Brahmani River; and the Belpata, Kumrabad, Lakshanpoor, and Salchala, to the W. of the Ramgarh hills. The Sankara range on the S.E., with its Singanmat peak, is a prominent landmark. The Ganges bed is 3 m. wide where the river skirts the district N. and S. The Gumani, joined by the Moral, the Bansloi, the Brahmani, the Mor, and the Ajai, rise in or pass through the district to join the Bhagirathi or the main Ganges lower down. None are navigable. The Teliagarhi pass, between the Ganges and the Rajmahal Hills, long formed the great military approach to Lower Bengal. The main and loop lines of the East Indian Railway enclose the district, the former sending off a branch to the coalfields in Hazaribagh. **Naya Doomka** (2500), chief civil station, on Sooree and Bhagalpoor road near the Mor. **Deogarh** (5000), only municipality in district, 4 m. E. of main railway, with popular shrine of Shiva known as Baijnath. **Rajmahal**, 3 m. from W. bank of Ganges, decayed but famous as Akbar's capital of Bengal from 1592 after Gaur and Tonda. The ruins extend 4 m. to W. of station. In 1860 Lord Canning here opened the upper section of the East Indian Railway, before the death of the Marquis of Dalhousie, its designer. Six m. S., in 1763, Major Adams defeated Meer Kasim at Oodanhala: the entrenched camps may still be traced at Rajmahal. **Sahibganj**, chief mart, on Ganges. The subdivisions are Naya Doomka, Rajmahal, Deogarh, and Godda.

III.—Chutia Nagpoor.

§ 42. Hazaribagh District, the N.E. district of the non-regulation Division of Chutia ("mouse") Nagpoor, is bounded E. by Manbhoom and Santalia, N. by Monghyr and Gaya, W. by

Gaya and Lohardaga, and S. by Lohardaga. Area, 7021 sq. m. Population, 1,072,486. On elevated central ridge rising W. to the plateau which forms Central India, forming the watershed between the Koel system of rivers on the W., and the Damodar on the E. From this ridge isolated hills rise to a maximum height of 2816 ft. in Chardwar, near Hazaribagh station, and 3057 in Jilinga. **Parasnath** hill (4479 ft.), between the trunk road and Manbhoom boundary, the eastern centre of the Jains, as Mount Aboo in Rajpootana is the western, is named after the second last of the 24 Tirthankaras or deified saints; the temples on its summit are a place of Jain pilgrimage in December, as the Samet Sikhara, or "peak of bliss." For some years it was a British military sanitarium. The Damodar river flows through the district for 90 m., receiving the Garhi, Haharo, Naikari, and Kunar, after that stream has been swollen by the Bokāro. The Barākar rises on N. face of elevated ridge, and flows through N. of district, uniting with the Damodar, 32 m. beyond the district. The Mohani Lilajan and Morhar pass into the Gaya district. **Hazaribagh** (11,500), chief town, lying in hills on central plateau; a cantonment also, with European Penitentiary; there are tea gardens in the neighbourhood. **Chatra** (9000), chief mart 36 m. N.W. of above, where the mutineers of the Ramgarh Battalion from Ranchi were defeated in 1857. **Pachamba**, 3 m. from Giridi railway station, centre of Free Church Mission; at **Karharbari**, Karanpura, Bokan, Ramgarh, Itkhuri, and Chope are the principal coal-fields. Mica, antimony, copper, tin, and iron have all been worked. There are 2 subdivisions—Hazaribagh and Pachamba.

§ 43. MANBHOOM DISTRICT is bounded on the E. by Bardwan and Bankura, N. by Hazaribagh, W. by Lohardaga, and S. by Singbhoom and Midnapoor. Area, 4147 sq. m. Population, 1,042,117. The Dalma hills in S. culminate in peak of same name (3047 ft.) Panchet or Panchkot (1600), in N.E., has ruined palace of old Rajas of Panchet. Gangabari or Gajloru, 20 m. S.W. from Puroolia, is highest peak on Baghmoondi plateau. The Barakar river skirts the N. boundary, and after receiving the Khudia falls into the Damodar, which receives Ijri and Guyai from the S. The Kasai (Cossye) flows through the district N.W. to S.E. for 171 m., receiving from the W. the Kumari, after that has been joined by the Tetka. The Subarnarekha ("streak of gold") skirts the Dalma hills S.E. before it passes into Singbhoom. **Puroolia** (6000), chief town close to the Kasai, near which are ruins of former Jain settlement. The district is in 2 subdivisions—Puroolia and

Govindpoor. In the latter are Missions of the Established and Free Churches of Scotland, and the Jharia coal-field.

§ 44. SINGBHOOM DISTRICT (Sangbonga = Kolarian name for God), is bounded E. by Midnapoor, N. by Manbhoom and Lohardaga, W. by Lohardaga, and S. by Orissa. Area, 3897 sq. m. Population, 551,348. The western hills form the Kolhan or original home of the Kols. In S.W. Saranda of the seven hundred hills rises to 3500 ft., and extends towards Cuttak in Orissa, and N. near Parahat falls to 850 ft., forming a gap through which a direct railway from Calcutta to Nagpoor in the Central Province is possible. Angarhari (2137 ft.), and Marmari (1861 ft.), near Chaibassa, are spurs of Saranda. On E. and S. of Subarnarekha the Kapargadi range runs S.E. to Tuiligar hill (2492 ft.), and Meghasani range in Orissa. The Subarnarekha flows through E. portion of district for 80 m., receiving several feeders. The Koel rises W. of Ranchi, drains the Saranda region, and after 36 m. passes into Midnapoor. The Baitaram touches the S. border for 8 m. **Chaibasa** (4500), civil station on right bank of Roro, with weekly market. Sepulchral and monumental stones of Monda and Ho or Larka Kols are found all over the district. The **Parahat** (54,374) chief, once called Raja of Singbhoom, never lost his independence, even to the Marathas, till, in 1818, he sought the protection of the British Government; he rebelled in 1857. A younger and loyal branch holds **Kharsawan** estate (26,280). **Saraikala** estate (66,347), is held by loyal descendant of chief who helped Lord Wellesley against Raghoji Bhonsla. Dhalbhoom estate (117,118), and the Kolhan or Ho-desam (150,904), form the administrative divisions of the district. There are Propagation Society's, Lutheran, and Roman Catholic Missions in Singbhoom.

§ 45. LOHARDAGA DISTRICT is bounded E. by Singbhoom and Manbhoom, N. by Hazaribagh and Gaya, W. by Mirzapoor and Chutia Nagpoor States, S. by these States and Singbhoom. Area, 12,044 sq. m. Population, 1,607,038. The central and S.E. portion consists of the elevated tableland of Chutia Nagpoor Proper which rises towards Central India and the Satpoora range. On the W. the high land runs towards the Vindhya range, and is marked by *pats* or hills of a nearly uniform height (3000 ft.), forming a horizontal stratum of trap rock. The subdivision of Palamau, the N.W. portion of the district, has an elevation of 1200 ft., with spurs of the Hazaribagh and Chutia Nagpoor plateaux running E. and W. The Subarnarekha river runs 10 m. S.W. of Ranchi, flows N.E., leaving the plateau in the waterfall, Hundrughagh (328 ft.), receives the Kanchi and Karkari from the W., and has a course of 100 m. before it passes into Singbhoom. The N. Koel, which rises in the Barwai hills, passes through Palamau to the Son. The S. Koel, which drains Chutia Nagpoor Proper, rises W. of Ranchi, when, joined by the Sankh beyond the district, 185 m. from its source, it becomes the Brahmani, and reaches the sea N.E. of Cuttak. The Amanat is the chief feeder of the N. Koel, from Hazaribagh, with which it forms the rich plain of Palamau. Nearly half the population are pure aboriginal tribes, and another fourth semi-Hindooised aboriginals. The Kolarian tribes are most numerous, Chutia Nagpoor Proper being the home of (1) the Moondas, Singbhoom of (2) the Larkas or Hos, and Maubhoom of (3) the Bhoomij Kols. The Kol and Chero empire seems to have covered Kikata, afterwards Maghada or Behar. The Ooraons are a Dravidian tribe mixed with the Kols; they are also known as Dhangars (hillmen). Gossner's, afterwards the German Lutheran Evangelical, Mission began in Lohardaga in 1845 among the Ooraons, and was divided with the English Propagation Society in 1869. Many thousand Kols and Ooraons have become Christians in several hundred villages, or more than one per cent of the whole district. **Ranchi** (12,500), chief town on central plateau (2100 ft.), and administrative centre of Chutia Nagpoor Division. Doranda, the cantonment for a sepoy corps, lies to the S. **Chutia** ("mouse" in Hindee), village 2 m. E. of Ranchi, ancestral seat of the Nagbansi Rajas of Chutia Nagpoor. **Daltonganj**, centre of Palamau subdivision on E. land of North Koel, named after Colonel Dalton, long the Commissioner of Division. Garwa, to the N.W., is chief mart. **Lohardaga**, 45 m. W. of Ranchi, administrative centre up to 1840. Ranchi and Palamau are the 2 subdivisions of Lohardaga.

§ 46. *SEVEN CHUTIA NAGPOOR STATES, between the Son and Upper Mahanadi, are bounded E. by Singbhoom and Lohardaga, N. by Mirzapoor and Rewa State, W. by Rewa and Bilaspoor in Central Provinces, and S. by Sambalpoor and Orissa States. Area, 16,025 sq. m. Population, 441,302. The States consist of hilly plateaux, marked by the flat-topped hills called *pats*. From the N. slope of watershed running E. to W., the Kanhar and Rehr streams join the Behar system; on the S. the Brahmani, Ib, and Mand flow to the Bay of Bengal. This feudatory territory, with similar States in the Central Province, was finally ceded by the Maratha Bhonslas of Nagpoor in 1817. The seven chiefs pay £467 as tribute, and are bound to supply military contingents. The people are pure or semi-Hindooised aborigines, Gonds, Cheros, Kols, Bhujias, and Karwars chiefly. **Bonai** (1297 sq. m., and 25,000 pop.), the most southerly State, watered by the Brahmani, on which, in lat. 28° 49′ and long. 85°, is Bonai Garh, the chief's fort (505 ft.). The people are Dravidians, Bhujias, speaking Ooriya, and said to have descended from Rama's Ceylon, army of apes in the *Ramayana* epic. **Gangpoor** (2484 sq. m., and 75,000 pop.), N. and W. of Bonai, a tableland (700 ft.) with the abrupt Mahavina range on the S., watered by the Ib, which joins the Mahanadi farther S., the Sankh, and South Koel. Coal is found at Hingir in the S., and there is gold-washing in the Ib. The Raja resides at Suadi on the Ib. The picturesque confluence of the Koel and Sankh is a legendary birthplace of Vyasa, compiler of the *Mahabharat* epic and *Vedas*. **Jashpoor** (1947 sq. m., and pop. 67,000), N. of Gangpoor, consists of elevated tableland called Uparghat on E., of lowlands called Hetghat on W. Above both, in N.W., is Khuria plateau, the watershed between the Ib and the Kanhar, which flows N. to the Son. The Raja's fort as at Jagdispoor, in centre of Uparghat. **Oodaipoor** (1051 sq. m., and pop. 28,000), W. of Gangpoor, shut in by Mainpat plateau in Sargooja to N., and watered by the Mand, on which are Rabkob, the Raja's fort, with gold mines and coal, and Shahpoor, the old castle. At Dorki, 24 m. S., is a mart. **Sargooja**, largest State (area, 6103 sq. m., and pop. 183,000), between Oodaipoor and Lohardaga, is surrounded by the Mainpat and Jamnapat (3781 ft.) plateaux and Korea forest tract, is watered by the Kanhar, Rehr, and Mahar, and forms one vast grazing (and coal) field for Behar and Mirzapoor. Bisrampoor in the centre, and Pratappoor farther N., are the two chief places. In the S., 8 m. W. of village of Lakhanpoor, are the temples of Ramgarh hill and other ruins, marking an early civilisation. **Korea** (1631 sq. m., and pop. 22,000), tableland E. of Sargooja, rising to 370 ft. at Deogarh, and watered by the Heshto, which rises near Sonhat, the Raja's fort (2477 ft). **Chang Bhakar** (906 sq. m., pop. 9000), most westerly State, with Reva on three sides, consists of wooded hills and ravines, watered by the Banas and Neoor streams, which flow into Rewa. Janakpoor, a mile above the Banas, is the residence of the Bhaya, a chief who administers justice under a tree. Rock-cuttings at Harchoka, on N frontier, show an early civilisation, swept away by the Marathas.

IV.—Orissa.

§ 47. Cuttak District (Katak = the fort), administrative centre of the Orissa Division of Bengal, is bounded E. by Bay of Bengal, N. by Balasor, W. by Orissa States, and S. by Poori. Area, 3516 sq. m. Population, 1,731,548. On the W. border hills rise to 2500 ft., generally crowned with Hindoo shrines or hollowed into Boodhist caves. Such are Naltigiri in the Assia range, Oodayagiri (sunrise peak) and Assiagiri, topped by a mosque. The Mahanadi waters the south, the Brahmani the centre, and the Baitarani the north of the district. The Mahanadi ("great river"), which has a course of 529 m. from its source in Raipoor and a catchment basin of 4500 m., enters Cuttak through the Naraj gorge 7 m. W. of Cuttak town, where it receives the Katjoori; after throwing off S. the Paika and N. the Biroopa to the Brahmani, and the Chitartala or Noon, which it again receives, it falls into the Bay of Bengal under its own name, and with the Jotdar channel as the Devi (goddess = Shiva's wife) estuary farther south at False Point. The Brahmani enters the district near Garh Balrampoor, receives the Kimiria from S. and Kharsua from N., and forms the Dhamra estuary, by which, and by the Maipara river, it reaches the Bay. The Baitarani enters Cuttak near Balipoor village, receives from N. the Salandi and Matai, and mixes with the Brahmani to form the Dhamra. To utilise the water of the Orissa rivers which, draining 63,350 sq. m., amounts to 2,760,000 cubic feet maximum discharge in flood and an average of 5360 in the cold weather, 4 Government canals have been cut: (1) the High Level, leaving the left bank of the Biroopa weir a mile from the Mahanadi, and designed to debouch opposite Calcutta 230 m. (the Midnapoor section of 53 m. is given under that district, above); (2) the Kendrapara Canal, 42½ m. from right flank of Biroopa weir to False Point Harbour, now open to Marsaghai within tidal range; (3) the Taldanda Canal for 52 m., to connect Cuttak with the main tidal branch of the Mahanadi; (4) the Machgaon Canal to connect Cuttak with the mouth of the Devi, starting from Birbati on the Taldanda Canal. When completed the canals will protect 1,600,000 acres from such famines as that of 1866. In Cuttak district are 680 m. of embankments to regulate 35 rivers or distributories.

Cuttak (51,000), chief town on peninsula formed by Mahanadi and Katjoori, one of the five ancient "forts" of

Odra-desa, with Fort Barabati opposite, seat of Government College and General Baptist Mission, and famous for filigree gold and silver work. **Tajpoor** ("city of sacrifice") (9500), on right bank of Baitarani, capital of province under the Kesari dynasty, now one of the 4 pilgrim regions of Orissa as the high place of Shivaism sacred to Parvati, with sun-worship monoliths and temples laid low by Islam. Kendrapara (11,000), N. of the Chitartala. The district has 4 subdivisions—Cuttak, Kendrapara, Jajpoor, and Jagatsinghpoor.

§ 48. BALASOR DISTRICT (Baleswar = young lord, *i.e.* Krishna, or Banesvar = forest lord) is bounded E. by Bay of Bengal, N. by Midnapoor, W. by Tributary States, and S. by Cuttak. Area, 2068 sq. m. Population, 942,414. This alluvial strip between the hills and the sea is watered by 6 streams. Subarnarekha ("streak of gold") winds through its N.E. corner to the Bay of Bengal at Pipli. The Panchpara, the Burabalang ("old twister"), the Janika, the Kainsbans ("*Kains* grass and bamboos") and Baitarani are the main channels of the many hill streams in order from N. to S. The 85 miles of coast have 7 ports—Subarnarekha, Saratha, Chanuya, Balasor, Larchanpoor, Churāman, and Dhamra. **Balasor** (18,500), on right bank of Burabalang, chief town; English port since 1642, when Surgeon Boughton obtained land here and at Hoogli from Emperor, whose daughter he had healed; here also French, Dutch, and Danes had factories. The trade and shipbuilding have decayed since the East India Company's monopoly ceased in 1832, and the salt manufacture ceased; but there is a coasting trade with Ceylon and the Laccadives. Seat of American Baptist Mission. **Pipli**, seat of earliest English settlement in 1634 and earlier Portuguese, on the Subarnarekha, now silted up; all traces of European settlements are washed into the river. **Jaleswar** (Jellasor), on left bank of Subarnarekha on Calcutta road, an East India Company's factory. **Chandbali**, on the Baitarani, a rising rice and pilgrim port, having steamer communication with Calcutta. There are 2 subdivisions—Balasor and Bhadrakh.

§ 49. POOREE DISTRICT is bounded E. by Cuttak, N. by Cuttak and Tributary States, W. by States and Ganjam (Madras), and S. by Bay of Bengal. Area, 2472 sq. m. Population, 885,794. A low range of hills in west, running to Chilka Lake, forms the watershed between the district and the Mahanadi valley. The Koyakhai, S. branch of Mahanadi, finds its way to the Bay of Bengal, on the N., through the Kusbhadra, with its branch, the Prachi, and to the Chilka lake, on the S., through the Bhargavi, Noon, and Dhaya. The district is protected from the floods of these rivers by 317 miles of embankments. The Sar Lake, N.E. of Poori town, is a backwater of the Bhargavi, 4 m. long by 2 broad. The **Chilka Lake**, a gulf or inland sea in S.E. corner of Orissa, salt or fresh and with area of from 344 to 450 sq. m. according to the season, and average depth of 3 to 5 ft. On E. side are the Parikood islands, partially silted up. **Poori** (Jagannath = "lord of the world") (22,500 resident population), chief town on the coast in N. lat. 19° 48′ 17″ and E. long. 85° 51′ 39″. Including the *kshetra* or idol precincts the whole town covers 1871 acres. Into the lodging-houses which form the main streets from 100,000 to 200,000 pilgrims are crowded, while sandhills arrest the natural drainage to the ocean. In spite of the sanitary precautions of the Government and the benevolence of the missionaries, it is officially calculated that at least 10,000 pilgrims perish every year in the town or when returning home across flooded streams and roads at the end of June. Poori, being an isolated and distant spot, was (1) the refuge of Boodhism and shrine of Gautama's golden tooth. The principal antiquities are at **Khandgiri**, half-way between Poori and Cuttak, with the snake, elephant, and tiger caves in sandstone; at **Dhauli**, a rock above the Dhaya, with Asoka's 11 edicts and 2 others; (2) a centre of Shiva-worship at **Bhuvaneswar** ("lord of earth"), S.E. of Khandgiri, under the Kesari or Sun dynasty till 1132 A.D., with temple dating from 500 A.D.; (3) an abode of sun-worship, chiefly at **Kanārak**, on the coast 19 m. above Poori shrine, where the "black pagoda" is a landmark, dating from 1237 A.D., on which, says Abul Fazl, Akbar's minister, the whole revenues of Orissa for 12 years were spent; its exquisite polygonal monolith now stands outside the lion gate of Jagannath's shrine; (4) headquarters of Vishnoo-worship under the form of Jagánnath; temple, finished by King Anang Bhim Deo in 1198 A.D. at a cost of half a million sterling, is almost a square (652 × 630 ft.), consisting of four chambers—the hall of offerings (bloodless), pillared hall for dancing girls, hall of audience, and towered sanctuary. Since 1840 the British Government has ceased to collect a pilgrim tax; when custody of the temple was left to Raja of Khoorda, banished in 1878 for murder, and now to the Ranee, under whom the place is neglected, and "the utter collapse of the whole system" is feared by the local Hindoo press. The car festival takes place about the beginning of the rainy season in June or July; the great car is 45 ft. high, 35 square, and on

16 wheels of 7 ft. diameter. The principal bathing spot, where as many as 40,000 pilgrims sometimes rush into the surf of the Bay of Bengal, the *swarga-dwara* ("gate of heaven") runs for $\frac{1}{4}$ m. along the coast. **Pipli**, on high road 25 m. N. of Poori, a mart and settlement of Baptist Mission. The district is in 2 subdivisions—Poori and Khoorda; the latter the scene of two insurrections, by the Raja in 1804, and the *paiks* or peasant militia in 1817-18, provoked by native revenue underlings.

§ 50. *The NINETEEN ORISSA STATES, the feudatory uplands between the Mahanadi delta and the Central Province, are bounded E. by three Orissa districts, N. by Midnapoor and Chutia Nagpoor, W. by Central Province States, and S. by Madras States of Goomsar and Kimidi. Area, 16,184 sq. m. Population, 1,624,310. From the first of three watersheds (1500 to 2500 feet), the valley of the Mahanadi, which bursts through the beautiful Barmool Pass, the hills rise to the second, running N.W. and S.E. (2000 to 2500) between Narsinghpoor and Baramba States, and feed the Brahmani on the other slope; from the N. bank of the Brahmani the third or Keunjhar watershed rises into peaks like Malaya-giri (3895 ft.) in Pal Lahara State, and slopes into the Baitarani on the S. and Burabalang and Subarnarekha on the N. **Angool** (881 sq. m., pop. 102,090), intersected by 85° E. long., was confiscated for rebellion in 1847; ex-Raja's family live at Angool village, and Chindipada is the chief mart. **Athgarh** (168 sq. m.) is on W. border of Cuttak, with Raja's village of same name, on road to Sambalpoor. Gobra, near E. border, is principal village, and Chagar, Baptist Mission settlement. **Athmallik** (730 sq. m.), E. of Angool, with chief's residence at Handapa in the centre. Kainta, on N. bank of Mahanadi, is principal village. **Banki** (116 sq. m., pop. 56,613), on W. border of Cuttak S. of Athgarh, confiscated since 1840 when Raja was convicted of murder, with principal village of same name on right bank of Mahanadi. **Baramba** (134 sq. m.), on opposite bank of Mahanadi, with Raja's residence of same name, and Gobnatpoor, on Mahanadi, principal village. **Bod** (2064 sq. m.), most W. of the States, including the Kond-mals under direct British administration, ceded in 1845 to suppress human sacrifices (*meriah*). Major S. C. Macpherson established the agency which has done much to civilise the Konds (Gonds or mountaineers). Bod village, on the Mahanadi, is the residence of the Raja; Jagatigarh is the only other large village. **Daspalla** (568 sq. m.), W. of Bod, with Barmool gorge of Mahanadi on N. border. The Raja lives at Kunjabana in the centre. Daspalla, on the E.

border, is the largest village. **Dhenkanal** (1463 sq. m.), W. of Cuttak border and Athgarh, home of the semi-Hindooised Savars or Sauras (the Suari of Pliny and Sabaræ of Ptolemy), and the best of the Orissa States, watered by the Brahmani. The enlightened Raja lives at village of same name. **Hindol** (312 sq. m.), between Dhenkanal and Angool, traversed by Sambalpoor road; the Kanaka Mountains (above 2000 feet) occupy the S. half. Raja's village is of same name in S.W. **Keunjhar** (3096 sq. m.), second largest of the States, to W. of Balasor. Baitarani rises in N. ranges. Road from Sambalpoor to Midnapoor crosses the State. Maharaja resides at village of same name on that road. **Khandpara** (244 sq. m.), W. of N. Poori, with principal mart at Kantilo on right bank of Mahanadi. **Morbhanj**, including Bamanghati (4243 sq. m.), largest and most N. State. Bamanghati is under direct British administration from Singbhoom. Meghasani Hill ("seat of clouds") is 3824 feet high in S. Wild elephants abound. Banpada in Burabalang and Daspoor on high road are the principal villages. **Narsinghpoor** (199 sq. m.), on N. bank of Mahanadi, between Baramba and Angool, with village of same name where Raja resides. Kanpoor, on the Mahanadi, is the principal mart. **Nayagarh** (5889 sq. m.), between Poori and Madras, well cultivated, with fine scenery. **Nilgiri** (278 sq. m.), between Balasor and Morbhanj, with village of same name where Raja resides. **Pal Lahara** (452 sq. m.), S.W. of Keunjhar, from which it was separated, with Malaya-giri (3895 feet) and other hills covered with finest oak timber. Lahara village is near the Sambalpoor road. **Ranpoor** (203 sq. m.), between Poori and Nayagarh, with Raja's residence of same name. **Talcher** (399 sq. m.), with coal, iron, and lime fields. Village of same name on right bank of Brahmani is Raja's residence. This State gives a name to a geological formation of the Gondwana system. **Tigaria** ("three forts") (46 sq. m.), smallest of the States, is S. of Dhenkanal, between Athgarh and Baramba, well cultivated and most densely peopled. Founded by Poori pilgrims, who took the land from the aborigines four centuries ago. The Raja resides at town of same name.

V.—*Protected States.

§ 51. *Bhootan and Towang.—**Bhootan State** (Boodhist) has had subordinate relations to the British Government since 1774, when it agreed to pay an annual tribute of five of its famous Tangun horses, and to restore the Raja of

Kooch Behar, in whose favour the Governor-General had interfered; but the State has also been a vassal of China for two centuries, since a body of Tibetan sepoys from Kampa ousted the Tephoo tribe, originally from Kooch Behar. Bhootia raids forced the British Government in 1841 and again in 1864 to annex the 18 *Dwars* ("doors") or passes which lead from the plains to the lofty terraces of which Bhootan consists, or Dalimkot, Zamarkot, Cheemarchee, Lukhee, Buxa, Bulka, Bara, Gooma, Reepoo Cheerung or Sidlee, and Bagh or Bijnee, along the Jalpaigori district of Bengal; Ghurkola, Banska, Chappagoree, Chappakamar and Bijnee, along the Kamroop district of Assam; and Boree, Gooma, and Kulling, along the Darrang district. Bhootan, as it now is, has an estimated area of 15,000 sq. m. and population of 20,000. It is divided into E. and W. Bhootan, running along Assam and Bengal for a distance of 220 m. The country, which has peaks S. of Chumalhari rising to 24,737 ft. at head waters of the Matichu, and to 20,965 and 20,576 at head of two others of the Manas affluents, is drained by three river systems into the Brahmapootra; the Manas, the Machu, and the Chinchu and Pachu, in the W. half which form the **Minagaon. Poonakha** is the winter capital on the Machu; **Tassisudon**, 24 m. W., is the summer capital. Wandipoor is an important castle in the Poonakha valley. The envoys Bogle and Turner, and the traveller Manning, entered Bengal by the Pachu valley. Eden proceeded from the Teesta by Dalimkot, the Tula-lap pass (10,000 ft.), the Am-machu, which flows through the Chumbi valley, and Paro to Poonakha, in 1863.

Towang, a small State E. of Bhootan, between the Deosham and Rowta rivers, leading directly from Assam to Tibet. Farther E. the frontier is occupied by the independent class of the Rooprai, Shergaia, and Thebengia Bhootias.

§ 52. *Nepal State, virtually protected by British Government, to which it paid a tribute like Bhootan, and the seat of a British Political Agent, though for a time also a vassal of China, occupies the loftiest Himalayan heights, from Sikkim W. to the Kumaun district, with an estimated area of 54,000 sq. m., population of 2 millions, and revenue of 1 million sterling. The E. two-thirds of the 500 m. of its S. border marches with the Behar districts of Bengal, and the W. third with those of Oudh. The chief route for traffic is from Patna N. through the Champaran district to Kathmandoo, the capital. Europeans not in the staff of the British Residency are not allowed to enter the State save with special permission. From the conquest of its Newar people and rulers by the Goorkhas in 1768, and the commercial treaty of 1792, the country was a scene of anarchy and bloodshed, varied by two wars with the British, till Maharaja Jang Bahadoor, its minister and virtual sovereign, visited England in 1850. After years of a firm and loyal administration, he died and was succeeded by his brother in 1877. The nominally ruling Maharaja is a Sesodia Rajpoot of the Oodaipoor family, married to Jang Bahadoor's daughter. The aboriginal tribes are Boodhist, but the Hindoos look on Nepal as the asylum of their faith, next to Benares. The Michi river separates Nepal from Sikkim on E., and the Kali from Kumaun on W. Four lofty ridges, running up into the peaks of Kinchinjinga, Gosainthan, Dhawalagiri, and Nanda-devi, divide Nepal into three natural provinces watered by the Kosi, Gandak, and Gogra. A fourth is the triangular valley of Nepal proper, wedged in between the Kosi on E. and Gandak on W., but watered by the Bhagmati, in which is the capital and seat of the British Resident. **Kathmandoo** ("wood building") (35,000 to 60,000), a mile from the base of Mount Nagarjoon, on E. or left bank of the Bishnmati, near its confluence with the Baghmati. The British Residency and barracks for a company of sepoys cover 40 acres of high ground on the N. of the parade, overlooking the Bishnmati. **Patan** (60,000), the largest city in Nepal, and old Newar capital, 1½ m. S.E. of Kathmandoo. **Kirtipoor**, capital of an old principality which overlooks Kathmandoo on N. and Patan on E., each 3 m. distant, where the Goorkha conquerors committed terrible atrocities and changed the name into Naakatapoor = "city of cut noses;" all the principal citizens being deprived of noses and lips, save those required as players on wind instruments for the conqueror's army. **Bhatgaon** (50,000), on E. side of same valley, 8 m. S.E. of Kathmandoo, on right bank of Hanooman under Mount Mahadeo Pokhra, long centre of a powerful principality. The lofty passes into Tibet from Nepal are these, from W. to E.—(1) Takla or Yari, midway between Nanda-devi and Dhawalagiri; (2) Mastang, 40 m. E. of Dhawalagiri; (3) Kerang, W. of Gosainthan Mountains; (4) Kuti E.,—the two last are the most frequented; the roads join at Tingri, where the Chinese defeated the Nepalese in 1792;—(5) Hatra; (6) Wallang.

CHAPTER V.

THE PROVINCE OF ASSAM.

§ 1. Assam Province. § 2. Products and Trade. § 3. Land Tenures. § 4. The People and Districts.

SOORMA VALLEY.

§ 5. Sylhet District. § 6. Cachar.

ASSAM VALLEY.

§ 7. Goalpara. § 8. Kamroop. § 9. Darrang. § 10. Nowgong. § 11. Seebsagar. § 12. Lakhimpoor.

HILLS.

§ 13. Garo Hills. § 14. Khasi and Jaintia Hills. § 15. Naga Hills. § 16. *Manipoor State.

§ 1. Assam Province (Aham, pronounced Asam = dominant tribe) has been the most north-easterly Government in British India since 1874, when it was cut off from Bengal. It is slightly less than England and Wales, having an area of 55,384 sq. m. (including Native States), with a population of 4,908,276 in the ordinary districts, an increase of nearly 19 per cent in the decade ending 1880. The Province consisting of the N. valley of the Brahmapootra and the S. valley of the Barak-Soorma with the Garo, Khasi, and Naga hills between, is situated between 28° 17′ and 24° N. latitude, and between 89° 46′ and 97° 5′ E. longitude, including Manipoor State. It is bounded E. by Upper Burma, with the Patkai Range between; on the N. by the S. section of the Himalaya, inhabited by Mishmees, Abars, Meeris, Daphlas, Akas, and Bhootias; W. by the Bengal district of Jalpaigori and State of Kooch Behar, by Maimansingh and Rangpoor; and S. by the Tipura and Chittagong, or Looshai Hill Tracts. While the outer frontier of the N.E. is still unsurveyed and undefined, the "inner line" of boundary has been laid down for the Nowgong, Seebsagar, Lakhimpoor, Naga Hill, and Cachar districts, across which no British subject is allowed to go to the wild tribes beyond without a pass. Of the three physical divisions of the Province, Assam proper on the N. is an alluvial plain 450 m. long and 50 in average breadth, watered by the **Brahmapootra** throughout its length. Going W. the first great river which breaks through the Himalaya from Tibet into the valley is the Subansiri, in E. longitude 94° 9′. The Dihong enters Assam in longitude 95° 17′, 20 m. below Sadiya, and is the true Brahmapootra, now considered to be identical with the Tsangpo of Central Tibet; it joins the Lohit, which enters Assam at the Brahmakoond. The Dibong joins the Dihong before its confluence with the Lohit. The second of the physical divisions consists of central hill tracts running transversely to the two river-valleys on either side, carrying the Roma and Patkai mountain systems from the Irawadi W. to the Brahmapootra, which turns S. when it rounds the Garo hills at Dhoobri. The third or **Barak-Soorma** forms the State of Manipoor and the districts of Cachar and Sylhet before joining the Brahmapootra and Ganges in the Megna estuary.

§ 2. PRODUCTS AND TRADE.—Coal of fine quality is found in five separate places in the Brahmapootra valley, and lime in the Sylhet district; but in places as yet difficult of access. Petroleum springs abound. Gold-washing is common in the Brahmapootra at Parghat, above Sadiya, in the Noa-Dehing and Hookong, and in the Dihong, "considered by the natives to be the richest in Assam." Not a fourth of the fertile area is yet cultivated, from want of population; coolies from Chutia Nagpoor and Santalia are imported. The food-growers are those of Bengal proper. Except where the permanent settlement of land-tax prevails in Sylhet and most of Goalpara, the State landlord makes an annual assessment. Part of the hill slopes used to be sold in fee simple, and half a million of acres is now held chiefly by Europeans. The great and growing culture of the Province is that of the indigenous and hybrid tea-plant. It is believed that the *Thea Assamiensis* is the original tea-plant introduced into China, where it has degenerated into the two varieties of *T. Bohea* and *T. viridis.* In 1780 Colonel Kyd formed a tea-garden in Calcutta with plants from Canton, but it was discouraged by the East India Company as likely to compete with their China monopoly. Since the rediscovery of the *T. Assamiensis* in Assam in a wild state in 1826, and its commercial cultivation from 1840, some 600,000 acres have been taken up for tea, of which 135,000 are under mature plants, 30,000 are under immature plants, and the rest is grass, forest, or waste, to be brought in. The out-turn, annually increasing, is about 40,000,000 lbs., of which 25 millions are from the Brahmapootra and 15 from the Soorma valley. The average yield is 282 lbs. per mature acre. There are 85 tea companies, of which 53 are registered in India. There are 1058 gardens. The import trade of the Province, chiefly from Bengal, is between 1¾ and 2 millions sterling in value, principally piece goods, salt, and rice. The export trade is valued at 3¾ millions, of which £30,000 only goes to the tribes across the border. Tea constitutes 80 per cent of the whole export; mustard-seed, lime, and limestone are the other principal articles. Wild elephants are caught in the Sylhet, Goalpara, Nowgong, and Naga forests; the revenue and royalty on captures is £6500 a year. In Sylhet town there is still one native carver of ivory, whose work is marked by ingenuity and taste. The silk and silver work and ivory mats of Manipoor State possess artistic merit. Marwari and Musalman merchants from Dacca are almost the sole traders in the Assam and Soorma valleys; of the natives, the Khasi and Jaintia hill-people alone are keen traders. Since Mr. D. Scott, in 1830, introduced the potato culture, that and the orange culture have long enriched that people.

The Province is partially opened up (1) by the Assam line of the River Steam Navigation Company from Calcutta, Kooshtea, or Goalunda to Dibroogarh, 661 m. The steamers touch at Serajganj, Kaliganj, Chilmaree, Dhoobri, Goalpara, Gauhati, Mangaldai, Tezpoor, Bishnath, Dunsiri Mookh, Kookeela Mookh, Dekoo Mookh, and Dehing Mookh, on their passage up the Brahmapootra; (2) by the Northern Bengal State Railway, which leaves the Eastern Bengal Railway at Damookdea Station (116 m. from Calcutta), and crosses the Ganges by steamer to Sara Ghat; at 113 m. from the Ganges at Parbatipoor, it sends off the Rangpoor branch line to Kaunia, whence a steamer crosses the Teesta, and communication is kept up by train and steamer with Dhoobri, 322 m. from Calcutta. From the Teesta a branch runs 14 m. to Mogulhat. A line of 75 m. will soon run from Dibroogarh to Sadiya, with 24 m. branch to coalfield.

§ 3. Land Tenures.—Except in waste lands and in 6116 square miles of permanently settled lands, long part of Bengal Province, the settlement of Assam is strictly "ryotwar," each cultivator being annually assessed by the officers of Government for the land actually occupied by him. The revenue is collected by officers called "mouzahdars," each of whom resides in his own circle, which is much larger than what is called a mouzah in other parts of India. The mouzahdar receives a commission on his collections, and this is the only expense incurred in realising the Government demand. Under this system the revenue is most punctually and satisfactorily gathered in.

VARIETIES OF TENURE HELD DIRECT FROM GOVERNMENT, 1880-81.

Nature of Tenure.	Number of estates.	Number of villages.	Number of holders or share-holders.	Gross area in acres.	Average area of each estate.
Small zameendars paying less than Rs. 5000 revenue . . .	603	...	3,101	217,900	361
Proprietary cultivating communities paying in common . .	9,741	366	89,625	387,536	40
Proprietary cultivators paying separately, including all small estates paying less than Rs. 100 . .	539,171	5,406	986,121	6,640,249	12
Holders of revenue-free tenures—					
In perpetuity .	914	65	2,672	85,835	93
For life . .	72	11	72	1,399	19
Grants held under the rules of 1838 and 1854	45	8	16	19,750	438
Landholders who have redeemed the revenue	2,424	96	3,765	279,724	115
Purchasers of waste lands . . .	330	193	251	205,792	629
Waste land leased under the Thirty-Years' Lease Rules .	448	56	295	163,804	365
Total . .	553,748	6,201	1,085,918	8,001,989	4,183

Of intermediate holders, or middlemen between the zameendar and ryot, there were in the same year 254 on permanent tenure, with an average rent of Rs. 9 for each holding, and 4192 on farming leases, with an average rent of Rs. 25 per holding. Since 1854, waste lands, for tea cultivation chiefly, have been granted on very favourable terms, under successive sets of rules —fee simple, thirty, ten and annual years' lease, and ordinary settlement. The Lease Rules of 1876, for the cultivation of tea, coffee, and timber trees only, are now in force.

§ 3. THE PEOPLE AND DISTRICTS.—The first synchronous census of Assam was taken on 17th February 1881, like the rest of the Indian Empire. The following shows the districts, areas, and population :—

	Districts.	Number of Judicial and Revenue Subdivisions.	Area in square miles.	Population.	Number of villages.	Total cost of officials and police of all kinds.	Revenue, 1880-81.	
							Land.	Gross.
Soorma Valley.	Sylhet . .	4	5,440	1,973,000	9,517	Rs. 31,95,484 or £319,548	Rs. 37,47,612 or £374,761	Rs. 81,83,291 or £818,329
	Cachar . .	2	3,750	356,705	555			
Assam Valley.	Goalpara . .	2	3,897	444,689	1,324			
	Kamroop .	2	3,631	644,843	1,649			
	Darrang . .	2	3,418	271,504	2,419			
	Nowgong .	1	3,417	308,889	1,725			
	Seebsagar .	3	2,855	365,300	1,950			
	Lakhimpoor	3	3,723	172,079	834			
Hill.	Garo Hills .	1	3,653	109,054	929			
	Khasi and Jaintia Hills	2	6,157	169,113	1,541			
	Naga Hills .	1	6,400	93,100	...			
	Total .	23	46,341	4,908,276	22,443			

Omitting the Manipoor State and Naga hill tribes, the proportion of males to females was 2,465,433 to 2,349,704. In Manipoor there were 72,688 males to 74,657 females. Of districts formerly censused the most remarkable increase in nine years occurred in Cachar, 52 per cent ; Lakhimpoor, 42 per cent ; Seebsagar, 23 per cent ; and Nowgong, 20½ per cent ; all of which are the chief tea-districts. Into these from 15,000 to 43,000 (in 1878) coolies, from Chutia Nagpoor chiefly, have been imported every year, by Dhoobri, and also by boat from Goalunda. The tea-garden population numbers about 200,000. Time-expired labourers often take up tea land for themselves. In 1880 the mortality among immigrant labourers was so low as 35·2 per mille ; and is now at the normal figure for an Indian population. The immigration and labour are regulated by Act I. of 1882.

The chief executive authority in the Province of Assam is the Chief Commissioner since 6th February and 12th September 1874. He is assisted by a Secretary with an Assistant ; two Judges ; Commissioner, Assam Valley Districts ; Conservator of Forests ; Deputy Surgeon-General, who is also Sanitary

ASSAM PROVINCE.

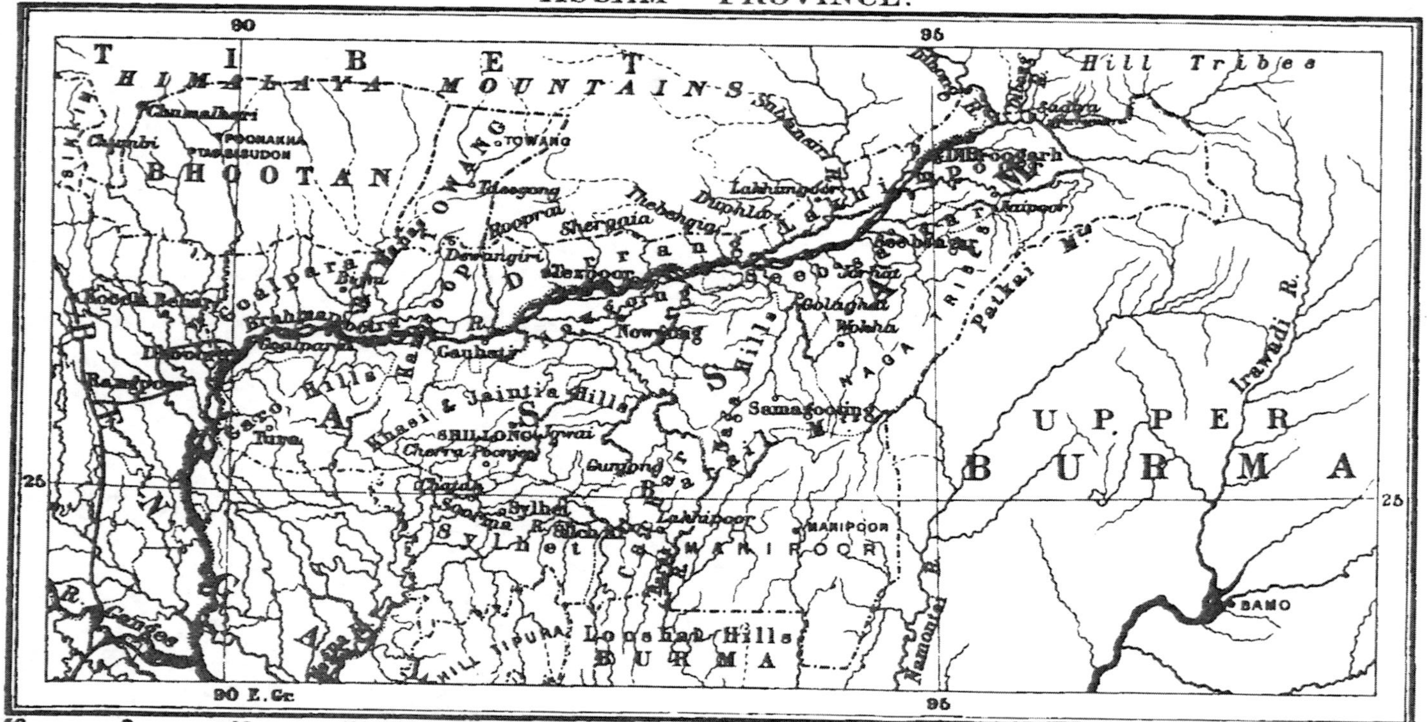

50 0 50 100 ENGLISH MILES

Stanford's Geog^l Estab^t

Commissioner; Inspector of Schools; Inspector-General of Police and Jails, who is also in Charge of Registration and Commissioner of Excise and Stamps; and Deputy-Commissioners.

Soorma Valley.

§ 5. Sylhet District (Srihatta), at the west end of the alluvial plain, 70 m. wide, of the Soorma or Barak, which constitutes the southern portion of Assam, is bounded E. by Cachar and Jaintia hills, N. by Jaintia and Khasi hills, W. by Maimansingh, and S. by Tipura. Area, 5440 sq. m. Population, 1,973,000. In the S. eight ranges of hills (600 to 1500 ft.) run into Hill Tipura, thus named, beginning W.—Dinarpoor or Satgaon, Baliseera, Banugach Rajkandi, Saragaj or Langla, Patharia, Duhalia or Pratapgarh, Sarishpoor or Siddheswar. The Ita hills, in centre of the district, rise to 600 ft. The level is otherwise broken by clusters of sand hillocks called *teelas*, rising from 20 to 80 ft., partially covered by the tea plant. The **Barak**, rising in Manipoor State and flowing through Cachar, where it becomes navigable in Sylhet at Banga, divides into the **Soorma** and Koosiara, which reunite at Ajmeriganj on the Maimansingh border. All the waters of the Barak system pass into the Dhaleswari and so into the Megna estuary, the tide of which extends to Lakai in S.W. of district. In S.E. is the wild elephant country, with six tracts reserved for hunting. **Sylhet** (18,000), chief town on N. bank of Soorma, where are the Europeans' houses and offices; a centre of the tea and lime industries. **Chatak**, on S. bank 35 m. below, the port for Khasi and Jaintia hills. **Sonamganj**, port lower down. **Ajmeriganj**, in S.W., below confluence of Soorma and Kalni. The district is in 4 subdivisions—Sylhet, Sonamganj, Habiganj, and Kareniganj. In 1776, when Sylhet was administered by the Dacca council, the district was under the Hon. Robert Lindsay as President, as described in detail in the *Lives of the Lindsays.*

§ 6. Cachar District is bounded E. by Manipoor State, N. by Naga hills, W. by Sylhet, and S. by Looshai hills. Area, 1285 sq. m. Population, 356,705. The district has high hills on three sides, and is intersected by the Barak, which drains these. To the south are the Hailakandi valley on W. and Chatla fen on E., divided by hills. The **Barail** range (2500 to 6000 ft.), in N., connects N. Manipoor with Khasi hills, and sends down the Jhiri, Chiri, Madura, Jatinga, Arang, Larong, Goomra, and Dhaleswari rivers, S.W. to the Barak. The

Bhoobans (700 to 3000 ft.) are on E. boundary S. of Barak. Rengti-pahar hills, N. and S. range between Sonai and Dhaleswari rivers. The Tilain range (100 to 500 ft.), running N. and S., is crossed by the Sylhet and Cachar road. The Sarishpoor or Siddheswar hills (600 to 2000 ft.) form W. boundary. The Hurang or Jujang hills, to the N. of Barak, are crossed by the road to Manipoor. The Barak, after a course of 180 m., becomes navigable for boats at Banskandi, and flows for 130 m. through Cachar. The Dhaleswari from the hills on the S. waters Hailakandi valley, forms the new channel called Katakhal, which 25 m. thereafter falls into the Barak, and under its old name reaches the Barail at Sialtekh Bazar. The other S. tributaries of the Barak are the Ghagra, which drains the Chatla fen, and the Sonai ("golden"), which reaches it at Sonarmookh. The whole district is one of forests, in which the caoutchouc was first discovered in 1862. Wild elephants, of the more valuable *kuemriah* (cost £110 for trained animal 7 ft. high), and of the *mirgia* and cross *doasala* varieties, are caught in N. and S. hills, in which four tracts are reserved. This district supplies one-third of all the tea exported from Assam (10½ million lbs. in 1881); the plant in its varieties of indigenous, hybrid (the best), and China, is best cultivated on the plateau spurs of the Barail range in the N., and in those of the Sarishpoor and Tilain hills S. of the Barak. **Silchar** (4000), chief town and cantonment, on S. bank of Barak, with trade suburb of Janiganj. **Lakhipoor** (or Lakshmipoor = city of goddess of fortune), 14 m. E. of Silchar, at confluence of the Chiri with the Barak, a centre of tea culture and chief mart of trade with Manipoor. **Sonai**, chief timber mart, on river of same name. **Hailakandi**, headquarters of second subdivision.

North Cachar subdivision (22,379), re-established at the close of 1880, is the tract between the Cachar plains on S., Nowgong on N., Naga hills E., and Jaintia hills W., inhabited by Kookras, Cacharees, and Kutcha Nagas; the two last were frequently attacked by the Angami Nagas, on their road to the plains. **Gunjong**, headquarters of subdivision, 20 m. N.W. of Asaloo in Naga hills. Four police posts at Asaloo, Hangrum, Ninglo, and Guilong, and an inner line nearer Silchar, of three stockades at Baladhan, Aisacherra, and Jaipoor, defend the frontier against the Angami Nagas. A Kooki militia act as scouts.

At **Maibong**, a forest valley in the Barail hills, on the brick ruins of the capital of the Cachari kings, who became Hindooised when driven S. by the Koch and Aham migrations.

Dimapoor ruins, a former capital of the same kings, in the Naga hills, are overgrown with jungle, but are distinctly traceable, along the Dhansiri river, with many monolithic pillars and splendid tanks of clear water.

ASSAM VALLEY.

§ 7. GOALPARA DISTRICT, western entrance to Assam valley, is bounded E. by Kamroop; N. by Bhootan hills; W. by Jalpaigori, Kooch Behar, and Rangpoor; and S. by the Garo hills. Area, including Eastern Dwars ("doors"), conquered in 1864 from Bhootan, 4433 sq. m., of which a tenth is forest. Population, 444,689. The Brahmapootra intersects the district and then finds its way south to Bengal proper, between the Bhootan range and the Garo hills. Low hills skirt the banks of the river, for which they occasionally form gorges. There are isolated ridges covered with forest; the highest is Bhairab Chura, 1600 ft. The Sri-Soorjya Pahar ("hill of the sun") is a supposed site of Hindoo observatory. The Brahmapootra, from the N., receives the Manas opposite Goalpara town, the Gadadhar or Gangadhar, from Jalpaigori, and the Sankos from Kooch Behar. Nine smaller streams, navigable only during the rains, fall into the Brahmapootra from the Bhootan and Garo hills. Three lakes, or inland sheets of water, covering from 7 to 12 sq. m. each, are the Tamranga, Upad, and Saras. **Goalpara** (5000), on hill on S. bank of Brahmapootra, with noble view of Himalaya and Garo hills; here is the American Baptist Mission. Gauripoor is a village on N. bank, residence of chief landholder. **Dhoobri**, now capital of district, steamer and labour port and military station on the N. bank, where the great river begins to turn south. **Bijni** and **Sidli**, two of the Eastern Dwars, rising centres of trade with Bhootan. The district is in 3 subdivisions—Goalpara, Dhoobri, and Eastern Dwars.

§ 8. KAMROOP DISTRICT is bounded E. by Nowgong and Darrang districts, N. by Bootan hills, W. by Goalpara district, S. by Khasi hills. Area, 3631 sq. m. Population, 644,843. The plain, rising N. and S. towards the hills, is divided from E. to W. by the Brahmapootra river, which receives from N. the Manas, falling into it opposite Goalpara, and is navigable by native craft; the Chaul-Koya, which drains the Pagla Manas, Saru Manas, Pahumara, Kaldiya, Noa-nadi, and Baraliya, and after sending off the Rorsa to the Brahmapootra, falls into the Manas just before that river reaches the Brahmapootra. The Lakhai-tara and the Bar-nadi also flow from the Bhootan hills to the Brahmapootra. From the south the Brahmapootra is fed by the Bata, Kulsi, and Singara. Most of these fifteen tributaries are navigable by native boats of two tons, but are fordable in the dry season. Marshes, termed *bheels* or *jheels* and swelling into small lakes, are numerous and may be reclaimed. There are large forest reserves, chiefly of *sal* (*Shorea robusta*), and plantations of caoutchouc and tea. There are 50 European land-holders. **Gauhati** (12,000), chief town and cantonment, on S. bank of Brahmapootra. Old capital of King Narak, called Pragjotishpoor in *Mahabharat* epic. Capital of Aham dynasty from 1615, with ruins of fortifications. Three shrines in the neighbourhood, Hindoo and Boodhist, attract thousands of pilgrims. Centre of American Baptist Mission. **Barpeta**, centre of second subdivision in N.W.

§ 9. DARRANG DISTRICT is bounded E. by Lakhimpoor; N. by Daphla, Aka, and Bhootia hills; W. by Kamroop; and S. by Nowgong and Seebsagar. Area, 3418 sq. m. Population, 271,504. This level district lies along N. bank of Brahmapootra for 126 m. with a breadth of 25 m. The Aham dynasty lent it to the hill Bhootias, for rice cultivation, during eight months every year. The Brahmapootra receives the Bhairavi, near Tezpoor, from the Aka hills; the Ghiladhari, Jeea Dhaneswari, Nonai, and Bar-nadi, all navigable streams, from N. The Bhola and Lakshmi, on leaving the hills, disappear for some miles in the porous soil. There are six large forest reserves, with rubber plantations; there are fifty-four non-Asiatics on tea estates. **Tezpoor** (2500), civil station, on right bank of Brahmapootra, on a plain between low hills, with ruins of palace of Ban Raja, described in *Prem Sagar*; a mile W. is a swamp, the legendary scene of contest between Krishna and the Raja, whence the ancient name, Sonitpoor = field of blood. Gigantic ruins of Shiva temples are near Tezpoor. Mangaldai, 50 m. W. of Tezpoor, head of second subdivision, and Bishnath, 26 m. E., are next in importance. Ndalgoori, N.W., is the principal annual fair, held at base of the hills, for trade with Bhootias.

§ 10. NOWGONG DISTRICT is bounded E. by the Naga hills, N. by Darrang, W. by Kamroop, and S. by Jaintia and Cachar hills. Area, 3417 sq. m. Population, 308,889. The district is a low plain along S. bank of Brahmapootra, sloping towards W. from Meekeer hills, which rise rapidly to 3500 ft., the highest peak, and extend 60 m. long by 40 broad. The Karnakhya hills in S.W., a small range, rise to 1500 ft. A shrine of Doorga is on the Karnakhya Parbat, cultivated with tea. The Brahmapootra sends off the Kalang in N.E., which rejoins it 15 m. above Gauhati. The Kalang receives from the S. the Mecha, Diju, Nanai, Kapili, and Kiling, and its old bed forms the two large lakes, Mari and Pota Kalang, S. of Nowgong station. The Sonai leaves the S. bank of Brahmapootra above Lookhoya, and flows S.W. to the Kalang, its old bed forming the lake Mar Sonai. The Kapili, which, from the Jaintia hills, joins the Kalang by one branch, flows W. to the Barpani, which falls into the Dimal, and that in its turn into the Kiling before its junction, as above, with the Kalang. The Deopanj, from the Naga hills, falls into the Diphlu. The Leteri, in the N., leaves the Brahmapootra opposite Tezpoor and reunites with it 24 m. lower down, after receiving several tributaries. The Dhaneswari, after bounding the district E., falls into the Brahmapootra. Besides these, navigable for nine months in the year, there are 110 streams navigable only in the rainy season. Besides the lakes mentioned there are the Garanga, Kachdhara, Mer, Udari Khangaria, and Pakaria. **Nowgong** (3000), chief place on E. bank of Kalang. Raha and Chapari-mookh are river-side marts near confluence of the Kalang, Dimal, and Kapili. Tea is largely cultivated by British capital.

§ 11. SEEBSAGAR DISTRICT is bounded E. and N. by Lakhimpoor, W. by Nowgong, and S. by Naga hills. Area, 2855 sq. m. Population, 365,300. The district lies along S. bank of Brahmapootra, to which numerous streams flow from the Naga hills. Besides the Dhaneswari above, forming part of its W. boundary, the Buri Dihing on N. border, the Disang, and Dikhu are navigable; in the rainy season the rivers navigable by boats of two tons are the Kakodanga, Disai, Kokila, Jangi, Dwarika, and Dimu. The island, or alluvial deposit, Majuli, is formed in the Brahmapootra at the junction of the Lohit. The lands inundated by the great river are, in the cold season, covered by vast herds of buffaloes. **Seebsagar** (5500), chief town, 12 m. S. from the Brahmapootra, picturesquely placed around a noble artificial lake covering 114 acres. **Rangpoor**, S., once a capital of Aham dynasty. **Garghaon**, fort and palace, on Dikhu river, once a capital of the Ahams, and seat of earlier civilisation. **Jorhat**, on the Desai, a centre of tea culture. **Golaghat**, on Dhaneswari, and head of steam navigation. Seebsagar district, second only to Cachar among the tea-growing districts of India, produces upwards of a million lbs. annually, and has 110,000 acres of waste land gradually coming under cultivation, largely by the Assam Company since 1859. The district is in 3 subdivisions—Seebsagar, Jorhat, and Golaghat.

§ 12. LAKHIMPOOR DISTRICT, head of Assam valley, the extreme N.E. district of India, running into China between Tibet and Burma, is bounded E. by Singpho and Mishmi hills; N. by Mishmi, Abar, Meeree, and Daphla hills; W. by Darrang and Seebsagar; and S. by the Lohit and the Patkai watershed. Area, 3723 sq. m. Population, 172,079. Between 28° 17′ 10″ and 26° 51′ 30″ N. latitude, and 93° 15′ 30″ and 97° 4′ 58″ E. longitude. The Brahmapootra, bisecting the district through its whole length, is fed principally by three rivers, which unite at latitude 27° 45′ and longitude 95° 30′. The southernmost, to which the Hindoos give the name of the main stream, comes out of the hills from 150 to 200 yards wide E. of the Brahmakoond (Brahma's well) valley, beneath the snowy range, receives the Kundel and Digaru from the N. Mishmi hills, and the Tenga-pani and Noa Dihing from the N.E. Singpho hills. The Dihong contributes the chief volume in continuation of the Tsangpo of Tibet. The Brahmapootra is navigable by steamer to Dibroogarh, and in the rains only to Sadiya, 100 m. farther, near the N.E. frontier. It receives the Dibroo from Lakhimpoor, the Buri-Dihing from the Patkai hills, navigable to Jaipoor, into which the Tingrai-nadi and the Sasoo fall. To the N. of the Brahmapootra the chief branches are the Lohit and Subansiri from Tibet. **Dibroogarh** (4000), chief station and cantonment, on the Dibroo, above its junction with the Brahmapootra, N. A railway is being laid 75 m. to Sadiya. **Lakhimpoor**, headquarters of subdivision. **Sadiya**, frontier military post, with annual fair for hill tribes. From this, in 1870, the late Mr. T. T. Cooper explored up the Brahmapootra, through the Mejoo Mishmee country, towards Bathang in E. Tibet; he reached within 10 m. of the first Tibetan outpost from Rooemah, near which Roman Catholic missionaries, Crick and Bouri, were murdered. **Jaipoor**, with extensive coal beds and petroleum springs. Here the indigenous tea plant discovered in 1826 by Mr. C. A. Bruce, who commanded a gunboat in first Burmese war, was cultivated by Government in 1835 in a garden sold to the Assam Company in 1840. There are now upwards of 120 plantations, exporting more than 2 million lbs. Silk culture once flourished in this district.

HILLS.

§ 13. GARO HILLS DISTRICT (Gaorana or Gawana = native name), most westerly of the ranges which divide the Brahmapootra from the Barak valley, is bounded E. by the Khasi hills,

N. and W. by Goalpara, and S. by Maimansingh. Area, 3653 sq. m. Population, 109,054. The hills rise from N. into the Tura range (4500 ft.), which runs W. and E. to join the Khasi hills, with two peaks, Tura and Kailas (Hindoo name), Bhim Tura (Garo), Manrai (Khasi), from which the snowy Himalaya are sometimes visible. The Arbela range runs N. of, and parallel with, the Tura. The five occasionally navigable rivers are the Krishnai, from the N. of Arbela range, passing into Goalpara; the Kalu (Garui = Garo name), from near Tura station, flowing W. into Goalpara, with Baranasi tributary; the Bhogai, from S.E. of station, flowing S. to Maimansingh, to old channel of Brahmapootra, with Noaranga tributary; the Netai, also from S. watershed of Tura, S. to the Kanks in Maimansingh; the Sameswari (Samsang = Garo name), the largest, flowing from N. face of Tura range, turns E. and S., receives the Rangkai, Rangai, and Chibok, and enters E. Maimansingh near Susang. Coal and limestone are found in its valley and elsewhere; there are picturesque gorges and caves in the limestone, especially above Rayak village. Wild elephants are caught for Government in *khedas* or stockades. The aboriginal Garos are similar to the Cacharis. The American Baptist Mission conducts the schools. **Tura,** chief village, on central spur of hill facing W., 2000 ft. from summit, and 40 m. from Singimari mart in Goalpara. Harigaon, 20 m. W. from Tura, on road through Goalpara to Maniker, on E. bank of Brahmapootra. The rainfall in 1878-9 was 177 inches, chiefly from June to September.

§ 14. KHASI AND JAINTIA HILLS DISTRICT (Ka Ri Khasi and Ka Ri Synteng = native names), headquarters of Chief Commissioner of the Province, is bounded E. by N. Cachar and Naga hills, N. by Nowgong and Kamroop, W. by Garo hills, and S. by Sylhet. Area, 6157 sq. m. Population, 169,113. The district is non-regulation, consisting largely of democratic States under nineteen native Seims ("soul" or "life") or chiefs. The Welsh Calvinistic Mission conducts the schools. The Shillong range rises to 6449 ft., the height of its principal peak; Dingili range, to 6400 ft.; Mao-thad-rai-shan, to 6297 ft.; Lao-syn-nia, to 5775 ft.; Lao-bah, to 4464 ft.; Lyng-ker-dem, to 5000 ft.; Loom-baiong, to 4646 ft.; and Mao-syn-ram, to 5810 ft. The Soh-pet-byneng ("navel of the sky") is believed by the Khasias to be the centre of the world; it is 4000 ft. The streams are mountain torrents, seven of which flow S. to the Soorma in Sylhet, and five to the Brahmapootra. Fine coal, iron, and lime abound; the "Sylhet lime" is supplied from the base of the S. mountains. The orange, cinnamon, cinchona, and potato flourish. **Shillong** (2500), capital of Assam since 1874, and cantonment; a sanitarium (4951 ft.), with its suburbs, Laban and Maokhar, belonging to Seim of Millyum. In 1878-9 the rainfall was 399·86 inches. Eight roads radiate from Shillong to Gauhatti (two days' distance), Sylhet, and Garo hills. **Jowai**, centre of 25 fiscal divisions of Jaintia hills, 26 m. from the plains. **Cherra-poonjee** ("village"), 30 m. S. of Shillong, near face of hills, with rainfall rising occasionally to 500 inches (805 in 1861), centre of coal-mining, with limestone caves; also at Roopnath, where one cavern is popularly believed to reach to China. **Nongklao** (3500 ft.), scene of rebellion in 1829; with a cinchona plantation since 1867. **Shella**, principal Khasi State, on lower hills, and a central station of Welsh Mission, with Normal School.

§ 15. Naga Hills District is bounded E. by the Singpho country and Seebsagar, N. by Nowgong, W. by Nowgong and Khasi and Jaintia hills, and S. by Manipoor and the Patkai and Saramete (12,822 ft.) ranges. Area, 6400 sq. m. Population, 93,100. All are forest tribes—Meekeer, Cachari, Kooki, Artanya, Angami, Sema, Rengma, Lhota, Hatigoria, and Kutcha Naga, who range from the comparative civilisation of the two first to the utter savagery of the last. The Nagas are the naked (Bengalee, *nangta*) or snake (Sanskrit, *naga*) tribes, who use the spear and *dao* or hatchet. The Rengma hills (2000 to 3000 ft.), drained by the Kabani, Sargati, and Dhaneswari rivers, are at present inaccessible. The Barail range (2000 to 6000 ft.), with trade routes from Manipoor, extends E. from Cachar to the Patkai mountains. The rivers, navigable by large boats in the rains only, are the Da-yang on E., flowing N. to S. to the Dhaneswari, which, rising in Barail hills, runs N. to the Brahmapootra. The Jamoona, rising in N., flows S. and E. along the Rengma base to the Kapili. Numerous swamps breed malaria. Coal, chalk, and limestone are found in the Rengma hills. **Kohima** (5000), latest headquarters and military station in S.E., with road to Golaghat in Seebsagar district. **Wokha**, subdivisional station in Singpho country, 62 m. S.E. of Golaghat. **Samagooting**, first headquarters station, 67 m. S.W. of Golaghat, with a school. The raids of the Angami Nagas for human heads, and the assassination of Survey officers, have caused eleven expeditions into the hills, with the result of a gradual occupation and pacification of the wild forest land up to the Patkai frontier, which marks off the Empire from the Hookoong valley of Upper Burma. To this valley there was an old trade route over a depression in the Patkai past the

Non-yang, or lake of Yang, which drains into the Kyendween, and that into the Irawadi. From Makoom, last outpost of Lakhimpoor, to the Kyendween is 90 m. of jungle track, followed by Mr. H. L. Jenkins in 1870. In March 1881 the Chief Commissioner traversed these hills. Entering them at Nichu Guard, he marched through the Diphu gorge to Zumha, and thence by the ordinary road, *via* Pherrima and Piphima, to Keruphima, whence he diverged to Sachema, Mezuma, and Khonoma. From Khonoma he travelled, *via* Jotsoma, to Kohima; thence he marched to Wokha by the country of the Rengma, Sema, and Lhota Nagas, and descended on the plains at Merapani.

§ 16. *MANIPOOR STATE (*Meithei laipak*, or Meithei country = local name; *Kathé* = Burman), Hindoo State with British Resident, is bounded E. by Kubo valley of Upper Burma, N. by Naga hills, W. by Cachar, and S. by the Looshai country. Area (unsurveyed), under 8000 sq. m. Population, 147,345. Manipoor valley, with an area of 650 sq. m., is an irregular oval 36 by 20 m., occupied by some 70,000 Meitheis, who trace the name Manipoor to the jewel "Mani" of the *Mahabharat.* The Raja ascribes his descent to the snake called Pakung-ba, which is the object of State worship, through male and female diviners called Maibees. All males between 17 and 60 work for the State ten days in every forty—a system called *lalloop*, practised among the Ahams of the Assam frontier. In Manipoor, with its fine ponies, originated the game of hockey on horseback (polo) three centuries ago; it is there played with great skill by all classes (seven on either side), from the Raja downwards. Of the mountain ranges, running N. and S., the principal are the Limatol (6500 ft.), and the Heerok (6000 ft.) or Roma to E., separating Manipoor from the Kubo valley, which was ruled by the Raja as far as the Kyendween river in the ten years ending 1834, when the British induced him to surrender it to Burma. On the W., the road of 103 m. from Silchar crosses the Hoorung hills at 800 ft., the Mookroo at 1500 ft., the Kala Naga or Owhynanglong at 400 ft., and the Limatol at 4900 ft., from the E. slope of which are seen the Logtak lakes, yearly lessening from the large lake which must have at one time filled the saucer-like valley. The Numbool and Numbol rivers from N. and N.W. fall into the lake, which sends out the Kortak to join the united Eempal, Eril, and Thobal from the N., and forms the Soogoono, which flows to the Kyendween below Gendat in Upper Burma. The Barak (Manipoori = Quaiy) rises in the Barail range, flows S.E., receiving the Mookroo, Erung, Tipar, and

Jiri, then N. and W. into Cachar, between which and Manipoor the Jiri is the boundary. **Manipoor** (Eempall = local name) (35,000), capital of the State, with portion of Raja's residence not destroyed by earthquake of 1869, and moat in which annual boat-races are held. The breed of ponies under 12 hands high is degenerating. Iron and limestone are found. Salt wells at Ningail and Chundrakong give an abundant supply, especially since the earthquake. Raw silk of good quality is produced. From Manipoor to Kubo the N. route (five to seven days' march) runs for 18 m. through the valley, and for 24 m. across the Roma range (5500 ft.), with indigenous tea-plants, to Sunjok, tributary village of Burma, now on right bank of Kyendween, from which is nine days' journey to Bamō, the Burma entrepot for China on the Upper Irawadi. **Kangjhupkool** is the British Resident's summer residence. The capital is now connected with all parts of Manipoor valley by roads. A cart road runs by Sengmai, 80 m., to Mao, on the border of the Naga hills district, and thence to Viswema in the hills; also from Manipoor to Kongal. The passes to Burma are closed to traders. The Manipoorees are famed in E. Bengal as carpenters, metal-workers, saddlers, and producers of blue cloth with a red border. The boundary between Manipoor and Burma, described in 1834 as an imaginary line drawn due N. from the Kubo valley, has just been laid down with pillars, so as to prevent or punish Kooki aggression, and fix the responsibility of the Shan population of Sumjok and the Burmese authorities, to whom they are subordinate.

CHAPTER VI.

THE PROVINCE OF BRITISH BURMA—GENERAL.

§ 1. Name, Size, and Position. § 2. Mountain Ranges. § 3. Rivers. § 4. Products, Railways, and Trade. § 5. Land Tenures and Taxation. § 6. The People and Districts.

§ 1. NAME, SIZE AND POSITION.—**British Burma Province** (Mram-ma, pronounced Bryam-ma = celestial beings, from Pali word Brahma), with an area of 87,220 sq. m., or slightly less than that of the Island of Great Britain, forms the eastern shore of the Bay of Bengal, from the Bengal district of Chittagong to Siam. Its population, which in 1881 was 3,736,771, increased 36 per cent in the previous decade, and has more than doubled since 1862, when Pegu, Arakan, and Tenasserim were first consolidated under a Chief Commissioner. Burma is the great Boodhist province along the Golden Chersonese or Malayan peninsula for 1800 miles. Lying between 92° and 90′ E. long. and 20° 50′ and 9° 55′ N. lat., it is bounded on the E. by a line of masonry pillars, uniting mountain and river from the crest of the Arakan to the Tenasserim Roma at Pakchan, separating it from Independent Burma and Siam; N. by the main crest of the Arakan Roma and the Naf estuary; W. and S. by the Bay of Bengal. This fertile strip of coast and river valleys, indented by estuaries and creeks, has been compared on the map to a bird flying S.E. with outstretched wings; Pegu, or the valleys of the Irawadi and Tsit-toung, forming the body, Arakan and Tenasserim the pinions. Fertile archipelagoes of Islands fringe the coast, of which the largest are Chedooba or Manoung, Ramree or Tan-myo, and Mergui.

§ 2. MOUNTAIN RANGES.—Four principal mountain ranges run N. and S. The **Arakan Roma** ("back-bone") or Yoma, Mons Mæandrus of Ptolemy, a meridian range starting from the Patkai between long. 93° and 94°, enclosing Manipoor, and stretching out W. to Tipura, contracts to a defined chain as it approaches Arakan and "700 m. from its origin in the Naga wilds, it sinks into the sea hard by Negrais, its last bluff crowned by the Golden Pagoda of Moodain, gleaming far to seaward, a Burmese Sunium. Fancy might trace the submarine prolongation of the range in the dotted line of the Preparis, the Cocos, the Andamans, the Nicobars, till it emerges again to traverse Sumatra, and the vast chain of the Javanese Isles (Yule's "Ava"). Its principal peaks are the Blue Mountain (4851 ft.), N. Arakan, throwing off W. to the coast at A-ngoo Maw, the watershed between the Naf and Mayoo; the Kyee ("ever visible"), the Nat-oo and the double Shwe-doung Mourg Hnitma ("golden brother and sister"). The passes are the precipitous Dha-let in N., the An in Kyouk-hpyoo to Meng-boo on the Upper Irawadi, 100 m.; and the Toung-goop in Sandoway, with a road to Padoung in Prome. The **Pegu Roma** or Yoma watershed between the Irawadi and Tsit-toung rises from the Re-me-theng plains N. of British territory, rises to 1200 ft. at frontier, increases to 2000 when it throws out spurs forming the valleys of the Pegu, Poozwon-doung and other rivers, forms at Rangoon the platform of the Shwe Dagon pagoda, and farther S. that of the Syriam Pagoda, and disappears in the dangerous rocks of the Hmawuon. The most northerly pass is the Za-diep-hpo ("nutmeg tree"). The **Tenasserim Roma, Pa-Wan** or Siam waterparting, starting from the waning Himalaya, trends S.E. between the Irawadi and Salween, 15 m. E. of the Tsit-toung it sends off the subsidiary Poung-loung range (2000 to 3000 ft.), 50 m. E. the main range rises to 8000 ft., and in Kareng-nee to 9000 ft., till one of its spurs almost reaches the sea near Martaban, where it parts the Salween from the big-mouthed Tsit-toung. Its principal peak in British territory is the Nat-toung ("spirit hill"). Six days' journey S.E. from the frontier station of Toung-ngoo, the Toung-goung-toon ("bald-headed mountain") rises to 8000 ft. The Tenasserim Roma, E. of Salween, forms the boundary between Tenasserim and Siam from the gorge through which the Thoung-yeng (16° 27′ 47″ N. lat., and 98° 50′ 50″ E. long.) flows towards the Three Pagodas, to the source of the Pakchan river which—down to Victoria Point—forms the S.E. boundary of the British Indian Empire. S. of the gorge the granitoid mass of Moo-lai-yit rises to 5500 ft.

§. 3. RIVERS.—The **Naf** in the N. is an estuary 30 m. wide at its mouth, and running 31 m. inland. Forty m. S. is the **Ma-yoo**, 4 m. wide, and broken in two, 10 m. up, by an island. The **Kooladan**, separated from the Ma-yoo by the island of Akyab, rises in the Arakan Roma, whence it flows S. over a rocky bed to a point 120 m. above Akyab, to which it is navigable by boats. Its mouth, protected by the Barongo and

Savage Islands, forms a spacious harbour which a bar renders difficult of entry. The Tsala, Rala, Kola, Palak, Kan, Mee, and Pee, are its tributaries. The other rivers on the Arakan coast are the Le-mro, Dha-let, An, Sandoway, and Khua. The **Irawadi**, from the snows of the S. face of the Langtang chain in 28° N. lat., and 97° 30′ E. long. in the gap of 80 m. of Singpho-Kampti country between India and China, has a course of 900 m. S.S.W. to the Bay of Bengal, of which 240 are in British Burma. Formed of what the Burmese call Myit-gee and Myit-ngay ("large and small river"), and receiving the Mogoung from the W., the Irawadi, after the first hundred miles of its course, is 900 yards broad when it enters the first defile (Tsheng-boo) of 150 yards. On emerging it becomes half a mile wide, passes Koung-toung-myo, where in 1769 the last army of Chinese mandarins was defeated, and below the old capital of Amarapoora enters the second Kyouk-deng ("defile") and below Tsampanago a third defile, below which, on the E. side, begins the valley of Ava, where it receives the Myit-ngay from the N. Shan country. After entering British territory it contracts between the spurs of the two Romas, passes through a fourth defile at Prome, where the delta begins, and below that has a discharge of 75,000 ft. The Irawadi sends off its first branch W. above Henzada at 90 m. from the sea, which, flowing past Bassein, receives the waters of the Panmawaddee and of the Penglaygalay, and bifurcating, enters the Bay of Bengal by two main mouths, the **Bassein** and the **Thekkay-thoung** rivers. This branch is navigable for large ships for 30 m., as far as Bassein; after passing Henzada it sends off a small branch to the eastward, which joins the Hlaing just above Rangoon. The main river then subdivides till it empties itself into the sea by ten mouths—the Yuay, Dayaybhyoo, Pyamaloo, Pyengazaloo, Dalla, Phyapon, Donyan, Thanhteat, and China Ba-keer rivers, and the Irawadi, which is between the Pyengazaloo and Dalla mouths. Its waters commence to rise in March and continue to rise till September from 37 to 40 ft. It is navigable for river steamers as far as Bamō, 600 m. beyond the British frontier. The velocity of its waters, when the river is full, is 5 m. an hour. The **Hlaing** rises close to Prome, where it is called the Myit-makat stream, and flowing in a southerly direction nearly parallel to the Irawadi, it gradually assumes the name of the Hlaing, and finally of the Rangoon river, and flows past the town of that name. Below Rangoon it is joined by the Pegu and Poo-zwon-doung rivers flowing from the E. and N.E. It is navigable for vessels of the largest size for some distance above Rangoon, but owing to the Hastings shoal, formed at the junction of the Pegu, the Poo-zwon-doung, and Rangoon rivers, vessels of more than 6 ft. draught cannot go up at low tide. The **Pegu** and the **Poo-zwon-doung** rise close together in the Roma range, about 58 m. above the town of Pegu. Here the Pegu river, which is almost dry during the hot season at low tides, is 105 yards broad; in its further course of 60 m. to the Rangoon river it rapidly increases in breadth, but, narrowing at its mouth, a bore goes up it, the effects of which are felt at Pegu. The Poo-zwon-doung river, which empties itself into the Rangoon river at the same spot as the Pegu river, is 50 yards wide at a distance of 35 m. from its mouth. The **Tsit-toung** rises far north of British territory, which it enters just above Toung-ngoo, where it is navigable with difficulty for large boats during the dry season; below Shwe-gyeen, where it receives the waters of the **Shwe-gyeen** river from the E., it slowly widens, till at Tsit-toung it is half a mile broad. Thence it curves backward into the Gulf of Martaban, from which the tidal wave sweeps up it as a bore with a curling crest 9 ft. high. The Tsit-toung has a course of 350 m., of which half is in British territory. A canal from the Pegu river to Myit-kyo, above Tsit-toung, facilitates communication between Rangoon and Toung-ngoo. The **Bheeleng** flows from the hills between the Tsit-toung and the Salween, 128 m., to the sea. The **Salween**, probably from the most E. spurs of the Himalaya, N. of Yunan, in 32° N. lat. (Lepper), after traversing the Shan and Kareng-nee States, crosses the British frontier, 300 yards broad, at 200 m. from its mouth. Thence it is navigable till it receives the Thoung-yeng, when it contracts to a torrent. On receiving the Gyaing and Attaran, it divides into two channels, of which the northern, known as the **Martaban** river, flows south past Maulmein to the sea at Amherst. The **Thoung-yeng** is the S. boundary of the Province for 198 m. from its source in the great E. chain. The **Tenasserim**, farther S., is navigable by boats, and the **Pakchan** by steamers, up to the junction of the Ma-lee-won.

The chief lakes or lagoons are—the **Engma** ("principal lake"), S. of Prome district, 10 m. long and 4 broad; the **Htoo** and **Doora**, in Henzada; and the **Sha-khai-gyee** and **Eng-rai-gyee** in Bassein.

§ 4. PRODUCTS, RAILWAYS, AND TRADE.—Tertiary coal occurs in Mergui and Thayit-myo, but not in sufficient quantity to constitute workable fields. Tinstone is the most important mineral found in the granite, which runs through the whole length of Tenasserim. In 1586 Mr. Ralph Fitch wrote of this division as supplying all India with tin; but neither to Chinese nor English has the mining been profitable of late. Oxide of iron, specular and brown, occurs chiefly in Tenasserim; copper and galena, manganese and antimony, also are there and near Toung-ngoo. Gold-washing, with results of slight economic importance, is carried on, mainly in bad seasons, in most parts of Burma, chiefly near Shwe-gyeen in Martaban, and in the bed of the Irawadi. Petroleum springs abound in the form of the clear limpid oil of Kyouk-hpyoo, like sherry, and the dark commercial oil from Re-nan-khyoung in Upper Burma. There also, and not in British territory, are found the finest Oriental rubies, sapphires, and emeralds. The true wealth of British Burma consists in its forests and rice. In this Province, first of all India, Lord Dalhousie began a system of forest conservancy under Mr. Brandis, Ph.D., in 1854, chiefly for the protection and extension of the teak tree. The Forest Act of 1865 applies to the forest reserves between the Irawadi and the hills E. of Tsit-toung, chiefly on the Pegu Roma range and the two Tenasserim circles, and regulates the import of timber from beyond the frontier. Cinchona and caoutchouc have been introduced; the first succeeds in the Succirubra variety alone, at the Than-toung-gyee plantation, 18 m. E. of Toung-ngoo (3700 ft.) The forests produce valuable oils (wood-oil chiefly), resins, gums, dyes, and fibres. The sesamum is largely cultivated for oil, on the flanks of the hills where cleared by fire, and on sandbanks occasionally submerged. Rice is the main crop, making Burma the granary of India during recent famines. It is raised chiefly in the delta of the Irawadi by five methods—on swamps, on levels occasionally irrigated, on occasionally submerged banks, on hill clearings, and on hot-weather lands from irrigation only. The culture of the first three commences with the rain monsoon in June; the harvest continues from November to January. Tobacco is raised everywhere, carelessly manufactured into cheroots, and largely exported. About 3 millions of acres are under rice every year; 180,000 under such fruit trees as the orange, lemon, doorian, mango, mangosteen, jack, cocoa-nut, custard-apple, and grape; 15,000 under oil-seeds; 5000 under sugar cane; 10,000 under cotton; 17,000 under tobacco; and 700 under indigo. Tea and coffee are grown to a slight extent in the Akyab district. The cultivators hold their land in plots of from 5 to 16 acres as peasant-proprietors, paying an annual tax to the State for cleared land, and farther paying a capitation tax in common with all adults. The foreign and coasting trade exceeds £18,000,000 in annual value, of which one-sixth is treasure. The inland trade with Upper Burma varies around £250,000 imports and £150,000 exports. Silk and cotton weaving and silk breeding, dyeing, preparation of cutch from the Acacia catechu for tanning, etc., of salt, of ngapee or salted fish and paste (the *balachong* of the Straits Settlements), pottery, lacquered ware, gilt teak boxes for tools, mats, gold and silver work, and steam-mills for rice and wood, are the chief manufactures. The Rangoon and Irawadi (State) Railway has, since 1877, run from Rangoon as far as Prome, 163 m. A line is being constructed 163 m. from Rangoon to Toung-ngoo, up the Tsit-toung valley, and has reached Pegu town, 48 m. It is about to be opened to Pycentaza, opposite the headquarters of Shwegyeen, and will be completed in 1884. The sea-borne trade alone in 1880-81 was £18,277,000 in value; and the land trade with Upper Burma £3,044,000, or £22,222,000 nearly equally divided between exports and imports. This is a growth of 117 per cent in ten years. The export of rice rose from 440,000 tons in 1870-71 to 892,262 tons in 1880-81, and was still higher in 1881-82. From Rangoon the Irawadi flotilla steamers reach Bamō in from 15 to 20 days; thence two English missionaries recently travelled unarmed, under the Convention of Chefoo, in 21 days to Talifoo, in 46 to the capital of Yunan, and in 68 days to the Yangtse river in S. Sechuen, 1765 m. from Shanghai, to which the Yellow River is open save for 100 m. of rapids and rocks between Quei-chow and Ichang.

§ 5. Land Tenures and Taxation.—Till 1879 the land revenue was assessed at a single rate per acre for whole villages or groups of villages, while the areas of holdings were roughly measured by rural revenue officers. In 1879 a cadastral survey of all the occupied lands was begun; and on results of that survey a new assessment of the land revenue for a term of 15 years is being framed. Fields are surveyed and their area ascertained with scientific accuracy; different rates of land revenue, varying with the fertility of the soil and the nearness of markets, have been fixed for each village or tract; and a careful record has been prepared of all rights in the land. Of three districts, Hanthawadi, Bassein, and Tharawadi, the total area surveyed is 1,924,146 acres, of which 505,727 acres are cultivated. The average area of each holding is 36 acres. The fiscal result is that lands which used to pay a land revenue of Rs. 4,04,587 will now pay a land revenue of Rs. 4,95,932 a year. The highest revenue rate is Rs. 3 (6s.) an acre, and the lowest is 12 annas (1s. 6d.) per acre. The average rate is Rs.

2-4 (4s. 6d.) per acre of cultivated land. The average gross value of the rice produced is about Rs. 21 per acre; and the cost of production, including the support of the cultivator and his family, is Rs. 16. The land-tax is thus one-ninth of the gross and less than one-half of the net produce. The average produce of ordinary lands is a little beyond 32 bushels per acre. Besides the land-tax there is (1) a local cess of 10 per cent on it for police, roads, schools, and rural post; (2) the capitation tax of Rs. 5 to Rs. 3 on each adult male; and (3) an export duty on rice of 6d. per cwt., which comes mainly out of the producer's profits. All this raises the land-tax to Rs. 3-14 (7s. 9d.) per cultivated acre; but Burman peasant-proprietors have no landlords, middlemen, or usurers, pay little salt-tax, and have excellent markets. That British Burma is progressively the most prosperous Province in Asia, is seen from the following comparative statement for ten years:—

			1871.	1881.
Cultivated area in acres . . .			2,090,386	3,518,685
Value of sea-borne trade—				
	1871.	1881.		
Exports .	£3,894,894	£9,478,143		
Imports .	3,903,144	8,802,273		
Total .	£7,798,038	£18,280,416		
Value of trade with Upper Burma, Siam, etc.			£2,341,009	£4,045,198
Total rice exports in tons . . .			487,162	892,262
,, tonnage of sea-going vessels entered and cleared			1,286,624	1,949,247
Approximate number of boats plying on the rivers			60,329	65,000
Approximate number of steamers plying on inland rivers for hire . . .			9	38
Miles of railway open for traffic . .			......	163
,, ,, under construction .			......	163
,, of canal open for traffic . .			......	39
Number of civil suits decided in the year .			31,804	31,026
,, of murders, dacoities, and robberies reported in the year . .			407	278
,, of children in Government and inspected schools . .			2,456	85,930
,, of patients treated in hospitals .			49,016	108,782
Land revenue			£331,944	£656,891
Fishery ,, ...			£66,084	£138,902
Forest ,, ...			£81,812	£151,661
Excise ,, ...			£98,781	£241,429
Capitation tax			£221,105	£288,804
Customs duties			£284,803	£595,656
Stamp ,, ...			£47,367	£78,499
Postal and telegraph receipts . .			£20,602	£36,238

	1871.	1881.
Total general revenue, exclusive of railway receipts	£1,232,066	£2,164,067
Municipal revenues	£106,094	£141,960
Local Fund ,,		£134,751
Port ,, ,,		£80,308
Net earnings of railways during year ending in June 1881	......	£60,696
Percentage of net earnings on capital cost of railway	......	4·597 per cent

§ 6. THE PEOPLE AND DISTRICTS.—The second census was taken in 1881 after an interval of 8½ years, during which the population of British Burma increased 36 per cent, or 4 per cent annually, largely from immigrants attracted by its fertile waste and high wages. The rate of increase varies greatly in the different tracts, ranging from 81 per cent in the fertile district of Hanthawadi to 3 per cent in the island district of the Arakan coast. The increase in population is divided among the chief races of the province thus:—

	Totals of 1872.	Totals of 1881.	Percentage of Increase.	Percentage of Decrease.
Burmans and Talaings	2,111,921	2,766,827	31·0	...
Karengs	331,706	518,294	56·2	...
Chins	51,117	55,015	7·6	...
Toungthoos	24,923	35,554	42·6	...
Shans	36,029	59,723	65·8	...
Other races of hill-men	31,242	27,598	...	11·6
Races from India	137,014	246,289	79·7	...
Chinese	12,109	12,962	7·0	...
Europeans and Eurasians	9,177	11,860	29·2	...
Total of all races	2,747,148	3,736,771	36·02	11·6

The census figures show that 541,743 of the inhabitants of British Burma were born outside the limits of the Province, and that of these 316,018 were born in Upper Burma. But the main causes of increase are probably the fecundity and healthiness of the population. The proportion of the population who are returned as under 12 years of age is 33·6 per cent, which is considerable for a country where there are many adult immigrants. The males are 53·28 per cent of the whole population, and 46·72 per cent are females. The surplus of men is partly due to the large number of immigrant labourers. Immigrants from India, in the first instance, come alone without their wives; while immigrants from Upper Burma are not allowed to bring their families. Among the Karengs and Talaings, whose numbers are rarely recruited by immigration, the distribution of sexes is less unequal. Among the Karengs there are 49·99 females to 50·01 males. Fifty-two per cent of all the males over 12 years of age, and 2·8 per cent of the women and girls over that age, are returned as able to read and write. According to the census returns, 66 per mille of the total population are under instruction, mostly at the monastic schools, which form an important feature in the social polity of Burma. The Educational Department has cognisance only of schools at which 24 per cent of the population are being taught. About 11 per cent of the population dwell in towns, and 68·56 per cent of the people live by agriculture. During five years the average surplus of imported over exported treasure has been £1,340,000 a year. The greater part of this silver and gold is converted into ornaments by the Burmans and Karengs. Every household of six persons in British Burma must have spent on the average about £12 during 1880-81 on imported articles and jewellery. The wages of unskilled labour range from 5s. a week at the slack season in Kyouk-pyoo to 25s. a week in the busy season at the rice-ports. The average wage over the whole of Burma is probably about 7s. 6d. a week as compared with an average of about 2s. 3d. a week in the rest of India. The earnings of ordinary cultivators are proportionately higher. Wealth, such as it is, is very widely distributed.

Men are wanted. Of 87,220 sq. m. only 5600 are cultivated. If the imperial and provincial revenues of all India were as heavy as they are in Burma, the general revenues of the Empire would be about 135 millions sterling. The total expenditure of British Burma in 1880-81 was—Civil, including railways and public works, £1,213,000; military, about £380,000. Thus British Burma, after paying interest on local railway capital, and a garrison maintained at war strength on account of political circumstances, yielded for the general purposes of the Empire a surplus of £767,000 in 1880-81. In this respect British Burma promises to be like Bengal, and proportionally to distance that Province.

CIVIL DIVISIONS OF BRITISH BURMA, 1881.

The chief authority in the Province of British Burma is the Chief Commissioner and Agent to the Governor-General, established on 1st January 1862. The Chief Commissioner is assisted by a Secretary, a Settlement Secretary, a Junior Secretary, and an Assistant to the Secretary, 3 Commissioners of Revenue and Circuit, 18 Deputy Commissioners, including 1 Superintendent of the Hill Tracts, Northern Arakan, and 32 Assistant Commissioners, 4 Collectors of Sea Customs, 4 Port Officers, a Director of Public Instruction, 2 Inspectors of Schools, an Inspector-General of Police, an Inspector-General of Jails, and 2 Conservators of Forests. The usual staff of officers in the Public Works Department is also attached to the Province. The Chief Commissioner exercises the powers of a local Government under the law, when such powers have been specially delegated to him by the Governor-General in Council; in all other respects, political and fiscal, he is the chief executive of the local Government, and under the Government of India. The judicial officers are the Judicial Commissioner, the Recorder of Rangoon, the Judge of the Town of Moulmein, and the Judge of the Small Cause Court, Rangoon.

The following is a statement of the area, population, revenue, etc., of the different Commissionerships, Deputy Commissionerships, and revenue subdivisions of the Province, omitting the Kareng-nee States:—

Commissionerships.	Districts.	Number of judicial and revenue sub-divisions.	Area in square miles.	Population, 1881.	Number of villages.	Total cost of officials and police of all kinds.	Revenue, 1880-81.	
							Land.	Gross.
						Rs.	Rs.	Rs.
Pegu.	Rangoon Town	1	22	134,176	..	74,306	10,853	43,79,439
	Hanthawadi .	3	4,236	427,720	1,393	3,15,614	21,50,685	34,49,358
	Thone-kwa .	4	5,413	264,063	976	1,89,447	5,76,309	19,30,728
	Bassein . .	3	7,047	389,419	1,697	3,92,080	7,78,613	44,58,381
	Henzada . .	2	1,948	318,077	1,228	1,22,474	4,62,225	10,72,021
	Tharawadi .	2	2,014	278,155	1,385	1,06,562	3,14,339	4,75,887
	Prome . .	3	2,887	322,342	1,647	1,47,130	2,83,423	8,12,032
	Thayet-myo .	2	2,397	169,560	870	99,887	1,09,831	8,82,792
	Total Pegu	20	25,964	2,323,512	9,196	14,47,442	46,86,278	1,69,60,638
Arakan.	Akyab . .	9	5,535	359,706	1,928	33,343	7,01,716	23,17,269
	Northern Arakan	1	1,015	14,499	195	55,104	3,192	6,706
	Kyouk-pyoo .	5	4,809	149,303	937	1,00,085	1,49,020	5,08,229
	Sandoway .	3	3,667	64,010	469	97,655	63,672	1,49,310
	Total Arakan	18	14,526	587,518	3,529	2,86,187	9,17,600	29,81,514
Tenasserim.	Moulmein Town	1	14	53,107	..	31,825	4,450	7,65,882
	Amherst . .	2	15,189	301,086	1,021	1,58,241	6,16,500	12,23,413
	Tavoy . .	4	7,150	84,988	290	1,12,554	1,08,150	2,42,455
	Mergui . .	5	7,810	56,559	199	72,824	82,848	2,14,810
	Toung ngoo .	8	6,354	128,848	835	1,10,556	52,097	5,04,496
	Shwe-gyeen	7	5,567	171,144	558	1,04,109	1,52,223	4,19,156
	Salween . .	1	4,646	30,009	209	75,093	9,601	28,584
	Total Tenasserim	28	46,730	825,741	3,112	6,65,202	10,25,869	83,98,796
	Grand Total	..	87,220	3,736,771	15,837	23,98,831	66,28,747	2,83,40,948

BRITISH BURMA AND ANDAMAN PROVINCES.

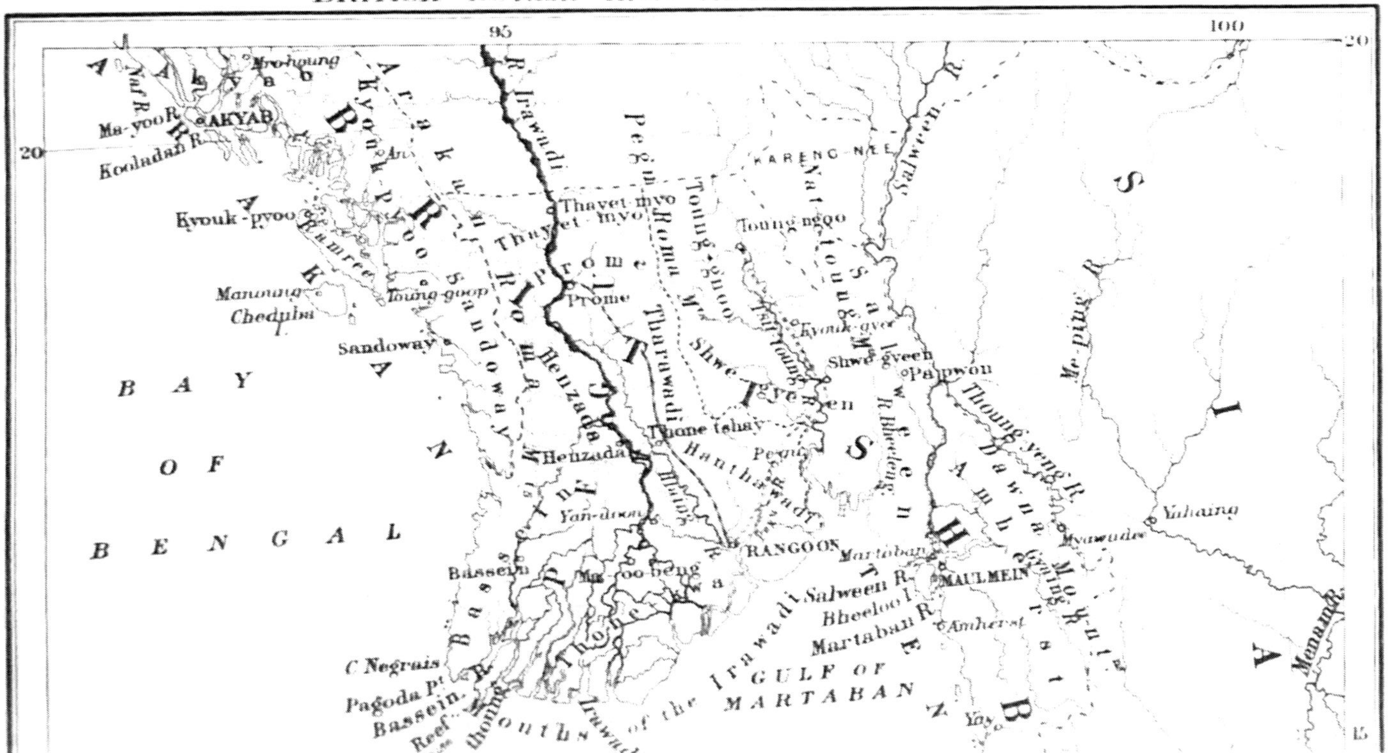

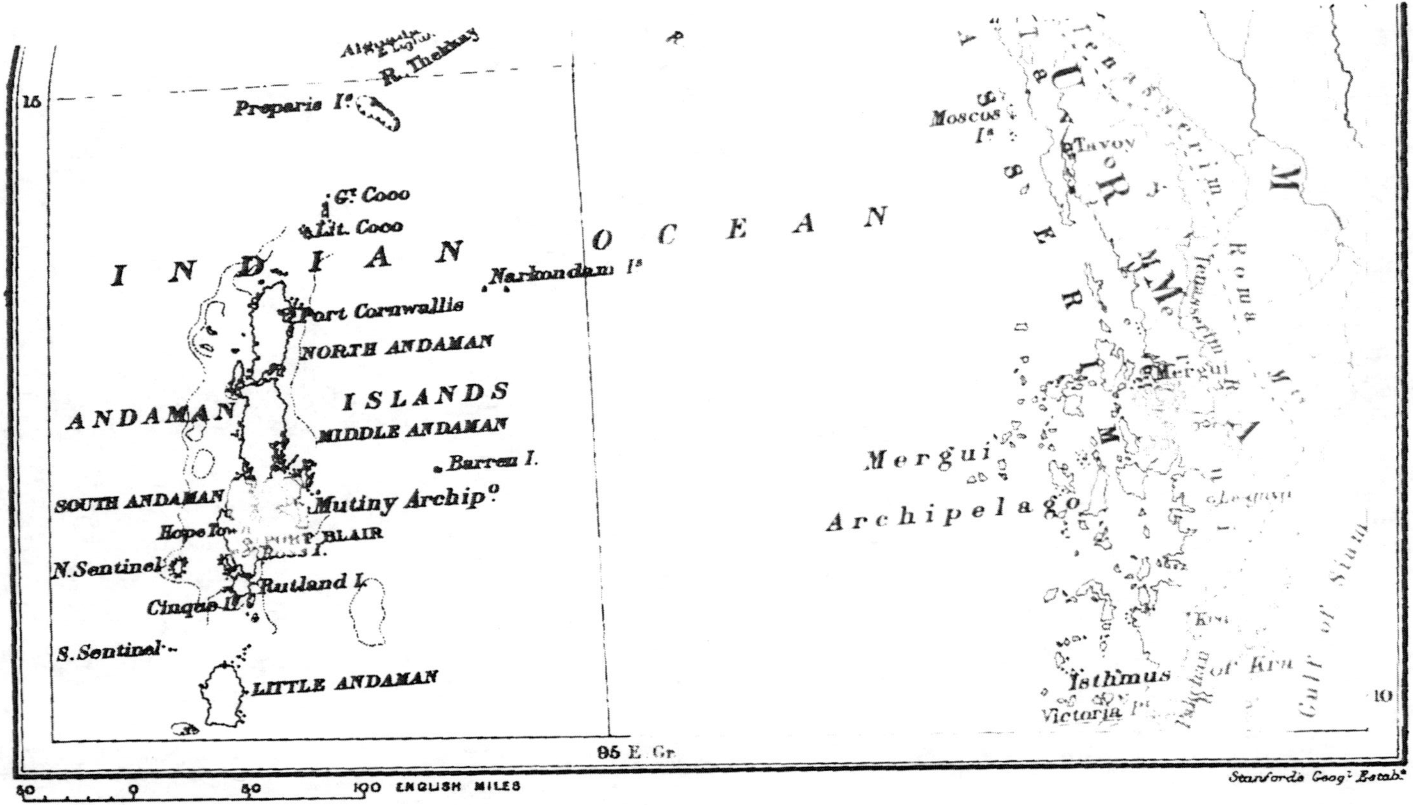

INDIAN OCEAN
Preparis I.
R. Thekhay
Gt. Coco
Lit. Coco
Narkondam Is
Port Cornwallis
NORTH ANDAMAN
ANDAMAN ISLANDS
MIDDLE ANDAMAN
Barren I.
SOUTH ANDAMAN
Mutiny Archipo
Hope Town
PORT BLAIR
Ross I.
N. Sentinel
Rutland I.
Cinque Is
S. Sentinel
LITTLE ANDAMAN
Moscos Is
Tavoy
Mergui
Mergui Archipelago
Isthmus of Kra
Victoria Pt
Gulf of Siam
15
10
95 E. Gr.
50 0 50 100 ENGLISH MILES
Stanford's Geog. Estab.

CHAPTER VII.

THE PROVINCE OF BRITISH BURMA—DISTRICTS.

PEGU.

§ 1. Rangoon. § 2. Hanthawadi. § 3. Thone-kwa. § 4. Bassein. § 5. Henzada. § 6. Tharawadi. § 7. Prome. § 8. Thayet-myo.

ARAKAN.

§ 9. Akyab. § 10. Northern Arakan. § 11. Kyouk-pyoo. § 12. Sandoway.

TENASSERIM.

§ 13. Maulmein. § 14. Amherst. § 15. Tavoy. § 16. Mergui. § 17. Shwe-gyeen. § 18. Toung-ngoo. § 19. Salween. § 20. *Karengnee States.

Pegu.

§ 1. Rangoon (Ran-koon, "end of the war") (134,176), the capital of British Burma since the second war in 1852. The city, 21 m. from the sea, occupies 22 sq. m. on the left bank of the Hlaing at its junction with the Pegu and Poo-zwon-doung rivers, with a suburb on the right bank. Founded, according to tradition of the Talaing or Telugoo settlers from N. Madras, about B.C. 585, by two brothers who deposited the hairs given by Gautama himself in the Shwe Dagon pagoda. The village of Dagon was conquered by the King of Pegu in 746-761 A.D., and called Aramana; was occupied by the Burmans in 1413; was distanced by Dala or Syriam on the opposite bank of the Pegu river; was conquered by Alompra or Aloung-bhoora, founder of the reigning Burman dynasty, in 1763, who gave it the present name; received an English factory and afterwards, in 1798, a British Resident, the result of the embassy to Ava of Colonel Symes; was held by the British 1825-7, during the first war, and was taken again by them in April 1852 on the outbreak of the second. Since it became the English capital Rangoon has been rebuilt. Between the strand, along the S. reach of the Hlaing and the old ditch, the city consists of square blocks with broad streets; the whole is divided into 11 quarters, of which the principal are Lam-ma-daw, Chinese town or Taroop-dan, N.E. town, N.W. town, S.E. town, and S.W. town containing the public offices and principal merchants' offices and shops. To the N. is the military cantonment enclosing the fortified **Shwe Dagon** ("golden log"), most venerated of Boodhist fanes by Indo-Chinese races, with the "Great Royal Lake" to the E., also a public drive, from which the city is supplied with good water. The other principal buildings are the law courts, town hall, Roman Catholic cathedral, and Tsoo-lai pagoda around Fytche Square, and the English church, Secretariat, Telegraph Offices, Bank of Bengal, and Custom House on the Strand road, where the Poo-zwon-doung joins the Hlaing. Monkey Point, crowned by a battery, sweeps the river and town. Here the last of the Great Mughul dynasty of Delhi, the titular Emperor Bahadoor Shah, died in captivity after the Mutiny of 1857, and some of his family are still State prisoners. **Rangoon** is the centre of American Baptist, S. P. G., and Roman Catholic missions; a Government High School, in which the learned missionary Dr. Mason was the first Professor of Pali, also prepares youths of all creeds for the examinations of the Calcutta University. Here Sir Arthur Phayre, the first Chief Commissioner, long resided. An Anglican bishopric was endowed privately in 1875. The Strand bank and the port are under a committee, who act as a Trust. The city is one of seven municipalities in the Province, and raises an annual revenue of about £50,000.

§ 2. HANTHAWADI DISTRICT, the fertile seaboard tract between the Tsit-toung and the China Ba-keer or To mouth of the Irawadi, is bounded E. by Shwe-gyeen district, N. by Henzada and Tharawadi, W. by Thone-kwa, and S. by Gulf of Martaban. Area, 4236 sq. m. Population, 427,720. The Pegu Roma rise to 2000 ft. in N. and run S. in two branches to the sea, dividing the valleys of the Hlaing and Poo-zwon-doung, and covered with forest, especially at the Bassein creek, where the Tdan-te Taw-gyee ("great forest") may be seen from Rangoon. The Hlaing enters the district as the Zay from Prome, and leaves it as the Rangoon river; from E. it receives the Ook-kan, Ma-ga-ree, Hmaw-bhee, which drain the W. slopes of the Pegu Roma, and at Rangoon the Pegu and Poo-zwon-doung, which drain the E. and S. flanks of that range. On the W. tidal creeks connect the Hlaing and Irawadi mouths; most of these are navigable, and in the rains are used by steamers. Besides Rangoon, the administrative headquarters, the principal places are **Pegu** (6000), on Pegu river, old capital of Talaing dynasty, which ruled from Bengal to Cochin China; captured by Burman Aloung-bhoora in 1756, now a village. On opposite bank are remains of pagodas, especially the **Shwe Hmaw-daw**, a solid pyramid of brick of 324 ft., rising from an octagonal base of 162 ft. long each side, on two terraces one above the other, which were the scene of sharp fighting in the war of 1852-3, and surrounded by 11 pagodas. **Twan-te**, a village, once an important town W. of Rangoon, 7 m. from mouth of Twan-te stream in the To river, with venerated Talaing pagoda, the **Shwe Tshan-daw**, and the ruins of Khabeng city in the neighbourhood. **Syriam** (corruption of Than-lyeng), on E. bank of Pegu river opposite Rangoon, the site of Portuguese, Dutch, and English factories, and scene of the impalement of the Portuguese Philip de Brito of Nicote by King of Burma in 1612, with ruins of Barnabite church and tombs. The district has 3 subdivisions—Hmaw-bhee, Syriam, and Pegu.

§ 3. THONE-KWA DISTRICT is bounded E. by Hanthawadi, N. by Henzada, W. by Bassein, and S. by Gulf of Martaban. Area, 5413 sq. m. Population, 284,063. The district is an alluvial tract intersected by muddy rivers and creeks communicating with the Irawadi, which traverses it from N. to S. To the E. it sends off the China Ba-keer or To, the Pya-poon, and the Kyoon-toon or Da-la, and reaches the sea W. of the Kyoon-toon. **Ma-oo-beng**, the civil headquarters, is a village infested by mosquitoes. **Yan-doon** (12,700), on left bank of Irawadi at W. mouth of Pan-hlaing creek, there called Gynoung-doung, a large mart 60 m. N.W. of Rangoon. **Pan-ta-naw** (6200), E. by S. of above, another mart chiefly for ngapee. **Donabyoo** (5000), on right bank of Irawadi above Gynoung-doung, from which Sir A. Campbell drove the Burmans in 1825 in the first war; Sir John Cheape, in 1853, in the second war, defeated a local rebel in a neighbouring stronghold after heavy loss. The district is in 3 subdivisions—Ma-oo-beng, Pan-ta-naw, and Gynoung-doung.

§ 4. BASSEIN DISTRICT is bounded E. by Thone-kwa, N. by Henzada and Sandoway, W. and S. by Bay of Bengal. Area, 7047 sq. m. Population, 389,419. The Arakan Roma pierce the whole length to the sea, at Cape Negrais and Pagoda Point, with Bhaw-me in N. (270 ft.), Kyoung-tha (381 ft.), Tsheng-ma (284 ft.), Nga-root, and Rwotpa passes, covered with mangrove and evergreen forest, with outcrops of limestone, and soapstone used for writing on the Burman *parabaik* or blackened fibre-paper. The rivers, chiefly dependent on the

Irawadi and the tide for their supply, are the Pyamalaw, with two mouths, forming E. boundary; the Rwe, with Daye-bhyoo mouth, and the Bassein, which, leaving the Irawadi above Henzada, is fed also from the E. slopes of the Arakan Roma, and is navigated by steamers up to the port of the same name (the Besygna of Ptolemy). **Bassein** (28,200), chief town and port 75 m. from sea, with fort enclosing conspicuous Shwe Moo-htaw pagoda and public offices; taken by assault in second war, since which it has become a great rice port, and has much trade with Madras. Seat of American Baptist Mission with Kareng normal and industrial schools, and of a Roman Catholic Mission. **Lemyet-hna** (5500), on Bassein river. **Regyee Pandaw** (5000), on creek of same name, a rice mart, where the Talaings were formally overthrown by Aloung-bhoora. **Ngathaing-khyoung** (4000), at N. entrance of Regyee creek, under Assistant Commissioner. **Negrais** or **Haing-gyee**, island at mouth of Bassein river, 3½ m. from Pagoda Point, of which Government of Madras took possession in 1687, with out-factory at Bassein town. In 1759 ten Englishmen were here treacherously murdered by the Burmans. On the opposite bank the new port of Dalhousie was formed, and was engulphed during a cyclone in 1856. Eight m. off is **Alguada**, Portuguese name for reef 10¾ m. S.S.W. from Diamond Island, on which is a fine lighthouse 144 ft.

§ 5. HENZĀDA DISTRICT is bounded E. by Tharawadi, N. by Prome, W. by the Arakan Roma, and S. by Thone-kwa and Bassein. Area, 1948 sq. m. Population, 318,077. With Tharawadi district, formerly a part of it, Henzada forms the head of the Irawadi delta. The Arakan Roma range rises to 4003 ft. in the latitude of Myanoung; N. it sends down to the Irawadi, at Akou-toung, a cliff (300 ft.) artificially caverned with statues of Boodha. Valuable forests clothe the hill slopes; embankments protect the town, and extend the rice cultivation along the Irawadi. **Henzada** (16,800), now chief town and municipality, on right bank of Irawadi to the S., with American Baptist, S. P. G., and Roman Catholic Missions. **Za-luon** (5000), rising town farther S. **Myanoung** (5500), headquarters of district till 1870, to the N. along Irawadi bank. **Kyan-kheng** (7600), farther N. on same river, a growing rice mart. **Kan-oung** (4000), 7 m. below Myanoung, founded by Aloung-bhoora. Mo-gnyo, Ta-pwon, and Tsan-rwe are rising towns.

§ 6. THARAWADI DISTRICT is bounded E. by Pegu Roma range, N. by Prome, W. by Henzada, and S. by Thantawadi. Area, 2014 sq. m. Population, 278,155. The Pegu Roma here rises to 2000 ft., and then branches out into the spurs which form the Pegu and Poo-zwon-doung valleys. The Hlaing from Prome enters the district as the Myit-ma-kha, and flows S. parallel with the Irawadi, receiving from the E. the Toung-myo, the Meng-bhoo, the Toung, the Meng-hla, the Tsheng-aing, the Toung-bho-hla, the Bheeleng, and the Thone-tsheng, all tapping a country rich in teak. The district was the appanage of the infamous Prince Tharawadi, who dethroned his brother in 1837. **Thone-tshay**, chief town, on stream of same name. **Meng-gyee** and **Re-kheng** (16,000), on left bank of Irawadi. **Ta-pwon**, headquarters of N. township, with valuable timber.

§ 7. PROME DISTRICT is bounded E. by Pegu Roma, N. by Thayet, W. by Arakan Roma, S. by Henzada and Tharawadi. Area, 2887 sq. m. Population, 322,342. These two Roma ranges send down forest-covered spurs; the western range is crossed by a road from Padoung to Toung-goop in Sandoway, by which the Burmese army in 1783 advanced to the conquest of Arakan, and dragged back to Ava an enormous statue of Boodha and a large cannon. The Irawadi divides the district, flowing N. to S. The S. Na-weng, falling into the Irawadi at Prome, drains the Pegu Roma, with its tributaries the N. Na-weng, Khyoung-tsouk, and Teng-gyee. The Hlaing, in its upper course known as Zay and Myit-ma-kha, carries off the surplus waters between the Pegu Roma and the Prome hills. The Eng-ma lake, 10 by 4 m., lies E. of the Prome hills in the course of the Hlaing; the Shwe-doung Myo-ma is a smaller lake on left bank of Irawadi, opposite Padoung. **Prome** (29,000), on left bank of Irawadi, once capital of kings of Prome, as Tha-re-kettra, 6 m. E., abandoned in second century A.D., now head of district, a flourishing municipality, terminus of the Rangoon railway, and on great north road. To S., on low hills, is the great pagoda **Shwe Tshan-daw** (80 ft.), covering area of 11,025 sq. ft., and surrounded by 83 shrines of Gautama. Centre of 3 Christian missions. The **Shwe Nat-daw Pagoda** rises to a great height on hills 14 m. S. of Prome. **Shwe-doung** (12,400), growing mart on river 8 m. below Prome. **Padoung**, 15 m. below Prome, on right bank, now of historic interest chiefly. **Poung-deh** (6800), 32 m. S.E. of Prome, on north road.

§ 8. THAYET-MYO DISTRICT, the most N. of Pegu, is bounded E. by Tonng-ngoo, N. by Upper Burma, W. by Arakan Roma, and S. by Prome. Area, 2397 sq. m. Population, 169,560. The Marquis of Dalhousie personally "examined and confirmed" the border line of masonry pillars running from 19° 29′ 3″ from the point on the left bank of the Irawadi, 6 m. N. of Mye-dai, the most advanced British post, due E. for 94 m. to the Pegu Roma at Tattay, down to Mai-haw on the Tsit-toung, and again due E. to the Poung-loung range. The district is broken by low hills where it does not swell into mountains, rising from the Irawadi which traverses its centre. The Tsaga-doung and Htoon-doung ("lime hill") are the most conspicuous; at the frontier the Myeng-ba range rises still higher. On the W. side the Irawadi receives the Pwon, Mah-toon, and Madekhyoung, on the E. the Kye-nee and Bwot-lay. **Thayet-myo** ("mango" or "slaughter city") (16,200), chief town and cantonment on high ground on right bank of Irawadi near frontier, with Asoka pagoda. **Allan-myo** (after Major Allan, who demarcated frontier) (6000), higher up on opposite bank, superseding Myedai, the old Burman town and customs station for frontier trade. **Rwa-toung** (4000), on Irawadi, opposite Thayet-myo cantonments. **Kama** and Gywon-doung, on either side of Ma-de river, where it enters the Irawadi, a pretty mart with Asoka pagoda. **Meng-doon** (4500), near the base of the Arakan hills, on stream of same name. The district grows much tobacco on the Irawadi sandbanks, and, like Prome, exports cutch largely. Iron and limestone, petroleum and brine springs, are found. The best cotton in Indo-China is produced here.

ARAKAN.

(Rakhaing = native name of Arakanese.)

§ 9. AKYAB DISTRICT is bounded E. by the Arakan Roma range, N. by Chittagong, W. by Bay of Bengal, and S. by Kyoukpyoo. Area, 5335 sq. m. Population, 339,706. From the Mayoo hills, forming the N. boundary, flows the Mayoo river to the sea; the Roma hills send down the Kooladan from the Blue Mountains to Akyab town, and the Le-mro to Hunter's Bay. The main river, the Kooladan, is navigable by boats of 400 tons 70 m. above Akyab, and by boats of 40 tons 50 m. higher to Dalekmai, in the Hill Tracts. **Akyab** (33,200), from *Akyatdaw* pagoda, a neighbouring landmark, once a Mugh fishing village, made chief station after first war of 1824-5, now a great rice port, with fine public buildings and high school. Savage Island lighthouse is at the harbour mouth. **Mro-houng** or Arakan ("old town") (3000), at the head of a branch of the Kooladan, 50 m. from its mouth, capital of the Arakan kingdom before its conquest by the Burmans, who carried across the Roma mountains the great metal statue of Gautama from the Ma-ha-moonee pagoda, 20 m. N: this was the Triglyphon of Ptolemy, named from the Boodhist trident or triglyph. Stormed by General Morison in first Anglo-Burmese war, and abandoned for its unhealthiness. Meng-ha, 20 m. S., centre of township of same name. Moung-daw, on the Naf estuary, on the road and with a ferry to Chittagong.

§ 10. NORTHERN ARAKAN DISTRICT is bounded E. and N. by Upper Burma, W. by Chittagong, and S. by Akyab. The unsurveyed territorial limits (area, 4483 sq. m.) include the Looshais, Shandoos, Chins, and Konesows, with whom we have political dealings without internal control. The administrative or inner line (area, 1015 sq. m.; population, 14,499) includes these six tribes—the Kamees or Kumees, Mros, some Chins, Choungthas, Chaws, and Koons. The Roma hills here consist of parallel ridges of sandstone covered by forest. **Kyouk-pandoung** (4000 ft.) and **Pogoung-toung** are hills fitted for sanitaria. The range is drained by the Kooladan ("foreigners' place," where the Arakan kings stationed Bengali slaves) and its tributaries, the Tsala, Rala, Kola, Palak, Kan, and Mee, which last receives the Thamie and Pay or Pee. The Le-mro, rising N. of Dalekmai, after 60 m. S. receives the Pee from E., the On from N., and the Peng or Wakrien, then the Wet, Tseng, and Roo. **Dalekmai**, on upper Kooladan, chief stockade, from which the frontier police (256 strong) patrol the whole length of the inner line weekly to **Prengwa** on Le-mro. At **Tsamee** on the Mee, and also on the Kan and Pee, are guard-houses. **Kooladan**, station below junction of Mee and river of same name. **Myouktoung**, mart near the plains, where the fine tobacco, sesamum and cotton of the tribes is sold to Akyab traders. In N. Arakan, on the Mee river, and in Akyab district, the American Baptist missionaries made a noble attempt to civilise the tribes, but were carried off by sickness.

§ 11. KYOUK-PYOO DISTRICT is bounded E. by Arakan Roma hills, N. by Akyab, W. by Bay of Bengal, and S. by Sandoway. Area, 4309 sq. m. Population, 149,303. This district comprises the strip of mainland from the An pass across the Arakan Roma range to the Ma-ee river, drained by the navigable An and Dha-let; and many islands, of which the largest are **Ramree** (with hills rising to 3000 ft.) and **Cheduba** ("four capes"), with mud volcanoes emitting marsh gas which lights up the sea for miles. **Kyouk-pyoo** ("white stone") (2300), on N. point of **Ramree** (3546), chief station, with offices on the beach. **Manoung** ("overcoming of the evil disposition"), on N.W. part of Cheduba, with oil wells. The largest volcano is Toung-nee ("red earth hill"), in centre of island. **An** (aeng), village and pass at W. foot of Arakan Roma range, and mart for Upper Burma. A detachment of Sir A. Campbell's force, returning from Yandaboo after the first war, traversed this pass (4664 ft.).

§ 12. SANDOWAY DISTRICT (Than-dwai = iron-bound) is bounded E. by Arakan Roma, N. by Kyouk-pyoo, W. by Bay of Bengal, and S. by Bassein. Area, 3667 sq. m. Population, 64,010. The Roma, rising in places to 5000 ft., fall to 3200 at Shouk-beng, where the Toung-goop pass crosses to Padoung in Prome. The rivers, which are mountain torrents not navigable till they enter tidal creeks, are the Ma-ee, Tan-lwai, Toung-goop, Sandoway, Kyien-ta-lee, and Khwa. **Sandoway**, 15 m. up river of same name, chief town and old native capital as Dwa-ar-wad-di. **Toung-goop**, 6 m. up stream, and at mouth of pass of same name. The district produces cretaceous limestone and steatite.

TENASSERIM.

§ 13. MAULMEIN (53,107), with an area of 14 sq. m., chief town of Tenasserim division since the first war in 1825 when it was waste land, stands on left bank of the Salween, at its junction with the Gaying and Attaran, and sheltered from the sea by the Bhee-loo-gwyon island, 107 sq. m. in extent. The town is made picturesque by low hills, the N. extremity of the Toung-ngoo range, which run through it N. to S., crowned by pagodas. Of the five quarters, four are on the W. between the Salween and the hills, from the mills and docks of Mopoon to the cantonment on the point formed by the Salween and Gaying, opposite Martaban, 6 m. off. Here are the offices and foreign residents. The Burmans and Talaings are chiefly in the fifth division, known as Daing-won-kweng, in the valley of the Attaran. **Maulmein** has long been the chief port for the shipping of teak and building of teak vessels. It has been the seat, since Judson's time, of American Baptist, Anglican, and Roman Catholic Missions. Salween House is the centre of the municipality. The site of the town was selected by Sir A. Campbell to command Martaban opposite.

§ 14. AMHERST DISTRICT is bounded E. by the Dawna chain, which shoots out from the Moolai-yit mass in the main range, N. by Shwe-gyeen, W. by Gulf of Martaban, and S. by Tavoy. Area, 15,189 sq. m. Population, 301,086. The **Dawna** chain (3472 ft.), extending N.N.W. for 200 m., divides the waters of the Houng-tharaw and the Hlaing-bhwai, which afterwards unite to form the Gyaing, from the Thoung-yeng. Across the Tenasserim Roma range in this district there is the pass from Burma to Siam, from **Myawadee**, on the left bank of the Thoung-yeng, to Rahaing in Siam, 45 m. due E., two days' journey, and thence down the Meinam to Bangkok in eight days. There are passes from the Houng-thraw and Menanda, its tributary, to Siam. The Three Pagodas pass leads from Kan-nee on the Attaran, by which the boat and elephant journey from Maulmein to Bangkok occupies twenty-five days. The **Toung-gnyochaw** rises N.N.W. from the Tsadaik hill of the Maw range to Maulmein. The Zwai-ka-beng is a small range of limestone hills N. of Maulmein and E. of the Salween. W. of the Salween, and crossed by two passes, one through the Gaw gap, a range runs N. from Martaban rising into the Koolamn-toung peak (above 3000 ft.) The Salween, Gyaing, Attaran, Thoung-yeng, and Bhee-leng are the principal rivers. The Salween is not navigable by sea-going vessels save at its mouth; it receives the Rwon-zaleng and Bhenglaing from the Hill Tracts. This is the great district for teak and other timber, and was long the border land in which Peguans and Siamese contended till the Burmans drove out both. **Amherst** (Kyaik Khamee = native name) (3200), sanitarium on the coast 30 m S. of Maulmein, on the Wakharoo, a navigable stream. **Martaban**, on right bank of Salween, opposite Maulmein, capital of a kingdom described by the Portuguese Faria y Sousa and Ralph Fitch as large and wealthy. In 1544 it was sacked by the Burmese, and in 1824 was taken by the British. **Bheeloo** island, shutting in Maulmein, has 60 pagodas, of which the Kalan is ascribed to Asoka. **Tha-tone** (3300), once a great Talaing capital and port, at which the Boodhist missionaries landed after their council of 241 B.C., now far inland. Other townships are Yay (2900), Moodone (2700), Yathabyin (2700), Poung (2400), Kaw-kareit (2300), and Kalo (2200).

§ 15. TAVOY DISTRICT is bounded E. by the Tenasserim range, N. by Amherst, W. by Bay of Bengal, and S. by Mergui. Area, 7150 sq. m. Population, 84,988. The main range rises to 5000 ft. between British territory and Siam, and is crossed by three passes—in the N. the Htandoung, by which the journey from Tavoy to Bangkok occupies 16½ days; S. the **Amya**, 12 days, but dangerous; and 38 m. farther S. the Mai-bhona, used only by the Karengs. The **Natyadoung Pass** is 50 m. higher up the frontier than the Amya Pass; by it the telegraph line runs to Bangkok. A spur rising into Na-wa-loo hill, 21 m. N.N.E. of Tavoy, forms the watershed between the Tavoy and Tenasserim rivers. The slopes are suitable for a sanitarium and coffee and cinchona culture. The Ma-hlwai spur, the N. boundary, sends off a low range forming the W. watershed of the Tavoy, which falls into the sea 40 m. below Tavoy town. The Tenasserim has two sources, separated by 80 m., and uniting at Met-ta; it flows into Mergui. The **Moscos** islands lie from 9 to 13 m. off the coast with a safe channel within and between the southern and middle groups. **Tavoy** (13,500), chief town; to the S. is island of same name, with a good harbour, Port Owen. To the N. are ruins of old Tavoy or Myo-houng, the ruler of which, in 1752, made overtures to the East India Company. In this and the next district there are the same equable climate and bountiful rainfall as in the Wainad and Ceylon, and land is offered on favourable terms.

§ 16. MERGUI DISTRICT is bounded E. by Tenasserim range, Pak-chan river, and Siam, N. by Tavoy, W. by Bay of Bengal, and S. by Lower Siam. Area, 7810 sq. m. Population, 56,559. From N. to S. the district is crossed by two parallel ridges with the **Tenasserim** river between them till it breaks through S.W. to the sea and a fine plain. The Palouk is a small stream in the N. with thermal springs. The Le-gnya rises in the E. or main range, flows N. past town of same name, and then W. to sea. The **Pak-chan**, rising in the main water-parting near the source of the Le-gnya, flows S.E. for 78 miles to Victoria Point, forming the boundary. At **Kra**, on the side of Siam, the isthmus is narrowest, and a project of cutting a canal has been broached. The chief pass between Mergui and Siam is the Mawdoung ("tired hill"), at the source of the Thien-kwon stream. Hence, S. to the source of the Kra, the people are Siamese, and there are 5 passes for pedestrians only. The **Mergui Archipelago** is a large and beautiful hilly cluster, extending S. from Tavoy island, and inhabited by the Selungs, a timid and neglected race who barter tripang with the Malays and Burmese for rice and spirits; the American Baptist Missionaries have reduced their language to writing. Maingy, in 12° 32′ N. lat., and St. Matthew's in 10° 52′, can be seen from 11 to 13 miles off. **Mergui** (8700), chief town and port on island at mouth of Tenasserim river, on site of the old city, in which 76 English merchants were massacred by the Siamese in 1695. Here the trigonometrical base line was laid down in 1880.

§ 17. SHWE-GYEEN DISTRICT is bounded E. by Salween district, N. by Toung-ngoo, W. by Tharawadi and Prome, and S. by Amherst. Area, 5567 sq. m. Population, 171,144. The district is shut in, in the Tsit-toung valley, between the Pegu Roma and Poung-loung ranges. Across the latter the N.

route runs up the valley of the Baw-ga-ta, and across the Thayet-peng-keng-dat hill to Kan-loo-doo, the N. post in Salween; the central route is up the valleys of the Moot-ta-ma and the Mar-dar to Pa-pwon; the S. passes from near the source of the Moot-ta-ma, across the high Thwot-ta-bat to Hpa-wa-ta, on the Bhee-leng river. The Poung-loung range rises to 4000 ft. in the Tsek-le hill opposite Shwe-gyeen town, and terminates in the Ke-la-tha hill above Keng-rwa, with a conspicuous pagoda. The passes over the Roma range are mere tracks. The **Tsit-toung**, called also the Toung-ngoo and Poung-loung, above Shwe-gyeen, enters the district from Upper Burma, at its N. border, and continues a tortuous course to the Gulf of Martaban, navigable throughout by steam launches, and famous for its tidal wave. Its affluents are small rocky streams, of which the chief are the Kwon, forming the N. border, and from the E. the Re-nwe, the Rouk-thwa, the Moon, and the Shwe-gyeen. The **Bhee-leng** from the Salween hills, the highway between Maulmein and the Tsit-toung in the rains, flows S. to the Gulf of Martaban, also with a tidal bore. There are 5 lakes, the picturesque Htoon-daw and Mwai-dweng, and the Tsaweng and Mee-kyoung-goung, in the Moon region; and the Nga-thwar-zoot, S. of the Bhee-leng. **Shwe-gyeen** (8000), chief town, at the junction of river of same name with the Tsit-toung, which sometimes floods it. **Kyaik-hto** ("royal boundary"), at the foot of the Poung-loung range on the Ka-dat, where it is crossed by the high road from Maulmein to Toung-ngoo. **Bhee-leng**, a river of same name, with ancient pagoda to N. **Tsit-toung**, on left bank of river of same name, taken by the British in first war. **Kyouk-gyee**, 34 m. above Shwe-gyeen, a betel-nut mart. Moon, to the N., with a traveller's bungalow. **Weng-ba-daw**, 7 m. below Tsit-toung, chief halting-place for boats, with manufacture of pots for salt-boilers.

§ 18. TOUNG-NGOO DISTRICT ("hill spur") (Nat-toung), is bounded E. by the "great watershed" of the Pa-Wan or Tenasserim Roma, N. by Upper Burma, from which it is marked off by Lord Dalhousie's line of masonry pillars, W. by the Pegu Roma, and S. by Shwe-gyeen. Area, 6354 sq. m. Population, 128,848. Besides two ranges, the Poung-loung trends E. through the district to meet the **Nat-toung** mountains; these tower into the crystalline granite peak (8000 ft.) between the Tsit-toung and the Salween, which bounds the empire farther E. Of the Tsit-toung the chief tributaries in the district, partly navigable, are the Ishwa, Kha-boung, Hpyoo, and the Kwon on the W., and on the E. the Bheng-byai, Kan-nee, Thouk-re-gat, and Rouk-tha-wa. This hilly country was a province of the Păgăn kingdom, with a capital on the Ishwa, 20 m. N. of the present chief town, and afterwards an independent kingdom, at war with both Pegu and Ava, the latter of which finally conquered it in 1512. The Karengs are numerous, among whom the American Baptist Missionaries have made many converts. **Toung-ngoo** (17,800), chief town and cantonment on right bank of Tsit-toung, 7 m. from frontier, 295 m. by water and 170 m. by land from Rangoon, with ruins of golden palace of Toung-ngoo dynasty. A railway of 163½ m. from Rangoon to Toung-ngoo is under construction. **Thandoung-gyee** (4500 ft.), experimental sanitarium on plateau 23 m. from Toung-ngoo, with cinchona plantation.

§ 19. SALWEEN DISTRICT is bounded E. by Zeng-mai in Siam, N. by Kareng-nee, W. by Toung-ngoo and Shwe-gyeen, and S. by Shwe-gyeen and Amherst. Area, 4646 sq. m. Population, 30,009. "The whole country is a wilderness of mountains;" the Poung-loung run N.W. and S.E. in three principal ranges drained by the Salween, Rwon-za-leng, and Bhee-leng, and traversed by Shan caravans to Rangoon and Maulmein. The Rwon-za-leng, rising in extreme N., is navigable to Pa-pwon, save in the rains, when the violence of the current forbids ascent, and almost descent. **Pa-pwon** (800), administrative headquarters, on the Rwon-za-leng, under an Assistant-Commissioner. This district is the base of the Maulmein foresters, who extract timber from the vast teak tracts across the Salween. It is inhabited chiefly by the Kareng (Karoon = native name) race, "among whom the results of the labours of the American Baptist Mission have the appearance of being almost miraculous."—(*Government Gazetteer of British Burma.*) The Karengs claim to have come from China, but Colonel Yule does not admit that they are from Yunan, the Carajan of Marco Polo. They are in three tribes—the Sgau, the Pwo (South Karengs), and the Bghai (Kareng-nee); they number nearly half a million.

§ 20. *KARENG-NEE STATES.—Protected by the British Government, and with independence guaranteed by its treaty of 1875 with King of Burma. Kareng-nee, the N.E. corner of British Burma on right bank of Salween. **Western** and **Eastern** or **Red Kareng-nee** are under chiefs, who call themselves Kara, of the Bghai tribe of Karengs; the **Gar-kho** are of the Pwo tribe, N. and E. of the Toung-ngoo district.

CHAPTER VIII.

PROVINCE OF THE ANDAMAN AND NICOBAR ISLANDS.

§ 1. The Fifteen Islands. § 2. Outlying Islands. § 3. Andaman Islands. § 4. Nicobar Archipelago. § 5. Larger Nicobar Islands. § 6. The Convicts.

§ 1. THE FIFTEEN ISLANDS.—This, the great penal settlement for life convicts from all India, was first occupied by the Government of India in 1789, was soon abandoned on account of unhealthiness, and was again occupied on 10th March 1858, chiefly for mutineers or determined rebels in the Sepoy War. Since October 1871 the local administration has been under a Chief Commissioner and Superintendent in direct correspondence with the Government of India. From the Negrais Point of the Arakan Roma range in British Burma to Acheen Head in Sumatra, 15 large and many small islands extend down the Bay of Bengal, at a distance of 700 miles from Calcutta, parallel with the Burman coast, off which they lie about 200 miles. The islands are in three separate groups: the **2 Cocos, 4 Andamans,** and **9 Nicobars.** They may be considered mountain-tops of the continuation of the Arakan Roma range, lying along the line of volcanic action which extends down to the N. of Australia. They all seem to indicate "a submarine range, stretching in a curve to which the meridian forms a tangent between Cape Negrais and Sumatra; and though this curved line measures 700 miles, the widest sea space is less than 90." (*Yule.*) The area is estimated at 3285 sq. m., and the population at about 30,000.

§ 2. OUTLYING ISLANDS.—The **Preparis Isles**, a small group, of which the Cow and Calf are the principal, lie S. of Point Negrais, from which they are separated by Preparis N. channel, in 14° 50′ N. lat. and 93° 25′ E. long. **Preparis Island**, the most northern, is a dangerous-looking place, from which coral reefs run out for 8 miles, with sandstones and unfossiliferous shales, roamed over by pigs and monkeys—the latter unknown in the Andamans—and without palms. **Coco** or **Keeling Isles**, two islands further S., are separated from the above by Preparis S. channel; discovered by Keeling in 1609, and named from the abundance of cocoa-palms which fringe the forests that cover their central elevation. **Great Coco**, the more northern, is 6 m. long and 2 m. broad, with low sandstone hills; visited in N.E. monsoon by Burmese to collect and dry cocoa-nuts. In 1849 (April), 4 Europeans and 8 Burmese settled here, but several died. Government offered a lease of the island for £2000 a year. Two miles off is Table Island, with light visible for 22 miles in clear weather, on S.W. end. **Little Coco**, 2½ m. long and 1 m. broad, to the S., consists chiefly of sandstones rising to an elevated plateau. **Narkondam**, 45 m. E. of Port Cornwallis, in 13° 24′ N. lat., and 94° 12′ E. long., is an extinct volcano with cone (1300 ft.) like Stromboli. **Barren Island**, in 12° 17′ N. lat., and 93° 54′ E. long., a volcanic island with circuit of 6 m., lies 36 m. S. of the Andaman Archipelago; the crater of the little cone (975 ft.) was very active in 1795, and still sends forth a thin column of white vapour and sulphurous fumes. There are sulphur deposits of little economic value. All these islands are uninhabited by permanent dwellers.

§ 3. The ANDAMAN ISLANDS are so named probably from the *Agathon Daimonos* Nésos of Ptolemy, corrupted into Andaman by the Arabs, who converted the Nésoi *Baroussai* or Nicobars into Baloos. Marco Polo calls the Andamans, which he passed, by the dual form Angamanin, or Two Andamans. The group lies for 156 m. between 10° 30′ and 13° 45′ N. lat. and 92° and 94° E. long. Area, 2700 sq. m. The people are woolly-haired naked Negritos, or Oriental negroes of small stature, in seven tribes, whom the British officers and chaplains are doing something to raise from the lowest stage of barbarism by "homes," and an orphanage. The language of the South Andamanese has been reduced, partially, to writing under the name of Bojingijida or Elakabeäda, into which the Lord's Prayer has been translated. The geological structure consists of sandstones of tertiary age like those in Arakan, with nests of coal, and serpentinous rocks in the high lands, all covered by forests of valuable woods and rare orchids; the whole surrounded by coral reefs. The scenery of the islets and channels is most beautiful. **North Andaman**, 57 m. long, with Saddle Mountain (2400 ft.), and Port Cornwallis, a landlocked bay on N.E. side, where Lieutenant Blair, in 1792, established a settlement which was abandoned in 1796 for Penang. Separated from this island by the Andaman Strait, a fetid creek, is **Middle**

Andaman, 59 m. long, with Kyd's harbour and Andaman "home" on E. side.

The principal island, separated from that by the narrow and navigable Middle Straits, is **South Andaman**, 49 m. long. Here, on the S.E., is the capital of the settlement, **Port Blair**, named after the Lieutenant of the Indian Navy, who in 1789 first surveyed and attempted to colonise it; a landlocked bay 7½ m. long, shut in by **Ross Island** (80 acres), the residence of the Chief Commissioner. Here tea has been successfully cultivated. Farther up, 2½ m., is **Chatham Island**, which Blair abandoned for Port Cornwallis; now depot of the artificer corps. Farther up, 2½ m., is **Viper Island**, reached through Navy Bay, where is the chain gang for violent convicts. On N. side of the bay is **Hope Town**, the landing-place where the Viceroy Lord Mayo was assassinated in 1871 by a Muhammadan fanatic, leading to **Mount Harriet** (1185 ft.), a sanitarium with magnificent views. At S. entrance of bay, fronting Ross Island, is the peninsula of **Aberdeen**, a farm clearing of male convicts, and **Haddo**, the female settlement. Two m. across from the head of the bay is **Port Mouat**, with Andamanese "home" and shore frequented by turtle, caught for the Calcutta clubs. Separated from the South Island by Macpherson Straits is **Rutland Island**, 11 m. long. These four islands are sometimes termed the Great Andaman, which is divided by Duncan Passage from the **Little Andaman**, 30 m. by 17 m.

Off the Middle and South Andamans, to the E., and divided from them by Diligent Straits, which is used by steamers during daylight, is the **Mutiny Archipelago**, with edible birds' nests farmed out to a Chinaman; the beautiful islands are named after Henry Lawrence, Havelock, Neil, Outram, and Sir Hugh Rose. Here the "Briton" and "Runnymede," with troops, were wrecked in 1844, in one of the cyclones which, originating in this region, sweep up to Bengal. Other islets are the **N.** and **S. Sentinel**, **Cinque**, and **Labyrinth**, off S.W. coast, and **Interview Island**, off N.W. coast; from the last the only untrained native who has yet been taken from the islands was removed to Calcutta, where, after some attempts to civilise him, he died.

§ 4. The NICOBAR ISLANDS are the Nakavaram of the Arab geographers, the Necuveran of Marco Polo, and probably the Nalo-kilo-chen (Narikela-dvipa) or cocoa-nut islands of the Chinese pilgrim, Hwen T'hsang. The name appears more distinctly in Nankouri, the principal island. The **Nicobar**

Archipelago, called by the Malays, who visit it for trade, the Sambillangs or Nine Islands, and consisting of nine large and eleven smaller islands, lies S. of the Andamans, between 6° 40′ and 9° 20′ N. lat., and 92° and 94° E. long. Area, about 736 sq. m. Population, 6000; said to be "fast dying out." Besides the Nicobarese of Malay origin, who fringe the coasts, there are aborigines in the interior of the Great Nicobar called Shobængs, and reported as of Mongolian origin. All attempts, spreading over more than a century, to form prosperous trading and missionary settlements on the island by the Danes and Americans, and by Moravians, Lutherans, and Jesuits, were frustrated by the unhealthiness of the sites selected, till 1869, when the repeated wrecking of vessels and destruction of crews forced the Government of India to take possession. Since that year Nankouri has been a penal settlement subordinate to Port Blair. The coast tribes live in raised beehive-like huts, as in lake dwellings, have abundant food from sea and land, with the same refuse heaps as in the Andamans, known as kitchen-middens. Professor Ball notices words and customs which they have in common with the Paharias or Dravidian hillmen of Rajmahal, the Savaras of Orissa, and the Garos who extend nearly to Negrais, and whose word for a freeman is Nakoba. The larger islands are surrounded by coral rocks forming raised beaches, and consist of magnesian claystones of tertiary age, with serpentinous rocks on the high lands, as in the Andamans.

§ 5. CAR-NICOBAR, the northmost of the chain, 80 m. E. of Little Andaman, from which it is separated by Ten Degrees Channel, is 6 m. long and 5 m. broad, and well peopled with six villages. There is a considerable trade in cocoa-nuts, fruit and hogs abound. Batti Malve, a wedge-like rock, hence sometimes called Quoin, to S., is uninhabited. Chowry is an orchard-like friendly island which supplies the group with pottery. **Terressa**, 6 m. S., where French Jesuit missionaries settled for a time, with Bompoka, 2 m. off, is also inhabited by fair Nicobarese. Tillangchong, to E. of above, is well wooded but uninhabited. Katchell, S.E. of Terressa, from which it is divided by a safe channel, is covered with wood, and has caves with guano deposits. **Nankouri** (4 sq. m.) island, and also harbour, formed like a cross, between this and the two neighbouring islands, Carmorta and Trinkat, is the chief station of the archipelago, under an Extra-Assistant Commissioner, with many villages, of which Malacca is the principal; here are graves of the Moravian missionaries. It is distant 225 m. from Port Blair, and 390 from Rangoon. At Cross Harbour was the Moravian settlement called Herman **Carmorta**, on N. side of harbour, 16 m. long and 2 to 5 broad. Here the stones of the Austrian factory of Maria Theresa, built by Bolts who defied Clive and was deported from India, were used to build the British magazine ; from this Denmark long tried to govern the archipelago, and here is the British convict settlement. **Trinkat**, small island fronting E. end of Carmorta, is covered with betel and cocoa-nut palms. Sombrero Channel shuts off the southernmost portion of the chain of islands. **Little Nicobar**, with good soil, rises to 1000 ft. **Great Nicobar**, separated from the above by St. George's Channel, is 30 m. long and 15 m. broad, with hill rising to 2000 ft. on N.E. to the Galatea river falling into Galatea Bay. This is the most southerly part of the Empire of British India, in 6° 40′ N. lat., and 80 m. N. of Acheen, in Dutch Sumatra, to which the life convicts on the Nicobars have sometimes escaped in an open boat. Kondul, Montschall, Treis, Track, and Merol, the other islands of this southern portion of the archipelago, are small and generally uninhabited.

§ 6. THE CONVICTS.—Since the occupation of Port Blair in 1858, and of Carmorta in 1871, above 20,000 convicts have been sent from India to these penal stations. The number there resident is now rarely above 8000. Every year some 500 life-term convicts are banished to these islands, which clearing and cultivation promise to make as healthy as they are beautiful. M. de Röepstorff, one of the officials, thus describes the penal system :—

"The murderers and other criminals who have escaped being hanged in their own Provinces are sent to Port Blair. On arrival a convict has heavy irons on ; these are at once taken off and lighter ones substituted. He is then put in a mess-gang, which, to a Hindoo, is a great punishment. After six months one leg-iron is removed, and the other at the end of another six months. If the man has behaved well during the first year, he may be allowed to cook his own food. Thus he remains until he has completed four years, when he is promoted to receive, besides his rations, 1s. 6d. per mensem. At the end of seven years, the convict, having completed his term of penal servitude, has his pay raised to 2s. per mensem, and he may then be promoted to a petty officership or servant, or put into a place of trust and better himself. After ten years he becomes a first-class convict, and he may then get a license, whereby he is allowed to build a house and take up some trade, and he may be allowed to marry. Finally, after twenty years, he may be pardoned and released. The convicts control themselves: to every 100 men 7 petty officers are allotted, who are responsible for them by day and night. Transportation improves them. Idleness is very often at the root of the evil that brought them into trouble. They have regular hours, are disciplined, and find out very soon that a plodding steady man can get on well. No serious plot could well be executed, for a Brahman would tell on a low-caste man, and a Musalman would not trust a Hindoo. There are fair-faced Persians and Kashmeeris, true Arabs, little sturdy hillmen, dirty Panjabis, dark-faced Tamils, slender Bengalis, Malays, Chinese, Burmese, Telingis, Cingalese, and many other nationalities mixed together. The prince and the beggar, the high-born Brahman considering himself the incarnation of the deity, and the outcast, all march together in the same file—the one is number 19,007, the other 19,008."

CHAPTER IX.

THE NORTH-WESTERN PROVINCE, WITH OUDH—GENERAL.

§ 1. Name. § 2. Size and Position. § 3. Physical Divisions. § 4. Canals. § 5. Railways. § 6. Products and Trade. § 7. Land Tenures. § 8. The People and Districts.

§ 1. NAME. — The **North-Western Province** including **Oudh, or Hindustan** proper, is known in the history of British India as the Provinces to the N.W. of Calcutta and Lower Bengal. They became British in the period from the cession of the Dewani or civil jurisdiction by the Emperor Shah Alum to Clive on 12th August 1765, to the conquests of Lake in 1801. They were organised under the Parliamentary charter of 1833 as a fourth Presidency governed from Agra, and then as a Lieutenant-Governorship, administered from Allahabad after the Mutiny of 1857-8. Oudh, which had been annexed in 1856 for the hopeless misrule of the Nawab Wazeers, whom we had made kings, was governed by a separate Chief Commissioner till 1877, when it was placed under the Lieutenant-Governor at Allahabad. For all geographical as well as most administrative purposes the two territories form one homogeneous Province. Since the formation of the "North-Western" Government the Indian Empire has extended over the Panjab much farther to the N.W.; but the only change which it is desirable now to make is to consider Oudh and that Government one, under the name, in the singular, of the North-Western Province.

§ 2. POSITION.—The N.W. Province is nearly the size of Italy, and not far short of that of the United Kingdom, with a much denser population than either. It has an area of 111,086 sq. m., and a population of 44,852,736. Oudh alone has an area of 24,213, and population of 11,407,625; the rest of the Province, or old North-Western Provinces, has an area of 86,873, including the two Native States of Garhwal and Rampoor, and a population of 33,445,111. The former has 12 the latter 37 districts, or 49 in all. The united Province, thus formed in

1877, lies between 23° 51′ 31″ and 31° 5′ N. lat. and 77° 4′ and 84° 45′ E. long. It is bounded E. by the Behar districts of Bengal Province, with the Karamnassa and portions of the Ganges, Gogra, and Gandak between; N. by Nepal, Chinese Tibet, and the Panjab State of Bashahr, with the Himalaya between; W. by the Panjab States of Jubal and Sirmoor, from which the Tons divides it, by the eastern districts of the Panjab, and the States of Bhurtpoor, Dholpoor, and Bhartpoor, from which the Jumna separates it; and S. by the Central Province division of Saugar, the States of Boondelkhand, Rewah, and the Chutia Nagpoor division of Bengal.

§ 3. PHYSICAL DIVISIONS.—The whole forms an alluvial plain sloping from the Himalaya mountains and from the Jumna with its N. affluent the Tons about the 77th parallel of E. longitude S.E. to the point (1) where the Ganges receives the Gogra near Godna or Revelganj in the Saran district of Bengal, and (2) where it begins to rise into the great plateau of Central India. The North-Western Province is thus the upper as Bengal is the lower basin of the Ganges and its tributaries, except the Brahmapootra. It consists of (1) the great plain of the **Doab** ("two waters") between the Ganges and the Jumna, once periodically swept by famines, but now protected by a network of canals and railways constructed since the great drought of 1833-5; (2) the **Himalaya** tract supplying the perennial waters from Garhwal State on the N.W. to the Gandak on the E., which divides Nepal into two; (3) the triangular plain of **Rohilkhand**, passing from the submontane tracts of *bhabar* or waterless jungle of boulder detritus, and *tarai*, or moist and malarious forest, into the alluvium of the river plains; (4) the semicircular tract of the Goomti and Gogra valleys forming **Oudh**, and the trans-Gogra districts; (5) the **Jumna - Chambal Plain** so far as not in the Panjab, or Muttra, Agra, and part of Etawah; (6) **Boondelkhand**, S.W. of the Jumna, which passes from the alluvium of the river plain S.W. into the stony and hilly outliers of the Vindhya and Kaimoor ranges; (7) the **Gangetic Valley**, from Allahabad eastward to the Gandak and Son, the densely-peopled and cultivated centre of Hindooism, of which Benares is the capital. Inferior to Bengal in resources and trade, and not so much of a rabbit-warren as the Hoogli district of Bengal, the North-Western Province stands at the head of all as the great Aryan land of the early Hindoo kingdoms and capitals, and the Hindustan of the Muhammadans, with their red stone cities and unsurpassed architecture. While Bengal and Burma are the rice, this Province is the wheat granary of Southern Asia, exporting chiefly to Calcutta, but more and more largely by two trunk systems of railway W. to Bombay.

§ 4. CANALS.—The mountains and principal rivers have been already described in Chapter II. There are ten systems of canal-works in this Province, all constructed or opened out since the great famine of 1837-8, and all protective so far that subsequent famines like that of 1860-1 were much modified in their disastrous influence. The ten systems have been constructed at a capital cost of 6½ millions sterling, and yield an annual gross revenue of not less than £300,000, or more than the interest charge. The great **Ganges Canal**, designed by Proby Cautley, and begun in 1842, was opened in 1854, and now consists of 654 m. of main stream, with upwards of 3000 m. of distributing channels. From the head supply at Hardwar it passes through Saharanpoor and Muzaffarnagar, whence it sends off a branch to Fatehgarh, sweeps W. through Meerut, then S.E. through Boolundshahr and Aligarh, and gives off the Etawah terminal at Akrabad. Continuing across the W. corner of Etah and through Mainpoori and Farukhabad, it reaches the Ganges at Cawnpoor; the other or Etawah terminal falls into the Jumna above Hameerpoor. The **Lower Ganges Canal** is a southward extension of the above to Allahabad, planned in 1866 and since 1873 under construction; starting from the headworks at Narora, on the border of Aligarh, 4 m. below the Rajghat station of the Oudh and Rohilkhand Railway, the canal follows the watershed between the Kali Nadi and Isan, and the Pandoo and Rind, and runs S. of the East Indian Railway to Allahabad. Both are navigable. When completed, the outlay on both will be 5 millions sterling. The **Eastern Jumna Canal**, opened in 1830, has 130 m. of main and 625 of distributing channels. The **Agra Canal**, opened in 1874, is 75 m. long. The **Dehra Doon Canals** extend for 67 m. The **Rohilkhand, Bijnaur, Boondelkhand, Boondelkhand Survey**, and **Eastern Ganges Canals** are protective and productive works of irrigation in local districts. For the generally well-watered districts of Oudh the Sardah and Betwa Canals only have been projected.

§ 5. RAILWAYS.—Besides the Grand Trunk Road, which passes through the whole extent of the Province to the S. of the Ganges, it is opened up by an annually extending system of railways. The **East Indian** sends off from Allahabad its Jubalpoor section of the main communication between Calcutta and Bombay, and at Ghaziabad, near Delhi, it joins the Sind,

Panjab, and Delhi system, which continues the iron line to Peshawar on the N., Sibi for Kandahar on the N.W., and Karachi on the W. From opposite Benares, and again from Cawnpoor, the **Oudh and Rohilkhand Railway** penetrates these districts, with main and branch lines. From Agra the **Rajpootana State Railway** proceeds by Bhartpoor to the Bombay and Baroda line on the W.; the **Sindia State Railway** runs through Dholpoor to Gwalior for 69 m.; **Cawnpoor to Farukhabad**, 87 m. Many light railways—like that, 29 m., from **Hathras to Muttra, Ghazipoor to Dildarnagar**, 12 m., **Muttra to Achneyra**, 22¾ m., and Bahraich to Patna, Bhanpoor to Kalpi, to connect Rohilkand directly with Bombay, and Bareli to Pilibheet—are under construction or survey.

§ 6. PRODUCTS AND TRADE.—Of all the great Provinces of India the North-Western is the least rich in minerals. In the beds of the Himalaya rivers, and even the streams of the sub-Himalaya rocks, the people wash for gold with poor results. The Son, a river of the Garhwal district, and the Ramganga, which it joins in the Palti Doon, are auriferous. There is tertiary coal in the Province of no economic value. There are iron mines in Kumaun leased to a company. Since the abolition of the export duty this Province has become one of the great wheat-producing regions. After supplying those of its own dense population who are able to afford wheat in addition to or in place of barley or the two millets *joar* and *bajra*, the Province exports an annually increasing quantity of wheat, which is limited only by the expense of railway transit, chiefly to Calcutta but also to Bombay. The two chief harvests of each year are the autumnal (*khareef*), sown in June and reaped in October-November, and the spring (*rabee*), sown in October-November and reaped in March-April. Tobacco is everywhere a homestead culture. The commercial crops exported, to the value of above 5 millions sterling a year, are—besides wheat—oilseeds, sugar, indigo, tea, opium, rice, cotton, and saltpetre. Tea, the China plant, is cultivated and manufactured, chiefly green, for export into Central Asia, on the slopes and valleys of Dehra Doon, Kumaun, and Garhwal. The imports, valued at 3 millions sterling, and chiefly from Calcutta by rail, are English piece goods, twist and yarn, rice for the Bengalee residents, and salt. Cawnpoor is the principal city of both export and import. Besides sugar, indigo, and coarse cotton cloth, and English rum and beer, the principal manufactures are ornamental metal-work, brocades, silk, wood and stone carved vases, carpets, leather, and tents. The trade with Tibet and Nepal is steadily increasing; it is of the annual value of a million sterling, of which one-tenth is with Tibet in borax, salt, and wool imports chiefly.

§ 7. Land Tenures.—(1) In the N.W. Province the Benares Division was put under the same **Permanent Settlement** as Bengal proper, and the other districts received the promise of a permanent settlement on certain conditions, which have been discussed up almost to the present day. Except the districts of Benares, the Province is under **Thirty Years' Leases.** Since the completion, in 1842, of Mr. R. M. Bird's first thirty years' settlements, the land-tax assessments have been again revised, after survey, and fixed for a farther period of thirty years in all the temporarily settled districts. A cadastral survey has been made of the four permanently settled districts. With few exceptions the land tenures may be divided into three great classes—*zameendaree*, *putteedaree*, and *bhyachara*. Zameendaree tenures are those in which the whole land is held and managed in common, and the rents and whole profits of the estate are thrown into one common stock, and divided amongst the several proprietors, whose rights are estimated according to fractional shares, whether of a rupee or of the local unit of land measure known as a beegah. Putteedaree tenures may be divided into perfect and imperfect putteedaree or bhyachara. Perfect putteedaree is that tenure wherein the whole lands are held in severalty by the different proprietors, all of whom are jointly responsible for the Government revenue, though each is theoretically responsible only for the quota represented by the proportion of the land he holds to the whole estate. Imperfect putteedaree is where portions of the land are held in severalty, and portions in common, with a joint responsibility for the Government demand. In this case the revenue is primarily made up from the rents of the common lands, and the remainder by a *bach* or cess proportioned to the holdings in severalty, and calculated either by custom or on a fixed scale. Talookdaree estates are those in which the profits remaining after the Government revenue has been paid are divided amongst different proprietors or classes of proprietors, the one superior and the other inferior. In such cases a subsettlement is usually made between the inferior proprietors and the superior, who is known as the talookdar. An estate may pass by the agreement of the sharers from one class to another, the joint responsibility remaining inviolate. The tendency is to increase the number of perfect putteedaree holdings by a partition of the common lands.

(2) In Oudh, before the Mutiny of 1857, the land system of the N.W. Province was attempted. As the tenants who had

been made proprietors invited the Talookdar landlords to resume their estates, Lord Canning made a settlement with 256 of the latter, preserving the rights of the subproprietors and tenants, to which subsequent legislation has been directed. The land tenures of Oudh, in their general features, resemble very closely those prevailing throughout Upper India; they may be broadly classified as held directly or indirectly from the State. The first may be subdivided into—(A) Talookdaree estates; (B) Zameendaree or Mufreed estates; (C) estates held in fee simple. Estates of the first class are held by the Talookdars, who were settled with immediately after the suppression of the Mutiny, and those of the second are the property of the ordinary zameendars, or small landowners of the country. It is with regard to the Talookdaree estates that the land tenures of Oudh differ chiefly from those of the N.W. Province. Whereas in the older Provinces the tendency was to set aside the large landlord and engage direct with the under-proprietors and tenants, in Oudh the position and rights of the Talookdar, as proprietor of the land, have been fully recognised. The Talookdars and zameendars alike possess the full right of property in their estates, which they can alienate or dispose of as they please; but they differ from each other in the degree of security on which their titles rest. Protected by Act I. of 1859, the title of a Talookdar is unassailable, except upon a cause of action which must have arisen subsequent to the settlement which was made with him after the reoccupation of the Province; whereas the zameendar is liable at any moment to be called on by the courts to defend a suit in which the cause of action may have arisen before annexation. By the same Act, too, the Talookdar has been freed from the provisions of the ordinary Hindoo Shasters and Muhammadan Shar'a which, except when overridden by a strongly defined family custom, usually regulate succession and inheritance among the Mufreed zameendars; and out of the 256 Talookdars of Oudh a large number have adopted the law of primogeniture. Subject to certain provisions, every Talookdar can bequeath by will the whole or any portion of his estate.

Omitting the two Native States, the whole revenue of which goes to the chiefs, the land of the N.W. Province with Oudh yields above 5¾ millions sterling, of which upwards of half a million is from estates paying a fixed tax. The State demand is nominally fixed at 50 per cent of the assumed rental; but cesses are levied at generally increasing rates for schools, roads, police, and other local objects. The 44 millions of the united Province paid a gross revenue of £7,202,663 in 1880-81, of which £5,631,200 was from land. The fiscal condition of the Province is thus seen :—

LAND SETTLEMENTS, NORTH-WESTERN PROVINCE WITH OUDH, 1880-81.

Nature of Settlement.	Area in sq. miles.	Annual revenue assessed.
		Rs.
Settled in perpetuity—		
N.W. Province	10,496	47,74,666
Oudh	1,908	8,74,576
Settled for 30 years or upwards—		
N.W. Province	54,381	3,44,81,825
Oudh	21,181	1,36,07,512
Settled for 10 years or under 30—		
N.W. Province	11,229	16,32,477
Oudh	40	5,133
Settled under 10 years—		
N.W. Province	1,051	4,56,566
Oudh	21	3,950
Settlement in progress—		
N.W. Province	4,081	17,35,803
Oudh	95	......
Total { N.W. Province . . .	81,238	4,30,81,337
Total { Oudh	23,245	1,44,91,471
Grand Total—N.W. Province with Oudh	104,483	5,75,72,808

§ 8. THE PEOPLE AND DISTRICTS.—The census of 1881 showed the population of Oudh to be 11,407,625, and of the old N.W. Province 32,699,493, an increase in Oudh of 1·67 per cent since the census of 1867, and in the N.W. Province of 6·27 per cent since the census of 1872, or of 5·4 per cent on the whole. There was a remarkable increase of population in some of the permanently-settled districts of the Benares Division, while in the upper districts, in which the effects of famine and fever had been most severely felt, there was little if any increase, and in more than one a falling off.

Adding the two Native States, the population in 1881 stood thus as to sex :—

	Males.	Females.	Total.
N.W. Province . . .	17,041,043	15,658,450	32,699,493
Oudh	5,860,960	5,546,665	11,407,625
*Rampoor . . .	282,985	260,916	543,901
*Garhwal . . .	102,044	98,479	200,523
	23,287,032	21,464,510	44,851,542

CIVIL DIVISIONS OF BRITISH TERRITORY, 1880-81.

Districts.	Subdivisions. Revenue.	Subdivisions. Judicial.	Area in square miles.	Population, 1872.	Number of villages.	Total cost of Officials and police of all kinds.	Revenue. Land.	Revenue. Gross.
						Rs.	Rs.	Rs.
Dehra Doon	2	1	1,193	116,945	482	1,04,544	[illegible]	2,81,625
Saharanpoor	4	2	2,221	884,017	1,917	3,08,709	12,07,235	15,21,367
Muzaffarnagar	4	2	1,654	690,107	1,046	46,170	12,19,833	15,02,394
Meerut	6	2	2,361	1,276,104	2,091	3,00,225	22,24,841	27,03,682
Boolundshahr	4	2	1,918	936,667	1,596	1,47,032	12,33,602	13,80,912
Aligarh	6	3	1,954	1,073,433	1,808	3,77,516	21,34,038	25,06,006
Kumaun	3	1	6,000	433,314	6,516	1,37,097	2,43,078	5,13,051
Garhwal	1	1	5,500	310,288	4,417	55,214	96,139	1,17,333
Tarai parganahs	3	..	920	188,358	591	62,061	4,28,851	4,93,349
Bijnaur	5	2	1,869	737,153	2,955	2,50,076	12,28,434	13,87,145
Moradabad	6	5	2,282	1,122,437	2,853	2,85,026	14,36,351	18,14,335
Budaun	5	4	1,986	934,386	2,358	2,05,449	10,36,250	12,05,446
Bareli	6	3	1,621	1,025,186	2,240	3,41,414	15,13,028	16,66,009
Shahjahanpoor	4	3	1,744	949,579	2,356	3,17,271	11,19,771	16,87,183
Muttra	6	2	1,453	784,780	1,038	2,01,548	15,04,566	19,72,046
Agra	7	2	1,845	1,008,653	1,228	3,07,774	17,83,954	22,77,380
Farukhabad	6	4	1,719	918,850	1,798	3,52,409	12,28,733	15,34,338
Mainpoori	5	2	1,697	765,845	1,442	2,01,472	12,60,499	14,45,711
Etawah	5	1	1,668	665,841	1,559	1,68,492	13,28,328	14,65,973
Etah	4	3	1,739	858,802	1,733	1,79,360	10,86,861	20,88,297
Jalaun	5	..	1,555	404,447	971	2,00,993	9,10,173	11,80,769
Jhansi	4	..	1,567	317,826	607	1,92,644	4,22,260	5,49,329
Lalitpoor	2	..	1,947	212,661	749	1,18,309	1,48,633	1,80,767
Cawnpoor	9	3	2,337	1,156,055	2,042	3,13,050	21,49,245	39,02,362
Fatehpoor	6	1	1,637	663,877	1,592	1,49,359	15,08,344	14,47,846
Banda	8	1	2,961	697,684	1,272	2,44,040	12,07,104	12,95,358
Allahabad	9	2	2,840	1,396,241	3,956	4,28,380	23,72,240	28,08,396
Hameerpoor	6	1	2,288	529,137	918	2,21,950	10,68,282	11,64,480
Jaunpoor	5	1	1,554	1,025,100	3,215	1,77,422	12,40,368	15,03,179
Gorakhpoor	6	3	4,585	2,019,361	8,391	2,94,602	17,01,712	21,12,255
Basti	5	2	2,758	1,473,029	7,524	1,60,402	13,14,331	14,52,697
Azamgarh	5	3	2,147	1,317,554	5,532	2,22,482	16,50,265	18,92,363
Mirzapoor	4	1	5,224	1,015,826	4,104	2,01,019	8,56,247	11,72,367
Benares	3	1	998	794,900	1,919	2,79,056	8,94,805	18,93,081
Ghazipoor	4	4	1,451	873,130	3,906	1,21,203	10,51,194	14,00,000
Balia	2	1	1,127	686,168	2,431	93,744	6,12,330	7,85,330
Pilibheet	3	2	1,350	482,933	1,308	1,36,656	7,18,458	9,24,429
Lucknow	3	2	979	778,195	956	2,56,940	6,08,765	10,81,169
Unao	4	4	1,768	945,955	1,766	1,86,431	12,03,696	15,26,023
Bara Banki	4	3	1,768	1,113,430	2,093	1,37,335	16,77,193	18,29,208
Sitapoor	4	4	2,215	932,959	2,365	1,51,008	13,34,052	15,92,094
Hardoi	4	4	2,300	932,322	1,980	2,71,036	13,78,939	16,37,263
Kheri	3	2	2,963	738,089	1,777	98,836	7,44,336	8,38,737
Fyzabad	4	2	1,688	1,024,652	2,569	1,64,844	11,12,711	13,77,486
Bahraich	3	1	2,740	774,640	1,944	1,03,575	9,77,177	11,80,657
Gonda	3	3	2,881	1,168,462	2,834	1,68,208	15,09,363	18,11,032
Rai Bareli	4	4	1,740	989,008	1,768	2,43,523	9,73,840	11,61,644
Sultanpoor	4	2	1,707	1,040,227	2,526	1,60,598	10,67,589	11,99,352
Partabgarh	3	3	1,434	784,156	2,214	1,04,336	9,74,542	19,49,085
Total	221	105	105,961	42,003,299	117,253	1,00,54,821	5,63,11,998	7,20,26,635

NORTH-WEST PROV

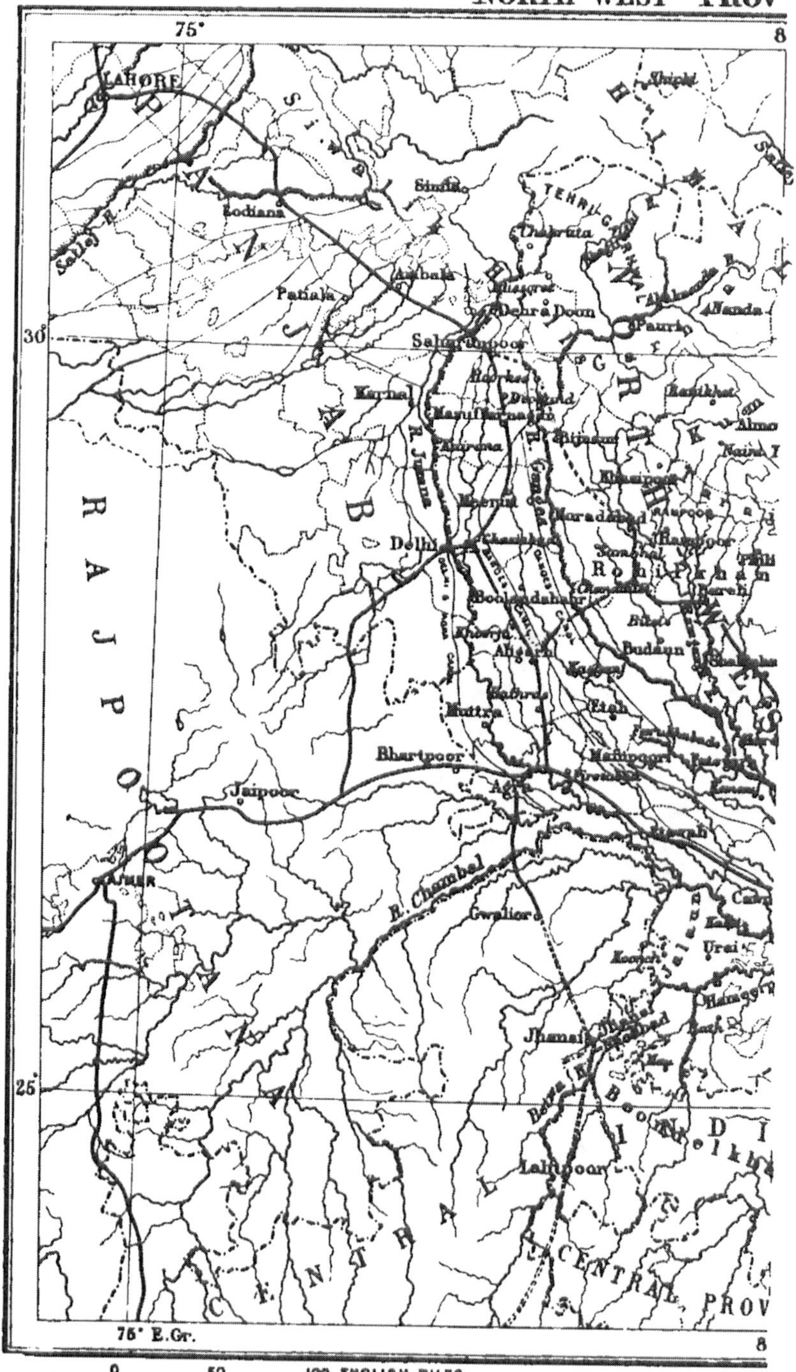

INCE, WITH OUDH.

Stanford's Geog' Est

CHAPTER X.

THE NORTH-WESTERN PROVINCE—DISTRICTS.

South-Eastern Districts.

§ 1. Allahabad City. § 2. Allahabad. § 3. Jaunpoor. § 4. Fatehpoor. § 5. Cawnpoor. § 6. Banda. § 7. Hameerpoor. § 8. Jalaun. § 9. Jhansi. § 10. Lalitpoor. § 11. Benares. § 12. Mirzapoor. § 13. Ghazipoor. § 14. Balia. § 15. Azamgarh. § 16. Basti. § 10. Gorakhpoor. § 18. Nepal Frontier.

North-Western Districts and States.

§ 19. Agra. § 20. Muttra. § 21. Mainpoori. § 22. Farukhabad. § 23. Etawah. § 24. Etah. § 25. Aligarh. § 26. Boolundshahr. § 27. Meerut. § 28. Muzaffarnagar. § 29. Saharanpoor. § 30. Dehra Doon. § 31. Garhwal. § 32. *Tehri-Garhwal State. § 33. Kumaun. § 34. Tarai. § 35. * Rampoor State. § 36. Bijnaur. § 37. Moradabad. § 38. Budaun. § 39. Bareli. § 40. Pilibheet. § 41. Shahjahanpoor.

South-Eastern Districts.

§ 1. Allahabad City ("city of Allah," the Prayag or "junction" of the Hindoos), capital of the N.W. Province since 1858, when the seat of government was removed from Agra, on the left bank of the Jumna at its confluence with the Ganges in N. lat. 25° 26′, and E. long. 81° 55′ 15″. Here Akbar built the noble red sandstone fort in 1575, calling the city by his own name; Jahangeer was governor, and his son Khusru died, and was buried in the mausoleum in the Khusru Bagh (garden). Ceded, with the district and Doab, to the British in 1801, Allahabad slowly prospered; when the Mutiny of 1857, in which the 6th Native Infantry murdered its officers and massacred the other Europeans till the arrival of General Neill, led Lord Canning to make it his own residence for a time and the centre of the provincial administration, from which Upper India was again brought under law. From that time the city has grown in size and beauty, covering the triangular area between the two great rivers. It is the headquarters of the most important military division S. of the Satlej from Dinapoor in Bengal to Cawnpoor. It is the centre of the railway system of N. India, being 564 m. from Calcutta and 89 m. from Benares to the S.E., 223½ m. from Jabalpoor and the Bombay line to the S.W., and 390 m. from Delhi to the N.W. The plain between the two rivers under the walls of the fort is the scene, every January, of the great fair, Magh Méla, where, at full moon, a quarter of a million of Hindoo pilgrims assemble to bathe at the Prayag, Tribeni, or confluence of the waters of the three rivers, the muddy Ganges, the clear Jumna, and the (invisible) Saraswati, which last disappears at Thaneswar, 400 m. N.W. In the fort is an underground temple of Shiva, the moisture on the walls of which marks, to the superstitious, the holy river; also a forked post or log, worshipped as the "undecaying Banian tree," seen by the Chinese Hwen T'hsang in the 7th century A.D., and before that the scene of human sacrifices. Within the gateway is an Asoka pillar with edict of 240 B.C., and inscription of Samoodra Goopta's victories in 2nd century A.D., to which Jahangeer added a Persian inscription on his ascension in 1605; in 1838 a British officer replaced the pillar as at present. Besides the Khusru Bagh, near the railway station, the most notable places are Government House, the public offices, and barracks, the Central College bearing the name of the scholar and former Lieutenant-Governor, Sir W. Muir; the Memorials of Lord Mayo, and the civil servants Thornhill and Mayne. The American Presbyterians and Episcopal Methodists, the Church and Baptist Missionary Societies, and Roman Catholics, have missions here. Allahabad is the third largest city of the Province (next to Lucknow and Benares), covers 22,202 acres, with 32,000 houses, has a growing population of 150,378, who yield a municipal revenue of £21,000 a year, or 2s. a head. Kydganj is the quarter inhabited by the wealthy natives.

§ 2. ALLAHABAD DISTRICT is bounded S. by Mirzapoor and Jaunpoor, N. by the Oudh district of Partabgarh, W. by Fatehpoor and Banda, and S. by Rewah State. Area, 2840 sq. m. Population, 1,396,241.[1] The district is in 3 portions —the central, between the **Ganges** and **Jumna**, alluvial, with its S. slope furrowed by ravines, draining into the latter; the northern, a rich plain N. of the Ganges; and the southern, a comparatively barren series of sandstone terraces rising towards the **Kaimoor** range, and drained by the S. **Tons** river,

[1] The population of all the North-Western Province districts is given according to the Census of 1872.

which flows from the Bandair hills of Boondelkhand to the Ganges at Sirsa, where it is spanned by a large railway bridge. Below Allahabad the Ganges is 3 m. broad, and up to this point it was navigated by inland steamers before the opening of the East Indian Railway. In extreme W. is the Alwara *Jheel*, a shallow lake 2½ m. by 2 m. The district is the Varanavata of the *Mahabharat* to which the Pandava brothers were exiled. It is traversed from E. to W. by the grand trunk road, and for 80 m. by the railway, which has 8 stations within the district. The Jabalpoor section to Bombay leaves the main line at Naini, and runs for 22 miles into Banda. At **Naini**, also, is the central jail. Besides the capital city the only town with more than 5000 inhabitants is **Mau Aima**, 17 m. to N. of it. **Katra**, 63 m. S.E. in a pass (1219 ft.) on the lower Kaimoor range, on the road to Mirzapoor. **Karra**, ruined town 40 m. N.W. of Allahabad on right bank of Ganges, from which Akbar removed the capital to Allahabad. Here in 1286 Muiz-ood-deen and his father met and united their forces against Delhi.

§ 3. JAUNPOOR DISTRICT is bounded E. and N.E. by Ghazipoor and Azamgarh; N. and N.W. by Oudh districts of Faizabad, Partabgarh, and Sultanpoor; W. by Allahabad; and S. by Benares and Mirzapoor. Area, 1544 sq. m. Population, 1,025,100. A rich and well-cultivated portion of the Gangetic plain, dotted with mounds and groves which cover the sites of old cities, traversed for 90 m. by the winding **Goomti**, an unfordable stream which through nodular limestone cuts its way to the Ganges, and by the Oudh and Rohilkhand Railway for 45 m. with 6 stations. The **Sai** (navigable), **Barna**, Pilli, and Basohi are the other rivers. There are numerous sheets of water in N. and S. On the Goomti and Barna stood great cities and temples, destroyed in the contest of Brahmanism with Boodhism, and in the Musalman invasion when, in 1194, Jai Chand, the Hindoo leader, was defeated by Shahab-ood-deen. In 1765 the battle of Buxar made it British, and ten years after it was permanently ceded by the treaty of Lucknow. In the Mutiny of 1857 the sepoys shot their officers and the magistrate and marched to Lucknow. **Jaunpoor** (24,000), chief town, on left bank of Goomti, 15 m. above its junction with the Sai, founded by Firoz Tughlak in 1360, whose now ruined fort was built of the stones of idol temples. Mosques, baths, and gateways in and around the town have left some fine ruins. The Jama Masjeed of Hassan is the chief ornament. Here was the capital of the Sharki dynasty of

"Eastern" sultans, who during the 15th century were the rivals of the Delhi emperors. Here the Church Missionary Society have a station. **Machlishahr** (9000), on a plain between the Sai and Pilli rivers, S. of Goomti.

§ 4. FATEHPOOR DISTRICT is bounded E. by Allahabad, N. by Oudh district of Rai Bareli, W. by Cawnpoor, and S. by Banda. Area, 1637 sq. m. Population, 663,877. The district is part of the alluvial plain between the Ganges and Jumna, with an elevated ridge passing through it from E. to W., and forming a watershed. There are three water-courses or rivers — the Pandoo, flowing N. to the Ganges, the Rind and Noon to the Jumna. The East Indian Railway runs through the district for 55 miles, and has 5 stations within it. After Baber's conquest in 1529 it was still loyal to the Pathan cause of Sher Shah against Hoomayoon. It became British in 1801, and speedily prosperous after the desolation of Musalman conflicts and Maratha raids. In the Mutiny of 1857 the Musalman mob murdered Robert Tucker, the Judge, who died a martyr's death; the other Christians had escaped. Three weeks later ten fugitives from Cawnpoor were here massacred. Havelock defeated the rebels at **Belinda** and **Aung**, and captured Fatehpoor, and Lord Clyde restored the district to peace. **Fatehpoor** (20,000), chief town on trunk road, 70 m. N.W. of Allahabad, and 50 m. S.E. of Cawnpoor, with two mosques of interest. Here the Bengalee confessor, Gopeenath Nundi, founded the American Presbyterian Mission. **Kora**, decayed town on old Mughul road from Agra to Allahabad, old provincial capital with some traces of former greatness. **Khajuha**, on old road from Kora to Fatehpoor, with fine ruins; here brass and copper vessels are made. Naraini is an agricultural mart, and Bindki, the chief market of the district, 5 m. S. of Mauhar railway station, where the Boondelkhand and Doab dealers meet.

§ 5. CAWNPOOR DISTRICT (Kanhpoor, or village of Kanh = a zameendar so named; also Kanh = Krishna) is bounded E. and N. by Fatehpoor district of Oudh, from which it is divided by the Ganges; W. by Farukhabad and Etawah; and S.W. by Hameerpoor, from which it is separated by the Jumna. Area, 2337 sq. m. Population, 1,156,055. Cawnpoor is a portion of the alluvial Doab between the Ganges and Jumna, exposed on its clay uplands to drought, which desolated it during the great famine of 1837, and from which it has since been protected by four branches of the Ganges Canal, with their distributing channels. The **Eesan** river passes through the N. of district to the Ganges. The **Pandoo** and **Rind** traverse its whole midland, and in the S. the Sengoor falls into the Jumna. After the conquest of Baber in 1529, and the struggle of his son Hoomayoon with Sher Shah, it was overrun by the Marathas and held by the Wazeer of Oudh, Safdar Jang, when the victories of Buxar and Kora led to the establishment of a cantonment at the new city of Cawnpoor, and at Fatehgarh. In 1801 it became British, with the whole lower Doab; in 1857-8 it was for a year the most notorious scene of the Mutiny outrages. **Cawnpoor** (125,000) stands on the right bank of the Ganges, to which the British cantonment was removed from Bilgram in the opposite district of Oudh in 1778; Ganges terminal of the great canal, as Etawah is the Jumna terminal; 628 m. N.W. of Calcutta, 130 m. above Allahabad, and 266 m. S.E. of Delhi. It is the seat of cotton mills and leather factories, and a considerable market for agricultural produce. Cawnpoor is notorious as the scene of Nana Dhoondoo Panth's five massacres of British officers, ladies, and children, most of whom, after their surrender in the entrenchments under General Wheeler, had survived the treacherous attack at the Sati Chaura Ghat on the boats in which they were promised safety. Memorial Gardens (50 acres) surround the well into which some two hundred, "the dying and the dead," were thrust, on the approach of Havelock's force, and the well itself is surrounded by a marble screen enclosing Marochetti's figure of the Angel of the Resurrection, with the palm of victory. A memorial church stands on the site of Wheeler's entrenchments. **Bithoor** (8000), 12 m. N.W. of Cawnpoor, on the Ganges, residence of Baji Rao, last of the Peshwas, and of his adopted son, the infamous Nana Dhoondoo Panth, whose palaces were destroyed by Havelock in 1857. The place has still a reputation for its Pandits skilled in Nagari caligraphy. **Shiurajpoor** (8000), 21 m. N.W. of Cawnpoor. **Bilhaur** (6000), also a centre of the Mutiny, on the trunk road, 35 m. N.W. of Cawnpoor.

§ 6. BANDA DISTRICT (from the sage Bamdeo) is bounded E. by Rewah State and Allahabad, N. by Fatehpoor, W. by Hameerpoor, and S. by the States of Panna, Chirkari, and Rewah. Area, 2961 sq. m. Population, 697,684. This is a poor district of Boondelkhand, sloping up from the Jumna S.W. to the Vindhya range, where are well-wooded hills rising to 2000 ft., from which the **Ken** and the **Bagain** flow S.E. to the Jumna. An aboriginal Naga dynasty ruled from Narwar, as a capital, or as viceroys of the Gooptas of Kanouj. The

Chandel dynasty, from 9th to 14th century, built fortresses like **Kalinjar** and Ajaigarh, temples and lakes, till overcome by the Muhammadans. The Marathas devastated the country, which in 1803 was ceded under the treaty of Bassein to the British, who recently gave it the light land-tax it needed. In 1857 the Nawab of Banda, after the mutiny of the 1st Native Infantry and murder of the Joint-Magistrate, was defeated by Whitlock. **Banda** (28,000), chief town, 1 m. E. of right bank of the Ken, a decaying place, with numerous Hindoo and Jain temples and mosques, and ruins of old and modern palaces; cantonments a mile from the town. **Rajapoor** (7000), cotton and produce mart on Jumna. Bargarh, Manikpoor, and Markundi are the three stations of the Jabalpoor railway in the district. Chilla, 48 m. from Banda, mart on the Jumna, with road to Fatehpoor. **Kalinjar**, old town and fort on Bindachal range (1230 ft.), 33 m. S. of Banda, mentioned in *Mahabharat*. Held by the British and the Raja of Panna throughout the Mutiny. Now of much archæological interest.

§ 7. HAMEERPOOR DISTRICT (Hameer Deo's place) is bounded E. by Banda, N. by Cawnpoor, W. by Baoni State, and S. by Alipoora, Chattarpoor, and Chirkhari States. Area, 2296 sq. m. Population, 529,137. Another poor and once over-assessed portion of the Boondelkhand plain stretching from the Jumna and Betwa to the Vindhya, among the outlying spurs of which are the noble artificial lakes of **Mahoba**, constructed by the Chandel Rajas. The **Betwa** river and the **Dhasān**, its tributary, are not navigable. **Hameerpoor** (7000), chief town, isolated on the triangle formed by junction of the above rivers with the Jumna, on the route from Banda to Cawnpoor. Here the 56th Native Infantry mutinied in 1857 and killed Europeans. **Mahoba**, in the S., old capital of Chandels, where, in 1183, Parmel, the last of these Rajas, was defeated by Prithvi Raja of Delhi; afterwards centre of power of the Boondela hero, Chatar Sal; with fine ruins. **Rath** (14,000), old town and mart in N.W. of district, with many ruins.

§ 8. JALAUN DISTRICT is bounded E. by Baoni State, N. by Cawnpoor and Etawah from which it is separated by the Jumna, W. by Gwalior and Datia States, and S. by Samthar State and Jhansi from which it is divided by the Betwa. Area, 1555 sq. m. Population, 404,447. The district is part of the plain of Boondelkhand, almost surrounded by the Jumna and its tributaries the **Betwa** and **Pahooj**; the last is the W. boundary. The **Non** flows through the centre, draining the district by numerous ravines. It forms part of the region of the same historical events as Banda, save that the Rajpoot clan of Kachwahas here took the place held by the Chandels in the E. From 1196, when Kutab-ood-deen took Kalpi, this tract became subject to the Muhammadans and then the Marathas. It finally lapsed to the British Government in 1840. In the Mutiny the 53d Native Infantry deserted their officers, the Jhansi mutineers overran the district, Sir Hugh Rose routed the rebels at Koonch and again at Kalpi in 1858, and since that time the land has been slowly recovering under a lighter assessment. **Urai** (7000), headquarters of district on Kalpi and Jhansi road. **Kalpi** (14,000), principal mart, on right bank of Jumna, 22 m. from Urai. Situated among rugged ravines, its fort was successively the central stronghold of the Musalmans and Marathas from the Dekhan and Bengal. Among several mausoleums the tomb known as the Eighty-four Domes is remarkable. **Koonch** (15,000), a declining mart, on open plain 19 m. W. of Urai; the staple industry of this and other towns is dyeing cotton with the red *al* of the root of *Morinda citrifolia*. From Urai and Jalaun a road crosses the Jumna at Shergarh to the nearest railway station at Phaphoond in Etawah.

§ 9. JHANSI DISTRICT is bounded E. by Hameerpoor, from which the Dhasān separates it; N. by Jalaun with the Betwa between; W. by the Datia, Gwalior, and Khaniya Dana States; and S. by Lalitpoor and the Orcha State. Area, 1567 sq. m. Population, 317,826. The district, much broken up by feudatory States, is part of the Boondelkhand hill plateau, with fine artificial lakes in the smaller hills, made by both the Chandel and Boondela princes, and enclosed or intersected by the Pahooj, Betwa, and **Dhasān** rivers, with their feeders, so as to be isolated during the floods of the rainy season. Here the Chandels gave way to the Khangars, who built Karar fort on the Orcha border, and were overcome by the Boondelas from the S. mountains under Roodra Pratap, founder of the Orcha family. Jhansi lapsed to the British in 1853 on the death of Gangadhar Rao, childless; but the Ranee, his widow, revolted in 1857 when the 12th Native Infantry seized the fort and massacred many Europeans, was defeated by Sir Hugh Rose, fled with Tatiya Topi, and finally fell in battle at Gwalior. **Jhansi Naoabad**, headquarters of district and cantonment, in extreme W. under the walls of Jhansi town, which belongs to Gwalior State. **Mau** (17,000) in S.E. **Rampoor** (7000), a Jain town on Jhansi and Naugaon road 5 m. W. of Mau, of which municipality it forms a part. **Gursarai** (6500), 40 m. N.E. of Jhansi on Jalaun and Sagar road, capital of Raja of same name. **Barwa Sagar** (6000), 12 m. from Jhansi on Naugaon road, on shore of picturesque lake; in the neighbourhood are an old castle last inhabited by the Rance of Jhansi, and remains of Chandel temple defaced by Musalmans. **Bhander** (6000), on left bank of Pahooj, 24 m. from Jhansi, fine old town with lake and Boodhist antiquities.

§ 10. LALITPOOR DISTRICT, nearly surrounded on all sides, save the south, by feudatory States, is bounded E. by Orcha State, and N. and W. by Betwa and Narayan rivers separating it from Gwalior, S. by Sagar district of the Central Province. Area, 1947 sq. m. Population, 212,661. This is the poorest district of the N.W. Province; sloping down from the Vindhya on the S. to the Jumna, its soil is drained off by numerous streams through rocky ravines. Of the old artificial lakes the largest is **Talbahat** in the N. hills. Held successively by the Gonds whose temples crown the Vindhya peaks, the Chandels and the Boondelas, the district was part of Chanderi State under Rajas descended from Roodra Pratap. Chanderi was taken by the Gwalior army under Baptiste in 1811, and was ceded to the British two years after the battle of Maharajpoor. In 1857 the Banpoor Raja revolted, the 6th Gwalior regiment murdered its officers, Sir Hugh Rose forced the passes to the S., and the district was subsequently reduced to order with difficulty. **Lalitpoor** (9000), chief town, near W. bank of Sahjad Nadi, on Jhansi and Sagar road; with Boodhist remains. **Talbahat** (5000), old town on lake of same name, 26 m. N. of Lalitpoor. Sir Hugh Rose demolished the fort in 1857.

§ 11. BENARES DISTRICT, the smallest and most densely peopled in the N.W. Province, sloping up from either bank of the Ganges, is bounded E. by Shahabad in Bengal, N. by Ghazipoor and Jaunpoor, W. and S. by Mirzapoor. Area, 998 sq. m. Population, 794,900. The Ganges is joined 16 m. below Benares city by the Goomti, and is 4 m. broad in the rainy season, where it leaves the district. The **Karamnasa** separates the district from Bengal on the S.E. The **Barna**, which gives its name to the city and district in the W. and **Nand** in the N. are small streams. Benares was under the Oudh viceroys during the Mughul period, who ceded it to the British in 1775. In 1737, Mansa Ram laid the foundation of the greatness of the family of the Maharaja of Benares; in 1778, Warren Hastings fined Chait Singh, whom the British had made Maharaja, half a million sterling for refusing to supply a contingent, and had to flee from the riot which followed; in 1799 the deposed Nawab of Oudh, Wazeer Ali, when residing at Benares, murdered

Mr. Cherry, the Government agent, and two officers; in 1857, the 37th Native Infantry mutinied and fled. **Benares** city (Varanasi or Banáras, "on the Barna") (207,570), the holy Kasi or metropolis of Hindooism, on the crescent-shaped left bank of the Ganges, 475 m. N.W. of Calcutta, 89 m. E. of Allahabad, 479 m. S.E. of Delhi. The first station of Gautama Boodha in the 6th century B.C., the headquarters of Brahmanism before and since, the residence of Sankar Acharjya the Shivaite teacher in the 7th century A.D., a scene of the iconoclasm of Aurangzeb whose mosque towers above its temples, the seat of Government and Christian Colleges, and of the missions of the Church, London, and Baptist Missionary Societies, this has always been the chief Hindoo city of N. India. Lying along the N. sweep of the Ganges is the native town; W. is **Sighra** suburb, the Christian missionary quarter; N. is **Sikraul** cantonment; S. of the Barna are the courts and the church, and N. of same stream is the civil station. **Rajghat** fort commands the city. **Ramnagar** (12,000), 2 m. S., on the right bank of the Ganges, has the Maharaja's palace, old fort, and garden, begun by Chait Singh. The principal Hindoo buildings in the city, all of freestone, are the Bisheswar, or golden temple of Shiva, covered with gold leaf by Ranjeet Singh; the observatory of Jai Singh, Jeypoor Raja, close by; the temple of Bhaironath, with his 4 ft. club; Tarakeswar shrine, fronting the well of Manibarnika, whose filthy waters represent the sweat of Vishnoo; the monkey temple at Doorga Koond; and Dasasameedh Ghat, one of the five places of pilgrimage. The incessant pilgrim traffic makes Benares a place of great trade, wealth, and luxury. Most of the greater Hindoo nobles of India have residences in the city. The *kinkob* or gold brocades, shawls, gold and brass work of its bazars are famous. **Sarnath** (Saranganath = "lord of deer"), first centre of Boodhism, is 3½ m. N. of modern site of Benares, where Gautama first preached. On a mound of ruins half a mile long and a quarter broad there are two stupas, and a third is near. Of these the Dhamek (Dharma = "the law") is a solid dome rising 110 ft. with a diameter of 93 ft., on the same site as Asoka's. The third stupa, called Chaukandi, is crowned by an octagon which commemorates Hoomayoon's visit in 1531. **Sakaldiha** and **Mughul Sarai** are the two stations of East Indian Railway, and Seopoor, Babatpoor, and Phoolpoor of the Oudh and Rohilkhand Railway. A Ganges bridge connects the two.

§ 12. MIRZAPOOR DISTRICT, the largest and most southern of the N.W. Province, is bounded E. by Shahabad and Lohardaga in Bengal, N. by Jaunpoor and Benares, W. by Allahabad and Rewah State, and S. by Sargooja State. Area, 5224 sq. m. Population, 1,015,826. The district stretches for 102 m. N. and S. from the Ganges plain to the Kaimoor and Vindhya ranges, which cross it from E. to W. with an average breadth of 52 m. The **Vindhya** hills send down sandstone spurs at Chanar and Kantit to the Ganges, which they overlook. Between these and the **Kaimoor** range, overhanging the **Son** valley, is the central plateau (600 to 800 ft.) The affluents of the Son are the **Rehand** and the **Pangan**, forming the Singrauli basin, with coal. Their history is associated with that of Benares and its Raja, and centres round Chanar. Khair-ood-deen Sabuktageen conquered the country from Prithvi Raja. Muhammad Shah put it under one of the Bahelia family, who retained the fortress till its surrender to the British in 1764. In 1857 the joint-magistrate and two planters were murdered, and Mr. Tucker twice defeated the insurgents. The East Indian Railway runs through the N. part of the district for 32 m., close to the Ganges and trunk road, with stations at Pahari, Mirzapoor city, and Gaepoora. The great Dekhan road, now nearly deserted, passes from Mirzapoor S. across the Vindhya at Tara Ghat. **Mirzapoor** city (67,000), on right bank of Ganges, 45 m. above Benares and 56 below Allahabad; long the greatest mart in Upper India for grain, cotton, shellac, and export produce. Mirzapoor has been affected by the through railway to Bombay and the rise of Cawnpoor. It is a fine stone city; a seat of the London Missionary Society. **Chanar** (10,000), an English-looking town on right bank of Ganges, 26 m. above Benares, with fine old fort still used as State prison and garrisoned from Allahabad. The stronghold, named from a deity of the heroic age, has been held by successive rulers—Hindoo, Muhammadan, and British. Once a settlement of European veterans and their families; still famous for its freestone. **Ahraura** (9000), grain mart, 10 m. S. of Ahraura Road Station on East Indian Railway.

§ 13. GHAZIPOOR DISTRICT is bounded N.E. by Balia, N.W. by Azamgarh, W. by Jaunpoor and Benares, and S.E. by Shahabad. Area, 1451 sq. m. Population, 873,130. The district consists of fertile uplands and low-lying tracts, and old river beds now forming lakes, of which **Suraha**, once a northern bend of the Ganges, is the largest. The Ganges, Gogra, **Sarjoo**, Goomti, and **Mandar** frequently inundate the country; the villages stand on raised ground. A portion of the Boodhist Asoka's empire, from the 4th century A.D. to the 7th, Ghazipoor was under the Goopta dynasty of Maghada. The Musalmans conquered it for the Ghori emperors, for the eastern sultans at Jaunpoor, for Baber again, for his son's rival Sher Shah, and for Akbar. From the deposition of Chait Singh in 1775 by Warren Hastings, to the present, the district has prospered. **Ghazipoor** (39,000), on left bank of Ganges, 64 m. N.E. of Benares, named from Masaood, the Ghazi or "champion of the faith," who founded it in 1330, under Tughlak. Here are tombs of the founder and of the Oudh Abdoolla, and Fazl Ali, and ruins of the Oudh palace of forty pillars. Here the Governor-General, the Marquis Cornwallis, died in 1805; a domed building covering his marble statue, by Flaxman, marks his grave. Has Government factory for opium monopoly. Here was Gossner's German Mission.

§ 14. BALIA DISTRICT is the land between the Ganges and Gogra, a new district formed from the above and the following districts. Often swept by the waters of the two streams. Bounded N.E. by Saran, W. by Azamgarh and Ghazipoor, and S. by Shahabad. Area, 1137 sq. m. Population, 686,368. **Balia** (9000), chief town, on left bank of Ganges, where it receives the Sarjoo, 42 m. E. of Ghazipoor; scene of a great bathing festival in October.

§ 15. AZAMGARH DISTRICT is bounded E. by Balia, N. by Gorakhpoor and Faizabad, W. by Jaunpoor, and S. by Ghazipoor. Area, 2147 sq. m. Population, 1,317,554. An alluvial portion of the Ganges plain, divided E. and W. by the Koonwar and the Tons. The **Gogra**, or Great Sarjoo, known also as the Debha or Dewa, forming the N. boundary, rolls along a great volume of water. The **Tons** pursues a tortuous course for 30 m. S.E. to Azamgarh town, from Mahool to Mau; its affluents are the Kunwar, Ungri, Majhui, Silhani, Kayar, and Saksui. The other rivers are the Little Sarjoo, Pharei, Basner, Mangai, Gangi, and Basoo. Some 20 lakes or swamps yield much fish. The Bhars, early possessors of the land, built the 35 vast forts in the Budaun and Sikandrapoor circles. Then came the Rajpoots, and Buinhars, and Muhammadans. When the Jaunpoor dynasty fell, Sikandar Lodi of Delhi built the **Sikandrapoor** fort on S. bank of Gogra. In 1801 the Oudh viceroy ceded it to the East India Company. In 1857 the 17th Native Infantry killed some of their officers, but Venables and the Goorkhas under Sir Jang Bahadoor restored order. **Azamgarh** (fort of Azam, a landholder) (16,000), on the Tons, 81 m. N. of Benares. Mau (12,000), on S.E., agricultural centre. Kopaganj (7000), sugar and indigo mart, on N. road. Mubarakpoor (6000), agricultural town.

§ 16. BASTI DISTRICT, Sub-Himalaya tract between Nepal and the Gogra, is bounded E. for 95 m. by Gorakhpoor; N. for 38 m. by Nepal hills, and N.W. for 98 m. by Gonda; W. and S. by Faizabad in Oudh. Area, 2788 sq. m. Population, 1,473,029. A *tarai* or marsh and forest land only 326 ft. above the sea, draining to S.E. Europeans have cultivated much of the waste jungle. The chief rivers are the **Rapti** (Irăvati = "the watery"), with its tributaries, the Arrah, Banganga, and Masidh, the Ami, the **Kouna**, and the **Gogra**. The largest lakes are the **Bakhira**, or Motee Jheel, on E. frontier, the Pathia, the Chaur, and the Chandoo. The history of the district belongs to Oudh and Gorakhpoor. The Oudh and Rohilkhand Railway skirts the S. border, and from the stations of Faizabad and Akbarpoor roads run into it; also from Basti, by Bansi, into Nepal; by Bhanpoor to Singarjot, and to Mendhawal. **Basti** (5500), on the Kouna, 43 m. from Gorakhpoor, 40 from Faizabad, and 112 from Benares. **Mendhawal** (8500), principal mart for iron and drugs from Nepal, 3 m. from the Rapti and 2 from the Motee Jheel = pearl lake. **Bansi** (3500), 32 m. N.E. of Basti, gives its name to the local Raja, whose seat is Narkatha, its N. suburb. The site of **Kapilavastu**, or Kapilanagora, capital of the Sakya clan, and birthplace of Sakya Mooni, the last Boodha ("intelligence"), has recently been identified with ruins at Bhuinla Tal (lake), near Rawai or Rohini river, N. of the Gogra, in Parganah Mansoorabad.

§ 17. GORAKHPOOR DISTRICT, with Basti the cradle of Boodhism, is bounded E. by Saran and Champaran, N. by Nepal, W. by Basti and Faizabad, and S. by Azamgarh, from which it is separated by the Gogra. A level plain of alluvium formed the hills, with much *sal* forest and *tarai* swamp, inhabited by the aboriginal Tharoos. Area, 4585 sq. m. Population, 2,019,361. The principal rivers are the tortuous Rapti, the wide Gogra navigable by steamers in the rains, the Great Gandak clear and rapid, the Little Gandak, the Rohini, Ami, and Gunghi. There are six large lakes—the Rungarh, Nandaur, Nawar, Bheuri, Chillna, and Amiyar. Once part of the Kosala kingdom, of which Ayodha was capital, this district is identified with the rise of Boodhism; its founder, born at Kapila, in Basti, near the border, died at **Kasia** (Kusinagara = city of the holy grass), 37 m. E. of Gorakhpoor, at N.W. corner of Ramabhar lake, where are a prostrate colossal statue, lofty brick mound called Devisthan, oblong mound with brick stupa, and other ruins. The country seems to have been held successively by the aboriginal Bhars; the Rhators, and other Aryan rivals; the

Musalmans, first under Akbar and then Oudh viceroys, who ceded it to the East India Company in 1801. In 1857 the Goorkhas under Sir Jang Bahadoor drove out the rebels. The Church Missionary Society has stations here. **Gorakhpoor** (52,000), on the Rapti, with mission settlement at Bisharatpoor ("evangel-town"), 8 m. off. Hence a good road runs to Benares by the Tucker embankment, 3 m. over the Amiyar and Bigra lakes. **Barhaj**, chief mart, on Rapti between Gorakhpoor and Ghatni Ghat; with **Gola** (5500) 1 m. E. **Padrauna** (5100), 49 m. N.E. of Gorakhpoor, the "Pava" of Chinese chroniclers, last halting-place of Boodha before Kasia; here is a large mound with ruins. **Roodrapoor** (9000) on Majhua, 23 m. S.E. of Gorakhpoor, with remains of large Rajpoot fort. **Pena** ("goad") (5500), near the Gogra, 44 m. S.E. of Gorakhpoor.

§ 18. *NEPAL FRONTIER. — The ordinary route to Kathmandoo, capital of Nepal, in a valley at the junction of the Bhagmati and Bishnmati rivers, is from Sagauli, on east side of Rapti in Champaran district of Bengal, 89 m. Of the N.W. Province part of the frontier, N. of Gorakhpoor and Basti, Mr. A. Swinton, commissioner, reported in 1861: The Goorkha town of Bootwal, situated at the base of the lower range of the Nepal mountains, is about 30 m. from Lotun, and there is a good road to it passable during the rains; there is a most eligible site for a sanitarium on the Tansein mountain (16,000 ft.); on its summit is a plateau well wooded and with plenty of water, 3 m. long and 1 m. broad; it is about 10 m. distant from Bootwal and accessible at all seasons. Between Sidonia Ghat and Bootwal is the Jurwa Pass, not far from the Urrah nadi, which is the boundary. It leads between Nawalgarh and Ghururbeer, and is 12 m. long. The Budgkayee Pass, the most open of the three, leads up the bed of a torrent and enters the Sonar valley. Its extreme length is 11 m., and the height of the crest is about 1000 feet above the plateau. The Koronia Sota Pass is 13 m. long, and winding (see pp. 100-1).

North-Western Districts and States.

§ 19. AGRA DISTRICT is bounded E. by Mainpoori and Etawah, N. by Muttra, W. by Bhartpoor State, and S. by Dholpoor and Gwalior States. Area, 1845 sq. m. Population, 1,068,653. Unequally divided by the Jumna; the smaller portion to N. is part of the Doab. The larger portion to S. is traversed by the **Utanghan**, and bounded by the **Chambal**; from both ravines rise into the plateau which ends in the

S.W. in the low sandstone outliers of the Vindhya. The **Agra Canal** fertilises the N.W. lands. From the time when the Lodi house settled on E. bank of Jumna, the district was connected with the history of the Delhi emperors, till it was held by the Jats of Bhartpoor and the Marathas alternately, from 1764 to 1803, or Lord Lake's victories. In 1857, on the mutiny of the Gwalior contingent, it was overrun by the rebels, with the exception of Agra fort, till after the fall of Delhi. Its Doab section is opened up by the East Indian Railway with stations at Firozabad, Toondla (junction for Agra), and Barhan. The capital is a terminus of the Rajpootana-Malwa Railway to Bhartpoor, Jeypoor, and Bombay, and of that to Gwalior. **Agra** (137,908), capital of Akbar's empire, and of the British N.W. Province from 1835 to 1858, on right bank of Jumna, 279 m. above Allahabad, 111 below Delhi, and 843 from Calcutta. The Lodi city was on the opposite bank; there Baber died in 1556. Akbar, his grandson, removed the capital from Delhi, to which Shah Jahan again transferred it; the great Emperor's mausoleum was erected at **Sikandra**, 5 m. distant, by his son Jahangeer; on the tomb the Viceroy, Lord Northbrook, placed a rich coverlet. To Akbar are due the fort and its palaces; to Shah Jahan, the pearl and great mosques, and Khas Mahal in the fort; but above all, the mausoleum of his wife, Mumtaz-i-Mahal ("exalted of the palace"), known as the **Taj Mahal**, where he too lies. For four months the British officials held the fort during the Mutiny till relieved by Colonel Greathed's column from Delhi. The Rajpootana and other railway communications, especially with Bombay, have given Agra new commercial importance. It is the seat of missions conducted by the Church Missionary Society and Baptists, and of a Roman Catholic establishment as old as Akbar's time. **Fatehpoor Sikri** (7000), Akbar's Windsor, 22 m. from Agra, where from 1470 he and Jahangeer held court. A wall 5 m. round encircles the ruins, among which are the great mosque and its gateway, the tomb of Shekh Salim Chisti, the house of Abul Fazl and his brother, of Akbar's Portuguese wife, Mariam, with Christian frescoes, and his state apartments. **Firozabad** (14,500), 25 m. E. of Agra, on road from Muttra to Etawah, with fine ruins; a station of East Indian Railway. Panahat (6500), near left bank of Chambal, 30 m. S.E. of Agra. **Batesar**, on right bank of Jumna, 35 m. S.E. of Agra, a great horse and bathing fair. Awah (5700), on road from Agra to Etah. Jalesar (15,700), 38 m. E. of Muttra or Doab plain, with railway station at Jalesar road.

§ 20. MUTTRA DISTRICT (Mathura) is bounded E. by Mainpoori and Etah, N. by Aligarh and Goorgaon, W. by Bhartpoor State, and S. by Agra. Area, 1453 sq. m. Population, 783,530. The district lies irregularly on either side of the Jumna; the level rises in S.W. to limestone hills of Bhartpoor. The portion W. of Jumna is the centre of the most numerous or Vaishnava division of Hindoos, as the grazing ground of Krishna and his brother Balaram; yet it is now a dry and treeless tract, and the whole district has suffered in almost every drought and famine. Muttra was afterwards a centre of Boodhism. Swept by Mahmood of Ghazni, its buildings suffered from the iconoclasm of Islam. It followed the fortunes of Agra historically even during the Mutiny, and was cleared of rebellion by Colonel Cotton's column. **Muttra** (60,000), on right bank of Jumna, 30 m. above Agra, great Brahmanical and Boodhist city till sacked by Mahmood in 1017, Sikandar Lodi in 1500, Aurangzeb in 1669, and Ahmed Shah Abdali in 1756. The buildings are chiefly of Jat and recent British times. Muttra is the centre of the Brajmandal of Vaishnava Hindooism, 42 m. long and 30 m. broad, where the pilgrims perform the Pari-krama or perambulation of Braj, visiting the 12 *bans* or woods, and 24 *upabans* or groves, besides the many ponds, wells, hills, and temples of Krishna. Most important of these still is **Brinda-ban** (21,000), 6 m. N. of Muttra, with temples, bathing ghats, and picturesque houses, all of stone. **Maha-ban** (7000), 6 m. S.E. of Muttra, with hill and old fort; in the neighbourhood is **Gokul** village, where Vishnoo first appeared as Krishna, and Vallabhi Swami, founder of the Maharaj sect, first preached. **Baladeva**, 6 m. beyond, with popular temple. **Gobardhan** ("nurse of cattle"), 13 m. W. of Muttra, pilgrim centre in limestone range, fabled to have been held aloft by Krishna on his finger for seven days to cover the people of Braj from the storms of Indra. **Kosi** (13,000), 29 m. N.W. of Muttra.

§ 21. MAINPOORI DISTRICT is bounded E. by Farukhabad, N. by Etah, W. by Muttra and Agra, and S. by Etawah. Area, 1697 sq. m. Population, 765,845. Mainpoori is a wooded plain with shallow lakes, and traversed by the main branches of the Ganges Canal. Between the **Kali Nadi** on the N.E. and the Jumna on the S.W. the lesser streams of the **Isan**, the **Arind**, the **Sengar**, and the **Sarsa** run S.E. in parallel courses. The Etawah branch of the canal is between the Sengar and the Arind, the Cawnpoor branch between the Arind and the Sarsa. The Aganga is a small drainage line, a tributary of the Sengar. Mainpoori was part of the kingdom of Kanauj, broken up into such petty principalities as Rapri and Bhongaon, formed a border land between the rival Musalman powers at Delhi and Jaunpoor, was occupied by Baber in 1526, and was ceded to the British in 1801. In 1857 the 9th Native Infantry mutinied, but the few Europeans held the capital for a time, and its citizens drove off the Jhansi rebels. The Chauhan Rajpoots, Phatak Aheers, and other castes, were long guilty of female infanticide till the Act of 1870 quartered special police on the "proclaimed" villages, of which there were 276 in 1875. The East Indian Railway runs through the S.W. corner with stations at Shikohabad and Bhadan. **Mainpoori** (from Main Deo) (22,000), on Agra branch of grand trunk road, 36 m. S.W. of Shikohabad railway station, a prosperous town in two portions.—Mainpoori proper and Makhanganj, with fine market called Raikesganj, and main street called Laneganj, both after recent officials. Seat of American Presbyterian Mission.

§ 22. FARUKHABAD DISTRICT is bounded E. by Oudh district of Hardoi, N. by Budaun and Shahjahanpoor, W. by Mainpoori and Etah, and S. by Etawah and Cawnpoor. Area, 1719 sq. m. Population, 918,850. The Ganges cuts off a small tract to N., watered also by the **Ramganga**; the main portion forms an upland plain to S., divided by the Kali Nadi, with the Arind and Isan streams. Here was Kanauj, the capital of the great Aryan kingdom of the Gooptas, which fell before Mahmood of Ghazni in 1018 A.D. The Rohillas here struggled long with the Musalman viceroys of Oudh, whom Warren Hastings assisted with a British force. Ceded in 1801, Farukhabad prospered till 1857, when the Nawab of Farukhabad was placed in power by the rebels, and the Europeans fled in boats from Fatehgarh to Cawnpoor, where they were murdered. The rebels were defeated at Kanauj, and again by Brigadiers Hope and Seton. **Fatehgarh** (14,000), civil and military headquarters, with gun-carriage factory in old fort, on right bank of Ganges, 83 m. N.W. of Cawnpoor, long an outpost against the Marathas under Perron and the Oudh viceroys. **Farukhabad** (80,000), principal native town, 3 m. W., with mud fort in which Nawab of Farukhabad resided. Seat of American Presbyterian Mission. **Kanauj** (17,000), 32 m. S., on W. bank of Kali Nadi, now 5 m. from its junction with Ganges, one of the most ancient capitals in the world, dating from prehistoric times, with brick ruins covering a semicircle 4 m. in diameter. Most notable are the shrines of Raja Ajaipal, whom Mahmood conquered, and the great mosque known as

"Seeta's kitchen," with early Hindoo carving. From Kanauj came the five chief Brahmanical Koolin clans of Bengal proper. **Kainganj** (10,500), 22 m. N.W. of Fatehgarh, noted for its mangoes and potatoes. Shamshabad (9000), on S. bank of Boodhi Ganga river, 18 m. N.W. of Fatehgarh.

§ 23. ETAWAH DISTRICT is bounded E. by Cawnpoor, N. by Farukhabad and Mainpoori, W. by Agra and Gwalior State, and S. by Jalaun. Area, 1698 sq. m. Population, 668,641. In this district the level Doab stretches across the Jumna valley to the Chambal gorges, which run up into the Vindhya. The portion N.E. of the Sengar is a fertile tract known as the *Pachar*, watered by the Etawah branch of the Ganges Canal. The opposite Trans-Chambal tract in the S., bounded by the **Kwari**, abounds in wild ravines, with scenery unsurpassed in the plains of India, and crowned by Bareh fort, near which, hence known as Panchnada or country of the five rivers, the Jumna, Chambal, Kwari, Sind, and Pahooj unite. The Chambal is here called Shivnad (Shiva's river). Etawah was almost always a purely Hindoo district, though conquered by Baber and opened up by his successful rival Sher Shah. After its cession to the British in 1801, Thuggee and the lawlessness of the landholders were gradually put down, and in the Mutiny of 1857 its people were the most loyal in Hindustan; the native officials kept up communication with the magistrate in Agra fort till Brigadier Walpole restored order. **Etawah** (31,000), pleasantly situated in ravines on left bank of Jumna, 70 m. S.E. of Agra, with fine square, high school, and American Presbyterian Mission. This town is the Itay described, 1631 A.D., by the Dutch author of "Vera India," De Laet. **Phaphoond** (6500), town with Musalman fair on old mound 36 m. E. of Etawah. **Auraiya** (7000), 42 m. from Etawah on Kalpi road; mart for Jhansi and Gwalior. **Jaswantnagar** (5500), trading town on East Indian Railway, N.W. of Etawah.

§ 24. ETAH DISTRICT is bounded E. by Farukhabad, N. by Budaun from which it is divided by the Ganges, W. by Agra and Aligarh, and S. by Mainpoori. Area, 1739 sq. m. Population, 833,892. Etah has 3 natural divisions—the lowlands between the **Burh Ganga** and the Ganges, the Middle Doab, and the country S. of the Kali Nadi. The Lower Ganges Canal will complete the water supply. The valley of the Kali was populous in Boodhist times, and as ruled by the Musalmans from Kanauj or Koil, was a lawless tract when it became British, prospered till it was temporarily in rebel hands in 1857, and was restored to order by Seton's column. **Etah** ("place of bricks") (8500), civil headquarters on trunk road, 9 m. W. of the Kali; the market-place is named Mayneganj, after a recent magistrate. **Kasganj** (16,000), chief commercial town near the Kali, 19 m. N. of Etah, once belonging to Colonel James Gardner. **Aliganj**, 34 m. from Etah on Farukhabad road; agricultural town. **Marahra** (9500), 12 m. N. of Etah, with Mayabasti suburb, chiefly Muhammadan. **Soron** (11,000), on Burh Ganga, 27 m. from Etah, an old Hindoo pilgrim centre. Atranji, famous mound, 15 m. S. of Soron, and 10 m. N. of Etah, with Brahmanical sculptures and coins, believed to have been visited by Hwen T'hsang. Patiali, old town mentioned in *Mahabharat*, on a mound on the old bank of the Ganges.

§ 25. ALIGARH DISTRICT is bounded E. by Etah, N. by Boolundshahr, W. by Muttra from which the Jumna separates it, S. by Muttra and Agra. Area, 1954 sq. m. Population, 1,073,353. A fertile district, through which the Ganges Canal runs from N. to S., dividing near Akrabad into the two branches which end at Cawnpoor and Etawah. The Lower Ganges canal is to start from the Ganges at Narora on the border, cross the Kali, run down the Doab between the Kali and Isan, turn the head of the Pandoo and keep between that river and the Arind to a point below Cawnpoor. The **Sengar** rises in Aligarh district near the Adhawan lake, flows S. for 190 m. into Etawah, Mainpoori, and Cawnpoor districts, and falls into the Jumna between Kalpi and Hameerpoor. There are several indigo factories; grain and cotton also are exported. Kutab-ood-deen in 1194 first imposed Islam on the Dor Rajpoots of Aligarh. On Aurangzeb's death, anarchy spread first under the Marathas; then under the Jats, whose leader took Koil in 1757, the year of Plassey; and also under the Afghans. From Lord Lake's victories in 1803 prosperity prevailed till 1857, when the Europeans fled, and Musalman excesses made the Hindoos welcome the restoration of British order. **Aligarh** (60,000 with Koil), civil headquarters and fort adjoining the old native city of **Koil** (where Balaram slew the demon Kol), in centre of district, with high site of Rajpoot stronghold, now crowned by Sabit Khan's mosque. Aligarh fort (740 ft.) was held by Perron for Sindhia, and stormed by Lake in 1803. East Indian Railway station, from which also the Oudh and Rohilkhand Railway diverges to Chandausi; the other stations are (East Indian Railway) Somna, Pali, and Hathras; (Oudh and Rohilkhand Railway) Rampoor and Raipoor. Here are the Aligarh Institute, founded by an enlightened Musalman, and the Post Office workshops. **Hardwaganj** (7000), 6 m. E., a trading mart.

Sikandra Rao (13,000), 23 m. E. of Koil on Cawnpoor road, near lake from which the Isan issues. **Atrauli** (16,000), 16 m. from Koil on Ramghat road to Ganges. **Hathras** (24,000), chief trading town, centrally placed 21 m. from Aligarh, 29 from Agra, and 24 from Kasganj, with railway to Muttra.

§ 26. BOOLUNDSHAHR district is bounded E. by Budaun and Moradabad, from which the Ganges divides it; N. by Meerut; W. by Delhi and Goorgaon, from which the Jumna divides it; and S. by Aligarh. Area, 1918 sq. m. Population, 936,667. This part of the Doab, 650 ft. above the sea, is traversed by three main branches of the Ganges Canal, one of which divides into two near Sikandarabad; from these run 626 miles of distributing channels. Waste land has thus disappeared, except the barren *oosar*, on which is the saline efflorescence known as *reh*. The principal local streams are the **Hindan and East Kali Nadi**. The district has formed a part successively of the territory of the Pandavas from Hastinapoor (mythical), the Goopta dynasty, Mahmood of Ghazni and his successors to Bahadoor Shah in 1707, and the Marathas and others who ruled from Koil. In 1803 it became British; when in 1857 the 9th Native Infantry mutinied, it was for a time restored to order by volunteers from Meerut, and finally rescued from Goojar and Musalman chaos by Greathed's column. The East Indian Railway passes through the district, with stations at Dadri, Sikandarabad, Chola, and Khoorja. In S.E. the Oudh and Rohilkhand line crosses the Ganges at Rajghat. **Boolundshahr** or **Baran** (15,000), on W. side of the Kali, with the ancient Baran on the raised bank, where coins of Alexander and the Indo-Bactrians are still found; there are Musalman tombs, and, in the new town, the Lowe memorial of a British magistrate. **Khoorja** (27,000), chief mart between Delhi and Hathras, 10 m. S. of Boolundshahr junction of Delhi and Meerut branches of trunk road, with new Jain temple. **Anoopshahr** (10,000), on W. bank of Ganges, a Hindoo bathing-place, where Ahmed Shah in 1757 operated against the Jats and Marathas. Rajghat, 9 m. S.E., is the railway station. **Sikandarabad** (19,000), on Delhi branch of trunk road, 10 m. E. of Boolundshahr, headquarters of Perron's Marathas, and Colonel James Skinner, after the battle of Aligarh. Here and at Boolundshahr are agencies of the Church Missionary Society. Indor Khera, 8 m. S.W. of Anoopshahr, is a very lofty mound which marks the site of Indrapoora, a city of the Goopta kings.

§ 27. MEERUT DISTRICT is bounded E. by Moradabad and Bijnaur, from which it is separated by the Ganges; N. by

Muzaffarnagar; W. by the Panjab districts of Panipat and Delhi, from which the Jumna divides it; and S. by Boolundshahr. Area, 2361 sq. m. Population, 1,276,104. This fertile upper portion of the Doab is watered by the Eastern Jumna Canal between the Jumna and Hindan, and by the Ganges Canal in two branches. On the **Burh Ganga**, or old bed of the Ganges, was **Hastinapoor**, the legendary capital of the Lunar race, the Pandavas, described in the *Mahabharat;* after that, under the descendants of Parikshit, as in the *Vishnu Purana*. Part of the Boodhist Asoka's empire, it was swept by Timoor, was the favourite resort of the Mughul Court, was held in the anarchy after Aurangzeb by the Luxemburg butcher and soldier of fortune, Walter Reinhardt, and his widow the Begam Samroo who died a British feudatory in 1836. In 1857 it was the first scene of the great Mutiny, which broke out on Sunday 10th May, when some of the 3d Bengal Cavalry refused to use the cartridges, and the massacre of the Europeans began. The district is traversed by the East Indian and Delhi and Panjab railways. **Meerut** (82,000), half-way between the Ganges and Jumna on the trunk road, ancient city restored to prosperity as a great military centre of British since 1806, with Musalman tombs and mosques, the Suraj Koond or monkey tomb, large church, and Church, Baptist, and Roman Catholic Missions. The cantonments were held all through the Mutiny by a few Europeans, and the surrounding country was kept in order. **Ghaziabad** (8000), junction of East Indian and Delhi and Panjab railways, with branch to Delhi; named after its founder in 1740, the brother of Salabat Jung of the Dekhan. **Bagpat** (8000), on left bank of Jumna, a sugar mart. Barot (7000), on E. bank of East Jumna Canal; Shahdwara (7000), or "king's gate," founded by Shah Jahan, near same canal; Hapoor, 18 m. S. of Meerut, and Pilkhuwa (6000), 19 m. S.W. of Meerut, purchased by Mr. Michel after the Mutiny, are the other municipalities. **Sardhana** (12,500), near Ganges Canal, 12 m. N.W. of Meerut, long capital of the notorious Reinhardt and Begam Samroo, whose private estates passed to their grandson's widow, only daughter of the second Viscount St. Vincent, and afterwards the wife of the third Baron Forester. The Begam's house, Roman Catholic cathedral and college, and old fort (N.) may be seen. **Garhmookhtesar** (8000), on right bank of Ganges, 4 m. below junction with Burh Ganga, ward of the legendary Hastinapoor, named from temple of goddess Ganga, and Brahmanical bathing centre.

§ 28. MUZAFFARNAGAR DISTRICT is bounded E. by Bijnaur,

with the Ganges between; N. by Saharanpoor; W. by the Panjab district Karnal from which the Jumna divides it; and S. by Meerut. Area, 1654 sq. m. Population, 690,107. The Hindan and Kali Nadi unite near the S. boundary. The Ganges Canal waters the uplands and sends off the Anoopshahr branch at Jauli village. The E. Jumna Canal waters the W. plateau between the Hindan and Jumna. Part of the Pandava kingdom, and then under Prithvi Raja, the Chauhan ruler of Delhi, the district was held by the Barha Sayyids during Mughul times. The Sikhs and then the Marathas were kept back by the Sardhana adventurer, George Thomas, who restored the Begam Samroo. In 1854 the 4th Irregulars mutinied. **Muzaffarnagar** (11,000), on road from Meerut to Landhaur, and station of Delhi Railway. Shamli (9500), 24 m. W. on East Jumna Canal, mart where Lord Lake relieved Colonel Burn when surrounded by a Maratha force in 1804, and a native official fell in 1857 fighting for British. **Kandhla** (11,000), on East Jumna Canal, 35 m. S.W. of Muzaffarnagar, an agricultural centre. **Kairana** (18,000), on Jumna, 31 m. S.W. of Muzaffarnagar, a municipality like the three previous towns. **Jalalabad** (7000), grain mart near little river Krishni, 21 m. N.W. of Muzaffarnagar, with ruins of famous Rohilla fort, Ghansgarh. Thana Bhawan (7000), 18 m. N.W. of Muzaffarnagar, old and decaying town whose Khazi in 1857 murdered 113 defenders of Shamli in cold blood. Khatauli (7000), prosperous mart and railway station, with Jain temples, 13 m. S. of Muzaffarnagar.

§ 29. SAHARANPOOR DISTRICT is bounded E. and N. by Bijnaur with the Ganges between, and Dehra Doon with the Siwaliks between; W. by Ambala and Karnal; and S. by Muzaffarnagar. Area, 2221 sq. m. Population, 884,017. The most N. district of the Doab in which the **East Jumna** and **Ganges Canals** begin at the base of **Siwalik Hills**. The former, planned originally by Shah Jahan's minister, Ali Murdan Khan, flowed for only one season, and was reconstructed by Sir P. Cautley, R.E., who designed the great Ganges Canal opened under the Marquis of Dalhousie in 1854. The history of the district is that of Muzaffarnagar, save that a Goojar revolt threatened in 1824, and there was a slight outbreak in 1857. **Saharanpoor** (45,000), on Damaula Nadi, headquarters of Jumna Canal, railway terminus for hill station of Mussooree, and junction of Delhi and Oudh railways. Here is a fine Botanic Garden, where early experiments were made in tea and cinchona culture. Seat of American Presbyterian Mission. **Deoband** (20,000), near E.

Kali Nadi, with Devikoond lake, a centre of Hindoo pilgrimage and many mosques; here the Pandavas passed their first exile. **Hardwar** (Hari-dwara = "Vishnoo's gate," or Hara-dwara = "Shiva's gate"), 39 m. N.E. of Saharanpoor, on right bank of Ganges, where it debouches through the gorge of the Siwaliks, most frequented of all Hindoo places of pilgrimage, and frequently a point whence cholera is carried over N. India. Every twelfth year, when Jupiter is in Aquarius, the *Kumbh-mela* attracts the third of a million, but of old as many as 3 millions. Here is the head of the Ganges Canal. Here the sage Kapila lived, and, in the 7th century A.D., Hwen T'hsang visited a Boodhist city 3½ m. in circumference. **Roorkee** (11,000), on ridge above the Solani, 22 m. E. of Saharanpoor, headquarters of Ganges Canal establishments, with Thomason Civil Engineering College, observatory, cantonment, Propagation Society's and American Missions. Gangoh (11,000), 23 m. S.W. of Saharanpoor; Manglaur (9000), 16 m. S.E. of Saharanpoor; Jawalapoor, 14 m. N.E. of Roorkee, with which it forms a municipal union; Rampoor (8500), 14 m. S. of Saharanpoor.

§ 30. DEHRA DOON (= Valley) DISTRICT is bounded E. and N. by Garhwal, from which the Ganges divides it, and Garhwal State; W. by Sirmoor and Ambala; and S. by Saharanpoor. Area, 1193 sq. m. Population, 116,945. This lovely and cool series of valleys, between the **Siwalik** (Shiva's) **Hills** and the Himalaya, consist of (1) the Doon proper, divided by ridge from Rajpoor to Mohun pass, into the Eastern Doon, which slopes to the Ganges and the Western Doon to the Jumna; and (2) **Jounsar Bawar**, a mass of rocks between the Tons on the W. and the Jumna on the E. and S. **Nuwada** or Nagsidh, the only isolated hill, is 5 m. S.E. of Dehra, where the Garhwal viceroys resided. The passes from the plains are the **Mohund** or Kheree, equidistant between the Ganges and Jumna, and the Timlee 7 m. E. of the Jumna. The **Ganges** enters the Doon at Tupoban, 165 m. from its source, and falls 23 ft. a mile to Hardwar, 15 m. below, at an elevation of 1024 ft., with a discharge of 7000-8000 ft. in the dry season. The **Jumna**, sweeping round Budraj mountain, enters the valley 110 m. from its source, falls 19 ft. a mile to the plains 21 m. away, and debouches 3 m. above Badshahmahal in Saharanpoor, old hunting seat of Delhi emperors, with a discharge of 4000 ft. The **Sooswa** and **Asun** torrents, rising near Bheem Tal, catch the mountain drainage, flow E. and W. respectively; the former receiving the Son from behind the spur of **Kalanga**, famous in the Goorkha War, falls into the Ganges; the latter, receiving the Tons, falls into the Jumna. The district is the legendary Kedarkoond or residence of Shiva, the retreat of Rama, and the route of the Pandavas to their immolation on the peak of Maha Panth. At Haripoor, on right bank of Jumna, is the Kalsi stone with Asoka's edict, believed to mark off India from China. Banjara traders first settled in 11th century in the valley, which was held successively by Garhwal, the Rohillas under the good Najeeb Khan, and the Goorkhas, from whom the British conquered it in 1815. In 1857 some Jalandhar insurgents passed through the district, but peace was not disturbed. The American Presbyterian Mission has successfully conducted missionary and educational work. European landholders pay one-fourth of the whole land-tax, and the population has increased fourfold under British rule. **Dehra** (7500) (2323 ft.), chief town, with fine Mission Schools; Ram Rae's temple, designed after Jahangeer's tomb, and a petrifying spring known as the Suhusra Dhâra ("place of the thousand drippings"), worshipped by Hindoos. **Annfield**, agricultural colony, established in 1857 by Church Missionary Society. **Mussooree** (Mansooree) (7433 ft.), sanitarium on lower range of same name, where the Himalaya bends back to enclose the Doon in an immense amphitheatre; in the season the population rises to 8000. **Landhaur** (7459 ft.), forming municipality with Mussooree; convalescent military depot since 1827, with many Christian institutions. There are 300 permanent European residents in the joint sanitaria. **Kalsi**, old mart of Jounsar Bawar. **Chakrata**, in same hill tract, a cantonment since 1859, reached from Kalsi.

§ 31. GARHWAL DISTRICT, so named from the "forts" of 52 petty chiefs, is bounded E. by Kumaun, N. by Chinese Tibet, W. by Garhwal State and Dehra Doon, and S. by Bijnaur. Area (estimated), 5500 sq. m. Population, 310,288. The district consists of the confused outliers of the main range of the Himalaya, rising into mighty peaks, and separated by ravines, of which Srinagar is the broadest. The waterless forest known as *bhabar* separates the base of the hills from the plains of Rohilkhand. The **Mana** (18,000 ft.) and **Niti** (16,570 ft.) passes lead through the valleys of the Saraswati and Dhauli into the Nari Khorsoom Province of China. Here the **Ganges** rises from two main sources, the **Alaknanda** and **Bhagirathi**, which unite at Deo Prayag, the most sacred spot of pilgrimage for Hindoos. The **Ramganga** rises near Lobha, flows through the district, and reaches the Ganges in Farukhabad district. In the 14th century Ajai Pal, first of the Chand dynasty, founded the Garhwal kingdom at **Srinagar**, on the Alaknanda, where the ruins of his palace are visible. In 1803 the Goorkhas introduced the merciless rule of Nepal, and in 1815 the British brought in peace and prosperity. **Pauri**, the administrative headquarters, above the valley of Srinagar. **Badrinath** and **Kedarnath**, the great Hindoo temples, are in the snowy range in the extreme N.W. At Chapra, near Pauri, there is a Christian mission. Sheep and goats from the Panjab State of Chamba carry the trade over the Niti (125 m. from Srinagar) and Mana passes. The nearest railway station is Saharanpoor, 100 m. S.W.

§ 32. *TEHRI-GARHWAL STATE is bounded E. and S. by the Alaknanda, separating it from Garhwal district; N. by Tibet; and W. by Dehra Doon. Area, 4180 sq. m. Population, 200,523. The State is formed of lofty ranges, and valuable deodar tracts, draining into the Ganges. The British restored the Raja after the Goorkha War in 1815, and he did good service in the Mutiny; his revenue is £11,300 a year. **Tehri** (4500 ft.), which sometimes gives its name to the State, is the capital towards the south. There are civil courts at Dehprag and Rowai also. The Raja pays no tribute, but is bound to give a passage to troops and assist the Paramount Power. Saharanpoor is the nearest railway station.

§ 33. KUMAUN DISTRICT is bounded E. by Nepal, N. by Nari Khorsoom Province of Tibet, W. by Garhwal, and S. by Moradabad and Pilibheet. Area, 6000 sq. m. Population, 433,314. The hill ranges run E. and W. and rise in elevation towards the N., till they culminate in 30 lofty peaks above 18,000 ft., within a tract of 140 m. long and 40 broad. The principal are—the **Trisool**, or trident mountain (23,382 ft.), on the border of Garhwal; **Nanda-devi** (25,700 ft.), to the N.E.; **Nandakot** ("Nanda's couch"), 22,538 ft.; Panichoola Peaks (22,673 ft.), farther E. From the Tibetan watershed beyond the rivers work their way down deep valleys; the principal are the Kali, Sarda or **Gogra**, which joins the Ganges in Bengal; its affluents, the E. Dhauli Goonka, Goriganga, E. Ramganga, and Sarjoo; and the Pindar and Kaliganga, which join the Alaknanda. The principal lakes are **Naini Tal** (4703 by 1518 ft.), Bheem Tal (4580 by 1490 ft.), Mankuchiya (3120 by 2270 ft.), Malwa Tal (5480 by 1833 ft.). The chief river plateaux are **Sameswar** and **Hawalbagh** on the Kosi, **Katyoor** on the Gaomati, and **Pali** watered by the Gagas and W. Ramganga. The south of the district consists of *bhabar* forest, under which the drainage finds its way to the *tarai*. This forest has been extensively cleared by the natives.

There are many European tea gardens, which export into Central Asia. Oranges and potatoes, limestone, iron, and copper add to the wealth of the district, the prosperity of which has been identified with the long administration of the Commissioner, Sir Henry Ramsay. The history is the same as that of Garhwal. **Almora** (5494 ft., 6600 pop.), chief town on crest of a ridge, and stronghold captured in 1815 by Colonel Nicholls. **Naini Tal** (6409 ft., 6000 pop.), European sanitarium, beautifully situated on lake of same name, and hot weather headquarters of North-Western Province Government. Here a disastrous landslip occurred in 1880. **Ranikhet** (5958 ft.), military sanitarium, with much level land, and easily accessible. Pithoragarh, Lohaghat, and Charal are level uplands. Champhanat village is the ruined capital of the Chand rajas. Ramnagar is a mart on the Kosi. The London Missionary Society has a station at Almora and Ranikhet, and the American Methodist Episcopal Church at Naini Tal.

§ 34. TARAI DISTRICT ("moist" land) is bounded E. by Pilibheet and Nepal, N. by Kumaun, W. by Bijnaur, and S. by Bareli, Moradabad, and Rampoor States. Area, 920 sq. m. Population, 185,658. From the line where the springs burst from under the *bhabar* forest at the foot of the hills, the district slopes down S.S.E., with an average breadth of 12 m. and length of 90 m. The streams drain into the Ramganga; the principal are the **Deoha**, which is navigable at Pilibheet; the Saniha, which joins the Sarda; the Sookhi ("dry"), which unites with the Bahgul to form part of the canal system; the flooded Kichaha or Ganla of the hills, and the Paha, Bhakra, Bhaur, and Dabka, between it and the Kosi. The Phika is the W. boundary. The district prospered only when Maratha and Rohilla conflicts drove the people of the south to its prairie lands. The resident tribes, the Tharoos and Bhooksas, ascribe their freedom from malarious diseases to their consumption of wild pigs and deer. The European officials reside at Naini Tal from May to November. The only towns are **Kasipoor** (13,500), 31 m. from Moradabad, station of transit trade from Tibet and Kumaun to plains, and of Hindoo pilgrims on way to Badrinath: the old Aryan city of Drona, hero of *Mahabharat*, and capital of the Govisana kingdom, and Jaspoor (7000), a small town.

§ 35. *RAMPOOR STATE (Musalman) is bounded E. and S. by Bareli, N. by Tarai, and W. by Moradabad. Area, 945 sq. m. Population, 543,901. The State is famous for the damask known as *khes*. The plain Rampoor *chadars* or shawls are from Rampoor, N.E. of Simla. It is traversed by the imperial road from the capital to Bareli and Moradabad. It is watered in the N. by the **Kosila** and **Nahool**, and in the S. by the Ramganga, after receiving the Kosila. The Nawab, with £158,657 a year, represents two Rohilla Afghan brothers who, in the 17th century, settled here in the service of the Delhi emperors. Maratha raids drove the family to seek the aid of the Oudh viceroys. The State having fallen under British guarantee, Warren Hastings assisted the Oudh viceroy to seat the rightful heir, defeating the usurper at Futtehganj, near Bareli, "but not before a Highland regiment had been almost cut to pieces by the Rohilla horse. A monument on the field commemorates the British loss, and the puppet-shows of Bareli still exhibit the slaughter of the flying redcoats by the cavalry of the Nawab."[1] In 1857 the present chief's father was most actively loyal. **Rampoor** (75,000), capital on left bank of Kosila, with lofty mosque, densely crowded streets, and tomb of Faiz-oolla Khan to N. **Badli Tanda** (12,000), a trading centre. **Shahabad** (8200) and Dhukia are famed for their sugar. Bilaspoor, Kaimri, and Nagulia Akal are rice marts trading with Delhi, which supplies goats for food. The State is politically under the Commissioner of Rohilkhand.

§ 36. BIJNAUR DISTRICT, running up between the Ganges and Sub-Himalaya, is bounded on N.E. by Garhwal; on N.W. by Dehra, Saharanpoor, Muzaffarnagar, and Meerut; and S., by Moradabad and Tarai. Area, 1869 sq. m. Population, 737,153. On N. the Siwalik range of Dehra throws out the low **Chandi** hills, with good sport. The fertile open upland is intersected in N. by many torrents between the hills and the Ganges. Famous in Boodhist times, Bijnaur was devastated by Timoor, and became involved in the history of the Rohillas, who concluded the treaty with the viceroys of Oudh at Lal Dhang in 1774 in this district. At Afzalgarh in 1803, Colonel Skinner defeated Ameer Khan of Tonk. In 1857-8 the mutinous Roorkee Sappers passed through, the Nawab of Najeebabad held sway for a time, though attacked by the Hindoos, and the rebels were defeated at Nageena. Bijnaur produces the best sugar in India. **Bijnaur** (13,000), 3 m. E. of Ganges, headquarters of the Jats; seat of American Methodist Mission. Six m. S. is Daranagar, great bathing fair on the Ganges. **Chandpoor** (12,500), Musalman town, 19 m. S. of Bijnaur, with fine old mosque. **Dhampoor** (7000), 22 m. S. of

[1] Memoranda prepared for the Information of H.R.H. the Prince of Wales during his visit to India.

Bijnaur, on road from Moradabad to Hardwar. **Nageena** (20,000), on same road, 38 m. N.W. of Moradabad, with Pathan fort, now a public office. Parasnath ruins are near, 6 m. in extent. **Najeebabad** (18,000), on the Malin, 31 m. S.E. of Hardwar, named after the Nawab who, in 1755, built Pathargarh fort, 1 m. E., and the tomb and palace in the town; a centre of the timber trade. **Mandawar** (7700), 8 m. N. of Bijnaur, a great Boodhist city in 7th century, now seat of papier-maché manufacture.

§ 37. MORADABAD DISTRICT is bounded E. by Rampoor State, N. by Bijnaur and Tarai, W. by Meerut and Boolundshahr, and S. by Budaun. Area, 2282 sq. m. Population, 1,122,437. Part of the great Gangetic plain, Moradabad is watered by the Ramganga and **Sot**; its many shallow lakes are utilised for irrigation. After Aheer and Boodhist times it was under the Jaunpoor sultans, till made a fief of Delhi by the Emperor Sikandar Lodi, who resided at Sambhal, then its capital. Like Bareli, it became the scene of the Oudh and British conflicts with the Rohillas. In 1857 the 29th Native Infantry mutinied and the Europeans found refuge at Meerut. The brigade of General Jones restored order. **Moradabad** (63,000, half Hindoos and half Musalmans), railway station on right bank of Ramganga, 10 m. from Rampoor border, named after son of Emperor Shah Jahan, with fort overhanging river, mosque, and tomb. **Sambhal** (47,000), 22 m. S.W. of Moradabad on Aligarh road, and 4 m. W. of Sot river; long a Musalman capital, on mounds of which the modern town stands. **Amroha** (35,000), old Musalman town 20 m. N. of Moradabad, on road between Bijnaur and Muzaffarnagar. **Chandausi** (24,000) railway station 28 m. S. of Moradabad, junction for Aligarh, sugar mart with lime deposits. **Dhanaura** (5500), agricultural town and sugar mart 33 m. W. of Moradabad. The Oudh and Rohilkhand Railway crosses the district with stations at Moradabad, Kharakpoor, Kundharki, Bilari, and Chandausi, from which the Aligarh branch diverges with stations at Bajhoi and Dhanari.

§ 38. BUDAUN DISTRICT is bounded E. by Shahjahanpoor; N.E. by Bareli and Rampoor States; N.W. by Moradabad; S.W. by Boolundshahr, Aligarh, Etah, and Farukhabad. Area, 1986 sq. m. Population, 935,856. Budaun is enclosed between the Ganges and Ramganga, and divided into two by the Sot. The other principal rivers from E. to W. are the Undhari, Areel, Mahawa, Choiya, and Nakta. In N.E., between the Sot and Ramganga, was the great forest which defied the Mughul armies; the jungles are still dense. Budaun, named after an Aheer prince Budh, gave two early emperors to Delhi, shared the fortunes of the Bareli district, was the scene of Hindoo and Musalman conflicts in the Mutiny, and was swept by Sir Hope Grant and the columns of Coke and Wilkinson. **Budaun** (34,000), picturesquely placed on banks of the Sot, with old fort, and fine mosque originally a Hindoo temple. **Bilsi** (5500), 13 m. N.W. of Budaun, principal mart; Kakora fair is near. **Ujhani** (8000), 8 m. S.W. of Budaun on Etah road, fine market town. **Sahaswan** (17,000), near Ganges, large town with site of old fort.

§ 39. BARELI DISTRICT (Bans or "bamboo" Bareli, to distinguish it from Rai Bareli in Oudh) is bounded E. by Shahjahanpoor and Pilibheet, N. by Tarai, W. by Rampoor State and Budaun, and S. by Budaun and Shahjahanpoor. Area, 1621 sq. m. Population, 1,023,186. The district is a level plain just below the slopes of the Himalaya, covered with groves, and watered by the Ramganga and **Deoha** rivers; the latter, rising in the Kumaun hills, is surcharged with lime, deposited in stalactites, which are an article of trade. The other streams are the Baigul, Nakatia, Dioramian, Sanka, Sidha, Dojoro, Kicha, and Areel, used for irrigation, and the inundations of which fertilise the soil. Bareli city is the great Rohilla capital of the whole country E. of the Ganges, now called Rohilkhand, but formerly **Kather**, a name restricted to the country E. of the Ramganga, where the Muhammadans made Budaun and Sambhal separate governments. The tract was occupied by civilised Aryans till the 11th century, when the hill and forest races—Aheers, Bheels, and Bhars—drove them out. When the Mughul empire broke up on Aurangzeb's death in 1707, Ali Muhammad Khan, a Rohilla Afghan, seized all Kather, the Rohillas fought with the Oudh viceroys aided by Warren Hastings, and ended by keeping only Rampoor State, under British influence. Mr. Henry Wellesley, the Governor-General's brother, was first President of Board of Commissioners at Bareli, when, in 1801, Rohilkhand was ceded with Allahabad and Korah in place of tribute. In 1857 the district and city were the last stronghold of the rebel leaders, who were driven into Oudh and Nepal on 7th May 1858. **Bareli** (105,000), on Ramganga, 96 m. above confluence with Ganges, 152 m. E. of Delhi, and 788 m. N.W. of Calcutta. Of the population there are almost as many Muhammadans as Hindoos. Founded by Barel (whence its name) Deo and Bas Deo in 1557, long a frontier stronghold of Mughul power; ruins of Barel Deo's fort in old town; modern fort overlooks cantonments. Headquarters of Rohilkhand Division and station of the American Methodist Mission. **Aonla** (11,000), old town and railway station, 16 m. S.W. of Bareli, on a branch of the Areel, with fine tomb of Ali Muhammad, the Rohilla leader who died in 1751. **Fatehganj East**, railway station 23 m. S.E. of Bareli, founded by Oudh viceroy, Shooja-ood-Doula, to commemorate British victory of 1774, by which he gained Rohilkhand. **Fatehganj West** ("mart of victory"), village 12 m. N.W. of Bareli, scene of British victory in 1796, with monuments marking the graves of East India Company's troops, and of two Rohilla chiefs. **Bisalpoor** (9500), municipal town, 3 m. E. of Deoha, and 24 E. of Bareli. Ramnagar or Ahichatra (2700), old capital, with great fort, Boodhist topes, and Jain temple, 8 m. from Aonla, mentioned in the *Mahabharat* as capital of north Panchala.

§ 40. PILIBHEET DISTRICT is bounded E. by Oudh district of Kheri and Nepal from which the Sarda divides it, N. by Tarai, W. by Bareli, and S. by Shahjahanpoor. Area, 1350 sq. m. Population, 483,953. The district, like Bareli, is watered by the Deoha and its affluents, of which the Kakra from Tarai is the largest. The Mala to the E. is a morass rather than a river, and is called Katna in its lower course. **Pilibheet** (30,000), on the Deoha, where the Kakra joins it, the two making the town an island when it was fortified. Famous for the fine white rice from Kumaun, which bears its name, and as a mart for the forest produce of Tarai and the hills. Jahanabad, village 27 m. N.E. of Bareli, and forming the ancient mound of Balarkhera, which covers an area of 1200 sq. ft.

§ 41. SHAHJAHANPOOR DISTRICT is bounded E. by Oudh districts of Hardoi and Kheri, N. by Bareli, W. by Bareli and Budaun, and S. by Farukhabad. Area, 1744 sq. m. Population, 949,579. The district, running up from the Ganges towards the Himalaya, is watered by the Goomti, the Khanaut which falls into the Deoha below Shahjahanpoor town, the Garai and the Ramganga, which last is the main waterway navigable to Kola Ghat, whence grain is shipped to the Ganges marts. The district was long the debatable ground between Oudh and Rohilkhand, inclining to the former. In 1857 the Europeans were attacked when in church, three were shot down, and the rest, aided by 100 faithful sepoys, escaped. Lord Clyde's force stopped the anarchy in April 1858. **Shahjahanpoor** (73,000), on left bank of the Deoha, founded during the reign of the emperor whose name it bears. Adjoining is Rosa sugar and rum factory. **Tilhar** (5500), 14 m. W. of Shahjahanpoor railway station, and local entrepot. **Pawayan** (6500), 17 m. N. of Shahjahanpoor. **Jalalabad** (7500), mart opposite Kola Ghat, head of navigation of Ramganga. **Miranpoor Katra** (6700), railway station 20 m. E. of Shahjahanpoor, where, in 1774, the British defeated the Rohillas.

CHAPTER XI.

OUDH SECTION OF NORTH-WESTERN PROVINCE—DISTRICTS.

§ 1. LUCKNOW CITY (261,485), capital after 1732 of the Persian soldier Saadat Khan, and the viceroys and kings of Oudh till 1856, then of a British Province till 1877, and now chief city of the Oudh section of the North-Western Province, called after Lakshman, half-brother and constant companion of Rama, whose capital of Ayodhya was fabled to have reached so far. The modern city covers the sites of 64 villages, an area now of 13 sq. m., the centre of which was Lakshmanpoor on the high ground topped by a mosque, and still known as Lakshman Tela (hill). Under the dissolute court of the Persian Sheeas during the disintegration of the Mughul empire, and even from the British victory of Buxar in 1764 down to annexation in 1856, the city grew in population, wealth, and luxury, till it contained nearly half a million of inhabitants. The Mutiny and the pure administration of British officials have resulted in giving its quarter of a million of citizens the advantages of education, science, and honest work. **Lucknow** is still the fifth city in the Indian Empire as to population, coming next after Calcutta, Bombay, Madras, and Haidarabad. The city lies on the west bank of the Goomti, with suburbs on the E., spanned by four bridges. It is, by railway, 42 m. from Cawnpoor, 80 from Faizabad, 104 from Shahjahanpoor, 199 from Benares, and 610 from Calcutta. It is 403 ft. above the sea. From the Machi Bhawan fort, inclosing Lakshman's hill, three military roads radiate through the city, and three branch out, one across the Goomti, and two along its banks. The abundance of *chunam* plaster, made from shells found in old lake-beds, gives a beauty to the buildings which in design are architecturally base even to vulgarity, but the *tout ensemble* is attractive at a distance. The whole is now redeemed by the greatest ornament of the city, the picturesque eminence which is crowned by the Residency with its memorial cross, and was held by the immortal garrison during the weary hot months of 1857, where Henry Lawrence and 2000 heroic men and women lie. "A magnificent banyan tree, the lofty tower and stately walls of the Residency covered with moon creepers and dense cloaks of dark foliage, rise grandly above the numerous ruins, interspersed with shrubbery, and bright with roses and oleanders. Near at hand is an artificial mound, whose sides are gay with parterres of flowers; and behind, half-hidden by groups of gigantic bamboos, their lofty heads feathering down almost to the ground, lies the graveyard," with its precious dust over which cypresses wave. Henry Lawrence died in the house built for Colonel Bailey's guard, close to the gate of the Residency enclosure, which the siege made famous as the Bailey-guard gate. Other sacred spots, marked by monuments, are that in front of the old Observatory called Tarawalli Kothi, where two parties of English women and other victims of the revolt were massacred, and their Hindoo and Muhammadan murderers were afterwards executed; the place where General Neill fell, advancing to the relief of the Garrison; the tomb of Havelock in the Alambagh garden on the Cawnpoor road. The principal Musalman buildings are the two mosques, the imambara, the four tombs—especially that of Haidar, and the Chatar Manzil and Kaisar Bagh palaces, the latter of which cost £800,000, and is partly in ruins though made over to the Oudh nobles. The Canning College, the Martiniére (for Eurasians), the Church and American Methodist Mission Schools, a convent for girls, and other schools supply education. Brocade in all its varieties, shawls, shoes, jewellery, glass, and clay moulding are the principal native manufactures, but they have declined since the court was driven out. The traffic of Oudh flows south through Lucknow from Bahramghat and Faizabad to Cawnpoor. The cantonments, covering nearly 12 sq. m., lie to the east of the old canal; the British troops generally consist of 3 battalions, 1 cavalry and 2 infantry regiments.

§ 2. LUCKNOW DISTRICT is bounded E. by Barabanki, N. by Seetapoor and Hardoi, W. by Unao, and S. by Rai Bareli. Area, 979 sq. m. Population, 778,195. The **Goomti**, entering from N., passes the capital E. into Barabanki, and receives the Barta and Loni streams on its right bank. The **Sai**, forming the S.W. boundary, runs parallel with the Goomti and receives the Nagwa and Bauk streams. Lucknow is a fertile level district of small proprietors. The Bhars, Passees, and other aborigines were overrun by Rajpoots and the Muhammadan settlers. It is well opened up by three lines of the Oudh and Rohilkhand railway system, extending for 52 miles. Besides Lucknow city only 3 towns contain more than 5000 inhabitants. **Kakori** (8500), old town 9 m. W. of Lucknow, the birthplace of several distinguished Musalman officials; with many tombs. **Malihabad** (8000), railway station, on Lucknow and Sandeela road, the families of which used to supply landholders with Afghan retainers. **Amethi Dungar** (7000), old weaving town 17 m. on road from Lucknow to Seetapoor.

§ 3. BARABANKI DISTRICT is bounded E. by Faizabad, N. by Seetapoor, W. by Lucknow, and S. by Rai Bareli and Sultanpoor. Area, 1768 sq. m. Population, 1,113,430. The district slopes gently seaward to S.E. with lateral inclinations to its main rivers the Gogra and Goomti. The Gogra is known as the Chauka till it meets the Sarjoo at Bahramghat. The **Kalyani** is the main affluent of the Goomti, draining several shallow lakes; between the two lies the most fertile tract. Traces of Naga or serpent and Boodhist worship are found, then of Rajpoot supremacy. At Satrikh, 5 m. S.E. of Barabanki town, the Musalmans first permanently settled in Oudh. The land was always turbulent, especially in the ravines with their strongholds along the Goomti and Kalyani. All the landholders joined the mutineers in 1857, and they sheltered the ex-Queen of Oudh. **Nawabganj-Barabanki** (14,000), 17 m. E. of Lucknow on road to Faizabad, with the stream Jamuriha between the native town Nawabganj and civil and railway station Barabanki. At Nawabganj Sir Hope Grant signally defeated the insurgents in 1857; the victor wrote, "I never witnessed anything more magnificent than the conduct of these zameendars," the Raikwar Rajpoots of Seetapoor and Bahraich. **Rudauli** (12,000), thriving mart 37 m. S.E. of Nawabganj. **Zaidpoor** (11,000), with cloth manufactures. **Fatehpoor** (7500), 14 m. N.E. of Nawabganj, an important place in Musalman days, and still a mart at the junction of four principal roads. **Daryabad** (5000), 24 m. east of Nawabganj on road from Lucknow to Faizabad, the former headquarters of the district.

§ 4. UNAO DISTRICT is bounded E. by Lucknow, N. by Hardoi, S.W. by Cawnpoor and Fatehpoor from which it is divided by the Ganges, and S.E. by Rai Bareli. Area, 1768 sq. m. Population, 945,955. This densely peopled tract is watered by the Sai and Kalyani streams from Hardoi, and by the Tinai and Loni, all draining into the navigable Ganges. The Rajpoots who supplanted the Bhars and Aheers are of two classes, those who accepted Musalman service and those who had fled from Upper India after defeat. The first Musalman invader was the nephew of Mahmood of Ghazni, Salar Masaood, the graves of whose followers in his disastrous march are still pointed out in the district. In July-August 1857 Havelock's small force of 1500 men, of whom 300 were Sikhs, with 10 guns imperfectly equipped and manned, fought several severe battles on his march from Cawnpoor to the relief of the Lucknow garrison, especially at **Unao** and **Bashiratganj**; his fortified camp was at **Mangalwar**, 6 miles from the Ganges at Cawnpoor. **Unao** (5500), chief town and railway station 9 m. N.E. of Cawnpoor, where Havelock gained his first victory on 29th July 1857. **Safipoor** (6750), 17 m. N.W. of **Unao**, on road to Hardoi. In 1425 the place was taken by the Zaidi Sayyids of Wasia, from whom the most important families in Upper India, the Barhah and Bilgram Sayyids, are descended. **Banjarmau** (8000), on same road, 31 m. from Unao, with 16 mosques; the ruins of old Hindoo village Newar are near. **Purwa** (10,000), 20 m. S.E. of Unao, formerly chief town, noted for shoe and leather work. **Mauranwan** (8000), 6 m. from Purwa, noted for jewellery and carpentry work.

§ 5. Rai Bareli District is bounded E. by Partabgarh and Sultanpoor, N. by Barabanki and Lucknow, W. by Unao, and S.W. by Fatehpoor from which the Ganges separates it. Area, 1740 sq. m. Population, 989,008. Named after the Bhars (Bharauli), this is one of the most beautifully wooded and fertile parts of the plain of Hindustan. It is divided into zones between the Ganges and Goomti by the Sai and the Loni. Brahmans form the bulk of the population. **Rai Bareli** (12,000), chief town on Sai, 48 m. S.E. of Lucknow, with suburb of Jahanabad. Here are the five forts of Ibrahim Sharki of Jaunpoor, who conquered the Bhars; the palace and tomb of Jahan Khan, Aurangzeb's governor, and four mosques, of which one is said to be a reproduction of that of the Kaaba at Mecca; the American Methodists have a mission here, as at other large towns in Oudh. **Jais** (12,000), old Musalman town, 36 m. from Sultanpoor, picturesquely built in mango groves. **Dalman** (6000), on right bank of Ganges, 16 m. S. of **Rai Bareli**, where Musalmans destroyed the Bhars. **Salon** (5000), decaying town on road to Partabgarh, in groves of mangoes and palms.

§ 6. SULTANPOOR DISTRICT is bounded E. by Jaunpoor, N. by Faizabad, W. by Rai Bareli, and S. by Partabgarh. Area, 1707 sq. m. Population, 1,040,227. A level land cut by ravines and watered by the Goomti and Sai. The main streams are the Khandu, Pili, Tengha, and Nandhia. The Bhars gave place to the Musalmans successively of the Ghori, Jaunpoor, and Mughul houses, and the Nawab Wazeers of Oudh. In 1857 three sepoy corps murdered some of their officers. **Sultanpoor** (6000), on right bank of Goomti, opposite site of Kusapoora, founded by Koosa, son of Rama, razed to the ground in Mutiny, then a cantonment, and now civil headquarters only. **Perkinsganj** (5000), named after first deputy commissioner, a rising mart near right bank of Goomti. **Amethi**, S.W. from Sultanpoor, residence and fort of the Raja Madho Singh, who saved Europeans in 1857. The Raja is head of the Bandalghoti solar clan, which occupies 299 sq. m. Of the population of 538 to the mile so many as 17 per cent are Brahmans.

§ 7. PARTABGARH DISTRICT is bounded E. and S. by Jaunpoor, N. by Rai Bareli and Sultanpoor, and W. by Allahabad. Area, 1434 sq. m. Population, 784,156. The Sai flows through the district, receiving small tributaries, and is navigable in the rains. The Ganges marks its W. and the Goomti touches its E. border. **Bela** (3000) and **M'Andrewganj**, civil headquarters, on road from Allahabad to Faizabad, with bridge over the Sai. **Partabgarh** (12,000 in municipality), 4 m. S. of Bela, with fort of its founder in 1617, Raja Partab Singh. **Manikpoor**, old ruined town, with historic associations, in groves on N. bank of Ganges; famous for residence of nobility from Akbar and Aurangzeb.

§ 8. FAIZABAD DISTRICT is bounded E. by Gorakhpoor, N. by Basti and Gonda from which it is divided by the Gogra, W. by Barabanki, and S. by Sultanpoor and Azamgarh. Area, 1688 sq. m. Population, 1,024,652. The Gogra, which forms the N. border for 95 m., is navigable even by steamers. The other rivers are the Bisoi and Madha, forming the Tons, and the Majhoi, which divides Faizabad from Sultanpoor. The Tons is navigable in the rains to Akbarpoor by 5-ton boats. The district is well watered, most fertile, and densely peopled. It contests with Tirhoot the honour of having given birth to Gautama Boodha; is, next to Pooree and Hardwar, the most frequented pilgrim place, as the birthplace of Ram; was devastated by Mahmood's general, Salar Masaood, in 1030 A.D., so that the peasants still believe a part of the high road to be crowded by the spirits of his headless troopers; and was the headquarters for a time of the Oudh viceroys. In 1857 the sepoys mutinied, but allowed the Europeans to flee to Gorakhpoor, and one Musalman landholder sheltered some of the fugitives in his fort. **Faizabad** (39,000), chief town on left bank of Gogra, 78 m. E. of Lucknow, forming, with the modern Ajodhya, one municipality, and built with that on the site of the ancient Ajodhya. The town was the provincial capital till, in 1780, the viceroy removed to Lucknow. Now frontier military station towards Nepal. The famous Bahu Begam's Dilkoosha palace, part of which was known as "the residence with the thousand doors," is now the Government opium factory. **Ajodhya** = "the unconquerable city of the creator," or "the city of the fighting Chattris," according to Dr. Wilson of Bombay, now part of Faizabad on the right bank of the Gogra, is frequented by at least half a million of pilgrims annually for the great fair of Ramnami, since the remarkable revival of Rama-worship 150 years ago, ascribed to the intolerance of Aurangzeb, the success of the Marathas, and the translation of the *Ramayana* epic into the vernaculars. The old city, now marked by ruins covered with jungle, which occupied 96 sq. m., was the capital of Uttar-Kausala or Kosala ("the northern treasure"), of the Soorajbans or solar race of kings, of whom Ram Chandar, the 8th *avatar* of Vishnoo, was the 57th. Since Raja Sumintra, the 113th and last, members of the oldest royal house on earth (out of Judaism) founded the comparatively modern Rajpoot sovereignties of Oodaipoor and Jaipoor. After the fall of the house of Dasaratha, Rama's father, Ajodhya's first revival took place under King Vikramaditya (57 A.D.). Baber and Aurangzeb erected three mosques, now in ruins, from the Janmasthan, a spot where the hero-king of the Hindoos was born; the Swargadwara, where his body was buried, and the Tareta-ka-Thakoor, where he offered his great sacrifice. In modern Ajodhya the resident population is under 8000; there are 63 Vishnoo and 33 Shiva temples, and 36 mosques. **Tanda** (14,000), near the Gogra, on the Faizabad and Azamgarh road, famous for cottons like those of Dacca. Jalalpoor-nahvi (6500), on the Tons, 52 m. from Faizabad, a weaving town. Singhauli (5500), on the Tons, opposite Akbarpoor, 36 m. from Faizabad.

§ 9. GONDA DISTRICT (the Gond or, perhaps, Gaur country) is bounded E. by Basti, N. by the crest of the lower Himalaya, dividing it from Nepal, W. by Bahraich, and S. by Barabanki and Faizabad from which it is separated by the Gogra. Area, 2881 sq. m. Population, 1,168,462. The district is like a vast English park studded with groves in pasture grounds, from which Dhawalagiri peak is clearly seen. It is watered by these chief rivers flowing from N.W. to S.E., the Bun Rapti, **Rapti**, Suwawan, Kuwana, Bisoohi, Chamnai, Manwar, Tirhi, Sarjoo, and Gogra. A belt of state forest skirts the base of the hills. Here was the kingdom of Sravasti, founded by Lava, son of the hero-king Rama; of Prasmaditya (6th century B.C.), who invited Boodha to Sravasti, and of the intolerant Brahmanist, Vikramaditya. The Musalman invasion of Mahmood's nephew was repelled by a Jain sovereign, Sohildeo, which gave place to a casteless Dom dynasty, of whom Ugrasen had a fort at Domriadhi. This was supplanted by the Rajpoot clans, Kalhausees, Janwaris, and Bisens, till the Oudh Nawabs enforced a semi-sovereignty, and their revenue officers exacted from the people till the British annexation in 1856 relieved the country. In 1857 the Raja of Gonda refused to submit, and the Raja of Balrampoor was actively loyal. **Gonda** (14,000), chief town, 28 m. N.W. of Faizabad, famous under native rule for the manufacture of shields; the Raja's palace is decaying. **Balrampoor** (14,500), largest town, on N. bank of Suwawan, 28 m. from Gonda. Residence of the Maharaja of Balrampoor, wealthiest of the Talookdars, with imposing palace. **Colonelganj** (10,000), rice and oil-seed mart between Gonda, Bahraich, and Barampoor, 2 m. N. of Sarjoo; headquarters of district in 1857. **Nawabganj** (6500), mart N. of Gogra, exporting to Patna and Cawnpoor. **Utraula** (6000), 3 m. S. of Rapti, with ruins of Rajpoot fort, tombs, and fine groves of Afghan conqueror's family. **Sahet Mahet**, fort and vast ruins, on S. bank of Rapti 10 m. from Balrampoor, marking Sravasti founded by Sravastu, 9th of the solar race from Manu, capital of Uttar Kusala, N. province of Rama's empire, and, in 6th century B.C., one of the six kingdoms of Madhyadesa or Central Hindustan. **Debi Patan**, village with temples in the aboriginal tract under the hills, one of the oldest seats of Shiva-worship and scene of a great fair.

§ 10. BAHRAICH DISTRICT (so named from the aboriginal Bhars, or from Brahm-aich = the "assembly of Brahma," who is said to have settled priests there) is bounded E. by Gonda, N. by Nepal for 80 m. parallel with the trend of the Himalaya, W. by Kheri and Seetapoor, and S. by Barabanki and Gonda. Area, 2740 sq. m. Population, 774,640. The watershed consists of a strip of elevated land running S.E. between the Gogra and the Rapti. The Gogra, which is called **Kaurlala** till it receives the Sarjoo, enters the district from the Nepal tarai at the N.E., where it is joined by the Mohan, and soon after by the

Girwa. The Sarjoo enters 22 m. E. and falls into the Kauriala at Katai ghat, having been turned into its present channel by a European timber-merchant. The Rapti enters the district from Nepal, at Sidania ghat, midway on the frontier line, and, after a course of 81 miles, passes into Gonda; it receives the Bhakla or Singhia above Sahet Mahet. The history of the district is identified with that of Gonda; but it was more terribly oppressed by the native tax-farmers before annexation than even Gonda. **Bahraich** (22,000), chief town on old Gogra bed, on road from Bahramghat to Nepalganj; the iron mart of Nepal. Here Mahmood's general, Masaood, was defeated by the Rajpoot confederacy, 1033 A.D., and slain; his shrine is the centre of an annual fair and pilgrimage of both Musalmans and Hindoos. Here the American E. Methodists have a mission. **Nanpara** (7000), 22 m. N. of Bahraich, a municipal town on Nepalganj road. Jarwal (5000), principal market of Hisampoor parganah, in S. Bhinga (4500), chief village of parganah of same name in N., on left bank of the Rapti.

§ 11. KHERI DISTRICT is bounded E. by Bahraich from which the Kauriala (Gogra) separates it; N. by Nepal, with the Mohan between; W. by Shahjahanpoor, with the river Sukheta; and S. by Seetapoor. Area, 2993 sq. m. Population, 738,089. The district consists of plateaux separated from each other by the following rivers, beginning E.—the Kauriala, Suheli, Dahawar, **Chauka**, Ul, Jamwari, Kathnu, Goomti, and Sukheta. The land N. of the Ul consists of unhealthy *tarai* and magnificent forests. In the old beds of the rivers are several large lakes surrounded by groves. After annexation in 1856, Kheri was in two districts, Muhamdi and Mallapoor; in 1837 the European officers in the former were massacred; those of the latter fled to the Nepal jungles, where fever cut them off. **Lakhimpoor** (7700), headquarters of district, picturesquely situated 1 m. S. of the Ul; the bazaar is Thurburnganj, built by deputy commissioner of that name. **Kheri** (5500), the only town in district, in lat. 27° 54′ N. and long. 80° 57′ E. **Muhamdi** (5000), 3 m. W. of the Goomti on road from Lakhimpoor to Shahjahanpoor; there are no brick-built houses, owing to a superstition of the people. The Hindoo village of Balimar Barkhar, 4 m. from W. bank of the Goomti, with extensive ruins, is popularly believed to have been the city of Raja Bairat, with whom the five Pandavas lived in the thirteenth year of their exile. Oel (3000), 8 m. S. of Lakhimpoor.

§ 12. SEETAPOOR DISTRICT is bounded E. by Bahraich, with the Gogra between; N. by Kheri; W. and S. by Hardoi,

Lucknow, and Barabanki, from which it is separated by the Goomti. Area, 2215 sq. m. Population, 932,959. A low ridge running parallel to the Gogra and Chauka rivers from N. divides this well-cultivated district. The Chauka, 8 m. to W. of the Gogra, joins it at Bahramghat in Barabanki. The principal cross streams connecting the two are, going W., the Gon, Oel, Kewani, Sarayan, and Goomti; the Gogra alone is navigable. In 1857 the sepoys in Seetapoor cantonments mutinied and murdered several officers and their families; on 13th April 1858 Sir Hope Grant routed the rebels near **Biswan.** **Seetapoor** (6000), chief town and cantonment on the Sarayan, half-way between Lucknow and Shahjahanpoor, among picturesque mango groves. **Khairabad** (16,000), largest town, 5 m. S.E. of Seetapoor, with 40 mosques and 30 Hindoo temples. **Laharpoor** (11,000), 17 m. N. of Seetapoor, on road to Mallapoor on Gogra. **Biswan** (7500), including Jalalpoor, 21 m. E. of Seetapoor, on road to Gonda and Faizabad. **Mahmoodabad** (6500), on road from Seetapoor to Bahramghat. **Paintepoor** (6000), rising town 3 m. W. of same road.

§ 13. HARDOI DISTRICT (named from Harnakas, a Thathera chief, or Hardeo, a devotee) is bounded E. by Seetapoor from which the Goomti separates it; N. by Kheri and Shahjahanpoor; W. by Farukhabad, with the Ganges between; and S. by Unao and Lucknow. Area, 2300 sq. m. Population, 932,322. This district, of the size of Perthshire, was, till annexation in 1856, the border land (1) between the rival Mughul and Afghan empires, as commanding the Ganges fords near Kanauj; (2) between the Rohilla Afghans and Oudh viceroys. From the Goomti (490 ft.) the country falls W. into the central plain of the Sai, with the Barta between. The rivers going W. are then the Sukheta, Garia, Ramganga, and Ganges, the three last of which are navigable. Of several lakes Sandi is the largest. **Hardoi** (7500), civil headquarters and railway station on Oudh and Rohilkhand Railway, 63 m. from Lucknow and 39 from Shahjahanpoor. **Shahabad** (18,000), on same road, 15 m. from Shahjahanpoor, formerly a great city. **Sandeela** (16,000), railway station, 32 m. N.W. of Lucknow, old capital of a Passee kingdom; the scene of two battles in Sepoy War, October 1858. **Bilgram** (12,000), near left bank of old Ganges, 15 m. S. of Hardoi, on the mound where Krishna's brother, Balaram, is believed to have slain the demon Bil. **Mallanwari** (12,000), former headquarters of the district, 21 m. S. of Hardoi. **Sandi** (11,000), on left bank of the

Garra, with cotton and carpet manufactures; an opium station. **Pihani** (7500), decaying town on Seetapoor and Shahjahanpoor road, with tomb of Sadi Jahan, Akbar's chancellor. **Gopamau** (6000), 2 m. W. of Goomti and 14 m. E. of Hardoi, the earliest of Masaood's conquests in Oudh, where *arsees* or thumb-mirrors of silver are made.

CHAPTER XII.

THE PROVINCE OF THE PANJAB—GENERAL.

§ 1. Name, Size, and Position. § 2. Rivers. § 3. Canals and Railways. § 4. Products and Trade. § 5. Land Tenures and Taxation. § 6. People and Districts.

§ 1. NAME, SIZE, AND POSITION.—The **Panjab Province** ("five waters"), the largest in extent, and in a military and political sense the most important of the Twelve Provinces, has been the highway of all the invaders of India, from the Aryan tribes of Iran, more than 1750 B.C., to the last Afghan raid of Ahmed Shah, about the same date after Christ, until the advance of the traders and troops of the British East India Company from the sea gave peace and prosperity to the whole land for the first time. This Lieutenant-Governorship alone is larger than the German Empire, is considerably larger than France, and falls little short of Austria-Hungary in area, with an extreme length of 800 miles from N. to S., and breadth of 650 miles. The Panjab, its Districts and States, leaving out Baloochistan, includes all India north of Rajpootana to Sind, between the Jumna on the E. and the Sulaiman mountains on the W., or between 27° 39′ and 36° 39′ N. lat., and between 69° 35′ and 80° E. long. The Province consists of 32 Districts, with an area of 107,010 sq. m. and a population of 18,842,264; and of 36 States, largely hilly and desert, with an area of 114,739 sq. m. and a population of 3,861,683. The area of the whole 68 Districts and States is thus 221,749 sq. m., and the population 22,703,947. Including 8153 troops in the Khaibar when the census of 1881 was taken, but excluding the population of the Hazara district and of the Lahaul and Spiti glens of the Kangra district, the whole population may be stated at 23 millions. The area of Kashmeer State, if accurately surveyed, would certainly raise the total extent of the Native States much higher.

This vast Province is bounded on the E. by the N.W. Province from which the Jumna divides it, and the Chinese tracts of Gartok and Rudok; on the N. by the Chinese Province of E. Toorkestan or Khotan, Yarkand, and Kashgaria, with the Kuenlun and the Karakoram ranges of the W. Himalaya between; on the N.W. by Chilas, Swat, and Pathan tribes dependent on Kabul; on the W. by the Pathan and Balooch tribes of the Sulaiman mountains, Afghanistan, and Baloochistan; and on the S. by Sind and Rajpootana. Sir C. U. Aitchison (*Treaties*) describes the North-Western Frontier line in 1876 as commencing from the head of the Khagan valley in Hazara district, whence it passes round the N.W. boundary of Hazara and along the left bank of the Indus to Torbaila, where it crosses the river and winds round the N. and N.W. boundary of the Peshawar valley to the Khaibar Pass. Leaving the Khaibar Pass it skirts the Afreedee hills as far as Kohat, and passes round the W. boundary of that district and along the Meeranzai valley. The Frontier then passes round the Wazeeree hills to Bannoo and the head of the Sulaiman range, thence down the base of this range to its termination on the upper confines of Sind and Khelat. On its outer side dwell a number of independent tribes, with about 170,000 fighting men.

§ 2. MOUNTAINS AND RIVERS.—The mountains and elevated tracts consist of (1) on E. and N. the **Western** or **Tibeto-Himalaya**, including the secondary formations of Spiti and the Kuenlun and Karakoram ranges; (2) The **Siwalik** and other subordinate groups running parallel to the Himalaya; (3) the **Salt Range** and the geologically related hills of Kalabagh, Shekh Budeen, and Balut; (4) on W. the **Sulaiman Range**; and (5) on S. the low sandstone outliers of the Aravali hills of Rajpootana in the Delhi and Goorgaon districts. From the Tibeto-Himalaya plateaux and snowy ranges, the Panjab plain slopes gently S.W. to the desert tableland of Rajpootana and Sind. As constituted since the Mutiny of 1857, the Province consists of seven great alluvial tracts, of which five are *doabs* ("two waters"), between the rivers which bring down the melted snows of the hills or catch the somewhat scanty rainfall. Beginning from the N.W. the (1) **Derajat** is a long and narrow strip between the Sulaiman and the Indus; (2) the **Sind Sagar Doab** lies between the Indus and the Jhelam; (3) the **Jetch** or **Chaj Doab** is between the Jhelam and Chenab; (4) the **Rechna Doab** is between the Chenab and the Ravi; (5) the **Bari Doab**, the most populous, lies between the Ravi and Beas; (6) the **Jalandhar Doab** is between the Beas and the Satlej; (7) the **Cis-**

Satlej and Delhi Districts stretch between the Satlej and the Jumna, and, as geographically outside the Panjab tract though like it in other respects, were part of the N.W. Province till the close of the Mutiny of 1857. Of these the Jalandhar is the smallest and most fertile doab. In all the seven, vegetation is most luxuriant in the submontane regions. Lower down, the rivers regulate the character of the soil, from the immediately adjoining lands fertilised by silt and inundations, though sometimes wasted by sand, to the high central tract that, as in the Bari, Rechna, and Jetch Doabs, is marked by *bar* or uncultivated soil covered with brushwood and stunted trees, used as fuel preserves and pasture; or, as in the Sind Sagar Doab, by *thal*, an undulating desert of sand.

The principal river is the **Indus**, the Sindh or Abba Sinh ("father of rivers") of the people, also the Atak of the Hindoos to go beyond which is to sin; also the Sintaw of the Chinese, of which Moore writes—"From the fair Sind or Attock's sacred banks." Issuing from the lion's mouth, whence its name Sinh-ka-bab, on the N. slope of Kailas, the Parnassus of the Hindoos, it crosses the E. border of Kashmeer after a N.W. course of 160 miles, during which it receives the Gar and Shaiok from Ladak. At Skardoh in Baltestan it bursts through the W. Himalaya by a gorge said to be 14,088 ft. deep, and enters the district of Hazara near Ghazee, between rocky banks, whence it emerges into the open plains dividing Yoosufzai and Chuch, where it becomes a mile broad with islands. At Atak it has run 860 miles, and thence to the sea its navigable portion is 942 m., a total length of 1802 m., in which it falls 20 ft. above Atak, 20 inches in 110 m. from Atak to Kalabagh, 8 inches thence 350 m. to Mithankot, and 6 inches onwards for 490 m. to the Arabian Sea. The basin drains 372,700 sq. m. It is the third of the rivers of N. India, next to the Ganges and Brahmapootra. Between the Indus and Jumna run the five rivers which give the Province its name. Next to the Indus, going S.E., is the **Jhelam**, the Sanskrit *Vitasta* or Bitasta, the Bidaspes of Ptolemy and Hydaspes of Alexander's annalists. Rising in the N.E. border of the Kashmeer valley, and receiving the Peer Panjal drainage, it forms the lakes of Srinagar, emerges by the Baramoola pass after a course of 170 m. of which 70 are navigable with a breadth of 420 ft., then receives the Kishn Ganga from Baltestan, marks off Kashmeer from Hazara to Rawal Pindi where it ceases to be navigable, becomes again navigable below Dangalli, 40 m. E. of Pindi, skirts the Salt Range in the district to which it gives its name, and, after 250

m. from the source, it enters the plains above Jhelam town. Dividing Jhelam district from Goojrat and Shahpoor, it turns S. into Jhang, and forms the Chenab at Timmoo Ghat, 10 m. S. of Maghiana, after a course of 450 m. The **Chenab**, from Kashmeer, enters Sialkot near Khairi Rihal village, receives the Tavi, forms the boundary between Sialkot and Goojrat and the W. border of Goojranwala, enters Jhang, unites with the Jhelam at Timmoo, receives the Ravi half-way down to Mooltan, and flows under the name *Trinab* to the Satlej, 50 m. above Mithankot. The Chenab is formed of the Chandra from Lahaul on the S.E. slopes of the Baralacha pass, and the Baghi, which joins it at Tandi, whence the name Chandrabagh, which the Greeks, fearing to Hellenise it into Sandrophagos = Alexandrophagos, of evil omen, called Akesines. The **Ravi**, the Hydraotes of Quintus Curtius, and both names from the Sanskrit *Iravati*, from Koolloo, passes through Chamba State S.W., forms the border of Goordaspoor, at Madhoopoor sends off the Bari Doab Canal, passes between Sialkot and Amritsar, leaves Lahore city a mile to the left, receives the Degh in Montgomery, passes into Mooltan, and then joins the Chenab after a course of 450 miles, 50 m. above Mooltan town. The **Beas** (the Sanskrit *Vipasa*, and Greek Hyphasis according to some), the sixth and smallest of the Panjab rivers, having a course of 290 m., rises in Koolloo, passes through Mandi State into Kangra at Sanghol, marks that district off from Hoshiarpoor, bends round the Siwalik, divides Hoshiarpoor from Goordaspoor, touches Jalandhar, and joins the Satlej at S. boundary of Kapoorthala State, at Hareeki above Firozpoor. The **Satlej** (generally considered the *Vipasa* or Hyphasis, also named Satadru, and Greek Sydrus or Hesidrus) rises on the slopes of the Kailas, the centre of the Indus and Brahmapootra head-waters, issues from the Rakas-tal or lake (15,200 ft.), crosses Guge plain, turns S. at Shipki, the frontier Chinese post, pierces the Himalaya to Rampoor N. of Simla, where it has fallen 3000 ft., receives the Spiti near Dablang, flows S.W. through the Simla States into Hoshiarpoor, turns S. round the Siwalik to the plains at Roopar, divides Hoshiarpoor from Ambala, and Jalandhar on the N. from Ambala, Lodiana, and Firozpoor, receives the Beas when the two united waters flow on to the three known as the Trinab, and the five form the **Panjnad** ("five streams"), which, after a course of 60 m. separating Muzaffargarh from Bahawalpoor, joins the Indus opposite Mithankot. The minor rivers are described in their respective districts hereafter, the **Kabul** and **Swat** in Peshawar, the

Kooram and **Looni** in Dera Ghazi Khan, the **Sohan** in Rawal Pindi, the **Saraswati** in Ambala and Karnal, and the **Markanda** and **Ghagar**, which, from Ambala, lose themselves in the Rajpootana desert.

§ 3. CANALS AND RAILWAYS.—The irrigating canals on the Panjab are the **Bari Doab Canal**; the **Western Jumna Canal**; the **Upper Satlej Inundation Canals**; the **Lower Satlej** and **Chenab Inundation Canals** in Mooltan district; the **Muzaffargarh Inundation Canals** from the Chenab, and the **Dera Ghazi Khan Inundation Canals** from the Indus. The **Sirhind Canal** from the Satlej at Roopar has just been opened; the **Swat River Canal** is under construction. The Bari Doab Canal leaves the Ravi at Madhoopoor, the main line runs for 247 m.; after sending off branches to Lahore, Kasoor, and Sobraon, it passes through Amritsar, and, crossing the Sind, Panjab, and Delhi Railway at Changamunga station, it again empties itself into the Ravi. The **Sind, Panjab,** and **Delhi Railway** (guaranteed); the **Panjab Northern** and **Indus Valley** (State) and the **Rajpootana** (58 m. only) open up the Province in all directions from Rewari and Delhi to Lahore and Peshawar in N., and from Lahore to Mooltan, Bahawalpoor, and Karachi S.W., and to Sibi towards Kandahar. There are above 700 m. of railway, 22,000 of road, and 2700 of water communications in the Province.

§ 4. PRODUCTS AND TRADE.—Rock salt, constituting the bulk of the Salt Range, on its S. slopes, is annually quarried to the value of half a million sterling. Slate, plumbago, and sulphur are worked to a profit in the Kangra and Chamba hills, Goorgaon and the Salt Range. Of metallic products, iron, antimony, and lead are found in Simla and Kashmeer States. Gold is washed for in the Indus at Kalabagh, and in the Bunhar river at the other end of the Salt Range, the present source being the tertiary sandstone formation. With a rainfall of 30 inches the Province has 12 millions of acres under spring crops, and 9 millions under autumn. The spring crops are chiefly wheat, barley, and gram (pea); the autumn crops are millets, maize, pulses, and sugar-cane. Of 6858 sq. m. of forest 3791 are reserved, of which 336 have been declared so under the Act. Less than one-third of the district area of 107,010 sq. m. is cultivated, while one-fourth is culturable and the remainder is barren waste. Of 11,622,036 acres cultivated in the spring of 1880-81 the number of millions under wheat was 6½, barley 2, gram and peas 2. There were 10,000 acres under tea; 11,000, poppy; and 79,000, tobacco. Of 10,376,342 acres of autumn cultivation, 4 millions were of millets, $1\frac{1}{2}$ of maize, $1\frac{1}{2}$ of pulses, nearly 1 of rice, nearly 1 of cotton and oil-seeds, one-third of sugar-cane, and 73,000 acres of indigo. The manufactures of the Province are estimated in annual value at $8\frac{1}{2}$ millions sterling, of which $2\frac{2}{3}$ are in cotton, $1\frac{1}{2}$ in gold and silver and jewel-work, and 1 million in leather. The inland trade is valued at upwards of 9 millions sterling in imports and 6 in exports. The exports to Kashmeer and Central Asia are valued at a million and a quarter sterling, and the imports at one-third less. The annual out-turn of manufactures of cotton, jewellery, leather, wood, silk, wool, etc., is estimated at £12,495,546 in value. There are 485 large factories, chiefly in Amritsar district, for wood, shawls, iron, oil, and silk.

§ 5. LAND TENURES AND TAXATION.—Under the Lawrences and officials of the school of R. M. Bird, the land system of the N.W. Province was introduced into the Panjab from its conquest in March 1849. But in the Panjab the old village communities are more perfect and numerous than in the older Province. Thus the great mass of the landed property in the Panjab is held by small proprietors, who cultivate their own land in whole or in part. The village communities have to a greater or less extent joint interests, and, under the British system of cash payments limited to secure a certain profit to the proprietors, are jointly responsible for the payment of the revenue. In some cases all the village land is in common, but it is much more usual for the proprietors to have their own separate holdings in the estate, and this separation may extend so far that there is no land susceptible of separate appropriation which is not the separate property of an individual or family. In an extreme case like this the right of pre-emption and the joint responsibility for the revenue, in case any of the individual proprietors should fail to meet the demand upon him, are almost the only ties which bind the community together. The separation, however, generally does not go so far. Often all the cultivated land is held in separate ownership, while the pasture, ponds or tanks, etc., remain in common. Trans-Indus, however, in the tracts of country inhabited chiefly by a Pathan population, periodical redistribution of holdings is by no means uncommon. Since the country came under British rule, every opportunity has been taken to get rid of periodical exchanges on a large scale by substituting final partitions or by adjusting the revenue demand according to the value of the lands actually held by each village; but the custom is in many cases still acted upon amongst the proprietors of the same village, though probably no cases remain in which it would be enforced between the proprietors of distinct villages. The relations of landlord and tenant are regulated by the Panjab Tenancy Act of 1868. One-fifth of the Province belongs directly to the State, but that is chiefly barren or in grass and wood. One-eighth of the whole land revenue is still assigned to the descendants of the old native families. In 1880-81, of the gross revenue of £2,726,455, exclusive of a quarter of a million from canals the land-tax yielded £1,901,615.

Nature of Settlement, 1880-81.	Area in Miles.	Annual Revenue assessed.
		Rs.
Settled in perpetuity	1,636	25,713
Settled for 30 years and upwards .	26,802	74,83,114
Settled for 10 years and under 30 .	53,256	93,01,816
Settled for under 10 years . .	60	22,264
Settlements in progress . . .	25,103	53,02,918
Total	106,857	2,21,35,825

§ 6. The People and Districts.—The second census of the Panjab, taken in February 1881, with the exception of Kashmeer recently desolated by famine, showed an increase at the rate of 7 per cent in 12 years.

Populations of 1868 and 1881 compared.

Divisions and States.	1868.	1881.	Percentage of Increase or Decrease since 1868.	
			Inc.	Dec.
Delhi Division	1,928,596	1,907,984	...	1·1
Hissar ,, ...	1,226,594	1,311,067	6·9	...
Ambala ,, ...	1,647,960	1,729,043	4·9	...
Jalandhar ,, ...	2,475,999	2,421,781	...	2·2
Amritsar ,, ...	2,743,659	2,729,109	...	0·5
Lahore ,, ...	1,888,945	2,191,517	16·0	
Rawal Pindi ,, ...	2,197,041	2,520,508	14·7	
Mooltan ,, ...	1,477,936	1,712,394	15·9	
Derajat ,, ...	988,897	1,137,572	15·0	
Peshawar ,, ...	1,033,891	1,181,289	14·3	
Khaibar Pass	...	8,173	...	
Total British Territory	17,609,518	18,850,437	7·06	
Total Native States .	...	3,861,683		
Total of Province .	...	22,712,120		

No trustworthy figures exist for the former population of the 36 Native States.

The nearly 19 millions in the districts occupied 2,716,914 houses or huts. Of the whole 10,202,083 were males, and 8,640,181 females. The average density was 175 to the square mile, varying from 497 in Jalandhar, 567 in Amritsar, and 504 in Delhi, to 48 in Dera Ismail Khan and 64 in Kohat. As to creed, 32,500 are returned as Christian; 112,260, Sikh; 7,127,489, Hindoos; 10,522,802, Muhammadan; and 71,713 of "other religions." Of the Christians, 26,876 appear as Europeans, 1821 as Eurasians, and 3823 as Natives. Oordoo and Hindee are the prevailing languages in the districts adjoining the North-Western Province, and Panjabee and Oordoo in the central districts; Pashtoo (Afghan) and Baloochee, Paharee (hill) and Lahaulee are spoken on the frontier.

CIVIL DIVISIONS OF THE PANJAB PROVINCE, 1880-81.

The Lieutenant-Governorship of the Panjab and its Dependencies was constituted on 1st January 1859.

Divisions.	Districts.	Judicial and Revenue Subdivisions.	Area in Square Miles.	Population, 1881.	Number of Villages.	Revenue.	
						Gross.	Land.
						Rs.	Rs.
Delhi	Delhi	3	1,258	643,515	808	11,56,863	7,55,145
	Goorgaon	5	1,938	641,848	1,264	13,68,454	12,41,674
	Karnal	3	2,396	622,621	922	7,64,793	5,87,581
Hissar	Hissar	5	3,540	504,183	658	5,08,443	4,24,237
	Rohtak	4	1,811	553,609	507	11,09,169	9,42,606
	Sirsa	3	3,116	253,275	659	2,21,870	1,72,411
Ambala	Ambala	6	2,570	1,067,263	2,310	11,10,701	7,82,621
	Lodiana	3	1,375	618,835	880	10,22,277	7,80,736
	Simla	3	18	42,945	270	1,43,563	13,592
Jalandhar	Jalandhar	4	1,322	789,555	1,272	17,65,270	12,11,588
	Hoshiarpoor	4	2,180	901,381	2,182	15,81,662	12,50,191
	Kangra	5	8,989	730,845	665	8,70,626	6,13,220
Amritsar	Amritsar	3	1,573	893,266	1,074	12,78,624	7,93,595
	Goordaspoor	5	1,822	823,695	2,355	13,67,050	10,46,777
	Sialkot	5	1,958	1,012,148	2,522	14,10,893	11,01,389
Lahore	Lahore	4	3,648	924,106	1,512	11,57,499	5,62,991
	Goojranwala	3	2,587	616,892	1,217	6,82,291	4,91,891
	Firozpoor	4	2,744	650,519	1,319	7,34,013	5,13,099
RawalPindi	Rawal Pindi	7	6,218	820,512	1,668	10,28,465	6,85,091
	Jhelam	4	3,910	589,373	976	9,70,404	6,91,217
	Goojrat	3	1,973	689,115	1,428	7,51,352	5,84,652
	Shahpoor	3	4,691	421,508	667	5,49,686	3,78,710
Mooltan	Mooltan	5	5,880	551,964	1,212	9,71,928	5,65,189
	Jhang	3	5,702	395,296	791	6,25,710	2,66,527
	Montgomery	4	5,574	426,529	2,279	5,81,571	2,75,512
	Muzaffargarh	3	3,186	338,605	722	6,90,694	4,12,011
Derajat	D. I. Khan	5	9,296	441,649	839	6,02,861	1,75,422
	D. G. Khan	4	4,577	363,346	672	4,93,767	3,37,658
	Bannoo	4	3,861	332,577	488	4,75,658	3,05,956
Peshawar	Peshawar	6	2,504	592,674	654	9,71,652	6,82,661
	Hazara	3	2,835	407,075	886	2,90,021	2,23,061
	Kohat	2	2,838	181,540	343	1,55,172	98,576
	Total	128	107,010	18,842,264	36,021	2,72,64,548	1,90,16,147

PANJAB PROVINCE,

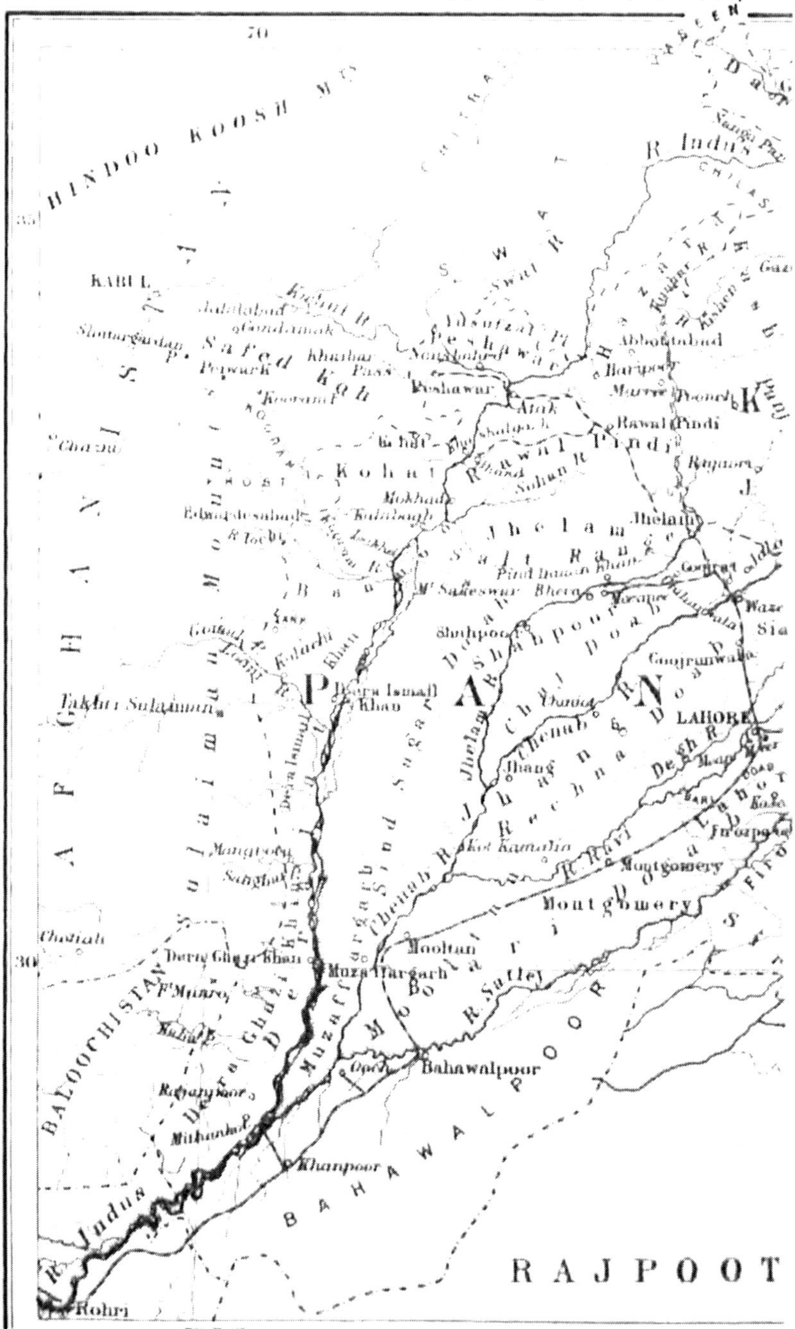

WITH FRONTIER STATES.

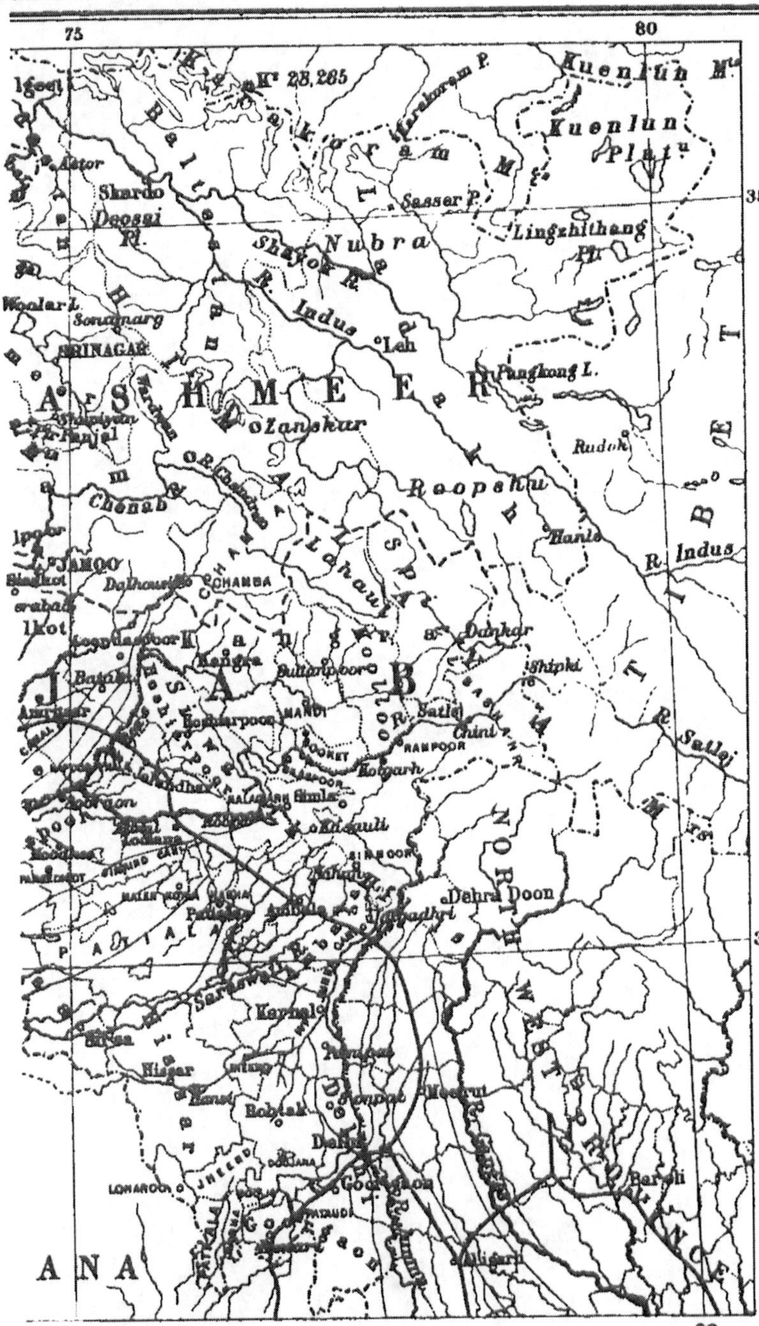

Stanford's Geog^l Estab^t

CHAPTER XIII.

PROVINCE OF THE PANJAB—DISTRICTS AND STATES.

South-Eastern Districts and States.

§ 1. Lahore City. § 2. Lahore District. § 3. Goojranwala. § 4. Firozpoor. § 5. *Fareedkot State. § 6. Amritsar. § 7. Sialkot. § 8. Goordaspoor. § 9. Jalandhar. § 10. *Kapoorthala, Mandi, and Sooket States. § 11. Hoshiarpoor. § 12. Kangra. § 13. *Chamba State. § 14. Simla. § 15. *Twenty Simla States, Maler Kotla and Kalsia. § 16. Lodiana. § 17. Ambala. § 18. Karnal. § 19. Delhi. § 20. *Pataudi State. § 21. Goorgaon. § 22. Rohtak. § 23. Hissar. § 24. Sirsa. § 25. *Loharoo and Dojana States. § 26. Patiala, Jeend, and Nabha States. § 27. *Bahawalpoor State.

North-Western Districts and States.

§ 28. Mooltan. § 29. Muzaffargarh. § 30. Montgomery. § 31. Jhang. § 32. Shahpoor. § 33. Goojrat. § 34. Jhelam. § 35. Rawal Pindi. § 36. *Kashmeer State. § 37. Hazara. § 38. Peshawar and the Khaibar Pass. § 39. Kohat. § 40. Bannoo. § 41. Dera Ismail Khan. § 42. Dera Ghazi Khan.

**Protected State.*

§ 43. *Baloochistan.

§ 1. Lahore City (131,000) = Lohāwar or Fort of Loh, son of Rama and of Seeta, who is still specially worshipped here, the capital of the Panjab Province, as it was of Ranjeet Singh's dominions till his death in 1839, and of the Mughul empire for a time till the reign of Shah Jahan, stands one mile S. of the Ravi which formerly washed its walls, amid the ruins of the ancient city which had a circuit of 16 miles, while the modern city walls have only 3. On the high road of invasion and war, few cities have suffered so much in the last 1½ centuries as what Milton called "Lahore of Great Mogul." The troops of Ahmed Shah Dooranee passed through it eight times. The Marathas and Sikhs have stripped the buildings of the Mughul period, and, being of brick, these crumble away. Still "Lahore can even now show an architectural *coup d'œil* worthy of an imperial city," in the tomb of Jahangeer, his palace and that of his successor Shah Jahan, the mosque of Wazeer Khan, the pearl mosque, the garden of Shalamar, and the Badshahi or imperial mosque of Aurangzeb; the mausoleum of Ranjeet Singh, with its curvilinear roof, projecting balconies, and details half-Muhammadan half-Hindoo; and in the once brilliantly enamelled front of the palace of the Mughuls, all overlooking a broad grassy plain. The best account of Lahore, compiled by Sir R. Montgomery's order in 1861, goes on to recall "the same palace front undisfigured by Sikh and English additions with its coloured frescoes fresh and vivid, the river flowing at its base, and eastward, as far as the eye could reach, a massive quay of masonry with flights of steps at intervals, and gardens extending to the water's edge; the now deserted suburbs filled with a thriving population and interspersed with tombs and terraces rising amid luxuriant gardens whose gates glittered with many-coloured porcelain," as when Lahore was the residence of Jahangeer. In his time Arjoon Mull, the Sikh leader who compiled the old or *Adi Grantha*, died in prison, and his shrine stands between the palace and Ranjeet Singh's tomb. Here, in 1849, Maharaja Dhuleep Singh transferred the kingdom and the Koh-i-noor diamond to the Queen and East India Company represented by Lord Dalhousie. When Commissioner Sir Charles Aitchison (Lieutenant-Governor in 1882) lowered the 30 ft. walls to 16 ft., and converted the trench into a garden. Outside to S. lies the civil station of **Anarkallee**, named from the lady whose tomb is used as the station church. From the Lohari gate the street of this name passes through the station with the public offices and Chief Court, and thence 3 m. S. by the Mall to the Lawrence Gardens and Government House in Donald Town, named after the good Lieutenant-Governor, Sir Donald M'Leod. The railway station and quarters lie N. and the suburb of Muzang S. of the Mall. **Meean Meer**, the military cantonment, is 3 m. E. of the civil station and 6 m. from the city. The other principal public buildings are the Panjab University, the Oriental and Government Colleges, the Mayo Hospital, the Medical School Museum, the Roberts Institute, and the Lawrence and Montgomery Halls. The city is the seat of an endowed bishopric, held first by the Church Missionary, Dr. French; of a native theological college founded by him; of a Union church; and of a vigorous mission of the Presbyterian Church in the United States of America. Lahore is inseparably connected with the career of Henry Lawrence and his brother John, Lord Lawrence, the first Chief Commissioner and Lieutenant-Governor of the Panjab, as the centre from which the most successful experiment in the government of an Eastern people was begun and directed, and the mutiny of the Poorbeah sepoys of the North-Western Province was first checked by disarming them, and then stamped out by the conquest of Delhi and the campaigns which followed. Lahore is 1225 m. N.W. of Calcutta, and 348 of Delhi, the centre of the lines of the Sind, Panjab, Delhi, and State railways, which connect it with Karachi on the Arabian Sea, the Indus and Central Asia on the N., and Delhi and the many lines to the S., S.E., and S.W.

§ 2. LAHORE DISTRICT is bounded N.E. by Amritsar, N.W. by Goojranwala, S.W. by Montgomery, and S.E. by Firozpoor, from which it is divided by the Satlej. Area, 3648 sq. m. Population, 924,106. A portion of the mainly level Panjab plain, Lahore District is divided into parallel belts which follow the S.W. direction of the three rivers, the **Satlej**, **Ravi**, and **Degh**. Between the two first lie the uplands known as the **Manjha** ("upland"), the upper part of which is the home of the Sikhs, "the Jut Sikhs of the martial sect of Gooroo Govind Singh, with long beards and tall stature," who furnished the flower of Ranjeet Singh's armies, and in 1857 sent forth hundreds to do battle for the British Government. The most important of these villages is Sobraon on the Satlej, opposite the battlefield on its left bank. Between the river and the high bank which bounds the Manjha to the S. is the fertile tract, Heetar. Between the Satlej and Ravi there run the **Bari Doab Canal**; the Hasli channel made by Shah Jahan's engineer, Ali Murdan Khan, which supplies Shalamar gardens; and the Katora, Khanwah, and Sohag inundation cuts from the Satlej. The history of the district centres in the capital, Lahore city, already described. Next to that in importance is **Kasoor** (17,500), on old bed of the Beas, 34 m. S.E. of Lahore, founded by Kush, brother of Loh the founder of Lahore, for some time an Afghan colony and aggregation of *kotes* or small fortified towns, subdued by Ranjeet Singh; now a place of trade. **Chooneean** (7500), on old bed of the Beas, S.W., a prosperous mart. **Path** (7000), agricultural town, 38 m. S.E. of Lahore. **Khem Kharan** (6000), on old bank of the Beas, 34 m. S. of Lahore, a municipality. **Sharakpoor** (4500), on the Degh, centre of a rice tract. Khudran (3000) is the only other municipality.

§ 3. GOOJRANWALA DISTRICT is bounded E. by Sialkot; N.W. by Shahpoor, from which the Chenab divides it; E. and S.E. by Jhang and Lahore. Area, 2587 sq. m. Population, 616,892. Goojranwala District, the central portion of the **Rechna Doab**, between the fertile plains of Sialkot and the desert tract of Jhang, is divided into the inhabited portion called *des*, and the now waterless but once well-irrigated jungle-land, *bar*. The Degh creates a small fertile belt in the S.E. corner; into that wend the Chenab watercourses, carrying off the surface drainage. Here was the Boodhist capital of the Panjab, Taki, the present village **Asaroor**, visited by Hwen T'hsang about 630 A.D. The chief town now is **Goojranwala** (23,000), on trunk road and railway 40 m. N. of Lahore, the birthplace and first capital of Ranjeet Singh, with tomb of his father, and cupola over a portion of the Maharaja's ashes. **Wazeerabad** (16,500), 22 m. N. of Goojranwala railway station, headquarters of Avitabile, Ranjeet Singh's general; near the projected bridge over the Chenab, with boat-building works; at the Dhonkal fair held in the neighbourhood 200,000 assemble. **Ramnagar** (8000), below the Chenab bank, 28 m. N.W. of Goojranwala, where in the second Sikh War in 1848 Gough first met the Sikhs under Sher Singh. **Eminabad** (7000), on trunk road 9 m. S. of Goojranwala, ancient town, with fine remains of Muhammadan architecture. **Akalgarh** (5000), near Ramnagar. Hafizabad, old town, 33 m. W. of Goojranwala.

§ 4. FIROZPOOR DISTRICT is bounded E. and S.E. by Lodiana and the States of Fareedkot, Patiala, and Nabha; N.E. by Jalandhar, from which the Satlej divides it; N.W. by Lahore, from which the united Satlej and Beas separate it. Area, 2744 sq. m. Population, 650,519. The Satlej flows N.W. from the point where it touches the district till it is joined by the Beas, when it turns S.W. with an abrupt cliff above its right bank, which once marked the frontier of the British Indian Empire, from the lapse of the Firozpoor State of Dhauna Singh in 1835. In 1839 Henry Lawrence administered this "ultima thule," rescuing it from barrenness, till now it is most prosperous, and trees abound. On 16th December 1845 the Sikhs crossed the Satlej opposite Firozpoor town, and the British victories of **Moodkee**, **Aliwal**, and **Sobraon** in this district followed each other. In 1857 one of the two sepoy corps at Firozpoor mutinied. **Firozpoor** (39,600 with garrison), named from the Emperor Firoz Shah in 1351-87, chief town, cantonment, and great arsenal on the old bank of the Satlej, 3½ m. from its present bed; the church to commemorate those who fell in the Satlej campaign was destroyed in the Mutiny and restored thereafter. **Firozshahr**, battlefield 12 m. E. of Satlej, where Hardinge and Gough attacked the entrenched Sikh camp, 21st December 1845. **Mooktsar** (5000), mart in W. of district; scene of a great festival, where the Sikh leader, Har Govind, fought the pursuing Muhammadans. **Dharmkot** (5500), 56 m. E. of Firozpoor, on road to Lodiana, a large grain mart. Zira (3000).

§ 5. *FAREEDKOT STATE (96,000), Sikh State under the immediate control of the Commissioner of Lahore Division, S.E. of Firozpoor District, and N.W. of Patiala State. The British protected the chief, head of the Barar Jat tribe, from Ranjeet Singh in 1809; he was loyal in the Sikh and Sepoy wars, and was made Raja with a patent of adoption. The area is 600 sq. m., and chief's revenue, £30,000. The chief town is **Fareedkot**, on the road from Lahore S. to Sirsa and Delhi. The chief's ancestors emigrated from Rajpootana at the same time with the Phoolkian branch of the tribe which now holds Patiala, Nabha, and Jeend.

§ 6. AMRITSAR DISTRICT is bounded N.E. by Goordaspoor, N.W. by Sialkot and Goojranwala, S.W. by Lahore, and S.E. by Jalandhar from which it is divided by the Beas. Area, 1573 sq. m. Population, 893,266. The district between the Beas and Ravi is a lower part of the Bari Doab or alluvial plain sloping E. to W. Its history is identified with the recent rise of the Sikhs; it is the centre of their original dissent from Hindooism, with which they are again almost identified. Here they fought the Delhi Mughuls and Ahmed Shah Dooranee, till Ranjeet Singh, after he seized Lahore in 1799, consolidated their power for fifty years to his death, after which, on the second Sikh War in 1849, the country became British. **Amritsar** (Amrita Saras = "pool of immortality") (152,000), centre of the Sikh dissidence from Hindooism, and chief commercial city N. of Delhi, was founded in 1574 by Ram Das, fourth Sikh leader, on a site granted by Akbar, 32 m. E. of Lahore, and midway between the Beas and Ravi. Destroyed by Ahmed Shah in 1761, it was soon restored. The sacred tank was the scene of the Gooroomata or yearly assemblage of the Sikhs, and the Golden Temple (copper gilt by Ranjeet Singh), where night and day the *Grantha* is recited, rose in greater splendour than when the Afghan marauders blew up its predecessor. It is called the Darbar Sahib. It consists of a square block with gilded dome on a rectangular platform, which a marble causeway joins to the land. Great fairs are held here in November and April. The Baba Atal is a lofty column which marks the grave of the son of Har Govind. The Church Missionary Society has here a vigorous mission. The city is the centre of the Kashmeer shawl manufacture and purchase, where many French and English firms have agents. It is an entrepot for the trade between Central Asia and India, having imports valued at 2 and exports at 1½ millions sterling annually. North of the city are the civil and railway stations, and beyond these the cantonment. North-west is the fort of **Govindgarh**, which Ranjeet Singh built. In 1857 the city was quiet and the people loyal. **Jandiala** (7000), railway station and mart on trunk road, 11 m. S. of Amritsar, named after Jand, son of the leader of the Jat colony which settled here. **Majeetha** (7000), 10 m. N.E. of Amritsar, named from its Jat founder. **Ramdas** (6000), near the Kirrān, with fine Sikh temple. **Tarn Tarn** (3000), 12 m. S. of Amritsar, named from a great tank supposed to cure leprosy, and with a leper asylum. Vairowal (5500), local mart and municipality.

§ 7. SIALKOT DISTRICT is bounded E. by Goordaspoor, N.E. by Kashmeer State, N.W. by Goojrat from which it is divided by the Chenab, W. by Goojranwala, and S. by Lahore and Amritsar. Area, 1958 sq. m. Population, 1,012,148. Forming the upper part of the Rechna Doab, between the Ravi and Chenab, **Sialkot District** has the character of a submontane and somewhat level tract, 20 m. from the lowest range of the Himalaya. The **Chenab**, a name formed by alliteration from the Chundra Bagh ("sun" and "moon") streams which join at Kisthwar to form it, has two tributaries here, both called Tavi; the one empties itself near Sydpoor on the left bank, the other joins the Chenab 12 m. lower down, forming the rich delta called Bujwant. In the interior, the Aik and Degh flow only during the rains. **Sialkot** (39,700), chief town and cantonment on N. bank of Aik, 72 m. N.E. of Lahore, founded by Raja Sal, uncle of the Pandavas in the *Mahabharat*, and restored by Salwahanna or Vikramaditya's son, Raja Rasalu, whose stronghold in the centre of the town is pointed out in a low circular eminence. In 1857 the Europeans bravely defended themselves in the fort, and Mr. Hunter, the founder of the Established Church of Scotland's Mission here, fell with his wife. Here are Tej Singh's Sikh temple, and many native paper mills. **Pasroor** (9000), 18 m. S. of Sialkot on Amritsar road, an old town with traces of Aurangzeb. **Zaffarwal** (6000), on E. bank of Degh, 27 m. S.E. of Sialkot on road to Dalhousie sanitarium; seat of American U.P. Mission. **Kila Sobha Singh** (5500), 23 m. S.E. of Sialkot, a colony of Kashmeeree shawl-weavers. Chawinda (5000), 14 m. S.E. of Sialkot, a rural centre.

§ 8. GOORDASPOOR DISTRICT is bounded E. by Hoshiarpoor from which the Beas separates it, and by Kangra; N. by Kashmeer and Chamba States; W. by Sialkot; and S. by Amritsar. Area, 1822 sq. m. Population, 616,892. This district is the submontane portion of the Bari Doab, between the Beas and Ravi, running up into the hill station of **Dalhousie** with military station of Bakloh, which crowns 3 peaks of the W. shoulder of the snowy Dhaola Dhar, in the main Himalaya range, separated by two minor ranges from the plains. The sanitarium was projected by Lord Napier of Magdala in 1851, the ground was purchased from the Raja of Chamba, and troops were stationed in the barracks in 1868. Dalhousie is 7687 ft. above the sea. The granite peak of Dain Khoond to the E. is 9000 ft. The station is 75 m. from Goordaspoor, and 52 m. W. of Pathankot. The Chakki torrent separates Goordaspoor from Kangra hills. The **Bari Doab Canal** is fed by the Ravi at **Madhoopoor** just S. of the hills, and opens out into three main branches. **Goordaspoor** (4500), chief town, 44 m. N.E. of Amritsar, on road to Pathankot; seat of American U.P. Mission. **Batala** (24,300), in centre of Doab, the principal place since the time of Shamsher Khan, the Delhi emperor's foster-brother, and now residence of descendants of Tej Singh, who led the Sikhs at Firozshahr and Sobraon. Seat of a Church of England Mission. **Dera Nanak** (8000), on the Ravi 13 m. N.W. of Batala, named from the founder of the Sikh sect who died in 1539 at Pakohi, a village opposite, and whose descendants, the Bedees, built the new town, with a temple dedicated to Baba Nanak. **Pathankot** (5000), old Rajpoot capital, on the road from Amritsar to Dalhousie, at which the carriage-way ceases 42 m. from Dalhousie; being connected with Amritsar 65 m. by rail. **Kalanam** (6000), on the Kirrān, 17 m. W. of Goordaspoor, old town where Akbar first assumed the title of Emperor. Deenanagar (7700), at the source of the Kirrān, named from Adeena Beg, the rival of the Sikhs in 1752, 6 m. N.E. of Goordaspoor. Soojanpoor (6000), at foot of hills 4 m. N.W. of Pathankot. Srigovindpoor (5500), on Ravi, 18 m. S.E. of Batala, a sacred Sikh place founded by Arjoon, who named it after his son.

§ 9. JALANDHAR DISTRICT is bounded N.E. by Hoshiarpoor, N.W. by Kapoorthala State, and S. by Firozpoor and

Lodiana from which it is separated by the Satlej. Area, 1322 sq. m. Population, 789,555. The Jalandhar Doab is the richest soil in the Province, and pays the highest land-tax; its fertility extends from the Satlej to the Beas. The torrents from the Siwalik hills, which pour through the submontane district of Hoshiarpoor, unite to form the **White** and **Black Ben** streams, the former in Jalandhar, the latter in Kapoorthala State. This Doab was once the Rajpoot kingdom of Katoch or Traigartha, dating from *Mahabharat* times; the descendants of its Rajas are now princes in the hills of Kangra, which was its stronghold. After the first Sikh War, the British formed the country between the Satlej and Beas into the Commissionership of the Trans-Satlej States, and adopted the fiscal system of the able Sikh, Misr Roop Lal. **Jalandhar** (52,200), chief town, cantonment, and railway station on trunk road, the old capital of Katoch previous to Alexander's invasion, with large suburbs; a centre of the American Presbyterian Mission. The cantonment, 4 m. distant, covers 7¼ sq. m., with a population of 12,000. **Kartarpoor** (11,000), 9 m. N. of Jalandhar, hereditary residence of Sikh leader since Arjoon obtained the site from Jahangeer in 1588. **Rahon** (11,800), on high bank of Satlej, 3 m. from its present channel, with cloth and sugar factories. **Phillaur** (8000), on right bank of Satlej, 27 m. S.E. of Jalandhar fort, commanding the passage of the river and depot of Sind, Panjab, and Delhi Railway. **Noormahal** (8000), 16 m. S. of Jalandhar, named after the Empress of Jahangeer, who restored it. **Nakodar** (9000), municipal town S.W. of Jalandhar.

§ 10. *KAPOORTHALA, MANDI, AND SOOKET STATES are directly under the control of the Commissioner of Jalandhar. **Kapoorthala State** covers an area of 800 sq. m., with a population of 251,917, along the left bank of the Beas before its junction with the Satlej. The chief is sixth of the Panjab feudatories in order of precedence, and holds estates in Oudh of still larger extent, as the reward of active loyalty in 1857. Randheer Singh, who was thus loyal, married a Christian wife, and for a time made his government Christian; his second son became a Christian. The State produces sugar, cotton, wheat, and maize, and yields a revenue of £100,000, of which £13,100 is paid to the suzerain Government. **Kapoorthala** town is 8 m. from the left bank of the Beas, and has a college founded in memory of Randheer Singh. The Jat family takes the name of Ahloowalia from Ahloo, the village of its founder. Phagwara and Sultanpoor are the other towns. **Mandi State,** bounded on S.E. by Koolloo, S. by Sooket, and W. by Kangra, has a mountainous area of 1200 sq. m., with 146,631 inhabitants, who pay £50,000 a year to the chief. Mandi is intersected by the two parallel ranges, the Goghar ka Dhar (7000 ft.) and Sikandar ka Dhar (6350 ft.), with salt mines at Goomah and Dirang. **Mandi** town (7500) is picturesquely placed on the Beas torrent (2557 ft.). The territory had 360 forts according to tradition, of which only 10 now exist, and Kamabgarh is the most famous. **Sooket State** lies on N. side of Satlej, which separates it from the Cis-Satlej States. Area, 420 sq. m. Population, 52,291. Revenue, £10,000, of which £1100 is tribute to the suzerain Government. Till 1200 A.D. Sooket was part of Mandi, after which incessant conflicts took place in the Bal valley, between the chief town Sooket and a point within 5 m. of Mandi.

§ 11. HOSHIARPOOR DISTRICT is bounded N.E. by Nalagarh State and Kangra, N.W. by Goordaspoor, S.W. by Jalandhar, and S. by Ambala. Area, 2180 sq. m. Population, 901,381. It lies between the W. slope of the Kangra hills running N. and S., and a parallel line of lower hills in the Jaswan Doon corresponding to Dehra Doon in the more easterly Siwaliks. Of the mountain torrents which intersect the plains, and fall into the Satlej and Beas, the principal is the **Soan**. This N. part of the Jalandhar Doab is most fertile and populous; it produces flax and linseed, and has the finest mango groves in the Province. **Hoshiarpoor** (21,500), chief town on broad torrent, 5 m. from foot of the hills; seat of American Presbyterian Mission. **Urmar** (14,000), local entrepot. **Meeanee** (8000), a mile from the Beas, and **Hariana** (8000), centres of trade. **Anandpoor** (7000), on left bank of Satlej, at base of Nina Devi peak, headquarters of Akali sect of Sikhs and residence of the Sodhis, or descendants of Ram Das, their leader. **Garshankar** (6000), on road from Hoshiarpoor to Roopar.

§ 12. KANGRA DISTRICT is bounded N.E. by Himalaya, separating it from Tibet; N.W. by Goordaspoor and Chamba State; S.W. by Hoshiarpoor; and S.E. by Bashahr, Mandi, and Bilaspoor States. Area, 8389 sq. m. Population, 730,845. Kangra lies on either side of the Sub-Himalaya chain, and consists of **Kangra Proper**, the submontane country; the central valleys of **Koolloo** and **Bangahal**, and **Lahaul** and **Spiti** on the Tibetan slope. It consists of three parallel lines of vast mountain ranges, with a transverse ridge. In each of these four basins a great river rises — the **Beas**, in the **Rotang** mountains N. of Koolloo; the **Spiti**, in the Tibetan valley of that name, and joining the Satlej in Bashahr State; the **Chenab**, from the slopes of Lahaul into Chamba State; and the **Ravi**, from the Bangahal valley into Chamba. The Katoch princes, each in his highland glen, held their own till 1009, when Mahmood of Ghazni, after defeating the Hindoos at Peshawar, seized Kangra fort and plundered Nagarkot temple. In 1360 Firoz Tughlak again overran the country, and sent the image to Mecca to be trampled on. Akbar himself was the first permanently to subdue the hill conntry. The Goorkhas swept the country from the Gogra to the Satlej, having defeated the Katoch princes at Mahal Mori in 1806, but were expelled by Ranjeet Singh. Kangra became British at close of first Sikh War, and was pacified after the victory of Goojrat. **Dharmsala** ("sanctuary") (3000), chief station and sanitarium and cantonment on spur of the Dhaola Dhar (6500 ft.), 16 m. N.E. of Kangra town, in beautiful scenery. Here the Viceroy, Lord Elgin, died in 1863; a monument covers his grave beside the church. The annual rainfall is heavy, 148 inches. Bhagsu is the military station. **Kangra** (6500), on both slopes of a hill above the Banganga torrent, ancient fort and capital, known as Nagarkot; "the Benares of the Panjab;" seat of the Church Mission. **Noorpoor** (10,000), on tributary of Chakki torrent (2000 ft.) 37 m. W. of Dharmsala, the principal commercial town, with Kashmeeree weavers of shawls inferior to those of Kashmeer and Amritsar only. **Jawalamookhi** (3500), ("fire-mouth") on Kangra-Nadaun road at head of Beas valley, with temple of Devi above jets of combustible gas issuing from the earth, and hot mineral springs; the centre of an annual fair. Opium from Koolloo is exported through this town. **Soojanpoor** with **Tira**, a palace of Katoch dynasty on the Beas, 15 m. above Nadaun. **Palampoor**, on outer slope of Dhaola Dhar, centre of tea culture of Palam valley; here, in 1868, Government established a fair for trade with Central Asia.

Lahaul is a subdivision of the Kangra district, with an area of 2119 sq. m., and a population of 6000, between the Chamba mountains on N.W. and Kanzam range on S.E., with Roopshoo subdivision of Ladakh on N.E. This lofty valley is traversed by the Chandra and Bagha torrents from the Baralacha pass (16,221 ft.), which unite at Tandi to form the Chenab. Kangser (11,345 ft.) is the highest inhabited village. At Kailang the Moravians have a mission to the Tibetan Boodhists, of whose language Dr. Jaeschke has published a grammar and dictionary. The other villages are Kardong and Kolang. The headman is termed *négi*. **Koolloo**, another subdivision with area of 1926 sq. m. and population of 91,000, is bounded N.E. and E. by the Central Himalaya, which separate it from Lahaul and Spiti. It is divided by the **Sainj**, which joins the Beas at Largi, into Koolloo proper and Sioraj, the latter of which is cut into inner and outer Sioraj by the Jalori or Sooket range. The head-quarters are Sultanpoor (1100), on right bank of Beas, in Koolloo proper, and Plach in Sioraj. Nagar is the old capital, a height 1000 ft. above the Beas. The road to Leh and Yarkund lies above the right bank of the Beas to Rotang pass, then up the Bagha to Baralacha pass, and then down to Ladakh. **Spiti**, subdivision with area of 2100 sq. m. and population of 3500 Tibetans under a headman called the *Nono*. Spiti is an outlying Himalaya valley in shape of a triangle, the apex of which is the point where the Kanzam ridge and Tibetan Himalaya converge, and the base is the transverse ridge of Manirang, dividing Kangra from Bashahr. It is drained by the **Li** or river of Spiti. The chief village is Dankar. The British Government, in 1846, kept Spiti as the road to the wool districts of Changthang, when it sold Kashmeer to Golab Singh.

§ 13. *CHAMBA STATE, N. of Kangra, is bounded on N. and N.W. by Kashmeer, and N.E. and E. by Lahaul and Ladakh. Area, 3216 sq. m. Population, 116,765. The State is locked in on almost every side by lofty mountain ranges; to E. is a region of snowy peaks and glaciers; on W. and S. are fertile valleys. The Ravi and Chandra-Bagha (Chenab) flow through it. The forests at Pangi on the latter, and Barmaur on the former, supply timber for public works. Iron, copper, and lead exist; fine slate quarries are worked; the climate is well suited for tea. Since the chief made over the sanitarium of Dalhousie, he pays £500 tribute out of a revenue of £24,400. Under a special officer as superintendent, Chamba has become a prosperous model State. **Chamba**, chief town, is in lat. 32° 29′ N., and long. 76° 10′ E. The Established Church of Scotland has a mission here.

§ 14. SIMLA DISTRICT has an area of 18 sq. m. and population of 43,000, on detached lands in the S. outliers of the Central Himalaya as they descend from Bashahr State to the plains at Ambala, between the Satlej and Jumna. The hills between the Satlej and Tons, S. and E., culminate in the **Chor** peak (11,982 ft.) The transverse spur between the Indus and Ganges river systems breaks into two ridges just N.E. of Simla sanitarium; one curves N.W. round the Satlej valley, the other, on which Simla stands, runs S.E. to the Subathoo and

Kasauli hills, where it meets the Sub-Himalaya range. The principal torrents are the Pahar, Giri Ganga, Gambhar, and Sarsa. The plots of territory, beginning with Simla site in 1816, have been acquired from the Hill States since the Goorkhas were driven back. **Simla** (16,000 in August, of whom 1600 are Europeans; 12,305 on 17th February 1881) is the Viceroy's summer resort since 1864, at a mean elevation of 7084 ft., 78 m. from Ambala and 57 m. from Kalka, at foot of the hills. In 1822 Lieutenant Kennedy built the first permanent house, and in 1827 Lord Amherst spent the hot season here. More than 300 houses dot the crescent-shaped ridge for a distance of 6 m., rising to Jako peak (8000 ft.) in E. and Prospect Hill in W., near which is Peterhoff, the Viceroy's house. The station has several European schools for boys and girls, churches, banks, sarai, markets, waterworks, and breweries. The deodar and rhododendron cover the ridges with beauty, set in the background of the snowy range. Jutogh cantonment is 4 m. to S.W.; Mahasoo, a retreat on the N. side of Jako, is on the N. road towards Kotgarh. **Kasauli** hill (6322 ft.) of Subathoo group, is a cantonment and convalescent depot overlooking Kalka valley, 32 m. S.W. of Simla, with Henry Lawrence Asylum for soldiers' boys at Sunâwar. **Dagshai**, cantonment on height 16 m. S. of Simla on Kalka road. **Subathoo** (4500 ft.), cantonment on extreme point of Simla range above Gambhar river, 9 m. from Kasauli, and 23 from Simla; a centre of American Presbyterian Mission. **Solan**, cantonment on S. slope of Krol mountain, 30 m. from Simla, on Kalka road. **Kalka** (2000 ft.), at foot of Kasauli hill, where mountain road to Simla sanitarium begins; a bazar and camping ground; about to be connected with Ambala by railway.

§ 15. *TWENTY SIMLA STATES, MALER KOTLA AND KALSIA are under the political supervision of the Commissioner of Ambala. The twenty Hill States around Simla lie between the Satlej and Jumna, and stretch from the plains of Ambala to the borders of China; or from lat. 30° 20′ to 32° 5′ and from long. 76° 30′ to 79° 1′. Area about 5441 sq. m. Population, 450,353, of whom the Kanets, a true Aryan tribe, form 60 per cent. The Goorkhas of Nepal subdued the country and its Rajpoot chiefs in 1803, and the British reconquered and restored it under Sir D. Ochterlony in 1815. (1) **Sirmoor** ("crowned head"), or Nahan (12,371 pop., 1096 sq. m.), on right bank of the Tons, traversed by the Giri from N.W. to S.E. Nahan is the Raja's residence. (2) **Bilaspoor**, or Kabloor (80,070 pop., 448 sq. m.), S. of Sooket State, traversed by the Satlej.

Kahloor is the Raja's residence. (3) **Bashahr** (64,422 pop., 3320 sq. m.), most easterly of the States bordered by Tibet, and traversed by the Satlej. **Chini**, one mile from right bank (9085 ft.), village with perfect climate, where Marquis of Dalhousie projected a sanitarium for convalescent troops. **Koonawar**, subdivision of Bashahr immediately S. of Spiti, in which these streams drain into the Satlej, Li or Spiti, Darbang, Peejar, Kozhang, Malgiri, and Yala on right; and Hocho, Tughlaghkur, Tidang, and Baspa on left. Sangnam and Kanum are the chief villages. The Koonawarees beat back the Goorkhas. **Rampoor**, on the Satlej, N.E. of Simla, with palace of Raja, who makes Saharan his summer quarters; the town is famed for the *chaddars* or plaids which bear its name. **Kotgarh**, 40 m. N.E. of Simla, on slope above the left bank of Satlej (6634 ft.). A Church Mission station, formerly a native capital and cantonment. The Raja lives at Bashahr, and is suzerain of Syree. (4) **Nalaghar**, or Hindoor (53,383 pop., 256 sq. m.), S.E. of Hoshiarpoor district. Raja's residence is of the same name; the fort is Maloun. (5) **Keonthal** (31,123 pop., 116 sq. m.), around Simla. The Raja lives in village of same name. His vassals are the Rana of **Koti**, and Thakoors of **Theog Madhan, Ghoond**, and **Ratesh**. (6) **Baghal** (20,643 pop., 124 sq. m.), with Raja's residence of same name. (7) **Baghat** (8339 pop., 124 sq. m.), with Raja's residence of same name. (8) **Jubbal** (19,916 pop., 288 sq. m.), S.E. of Simla, with Rana's residence of same name. (9) **Koomharsain** (9574 pop., 90 sq. m.). The Rana's village of same name is 40 m. E. of Simla, above left bank of Satlej. (10) **Bhajji** (12,106 pop., 96 sq. m.), with Rana's residence of same name. (11) **Mailog** (9147 pop., 48 sq. m.), with Thakoor's residence of same name. (12) **Balsan** (5190 pop., 57 sq. m.). (13) **Dhami** (3322 pop., 27 sq. m.). (14) **Kothar** (3648 pop., 20 sq. m.). (15) **Koonhiar** (1932 pop., 8 sq. m.). (16) **Mangal** (1060 pop., 13 sq. m.). (17) **Beeja** (1158 pop., 4 sq. m.). (18) **Darkooti** (590 pop., 5 sq. m.). (19) **Taroj** (3216 pop., 67 sq. m.), and (20) **Sangri** (2593 pop., 16 sq. m.), are the other States, each with a village of the same name, in which the chief resides. **Maler Kotla** (71,035 pop., 165 sq. m.), is a Cis-Satlej State under an Afghan Nawab. **Kalsia** (67,649 pop., 155 sq. m.), Cis-Satlej Sikh State.

§ 16. LODIANA DISTRICT is bounded E. by Ambala; N. by Jalandhar from which the Satlej separates it; W. by Firozpoor; and S. by Patiala, Nabha, and Maler Kotla States. Area, 1375 sq. m. Population, 618,835. A branch of the Sirhind

Canal from Ambala irrigates the W. portion. In *Mahabharat* times the district possessed great cities. The Rais of Raikot, Rajpoots who became Musalmans, held it from 1445; and George Thomas, the Irish adventurer, helped them against the Sikhs. In 1480 two of the Lodi princes at Delhi founded **Lodiana** (44,200), chief town, railway station, and fort, 8 m. S. of high bank of Satlej, held by British since, in 1809, Ochterlony occupied it as a cantonment, and residence of exiled family of Shah Soojah of Kabul, pensioned by the British since 1840. Chief centre of American Presbyterian Mission since 1834. Adjoining are the brick ruins of Soonet, old Hindoo town. **Raikot** (10,000), 30 m. S.W. of Lodiana, walled town and old capital of Musalman Rajpoot Rais. **Machiwara** (6500), old Hindoo town mentioned in *Mahabharat*, on Satlej bank 23 m. S. of Lodiana, with sacred Sikh shrine. **Jagraon** (16,900), grain mart, 29 m. S.W. of Lodiana, on Firozpoor road. Bhilolpoor (3500), old town of Hindoo dynasty called Muhbpoora.

§ 17. AMBALA DISTRICT is bounded on E. by Simla States; N. by Hoshiarpoor from which it is divided by the Satlej; W. by Lodiana and Patiala; and S. by Karnal and Saharanpoor, with the Jumna between. Area, 2570 sq. m. Population, 1,067,263. The Kotaha tract in the centre of the district, consisting of two parallel ranges, is covered by the forest of Morni, in which are two lakes divided by a hill but communicating with each other below. The **Ghaggar**, which rises in Sirmoor, crosses the district into Patiala State. The land between this and the **Sarsootee** (Saraswati) was the first settled abode of the Aryan Hindoos, and is a centre of pilgrimage from all N. and E. India. Debouching from the hills at the pilgrim spot Yad Budree on the Sirmoor border, the Sarsootee flows to Chotee Pabnee where it unites with the Choutoung, but is fabled to disappear till it reaches Thaneswar and Pihoia towns. Here was the scene of the conflict between the Pandavas and Kauravas; and Hwen T'hsang, in the 7th century, found a civilised kingdom with Srugna, the modern village Sugh, as its capital. The other streams of the district are the Chutang, Tangri, Baliali, Markanda, Begana, Sukhia, and Sombh. At Hathni Koond, where the Jumna leaves the hills, the **Western Jumna Canal** begins, and the **Sirhind Canal** passes through a portion of the district. Under the treaty of 1809 with Ranjeet Singh, the British Government protected the Cis-Satlej chiefs, who, after the second Sikh War in 1869, lost sovereign rights. The nucleus of the district lapsed in 1823, and **Ambala** (67,500), city and cantonment (in 1843), became an important centre of British administration; 3 m. E. of the Ghaggar on plain (1040 ft.), founded by Amba Rajpoot, whence its name. Cantonments lie 4 m. S.E. of city and cover 7220 acres. A commercial centre at point where Sind, Panjab, and Delhi Railway crosses trunk road, with fine church, club, hotels, and shops, and American Presbyterian Mission. Here in 1869 the Viceroy, Lord Mayo, received in Darbar the Afghan Ameer, Sher Ali. The city is 1020 miles N.W. of Calcutta. **Roopar** (10,500), old town (Roopnagar), commanded the Satlej, on S. bank of which it stands 43 m. N. of Ambala and head of Sirhind Canal; here Lord W. Bentinck received Ranjeet Singh in 1831, amid great splendour. **Jagadhri** (12,300), W. of Jumna, 37 m. S.E. of Ambala, destroyed by Nadir Shah, now a flourishing town with metal manufactures. **Buriya** (8500), near W. bank of Jumna Canal, with Sikh fort. **Mani Majra** (6000), Sikh Raja's residence at hill-foot, 23 m. N. of Ambala. **Sadhaura** (10,800), old town at hill-foot, 26 m. E. of Ambala. **Thaneswar** (8000), on the Sarsootee, 25 m. S. of Ambala, old Hindoo capital in *Mahabharat* times, sacked by Mahmood of Ghazni in 1011. The sacred pool of the Sarsootee, fabled to be visited by all other holy waters during eclipses of the moon, is the centre of 360 pilgrim cities, and of the most attractive Hindoo bathing festival, which is, however, fast declining. **Shahabad** (10,300), old brick town, midway between Thaneswar and Ambala, an agricultural centre.

§ 18. KARNAL DISTRICT is bounded E. by Meerut and Muzaffargarh from which it is divided by the Jumna, N. by Ambala, W. by Patiala and Jeend States and Rohtak, and S. by Delhi. Area, 2396 sq. m. Population, 622,621. The district is watered by the W. Jumna Canal in three channels towards Delhi, Hissar, and Rohtak. It is traversed S. to N. by trunk road from Delhi to Ambala, and has been the scene of the Aryan War sung in the *Mahabharat*, and of three great conflicts with successive Musalman powers. **Karnal** (23,200), in N., on old bank of Jumna, now 7 m. E., founded by Karna, the Raja who was champion of the Kauravas, held successively by Jeend Rajas and George Thomas, and bestowed on an Afghan Nawab by Lord Lake in 1803. Civil station lies W. where old cantonment was; here is a Government stud farm. **Kaithal** (15,000), old town, 40 m. W. of Karnal, on artificial lake, said to have been founded by Yudistheera; the Kapisthal of Sanskrit writings. Memorable as the scene of Henry

Lawrence's earliest success in civilising. **Panipat** (25,022), on trunk road 53 m. N. of Delhi, near old bank of Jumna. The modern town stands on mound of ruins of the historic capital. Old Panipat was the pledge claimed by Yudistheera from Duryodhan as the price of peace in the Kaurava and Pandava war; the scene of Ibrahim Lodi's defeat by Baber, who thus established the Mughul dynasty in May 1526; the field on which, in 1556, Akbar, his grandson, restored that power by defeating Hemoo, Hindoo general of the Afghan Sher Shah; the city beneath whose walls Ahmed Shah Dooranee, the Afghan, on 7th January 1761, destroyed the confederation of Marathas, four years after the British victory of Plassey. **Sewan** (6500), 14 m. N. of Kaithal. **Kunjpoora** (5500), 10 m. N.E. of Karnal.

§ 19. DELHI DISTRICT is bounded E. by Meerut and Boolundshahr from which the Jumna divides it, N. by Karnal, W. by Rohtak, and S. by Goorgaon. Area, 1258 sq. m. Population, 643,515. The Jumna has slowly gone E. from its old bed beneath a cliff now far to the W., but at Delhi city it washes the base of the stony tableland (500 ft. above the lowlands), which is an offshoot of the **Mewat** hills, the N. outlier of the Aravali range of Rajpootana. Torrents in the rainy season flow through the ravines to the plains below; in the S.E. of the district the **Najafgarh** lake covers about 27,000 acres in October. The Jumna is fordable except during the rains, its waters having been drained off by the canals before reaching Delhi district; at Okhla, below Delhi city, it supplies the **Agra Canal**.

Delhi City (*Dehli*).—On the 35 sq. m. of this plateau, where it is washed by the Jumna, the successive Asiatic capitals of India have been built from 1500 B.C. to 1857 A.D., when the Mutiny resulted in the banishment of Bahadoor Shah, the last titular Great Mughul, to Rangoon, where he died 7th November 1862. The imperial ruins have a circumference of 20 m. at the present day. (1) **Indraprastha** ("field of Indra"), now called Indrapat and Poorana Kila or Old Fort, 2 m. S. of modern Delhi, between the Delhi gate and Hoomayoon's tomb; founded by Yudistheera and the Pandavas from Hastinapoor, whose line after 30 generations was succeeded by Visarwa, minister of the last Pandava; and his, after 500 years, by fifteen Gautama rulers. (2) Five m. below the modern capital, about 50 B.C., the first Delhi was built and named either from Raja Dilu, successor to the Gautama line, or from the fact that the iron shaft of Raja Dhava, set up in 3d and 4th centuries A.D., remained loose (*dhila*), when

Anang Pal, founder of the Tuar Rajpoot dynasty, dug it up and replaced it. The only historical fact is that, in 1052 A.D., Anang Pal II. "peopled Dilli," or restored it as the Tuar capital; and a century after it became subject to the Chauhan ruler of Ajmer. From an alliance between the two sprang Prithvi Raja, who in 1193 fell as the last champion of Hindoo independence against Shahab-ood-deen, whose viceroy and successor, Kootab-ood-deen, made this Hindoo city the first Musalman capital. Anang Pal's fortifications and Prithvi Raja's outer wall (Lalkot and Rai Pithora's Fort) may still be traced around the **Kootab Minar** or Muazzam's pillar of 238 ft., in five stories rising from a diameter of 47 to almost 9 ft., which the conqueror built beside the mosque described a century and a half afterwards by the traveller from Tangiers, Ibn Batuta, as unequalled for beauty and size. (3) **Tughlakabad**, 4 m. E. on a rocky eminence, a half hexagon with circuit of 4 m., built in 1321 by Ghiyas-ood-deen, whose son Muhammad Tughlak ordered it to be deserted, as we still see it, for Deoghar 800 m. south, in the Dekhan, to which he caused a road to be planted with full-grown trees. (4) **Firozabad** was founded (1351) by his nephew and successor, the wise builder of cities, canals, and colleges, on the ground between the Ridge and Hoomayoon's tomb, outside the modern Delhi Gate; here stands Asoka's pillar, a sandstone monolith, 42 ft. high, with inscription transferred by Firoz Shah, whose *lathi* or club it is called, from Khizrabad on the Upper Jumna. (5) **Modern Delhi** or Shahjahanabad. Timoor's invasion, the succession of the Sayyid dynasty till 1444, and of the Afghan Lodi, overthrown at Panipat by Baber, led to the Mughul dynasty. Baber lived chiefly at Agra; his son Hoomayoon restored Indraprastha as Poorana Kila, his capital; his rival Sher Shah followed him there and has left his mark in Salimgarh, the fort adjoining modern Delhi, called after his son. Agra, Lahore, and Ajmer were from time to time the capitals of Akbar and Jahangeer till Shah Jahan built Delhi as it is, with the Jama Musjeed and W. Jumna Canal. Under Aurangzeb it reached its height of splendour, gradually since dimmed by the Marathas, by the Persian Nadir Shah, its conquest from the Marathas by Lord Lake in 1803, the massacre of more than 50 Christian women and children in its palace-fort, and the extinction of the line of titular emperors in the captivity and death of Bahadoor Shah. In 1857, after the battle of Badli-ka-sarai on 8th June, the British held the historic Ridge N.E. of the city whence some

5000 men, after a siege which lasted till 20th September, took the city and checked growing anarchy over Hindustan proper. On 1st January 1877, on a turf-covered plain 4 m. N. of Delhi and E. of the Karnal road, the Queen, whose direct administration had been established on the cessation of the East India Company on 1st November 1858, was proclaimed, under Act of Parliament, **Empress of India.** **Delhi city** (173,393), stands on right bank of Jumna, by a fine bridge across which it is entered through a corner of the Salimgarh fort by the railway (East Indian and Sind, Panjab, and Delhi), which passes out on S.W. to Bombay as the Rajpootana-Malwa Railway. Shah Jahan's walls on three sides, in addition to the river face, have a circuit of 5½ m., with 10 gates, of which the Sepoy War has made the Kashmeer gate and Mori bastion renowned; outside these, in the cemetery, lies the dust of the hero, John Nicholson. Of the ten main streets, the finest, perhaps in Asia, is the Chandni Chouk, or Silver Street, running for ¾ m., 74 ft. broad, E. from the fort to the Lahore gate. Shah Jahan's palace—now the fort—and great mosque of marble and red sandstone are still among the greatest architectural glories of the Mughuls, although military necessities have somewhat impaired the former. The Queen's Gardens, Institute and Museum, College, Residency, church built by Colonel Skinner, Propagation and Baptist Societies' Missions, are the principal public institutions. But in all save historical interest, Delhi, like Cawnpoor, stained by the blood of the Mutiny massacres, is subordinated to the capital, Lahore, from which it is distant 348 miles; from Agra, 113; from Allahabad, 390; from Calcutta, 954; and by Ahmedabad from Bombay, 689.

Sonpat (13,100), 25 m. N.W. of Delhi, ancient town on hill of ruins. **Fareedabad** (7500), 16 m. S. of Delhi, confiscated for rebellion from Raja of **Ballabgarh** (6500), former capital of State of same name, on Muttra road, 21 m. S. of Delhi; a grain mart.

§ 20. *PATAUDI STATE (50 sq. m., pop. 17,850), Musalman State under the Commissioner of Delhi, is surrounded by the district of Goorgaon, 40 m. S.W. of Delhi, pierced by the Rajpootana-Malwa Railway to Bandikhui junction. Lord Lake granted the State to Faiztalab Khan for military service against Holkar. The revenue is about £10,700.

§ 21. GOORGAON DISTRICT is bounded E. by Aligarh and Boolundshahr; N.E. by Delhi; N. by Rohtak; W. by Jeend, Nabha, and Alwar States; and S. by Muttra. Area, 938 sq. m. Population, 641,848. Goorgaon, the most S. portion of the Panjab plain, stretches S. to the Rajpootana tableland, from which two ridges (600 ft.) strike through it, the W. separating it from Alwar, and the E. running up to the walls of Delhi. Salt is made from wells and the Rohtak banks of the Najafgarh lake. Iron is found in the extreme S. at Firozpoor, with copper, plumbago, and ochre. At Sonah, the base of the W. range, there is an efficacious sulphur spring. Goorgaon, the Mewat of the Musalmans, the land of the marauding Meos, has been gradually civilised since Lord Lake's conquest in 1803. In 1857 anarchy raised its head, but a loyal native preserved the public property at Bharawas cantonment, near Rewari, then the civil station, and, after the fall of Delhi, order was at once restored. **Goorgaon** (4000), civil station since 1821, formerly part of the Begam Samroo's estates, and an old cantonment; railway station, 21 m. S. of Delhi. **Rewari** (24,000), 34 m. S.E. of Goorgaon, a railway station and chief entrepot between Panjab and Rajpootana; an old Hindoo town with ruins of Gokalgarh fort of the semi-independent Rajas. **Nuh** (5000), 30 m. S. of Goorgaon, centre of coarse salt manufacture. **Palwal** (10,650), 30 m. S.E. of Goorgaon, the "Apelava" of the Pandava kingdom of Indraprastha. **Firozpoor** (9500), prosperous mart in extreme S., a cantonment of Emperor Firoz Shah. **Hodal** (7000), local mart S. of Palwal on Delhi and Agra road. **Farukhnagar** (11,000), centre of salt manufacture on banks of Najafgarh lake; branch railway station.

§ 22. ROHTAK DISTRICT is bounded E. by Delhi and Doojana State, N. by Karnal, W. by Hissar and Jeend State, and S. by Goorgaon. Area, 1811 sq. m. Population, 553,609. Rohtak formed part of the region known as Hariana, extending from the swamps on the Delhi border to the Rajpootana desert. The **Sahibi** stream, from the Ajmer hills, flows through a corner of the level district; the N. portions are watered by the Rohtak and Batana branches of the W. Jumna Canal. Unlike the rest of India, in Hissar the people are gathered into many towns, originally for security. **Rohtak** (15,700), chief town on Hissar road, 42 m. N.W. of Delhi; to N. lies old site of Khokrakot. **Jhajar** (11,650), 35 m. W. of Delhi, old capital of State confiscated for rebellion. **Beri** (10,000), N.W. of above, trade and pilgrim centre. Majra (8000), Bahadoorgarh (7500), 18 m. W. of Delhi. Gohana (7000), Maheem (6700), are other towns. Georgegarh, near Jhajar, fort built by George Thomas, who fought his way through the Maratha besiegers to Hansi, where he was overthrown.

§ 23. HISSAR DISTRICT is bounded E. and S. by Jeend

State and Rohtak, N. and N.W. by Patiala State and Sirsa. Area, 3540 sq. m. Population, 504,183. Hissar, a sandy plain on E. border of Bikaner desert, with hills on S. (800 ft.). The Ghaggar passes through it in two branches into Sirsa, and it is further watered by the W. Jumna Canal, E. to W. A tract of 43,287 acres, forming the Government cattle stud, is near **Hissar** (14,170), chief town on the canal, 102 m. W. of Delhi; favourite residence of its founder, the emperor Firoz Shah; restored by George Thomas after the famine of 1783. **Bhiwani** (33,800), chief commercial centre for N. Rajpootana States and Panjab, 37 m. S.E. of Hissar. **Hansi** (12,660), on W. Jumna Canal, 16 m. E. of Hissar, chief town of Hariana till famine of 1783, thereafter headquarters of George Thomas, and British cantonment till 1857, when there and at Hissar the sepoys murdered the Europeans who did not at once flee. Fatehabad (4000), 30 m. N.W. of Hissar, with pillar of its founder, Firoz Shah. Agroha (1100), 15 m. N.W. of Hissar, old centre of Agarwala Banias, the wealthiest guild in India. Tosham, police station 23 m. S.E. of Hona, rocky elevation (800 ft.), with rock inscriptions not yet deciphered.

§ 24. SIRSA DISTRICT is bounded E. by Hissar; N.E. by Patiala State and Firozpoor; W. by Googaira, from which it is separated by the Satlej and Bahawalpoor State; and S.W. and S. by Bikaner State. Area, 3116 sq. m. Population, 253,275. Sirsa is a sandy but increasingly-cultivated plain between the Ghaggar and Satlej, a transition from the desert of Bikaner to the pasture lands of the Satlej tract. **Sirsa** (12,300), chief town, founded in 1837 on N. side of a dry bed of the Ghaggar; great wheat market; ruins of old Sirsa (from Raja Saras, or Sarsootee) are near. Rania (5000), on right bank of the Ghaggar, 13 m. W. of Sirsa. Ellenabad (3500), on the Ghaggar, 23 m. W. of Sirsa, frontier trade town for Marwar, with ruins of old town of Kharial on opposite bank. Fazilka (3500), entrepot on Satlej, through which trade passes to Karachi.

§ 25. *LOHAROO AND DOOJANA STATES are petty Musalman principalities under the superintendence of the Commissioner of Hissar. **Loharoo**, on the E. edge of the Bikaner desert S. of Hissar, has an area of 285 sq. m., population of 13,846, and revenue of £6200. It was granted by Lord Lake to the Musalman agent of the Raja of Alwar for diplomatic services, and was transferred to his nephew when his son was executed for the murder of Mr. Fraser at Delhi in 1834. The chief town of the same name is in the south. **Doojana**, in the heart of Rohtak district, has an area of 100 sq. m., population of 16,621, and revenue of £7720. Lord Lake granted it to the Afghan Nawab for service. The chief town of the same name is 37 m. W. of Delhi.

§ 26. *PATIALA, JEEND, AND NABHA STATES, Sikh principalities Cis-Satlej held by nobles of the Phoolkean clan, founded in Nabha by Phool, an agricultural notable, in the 17th century, are under the direct control of the Lieutenant-Governor of the Panjab. **Patiala** lies chiefly in the plain S. of the Satlej, but also in the hills stretching to Simla, which was exchanged by the Maharaja for other territory, where there are slate, lead (Subathoo), marble, and copper mines (Narnaul). Area, 5412 sq. m. Population, 1,467,412. The gross revenue is about half a million sterling. A branch of the **Sirhind Canal** traverses the principality. **Patiala**, the capital, was built in 1752, and to it most of the population of Sirhind was removed; it is E. of Ambala, with a college. The State has been increased from time to time by the Paramount Power for the active loyalty of its chief. The request of Maharaja Narindar Singh, and his brother chiefs, occasioned the adoption policy of Lord Canning after the Mutiny. **Jeend**, consisting of scattered tracts E. of Satlej and S. of Patiala, has an area of 1236 sq. m., population of 251,231, and gross revenue of £60,000. The capital of the same name is between Karnal and Hansi road and Chautung stream in lat. 29° 19′ N., and long. 76° 23′ E. The Raja has been frequently rewarded for his loyalty. **Nabha**, with chief town of same name E. of Patiala town, stretching S. of Lodiana into the Patiala State, has an area of 863 sq. m., population of 261,563, and gross revenue of £65,000. Since the first Sikh war the family has been distinguished by its active fidelity.

§ 27. *BAHAWALPOOR STATE, a Musalman principality, next to Kashmeer and Patiala in precedence, stretches for 300 m. along the Satlej, Panjnad, and Indus rivers from near Fazilka in Sirsa S.W. to Khairpoor in Sind. On the E. and S. it is bounded by the Bikaner and Jaisalmeer States. Area about 22,000 sq. m. Population, 573,134. The strip of alluvium extends from the rivers for 8 or 14 m. to an elevated belt in the centre 20 m. wide, to the E. of which is the desert stretching into Rajpootana. After long anarchy the British Government administered the State from 1866 till 1879, creating £200,000 of revenue, chiefly from 810 m. of inundation canals. The Indus Valley State Railway passes into the State from Mooltan and Adamwahan by the fine Empress bridge across the Satlej to the capital. **Bahawalpoor** (20,000), 2 m.

S. of the Satlej, with silk manufactures; the Nawab's palace is near. **Khanpoor** (10,000), on the Ikhtiarwah navigable canal, a railway station and prosperous mart, with ruined fort.

North-Western Districts and States.

§ 28. MOOLTAN DISTRICT is bounded E. by Montgomery, N. by Jhang, W. by Muzaffargarh, from which the Trinab divides it, and S. by Bahawalpoor, with the Satlej between. Area, 5880 sq. m. Population, 551,964. Near the confluence of the river system which centres in the Indus, and surrounded by the Ravi, Chenab, and Satlej, Mooltan was a populous garden in the days of Alexander and the Boodhist supremacy, when it was the centre of the Malli, from whom it has its name. Changes in the courses of the rivers, but especially successive waves of invasion and conflict, have left it a barren, hot, and almost rainless tract save along the banks of the three streams. **Mooltan** (68,674), formerly on the Ravi river 30 m. N., now 4 m. from the Chenab, the junction of the Sind, Panjab, and Delhi Railway with the Indus Valley State Railway. Believed to be the Kaspeiræa of Ptolemy, or Kasyapapoor, named from the father of the Hindoo sun-gods, from whose temple some derive the name (*Molosthana*). Dismantled after its capture in 1849 from Moolraj, son of Siwan Mull, the murderer of Vans Agnew and Lieutenant Anderson, whose monument, an obelisk, is in the fort. The tomb of Rukn-ood-deen, a Musalman saint, is visible for 14 m. from the city. This is a station of the Church Missionary Society. It is the entrepot of the trade of the Panjab for Karachi; **Sher Shah**, on the Chenab, is its port. **Shoojabad** (6100), 3 m. from Chenab, and **Khror** (5100), 4 m. from the Satlej, are local trade centres. **Atari**, village with ruins, 20 m. S.W. of **Talamba**, old city, near the Ravi, identified with the "city of Brahmans" taken by Alexander.

§ 29. MUZAFFARGARH DISTRICT is bounded E. by Mooltan, with the Trinab between; N. by Dera Ismail Khan; W. by Dera Ghazi Khan, with the Indus between; and S. by Bahawalpoor from which it is divided by the Panjnad, or collected Five Rivers, before their junction with the Indus. Area, 3136 sq. m. Population, 338,605. The district forms the thin end of the Sind Sagar Doab. It is most fertile where irrigated, as in the middle tract, or inundated by the Indus and Trinab, which in Timoor's time united at Uch, 60 m. above Mithankot, their present confluence. The camels of the Povindah carriers from Afghanistan graze on the sandy wastes. **Muzaffargarh**

(3200), 6 m. from the Chenab on the Mooltan and Dera Ghazi Khan road, the administrative centre. **Khangarh** (4500), 11 m. S. of Muzaffargarh. The district exports indigo to Afghanistan and cotton to Sind.

§ 30. MONTGOMERY DISTRICT is bounded N.E. by Lahore, N.W. by Jhang, S.W. by Mooltan, and S.E. by Bahawalpoor and Sirsa from which the Satlej divides it. Area, 5574 sq. m. Population, 426,529. The district is a portion of the Bari and Rechna Doabs, fertile along the Satlej and Ravi, but barren and saline in the centre, or covered with impenetrable jungle. Here the Malli flourished, as in Mooltan, and the land was populous before war desolated it. Here alone, N. of the Satlej, was there a rising in 1857, when the turbulent Kharrals were put down by Colonel Paton with a force from Lahore. **Montgomery** (3000), headquarters and railway station midway between Lahore and Mooltan on central ridge of the Bari Doab. **Pak Pattan** ("ferry of the pure") (6500), 30 m. S. of Montgomery, junction of W. roads from Dera Ismail and Ghazi Khan, now 10 m. from Satlej, of which it was the chief ferry crossed by Mahmood and Timoor, and old travellers; a popular shrine of Fareed-ood-deen, who spread Islam over S. Panjab—whence its name. **Kot Kamalia** (6000), 40 m. W. of Montgomery, with ruins of the town taken by Alexander from the Malli; sacked by insurgents in 1857. Harappa, 16 m. S. of Kot Kamalia, with extensive ruins of another town taken by Alexander. Chichawatni, railway station, on the Ravi, where Major Chamberlain was besieged in 1857.

§ 31. JHANG DISTRICT is bounded S.E. by Montgomery, N.E. by Goojranwala, N. by Shahpoor, and W. by Dera Ismail Khan. Area, 5702 sq. m. Population, 395,296. The district lies in the Rechna, Chach, and Sind Sagar Doabs; the Jhelam and Chenab unite below the chief town. The Ravi touches its S. border. On its Goojranwala border stood the hill and lake of Sakala, the Aryan capital of Madrades in *Mahabharat* times, the Sangala of Alexander and the Sagal of the Boodhist legend of King Kusa. Sherkot, in the Chenab lowlands, was another town of the Malli taken by the Greeks. **Maghiana** *cum* **Jhang** (21,630), chief town, 3½ m. from the Chenab, and 10 to 13 m. N.W. of its junction with the Jhelam. The public offices are in Maghiana. **Chiniot** (10,731), 3 m. W. of Chenab on road from Jhang to Wazeerabad, "famous for native painters and artificers."

§ 32. SHAHPOOR DISTRICT is bounded by Goojranwala from which the Chenab separates it, and Goojrat; N. by Jhelam, with river of same name between; W. by Bannoo and Dera Ismail Khan; and S. by Jhang. Area, 4691 sq. m. Population, 421,508. This still somewhat barren district stretches from the Chenab across the Jhelam, which divides it, over the Sind Sagar Doab up to the **Salt Range** rising to its greatest height (5000 ft.) in Mount Sakeswar, and enclosing small alluvial basins and lakes. Here also water changes and wars have desolated a tract populous from Alexander to Akbar. **Shahpoor** (5000), civil station on left bank of the Jhelam, opposite **Khushal** (8500), on road from Lahore to Dera Ismail Khan, a flourishing mart for the trade of the Salt Range. **Meeanee** (7000), centre of salt trade on left bank of Jhelam, opposite Pind Dadan Khan, through which the produce of the Mayo Mines passes. **Bhera** (15,165), the largest mart on left bank of the Jhelam; old capital of Sopheites, Alexander's contemporary, the ruins of which are called Jobnathnagar. **Sahiwal** (9000), 20 m. S. of Shahpoor, an agricultural centre.

§ 33. GOOJRAT DISTRICT is bounded N.E. by Kashmeer, N.W. by Jhelam, W. by Shahpoor, S.E. by Goojranwala and Sialkot, from which it is divided by the Chenab and Tavi. Area, 1973 sq. m. Population, 689,115. This is a Sub-Himalayan district between the Chenab and Jhelam, well wooded, but partially cultivated. The low **Pabbi Hills** (1400 ft.) pass into the N. angle from Kashmeer State, which begin 5 m. below Bhimbar and run S.W. to the Jhelam, whence they trend N. to the Salt Range. The **Tavi** is an affluent of the Chenab in the N.E. corner. From Alexander to the Marquis of Dalhousie the district is historically prominent. The valley of Mong or Moga, in lat. 32° 39′ N. and long. 73° 33′ E., named after Raja Moga, the Moa or Manas of the coins, was the site of **Nikæa**, and Alexander's field of battle with Porus after the passage of the Jhelam. In the old mound of ruins, 6 m. W. of Pabbi range, many Greek and Indo-Scythian coins are found with the monogram **Nik**. At Bahlolpoor, on the Chenab, 24 m. N.E. of Goojrat, the Delhi emperor, Bahlol Lodi, fixed the seat of government (1450-88), but Akbar reverted to Goojrat as the chief town. In the second Sikh war Sher Singh's army on N. bank of Chenab was outflanked by Sir Joseph Thackwell from the Wazeerabad ferry, and was defeated by Lord Gough at Sadullapoor. Retreating N. between the Jhelam and Pabbi hills the Sikh general was driven off the doubtful field of **Chilianwala** (13th January 1849). The ten years' wars, which had begun with the first Afghan campaign, were closed by the British victory (22d February) of **Goojrat** (18,750), on an old site of two successive cities, a little to N. of Chenab, so named from its Goojar founders. Akbar's fort is in the centre of the town, and the public offices to the N. The place has given its name to the inlaid work in gold and iron known as Goojrat ware. **Jalalpoor** (12,840), 8 m. N.E. of Goojrat, chief mart, with shawl manufactures. **Kunjah** (6000), local mart, 7 m. N.W. of Goojrat.

§ 34. JHELAM DISTRICT is bounded E. by Kashmeer State from which the Jhelam divides it, N. by Rawal Pindi, W. by Bannoo, and S. by Shahpoor. Area, 3910 sq. m. Population, 589,373. The Himalaya send out a rugged spur into the Sind Sagar Doab, consisting of the **Salt Range**, a treble line of parallel hills of red sandstone and carboniferous rocks running E. and W., with a strip of fertile plain along the Jhelam river. This is Jhelam district, of great beauty, with the **Kallar Kahar** lake on a plateau among the lower ridges. From the Salt hills the country runs in an elevated plateau into the Rawal Pindi mountains. The watershed, running N. and S., sends the western streams into the **Sohan**, and finally the **Indus**, and the eastern into the **Jhelam**, which is navigated by flat-bottomed boats above the town of that name. The Salt Range was the home of the exiled Pandavas, and is described in the *Mahabharat.* The much-disputed question as to the point at which Alexander crossed the Jhelam ("Hydaspes," from Sanskrit *Vitasta*) has been settled in favour of **Jalalpoor**, as the site of Bukephala, opposite Mong and close to Chilianwala, where Porus or Purusha was defeated. The main route of invaders from the north has lain through this district, whence its many fastnesses and its warlike tribes. **Jhelam** (21,107), on N. bank of river, 103 m. from Lahore, chief civil, military, and railway station, with bridge; seat of American United Presbyterian Mission. **Pind Dadan Khan** (16,724), chief town, 1 m. from N. bank of Jhelam river and 5 m. from foot of Salt Range, of which it is the emporium, named from Dadan Khan, the founder, in 1623. **Chakwal** (6000), grain mart and shoe factory, midway between the above town and Rawal Pindi. Talaganj (6000), 80 m. N.W. of Jhelam, with shoe manufactures. Lawa (5500), agricultural centre, N. of Salt Range and Mount Sukeswar.

§ 35. RAWAL PINDI DISTRICT is bounded E. by Kashmeer with the Jhelam between, N. by Hazara and Peshawar, W. by Peshawar and Kohat with the Indus between, and S. by Jhelam district. Area, 6218 sq. m. Population, 820,512. Like the above, this district forms part of the Himalaya spur which runs down into the Sind Sagar Doab. Its E. or Jhelam side consists of the sandstone **Marree Hills**, with fine forests, cultivated dales, and much beauty. Its W. mountains belong to the limestone system Trans-Indus, the chief range of which is named the white hill or **Chitta Pahar** (also Kala Chitta Pahar). The barrenness of this tract is relieved by the **Chach** oasis to the N. The **Indus** from Hazara opens out to a breadth of more than a mile containing wooded isles, contracts at Atak under the black rocks of Jalalia and Kamalia, again opens out into the **Bagh Nilab** ("blue lake"), and is once more narrowed at the gorge of the **Mokhad Hills**, its highest navigable point. The **Sohan** rushes down from the base of the Marree mountain, receives the Khird, Aling, Koorung, Leh, two Seels, and Vurala, and falls into the Indus. The **Haroh**, from one source at N. base of Marree mountain and another from Mochpooree mountain in Hazara, reaches the Indus near the Bagh Nilab. The **Resh** carries off the surface drainage from the Chitta Pahar to the Indus. On the Greek invasion the Turanian Takkas held the country under their own name of Takshasila, the Taxila of Alexander, now the ruins of **Shah Deri** or **Dera Shahan**, N. of the Margala pass, where also the Boodhist Asoka, when a prince, put down rebellion. In the Chach valley Mahmood of Ghazni defeated the Rajpoot federation under Prithvi Raja and the turbulent Ghakkars, non-Aryan, whose capital of **Pharwala** on the Sohan, now a fort, Baber took as described in his Memoirs. The Sikhs did not reduce the Ghakkars of the Marree hills till 1830, and in 1857 the old feud threatened rebellion, which the authorities, warned by a faithful native, nipped in the bud. John Lawrence took up his position here to organise measures for the peace of the Province and the fall of Delhi. The district was under General John Nicholson, to whose native aide-de-camp Lord Dalhousie made over the garden of **Wah**, in the valley of Hassan Abdal, watered by the Chiblat feeder of the Haroh, and extolled by Akbar for its beauty; Wah was a resting-place of the emperors on their way to Kashmeer. **Rawal Pindi** (53,000), chief town and cantonment (7000) on the Leh, 174 m. from Lahore, on the Jhelam valley road to Kashmeer, railway junction for Kohat, and seat of an American Presbyterian Mission. **Marree** (7057 ft.), sanitarium for Panjab officials and troops since 1853, on a ridge of the Marree hills, five hours' journey from Rawal Pindi, with magnificent views. For a population of above 11,000 in the season there are several churches, hotels, and shops, a successful brewery, and a Lawrence Asylum. **Atak** (3500), town and fort, built by Akbar, overhanging the Indus, opposite the infall of the Kabul river. This is the Atak Benares of the Muhammadan writers, as distinguished from Katak Benares in Orissa. Here were a bridge of boats and ferry till the railway to Peshawar was completed; also a tunnel, half constructed under the river and abandoned. **Hazro** (7500), in Chach plain, commercial centre, with snuff manufactures. **Campbellpoor** is a cavalry cantonment, S.E. of Atak.

§ 36. *KASHMEER STATE, including **Jamoo, Ladakh, Baltestan**, and **Dardestan**. **Kashmeer** (Kashuf-deo = the legendary gin of Kasyapa, the Hindoo sage said to have drained the valley) is the name of the famous Vale popularly applied to the whole tributary State now held by the son of the Rajpoot trooper, Golab Singh, to whom Ranjeet Singh gave the principality of Jamoo, and to whom Lord Hardinge, the Governor-General, sold Kashmeer and the hill country between the Indus and Ravi, for £750,000. The gross revenue is £450,000 a year. The area is 68,000 sq. m., and the population was estimated at 1,534,972 before the desolating famine of 1880. The State now includes Jamoo, Kashmeer proper, Baltestan, and the Gilgeet portion of Dardestan, up to N. lat. 36° 30′ at a peak 19,325 ft. high in Yaseen, and Ladakh to the Kuenlun plains and Changchenmo valley. The whole is bounded E. by Chinese Tibet (Gartok and Rudok), N. by the Kuenlun Range, Kashgaria again under the Chinese, and Yaghistan, reaching to the Pamir Steppe; W. by Yaseen, Chitral, and the independent republics stretching to Afghanistan, by Hazara, Rawal Pindi, Jhelam, and Goojrat; and S. by Sialkot, Goordaspoor, Chamba State, Lahaul, and Spiti. The State extends 240 m. from N. to S., or lat. 32° 30′ to 36° 30′; and 400 m. from E. to W., or long. 73° 30′ to 80° E. Rising from the great plain of the Panjab (1000 ft.), the two outer ridges of bare sandstone reach 4000 ft. above the sea. Farther in are the Middle Mountains, with forest and pasture rising to 8000–10,000 ft. Then the great chain of snowy mountains, running S.E. and N.W. from 15,000 to 27,000 ft., divides the drainage of the Chenab and Jhelam from that of the higher feeders of the Indus. Branches of this chain (the **Pansal, Peer Panjal, Darwar, Haramook**, and **Sonamarg**) enclose the valley or plain of Kashmeer, with hills sloping down from 15,000 to 5000 ft. To the N. and E. the Tibetan mountain system stretches over the high level of Baltestan (little Tibet), Gilgeet, and Ladakh, the summits varying from 17,000 to 22,000 ft., and one unnamed peak, K 2 of the Trigonometrical Survey, being 28,265 ft., the second highest yet known. The valleys here vary from 5000 to 15,000 ft.; the plateaux of Deosai, Lingzhithang, and Kuenlun in the N.E., stand at from 13,000 to 17,000 ft. above the sea. In Baltestan and Ladakh the people are Turanian Tibetans; in the lower and more Indian regions they are Aryans, viz. Hindoo Dogras and Muhammadan Chibhalis in the outer hills, Hindoo (chiefly) Paharees or highlanders in the middle mountains, Muhammadan (chiefly) Kashmeerees in the valley, and Muhammadan Dards between the Tibetans and Afghans. The **Jhelam** intersects the valley which it has created; in the S.E. end, in which it rises, the stream is navigable for 60 m. from Islamabad to Baramoola. The **Kishen Ganga** from the Deosai plains flows N.N.W. to Shardi, then S.W. till it joins the Jhelam below Muzaffarabad. The **Maru Wardwan**, from valley of the same name, flows S. to the Chenab above Kistawar. The **Chenab** passes through Kistawar and Badrawar to the plains W. of Jamoo. Of the many and beautiful lakes in the valley, the chief are the **Dal** or city lake, the **Anchar**, the **Manasbal** (finest), and the **Woolar**, through the largest part of which the Jhelam flows, all near Srinagar city. Of the mountain lakes, the **Konsa Nag** is on the top of the Peer Panjal range; the **Shisha Nag** above the head of the Lidar valley; and the **Gangabal** and Sarbal Nag on Harāmook, which looks down on the N.E. shore of the Woolar.

To reach the summer capital from the Panjab, there are four public routes with accommodation for travellers. Two from Goojrat railway station go (1) by Peer Panjal pass, and (2) by Poonch; two from Rawal Pindi go (1) by Marree, and (2) by Abbottabad (from Peshawar). The most frequented and historical, though not the easiest, is the imperial *Goojrat and Peer Panjal Route* used by the Mughul emperors, once cared for by Ali Murdan Khan, and still the commercial highway. There are 15 stages. From Goojrat it is 28½ m. to **Bhimbar**, town with old fort near river of same name; the last Raja's eyes were put out with a red-hot needle by Golab Singh. Thence over the Aditak and Kaman Goshi ranges, 55 m. to **Naoshera**, above the Tavi, taken by Ranjeet Singh. **Rajaori**, 28 m. farther up the Tavi, is the largest town on the route, and old capital of a State. **Baramgalla**, in Poonch, 25 m. farther, is reached after crossing the Rutten Peer pass (8200 ft.), above the Sooran river; here Jahangeer died, and Noormahal removed the remains to Shahdera, near Lahore. Fourteen miles farther on, amid grand scenery, the Peer Panjal range is crossed at 11,500 ft. **Shupiyan**, 20 m. farther, is the mart for the Panjab and the largest town on the Kashmeer side. When the Peer Panjal pass is closed by snow, the second or *Goojrat and Poonch Route* is followed from the 98th m. at Thana Mundi. **Poonch** is a town of 500 houses on the Sooran; 57 m. farther on beyond Haidarabad is the finest waterfall in Kashmeer. **Baramoola**, 40 m. farther, on right bank of Jhelam, has 250 houses; from this **Goolmarg**, a mountain "down," may be visited.

Two marches off, or 31 m. by land or water, is **Srinagar** (150,000) (Suryanagar = "city of the sun"), on either side of the Jhelam, spanned by seven of the peculiar Kashmeer bridges, midway in the valley (5200 ft.). This is the summer residence of the British Political Agent, Church medical missionary, chaplain, and doctor; and of hundreds of military officers, sportsmen, and travellers, for whom the Maharaja courteously provides bungalows in orchards above the city, and camping-grounds in the groves on the apple-tree canal (*sunt-i-kool*), opening into the Jhelam opposite the palace. The Sher Garhi, a city fort and palace of stone, is the chief building. The Badshah, a noble ruin, is the tomb of the eighth Musalman king who introduced the first shawl-weavers from Toorkestan. The great mosque was built by Shah Jahan. Around the city the chief objects of interest are the floating gardens, covering much of the Dal lake; the Char Chenar of Jahangeer's wife, described by Bernier and Moore, a mass of masonry in the same lake, formerly with a plane tree at either corner to give shade during the siesta, and a garden in which was a tablet, now gone, erected in 1835 by "three travellers, Baron Carl von Hugel, from Jummoo; John Henderson, from Ladakh; and Godfrey Thomas Vigne, from Iskardo," who caused these names of their predecessors to be engraved—"Bernier, 1633; Forster, 1786; Moorcroft, Trebeck, and Guthrie, 1823; Jaquemont, 1831; Wolff, 1832: of these, three only lived to return to their native country;" the Shalimar Bagh, Jahangeer's pleasure garden, in which Moore's *Lalla Rookh* pictures Shah Jahan and Noormahal's reconciliation; the Takht-i-Sulaiman hill, 1038 ft. above the city; and the Ham Parbat, 250 ft., which Akbar crowned by a vast fort. **Jamoo**, the Maharaja's winter capital, is not far from Sialkot on the Tavi.

In E. Kashmeer the chief places of interest are the ruins of **Awantipoor**, an old capital, 17 m. above Sialkot, partly excavated at Bishop Cotton's suggestion; **Islamabad**, the ancient Anant Nag, a mile from right bank of Jhelam; **Martand** or **Mattan**, 5 m. to N., a massive ruin of a temple of the sun, with a magnificent view; the **Bhoomjoo** caves; **Vernag** spring, the Jhelam source; **Ambernath** cave (above 16,000 ft.). On the road to Leh is **Sonamarg** ("golden meadow"), 5 marches E. from Sialkot, a popular sanitarium. Thence the track proceeds through the pass from the Sind to the Dras valley, 3 marches to Kargil, then 4 marches to Khalsi in the valley of the Indus, spanned by a wooden bridge, then 4 marches to **Leh**, capital of Ladakh, residence of the British Commissioner, and of the Maharaja's English Governor. The district of **Zanskar** lies S.W. To **Nubra**, along the Shayok river, the Khaidong pass (17,229 ft.) leads through the Leh range. **Roopshu**, with its salt lake, is a high district at S.E. end of Ladakh, ending in the valley of **Hanle**, near the Tibetan border. To E. of Leh, the **Pangkong** is the lowest (13,900 ft.) of a series of lakes passing into China towards Rudok for 90 m., and navigated by Captains Trotter and Biddulph. The commercial treaty of 1870 abolished transit duties on goods to and from E. Toorkestan, and a British Mission in 1873-4 to the Ataligh Ghazi of Kashgar opened up the trade route over the **Sasser** (17,800 ft.) and **Karakoram Passes** (18,550 ft.), to Yarkund and the country since reoccupied by the Chinese Government. **Changlung**, in the Nubra valley, is the last habitation on the Ladakh side of the British frontier S. of Karakoram.

In Baltestan the chief places are **Skardo** (7440 ft.), with a fort taken by the Dogras in 1840; **Shigar** (8000 ft.), pleasantly situated; Basha, Braldu, Rondu, Deosai. To **Gilgeet**, in Dardestan, 230 m. from Srinagar, and centre of a British Political Agent till recently, is 22 days' march by **Astor** (14 marches), with the **Nanga Parbat** peak in view. Lieut. G. W. Hayward, sent by the Royal Geographical Society to explore Pamir from this side, was, with his five servants, murdered at Darkoot, beyond Yaseen, on the Upper Chitral road to Badakshan, and 20 m. from Sarhadd in Wakhan, by Meer Wullee, who had hoped to use him for the restoration to himself of Gilgeet by the British Government. In 1874 part of the British Mission to Kashgar explored the **Pamir** ("waste") route S.W. from that city to Afghanistan by the **Sirikol Valley** (10,250 ft.) ("head of the mountain"), and over the **Bam-i-dunya** ("roof of the world"), to **Kila Panja**, or the five forts on the Oxus left bank, there 60 yards broad in 37° N. lat. and 72° 30′ E. long. in Wakhan, crossed by Marco

Polo in 1272, and by Benedict Goes in 1602. The Mission returned by the Great Pamir or **Wood's Victoria Lake** (13,900 ft.), which was frozen over on 1st May. The watershed is 14,300 ft. above the sea.

The annual tribute of the Maharaja of Kashmeer is 1 horse, 12 shawl-goats, and 3 pairs of shawls; the last is submitted by the Viceroy to the Queen-Empress.

§ 37. HAZARA DISTRICT, most N. of the Indian Empire, reaching to 35° N. lat., is bounded E. by Kashmeer, N. by Chilâs, and S. by Rawal Pindi. From the **Kaghan Glen** (6610 ft.), separating Hazara from Kashmeer, the N.W. frontier-line passes down between Hazara and the **Hussunzai** Afghans in the Cis-Indus strip of rugged hills containing the **Black Mountain, Torbaila,** and **Mount Mahaban,** the Aornos of Alexander, held by the Judoons, near whom was the fanatic colony of **Sitana.** From Torbaila, the Indus forms the W. boundary, separating Hazara from the Yusufzai Afghans. Area, 2835 sq. m., of which hardly 300 are level. Population, 407,075. The district, piercing the outer Himalaya, whose peaks rise to 17,000 ft., is a valley 56 m. wide at its opening from Rawal Pindi, and narrowing to a point in the dark gorge and still lakes of Kaghan, through which the **Kunhar** rushes to the Jhelam. Other valleys are Agroz, drained by the Unar, Mansahra by the Sirhan, Abbottabad by the Dor, and Khanpoor by the Haroh, all into the Indus. Pakli and **Haripoor** are well irrigated plains, the latter (4500) the seat of the Sikh Government and British outpost now. Lieutenant Abbott tamed the district for the first time in history; in 1868 local disturbances in **Agroz** (British outpost) led to the Black Mountain expedition. **Abbottabad** (1200) (4166 ft.), on the Dor, chief station and headquarters of frontier force, established by James Abbott, 124 m. E. of Peshawar. Baffa (4500), on the Sirhan or Pakli plain, chief mart of N. Hazara and the Swat border. The road from Hasan Abdal in Rawal Pindi to Srinagar in Kashmeer passes Haripoor, Abbottabad, and the local mart of Mansahra, and crosses the Kunhar by an iron suspension bridge, and the Jhelam by a ford.

§ 38. PESHĀWAR DISTRICT is bounded N.E. by the Bonair and Swat hills, N. and W. and S.W. by hills linking the Safed Koh to the Hindu Koosh, and inhabited by Ranizais, Osman-Kheylis, Upper Momands, and some Afreedees; and on the S.E. by Hazara and Rawal Pindi, with the Indus between. Area, 2504 sq. m. Population, 592,674. Peshawar district is a valley, the old bed of a post-tertiary lake, opened to the

Indus by the **Kabul River**, and surrounded by the hills (3000 to 5000 ft.) of independent Afghan tribes. Across the valley of the Kabul the range rises to 7060 ft., the height of **Moolla Ghar**, the principal peak, and is opened by 28 miles of the **Khaibar Pass**. North of this stretching by the **Swat Mountains** into the **Hindu Koosh**, and to the S. of these mountains—forming part of the great Peshawar basin, down to Atak on the E.—is the **Yusufzai Plain** or *samah*, extending 64 m. S.E. to N.W., and 46 m. N. to S., with an area of 3200 sq. m. and a population of 150,000, partly within and partly beyond the British frontier. The **Kabul River**, believed to rise from a spring, Sar-i-Chasmah, in Afghanistan (8400 ft.), lat. 34° 21′ N., long. 68° 20′ E., is fordable for 60 m. to Kabul city, below which it receives the Logar; 40 m. S. of Kabul, the Panjsher; 15 m. farther, the Tagao; 20 m. below, the united Alingar and Alishang; 20 m. farther, at Balabagh, the Soorkhab; and 2 m. below Jalalabad, the Koonar; thence, by the N. base of the Khaibar range, it enters the Peshawar valley at Michnee, where it divides into the Adoozai and Nagooman, which reunite at Doobandi, whence the river flows 40 miles to the Indus at Atak, after a course of 300 miles, navigable on inflated skins below Jalalabad. The **Swat River**, which falls into the Adoozai branch at Nisatha, rises in the hills dividing Panjakora from Swat and enters Peshawar N. of Michnee. The W. and central lands along these rivers are well cultivated and beautiful; the E. or Yusufzai plain and Khattak hills are bleak. The Bara, from the S., joins the Kabul river. The Kalpani, from the N.E., falls into that stream near Naushahra. Peshawar, or Parashawara, is the Gandhara of the Sanskrit, of which the Pukelas of Arrian, or Pushkalavati, was the capital taken by Alexander's general, Hephaistion, and now represented by the vast ruins of **Hashtnagar** ("eight cities"), on the left bank of the Swat. It became Boodhist till the appearance of the Pathan or Afghan "infidels," before the 8th century. In 978, Jaipal, Raja of Lahore, who held it, was defeated by Sabuktageen, the Samani governor of Khorasan, and his famous son Mahmood, as Sultan, began his series of conquests at Peshawar in 999, converting the Pathans to Islam. From that time to Nadir Shah in 1738, the valley was under Delhi; thereafter it was part of the Dooranee Afghan empire, or Sikh kingdom of Ranjeet Singh, and in 1849 it was made by Lord Dalhousie the British frontier, rather than the Indus. In 1857 the 55th Native Infantry mutinied at Naushahra and Hoti-Mardan, but were chased by Nicholson into the Swat hills; Edwardes held this Gate of the

Empire all through the crisis. **Peshawar City** (57,000), and **Cantonment** (23,000), near left bank of the Bara, stands 13½ m. S.E. of junction of Swat and Kabul rivers, and 10½ m. from **Jamrood** fort at the mouth of the Khaibar pass; 15 m. S. of **Michnee**, its other frontier-post on left bank of Kabul river; 190 m. S.E. of Kabul city; and 282 N.W. of Lahore. A mud wall, 10 ft. high, surrounds the city; the Goz Khatri, successively a Boodhist monastery and Hindoo temple, is now a sarai, and contains the public offices. Much trade passes through the city from Bokhara and Kabul to Amritsar and the S.; but the attempt to establish an annual fair has failed. Outside to N. the Bala Hissar quadrilateral fort commands the place. **Peshawar Cantonment** lies W. of the city, from which the Sadr Bazar divides it, on one of the highest slopes of the valley overlooking the Khaibar, and covering an area of 3½ by 1¾ miles. The Church Missionary Society has a large mission to the Afghans in the city. **Naushahra Kalan** (13,000), cantonment and railway station on right bank of Kabul river, opposite Naushahra cantonment, with bridge of boats, 19 m. W. of Atak, and 26 m. E. of Peshawar. **Charsada** (7500), agricultural and administrative centre of Hashtnagar, on the Swat, 15 m. N.E. of Peshawar, with adjoining village of Prang. Charsada was the **Peukelas** of Alexander's time, and the scene where Boodha pulled out his own eyes. **Hoti-Mardan**, two villages forming cantonment of corps of Guides on right bank of Chalpani, 16 m. N. of Naushahra, and 33 N.E. of Peshawar; from this place Yusufzai is administered. Tangi (7500), N.E. of Peshawar, near the Swat river and Mohmund frontier. **Cherat** (4500), hill cantonment on Khattak range, between Peshawar and Kohat districts; 34 m. S.E. of Peshawar city; used as a sanitarium by the troops since 1861. Fort **Mackeson**, near the mouth of the Khaibar pass, at foot of Khattak range. **Shabkadar**, fort and town, 17 m. N.E. of Peshawar.

Khaibar Pass (pop. 8173, of whom 7970 are males, and 203 females). —"In September 1880 the army which had been in occupation of N. Afghanistan returned to India through the Khaibar pass. Garrisons were for a time maintained at Landi Kotal and Ali Masjid, but it was decided to withdraw the troops entirely from foreign territory. The British Government recognise the independence of the Afreedee tribe, who in return pledge themselves to accept no other interference in their political relations; and also, in consideration of certain subsidies, undertake the entire responsibility for the security of the Khaibar pass, and maintain a body of Jezailchis with this object. The arrangements were completed in December 1880.

"The right to levy tolls on caravans making use of the Khaibar was reserved by the British Government, in consideration of the large subsidies paid to the tribe ; and a scale of tolls has now been formulated, and dues in accordance with this scale are levied from the caravans."—*Lieutenant-Governor's Report*, 1880-81.

§ 39. KOHAT DISTRICT is bounded E. by Rawal Pindi, with the Indus between ; N. by Peshawar and the Afreedee hills ; N.W. by the Orukzai country ; W. by the Zaimookht hills, Kooram river, and Wazeeree hills ; and S. by Bannoo. Area, 2838 sq. m. Population, 181,540. This Trans-Indus district consists of barren hills rich with rock-salt, and with unfrequent patches of cultivation. The hills in the E. or Khattak country are divided N. and S. by the **Teri Toi** river, which rises in Upper Meeranzai and flows E. to the Indus, 12 m. N. of Makhad ; N. the **Kohat Toi** flows parallel with it. In the W. the Meeranzai valley is more fertile. The frontier hills, which run into the Safed Koh, rise into two peaks, **Dupa Seer** (8260 ft.) and **Mazeo Garh** (7940 ft.). The **Wazeeree Hills**, to S., run in between the Kohat and Bannoo districts, and do not rise above 4000 ft. The **Afreedee Hills**, between the Kohat and Peshawar districts, are crossed by two principal passes connecting the two districts, the **Jawaki** and **Kohat Passes**. The Kohat pass or *guli* has been kept open by British influence since 1849, a mounted guard being maintained on the crest or *kothal ;* here Sir C. Napier led a punitive expedition. On the Peshawar side Fort Mackeson commands the mouth of the Kohat Pass, and is connected with a post near the mouth of the Jawaki pass. The **salt mines** lie along either side of the Teri Toi in bluish-gray rock, quarried at intervals of 40 m. The vein, one of the largest in the world, is a quarter of a mile wide, 1000 ft. thick, and sometimes rises in hills of 200 ft. The five mines now worked are at Jatta, the headquarters, and Malgin, 9 m. E., both on N. bank of Teri Toi ; and on the S. side Narri, 31 m. S.W. of Malgin, Bahadoor Khel, and Kharrak. There are petroleum springs at Panoba, 23 m. E. of Kohat, and sulphur in N. range. **Kohat** (18,200), chief town, cantonment, and fort, near N. bank of Kohat Toi, 2 m. from S. base of Afreedee hills, 37 m. S. of Peshawar. Hangu is the capital of the Upper Bangash tribe of Pathans, and Teri of the Khattaks.

Kooram.—"The evacuation of the Kooram Valley took place in October 1880. During its occupation by the British forces, a portion of the valley which adjoins the district had been made over temporarily to the political control of the Deputy Commissioner of Kohat, and a question arose regarding the boundary which should be maintained after the retirement of our troops. It was settled that the Kooram river should remain, as before, the boundary. The administration of the valley is in the hands of two delegates appointed by the tribal council of the Turi tribe, which constitutes its principal population; and, notwithstanding that some interference was at one time attempted on the part of the Ameer of Kabul, the new arrangement has, on the whole, worked well and smoothly."—*Lieutenant-Governor's Report*, 1880-81.

§ 40. BANNOO DISTRICT is bounded E. by Shahpoor, Jhelam, and Rawal Pindi; N. by Kohat; W. by the Mahsood Wazeeree hills; and S. by Dera Ismail Khan. Area, 3831 sq. m. Population, 332,577. The Indus, from Kalabagh on N., opens out and divides the district. On E. the Salt Range from Shahpoor meets the Indus at Mari, opposite Kalabagh, and the land is like the rest of the arid Panjab plain. On the W. the plain rises into the **Khattak-Niazar** or **Maidani** hills, with the peak Sukha Ziarat (4745 ft.) Hence the oval valley of Bannoo stretches for 40 m. W. and 60 N. to the border on which the Peer-ghul and Shiwadar peaks of the Wazeerees look down, with the Safed Koh as a background. The **Kooram** and **Tochi** or Gambeela, which unite beyond Laki town, drain the valley to the Indus. The Kooram, rising in the Safed Koh, passes through the beautiful **Kooram Valley**, which is 60 m. long and 3 to 10 wide, with a population of 78,000 in 36 villages, which supply 20,000 fighting men; enters Bannoo district at N.W. corner, 5 m. from the headquarters, and falls into the Indus 4 m. S. of Isakhel. The **Kooram Pass** to Kabul lies along the course of the river; here General Roberts won the victory at **Peiwar Kotal** in December 1878. **Edwardesabad** (4000) is the chief town and cantonment in N.W. corner, close at the entrance to the Kooram Valley, and on the Kooram river just below its junction with the Shaml, and about 50 m. above its junction with the Indus. Founded by Herbert Edwardes, who reduced the wild tribes to order. The cantonment lies around the fort of Dhuleepnagar, so named from Maharaja Dhuleep Singh. Edwardesabad is a station of the Church Missionary Society. **Laki** (4500), on right bank of Tochi, 32 m. from Edwardesabad. Ten m. from Edwardesabad is the Kooram post at the entrance to the valley, at the end of the spur of hills which divides the Kooram and Khost valleys, through which the Kooram and Shaml rivers respectively flow. **Kalabagh** (6500), on right bank of the Indus, at foot of Salt Range, 105 m. below Atak, picturesquely built in the salt cliffs, and with manufactures of iron. Mianwali (4700), on left bank of the Indus. Isakhel (7500), on right bank of the Indus, 42 m. S.E. of Edwardesabad.

§ 41. DERA ISMAIL KHAN DISTRICT is bounded E. by Jhang and Shahpoor, N. by Bannoo, W. by Sulaiman range, and S. by Dera Ghazi Khan and Muzaffargarh. Area, 9296 sq. m. Population, 441,649. The district extends W from the centre of the Sind Sagar Doab to the **Sulaiman** mountains, which culminate near the chief town in the two peaks of **Takht-i-Sulaiman** (11,295 and 11,070 ft.), and are held by the Wazeeree, Sheorani, Ushtarani, Kasrani, and Bozdar tribes of Pathans. The range forms a staircase from the plains of India to the plateau of Afghanistan, intersected by about a dozen passes between Dera Ismail Khan and Jacobabad, and all of growing military importance. They are connected with the Zhob valley route from Pisheen, and the Bori valley and Ason Ali roads farther S. The **Gomal Pass**, between Kulachi and Tank, through the range, is the caravan highway of the Povindah carriers from Kabul and Kandahar; it follows the **Gomal River** or Looni. The **Shaik Budeen** range in N., with sanitarium (4516 ft.), separates Dera Ismail Khan from Bannoo. The **Khisor Hills** lie between that and the Indus, which divides the district. The ruins of Kafir Kot, two forts on the N. border, point to the civilisation of the Derajat in Græco-Bactrian times. From the end of the 15th century, when Malek Sohrab settled with his Baloochees here, and his sons Ismail Khan and Fateh Khan founded the towns of these names, this Kot family ruled till the Afghan Ahmed Shah took it about 1750, and the Afghan governor afterwards built a capital at Mankera, between the Indus and Jhelam, which Ranjeet Singh took. Edwardes so civilised the people as to take levies from it to Mooltan. **Dera Ismail Khan** (19,000), 4½ m. from the right bank of the Indus, chief town and cantonment, built since 1823, when the Indus flood swept the old town away, with fort of Akalgarh; a Church Missionary Society's station. Here is the tomb of Sir Henry Durand. **Kulachi** (10,000), centre of transit trade by Ghwalari pass, on right bank of Looni, 37 m. N.W. of Dera Ismail Khan. **Leiah** (6000), old capital E. of present bed of Indus, in S. **Bhakkar** (5000), farther N. **Tank** (3400), 42 m. N.W. of Dera Ismail Khan, on ravine issuing from Tankzaru pass; here Sir Henry Durand, when Lieutenant-Governor, was accidentally killed.

§ 42. DERA GHAZI KHAN DISTRICT is bounded E. by Bahawalpoor and Muzaffargarh, with the Indus between; N. by Dera Ismail Khan; W. by the Sulaiman mountains; and S. by Jacobabad in Sind. Area, 4377 sq. m. Population, 363,346. The Balooch tribes begin on the N. and W. borders of this narrow strip of sandy soil between the Indus and Sulaiman (7462 ft. here) under the names of Khosahs, Logharees, Goorchanees, Marrees, and Boogtees, who hold the Sanghar, Sakhi-Sarwar, Kalia, Chachar, and Sori passes under the British Government. Of the hill torrents the **Kaha** and **Sanghar** alone are perennial, so that in the hot season the people desert the "Pachad" or W. portion of district for the hills or the Indus lowlands termed the "Sind." In 711 A.D. the Arab Muhammad Kasim, the first Musalman invader, took the country, which became part of the Mooltan administration from Delhi. Following Malik Sohrab came the second Balooch invader, the Makrani chief, Haji Khan, whose son founded and gave his name to **Dera Ghazi Khan** (19,000), in pleasant groves 2 m. W. of present bed of the Indus, and skirted by Kastoori Canal. The old town was swept away in 1857 by Indus floods, from which a massive dam protects the new station; centre of Church Medical Mission to Baloochees. **Mithankot** (3500), below junction of the Indus with the Panjnad or united Five Rivers, once the commercial capital. Dajal (6500), decaying town in centre of district. Jampoor (8000), 32 m. S. of Dera Ghazi Khan, noted for wood-turning industry. **Rajanpoor** (4000), cantonment and town, 73 m. S. of Dera Ghazi Khan, just N. of Mithankot. **Mangrota** (4500), on the Sangarh, 45 m. N. of Dera Ghazi Khan, fort and military station. Harrand Fort, military outpost, formerly the most W. possession of Ranjeet Singh.

*BALOOCHISTAN.

§ 43. *BALOOCHISTAN STATE (by the treaties of 1844 and 1876 bound to receive a British garrison, controlled by the Governor-General's Agent, and opened up by a British railway and telegraph) was peacefully reduced to order in 1876 by Sir Robert Sandeman, from his experience as Commissioner of the adjoining Derajat, and is free from allegiance to Afghanistan or Persia. The State is bounded E. by Sind, N. by Afghanistan, W. by Persia, and S. by the Arabian Sea. Since Sir F. Goldsmid's joint commission fixed the boundary in 1871 in order to arrest continued encroachment by Persia, from Gwadur Bay, about 61° 36′ E. long. N. to lat. 26° 15′ N., when it turns E. to Nihing river, follows that to its source and to 63° 12′ E. long., whence it goes N. to Jalk, Baloochistan may be stated to have an area of 106,500 sq. m., and the population is estimated at nearly 500,000, while the Khan's revenue is only £30,000.

More loosely, the tract of Baloochistan covers 148,000

sq. m., divided thus—Panjabi Baloochistan, 8000; Kalati Baloochistan, 80,000; Persian Baloochistan, 60,000 or less. Kalati Baloochistan is the region between the longitudinal lines 57 and 67, bounded S. by the sea and N. by a line sufficiently above lat. 28° to take in the Kuh-i-Basman and Kuh-i-Nushadir, according to Sir F. Goldsmid. The line of demarcation between W. or Persian, and E. or Kalati Baloochistan, is N. at the Mashkid river, and S. at the fishing village of Gwettar.

From Gwadur Bay, which is the most W. point of India, the coast runs E. for 600 miles to Cape Monze or Ras Muari where Sind begins. From W. to E. the headlands are—Cape Zegin, the W. extremity of Gwadur Bay; Ras Juni, its E. point; Ras Nu, W. point of Gwadur Bay; Ras Pashi; Ras Arubah; Gurab Sinh and Ras Muari, E. headland of Sonmeani Bay, N. of Karachi. Alexander's admiral, Nearchus, coasted this land of the Ichthyophagi and date-eaters from the Indus to the head of the Euphrates, while he himself led his army back through the Oritae and Gadrosii. The Brahooees ("on the waste" = shepherds) and Baloochees, both Muhammadan Soonnees, now form the population, the former having become dominant under Kumber, the shepherd head of the chief tribe, the Kumbarani. The Kohistan or mountain land is the E. portion between Kalat the capital and Kach-Gandava, enters Baloochistan from Afghanistan from the N. of the Bolan pass, as the **Herbui Mountains**, throws off a spur to the Indus at Sewan, and strikes the sea at Cape Monze as the **Khirthar Mountains.** The Bolan and the Moola are the two principal watercourses which drain the Kohistan. The **Bolan River** rises 60 m. N.E. of Kalat, and discharges itself into the Kach plain at Dadar. The **Moola River** rises 45 m. S. of Kalat, and ends in Kach at Kotra, near Gandava. Each gives its name to a pass. The **Bolan Pass** begins 5 m. N. of Dadar, and rises for 60 m. N.W., 90 ft. in the mile, to the broad plain Dasht-i-Bidaulat (8500 ft.), 10 miles from the Seer or head of the pass. A British detachment was lost here in a flood in 1861; in 1839 a column, with artillery, went up in six days. Quetta is 25 m. from the head of the pass; in 1878 a railway was planned here. The **Moola** or **Gandava Pass**, entered at Peer Chatta, 9 m. from Kotri, at Taphoi 9 m. S. of Kotri and at Gatti (very difficult), leads from Kach-Gandava to the tableland of Jhalawan (5250 ft.), 102 m. from Peer Chatta. The Gaj and Nana streams, S. of the Moola, are absorbed when they reach the plains. To the W. of Kalat the mountains are lower up to the desert west of Kharan; the Dasti or Moolani is the chief watercourse.

Baloochistan is divided into seven districts. **Kalat**, in N. of which Kalat is the chief town and capital of the whole country. **Sarawan**, surrounding Kalat, on N.; Mustoong is chief town, and Quetta the fort. **Jalawan**, S. of Kalat; Kozdar, chief town. **Lus**, to S. on the coast; Beyla, chief town. **Kach Gandava**, E.; Bagh, Dadar, and Gandava, chief towns; and **Sibi**, terminus of Kandahar State Railway, 133 m. from Ruk, in the valley of the Nari, 12 m. N. of Mitri, rapidly laid down during the second Afghan war. **Mekran**; Kej, chief town. **Kohistan**; Jalk, chief town. **Kalat City**, the capital (7000 ft.), stands on the W. side of a well-cultivated valley, 8 m. long, and 2 to 3 broad, surrounded by a mud wall and hill on which is the Khan's citadel, stormed in a few minutes by Willshire in 1839, and occupied by Nott in 1840. **Quetta** (Kwatta = Afghan name) or **Shal** (Brahooee, meaning "the fort") is the British capital (5800 ft.), the residence of the Governor-General's Agent, and, in the second Afghan war, the base of the southern column which advanced to Kandahar. Quetta, at the N. end of valley of same name, on the Bolan route from Jacobabad to Kandahar, and 103 m. N. of Kalat, is surrounded by mud walls and dominated by a fort on an artificial mound in the centre. The railway may be continued from Sibi through the Nari pass to Harnai (3500 ft.), thence through the Chapar hill to the valley above and on to Quetta and Pisheen. There is "an alternative route to the Upper Chapar valley on the sides of the Adeena hills, by which the line would pass 12 m. from Quetta, and over the river Lora to Kandahar."

Pisheen and **Sibi**, included in the Panjab frontier by the Gandamak treaty, were made over by the Tripartite treaty of 1838 to Ranjeet Singh, and were overrun by the Marrees. The boundaries of **Sibi** are E. the Panjab and Sulaimans, N. Pisheen and the country of the Dumar Pathans, W. the Bolan pass, S. Kalat. The great caravan routes between Kandahar, Dera Ghazi Khan, Mooltan, and Rajpootana *via* Bahawalpoor, traverse these two districts, and have been open to peaceful trade since the second Afghan war. **Pisheen** is a continuation of Sibi to the **Amran** mountains, including Shorawak, and is separated from Kandahar province by a desert 70 m. wide. The Kalat district of **Nushki** joins Pisheen at Shorawak and bounds it W.; Quetta and Sibi bound it S.; the Khakar hills and the Zhob and Borj country E.; and Kandahar desert N. British officers administered Pisheen for a year before it became British under the Treaty of Gandamak and it was administered from Quetta. The aborigines are the Tarens, who have been most loyal. Through this country lies the great highway of **Thal-Chotiali** (3000 ft.) from Fort Munro (6240 ft.) on the Sulaiman range past Vitakri, along the Looni and Bori valleys to Balozai N. of Quetta. The old Balooch frontier, held by troops and police, runs for 700 m. by Rajanpoor and Jacobabad to Karachi.

The Gandamak treaty frontier, commencing also at Dera Ghazi Khan, runs in a straight line to Thal-Chotiali, Pisheen, Sibi, the Amran range at Chaman, Shorawak, and Nushki, whence the Baloochistan frontier runs to the Persian Gulf at Gwadur. **Sewestan** is now defined as including all the district drained by the Nari and its affluents. Its rugged ranges of sandstone and limestone running S. and W. culminate in the Zarghoon Mountain (11,730 ft.), the highest in S. Afghanistan, to be pictured only by some of Gustave Doré's illustrations to the *Inferno*, according to the Survey Report.

CHAPTER XIV.

PROVINCE OF BOMBAY—GENERAL.

§ 1. Size. § 2. Position and Physical and Historical Divisions. § 3. Mountains and Rivers. § 4. Canals and Railways. § 5. Products and Trade. § 6. Land Tenures and Taxation. § 7. The People in Districts and States.

§ 1. Size.—**Bombay Province** (still a "Presidency" in the military sense, so long as the European and native garrison of 40,000 men are under a local Commander-in-Chief) corresponds in size, population, and position very nearly with the Peninsula of Spain and Portugal in Europe. Without Baroda State it has an area of 191,847 sq. m., one-third of which consists of Feudatory States or 66,408 m., and a population of 23,273,786, nearly a third of whom, or 6,784,482, are in these States. As nearly coextensive with Western India, with a great length of coast line and with such harbours as Bombay city and Karachi, though not opened up by great navigable rivers such as those of which the metropolis, Calcutta, is the mouth, the Province of Bombay has a seaborne or foreign and coasting trade of £71,695,017 (1880-81). The completion of the railway through Rajpootana, which connects Bombay harbour directly with the great cities and fertile plains of Hindustan, is increasing the trade. The Province yielded a gross imperial and local revenue of £11,894,830 in 1880-81. Its northern section of Sind belongs geographically and historically to the Panjab, with which it has long been proposed to connect it; but when that is done the Central Province will doubtless be added to Bombay, to which it more properly belongs than to any other local administration.

§ 2. Position and Physical and Historical Divisions.—The Western Province of India is bounded E. chiefly by a series of States reaching from Mysore N. to Haidarabad, Berar, the Central Province, Indore, Baroda, Rajpootana, and the Derajat of the Panjab; N. and N.W. by Baloochistan; W. by the Arabian Sea; S. by the S. Kanara District of Madras and by Mysore State. The Province extends from the most N. point of Sind, 28° 47′ N. lat. to 13° 53′, and from the most W. point of Sind, 66° 40′ E. long. to 76° 30′, the E. extremity of Khandesh. Within this is the small territory of the Portuguese in Goa, Daman, and Diu, with an area of 1062 sq. m.; its population of 444,987 is not included in the above.

The great natural, and to some extent historical, divisions of Western India from N. to S., are these: **Sind**, or the lower Indus valley, fertile only where irrigated; **Goojarat**, or the peninsulas of Kach and Kathiawar, consisting chiefly of rich alluvial plains, industriously cultivated by the Goojars, who give the country its name; the **Konkan**, N. and S., or the three moist and densely peopled coast districts of Thana, Kolaba, and Ratnagiri, between the Sahyadri range and the Sea; the **Dekhan** tableland, sloping away E. from the watershed of that range, scored by the great rivers which find their way to the Bay of Bengal; and the **W. Carnatic**, or fertile black land S. of the Kistna river. Historically viewed, Sind is the Indus land through which the Musalman invaders poured to the rich plains of Goojarat, where the Boodhist Asoka carved his edicts on the rock, and Rajpoot dynasties had ruled for fifteen centuries, till Mahmood of Ghazni sacked the shrine of Somnath (1024 A.D.), the Toorks of Delhi under Alaf Khan destroyed the Rajpoot capital, Patan (1297 A.D.), and, in 1403, their governors became independent sovereigns of Ahmedabad. The Kathiawar portion of Goojarat was the **Saurashtra** of the earlier Hindoos. In the Dekhan, the most powerful Rajpoot dynasties ruled from Walabhi and Goolbarga till the Bahmani house fell in 1490. **Maharashtra** gave birth to the soldier peasants whom Shivaji (born in 1627) united into a confederacy from Poona as a capital in 1749, which swept all India till overthrown by the Afghans at Panipat, and then yielded to the British, who, in 1818, finally reduced to order the Peshwa or hereditary "mayor of the palace," the Gaekwar of Baroda, Holkar of Indore, Sindia of Gwalior, and Bhonsla of Nagpoor. Bombay, the first part of India to become British, was the latest to grow into dimensions worthy of one of the three old Presidencies, which it became in 1668. It was subordinated to the Governor-General in 1773, but, like Madras alone, with a Council and Commander-in-Chief, and with the power of corresponding direct with the home authorities, who have always directly appointed its Governor. Maharashtra is the country of the aboriginal Mahars, or the "great country," and its people are still the ablest in India. The **Parsees**, who do not exceed 73,000 in number, are the descendants of the ancient Persians of the empire of Cyrus, who, after the defeat at Kadseah (658 A.D.) of Yezdijird III., the last of the Sassanians, landed in W. Thana district in 717, and have since prospered in Goojarat, Surat, and Bombay city. The many Jews in the Konkan who call themselves **Beni-Israel** are believed to be descendants of the remnant of the captivity who fled into Egypt, and, according to the warning of Jeremiah, were sent captive to Yemen, were reinforced after the fall of Jerusalem, and thence reached the S. Konkan of Bombay at Rajapoora.

§ 3. MOUNTAINS AND RIVERS.—The chief mountain ranges run N. to S. In N. on the right bank of the Indus, are the **Khirthar Mountains**, a continuation of the Sulaiman between Baloochistan and Sind. Passing S. by ridges of low sandhills in the Indus deserts and the isolated hills of Kach and Kathiawar, we reach the **Western Aravali Chain** ("line of peaks") which, stretching from Mount Aboo to the valley of the Narbada, separates Goojarat from the Central India States. From the rugged country S. of the Tapti spring the **Sahyadri Mountains** or **Western Ghats**, which run parallel to the sea at a distance of 40 to 50 m., with an average elevation of 1800 ft., but send up single peaks to double that height. This range of basalt and trap extends S. for 500 m., covering a belt of country 20 m. broad, abrupt at their W. declivity on which the clouds of the S.W. monsoon break with fury, in May-June every year, and sloping eastwards towards the Coromandel coast. The **Satpoora** and **Satmala** or **Ajanta Hills** run E. at right angles to the Ghats. The Satpoora (5434 ft. at Toran Mall), stretching from the E. of Goojarat to the Aseergarh fort, separate the valley of the Tapti from that of the Narbada, and Khandesh from Indore. The Satmala, which form the N. slope of the Dekhan plateau, separate Khandesh from Haidarabad State.

(For **Indus** river see pages 28 and 194.) The **Sabarmati** and **Mahi** rivers of Goojarat rise in the N. and S. respectively of the Mahi-kantha spurs of the Aravali and reach the Arabian Sea near the head of the Gulf of Kambay. The largest river which finds the sea at Goojarat is the **Narbada** or Narmada or Rewah (Namadus of Greek geographers), the traditional boundary between Hindustan proper and the Dekhan. It flows for 80 m., from Amarkantak Hill in Rewah State to the Gulf of Kambay below Broach. Running W. through the

Central Province, in which it forms lovely reaches or pools (*dohs*), and falls over the Marble Rocks 9 m. S.W. of Jabalpoor, it flows between the Satpoora and Vindhya mountains, then past coal and iron mines, cotton and millet fields, through the jungles of Nimar and round the idol island of Mandhata, receiving many tributaries, chiefly from the S., till it enters Goojarat at Makrai. There it separates Baroda from Rajpeepla State, winds through Broach from half a mile to a mile broad, and widens into an estuary which opens out into the Gulf of Kambay. It drains but does not irrigate 36,400 sq. m., and discharges a maximum volume of 2,500,000 cubic feet a second. In superstitious sanctity the Narbada comes second only to the Ganges; thrice its railway bridge near Broach city has been injured or carried away by floods. The **Tapti**, from the Betool district of the Central Province, cuts through the Satpoora, which hem it in for 150 m.; crosses the upland plain of Khandesh for 180 m., where it receives several tributaries, descends to the lower level of Goojarat by the narrow Haranphal or "deer's leap," towards the Dang forests for 50 m., and for the final 70, of which 32 are tidal, winds through Surat, passes the city and falls into the Gulf of Kambay, after a course of 450 m., in which it drains 30,000 sq. m. and covers a volume varying from 120,000,000 cubic yards in flood to 25,000 at the close of the dry season, in hourly discharge. The Tapti is commercially the most valuable of the Goojarat rivers, but surveys have proved that its broken channel and rapid current forbid it to be the highway for the produce of Khandesh and the Central Province, which depend on railways. The other streams flowing W. to the ocean are mountain torrents or creeks, from the Sahyadri of which the Shiravati in N. Kanara is the most notable for the **Gersoppa** succession of falls through the W. crest of the Ghats, the chief of which is 890 ft. in height. The Sahyadri give birth to the great eastward rivers of the Dekhan, the Godavari from above Nasik and the Kistna from Mahableshwar, which more fully belong to Madras.

§ 4. CANALS AND RAILWAYS.—**Canals** are not numerous or extensive in this Province, except in Sind, where by a network of channels the Indus supplies nearly the whole cultivation. In Goojarat and the Dekhan there are 24 small but locally important works of irrigation, fed from the Sahyadri range by permanent storage, as in the Mutha canal system; by rivers with a supply lasting to December only, in 9 cases; by 3 rivers rising elsewhere with large catchment areas, and by 9 rivers with smaller areas. The most important are the **Kistna**

Canal, in Satara; the **Ekrook Tank**, in Sholapoor; and the **Kirkee** waterworks, near Poona. Others are the **Palkher Canal**, in Nasik; the Ojhar and Lakh, in Ahmednagar; the **Neera**, in Satara; and the **Gokak**, in Belgaum. The capricious rainfall of the E. Dekhan, where the famine of 1876-8 was most severe, can best be improved by reclothing the Sahyadri hills with forests. The area under forest conservancy is about 13,230 sq. m., of which 7771 are reserves. The Indus Conservancy Department keep the river clear, from which the Inundation Canals supply Sind, or the Desert, Begari, Sukkur, and Thar Canals. The most important work is the maintenance of the irrigation channels during the yearly inundation. There are no navigable canals in Bombay.

Bombay is the western focus of the Indian railway system. Within its limits are upwards of 3500 miles of railway, of which the **Great Indian Peninsula line** has 1288, stretching from Kalyan junction towards Calcutta and Madras; the **Bombay, Baroda, and Central India** has 422, running N. through Goojarat to Wadhwan for Kathiawar, and Ahmedabad for Rajpootana and Delhi; the **Rajpootana - Malwa** has 1116. The principal branches and connecting links are the **Bhaunagar - Gondal** line, 104 m. from Wadhwan, with branch from Dhola junction, 31 miles, to Dhoraji in W. Kathiawar, 119 m.; the **Holkar** and Sindia-Neemach, with Oojain branch, 289 m.; the Neemach-Naseerabad continuation, 101 m.; and four small Baroda lines, of which **Dabhoi** is the centre. Under survey or construction are the **Eastern Dekhan**, 173 m. from Hotgi to Beejapoor and Bagalkot, and the Barsi Road to Pandharpoor (33 m.) and Bansi (20 m.) branches. The **S. Maratha** or Marmagao-Hoobli line will connect Goa with N. Madras, running 49 miles to the British frontier, thence to Dharwar, Hoobli, Guddak, and Bellary, in tracts lately afflicted by famine.

§ 5. PRODUCTS AND TRADE.—Bombay Province, as it is, has no coal; but may be supplied from the Central Province, where the fuel abounds in the Satpoora region and Godavari valley. Iron is mined and smelted at Teagar, in Dharwar. Gold exists in the quartz of the Dambal hills of the same district, and is washed by the natives out of the streams which feed the Upper Malprabha, especially the Soortoor. The Province produces fine building stone, limestone, and slate, from which modern Bombay city has been built. Of the occupied area of Bombay 85 per cent is under crops, chiefly the great and spiked millets in the Dekhan, known as *jowari* and *bajri*; rice in the

Konkan, and wheat in Goojarat and Sind, and cotton. Since 1825 cotton has been exported from Bombay; but in 30 years the value of the export had not increased to more than 2½ millions sterling (1853-54). In 1864-65, during the civil war in the United States, the value rose to 30⅓ millions, and it now stands at about 10 millions a year. The area planted annually is about 4½ millions of acres, of which half a million is under the exotic plant in Dharwar, Khandesh, and the S. Maràtha States. The out-turn is about 1,900,000 cwts. Gradually steam manufacture is restoring a local manufacturing trade. There are 42 mills, of which 32 are in Bombay city, with 1,158,570 spindles and 12,310 looms, consuming upwards of 1 million cwts. There are experimental farms in Sind, and at Bhadgaon in Khandesh. Silk-weaving flourishes at Ahmedabad, Surat, Nasik, Yeola, and Poona; carpet-making at Ahmednagar. Sind produces woollens, leather-work, and the best pottery in India. Bombay city, Nasik, and Poona are famous for brass-ware. Ahmedabad is unrivalled in ironwork and perforated brasswork; Kach in cutlery, armour, and embossed gold and silver work; Koompta in sandal-wood carving; and Kathiawar, as well as Kach, in stone-cutting. Omitting re-exports, the value of the export trade of Bombay in 1880-81 was £34,924,270, of which £27,473,096 went to foreign external ports, £1,762,228 to foreign Indian ports, £4,345,766 to British ports in other Provinces, and £1,343,179 to other Bombay ports. The imports amounted to £34,738,476. The value of the cotton crop exported was £9,777,185, and of the grain (chiefly wheat) and pulse was £2,278,393, an extraordinary increase over previous years. The Malwa opium export to China fell to £5,903,113.

§ 6. LAND TENURES AND TAXATION.—Settlement is always for thirty years, except in Sind, where, owing to the still imperfect condition of irrigation, it has been thought desirable to adopt the shorter period of ten years. The advantages enjoyed by the occupant of land under the survey settlement are—(1) Fixity of tenure conditional on the due payment of the Government demand. (2) His occupancy is heritable, and transferable by gift, sale, or mortgage, without other restriction than the requirement to give notice to the authorities. (3) His assessment is fixed, but subject to revision after periods of thirty years. The right of occupancy is not affected by the expiration of a term of settlement, being conditional solely on the payment of the assessment imposed. (4) He is at liberty to resign his entire occupancy, or any part of it, defined by the survey in any year, provided notice be given by a fixed date. If waste land be available, he may enlarge his holding at pleasure on application to the district officials. (5) He may sublet his lands, and Government aids him, under certain limitations, in recovering rents from his tenants. (6) His holding cannot be encroached on by his neighbour, every field in it being clearly defined by boundary marks, and susceptible of immediate identification by means of the village maps. Further, the fact of his possession of any field can be traced without difficulty in the village records year by year up to the date of the introduction of the first survey settlement.

The tenures on which land is held in Sind are of the simplest character. Doubtless in the ancient times of Hindoo nationality, and under Brahman dynasties, the same complexity of land tenure prevailed in Sind as in other Provinces of India; but as successive waves of Muhammadan invasion and conquest passed over the Province, and when finally the bulk of the population forsook the old faith to profess that of Islam, the ancient institutions must have gradually decayed and given way to those brought in by the conquering race. The land in Sind is held by a large number of peasant occupants and by a comparatively small body of large proprietors. Probably half the entire number of holdings do not exceed 5 acres in area, and not more than a quarter exceed 30 acres. Yet there are not wanting indications that in times not distant from the present nearly all the land was held by large proprietors. In course of time the zameendaree rights in the land were purchased by the tenant, or lapsed on demise without heirs, or otherwise fell into disuse, and thus has sprung up the present large peasant proprietary.

The gross land revenue of Bombay Province was £3,812,385 in 1880-81. Of this 18 per cent is alienated, or £680,895 in the same year. The revision of the thirty years' settlement up to the same time cost £206,744, and added £879,621 in all to the revenue; the annual increase was £147,120. In 1879 and 1882 the Dekhan Agriculturists' Relief Acts were passed, to protect the peasantry from usurers by means of village registrars, and keep them from litigation by "conciliators." There are, besides the land-tax, the same cesses as in other Provinces for schools, roads, and police.

§ 7. THE PEOPLE IN DISTRICTS AND STATES.—Besides Aden and Perim (34,890) and the Native States (6,941,631), the census of 1881 showed that the total population of ordinary British territory (districts) was 16,454,414, of whom 8,497,718 were males and 7,956,696 females. The number of males to

100 females is 106·7, if Sind be included; but, excluding that division, the circumstances of which, as regards the relative proportions of the sexes, are very different from those of the rest of the Province, and excluding, also for similar reasons, the city of Bombay, the ratio is reduced to 102·5, varying between 90·2 in Ratnagiri—where the male population is generally given to spending the fair season in Bombay in search of work—and 112·8 in Kaira. Distributed according to the main religions, the population comprises 12,308,111 Hindoos, 3,021,112 Muhammadans, 216,224 Jains, 138,329 Christians, 127,100 Sikhs, 72,065 Parsees, 562,678 persons belonging to forest or aboriginal tribes, and 8395 of other religions, chiefly Jews. The ratio of each religion to the total population is, per 10,000 —Hindoos, 7480; Muhammadans, 1836; Aboriginals, 342; Jains, 132; Christians, 84; Sikhs, 77; Parsees, 44; Jews, 4·8; and others, 0·2. In ten years the population has increased by only 168,778, or 1·03 per cent. This result includes a decrease in males of 0·28 per cent, with a balancing increase in females of 2·48. In Goojarat, Broach is the only district that shows a diminished population, or 6·67 per cent, due to a severe epidemic of fever and other disease in 1878-9. In the Konkan the districts of Thana and Kolaba show an increase respectively of 7·21 and 8·91. The population of Ratnagiri fell off by 2·16 per cent. In the Dekhan the large district of Khandesh has increased from a population of 1,030,036 to 1,237,231, or a difference of 20·11 per cent. This change is due to the advance of the district in well-being, as the amount of fertile and available land attracts cultivators from the older colonies of Goojarat and the Central Dekhan. The rest of the districts, except Nasik which has increased by 5·88 per cent, show a decrease, most of which must be attributed to the famine and accompanying sickness and emigration that took place in 1876-78. The variation is from 2·25 in Poona, where the city has some counterbalancing effect on the rate of change, to 19·02 in Sholapoor. In Satara, however, where the famine affected but a portion of the district, the population may be called stationary, as the decrease is of ·02 only, and it is not improbable that even this may be due to the absence of large bodies of the lower classes on the railway works and in Bombay. The Kanarese division shows an increase of 5·88 per cent in N. Kanara; but in the Dekhan, or tableland of this tract, the decrease ranges from 21·77 in Kaladgi to 8·56 in Belgaum. In Sind the increase has been universal, and ranges from 4·24 in Haidarabad to 29·91 in the Jacobabad district.

PROVINCE OF BOMBAY.

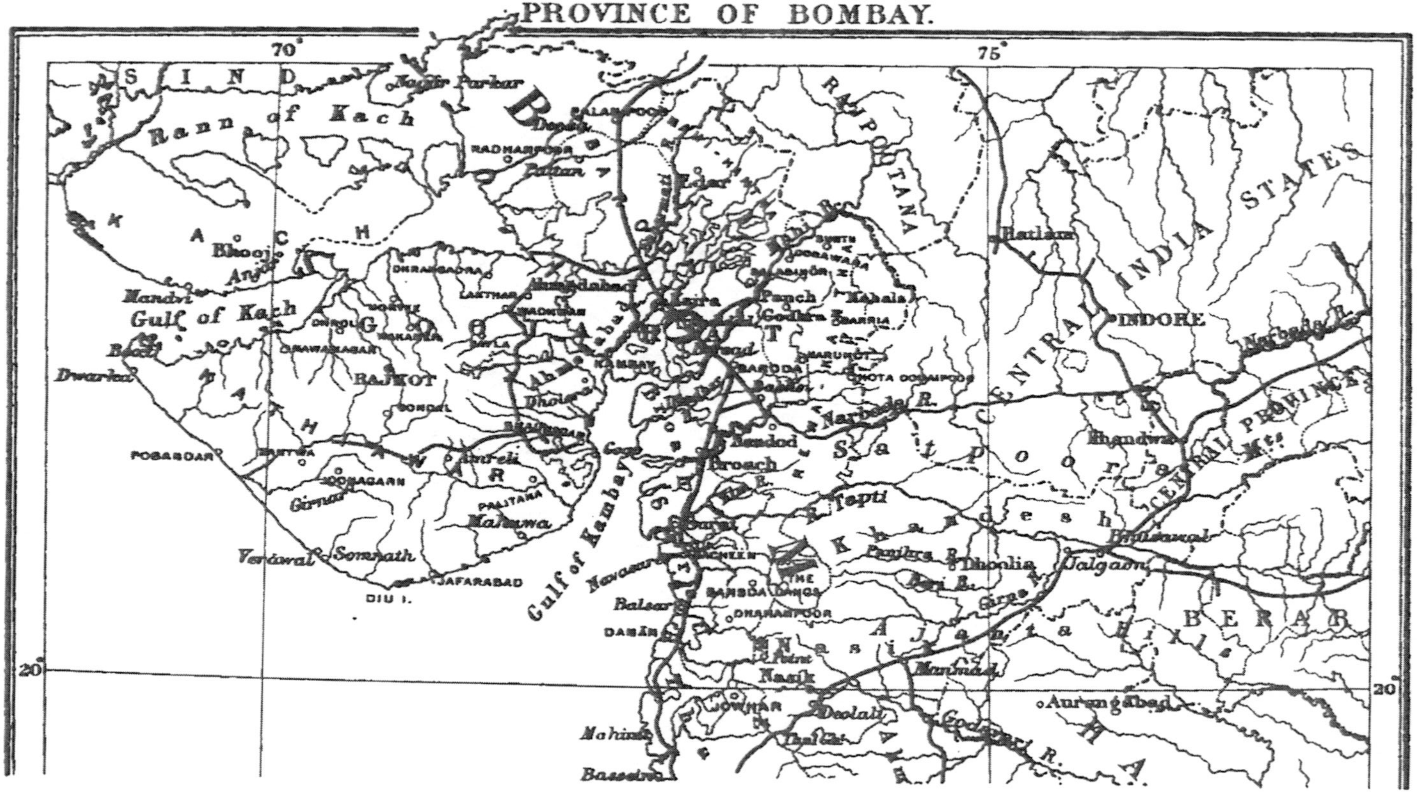

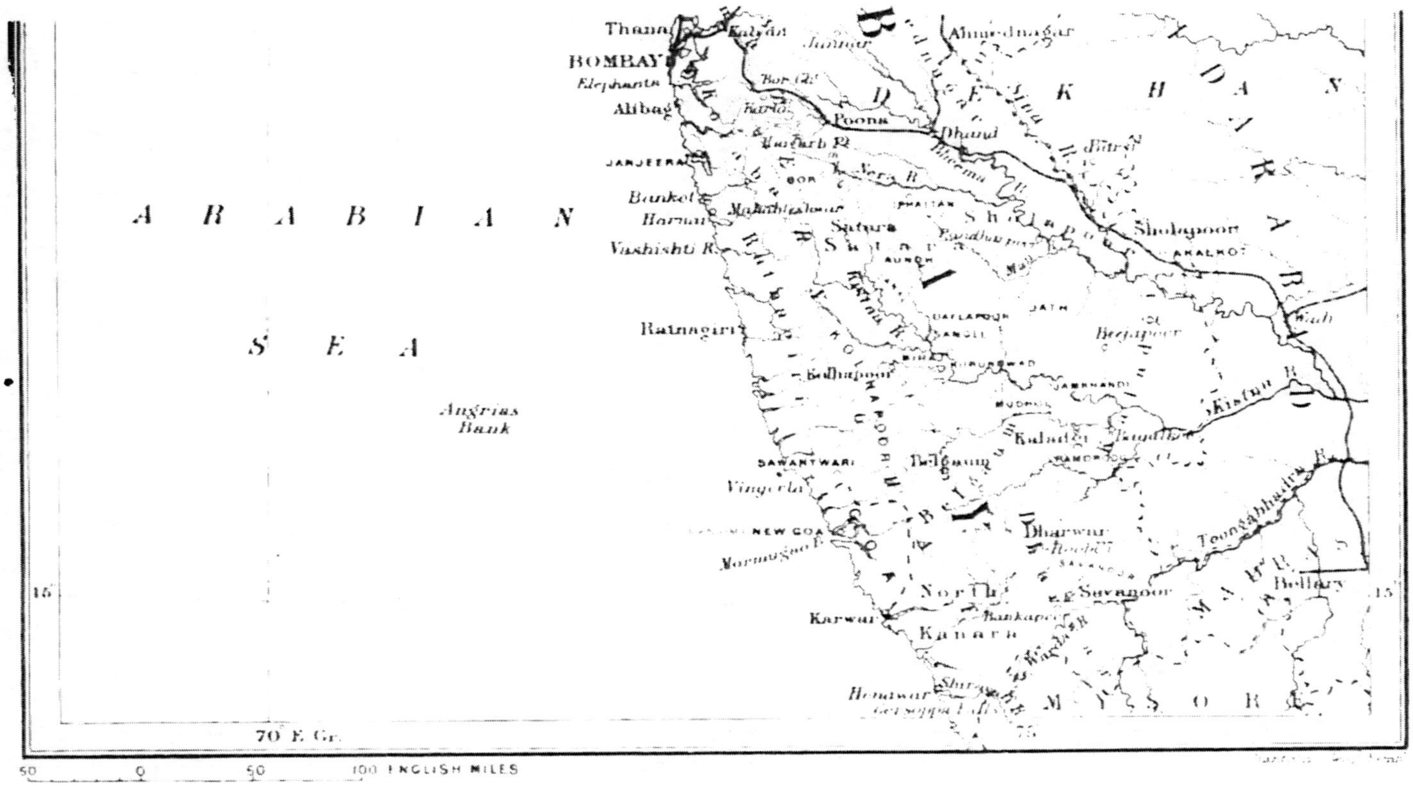

ARABIAN
SEA
Angrias Bank
Thana
BOMBAY
Elephanta
Alibag
JANJEERA
Bankot
Harnai
Vashishti R.
Ratnagiri
Kalyan
Junnar
Ahmednagar
Poona
Dhaund
Bhima
Nera R.
BOR
PHALTAN
Satara
Sholapoor
AKALKOT
AUNDH
JATH
DAFLAPOOR
SANGLI
Beejapoor
KURUNDWAD
Kolhapoor
JAMKHANDI
MUDHOL
Kistna R.
Kaladgi
RAMDROOG
Belgaum
SAWANTWARI
Vingorla
NEW GOA
Marmagao
Dharwar
SAVANOOR
Savanoor
Toongabhadra R.
Bellary
Karwar
Bankapoor
Kanara
Honawar
Gersoppa Falls
MYSORE
North
70 E. Gr.
75
15
50 0 50 100 ENGLISH MILES

CIVIL DIVISIONS OF BRITISH TERRITORY, 1881.

Divisions.	Executive District.	Executive Subdivisions.	Area in Square Miles.	Population, 1881.	Number of Villages.	Total cost of Officials and Police of all kinds.	Imperial Revenue.	
							Land.	Gross.
						Rs.	Rs.	Rs.
	Bombay City	..	22	778,196	..	....	2,59,394	7,98,083
Northern.	Ahmedabad	8	3,821	856,324	884	8,99,588	14,11,814	19,17,611
Northern.	Kaira	7	1,608	804,800	589	6,31,747	20,08,738	23,11,461
Northern.	Panch Mahals	5	1,613	255,479	719	3,08,918	2,89,212	3,62,930
Northern.	Broach	6	1,453	326,930	423	3,89,626	22,42,786	25,35,810
Northern.	Surat	8	1,662	614,198	853	7,73,732	26,33,202	29,45,146
Northern.	Thana	11	4,242	908,548	2,263	8,91,739	14,98,689	19,35,466
Northern.	Kolaba	5	1,496	381,649	1,064	2,88,192	7,26,417	9,48,675
Central.	Khandesh	22	10,337	1,237,231	3,303	12,43,044	32,46,642	41,79,118
Central.	Nasik, including Peint	12	5,940	781,206	1,696	6,74,850	12,82,071	17,30,119
Central.	Ahmednagar	11	6,666	751,228	1,362	8,09,402	12,40,330	17,44,153
Central.	Poona	11	5,347	900,621	1,201	18,85,375	14,67,408	18,88,785
Central.	Sholapoor	7	4,521	582,487	716	5,45,156	10,60,577	12,39,652
Central.	Satara	11	4,987	1,062,350	1,356	8,09,844	16,28,362	20,45,262
Southern.	Belgaum	7	4,656	864,014	1,133	6,95,927	12,48,603	17,93,700
Southern.	Dharwar	14	4,534	882,907	1,436	7,24,808	23,61,557	26,20,651
Southern.	Kaladgi	8	5,757	638,493	1,204	6,18,929	16,10,014	17,69,847
Southern.	Kanara	11	3,910	421,840	1,201	7,17,798	7,50,435	12,19,595
Southern.	Ratnagiri	9	3,922	997,090	1,337	7,63,326	9,73,049	11,76,591
Sind.	Karachi	8	16,109	478,688	3,958	6,47,579	6,88,349	17,07,062
Sind.	Thar and Parkar	7	12,729	203,344	1,750	2,12,516	2,29,867	2,95,756
Sind.	Haidarabad	4	9,052	754,624	1,104	7,35,220	13,18,105	14,31,303
Sind.	Shikarpoor	4	8,809	852,986	4,060	6,74,580	19,46,601	24,18,271
Sind.	Upper Sind Frontier	8	2,225	124,181	138	25,309	2,52,728	2,63,556
	Aden	..	85	34,890	2	2,70,423	....	1,836
	Total	194	125,453	16,489,274	33,752	1,62,37,623	3,23,83,950	4,12,80,454

CHAPTER XV.

PROVINCE OF BOMBAY, WITH SIND AND ADEN.

Sind Districts and State.

§ 1. Karachi. § 2. Haidarabad. § 3. *Khairpoor State. § 4. Shikarpoor. § 5. Upper Sind Frontier. § 6. Thar and Parkar.

Northern Districts and States.

§ 7. Bombay City. § 8. Thana. § 9. *Jowhar State. § 10. Kolaba. § 11. *Janjeera State. § 12. Surat. § 13. *Surat States. § 14. Broach. § 15. Kaira. § 16. *Kambay State. § 17. Panch Mahals. § 18. *Narukot State. § 19. Ahmedabad. § 20. *Kathiawar States. § 21. *Kach State. § 22. *Pahlanpoor and Radhanpoor States. § 23. *Mahi-Kantha States. § 24. Rewa-Kantha States.

Central Districts and States.

§ 25. Khandesh. § 26. *The Dangs. § 27. Nasik. § 28. Ahmednagar. § 29. Poona. § 30. Sholapoor. § 31. Satara. § 32. *Satara States.

Southern Districts and States.

§ 33. Kaladgi. § 34. Belgaum. § 35. Dharwar. § 36. *Southern Maratha States, Savanoor, and Akalkot. § 37. *Kolhapoor State. § 38. *Sawantwari State. § 39. Ratnagiri. § 40. North Kanara.

Portuguese Territory.

§ 41. Goa Province, Settlement, and City.

Aden, Perim, and Allied Ports.

§ 42. Aden Settlement. § 43. Perim Island; adjoining African and Arab Ports. § 44. Sokotra.

Sind.

§ 1. KARACHI DISTRICT is bounded E. by Haidarabad with the Indus between, N. by Shikarpoor, W. by Baloochistan, with the Sulaiman range and Habb river between, and S. by the Arabian Sea and Kori creek separating it from Kach. Area, 16,109 sq. m. Population, 478,688. Stretching for 200 m. from

SIND AND BALOOCHISTAN.

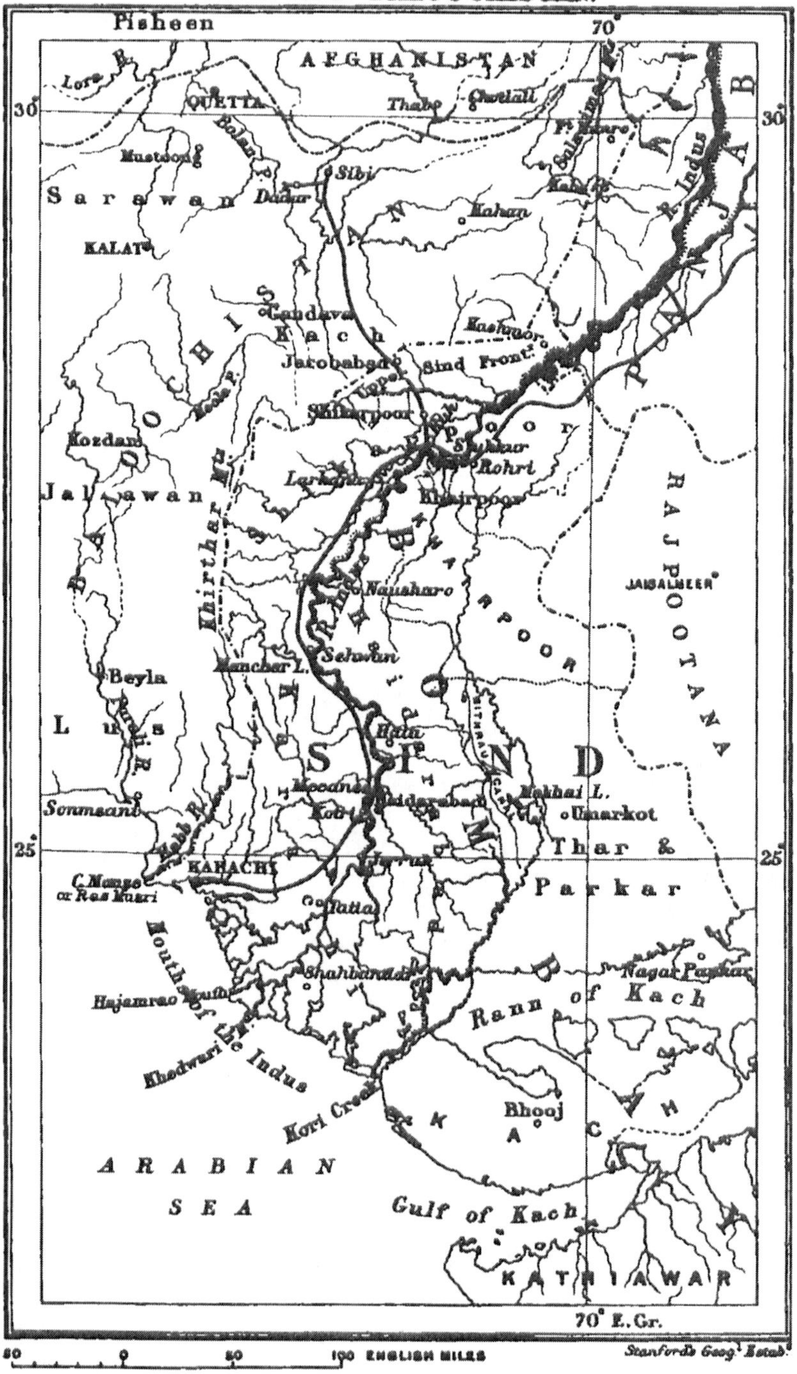

the mouth of the Indus to the Balooch border, Karachi is a varied district of hill and delta and swamp. The **Khirthar Mountains** send out the **Lakki Range** into the Sehwan subdivision, containing the **Manchar Lake**, the only large sheet of water in Sind and ending in Cape Monze (Ras Muari). The **Habb** river, said to rise in Las—by others, near Kalat—forms the W. boundary for above 100 miles after it issues from the Pabb mountains, and is the only permanent river in Sind besides the **Indus**. The Balan and Maler, in W., are mountain torrents. Of springs, the most notable is the Peer Mangho, generally known as "Muggur Peer," 7 m. N. of Karachi town, visited on account of its many alligators, which are different from the long-snouted ghaviāl of the neighbouring Indus. **Karachi** (58,000), chief town of Sind and port of the Panjab, on a bay formed by Manora Point near Cape Monze, into which the Layān river discharges, at the extreme N. end of the Indus delta. The opening of the bay between Manora Head and the sanitarium of Clifton is 3½ m. wide, and is blocked by the Oyster Rock and Island of Kiamāri farther up. From Kiamāri, the landing place and railway station of the Sind, Panjab, and Delhi Railway, the Napier Mole runs for 3 m. to the custom-house, whence the Bandar and M'Leod roads lead through the town to the cantonments. The harbour and dense native quarter lie along the former; the latter passes the courts, banks, ironworks, cotton presses, and caravanserai for the Kandahar trade to the military quarter, half a mile from which is the Government garden of 40 acres. The Church Missionary Society has long had a centre here, where Dr. John Wilson was the first, in 1850, to preach Christianity in the vernacular. The churches, schools, Frere Hall, and Government House are the principal public buildings; in Government House grounds is a monument erected by Sir Charles Napier in 1849 to those of H.M. Cheshire (22d) Regiment who fell in the Sind campaign. A mere fort, dating from 1725 to 1842, when the Talpoor Meers ceded it to the British, Karachi has grown to be a great seaport, with an annual sea-borne trade valued at £4,000,000, chiefly since the expenditure of £450,000 on its harbour. **Kotri** (8000), on the right bank of the Indus, 106 m. N. of Karachi town, terminus of Sind Railway, and of its Indus Steam Flotilla to Sukkur, 270 m., Mithankot, 430 m., and Mooltan, 570 m., being superseded by through railways. Here, in 1839, the Bombay division of the army advancing on Afghanistan encamped. **Sehwan** (5000), ancient town near right bank of Asal, where it flows from the Manchar lake into the Indus on the road to Kalat and Kandahar; probably the *Sindomana* of Arrian, with old fort of Alexander on a mound surrounded by ruins. **Tatta** (8000), old town, now 4 m. W. of right bank of Indus, and 50 m. E. of Karachi. At the foot of the Makli hills, with fine mosque begun by Shah Jahan, and ruins of Akbar's fort. Boobak (6000), on Manchar lake, 9 m. W. of Sehwan, with carpet manufactures. An English factory existed here for a time after 1758. **Jerruk** or Jhirak (2000), 24 m. S. of Kotri, above the Indus, preferred by Burnes and Napier as an English station to Haidarabad. Shahbandar ("king's port"), now decayed, formerly station of Sind rulers' fleet in the Indus delta, and seat of an English factory.

§ 2. HAIDARABAD DISTRICT is bounded E. by Thar and Parkar, N. by Khairpoor State, W. by Karachi with the Indus between, and S. by the Arabian Sea, the Kori creek separating it from Kach. Area, 9052 sq. m. Population, 754,624. The district is an alluvial plain, lying along the Indus, from which it passes E. into sandy wastes. The **Ganja Hills** (100 ft.), a limestone range, run parallel to the Indus for 13 m. S. of Haidarabad town. In the N. are the Rohri canals, in the S. the Tuleli, and in the E. the Nara. There are 317 canals, of which 300 are State and 50 tap the Indus directly. **Haidarabad** (36,000), chief town, cantonment, and former provincial capital on the Ganja hills, 3½ m. E. of the Indus at Gidu-Bandar, whence is a steam ferry to Kotri railway station. The fort with arsenal, palaces and tombs of the former Meers of Sind, and Residency which Outram held against the Baloochees in 1843, are notable. Here is a Church Mission. The fort was the site of the old town of Nerankot. **Meeanee**, small place 6 m. N. of Haidarabad, where Sir C. Napier defeated a Balooch army on the banks of the Tuleli. He again defeated the Meers at the village of **Dabo**, near Haidarabad, and took the fortress of Umarkot in the desert, after which he wrote in answer to the charge of injustice, "Peccavi" = I have sinned (Sind). **Hala** (4500), on the Aliganj canal, 2 m. from old Haidarabad, famed for its glazed pottery and tiles. **Nausharo** (3000), on main road from Haidarabad to Rohri. **Adam-jo-Tando** (4000), 14 m. E. of Hala on the Sangrowah canal. Meerpoor (1500), decayed town on Letwah canal, 41 m. N.E. of Haidarabad.

§ 3. *KHAIRPOOR STATE is bounded E. by the Jaisalmeer State of Rajpootana, N. and W. by Shikarpoor with the Indus between, and S. by Haidarabad and Thar and Parkar. Area, 6109 sq. m. Population, 129,174. The Rajpoot dynasty in

Sind was supplanted by the Muhammadan Arabs in 711, and these by Mahmood of Ghazni in 1025; Akbar incorporated Sind into the Delhi Empire in 1591. After Nadir Shah's invasion in 1740, the Dooranee rulers of Kandahar became suzerains of Sind, then ruled by the Kaloras, a religious sect under whose chief the English established the Tatta and Shahbandar factories. The tyranny of the Kaloras led to their overthrow in 1783 by three chiefs or Meers of the Talpoor Baloochees. In Napier's war with these the Haidarabad and Meerpoor Talpoors were deprived of power, and their descendants are pensioned. The Khairpoor family, loyal to the engagement made with Sir A. Burnes in 1838, retained its territory as a Feudatory State. The alluvial plain is fertile where watered by the Indus and **Eastern Nara** canal in the old Indus bed, but arid elsewhere. To the N. are the **Ghar** limestone hills, which run for 40 m. from Rohri. On a W. spur of these is the fort of **Diji**, 12 m. S. of the chief town of **Khairpoor** (7500), on the Meerwah canal, 15 m. E. of the Indus, a mart for the indigo and grain raised in the State, with manufactures of cloth and arms. The Meer has an annual revenue of £45,350. The State is divided into the six districts of Meerwah, Wadi Goghri, Nandi Goghri, Ladho Gagan, Nara, and Jabo. The largest town is Raneepoor (6500), on the road from Haidarabad to Rohri, from which it is 45 m. S.W. There is much good land, but it is kept as a game preserve.

§ 4. SHIKARPOOR DISTRICT is bounded E. by Jaisalmeer and Bahawalpoor States, N. by the Frontier District, W. by the Khirthar mountains, and S. by Karachi and Khairpoor State. Area, 8809 sq. m. Population, 852,986. The plain of the Indus, which intersects the district, is broken at Sukkur and Rohri by limestone hills, which enclose the river. The **Khirthar Range**, on the W. border, rises to 7000 ft. The sandhills of Rohri, termed the "Registhan," are bold in outline and largely covered with forests which extend over 207 sq. m. The district is often flooded. **Shikarpoor** (39,000), chief town, and entrepot for transit trade between the Bolan Pass and Karachi, 18 m. W. of the Indus, between the Chota Begari and Raiswah branches of the Sind Canal, in the midst of a fertile tract. Shikarpoor is 10 m. from Ruk on the Sibi railway. It is 22 m. N.W. of **Sukkur** (13,000), railway station on right bank of Indus, opposite Rohri, 330 m. from Karachi; with **Bukkur**, an island fortress between, and the principal British arsenal during Sind and Afghan campaigns, now a jail. A little below Sukkur the Indus will be crossed by a railway bridge costing £270,000.

Ruk junction, 315 m. from Karachi, is the station for Sibi, 133 m. N.W., and Kandahar. **Rohri** (9000), railway station on left bank of Indus, on a limestone eminence; the mouth of the E. Nara channel is on N. side of town, a picturesque place with many Muhammadan mosques; the ancient Loharkot. **Reti**, railway station on E. border, 4 m. S. of which are the vast ruins of Vijnot, a chief city before the Moslem conquest. Seorai Fort ruins lie 3 m. N.W. of Wulhar station in Bahawalpoor. **Larkana** (11,000), the "Eden of Sind," on S. bank of Lar canal, in the centre of the finest part of Sind, 40 m. S.W. of Shikarpoor, a grain mart, with manufactures of cotton, leather, and metal. Mehar (1300), a pretty town 36 m. S.W. of Larkana, on the Kakol canal. The old Rajpoot capital was at Aror, captured in 711 by Muhammadans, 5 m. E. of Rohri.

§ 5. UPPER SIND FRONTIER DISTRICT is bounded S. by Rohri subdivision of Shikarpoor and Bahawalpoor from which it is divided by the Indus, N. by Dera Ghazi Khan and Baloochistan, W. by Baloochistan, and S. by Shikarpoor. Area, 2225 sq. m. Population, 124,181. The extreme N. point is **Gyandari Hill**, a stream from which to Mithri is the boundary between Sind and the Panjab. From the same hill its Balooch border runs W. to the Lehni tower. Hilly in the N.E., the district is otherwise a strip of plain with high sandhills, and half of it subject to inundation. Six canals draw off the Indus to fertilise the soil. The **Begari**, from the Indus, forms the S.E. boundary with Shikarpoor for 85 m., and sends off the **Noorwa** (which again has the short **Budwa** branch), the **Sonwa**, and the Mirzawa. The **Desert Canal** runs 35 m. into the desert W. of Kashmor. **Jacobabad** (11,000), chief town and military frontier station, founded by General John Jacob, who tamed the frontier tribes, and is buried here. It is 26 m. from Shikarpoor on the trade route to Kandahar by the Bolan Pass, and 36 m. from Ruk on the railway to Sibi. **Thul** (1200), 23 m. E. of Jacobabad. **Kashmor** (1000), 86 m. N.E. of Jacobabad, on a canal near the Indus, often destroyed by floods.

§ 6. THAR and PARKAR DISTRICT, under a Political Superintendent, is bounded E. by Malani State in Rajpootana, N. by Khairpoor State, W. by Haidarabad, and S. by Kach. Area, 12,729 sq. m. Population, 203,344. The plain of the **Eastern Nara** is fertile, including Umarkot subdivision, but the rest is *Thar* or desert; *Parkar* is the peninsula S.E., which runs into the salt marsh known as the Rann of Kach, and is intersected by low ranges (380 ft.) rising into the **Kalunjhar**

Hills. The **Mithrau Canal** for 123 m. irrigates the W. tracts which the Nara does not reach, and there are twelve smaller canals. The **Mokhal Salt Lake** is in the Thar. **Umarkot** (4000), chief town, on a canal on the edge of the E. desert, where the great Akbar was born in October 1542, when his father Hoomayoon was an exile on his way to Afghanistan; a stone slab with an inscription marks the spot. In 1591 Akbar marched through the town to conquer Sind. **Nagar Parkar** (2500), 120 m. S.E. from Umarkot, on N.E. corner of the Rann of Kach, an old town. Nabisar, Khipra, Sanghar, Chachra, Gadra, Mitti, Islamkot, Virawah, and Dipla, are village municipalities with fewer than 2500 inhabitants. From Umarkot to Haidarabad there is a road, but elsewhere the sandhills make travelling difficult.

Northern Districts and States.

§ 7. BOMBAY CITY (773,196) (named from Mumba, the chief goddess, whence the Maratha name Mumbai or Mahima = "great mother," Tanna-*Mayamba* = name of Konkan kingdom in 16th century, and Maimbi = Portuguese name), capital of Bombay Province, chief city of Western India and finest harbour in S. Asia. Formerly one of a group of islands off the Konkan coast on the Indian Ocean, Bombay has long been connected by causeway with Salsette, and that with the mainland. Bombay is a great city scattered over 22 sq. m., in 18° 58′ N. lat. and 72° 52′ E. long. Charles II. received Bombay island from Portugal in 1661 as part of the Infanta Catherina's dowry, and in 1668 transferred it to the East India Company, whose agents in Surat had long coveted it for naval and commercial purposes. From the first an asylum for all the races around the Indian Ocean, Bombay grew chiefly within the walls of the Fort till 1863-66, when the American Civil War gave it the cotton supply of the world, the Fort walls were removed, and much of the wealth was used to extend and adorn the city with public buildings, in spite of a time of financial panic. From N. to S. the connected islands, of which Bombay is the most exposed to the Indian Ocean, and which are probably the Heptanesia of Arrian, are these—(1) Bassein; (2) Dravi; (3) Versova; (4) Salsette; (5) Bombay; (6) Old Woman's Island; (7) Kolaba; then within the harbour between these and the mainland, (8) Trombay; (9) Elephanta; (10) Butcher's Island; (11) Gibbet Island; (12) Karănjā. Bombay stretches N. for 11½ m. from Kolaba point to Sion causeway which connects it with Salsette, and is from 3 to 4 m. broad, in trapezoid form. It consists of a low plain or "Flats" between two parallel ridges which run out into the sea. The outer and shorter is Malabar hill, the favourite residence of the wealthy Europeans and Parsees, on the summit of which are the Parsee "towers of silence;" at the point is the Governor's summer house. The longer is Kolaba, with barracks, docks, and factories, and lighthouse on the Prongs, a reef to S., rounding which the noble harbour is gained, with the Prince's Dock. Between Malabar and Kolaba points lies the shallow tidal Back Bay, much of which was reclaimed during the cotton speculative mania. On the N.E. side are the esplanade and principal public offices erected at that time, the Secretariat, the University, the Courts, and the Sailors' Home adjoining the Apollo Bandar, or Palawa landing-place on the E. or harbour side, whence the mail-steamers, after landing the mails, pass N. to the head of the harbour at Mazagaon. N. of the Apollo Bandar and E. of the Esplanade is the city proper or fort, where are the Town Hall with the Elphinstone circle of mercantile offices on either side; St. Thomas's Cathedral, the oldest Protestant church in India (1718), where lies Jonathan Duncan, the Governor who put down infanticide in Benares and Kathiawar; the mint, custom-house, dockyard, and cotton green. Farther N., between Girgaum quarter, at the head of Back Bay and the new wharves on the harbour, is the densely peopled native city, with picturesque streets, new markets, railway stations, hospitals, and colleges. At Ambrolie are the Free Church Institution, Maratha church and girls' schools, built by John Wilson, D.D., who was buried in the Scottish Cemetery, now closed, after a missionary career of forty years. N. of the Native City, across the breadth of the island from W. to E., are Breach Candy, a favourite European quarter, on the Indian Ocean; the racecourse, Byculla with the club, many English and Native houses, Elphinstone College, Victoria Gardens, and the marine quarter of Mazagaon, the point of departure of the mail-steamers. At Parell, still to the N., is Government House since 1771, formerly a Jesuit establishment, with paintings and busts of several public men; the statues of such are to be found chiefly in the Town Hall. There are 30 cotton mills at work with about a million spindles. Since their flight from Persia and its foundation, Bombay has been the headquarters of the enterprising and loyal Parsees. Hardly less active as traders are the Hindoo Banias of Goojarat and Marwarees of Central India; and the Musalman Bohoras,

Khojas, and Memons, all of whom trade along the E. coast of Africa and S. and E. coasts of Asia, from Zanzibar to Shanghai. The municipality has a revenue from somewhat heavy taxation of about the third of a million sterling. In a military sense Bombay is under Poona, where are the headquarters, but is the place of landing and departure for all the British troops. The principal Missionary Societies have colleges, schools, and establishments here since the charter of 1813 granted toleration. Mountstuart Elphinstone was Governor in 1819, Sir John Malcolm succeeded him in 1827, Sir Robert Grant in 1835, Sir George R. Clerk in 1847 and again in 1860, and Lord Elphinstone in 1855. Of most of these there are public memorials in Bombay, also of the Queen-Empress. The naturalist Victor Jacquemont died in Bombay, from which his remains were lately removed to France. The city draws its water from **Vihar Lake** (1400 acres), 15 m. N., near Bhandoop railway station, and **Toolsi Lake**, N. of Vihar.

In 1880 the number of births registered, excluding still-born, was 17,247, being 22·84 per mille on the population at the census of 1881. Of these, 9388 were males and 7851 were females. The number still-born was 1253, against 1113 in 1879. The number registered is considerably in advance of the previous year, but these returns are manifestly imperfect. Exclusive of still-born, 21,146 deaths were registered, being 1381 fewer than in 1879. The death-rate, calculated on the rough total at the census of 1881, was 28·01 per 1000. The death-rate varied from 12·27 in the southern division of the Fort to 48·86 per 1000 in Khara Talao and 54·15 per 1000 in Kamathipoora. Of the total number of deaths, 11,180 were of males and 9966 were of females. Seven thousand five hundred deaths from fever of all kinds were registered; 30 cases of cholera proved fatal out of 50; 207 deaths were registered due to smallpox; 2710 due to phthisis, against 2949 in 1879; 2304 deaths occurred from diseases of the digestive system; 1973 from diseases of the respiratory system; 56 as against 36 from syphilis, including its after effects; and 345 deaths from accidents and violence. Measles assumed an epidemic form, causing 3365 deaths. Of the numerous races in the city of Bombay, the lowest rate of mortality was among the Parsees. This was the case in the two previous years also.

Elephanta Island, so named by the Portuguese from the stone elephant formerly there, but called by natives Gharapoori ("place of the rock" or of "purification"), 6 m. E. of Bombay, and 4 W. of mainland, with a circumference of 4½ m., is much visited for its great cave in W. hill (250 ft.), where from the compact trap several remarkable Brahmanical shrines were cut about the 8th century A.D. The largest measures 130 ft. back from the entrance, and forms, in its central area, a square of 91 ft. supported by six rows of columns six in each row, save at the sacellum. The most famous sculpture is the colossal Trimoorti, or three-faced bust of the Hindoo triad.

Salsette Island (Shatshashthi), stretching N. from head of Bombay harbour 16 m. to Bassein inlet, with an area of 150 sq. m., long a favourite settlement of the Portuguese, and peculiarly rich in rock-temples, the most famous of which are the 109 Boodhist caves of **Kanhéri**, 6 m. W. of Thana, excavated in volcanic breccia which rises to 1550 ft. The other groups of caves are at Marol to S. and at Magathana, Mandapeswar (Montpezor), and Jogeswari, in N.W. Their age ranges from before the Christian era to the end of the 9th century A.D.

§ 8. THANA DISTRICT, or the N. Konkan, is bounded E. by Poona, Nasik, and Ahmednagar; N. by Portuguese Daman and Surat; W. by the Arabian Sea; and S. by Kolaba district. Area, 4242 sq. m. Population, 908,548. Thana district consists of Salsette, a Konkan strip of coast, and the slopes of the **Sahyadri** or **W. Ghats** to the tableland of the Dekhan (2500 ft.), reached by the **Thal** pass (1912 ft.), and railway incline to N.E. for Allahabad, and Calcutta, and **Bor** pass (1798 ft.), and incline to S. for Poona and Madras, both great engineering works. This district forms the transition from the Marathee to the Goojaratee tracts, which are marked off by the **Vaitarani** river, navigable for 20 m. from its mouth. The navigable **Bassein Creek** separates Salsette from the mainland. The **Thana Hills** run through Salsette N. to S.; the **Matheran** ("wooded head"), outlier of the Sahyadri range, has a sanitarium, within 4 hours of Bombay, reached from Neral railway station, 54 m. from Bombay. The **Damān** range, with Toongar, and a range running N. to S. between the Vaitarani and Bassein creek, Mahooli, and Malangarh, are the other considerable hills. **Thana** (15,000), chief town, port, and railway station in Salsette, on Thana creek, 20 m. S. of Bombay, many of whose merchants reside here; seat of a Free Church Medical Mission, and once of a Nestorian bishop. In 1320 four companions of the Italian friar, Odoricus, became martyrs here. **Kalyan** (13,000), port and railway station, 33 m. N.E. of Bombay, junction of the N.E. and S.E. lines of Great Indian Peninsula Railway, seat of a Nestorian bishop mentioned by

Cosmas Indicopleustes. In 1673 Fryer "gazed with astonishment on ruins of stately fabrics." Four m. distant is the old Shaivite temple, **Ambarnath** ("immortal lord"). Wasind, 50 m. N.E. of Bombay, at which the ascent by the Thal Ghat begins by gradient of 1 in 37 to Igatpoori (1992 ft.), 85 m. from Bombay at top of ghat, a sanitarium with locomotive works in Nasik district. Returning to S., the Bombay, Baroda, and Central India Railway, which starts from Kolaba, passes by a causeway into Thana district, or Salsette, at **Bandora** (7500), 10 m. N. of Bassein. This port is a centre of the descendants of Xavier's caste converts in the 16th century, who bear Portuguese names, but differ from the Goanese Christians in refusing domestic service. **Bassein** (4500) (Wasai), Portuguese port for two centuries from 1534, during which it was their "Court of the North," where the Dons and Hidalgos reproduced Lisbon, and none but Christians were allowed to sleep. Captured from the Marathas by General Goddard in 1780, but not incorporated with British territory till the defeat of the last of the Peshwas in 1818. The walls and some ecclesiastical ruins of old Bassein remain. Under the Bassein treaty of 1802 the Peshwa agreed to maintain a British subsidiary force, which led to the dissolution of the Maratha confederacy in 1818. **Mahim** (7500), 56 m. N. of Bassein and 5 W. of Palghar, railway station. Sanjan, old town, now village, 70 m. S. of Surat, where the Parsees first landed in India. Five m. N. of Bassein are the ruins of Supara, old capital of the Konkan, B.C. 250 to A.D. 1265, recently identified; a great port from the times of the Greek navigators to the 10th century. **Panwel** (11,000), most S. town, 16 m. S.E. of Thana town, port for the mainland from Bombay before railway.

***Damān** ("border") (41,000), Portuguese port and settlement of 82 sq. m., 100 m. N. of Bassein, intersected and surrounded by British territory, contiguous to Thana district, with an annual revenue of £8000, under a Governor, subordinate to Goa.

§ 9. *JOWHAR STATE, in N. of, and under Thana, which surrounds it, has an area of 538 sq. m., population of 38,000, and revenue of £9600, with village of same name 44 m. N. of Thana town. The chief is of the Kolee tribe; the people are principally Waralees, Kulkurees, and casteless tribes. The nearest railway station is Dahánu.

§ 10. KOLABA DISTRICT, or S. Konkan, is bounded E. by Satara and Poona; N. by Amba river, Thana, and Bombay harbour; W. by the Arabian Sea; S. by Janjeera State and

Ratnagiri. Area, 1496 sq. m. Population, 381,649. This strip of the S. Konkan immediately S. of Bombay city consists of a series of ranges running N. and S. between the Sahyadri Ghats and the sea, with rice plains at their base, and a sea frontage of 20 m. Of the Sahyadri the most remarkable peaks are **Raigarh**, once capital of Shivaji, where he died at 53, now in Mahad subdivision; and the Trigonometrical Survey Station of **Meeradongar.** From the hills small streams pass to the sea; and there are many tidal inlets, of which the principal are from N. to S.—**Nagotna, Roha** or **Chaul**, and Bankot. The forests are rich in the blackwood from which the famous Bombay furniture is made, and in teak second only to that of Calicut. The fertile coast lands are owned chiefly by Brahman middlemen or *khots*. There are many Beni-Israel, or descendants either of the Jews who fled to Egypt and Arabia at the Captivity, or of the Ten Tribes. **Alibag** (6000), chief town and harbour, 19 m. S. of Bombay, with a fort on a rocky island; old stronghold of Shivaji, and afterwards of the Maratha pirate Angria, whom Clive attacked. The town is the centre of a Free Church Mission. **Nagotna**, town 20 m. up the Amba river, 40 m. S.W. of Bombay and 70 from Mahableshwar, on an old and frequented route to Poona; long the northern limit of the kings of Beejapoor. **Pen** (6500), 16 m. N.E. of Alibag. **Rewadanda** (6000), port 6 m. S.E. of Alibag. **Mahad** (6700), 53 m. S.E. of Alibag, with many Boodhist caves. **Khuda**, N.W. of Mahad, has 22 caves.

§ 11. *JANJEERA STATE, supervised by the Collector of Kolaba since 1867, up to which time it had been practically independent of all control, lies between the Rewadanda creek in Kolaba on N., and the Bankot creek of Ratnagiri on S., a narrow strip of mainland with the small island Janjeera, on which is chief town of same name. Area, 325 sq. m. Population, 75,194. Revenue, £32,879. It is named from the Arabic *Jazwah* = an island, and also Habsan from the African or Abyssinian origin of the Nawab or Seedee. In 1489 a party of Abyssinians seized Janjeera island by stratagem, and held it and the mainland, now as admirals of the Beejapoor and now of the Mughul fleets, but always as pirates, independent of the Marathas, though respecting English ships. The Nawab, under an arrangement with the Marathas, holds Jaffnabad in Kathiawar, also **Janjeera**, chief town, on island 44 m. S. of Bombay; 3 m. off is Murud, where the Assistant Political Agent resides. The three Janjeera ports are connected by coasting steamers with Bombay, which receives from them large supplies of firewood.

§ 12. SURAT DISTRICT is bounded E. by Dharampoor, Bansda, Baroda, and Rajpeepla States; N. by Baroda State and Broach; W. by Arabian Sea; and S. by Thana and Portuguese Damān. Area, 1662 sq. m. Population, 614,198. Surat has a coast-line of 80 m. from the Damaganga river N. to the Kim. Narrowing into the Gulf of Kambay, and with the Sahyadri hills approaching the sea, the alluvial strip of coast is only 15 m. broad on S., but is spread out to 60 m. by delta which the Tapti forms. On the N.E. the plain passes into the wild hills and jungle of the **Dangs**, the outcome of the trap plateau of Central India. The **Rajpeepla** range shoots out flat-topped hills (200 to 300 ft.) between Surat and Broach, and the Sahyadri hills slope between Surat and Khandesh. To the S. are isolated hills, one near **Mota**, seven others near **Doongri**, 6 m. from the coast, and **Parnera** (500 ft.), 12 m. farther S. The Tapti and Kim in N. are the only large rivers, but the S. streams ending in navigable estuaries are valuable commercial channels. The **Tapti** (Tapi, correctly), rising in W. of Satpoora plateau of Central India, flows W. for 150 m. till it enters the plain of Khandesh below Boorhanpoor, then for 180 m. it flows along that plain; then for 50 m. it forces a way through the hills to the plain of Goojarat, and then for 70 m. more it traverses Surat plain to the sea 14 m. below Surat town: it receives the Wareli from the W. spurs of Rajpeepla hills, and is navigable for only the last 20 m. of its course. The **Kim**, from the Rajpeepla hills, with a course of 70 m., during which it drains 700 sq. m., forms the N. boundary of Surat, and falls into the Gulf of Kambay 20 m. N. of the Tapti estuary. **Surat** (110,000), (the "good country"), on the S. bank of the Tapti, "prime mart" of India under Akbar, Jahangeer, and Shah Jahan, where first the English Captain Hawkins and then Sir T. Roe landed in 1608-15; opened to trade in 1612 by treaty, along with Kambay, Ahmedabad, and Gogo; seat of an East India Company's Presidency before Bombay, which superseded it after 1687; the "gate of Mecca" for Musalman pilgrims, till plundered for three days by the Maratha Shivaji; still the local commercial centre of Goojarat, and seat of Irish Presbyterian Mission. The castle, now used for public offices, is still the chief feature of the city; the English cemetery is the most interesting, with its tombs and inscriptions, especially those of the brothers Oxindon (1669), Angier (1677), the Dutch Van Reede (1691), "the Mæcenas of Malabar." Vaux's tomb on right bank of Tapti, near mouth of river, is a landmark. **Suwali**, seaport of Surat, and the "Swally" of the old travellers, is 12 m. W. of the city, outside the mouth of the Tapti; Tom Coryate, the eccentric traveller, died here in 1617. **Rander** (11,000), on right bank of Tapti, 2 m. above Surat, with which it is connected by a bridge, an old commercial capital. Balsar (Walsad) (12,000), timber port, 40 m. S. of Surat and 115 N. of Bombay, on the estuary of the navigable Auranga. Pardi (5000), farther S., near which is Umarasari, with the oldest Parsee temple in India. **Olpad** (4300), N.W. of Surat. **Mandvi** (4500) and **Bardoli** (4500), in N.E. corner of district, where there is much waste land.

§ 13. *SURAT STATES, SACHEEN, BANSDA, AND DHARAMPOOR. **Sacheen** (43 sq. m., pop. 18,154) consists of 20 villages, chiefly within Surat district, yielding the Nawab £18,350 a year. The chief village, Sacheen, is 9 m. S. of Surat. The Nawab is the descendant of the elder branch of the Habshi or African Seedees of Janjeera, or admirals of the Beejapoor and Mughul rulers. The elder branch accepted Sacheen from the Marathas in exchange for Janjeera, which, however, the younger branch never surrendered, and still hold. The other villages of any note are Dumas (5000), near the mouth of the Tapti, a sanitarium of the Europeans in Surat, and Bhimpoor, a mile distant, with a temple of the monkey-god. **Dharampoor** (794 sq. m., pop. 74,592), E. of Balsar subdivision of Surat, yielding £250,000 a year to the Rajpoot Raja, who has second class powers. The chief town (3500) is of the same name, just S. of the Auranga. Naga, the old capital, is 24 m. S.W. **Bansda** (384 sq. m., pop. 32,154), to N. of Dharampoor, yielding £15,740 a year to the Rajpoot Raja, who resides at the chief village of the same name, in the centre of the State. Unai, on N. border, has a hot spring, the centre of a fair. These three States are immediately controlled by the Surat Political Agent.

§ 14. BROACH DISTRICT (Bharuch) is bounded E. by Baroda, N. and W. by Kambay Gulf, and S. by Surat. Area, 1453 sq. m. Population, 326,930. This alluvial plain, 54 m. along the Gulf of Kambay, with a breadth of 20 to 40 m., lies between the Kim on S. and the **Mahi** on N. Between these are the Dhadhar, 20 m. S. of the Mahi, and the Narbada. The **Dhadhar** rises behind Champáner in a western spur of the Vindhyas, and flows for 70 m. into the Gulf of Kambay, 20 m. S. of the estuary of the Mahi; it receives the Vishwamitri, on which the city of Baroda stands. The **Narbada** (also named Rewa) rises at the hill of Amarkantak in Bilaspoor district of Central Province, and for 500 m. flows W. between the Vindhyas and Satpooras. It is half a mile broad where it enters this district, and a mile near the town of Broach. On the left it receives the Kaveri, opposite **Sukaltirth** (place of pilgrimage), and the Amravati; on the left it is joined by the Bhooki. When in flood it forms islands; the flat near Sukaltirth, 10 m. from Broach, has still the stump of the venerable banian tree of the reformer Kabeer. **Broach** (37,000), the ancient Barygaza, on right bank of Narbada, 20 m. from its mouth; a walled town picturesquely situated on a mound, and named from its patron sage Bhraju Rishi. Long under the Musalman dynasty of Ahmedabad, and famed for its fine calicoes, it was twice plundered by the Portuguese, and again by the Marathas. The British established a factory here in 1616, besieged and took the town in 1772, when Brigadier Wedderburn fell, and again took it in 1803. Many Parsees and wealthy Jains still maintain its commercial reputation as a coasting port like Surat, and as the seat of cotton mills and handlooms. **Ankleswar** (9000), 6 m. S. of Broach, a chief mart, and once celebrated for its paper manufactures. **Jambusar** (15,000), 5 m. N. of the Dhadhar, a decaying cotton port; like Tankari, 10 m. S.W., once chief port for Malwa opium and indigo. **Amod** (5500), 21 m. N. of Broach, with ironworks. **Kavi** (4500), on left bank of the Mahi, on the Jain pilgrim route to Palitana, Girnar, and Gogo. Of the culturable land in this district 95 per cent is occupied.

§ 15. KAIRA DISTRICT (Kheda, correctly) is bounded E. by Baroda State and Panch Mahals district, from which the Mahi separates it; N. by Balasinor and Mahi-Kantha States; N.W. and W. by Ahmedabad; S.W. by Kambay State; and S. by Broach. Area, 1609 sq. m. Population, 804,800. The **Mahi**, the third river of Goojarat, rises in the Malwa State of Amjhera, in the Mahad lake, in Western Vindhyas; flows N. for 140 m. till the Bagar hills turn it W., and the Meynar mountains S.W. to the Goojarat plain, where it forms the S.E. and S. boundary of Kaira, and falls into the Gulf of Kambay. Between it and the Sabarmati, the W. boundary, the smaller Shedhi forms the line of drainage. The Khari, from Edar State, falls into the Sabarmati after irrigating rice land by dams. The whole plain sloping S.W. is fertile, and yields the best tobacco in Western India. **Kaira** (13,000), chief town, 5 m. S.W. of Mehmudabad railway station, an old city with brick wall, and the frontier military station till 1820, when Deesa superseded it. **Nadiad** (25,000), largest mart and railway station, 29 m. S.E. of Ahmedabad. **Mehmudabad** (8500), old pleasure capital of Muhammadan rulers of Goojarat, 18 m. S.E. of Ahmedabad. **Anand** (9000), railway station, 40 m. S. of Ahmedabad; to W. is the Wartal monastery of the reformer, Narayan Swami. **Borsad** (13,000), 12 m. W. of Wasad railway station and 24 N.E. of port of Kambay; seat of Irish Presbyterian Mission. **Dakor** (8000), centre of Krishna-worship on Pali branch of Bombay, Baroda, and Central India Railway. **Kapadwanj** (14,000), fortified town on E. bank of Mohar, 36 m. N.E. of Khaira, and old mart on one of the main routes between Central India and coast, with many prosperous Musalman merchants of the Bohora division of Sheeas; agate and moss pebbles are found in Majam river, 15 m. distant.

§ 16. *KAMBAY STATE (Khambhat = Stambhatirth = pool of the pillar-god, Mahadeva), Musalman principality controlled by the Collector of Kaira, at the head of Kambay Gulf, is bounded E. and N. by Kaira, W. by Ahmedabad from which the Sabarmati separates it, and S. by the Gulf. Area, 350 sq. m. Population, 85,000. The Nawab, descendant of the last but one of the Muhammadan Governors of Goojarat, has a revenue of £35,000, and first class administrative powers. Kambay is a gently waving alluvial brackish plain between the two tidal rivers, Mahi and Sabarmati. **Kambay** (34,000), the capital, is now a decaying town, straggling over 4 sq. m., with Nawab's palace and the old English factory. From 13th to 16th century it was one of the two chief ports of India, till the Portuguese seized control of the trade from the Goojarat kings. It was famed for the polishing and export of the Kambay stones, or carnelians, the agates found within a radius of 120 m., and the foreign stones sent to its lapidaries, as in Europe to Amsterdam. Queen Elizabeth's letters, carried by Fitch Leedes and Newberry in 1583, were addressed to Akbar as "King of Kambay." The English suffered there, as at Surat, till Bombay was founded. The Parsees who, when driven from Persia, settled at Sanjan, 70 m. S. of Surat, spread thence to Kambay, seized it, and were driven out by the Hindoos, who held it till the Musalman conquest in 1297. Kambay is 52 m. S. of Ahmedabad, and now exports only cotton, printed *sarees*, and agates.

§ 17. PANCH MAHALS DISTRICT, or five subdivisions under non-regulation administration, on extreme E. of Goojarat, form two groups separated by the forest-clad hills of Baria State in Rewa-Kantha. Area, 1613 sq. m. Population, 255,479. In S.W. group the **Pawgarh Hill** (2600 ft.), of historic interest, is the centre of a fertile tract; in N.E. the country is more like the neighbouring Malwa. The Mahi touches a few villages in N.W. The inhabitants are of the aboriginal class—Naikras,

Bheels, and Kolees; the Goojarat Bheel corps keep the peace. The chief town is **Godhra** (11,000) ("cows' lake"), 17 m. E. of Pali, terminus of branch railway, with lake and fort to N.E. covered by Muter's force when in 1857 Tatia Topi was prevented by Park and 72d Highlanders (on camels) from rousing the Marathas after his defeat at Gwalior, through the Panch Mahals. **Champaner**, a mile N.E. of Pawgarh hill, now deserted and unhealthy, formerly capital of the Goojarat kings, taken by Hoomayoon himself in 1535, surrendered to British in 1802 by Sindia; ruins of tombs, mosques, palaces, and walls abound. **Dohad** (11,500) ("border"), 43 m. E. of Godhra, at mouth of chief pass between Goojarat and Malwa.

§ 18. *NARUKOT STATE (143 sq. m., pop. 5517), in S.E. of Panch Mahals, whose administrator controls it. The chief is a Hindoo of the Kolee tribe, and the people are the once turbulent and now contented Naikras. Jambughoda (500), 20 m. E. of Baroda, is headquarters of the State; the chief lives at Jhotvar, half a mile N.W.

§ 19. AHMEDABAD DISTRICT is bounded E. by Kaira and Balasinor State, N. by Mahi-Kantha and Baroda States, W. by Kathiawar State, S. by Gulf of Kambay. Area, 3821 sq. m. Population, 856,324. Lying between the Gulf of Kambay and Rann of Kach, this tract has been recovered from the sea and is still flooded in high tides. In extreme N.E. the plain rises into ridges of metamorphic rock (500 ft.), and in S.W. at Gogo, the Khokra range (96 ft.) runs parallel with the shore. The **Sabarmati**, the fourth river of Goojarat, rises as the Sabar in S.W. spurs of Aravali hills, flows S. through Mahi-Kantha to N.W. corner of Ahmedabad district, where it is joined by the Hathmati, takes the name Sabarmati, and after a course of 200 m., draining 9500 sq. m., falls into the Gulf of Kambay. It receives smaller tributaries both above and below Ahmedabad city. As the chief manufacturing district of the whole Province, Ahmedabad contains many large towns; 13 have more than 5000 inhabitants. In all, trades-union or caste guilds regulate manufactures and trades; half the agricultural land is held by talookdars or large holders. **Ahmedabad City** (118,000), second only to Bombay, from which it is 310 m. N., covers 2 sq. m. on raised left bank of the Sabarmati. Founded on site of Ashanal, in 1413, by Ahmed Shah, it was taken by Akbar, was one of the most splendid centres of India in the 16th and 17th centuries, when it had nearly a million of souls, and its merchants made fortunes of a million sterling. Maratha anarchy reduced it, but its prosperity still "hangs on three threads"—

silk, gold, and cotton manufactures; also paper and pottery. Headquarters of N. division of Bombay army, the cantonments being 3½ m. N. of city. Seat of Irish Presbyterian Mission. Mosques, tombs, palaces, and gateways abound, illustrating the finish of Jain or Chalookyan architecture with the largeness of conception of the Saracenic. Terminus of Bombay, Baroda, and Central India Railway from Bombay, and starting point of Rajpootana-Malwa Railway to Delhi, which is 890 m., and Agra, which is 848 m. from Kolaba station in Bombay, by this route. Five m. S.W. is the Presbyterian Mission settlement of Shahavadi. **Dholera** (13,000), mart on Kambay Gulf, which gave its name to a variety of cotton in Lancashire, now 12 m. from sea. Cotton season lasts from November to end of December, when balance of old crop is sent off, and from January to June, when the new crop from N.E. Kathiawar is despatched. **Gogo** (101,000), port in S., 40 m. from head of Gulf, the "Caga" of Friar Jordanus in 1321, still a nursery of lascar seamen, but rivalled by Bhaunagar, 8 m. nearer the cotton districts; 11 m. S.W. is Wallacepoor Presbyterian Mission settlement. **Dhandooka** (10,000) and **Dholka** (21,000), two towns between Ahmedabad and Dholera; the latter is on the Sabarmati and the ancient Viratpoor, which the Pandavas in their wanderings (1400 B.C.) found to be ruled by a Bheel queen. **Viramgam** (20,000), on the Dhola-Wadhwan Railway, 38 m. W. of Ahmedabad, a growing mart. **Parantej** (8500), on the Bokh in N., with soap factories.

§ 20. *KATHIAWAR STATES are bounded E. by Gulf of Kambay and Ahmedabad, N. by Rann and Gulf of Kach, W. and S. by the Arabian Sea. Area, 20,338 sq. m. Population, 2,348,325. Chiefs' revenue about £1,125,000. Kathiawar (country of the Kathi immigrants from Kach), Saurastréné of the Greeks, Surashtra or "good land" of the Hindoos, and Sorath of Hindoos and Muhammadans, forms nearly the whole of the peninsula of Goojarat, 220 m. long and 165 broad. The undulating surface is broken by such low ranges as the **Tangha** and **Mandhav Hills** in Jhalawar; hills in Hallar; the **Gir** range in S., parallel with coast to **Girnar**, with Asoka edicts 260-223 B.C.; opposite Girnar is **Osam Hill**, and farther W. is the **Barada** group. Of the rivers the chief is the **Bhadar**, from the Mandhav hills, 115 m. S.W., to the sea at Navi Bandar. From the same hills another Bhadar flows E. to Gulf of Kambay; the Aji, Machu, and Satrunji are the other rivers. The States export much of the best Indian cotton. The finest Indian lions are found in Kathiawar.

The peninsula contains 186 States, ranging from 3800 sq. m.

to a village, grouped in seven classes according to the jurisdiction of their chiefs. Since 1817, when the Peshwa ceded his rights, and 1820, when the Gaekwar of Baroda engaged to act in Kathiawar only through the British Government, that Government has administered Kathiawar, under a Political Agent and five assistants, from **Rajkot**. In 1863 the country was divided into the four old "prants" or counties, each under a British officer. *Jhalavad*, in the north-east, comprises 1 first class State (Dhrangadra), 3 second, 3 third, 2 fourth, 2 fifth, and 6 thana circles, with 229 villages. *Hallar*, to the north-west and centre of the peninsula, comprises 1 first class State Nawanagar, 4 second, 3 fourth, several minor ones, and 2 thana circles, with 94 villages. *Sorath*, south-west and south, contains Joonagarh, a first class State, 1 second, 2 third, a number of petty estates, and 3 thana circles, with 50 villages. *Gohelwad*, to the east and north-east of Sorath, contains a first class State Bhaunagar, 1 second, 2 third, 1 fourth, and 5 thana circles, with an aggregate of 147 villages. The States, under management of their chiefs, occupy an area of 18,400 sq. m., with a pop. of 2,056,820. Those administered by Government comprise an area of 1900 sq. m., and a pop. of 263,809. The railway has extended as far as Bhaunagar and Dhoraji; and this peninsula, a generation ago the scene of anarchy and oppression, has become prosperous. Infanticide among the Rajpoot tribes has been put down. Kathiawar was a Province of Asoka and the Maurya kings, then of the Sah dynasty, who ruled over Malwa and N. Dekhan, of the Gooptas of Kanauj, of the Goojarat Chalookya kings, then of the Valabhi kings. Mahmood of Ghazni sacked Somnath in 1024; then the Ahmedabad dynasty ruled; the Portuguese took Diu (1536); Akbar conquered Goojarat; and by 1760 the Marathas firmly held it till in 1807 the East India Company's and the Gaekwar's forces enforced peace. There are 4 chiefs in the first class; 20 in the second, third, and fourth; and 78 in the other three.

1. **Joonagarh** (3800 sq. m., 400,000 pop.), with capital (20,000) of same name ("old fort"), 60 m. S.W. of Rajkot, under a Nawab, descendant of the soldier of fortune who seized the State in 1735. Ten m. from the capital is the **Girnar** group of hills (3500 ft.), with Jain temples, and at the base the conical granite boulder, 12 ft. high and 75 in circumference, on which are the 14 edicts of Asoka first deciphered by Dr. John Wilson and James Prinsep. The port of the State is **Veráwal** (11,000), 2 m. from which is the Phallic shrine of old **Somnath**, the supposed sandal-wood gates of which Lord

Ellenborough caused to be brought back from Ghazni, but they lie in Agra arsenal.

2. **Nawanagar** (3395 sq. m., 315,500 pop.), with capital and port (35,000) of same name, 310 m. N.W. of Bombay, where is an inferior pearl fishery, under the Jam, a Jareja Rajpoot, connected (194 m.) with Wadhwan by railway. Stone and iron abound. **Jorya** (6600), a fortified port on S.E. shore of Gulf of Kach, 145 m. W. of Ahmedabad. On the extreme W. is the district of **Okhamandal**, directly under the Gaekwar of Baroda, with famous shrines of Krishna at the once pirate stronghold of **Beyt** ("island") island, whence conch shells are exported for temple use, and **Dwarka** ("door"), fortress-shrine, centre of more than one Wagher war; the place is to W. what the Jagannath shrine of Poori is to E. India.

3. **Bhaunagar** (2784 sq. m., 400,500 pop.), with capital and port and railway station (36,000) of same name on N. shore of Gulf of Kambay, under Thakoor Saheb, a Gohel Rajpoot. The other port is **Mahuwa** (14,000), at the mouth of the Gulf of Kambay. An Irish Presbyterian Mission station.

4. **Dhrangadra** (pop. 91,000), with fortified capital (11,000) of same name, 75 m. W. of Ahmedabad, an inland State, the nearest port to which is Dholera, 70 m. S.E. The State is under the Raja Saheb.

The next 20 States in order of political importance are **Morvee** (1062 sq. m., pop. 91,000), under Thakoor Saheb, with capital (13,000), on Machu river, which falls into Gulf of Kach; Wawanya is the port. **Wankaner** (376 sq. m., pop. 29,000), inland State under Raja Saheb, with capital (5500) of same name. **Palitana** (99 sq. m., pop. 52,000), under Thakoor Saheb, with capital at E. base of famous Jain **Satrunjaya Hill**, 120 m. S.W. from Ahmedabad and 190 N.W. from Bombay, sacred to Adinath, deified priest of Jains, covered with splendid temples of modern origin, grouped as neither Boodhists nor Hindoos have done—"one almost feels the place a satanic mockery of that fair celestial city into which naught may enter that defileth." Dr. John Wilson pronounces the temples the most costly in India, and inferior only to Elura; they are built of sandstone or basalt with marble and colossal images, and are guarded by Muhammadans. **Dhrol** (400 sq. m., pop. 19,000), inland State under Thakoor Saheb, with chief town of same name, and exporting from Jorya fort. **Limree** (280 sq. m., pop. 46,000), under Thakoor Saheb, with capital (13,500), not far from Wadhwan railway station. **Rajkot** (479 sq. m., 37,000 pop.), inland State under Thakoor Saheb, an offshoot of Nawanagar, with capital and cantonment (12,000), in which the Political Agent has headquarters, and there are the Rajkoomar college for W. India chiefs and Irish Presbyterian Mission. **Gondal** (699 sq. m., pop. 138,000), an offshoot of Rajkot, under Thakoor Saheb, with fortified capital (13,000). **Wadhwan** (238 sq. m., pop. 46,000), under Thakoor Saheb, with chief town a railway station. **Porbandar** (535 sq. m., pop. 71,000), on W. coast, under Rana with third class powers; the capital of same name exports famous limestone from Barda hills; the other ports are Madhoopoor and Miani. **Lakthar** (20,500 pop.), under Thakoor, with chief town and railway station, famous for pottery, 13 m. N. of Wadhwan. **Sayla** (16,500 pop.), under Thakoor, with chief town; exports through Dholera. **Choora** (14,000 pop.), under Thakoor, with chief town; exports through Dholera. **Wala** (88 sq. m., pop. 17,500), an offshoot from Bhaunagar, under Thakoor, with chief town on site of **Valabhi**, ancient capital of the Valabhi kings, where copper plates and coins are dug up. Jasdan (32,000 pop.), whose chief is a Kathi, with town of same name. **Bantwa** (208 sq. m., pop. 41,000), an offshoot of Joonagarh, under Muhammadan chief, who resides at Manawadar; with chief town of same name. The Thakoors of **Lathee**, **Virpoor**, and **Mallia**, and the chiefs of **Mooli** and **Bujana**, have fourth class powers. **Jafarabad** (53 sq. m., 10,500 pop.), second class State held by the Nawab of Janjeera, 192 m. S.E., with port of same name on the estuary of the Ranai, the most accessible on the coast. West of this port is the Portuguese island, port, and fort of **Diu** (11,000), near entrance of Gulf of Kambay, 6½ m. long and 1 broad, a decaying place with ruins; on the mainland the Portuguese possess the village of Gogola and the fort of Simbor on an islet 12 m. from Diu.

§ 21. *KACH STATE, almost an island, being surrounded by the salt marshes known as Great and Little **Rann** (Sanskrit Aranya = forest or desert), is bounded E. by Palanpoor, N. and W. by Sind, S. by the Gulf and Kathiawar. Area (without Rann) 6500 sq. m. Population, 500,000. From the S. coast a plain 20 to 30 m. stretches to the **Dora** range, running E. and W., with the **Nana** peak (800 ft.) That is connected by another fertile plain with the **Charwar** hills, parallel to it, having the Indria peak (900 ft.), from which a low belt of rich pasturage ends in the Great Rann desert, whence rise 4 hilly islands, **Patcham Peer** (1450 ft.) the highest. Only in the rains do these two ranges send streams N. to the Rann and S. to the Gulf. The **Rann**, covering 9000 sq. m., and varying in breadth from 25 to 35 m. on N. to 2 m. on E., is the raised bed of the sea covered in the dry season with a hard surface of stone, shingle, and salt. The State was crossed by earthquake waves four times between 1819 and 1864; in the first year every fort was shaken and many levelled. Iron is found, but not worked; the coal in the Charwar hills is worthless. The Rao of Kach emigrated from Sind in 15th century, and is head of the Jareja Rajpoots. Rao Desal, the most enlightened, was trained by Rev. James Gray, friend of the poet Burns, whose monument stands in the capital. **Bhooj** (24,000), at foot of a fortified hill, with cantonment; **Mandvi** (36,000), chief port, 36 m. S. of Bhooj on N. coast of Gulf of Kach, to which till 1836 a brisk trade in slaves from Zanzibar went on. The people are still the best sailors and capitalists on the shores of the Indian Ocean, and are famed for their embroidery and silverwork, and manufactures of silk and cotton. Mundra, Anjar (13,000), Naliya, and Jakhan are the other 4 municipalities in Kach.

§ 22. *PALANPOOR AND RADHANPOOR STATES, forming the Palanpoor Political Agency (8000 sq. m., pop. 578,732), are bounded E. by Danta and Sirohi States with the Aravali range between, N. by Sirohi and Marwar, W. by Kach, and S. by Baroda. **Palanpoor** (2384 sq. m.), under Dewan, of Afghan descent, with capital of same name, a station on State Railway, 393 m. N. of Bombay and 498 S.W. of Delhi. **Deesa** (6000), cantonment on left bank of Banas, to W. of Palanpoor. **Danta**, 36 m. E. of Deesa, is a vassal State of Palanpoor. **Radhanpoor**, under Nawab of the Persian Babees, who accompanied Hoomayoon on his restoration, with capital (14,000) of same name. Munjpoor and Samee are the other chief towns.

§ 23. *MAHI-KANTHA STATES ("bank of the Mahi") form a Political Agency, which is bounded N.E. by Oodaipoor and Doongarpoor States, W. by Baroda and Palanpoor, S. by Kaira, and S.E. by Rewa-Kantha. Area, 4000 sq. m. Population, 517,485. This tract, named from the Mahi river which traverses it, contains 58 chiefships, of which the only important one is that of Edar and Ahmednagar. On the border between Mahi-Kantha and Rajpootana Sir J. Outram did much to civilise the wild Bheels and Kolees. **Edar** (218,000 pop.), under Maharaja of the Rathore Rajpoots, with chief town of same name, traditionally known as Eeldoorg, 64 m. N.E. of Ahmedabad. Large fairs are held at Samlaji and Brahma Khair.

§ 24. *SIX REWA-KANTHA STATES ("bank" of the Narbada or "Rewa"), forming a Political Agency, scattered among the

Panch Mahals, Baroda, and Surat States, have an area of 4792 sq. m. and population of 510,000. The only chief with first class powers is the Maharana of **Rajpeepla** (1514 sq. m., pop. 121,000), lying along S. bank of Narbada; the hills (2000 ft.) are a continuation of the Satpooras, and form a watershed between the Narbada and Tapti. **Nandod** is the capital. **Chota Oodaipoor** (873 sq. m., pop. 63,000), lying between Baroda W. and Ali Raipoor E., is under the Maharawal. The capital of same name (3000) is on high road from Baroda to Mhow, before which Tatia Topi was defeated in 1858. Mohan town, which sometimes gives its name to the State, commands the passes. **Barria** (813 sq. m., pop. 53,000), N. of above, a Bheel State under Maharawal, of which Deogud Barria is capital. **Loonawara** (388 sq. m., pop. 75,000), immediately S. of Rajpoot State of Doongarpoor and Mahi river, under Maharana, with fortified capital of same name 4 m. E. of confluence of Mahi and Panám. **Balasinor** (150 sq. m., pop. 42,000), S. of above and N. of Kaira, under Nawab, with chief town (9000) of same name on Sheri river, between Baroda and Neemach. **Sunth** (394 sq. m., pop. 50,000), W. of Loonawara, a wild Bheel country under Maharana, with chief town of same name.

Central Districts and States.

§ 25. KHANDESH DISTRICT is bounded E. by Berar and Nimar, N. by Holkar's and the Barwani States, N.W. by Rewa-Kantha, W. by Baroda and the Dang States, and S. by Nasik and Haidarabad State. Area, 10,338 sq. m. Population, 1,237,231. Khandesh is an upland basin, the most northerly section of the Dekhan tableland, stretching about 160 m. along the Tapti. The N. frontier consists of the **Satpoora Mountains**, a range from 30 to 40 m. wide, through which the Sindwa pass on the Agra road leads to Holkar's State. On S. the **Ajanta**, **Satmala**, or **Chandor** range, with the famous caves, marks off Khandesh from Haidarabad State. On S.W. the Arva or **Laling** and **Galna** hills separate Khandesh from Nasik, whence the frontier crosses the Sahyadris to Songad town. The **Hatti** hills are in S.E. The **Tapti**, which flows through Khandesh for a third of its whole course of 450 m., receives many tributaries from both sides; of those the chief are the **Girna** from Nasik, which falls into the left bank near Nander; the **Bori**, 20 m. N., and parallel to the Girna; the **Panjhra**, from the crest of the Sahyadris at Pimpalner to the Tapti near Thalner; and the Borai, N. and parallel to the Panjhra. The **Narbada** skirts the N.W. corner for 45 m., and carries the timber of Khandesh to the coast. The 20 forest reserves cover 2326 sq. m. in three groups. This compact district is named Khandesh, as "the Khan's land," or "Krishna's (Kanha) land," or "the land of the pass or gap," and is the Khandav forest of the *Mahabharat*. The chief town is **Dhoolia** (13,000), on S. bank of Panjhra, 30 m. N. of **Chalisgaon** (4000), railway station on Bombay-Agra road, with lines for the Bheel corps; 6 m. distant are the hill and fort of Laling, commanding the Agra road and Avir pass to Malegaon. **Bhamer Fort** and **Caves** are 35 m. N.W. of Dhoolia, near **Pimpalner** (3000), on the Panjhra, an old town and mart for the Dangs. **Balsáne**, 14 m. E. of Pimpalner, has a well-preserved series of old temples and caves like those of Elura. **Amalner** (7600), 21 m. N. of Dhoolia, with old fort, now a grain mart. **Bhadgaon** (6500), on an island formed by the Girna, 34 m. S.E. of Dhoolia; 2 m. N. and 10 m. N.E. of Kajgaon railway station is the Khandesh Government Farm, started in 1869. **Pachora** (3000), 231 m. from Bombay, is nearest railway station to the Ajanta Caves, 28 m. off. **Jalgaon** (8000), railway station; 30 m. farther on is the English capital of the district and centre of its cotton trade since the American civil war (1862-5). **Bhusawal** (8000), a mile from the Tapti, crossed by large viaduct, and 2 m. W. of junction of Nagpoor and Jabalpoor lines of Great Indian Peninsula Railway, with large railway works. **Dharangaon** (12,000), 35 m. N.E. of Dhoolia, an old cloth mart, where the English planted a factory in 1674, which Shivaji plundered. Here (1825-30) Outram raised his Bheel (billa = "a bow") corps, and his Bungalow is still the public headquarters. In 1844 Government began cotton-gin experiments here under two American planters; Jalgaon is the railway station. **Erandol** (11,000) walled town above the Anjni river, 8 m. from Dharangaon, with paper manufactures. **Nandoorbar** (7500), 32 m. N.W. of Dhoolia; oldest town in district, where in 1666 an English factory was established. **Parola** (12,500), 24 m. E. of Dhoolia, an old cotton cloth mart. **Yaval** (9000), 9 m. N.W. of Bhusawal railway station, with fine view from old fort.

§ 26. *THE DANGS are 16 Khandesh States in the three groups of the Dangs, Mehvas, and Surgana, in the wild Bheel country below the Ghats, between Khandesh and Nasik on N.E., Rewa-Kantha and Bansda State on W. Area, 3840 sq. m. Population, 60,270. The country is a mass of steep wooded flat-topped trap hills running W. from the foot of the Sahyadris, and forms the first step into the Dekhan plateau. The Purna and Amlika are the chief rivers. The country is rich in teak timber, second only to that of Kanara, but is most unhealthy. Outram tamed it in 1830, and he alone of the force escaped sickness by sleeping with his head and face covered with fine gauze. The Collector of Khandesh visits the States once a year. **Gharvi** is the central post; its chief and those of Der-Chaoti, Amála, Pimpri, and Vasurna, claim the title of Raja; the other chieftains are Naiks; all follow the Gharvi standard. Of the Mehva group the only school is in **Kathi**. In the S.W. corner is **Surgana**, which has one school, often closed for want of pupils.

§ 27. NASIK DISTRICT (including Peint) is bounded E. by Haidarabad State, N. by Khandesh, W. by the Dangs and Thana, and S. by Ahmednagar. Area, 5940 sq. m. Population, 781,206. This tableland (1300 to 2000 ft.) is hilly on W. or *dang* portion, and well cultivated on E. or *desh* side. The **Chandor Hills** form the watershed. To S. the streams are tributaries of the **Godavari**; the chief are Darna, Kadwa, Deo, and Maralgin. To N. the Girna and its tributary, the Mosam, flow into the Tapti. The Sahyadri mountains run N. to S., the other hills E. to W. The hills are crowned with forts famous in the Maratha wars. **Nasik** (23,000), on the Godavari, 30 m. from its source at Trimbak village, 4 m. N.W. of the Great Indian Peninsula Railway station, the Benares of W. India, dotted over with temples and shrines, a capital of the Maratha Peshwas and British since 1818. It is the Nasika of Ptolemy. Occupied by Church Missionary Society; their settlement of Sharanpoor, with industrial school for freed Africans, is near. Five m. S.S.W. of town are the 17 *Nasik caves* (Pandu Lena) of Boodhist origin, and of the same date as those of Kanheri, or the time of the Andhrabhritya kings of the Dekhan, about 1st century A.D. Two of the *viharas* are "very far in advance of any yet met with" in richness of decoration. **Deolali** (2000), railway station and depot for British troops on the way to and from England, 113 m. from Bombay. **Lasalgaon**, chief mart and railway station, 146 m. from Bombay. **Vinchoor** (5500) fort is 3 m. off. **Yeola** (18,000), 161 m. from Bombay, with large silk and cotton manufactures. **Manmad** (4000), junction with Dhond and Manmad State Railway, which forms a chord line between N.E. and S.E. sections of Great Indian Peninsula Railway; caves are near. **Sirmar** (10,500), 17 m. S.E. of Nasik, on Poona road, a rural centre. **Malegaon** (10,000), cantonment on Bombay and Agra trunk road, 24 m. N.E. of Manmad railway station, captured by the British in 1818 from

Pindari Arabs. **Chandor** (6000), at foot of old fort, commanding passage from Khandesh to Bombay, with a palace of Holkar's. **Peint**, 32 m. N.W. of Nasik, and Haisul, 10 m. S. of Peint, residence of Begam of Peint, a lapsed State.

§ 28. AHMEDNAGAR DISTRICT is bounded E. by Haidarabad State from which the Godavari separates it on N.E., on N. by Nasik, W. by Thana and Poona from which it is divided by the Bheema and Kera, and S. by Sholapoor. Area, 6666 sq. m. Population, 751,228; a decrease on the census number of 1871, due to the famine of 1877 in this and six southern districts. The **Sahyadri** hills, which form the W. border, throw spurs E., the valleys forming the beds of the **Prawara** and **Moola** rivers, whence the district stretches in hill and tableland to the **Gor** in S. In N.W. the **Kalsubai** hill rises above 5000 ft.; 18 m. W. of Ahmednagar city, **Parner** hill stands at 3240 ft., or 500 above the tableland. The **Godavari** forms the N. boundary for 40 m., receiving the united Prawara and Moola, and thereafter the Dhor. In S. the **Sina** and **Kera** flow into the **Bheema**. **Ahmednagar City** (33,000), third city of the Dekhan, covering 3 sq. m. on left bank of Sina, 12 m. from its source, on the Dhond and Manmad State Railway, 51 m. from Dhond. Founded in 1494 by Ahmed Nizam Shah, who made himself independent, Ahmednagar was taken by the Beejapoor kings, and was heroically defended in 1595 by Chand Bibi, the "noble queen" of Meadows Taylor's story, against Akbar's son, who captured it. It surrendered to General Wellesley in 1803, and became British finally in 1818. Ahmednagar is a station of the American Mission Board, the Vernacular Education, and the Propagation Societies. **Sangamner** (10,009), 49 m. N.W. of Ahmednagar. **Pathardi** (7200), 25 m. E. of Ahmednagar. **Kharda** (7000), 56 m. S.E. of Ahmednagar, scene of a Maratha defeat by the Nizam in 1795. **Srigonda** (6000), 28 m. S. by W. of Ahmednagar. **Bhingar** (5800), a municipality.

§ 29. POONA DISTRICT is bounded E. by Sholapoor and Ahmednagar, N. by Ahmednagar and Nasik, W. by Bhor State, S. by Satara and Phaltan State from which it is divided by the Neera. Area, 5348 sq. m. Population, 900,621; a decrease since 1871, due to famine of 1877. Poona and the adjoining districts of Satara and Sholapoor, emphatically Maharashtra = the Maratha country, are bounded on W. for 150 m. by the Sahyadri range, under which the great Maratha capitals of Poona, Satara, and Kolhapoor nestled, while the Musalman capitals of Ahmednagar, Beejapoor, Bedar, and Goolbarga lay to

W.; walled cities in the plains. From Paitan on the Godavari the great Salevahana ruled Maharashtra early in the Christian era; then from Kalliani, near Sholapoor, the Chalookya Rajpoots ruled till close of 12th century, when the Deogiri or Doulatabad Rajas succeeded, to be extinguished by the Musalmans in 1312. In 1345 the Bahmani dynasty, founded by Musalman nobles who revolted from M. Tughlak, ruled from Goolbarga and then Bedar till 1491, when the Dekhan was divided by the kings of Beejapoor, Ahmednagar, and the Nizam Shahi, who in 1565 destroyed the Hindoo dynasty of Beejanagar at Talikot. Under the Beejapoor kings the Marathas became powerful, led by Shivaji, son of Shahji Bhonsla, whose empire fell only in 1818 with Baji Rao, last of the Peshwas. Even in 1857 peace prevailed, save at Kolhapoor, where that Peshwa's adopted son, Nana Doondoo Pant, produced incipient mutiny. The **Bheema** river passes through Poona district from N.W. to S.E., receiving the streams from the Sahyadris. The **Khadakuasla Lake** ($5\frac{1}{2}$ sq. m.) is 10 m. S.W. of Poona city, which it supplies. **Poona City** (120,000 on 4 sq. m.), with **Kirkee** ("window"?), headquarters of Bombay Artillery, 4 m. N.W., 119 m. S.E. of Bombay, on right bank of Moota, near its *sangam* or confluence with the Moola, 1850 ft. above the sea, and seat of the provincial Government in the rainy season. To S. is the peak of Parvati with temple, and public garden Heerabagh below. The Bund, along the Moola-Moota river, with gardens, and the road from the city W. to Kirkee, form the European quarter. The principal buildings are the Government House at Ganesh Khind ("ravine of Ganesh"), N.W. of Parvati, the Council Hall, Dekhan and Engineering Colleges. The Judges' Chambers, near the last, are on the site of the Residency of the British Agent, from which Mountstuart Elphinstone retired to Kirkee before the battle, and still identified by the natives with the Peshwa's rule, though his residence was in the Fort. The Free Church of Scotland has had a mission in Poona since the city was open to Christians. The native town is divided into seven quarters, each named after a day of the week; the Shanwar or Saturday division contains the walls of the Junawada, or "old palace" of the Peshwa, near the street in which he witnessed offenders trampled to death by elephants. In the Boodhwar or Wednesday division are the public offices and former residence of Nana Farnavees. Poona was granted by Sultan of Ahmednagar to Shivaji's grandfather. By treaty of Bassein in 1802 a British force was stationed there. The victory of Kirkee over Baji Rao, the last Peshwa, on 5th November 1817, and Elphinstone's settlement of the ceded territories for the first time gave peace and prosperity to the Dekhan.

Singar (4162 ft.) ("the lion's den"), scene of Shivaji's exploits, Maratha fort and popular sanitarium, 12 m. S.W. of Poona, on E. side of the Sahyadris, where there branch off into the Dekhan the hills of **Poorandhar** (4472 ft.), forts and town 16 m. S. of Poona, commanding pass of same name, one of the first places taken by Shivaji; surrendered to British in 1818. **Saswad** (6500), on left bank of Karha, 16 m. S.E. of Poona, with old palaces of the Peshwa and Poorandhar Brahmans; seat of Scottish Free Church Mission. **Indapoor** (8000), 84 m. S.E. of Poona, another station of same mission. **Karla**, or Karlen, village on Bombay and Poona road, near which are the famous **Karlé Caves.** The great central group of Western Caves, which are architectural, as the Kathiawar group are unornamented and the Orissa group are sculptural, are near the head of the **Bor Ghat** (1798 ft.), the pass 40 m. from Bombay and Poona, once the key to the Dekhan, now ascended by the railway. Karlé, which has the largest and finest *chaitya* in India, is near Lanoli (Lenavali = "grove of the caves") railway station. The Bhaja Caves are on the opposite or S. side of the railway. The Bedsa Caves are on the S. side of the hills, in which Bhaja is. The caves at Kondané, Jambroog, and Ambivalé, are in the lower scarps of the Sahyadris, near Karjat railway station (in Ahmednagar). Karlé is reached also from Khandala railway station (2000 ft.), sanitarium near head of Bor Ghat. From Talegaon (5000), railway station 20 m. N.W. of Poona, the town of **Junnar** ("old town") (10,500) is distant 26 m., with 57 Boodhist excavations around it, comprising almost every variety of rock-cut temples, and forms not found elsewhere, intermediate between the simplicity of the Kathiawar group and the richness of those of a subsequent age. **Shivaneri**, or Sewnar, hill-fort 1½ m. S.W. of Junnar, was the birthplace of the great Maratha, Shivaji Bhonsla, in 1627.

§ 30. SHOLAPOOR DISTRICT is bounded E. by Akalkot and Haidarabad States; N. by Ahmednagar; W. by Poona and Satara, and Pratinidhi and Phaltan States; and S. by Kaladgi. Area, 4521 sq. m. Population, 582,487; a decrease of 19 per cent, due to famine of 1876-77. The **Bheema** and its tributaries, the **Man, Nera,** and **Sina,** flowing S.E., are the chief rivers. There are great reservoirs at Ekrook and Siddheswar, near Sholapoor town, at Korégan and Pandharpoor. **Sholapoor** (50,000), on plain of Sina, 150 m. S.E. of Poona. Since it was stormed by General Munro in 1818, Sholapoor has become a prosperous seat of silk and cotton manufactures, and entrepot for Poona and Haidarabad. American Board's Mission station. Beejapoor, 58 m. off, is best reached from Sholapoor. **Barsi** (18,700), mart, 20 m. from Barsi Road Railway Station, 43 m. N. of Sholapoor. **Pandharpoor** (16,500), on right hand of Bheema, 38 m. W. of Sholapoor, and 31 m. from Barsi Road Railway Station, with popular shrine of Vithoba. **Karmala** (7000), 69 m. N.W. of Sholapoor, and 71 from Jeur Railway Station. **Vairag** (7000), 28 m. N. of Barsi.

§ 31. SATARA DISTRICT is bounded E. by Sholapoor, N. by Bor and Phaltan States and Poona from which the Neera divides it, W. by Kolaba and Ratnagiri with Sahyadris between, and S. by Kolhapoor and Sangli States from which it is separated by the Varna. Area, 4968 sq. m. Population, 1,062,350. The **Sahyadri** main range running S., and the **Mahadeo** range E. and then S.E., start from **Mahableshwar** (4717 ft.) in N.W. corner of district, with spurs and streams that form the head-waters of the **Kistna** river. There are irrigation works on the Kistna near Karad, on the Neera near Malshuas, and on the Man. The Sahyadris are crossed by 15 roads or bullock tracks, of which the chief are the Kamatgi, Pasarni, Kumbharli, Varandha, and Fitzgerald. **Satara** (25,000), in the highlands, near confluence of Kistna and Yena, chief town and famous fort named from its 17 walls, towers, and gates, given up by British to last representative of Shivaji during 1818-1848; pronounced "the most lovely station" in W. India. **Mahableshwar** (Arthur's Seat), chief sanitarium (except in rains, when 240 inches fall) in Bombay, reached generally by horse or post carriage from Poona (74 m. S.) by the Katraj and Kamatgi or Pasarni ghat, or by sea from Bombay to Dasgaon near mouth of the Savitri, and thence by old road (35 m.), established in 1829 by the Governor whose name survives in Malcolm-pet (Nehar), 3½ m. E. of Mahableshwar. **Wai** (11,000), at foot of Mahableshwar, 15 m. E., a Brahmanical town. **Karad** (11,500), 31 m. S.E. of Satara; Tasgaon (10,500), 60 m. S.E.; **Urun** (8500), 48 m. S.E.; and **Ashta** (10,000), on right bank of Kistna, 64 m. S.E.; all municipalities.

§ 32. *FIVE SATARA STATES of Bor, Phaltan, Aundh, Jath, and Daflapoor, under the supervision of the Collector of Satara, which adjoins or surrounds them. **Bor**, under the Pant Sachiv, a Brahman, has an area of 1491 sq. m., a population of 137,000, and a gross revenue of £71,507. The chief town is Bor (4000), 25 m. S. of Poona. The State lies between

Satara and the Sahyadris, with Kolaba on W. **Phaltan**, under the Nimbalkar, a Rajpoot, has an area of 397 sq. m., population of 47,800, and revenue of £26,600. The chief town is Phaltan (10,000), 37 m. N.E. of Satara. The State lies between Poona and Satara. **Aundh**, under the Pant Pratinidhi ("representative of the Raja," or Shivaji), Brahman, has an area of 213 sq. m., population of 68,335, and revenue of £21,555. The chief town is Aundh, 26 m. S.E. of Satara. **Jath**, under a Deshmookh, a Rajpoot, has an area of 885 sq. m., population of 64,000, and revenue of £12,900. The chief town is Jath, 88 m. S.E. of Satara. **Daflapoor**, under a Deshmookh, has an area of 40 sq. m., population of 5000, and revenue of £920. The chief town of Daflapoor is 80 m. S.E. of Satara. The total population of these States in 1881 was 313,813.

Southern Districts and States.

§ 33. KALADGI DISTRICT is bounded E. by Nizam's States; N. by Sholapoor and Akalkot State from which the Bheema divides it; W. by the Jath, Jamkhandi, and Mudhol States; and S. by Dharwar and Ramdroog State with the Malprabha between. Area, 5757 sq. m. Population, 638,493; a loss of 22 per cent since 1871, due to the famine of 1866-68, from which this district suffered most. N. of the Kistna, the section from the Bheema is a treeless plain of black soil, interrupted only by the Sina and Don. S. of the Kistna to W. lines of hills break the level; the Badami cliffs of sandstone are chief. The other chief rivers are the Ghatprabha and Malprabha. **Kaladgi** (6500), chief town, 104 m. S. by W. of Sholapoor Railway Station. **Bagalkot** (14,000), on Ghatprabha, 15 m. E. of Kaladgi, a mart with silk and cotton manufactures. **Beejapoor** (13,000), 52 m. N.E. of Kaladgi and 160 S.E. of Poona, old capital of famous Musalman kingdom founded by Yusuf (died 1510), son of the Osmanli Sultan, Murad II., under one of whose descendants Shivaji rose to power, and extinguished by Aurangzeb in 1686. The splendid architectural remains have been preserved by the British Government since 1818—the walls 6¼ miles in circumference, domed mosques, tombs, and seven-storied palaces. **Hungund** (6500), good market, 40 m. S.E. of Kaladgi. **Gooludgad** (10,700), manufacturing town, 22 m. S.E. of Kaladgi; German Mission station. **Ilkal** (10,000), mart, 8 m. S.E. of Hungund; the Nizam's cantonment, Lingasagar, 24 m. E., is supplied from Ilkal. **Gajandragad** (7700), 41 m. S.E. of Kaladgi. **Talikot** (7500), 60

m. N.E. of Kaladgi, where the Musalman kings of the Dekhan destroyed the Hindoo empire of Bijaynagar in 1565. Keroor (7000), 14 m. S.E. of Kaladgi, and Amingarh (7500), 32 m. S.E., are municipal marts.

§ 34. BELGAUM DISTRICT is bounded E. by Mudhol and Jamkhandi States and Kaladgi, N. by Miraj State, W. by Kolhapoor and Sawantwari States and Goa, and S. by Dharwar and N. Kanara. Area, 4737 sq. m. Population, 864,014; a loss of about 11 per cent since 1871, due to the famine of 1876-78. The plain sloping from the Sahyadris to Kaladgi is dotted with peaks and low ranges covered with forest. The **Kistna** flows through centre and **Malprabha** through S. of district from the spurs of the Sahyadri. **Belgaum** (27,000), chief town and cantonment (2500 ft.), on the Bellary affluent of the Markandi, which flows into the Ghatprabha tributary of the Kistna; the old Kanarese name was Vennugrama, from the numerous bamboo groves; seat of London Missionary Society. **Gokak** (13,000), 30 m. N.E. of Belgaum, known for its toy and paper manufactures. E. 3½ m. are the **Falls of Gokak**, by which the Ghatprabha river precipitates itself 176 ft. into a fissure as it issues from the W. Ghats on to the Dekhan plateau. In July 100,000 cubic ft. per second is thus hurried over with a deafening noise. **Athni** (11,700), chief mart, sending grain and cotton W. 24 m. to Miraj State. **Nipani** (9500), 45 m. N.W. of Belgaum. **Hongal** (9000), manufacturing place. Sankeshwar (9000), 27 m. N.W. of Belgaum, residence of great *Swami* of W. India, with fair of the reformer, Sankar Acharya. **Saundatti** (8000), 41 m. S.E. of Belgaum, with ruins of hill-fort of Parasgad. **Badami**, early capital of the Chalookyas, with caves. **Murgod** (7000), mart, 27 m. E. of Belgaum. The S. Maratha Railway will open up this district to Poona.

§ 35. DHARWAR DISTRICT is bounded E. by the Madras district of Bellary from which the Toongabhadra divides it, N. by Kaladgi and Belgaum, W. by Goa and N. Kanara, S. by Mysore. Area, 4535 sq. m. Population, 882,907; a reduction of nearly 11 per cent since 1871, owing to the famine of 1876-78. The Poona and Harihar (Mysore) road divides this famous cotton tract into two parts; to N. and N.E. is the black soil plain with rich crops of cotton, in S.E. are the **Kapad Hills**, (gold-washing), more cotton soil, and then an undulating country of red soil down to Mysore. To W. the land rises into the hills of N. Kanara, with fine forest reserves. Of 7 chief streams which flow from this watershed, one descends the Sahyadri Ghats to the Indian Ocean, the Birti. These six flow S. to the Bay of Bengal: the Malprabha on N., dividing Dharwar from Kaladgi; the Bennihalla, its tributary; the **Toongabhadra** on S.E. border, dividing Dharwar from Mysore, Bellary, and Haidarabad State; the Wardha and Koomadwati, its tributaries. After the battle of Talikot, Dharwar became a portion of the Beejapoor kingdom; was seized by Shivaji, then by Haidar Ali, when the British helped the Marathas to recover it in 1791; in 1818 it became British with the rest of the Maratha empire. The Basel Evangelical Society and the Romish and Goanese Catholics have missions in the towns and villages. Kanarese is the vernacular. The S. Maratha Railway is opening up the district from Bellary, on a branch of the Madras and Bombay trunk line, to the W. coast, where are the ports of Koompta, Karwar, and Vingorla. **Dharwar** (27,500), chief town and ruined fort on Poona road, to W. of the last spurs of the Sahyadris; with hill of Mailargood 1½ m. to S. **Hoobli** (38,000), centre of cotton trade, 13 m. S.E. of Dharwar, 90 m. from Karwar port, and 132 from Bellary; Shivaji plundered the English factory here in 1673. **Raneebennoor** (12,000), 80 m. S.E. of Dharwar, prosperous manufacturing mart. **Gadag** (10,500), mart, 45 m. E. of Dharwar, forming a municipality with **Betigeri** (8700). **Nargoond** (10,000), entrepot, 32 m. N.E. of Dharwar, where, when a Feudatory State, the Maratha chief in 1857 murdered Mr. Manson, the commissioner. **Nawalgund** (9500), 24 m. N.E. of Dharwar, with cotton, carpet, and toy manufactures; once taken by Tipoo from the chief called Desai. **Annigeri** (7000), mart, 29 m. E. of Dharwar on Bellary road. **Mulgund** (7000), 38 m. S.E. of Dharwar.

§ 36. *EIGHT SOUTHERN MARATHA STATES, SAVANOOR AND AKALKOT STATES, form with Kaladgi, Belgaum, Dharwar, and Kolhapoor States, the Maratha division of the "W. Karnatic" or "Doab" between the Kistna and its tributary the Toongabhadra. **Mudhol**, under the Ghorpade, a Maratha Raja, is traversed by the Ghatprabha river between Kaladgi and Belgaum, has an area of 362 sq. m., pop. 60,000, and rev. £14,647. The chief town (6500) is of same name. **Sangli**, under a Rao Saheb, has an area of 896 sq. m., pop. 224,000 (rev. £76,400), scattered over six divisions, from chief town (13,000) of same name on the Kistna near its junction with the Warna, to the Toongabhadra in Dharwar. **Miraj** (senior branch), under a Rao Saheb, has an area of 340 sq. m., pop. 82,500 (rev. £27,946), scattered over three divisions from the Kistna, near which is the chief town (23,000), S.E. of

Sangli town to Dharwar. **Miraj** (junior branch) has an area of 208 sq. m., pop. 35,700 (rev. £15,944), scattered over four divisions in Dharwar, Satara, Sholapoor, and Poona; the chief resides near Miraj town. **Jamkhandi**, under a Rao Saheb, has an area of 492 sq. m., pop. 103,000 (rev. £38,680), scattered over three divisions, on the Kistna N. of Mudhol, and in Dharwar S. of Hoobli; chief town (12,500) of same name is 162 m. S. of Poona city. **Kurundwad** (1 senior), under a Rao Saheb, has an area of 182 sq. m., pop. 40,000 (rev. £10,000), scattered over the country, traversed by the Kistna S.W. of Miraj; at the town of same name (8000) the chief résides, also the two younger branches whose estate (2) of 114 sq. m., pop. 30,000 (rev. £10,283) is divided between the Nizam's border and S. of Belgaum. **Ramdroog**, under a Rao Saheb, with area of 140 sq. m., pop. 38,000 (rev. £10,404), lies between Kaladgi E., Dharwar S., and Kolhapoor N. and W., and is bisected by the Malprabha. The chief town and fort of same name (6500) was with Nargoond one of the two strongest in the Karnatic, and was besieged for 7 months by Tipoo. **Mhaisal** has an area of 21 sq. m., pop. 2700 (rev. £1600). **Savanoor** has an area of 70 sq. m., pop. 14,751 (rev. £7327), in Dharwar, under a Nawab related to Tipoo, but plundered by him and protected by the Marathas and General Wellesley. Chief town of same name (8700) on Poona road S.E. of Dharwar town. **Akalkot**, between Sholapoor W. and the Haidarabad State E., has an area of 498 sq. m., pop. 81,000 (rev. £28,283). The chief town of same name (8580) is 250 m. S.E. of Bombay.

§ 37. *KOLHAPOOR STATE, under Shivaji IV., representative of the younger branch of the great Shivaji, as the now extinct Raj of Satara was of the elder, is bounded S. and E. by Belgaum, N.E. by Kurundwad, Miraj, and Sangli States from which the Kistna divides it, N. by Satara with the Warna between, W. by Ratnagiri and Sawantwari with the Sahyadri mountains separating them. Area, 2778 sq. m. Population, 800,267. Revenue, £164,408. This principality consists of a succession of hill and dale (1790 ft.), running in parallel lines E. from the Sahyadri range, dotted with numerous hill forts (3000 ft.), with high westward scarps. Of these now pleasant and once impregnable retreats the chief are Panhala, Vishalgarh, Baura, Bandargarh, and Rungoona. **Kolhapoor** (40,000), the capital, picturesquely situated opposite a gap in the Sahyadri range, through which the sea-breeze blows. A new palace is being built for the Raja. Shivaji III. died in Europe in 1870, and his body was burned with Hindoo rites at Florence, where there is a memorial of him. Kolhapoor has a college, schools, and Christian Missions of the Gospel Propagation and American Presbyterian Societies. There are 11 vassal chiefs of Kolhapoor whose estates are included in its area. Of these **Vishalgarh**, with Mulkapoor as the residence, has 280 sq. m., from which Shivaji marched 100 m. to Mudhol in one night, plundered it, and returned to hold it against the Muhammadans; here are noble cascades in the rainy season. **Baura**, 26 m. S.E. of Kolhapoor, has 83 sq. m., and **Inchal-Karanji** 201. The others are Kapshi, Kagal, Juchal Karanji, Torgal Datwad, Himmat Bahadoor, Kagal (senior), Sar Lashkar Bahadoor and Patan (in Satara).

§ 38. *SAWANTWARI STATE, 50 m. long and 10-30 broad, lies between the Sahyadri range which separates it from Kolhapoor State and Belgaum on E., and a narrow strip of the coast of Ratnagiri on W. which shuts it off from the Arabian Sea, on N. it is bounded by Ratnagiri, on S. by Portuguese Goa. Area, 900 sq. m. Population, 174,412. Revenue, £32,634. In this land of hills and streams, rising rapidly from the coast, the river mouths and backwaters are navigable for a short distance only. The chief streams are the **Karli** or Sarambal on N., which flows from the village of Shivapoor on the Sahyadri range 35 m. S.W. to the sea at Malvan; and the **Terakhol** or Banda, which, rising in the same range S. of the Karli, marks off the State from Goa, and is tidal and navigable to Banda 15 m. from the sea. The country rising to the Sahyadris is strikingly beautiful, dotted with groups and peaks from 300 to 3000 ft. high, covered with forts of historic fame, such as Manohar and Mausantosh. The range is crossed by 7 chief passes, of which the **Amboli** and Ram are fit for carts. Sawantwari ("the Sawant's" or "the beautiful garden") (8500), chief town in palm groves (367 ft.), 19 m. W. of base of the hills and 17 E. of Vingorla fort, with beautiful Motee Talao ("pearl lake") and fort. Banda (2500), 6 m. S. of Sawantwari, on right bank of Terakhol, a great port in 16th century, with ruins of mosques and tombs. Kudal (2700), on Karli, 13 m. N. of Sawantwari, a Chalookya capital in 6th century. Here in 1748 Jayram Sawant defeated the pirate Angria.

§ 39. RATNAGIRI DISTRICT is bounded E. by Sawantwari and Kolhapoor States and Satara with the Sahyadris between, N. by Kolaba and Janjeera State, W. by Arabian Sea, and S. by Portuguese Goa. Area, 3922 sq. m. Population, 997,090. This narrow strip of low land between the Sahyadris and the sea has a dangerous coast-line of 160 m. from Bankot on N. to Fort Redi on S., opposite Fort Terakhol, the Portuguese limit. The promontories and rocky islands are crowned with old Maratha forts, as at Suvarndroog and Malvan. The hills are crossed by many passes up to the Dekhan tableland, amid grand scenery. The principal hills are the hog-backed **Mandangar**, a fort 14 m. from the sea at Dapoli, a conspicuous landmark, which commands a view of Mahableshwar; S.E. are **Palgar**, **Mahipatgar**, facing the Hatlot pass; and Makarandgar (in Satara), the famous "saddle-back" of visitors to Mahableshwar, **Sumargar**, and **Rasalgar**. The **Savitri** or Bankot river forms the N. border for 24 m., one of the 5 streams (*panch* **ganga**) which rise in the village of old Mahableshwar, and flow for 50 m. to the sea. The **Vashishti**, the largest stream, flows 30 m. S. and parallel to the Savitri from the Tivra pass to the port of Anjanvel, a mile below the famous old port of Dabhol. The Shashtri flows from Prachitgar in the hills 40 m. to the seat at Jaygar promontory, past Sangameshvar. The Ratnagiri, 25 m. S. of the above, flows from the Amla pass 40 m. to the Ratnagiri promontory. The Muchkoondi, the Jayatapoor, on which was the old town of Rajapoor, where the English and French had factories; the Vijyadroog, the Devgad, the Achra, and the Kalavli, succeed in order from N. to S. till the S. border is reached in the **Karli**, which flows for 30 m. from Manohargar in Sawantwari to the sea, 8 m. S. of Malvan. This Southern Konkan has always been the chief recruiting ground of the Bombay army, and has many pensioners and Portuguese Catholic "Christis" or caste Christians, who avoid menial service, like those of Goa, but are clerks and shopmen. The peasants on the uplands have suffered much from famines, and the land tenures, especially those of the *khots*, or large middlemen, have led to much litigation. **Ratnagiri** (11,000), chief town, facing the sea, 136 m. S. of Bombay, centre of the sardine fishery, with fort and lighthouse; here is an American Presbyterian Mission. The other 8 ports in order from N. to S. are these: **Bankot**, or Fort Victoria (4000), earliest British possession in Western India next to Bombay, from which it is 73 m. S.E., surrendered in 1755 to Commodore James, and used chiefly as the beef-market of Europeans and Musalmans in Bombay. Here in 1822, and at the next port of **Harnai** (6000), with the island fortress of **Suvarndroog** ("golden fortress"), long the stronghold of Angria's pirates, the Scottish Missionary Society, under Rev. D. Mitchell, formerly a British officer, opened their first Mission, which, in 1829,

Dr. John Wilson joined. **Chiplun** (6000), on S. bank of Vashishti, near entrance to Kumbharli pass, on an easy road to the Dekhan; the first home of the Konkanast or Chitpávan Brahmans; here and at Mhar, on the Savitri, at Dabhol, and at **Sangamesvar**, are Bhoodhist cells or caves; in the S. Konkan there are in all 150 separate excavations. After Ratnagiri and Rajapoor, already noticed, come **Kharepatan** (3000), leading to the Phonda pass, and being silted up, once a famous fort; and **Malvan** (14,000), with Shivaji's fortress and coast capital, **Sindhudroog** ("ocean fort"), on a low island a mile from the shore, long a pirate nest, and considered by the Marathas the cenotaph of Shivaji, in which his stone image, covered with a gold or silver mask, is worshipped. **Vingorla** (15,000), a mile E. of mouth of a swampy creek, a rising port, because nearest to the cantonments of Belgaum and Dharwar, to which a splendid cart road leads over the Parpoli pass, 75 m. to Belgaum. Here were early Dutch and British factories. Nine m. N.W. are the **Vingorla Rocks** or **Burnt Islands**, a group of ten, 3 m. from the shore, believed by some to be Ptolemy's Heptanesia and the Sesikreienai of the Periplus. **Vijayadroog** ("Fort Victory") or **Gheria** ("the enclosure"), 170 m. S. of Bombay, on entrance to Vaghotan river, one of the best harbours (2300) on the W. coast, the steamers calling at Jaytapoor, 6 m. off; in 1698 the pirate chief Angria made Vijayadroog his capital, and it was not taken till 1756 by Clive and Admiral Watson. The Marathas again made it a centre of piracy till 1818, when it became permanently British.

§ 40. NORTH KANARA DISTRICT, transferred from Madras because of its commercial relations with Bombay, of which it is the most S. district, is bounded E. by Mysore and Dharwar, N.W. by Goa, W. by Arabian Sea, and S. by South Kanara. Area, 3911 sq. m. Population, 421,840. The Sahyadri range, running N. and S., divides the district into the Balaghat or uplands (3000 sq. m.), and Payanghat or lowlands. The coast is broken by the Karwar headland and 4 estuaries of the **Kali** in N., the **Ganganali** and **Tadri** in centre, and the **Shiravati** in S. The last, falling over a cliff 825 ft., just above the old capital of Gersoppa, captured successively by the Portuguese, Haidar Ali and Tipoo, and General Matthews, divides into several channels, and forms the famous **Falls of Gersoppa**, 35 m. above Honawar (see Mysore). Two streams flow E. from the Sahyadri watershed, of which the **Warda** tributary of the Toongabhadra is alone important. The teak forests of this district, above and below the Ghats, are valuable. Of 12 ports these 5 are the chief. **Karwar** (13,500), chief town, 295 m. S.E. of Bombay, the only safe harbour all the year between Bombay and Cochin; a factory of the East India Company in 1663. **Ankola**, a small port to S. **Koompta** (11,000), on a creek 328 m. S.E. of Bombay, the chief mercantile town; it is 410 m. N.W. of Madras. **Bhatkal** (5300), 64 m. S.E. of Karwar, centre of the Nawayat ("newly arrived") Musalman seamen and traders driven from Bagdad by Sheea persecution, and a famous port for two centuries, from 1321 till Goa supplanted it. **Honawar** (5300), 40 m. S.E. of Karwar, on N. of the large estuary which receives the Shiravati, a great city in 13th century, taken from Haidar Ali by Matthews in 1783. Sadashivgarh port is a village between two ruined forts at the entrance of Kali river.

Portuguese Territory.

§ 41. GOA PROVINCE consists of Goa Settlement, Daman (already described) on N. of Thana district, and Diu island (already described) off S. Kathiawar, and comprises 1096 sq. m., with a population of 407,700. The Province, under a Governor-General on Rs. 18,000 a year, constitutes, with Mozambique, Macao, and Timor, one judicial district, divided into Comarcas, these into Julgados, and these into Tregulsias or parishes.

Goa Settlement, lying between 14° 53′ and 15° 48′ N. lat., and between 73° 43′ and 74° 24′ E. long., is bounded E. by Sahyadri Ghats, which separate it from Dharwar, N. by Sawantwari State and Ratnagiri with the Terakhol or Aurandem river between, W. by the Arabian Sea, and S. by N. Kanara. With an extreme length of 62 m. N. to S., and breadth of 40 m. E. to W., the area is 1062 sq. m., and the population 392,234. By recent treaty the Madras Railway N.W. to Bellary (305½ m.) is being continued by Hoobli through Goa Settlement to Mormugao. Isolated peaks of the Sahyadris are Sonsagar (3827 ft.), Catlanchimanli (3633 ft.), Vagnerim (3500 ft.), Morlemchogor (3400). After Terakhol on N., the 7 principal rivers which flow W. to the sea are the **Chapora** or Colvalle, for 18 m.; the Baga, 1 m.; the Singuerim, 3½ m.; the **Mandavi**, 38½ m. from Parvar Ghat to Nova Goa and Bay of Aguado; the Juari, 39 m. from Digny Ghat to Mormugao Bay; the Sal, 15 m.; and the Talpona, 7 m. The Settlement is divided into the old (velhas) and new (novas) conquistas, forming the 3 judicial Comarcas of the Ilhas, Bardez, and Salsette. The Ilhas are in

2 Julgados, Panjim, and Ponda. Bardez comprises 4—Mapuça, Calangute, Pernem, and Bicholim; Salsette has 3—Margao, Chinchinim, and Quepern. **Mapuça** (12,200) and **Margao** (20,000) are the principal towns next to the capital.

Nova Goa, comprehending **Panjim** (14,200), **Raibandar**, connected with it by a causeway, and **Velha Cidade de Goa**, covers 6 sq. m. on left bank of Mandavi river, 3 m. from its mouth. The port of Goa, 250 m S. of Bombay, from which it is reached by a voyage of 32 hours, is formed by Aguado point N., and Mormugao point S., the future railway terminus. Panjim is 5 m. from the harbour's mouth, and Raibandar 2 m. farther. The viceroy's palace was the fort of the Beejapoor King Adil Shah, when Vasco da Gama landed at Calicut in 1498. Albuquerque captured Goa first in 1510, and Goa Dourada ("golden Goa"), founded by Musalmans in 1479, became the metropolis of an empire said to cover 4000 leagues, till the Dutch, and then the English, came. Now Old Goa is only the ecclesiastical capital, the seat of the Portuguese Primate of the East. The Cathedral of St. Catherine is still majestic amid the ruins; and the Church of Bom Jesus, with the body of Francis Xavier (died 1552), shrunken to 4½ ft., and minus two toes bitten off by a relic-hunting lady, attracts many pilgrims. Three-fourths of the whole population are caste Christians. The Convent of St. Cajetan resembles St. Peter's, Rome. The site of the Inquisition, founded in 1560 and suppressed in 1812, is between this and the cathedral. The Convent of St. Monica was built by the infamous Archbishop Menezes. The island of Goa, 9 m. long and 3 broad, projects between the promontories of Bardez and Salsette, dividing the harbour into the two anchorages of Aguado and Mormugao. Goa Proper, or the Velhas Conquistas, is divided into Ilhas (48 sq. m.), Salsette (102), Bardez (72). The Novas Conquistas comprise Parnem (73 sq. m.), Batagrama (67), Satari (144), Ponda or Antray (79), Kanakona (113), Embarbarcem (186), Kakoran (5), Chandravadi (37), Babb (57), Astrogar (77), Anjadive (1), and Terakhol (1). The annual revenue is £77,000, and expenditure £26,500.

Aden, Perim, and Allied Ports.

§ 42. ADEN SETTLEMENT, the Adané, Athana, and Arabia Felix of classical geography, and believed by some to be the Eden of Ezekiel xxvii. 23, is a fortified peninsula on S. coast of Yemen in 12° 47′ N. lat., and 45° 10′ E. long. The British territory which has an area of 37 sq. m. and population of 35,000, of whom 4000 are the garrison, consists of the two peninsulas of Aden (Jebel Shumshum) and Little Aden (Jebel Ihsan), to the W. between which is the harbour or West Bay or Back Bay (Bandar Tawayih), 8 m. from E. to W. and 4 from N. to S., divided into two by a spit of land, and dotted with islets. Aden is a vast cinder or volcanic crater (1775 ft.), forced up through limestone, and consisting of vesicular lava and rocks, from which pumice-stone is exported. The crater throws out many spurs to the sea, with valleys radiating from it. The inhabited portion, or Aden proper, is an irregular oval, 15 m. in circumference, connected with the mainland of Yemen by a narrow neck 1350 yards broad, along which are a causeway and the Sheikh Othman aqueduct, but for which it would be an island. The N. boundary is the Khor Maksar creek, 2 m. N. of the defensive works across this isthmus. As the entrepot between the Mediterranean empires and the East, Aden was a great city, was destroyed by Aelius Gallus under Augustus, received the Christian embassy of Constantius (324), flourished under Himyarite, Abyssinian, and Islam influences till eclipsed by Mokha, became independent under its own Imams and local chiefs (932), who beat off Albuquerque (1513), fell before Solyman the Magnificent (1538), declined under the Imams of Senaa, who expelled the Turks (1630), and were in turn driven out (1735) by the native Arab tribes, of whom the chief are the Abdalees under Sultan of Lahej, Fadhlees, Akrabees, Owlakees, Subaihees, Yaffaees, Howshabees, Alawees, and Ameers. In 1839 the plundering of British vessels forced the Bombay Government to conquer and annex the place, which had degenerated into a pirate village. Since that time Aden has been administered by a Political Resident, who is also Military Commandant, and it is legally part of India. The opening of the Suez Canal has gradually increased the total trade of this free port to nearly 4 millions sterling annually. The land trade carried by 250,000 camels is about £350,000 in value. It is the port of transhipment for Zanzibar and the E. coast of Africa; 2515 steamers and craft touch at it annually. Here is a Roman Catholic Mission. **Aden Town** and cantonment lie within the crater, which opens on the E. face. To N. is the Main Pass, from which the road passes Maala village with the customhouse, and reaches the harbour at "Steamer point," where are the principal hotels, shops, and consuls' houses. On the Ras Tarshyne headland beyond are the Residency and artillery quarters. At Ras Baradlee to S. is the Eastern Telegraph

Company's Office, 1818 m. from Bombay, and 1465 m. from Suez. Of the 50 old tanks and reservoirs to store rain-water, 13 have been restored. Of the population, one-half are Arabs, one-fourth Africans, and one-fourth Muhammadans, Jews, Hindoos, and Parsees from India. Aden is best defended by iron-plated monitors. In 1882 the village of **Sheikh Othman**, 6 m. beyond the isthmus, and commanding the roads leading to Aden, was purchased from the Sultan of Lahej. From its wells the garrison and shipping at Aden obtain large supplies of excellent water. The place was twice captured by the British: in 1841, when an attempt was made by the combined Abdalee and Fadhlee tribes to recapture Aden; and in 1858, in consequence of several outrages on British subjects committed by the Abdalee, under the Sultan of Lahej, when the fort was blown up with the ammunition found there.

§ 43. PERIM ISLAND (245 ft.), outpost of Aden in Straits of Bal-el-Mandeb, the Mayoon of the Arabs, waterless, of volcanic origin, with lighthouse since 1861, and quarters for detachment of 50 sepoys and officer. The island, 3½ m. long and 1¼ wide, is nearly 1½ m. distant from the Arabian coast, where is the "small strait" usually taken by steamers, and 9½ from the African coast, where is the "broad strait." The harbour facing S.W. has natural advantages which could be increased by the formation of "the spit" into a pier. Perim is the Perantonomasiam ("extending across to Asia") of Ptolemy and the Diodorus of the Periplus, and was seized by the Abyssinians during their conquest of Yemen, A.D. 575. The Portuguese under Albuquerque landed on Perim in 1573, and named it Vera Crux. In 1799 a Bombay garrison under Colonel Murray took possession of Perim, to prevent the French troops in Egypt from seizing it and joining Tipoo. The British reoccupied it in 1857. On the African coast opposite Aden the British possess the **Massah Islands** in the Bay of Tajoora, and the island of **Eibat** near Zaila, which they purchased in 1840, but have not occupied. In 1854 the Imam of Muskat ceded the **Kooria Mooria Islands** on the Mahra coast of Arabia, valuable for their guano.

To prevent the slave trade and piracy, and anticipate the interference of other Powers, the Government of India have engagements with not only the Sultans of Lahej, Fadhlee, and the other chiefs around Aden, but with these ports on the African, Dankali, or Somali coasts, opposite Aden, going W. to E.—Tajoora, Zaila, Bulhar, and Berbera, also with Shoa and Zanzibar. On the Arabian coast the Indian Government has similar engagements with the Imam of Muskat, and with the Nukeebs of Makalla and Shehr, the two principal ports on the Hadramaut or S. coast, the former 250 m. N.E. of Aden, and the latter 20 m.

Assab (177, of whom 7 are Italians) is a bay and settlement on the S.W. coast of the Red Sea, in Straits of Bab-el-Mandeb, recently purchased by the Rubattino Company.

§ 44. SOKOTRA (1520 sq. m., and 5000 pop.), a British feudatory island 148 m. off Cape Gardafui, and 500 m. from Aden, 82 m. long and 20 wide, held by the Sultan of Kisheen on the Mahra coast of Arabia. In 1834 the British obtained the right to land and store coal there; in 1876 the Sultan bound himself and successors never to cede, sell, mortgage, or give for occupation, save to the British Government, Sokotra or any of the neighbouring islands. Sokotra is the Dioscorida (Dwipa Sakhadara = "island of the abode of bliss") of the ancients, was inhabited by Nestorian Christians in the 13th and 15th centuries, who were oppressed by the Mahra Arabs, was held by the Portuguese when Xavier visited it, was explored by Lieutenant Wellsted in 1834, and having no safe harbour was superseded by Aden. The capital is Tamarida (100), on N. coast, with ruins of old capital. Hadibu to E., Kathub, and Golonsir are the other villages on bays of same name. Between Ras Shaal, the W. point, and Cape Gardafui on the African mainland, are islands, of which the chief are The Brothers (10 sq. m.), Abdal Kuri (65 sq. m.), and Bander Saleh (10 sq. m.). Sokotra has been famed from of old for the Aloe (*Aloe Sokotrina*) and dragon's-blood gum.

CHAPTER XVI.

PROVINCE OF AJMER.

§ 1. Ajmer-Merwara generally. § 2. Ajmer. § 3. Merwara.

§ 1. AJMER-MERWARA (Sansk. *Meru* = hill) is a small isolated Province in the heart of the States of Rajpootana, and the highest plateau of Hindustan. Formerly a district of the North-Western Province, it is now under the Governor-General's Agent for Rajpootana as Chief Commissioner, and is directly administered by a resident Commissioner, with one assistant for Ajmer and one for Merwara. It lies between 25° 36′ and 26° 46′ N. lat., and between 73° 45′ and 75° E. long., and is bounded E. by the States of Kishangarh, Marwar, and Jaipoor; N. by Kishangarh and Marwar; W. by Marwar; and S. by Mewar. The area is 2710 sq. m., and the population 460,722. The Province forms the crest of the great Rajpootana watershed, from which the scanty rainfall of 20 inches, diminishing to 5½ in the famine of 1868, finds its way by the Loni into the Gulf of Kach, and by the Chambal into the Bay of Bengal. The **Aravali** chain crops out here in several parallel ranges, on the highest of which (2853 ft.) is **Taragarh Fort**, with Ajmer city at its base; 3 m. W. is the **Nagpahar** ("serpent-hill"). The hills form a double ridge at Beáwar in Merwara, where they enclose its valley. The principal stream is the **Banas**, which, rising in the Aravali 40 m. N.W. of Oodaipoor, skirts the S.E. border. The Khari, Dar, Sabarmati, and Saraswati, are swollen into torrents only by heavy rain. The land is irrigated from 419 tanks embanked by damming up hill streamlets, which, drying by March, yield spring crops. Of four natural reservoirs, **Pushkar** lake deserves notice as a place of pilgrimage. Reboisement is carefully carried on over the arid hill-sides; 101 sq. m. are forest reserves. The Rajpootana-Malwa Railway passes through the N.W. section from Bombay to Agra and Delhi, and from Ajmer 192 m. S. by Naseerabad to Indore and

PROVINCE OF AJMER; BARODA, RAJ

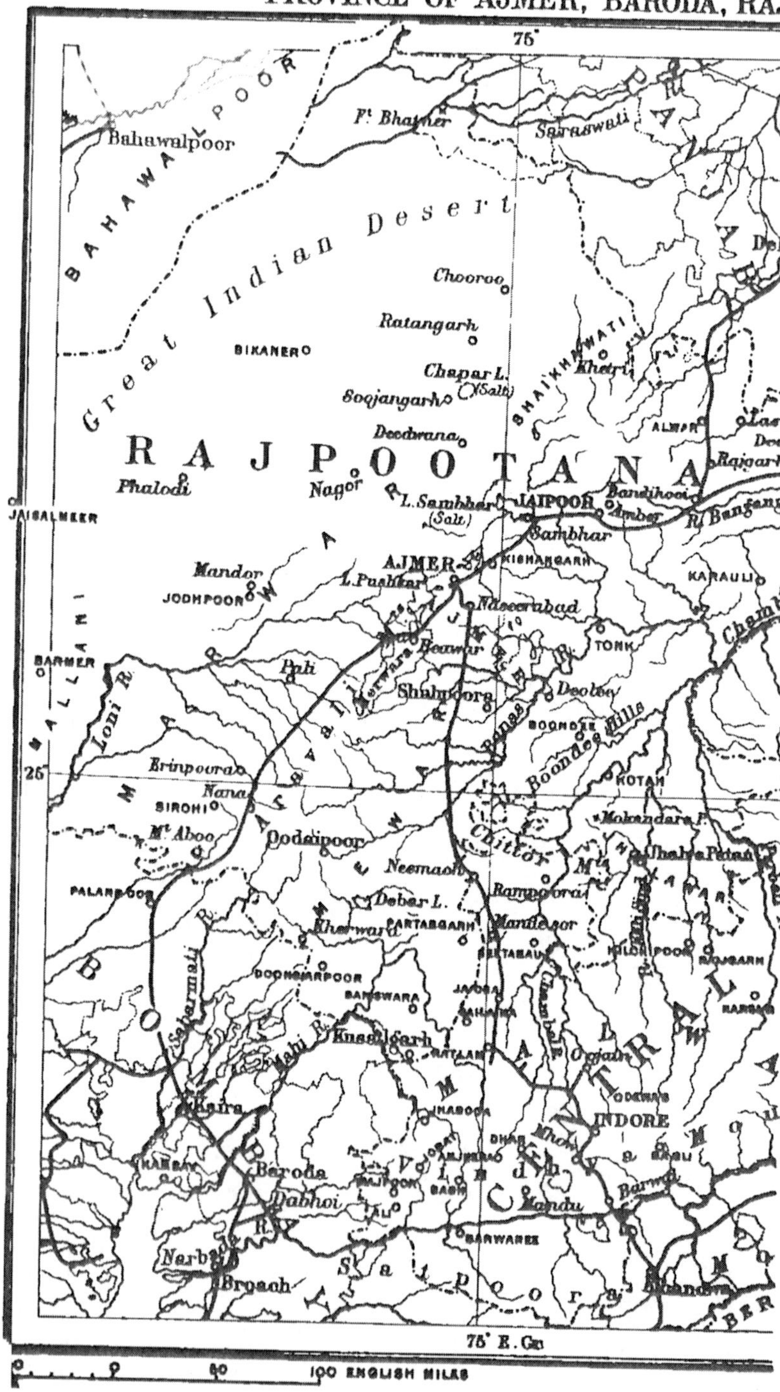

POOTANA AND CENTRAL INDIA STATES.

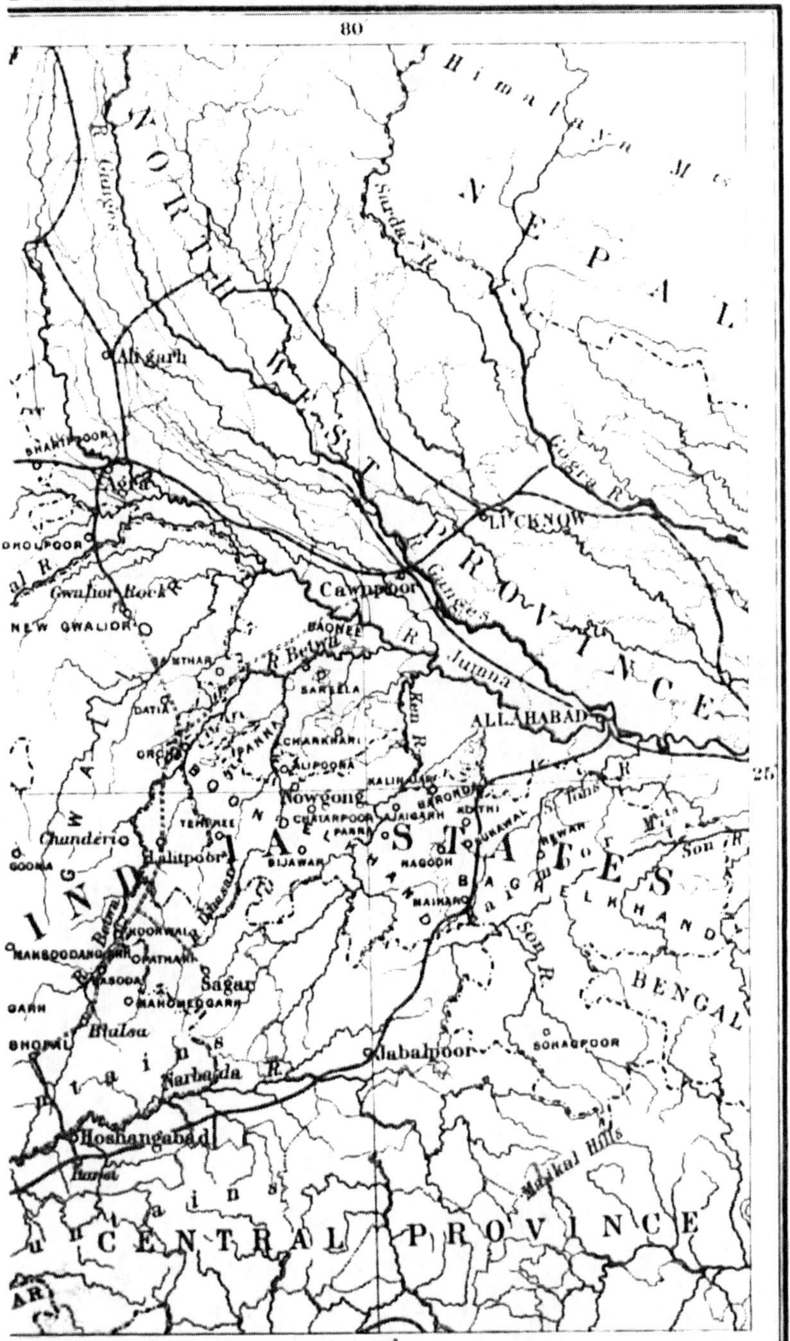

Stanford's Geog[l] Estab[t]

Khandwa on the Great Indian Peninsula line. Barley, millets, teel, and cotton form the chief crops; the poppy, for opium, is grown in Beáwar and Todgarh. When both the S.W. and N.E. monsoons fail, Ajmer, like the rest of Rajpootana, is exposed to the "treble famine" of grain, grass, and water, as in 1868-9 when cows were offered at a rupee each. The United Presbyterian Church of Scotland occupies the Province, and has six stations. Since Sindia ceded it in 1818, as for six centuries before, "Ajmer has been the symbol of political predominance in Rajpootana, and has contained the garrison by which the masters of N. India have enforced their jurisdiction" over the clans.

§ 2. AJMER ("Aja's hill") (27,000), the land of the eponymous chief Aja, who built Taragarh Fort, and in the valley below, Indurkot, founded **Ajmer City**, 145 A.D. It is 615 m. N.E. of Bombay, 276 S.W. of Delhi, and 228 W. of Agra. In 685 the Chauhan Rajpoot chief was defeated by the Arab conqueror of Sind, and his successor founded Sambhar. In 1024 Mahmood of Ghazni swept through to Goojarat and Somnath, sacking the city, whose Rajpoots led him astray into the desert on his return and had their revenge. Prithvi Raja, the last of the Chauhan dynasty, was adopted by Arang Pal, and became ruler of Delhi also. With Kanauj and Oojain, Ajmer fell before the Musalman house of Ghori in 1193. In the Taragarh is the "treasury of martyrs," the tomb of Saiad Husain and the garrison who were massacred by the Rajpoots in 1210. To this Akbar walked on foot to offer thanks for the birth of his son Salim (1570 A.D.) For two centuries Ajmer was a favourite residence of the Mughul emperors; here Sir Thomas Roe, the envoy of James I., was received, and the eccentric Coryate wrote (1616 A.D.) Sindia ceded the district to the British in 1818, and it has remained Hindoo in spite of long Musalman supremacy. Ajmer is a walled town with five gateways. On N. is Akbar's palace, now the treasury; on S. the dargah or shrine of a popular Musalman saint. There are a Government College, the Mayo College for the Rajpoot nobles, and the United Presbyterian Scottish Mission. Here are the headquarters of the Merwara Battalion. **Pushkar** or Pokhir (4000), pilgrim centre and lake, a few miles W. of Ajmer, where the Rajpoot nobles have houses, and 100,000 Hindoos crowd in October to wash away sin on the spot where they are taught that Brahma performed the *yajna* sacrifice. **Naseerabad** (18,000), railway station, and cantonment of Bombay army, 14 m. S. of Ajmer, where two Bengal regiments and a battery mutinied in 1857 without hurt. The sanitarium is **Taragarh** (2855 ft.) since 1860, beside Ajmer city. **Kekri** (5000), 50 m. S.E. of Ajmer, is a decaying mart.

§ 3. MERWARA ("hill-land") forms the S.W. narrow strip of the Province, 70 m. long and 1 to 15 broad (602 sq. m.), the aboriginal people of which Colonels Hall and Dixon redeemed from wild savagery and made loyal and prosperous. The Mers are the descendants of the mixed aborigines and refugees who found an asylum in the fastness of what they term the Mugra or highlands, and to whom the villagers of Marwar and Mewar plains paid black-mail. In 1836 Colonel Dixon founded the "new town," which he called Nya Nagar, beside the cantonment of **Beawar** (12,000), 36 m. S.W. from Ajmer and 32 m. from Naseerabad, which is a growing cotton centre, with a stone wall and four gateways; has iron and dyeing industries; and is the first seat of the United Presbyterian Scotch mission. Todgarh (named from Colonel J. Tod) is a mission station in S., where the highest peaks of the Aravali rise to 2853 ft., and the average level of the valleys is 1800 ft. Three passes here cross the upper part of the range.

CHAPTER XVII.

BARODA, RAJPOOTANA, AND CENTRAL INDIA STATES.

**Baroda State.*

§ 1. Position, People, and Taxation. § 2. Central Baroda. § 3. Northern. § 4. Southern. § 5. Kathiawar Vassals.

**Rajpootana States.*

§ 6. Rajpootana generally. § 7. Land Tenures. § 8. Siróhi. § 9. Mewar. § 10. Doongarpoor. § 11. Banswara. § 12. Partabgarh. § 13. Marwar. § 14. Jaisalmeer. § 15. Bikaner. § 16. Jaipoor. § 17. Kishangarh. § 18. Alwar. § 19. Bhartpoor. § 20. Dholpoor. § 21. Karauli. § 22. Boondee. § 23. Kotah. § 24. Jhalawar. § 25. Tonk.

**Central India States.*

§ 26. Central India Agency. § 27. Malwa. § 28. Boondelkhand. § 29. Indore. § 30. Dewass and Bagli. § 31. Gwalior. § 32. Bhopal. § 33. Rajgarh, Narsingarh, Koorwai, Maksoodangarh, Kilchipoor, Basoda, Mahomedgarh, and Pathari. § 34. Jaora, Ratlam, Sailana, and Seetamau. § 35. Bheel Agency States. § 36. Raghoogarh and Paron. § 37. Boondelkhand States. § 38. Baghelkhand States.

§ 1. Position, People, and Taxation.—**Baroda State** (Wadodra) is the most W. of the four great principalities or groups of States, directly controlled by an Agent of the Governor-General, and surrounded by the Bombay, Panjab, North-West, and Central Provinces, with the small Province of Ajmer-Merwara in the centre of the whole. Baroda, or the Gaekwar's State, is scattered over N. Goojarat between 21° 51′ and 22° 49′ N. lat. and 72° 53′ and 73° 55′ E. long., with an area of 8570 sq. m. and population of 2,185,005, yielding the Gaekwar a gross annual revenue of 14,382,129 *Baroda* rupees, of which 114½ = 100 British rupees or £10. The whole State is divided into four districts, rich and populous, drained by the Narbada, Tapti, Mahi, and their tributaries, and with the black soil which produces luxuriant crops of cotton, tobacco, sugar-cane, oil-seeds, and grain. Everywhere signs of former prosperity are seen, checked by Maratha rule, and reviving since British interference to prevent oppression. Baroda is one of the still existing principalities, Indore and Gwalior being the other two, which Maratha soldiers carved out of the debris of the Mughul empire first under Shivaji and then under the Peshwas. Peelajee, the first Gaekwar ("cowherd"), was the Peshwa's second in command till 1731, after which his successors acquired the whole of Goojarat. British influence, as suzerain, began in 1780, a subsidiary force was formed, and a Resident was appointed. After a succession of crimes and the misrule of a century, the State was in 1881 placed under the young Gaekwar adopted by the widow of Khandi Rao, who had died in 1870. During his minority much progress was made under the British Resident and Sir T. Madhava Rao, the late prime minister. The population increased to 180,563 in the decade ending 1880. The Gaekwar's new title is Farzand i Khas i Daulat i Inglesia = "own favoured son of the British Empire." The troops and armed police number 17,000. The regular force of 3126 is organised on the British system. Of the five batteries of artillery, two consist of two gold and two silver 3-pounder guns. On regulars and irregulars, or police, nearly one-third of the revenue is spent. During 1879-81, the last two years of the present Gaekwar's minority, the finances stood as on the next page; the details form a curious contrast to those of the British Government's balance-sheet, especially in the items of palace expenditure and religious allowances to Brahmans.

Baroda has 1⅓ millions sterling invested in the Government of India's Securities, or one year's revenue; has a State railway and no debt. Sir Madhava Rao writes of this investment :—"The investment by Native States in British securities affords proof of confidence in the justice and durability of the British Government. It is a substantial security for the incessant loyalty of the Native States. It materially raises the value of the British Government securities in the market. And it benefits the general public by putting in circulation wealth which would otherwise lie inert in the shape of buried treasure or useless jewellery."

Besides this the State had a working balance of £801,870.

RECEIPTS.

	Baroda Rupees. 1879-80.	Baroda Rupees 1880-81.
Land Revenue	1,01,01,413	97,42,082
Tributes (called Ghasdana) and fixed Jamabandi	6,53,952	7,43,590
Abkari (sale of spirituous liquors and drugs)	2,19,133	2,45,729
Miscellaneous Taxes . . .	3,07,594	3,61,266
Customs and town duties . . .	9,89,331	10,76,823
Opium	4,92,034	4,06,147
Stamps	1,95,624	2,26,338
Mint	10,500	9,300
Judicial Fees, Fines, etc. . . .	1,13,822	1,28,892
Education	10,511	15,171
Interest	5,15,517	8,10,233
Railway (State lines) net receipts . .	36,124	74,900
Miscellaneous Receipts . . .	3,45,777	5,41,608
Total Receipts . .	1,39,91,445	1,43,82,129

DISBURSEMENTS.

	1879-80.	1880-81.
Palace	11,59,669	12,21,422
Huzoor Katcherri Establishments . .	4,52,637	4,96,740
Land Revenue Department . . .	9,78,610	11,15,073
Opium Department (purchase of opium) and cost of establishments, etc. . .	4,47,610	12,69,345
Other Civil Establishments . . .	2,32,976	2,74,871
Judicial Establishments . . .	2,91,365	2,91,010
Police	8,11,782	8,21,605
Jails	1,03,793	72,678
Military Department . . .	30,94,138	31,90,250
Assamdars, Nemnookdars, Pensions, and Miscellaneous Allowances . .	7,34,432	8,24,083
Public Works	11,95,284	16,31,498
Education	1,71,423	1,94,519
Medical Department . . .	1,25,844	1,33,804
Municipalities	2,72,415	2,68,046
Religious and Charitable Allowances .	7,96,408	8,75,852
Miscellaneous	1,94,243	3,31,786
Extraordinary Charges . . .	7,80,292	44,790
Total Disbursements . .	1,18,42,921	1,30,57,372

The second census of Baroda State, taken in 1881, showed an increase, save in the capital, which, like Lucknow after the fall of the ex-king of Oudh, lost the large class who feed on the vices of a corrupt court. As in the rest of Goojarat, the people are chiefly peasantry of the Bhathela clan of Brahmans, Koonbees, Rajpoots, and Kolees. The Maratha bankers and merchants are wealthy. The Parsees are numerous.

AREA AND POPULATION OF BARODA STATE, 1881.

Districts.	Approximate Area in Square Miles.	Population, 1881.			No. of Persons per Sq. Mile.
		Males.	Females.	Total.	
Amreili, Kathiawar . .	1,560	77,048	70,420	147,468	95
Kari, North .	3,158	509,954	478,533	988,487	313
Navasaree, South	1,940	146,477	141,072	287,549	148
Baroda, Central	1,906	349,283	305,706	654,989	344
Baroda City .	5	53,871	47,947	101,818	20,364
Total .	8,569	1,136,633	1,043,678	2,180,311	254
Baroda Cantonment . .	1	2,879	1,815	4,694	4,694
Grand Total	8,570	1,130,512	1,045,403	2,185,005	255

§ 2. CENTRAL BARODA consists of the country around the capital. Area, 1906 sq. m. Population, 654,989. **Baroda City** (101,818), E. of the Vishwamitri, over which 4 bridges lead from the cantonment to the city. The Residency is in S. part of cantonment, where is the church consecrated by Heber, and, opposite it, the magistrate's office in which the deposed Gaekwar, Mulhar Rao, was tried. E. of the Residency is the new palace, of great size, and erected at a cost of a quarter of a million sterling. Near the city is the **Naulakhi Baori** or Nine Lakhs Well (£90,000), now the chief sight of the place, "with grand flights of steps descending to the water through rows of stone pillars and pilasters," as described by James Forbes a century ago. Baroda is 248 m. N. of Bombay and 62 S. of Ahmedabad. **Miyagaon**, railway station, 19 m. S. of Baroda, with branch railway to **Dabhoi** (15,000), 15 m. S.E. of Baroda, the Darbhavati fortress of 11th century, a walled city 2 m. square, with fine Diamond Gate, surrendered to General Goddard in 1780. **Chandod**, pilgrim centre, 30 m. S.E. of Baroda, on Narbada; terminus of railway from Baroda and Dabhoi. Bahadoorpoor, branch railway station, 9½ m. from Dabhoi. **Padra** (8000), 8 m. S.W. from Baroda, with Gaekwar's state prison. Vishwamitri, railway terminus of branch line from Goa Gate, Baroda.

§ 3. SOUTH BARODA, chiefly in Surat, fringed on S. by Rajpeepla hills. Area, 1940 sq. m. Population, 287,549. The principal place is **Navasaree** (15,000), port and railway station, on left bank of Poorna, 12 m. from sea, 18 m. from Surat; a colony of the Parsees, with large fire-temple and many priests. **Songarh**, old Maratha fort and Peshwa's capital S. of Tapti, in hills of same name, commanding ascent to Khandesh uplands; with fine stone for building. **Roopgarh**, fort, 10 m. S. **Wajpoor**, on Tapti. Sáler, hill fort in S.E. corner. Bilimora (5500), railway station, N. of Navasaree.

§ 4. NORTHERN BARODA, or Kari (area, 3158 sq. m., pop. 988,487), consists of the subdivisions of Pattan, Kari, Beejapoor, Beesnagar, Debgaon, etc. **Pattan** (32,000), the famous Anhilwara Pattan or Rajpoot capital of Goojarat (746-1194 A.D.), on the Saraswati branch of the Banas, now a town of Jain temples and libraries, known for its cutlery and pottery.

§ 5. KATHIAWAR BARODA. Area, 1560 sq. m. Population, 147,468. **Amreli** (16,000), 139 m. S.W of Baroda. **Okhamandal**, military station in N.W. corner of peninsula of Kathiawar, separated from the mainland by the Rann of Kach, centre of a territory of 334 sq. m., and long a pirate stronghold.

The British Government has the right of opening new ports, and it controls salt-works in Baroda State; it has enforced the prohibition of *suttee*, the sale of children, and slavery since 1840.

**Rajpootana States.*

§ 6. RAJPOOTANA (Raet'hana, Rajasthan or Rajwara = "dwelling of princes"), consisting of 19 principalities, besides Ajmer-Merwara, is larger than Italy, and has less than half its population. The approximate area is 130,934 sq. m., and population 11,005,512. This half-desert territory, to which the Hindoo chivalry were gradually driven from the rich plains of Goojarat and Central India, lies between 23° and 30° N. lat., and 69° 30′ and 78° 15′ E. long. It is enclosed between the Indore and Gwalior States on S.E., the North-Western and Panjab Provinces on N.E., Bahawalpoor State on N.W., Sind on W., and Baroda and Bombay on S.W. It is traversed from S.W. to N.E. by the State railway, which links on Bombay to Delhi and Agra, and from the S. to that railway at Ajmer, by the Malwa railway from Khandwa on the Great Indian Peninsula line through Indore. The **Aravali** range ("row of peaks") (3450 ft.) intersects the country from the ridge of Delhi on N.E. to **Mount Aboo** on S.W., marking off three-fifths, chiefly desert, to N.W., and two-fifths on S.E.

(1) The North-Western division, comprising the vast tract from Sind on W. along the S. Panjab border to Delhi, is uniformly sandy, with an annual rainfall of 5 inches; it consists of the Great Desert (of Bikaner), stretching from the Rann of Kach N.E. beyond the Loni river, and the Little Desert (of Mallani) farther E., with limestone ridges between. The **Loni** ("salt") river flows for 200 m. from the Pushkar valley near Ajmer to the Rann in a course nearly parallel with the Aravali range. (2) The south-eastern division is protected from the desert by the Aravali watershed, save where in the N.E. the sand has drifted through its gaps, as against the hills that surround Jaipoor city. This division consists of wide vales, fertile plateaux, and great breadths of good soil, with forests and artificial lakes. The whole is watered by the drainage of the **Vindhyas** carried N.E. by the Chambal and Banas rivers. The **Chambal** is the largest river in Rajpootana, through which it flows for one-third of its course of 560 m., and forms the boundary for another third. Rising near the summit of the Vindhyas in Malwa it enters Rajpootana at Chaurasgarh in Mewar, breaks through the Patar plateau, meets the Bamni at Bhainsrogarh after a succession of small cataracts known as *chulis*, receives several large streams in Kota, then farther N. the Parbati from right and Banas from left, and passes through Karauli and Dholpoor States into the Jumna. The **Banas**, from Kankraoli in Mewar, which State it drains, receiving the Berach and Kote Sari from the Aravalis and the Dhoond from Jaipoor, flows for 300 m., chiefly N., and after rounding the Patar plateau it joins the Chambal beyond N.E. end of Boondee State. The W. Banas and Sabarmati, which rise among the S.W. hills of Mewar and flow S.W.; and the Mahi, which passes through Partabgarh and Banswara, receiving the Som, drain the S.W. corner of Rajpootana through Goojarat into the Gulfs of Kach and Kambay. The **Sambhar Salt Lake** is the only natural sheet of water in Rajpootana; it is shared by Jaipoor and Marwar; artificial lakes abound chiefly in Mewar.

In Rajpootana, as it now is, British influence alone has preserved the ancient dynasties and clans, to which every successful Hindoo chief seeks to trace his ancestry. The Rahtor Rajpoots of Kanauj, who ruled as far S.W. as the Tapti and are still in Marwar, the Chauhans of Ajmer, the Solankhyas of Anhilwara in Goojarat, the Gehlots with the Sesodia sept still in Mewar, and the Kachwáhas still in Jaipoor, were the tribal dynasties of Rajpoots, gradually supplanted by the Musalman invaders of the 11th century, and weakened by internal feuds.

At the beginning of the 16th century the Sesodia chief, Rana Sanga, aided by Medni Rao of Chandéri, caused the Rajpoot power to revive, but only to be overthrown by Baber at Fatehpoor Sikri in 1527. The Sesodias were the last to submit, to Jahangeer in 1616, after which Akbar incorporated the Rajpoot nobles in his imperial system. Aurangzeb's death and Nadir Shah's invasion led the Sesodias, Rahtors, and Kachwáha clans to form a federation, which internal jealousy so weakened that the Marathas took Ajmer in 1756. The Rajpoots were saved by Lord Wellesley, and by Wellington and Lake, till the policy of non-interference introduced by the second administration of Lord Cornwallis reopened the floodgates of anarchy for ten years. By 1818, under Lord Hastings, Rajpootana was politically formed as it now is, 16 States remaining Rajpoot, and two Jat (Bhartpoor and Dholpoor), while the scattered districts of Tonk were left in the hands of the Musalman freebooter Ameer Khan, as Nawab. Most of these chiefs pay tribute, and three support local corps. So effective has been the British peace that although there was not a British soldier in Rajpootana when the Mutiny of 1857 began, and of the sepoys the Mers and Bheels alone were faithful, the chiefs rendered active assistance. Of the 16 Rajpoot States, 3 are ruled by the Rahtor clan—Marwar, Bikaner, and Kishangarh; 4 by the Sesodia—Mewar (with Shahpoora), Banswara, Doongarpoor, and Partabgarh; 3 by the Chouhan—Boondee and Kota by the Hara sept, and Siróhi by the Deoria; 2 by the Bhatti sept of the Jadoor clan—Karauli and Jaisalmeer; 2 by the Kachwáhas—Jaipoor and Alwar by its Narooka sept; and 1 by the Jhala—Jhalawar. Geographically all the States are thus grouped, beginning from the Bombay side S.W.: (1) SOUTHERN—*Siróhi*, *Mewar* (with Shahpoora), *Doongarpoor*, *Banswara*, and *Partabgarh*; (2) WESTERN AND NORTHERN—*Marwar*, *Jaisalmeer*, *Bikaner*; (3) EASTERN—*Jaipoor*, *Kishangarh*, *Alwar*, *Bhartpoor*, *Dholpoor*, *Karauli*, *Boondee*, *Kota*, *Jhalawar*, and scattered *Tonk*. In the centre is Ajmer Province, and the whole is administered from Mount Aboo in the south.

§ 7. LAND TENURES.—(1) The hereditary feudal or clan system of the early Hindoos, broken down by Musalman centralisation elsewhere, still prevails in Rajpootana, especially in the W. and S.W. A very great proportion of the land is held on freehold tenure by the kinsmen and clansmen of the chief and by other clans of Rajpoots. The word "freehold" is here used to denote the holding of a free man by service not unbecoming his birth, and under payment of the customary share of the produce of the soil in which chief and clan are coparceners, the "fruits of worship," as it is devoutly expressed. There are also, here and there, some assignments or grants of land of the nature of *jágeers* proper,—that is, the revenue was allotted to certain persons merely as a convenient way of paying the estimated actual cost of civil or military establishment or services. All large estates are held under the implied condition of keeping up the police within their borders, protecting traffic, preventing heinous crimes, and pursuing offenders hot-foot when the hue and cry is raised, or when the tracks of flying brigands are run into the boundaries. In some parts of the country the estate passes in block to one heir, and others are entitled to maintenance; in others the tendency to divide the land as the family increases and branches out is more marked; while in other parts division among brothers is imperative, and of course the *morcellement* of the freeholds is in proportion as the custom of subdividing the land among the clansmen may prevail. The smaller plots are usually held on the *bhoom* tenure, which is thought a better title than any, because the *Bhoomia* and his heirs hold for ever on condition of some peculiar service, such as watch and ward, guard of the roads, or attendance at specified occasions, and are not, like the petty kinsmen and clansmen of a family chief, portioned off upon lots of the family domain which might be resumed if the chief and his folk quarrelled. Some of the groups of cultivating Rajpoots who hold on the *bhoom* tenure have occupied from time immemorial, paying, not rent, but customary rates and services, and are very proud of having held the land before its conquest by the ruling family. All these freeholding classes are distinct from the mass of cultivating peasantry. (2) The cultivator is understood to have a permanent hereditary right to his holding so long as he pays the rent demanded, and to evict a man is a hard measure; but in a country where the irresponsible exactions of the native tax-collectors are checked only by the scarcity of tenants, the precise strength of the tenure depends really on the balance between these two opposing considerations, the desire to squeeze the tenant and the fear of losing him. On the whole, it may be said that the demand for tenants prevails, and a good cultivator has a firm root in his soil, which can be mortgaged or sold, and which passes by inheritance; a distinction is recognised, naturally, between lands which have come to a cultivator by inheritance, or which he has himself cleared or improved, and lands which have changed hands recently, or which have been assigned in an ordinary farming way. The real point of importance, however, is, of course, not the nature of tenure, but the limitation of rent demand, and this is practically unfixed, except where the English officers have prevailed upon a chief to accept and uphold a regular land revenue settlement. In rack-renting States all particular tenures are loose and undefined; and though the village community, as a body, generally sticks to the township, yet, between the rent-collector and the money-lender, the peasant is apt to sink into the condition of a predial serf rather held to, than holding by, the land. There are, speaking broadly, no middlemen in Rajpootana between the tax-collector and the rent-payer, though the headman of a village often contracts for a fixed payment for a short term of years.

§ 8. SIROHI STATE (Sirnoe) is bounded E. by Mewar, N. and W. by Marwar, S. by Palanpoor, and by Edar and Danta States of the Mahi-Kantha. Area, about 3200 sq. m. Population, 60,000. Revenue, £11,000 to the Rao, of which £688 is tribute to the British Government. Divided by Aravalis from N.E. to S.W., the drainage parts into the Loni and W. Banas. **Sirohi**, the capital, N. on Ajmer and Ahmedabad road. **Aboo** (railway station, Aboo Road, 425 m. N.E. of Bombay and 465 S.W. of Delhi), sanitarium since 1845, and headquarters of Governor-General's Agent for the Resident and Chief Commissioner of Ajmer; with Lawrence Military Asylum, barracks on undulating plateau of **Mount Aboo** (ancient Arbooda), a cluster of hills 7 m. from W. face of Aravali range with peak rising to 5653 ft., and Gem Lake (Nakhi Talao), compared by Tod to that above Andernach on the Rhine. One of the chief western—Parasnath in Bengal is the E.—spots of Jain pilgrimage, with exquisite marble temples of which Virnala Sah's erected in 1032 A.D. is the most complete, also to E. and 1 m. N. of sanitarium at Delwara ("place of temples"). The usual ascent is from Anadra on S.W. At the base are the marble ruins of Chandravati, now nearly removed for temples in Goojarat. The marble is from the village of Jariwao on S.E. border. Kine may not be killed on the mountain which, till 1836, no chief was permitted by the Rao to visit. **Erinpoora**, cantonment, with railway station at Erinpoora Road, 52 m. N.E. of Aboo Road and 477 from Bombay. Nana is an important railway station between Aboo and Erinpoora.

§ 9. *MEWAR STATE, or OODAIPOOR (from the capital). The Maharana stands first of all Rajpoots as heir to the throne of the legendary Rama, representing the elder branch of the Sooryabansee or "children of the sun," and never having given a wife to the Musalman emperors. By adoption of heirs, the House of Mewar is the oldest sovereign line outside of Judaism. Mewar is bounded E. by Jhalawar, Kota, and Boondee; N. by Jaipoor and Ajmer; W. by Marwar and Sirohi; and S. by Doongarpoor, Banswara, Partabgarh, and Holkar's States. Area, 13,674 sq. m. Population, 1,200,000. Revenue, £640,000, of which £20,000 is paid as tribute to the British Government. A section of the Aravalis extends from S.W. and Sirohi N. between Mewar and Marwar to Merwara, and contains iron, lead, zinc, and copper. **Oodaipoor** ("city of sunrise"), the present capital in the valley of the Girwa, picturesquely built on a ridge (2064 ft.) overlooking an embanked lake, with an imposing palace; here Oodai Singh founded the city after Akbar's capture in 1568 of **Chittor** to E., the sacred fortress first sacked by Bahadoor, Sultan of Goojarat, when 1300 Rajpoot females were immolated; now a station on Malwa railway, 277 m. N. of Khandwa. Saloombar, Nathdwara, Deogarh, and Jahzapoor are places of local importance, also Amlee, Banera, Bednor, Bhinda, Dabla, Goosa, Gungapoora, Koorabur, Raipoor, Rajgarh, Rajnagar, Rashmoo, Rohera, Sanganeer, and Sawa. A road runs from Oodaipoor to the **Dasoori Pass**, the only pass for wheeled carriages for 250 m. from Barh near Ajmer to S. of Sirohi. **Debar Lake**, 20 m. S.E. of the capital, the largest artificial lake in India, 30 m. in circumference, constructed by Jey Singh in 1681. **Kankraoli Lake**, formed by marble dike in famine of 1661 at a cost of nearly a million; 12 m. in circumference. **Kherwara** (1200 ft.), in S., is the cantonment for local troops.

Shahpoora, in N.E., chief town of the fief of same name, held from the Maharana of Oodaipoor by the Raja, who pays tribute to the British Government also.

§ 10. *DOONGARPOOR STATE is bounded E. by Mewar and the Mahi separating it from Banswara, N. by Mewar, W. by Rewa- and Mahi-Kantha, and S. by the Mahi. Area, 952 sq. m. Population, 100,000. Revenue to the Maharawal, a Sesodia offshoot of Mewar, £15,000, from a country which softens down from the forest-clad hills of Mewar to the rich plains of Goojarat. Toys, drinking-vessels, and images made of a greenish-gray stone, form specialties of the State. The Mahi and Som are the only rivers, meeting near the Baneshar temple, where there is a fair. **Doongarpoor** (5000), 139 m. S.W. of Neemach, on route to Deesa, at the base of a hill (700 ft.), crowned by the palace, and with a lake at its foot. Galliakot and Sagwara have each 3000 inhabitants.

§ 11. *BANSWARA STATE, the most S. of Rajpootana, is bounded E. and N.E. by Partabgarh, N. and N.W. by Doongarpoor, W. by the Rewa-Kantha, and S. by Central India States. Area, 1500 sq. m. Population, 150,000. Revenue to the Maharawal, formerly of Mewar, £30,000. The aborigines are Bheels. The Mahi river enters from Ratlam. Madria and Jagmer are hills, and the Bai an artificial lake near the capital **Banswara** (6200), a walled town. Due W. is the Talwara pass, 6 m. through the hills. **Kusalgarh,** chief village of petty chiefship of a Rao, to S.W. Kalinjra is the only other town.

§ 12. *PARTABGARH STATE is bounded E. by Ratlam, Jaora, and Gwalior States; N. and N.W. by Mewar from which it is an offshoot; and S.W. by Banswara. Area, 1460 sq. m. Population, 150,000, chiefly Bheels. Revenue to the Maharawal, £60,000. **Partabgarh** (1700 ft.), the capital, is in the centre of the State.

§ 13. *MARWAR STATE OR JODHPOOR is bounded E. by Kishangarh and Jaipoor; N. by Jaipoor, Bikaner, and Jaisalmeer; W. by Sind and the Rann of Kach; and S. by Sirohi, Mewar, and Ajmer-Merwara. The largest of the States of Rajpootana, Marwar has an area of 37,000 sq. m., chiefly of sandy plain with isolated red sandstone hills of the Aravali type. Population, 2,000,000, yielding £250,000 gross revenue to the Maharaja, chief of the Rahtor Rajpoots, and like Mewar claiming descent from Rama. The **Loni** river, called the Sagar Matti at its source in Ajmer lake, is joined at Govindgarh by the Sarsooti from the Pushkar lake, and thence flows S.W. through Marwar to the Rann of Kach. Receiving the drainage of the Aravalis it often inundates Mallani district with the *Rel* or overflow, which fertilises the soil. Its tributaries are the Tojri from the Merta district, the Sookri from the Sojat district, the Gooea Bala from the Kapura hills in Sojat, the Reria or Pali from near Sojat, the Bandi from the Aravalis near Siriari, and the Juwai which passes Erinpoora cantonment. The Sambhar lake, described under Jaipoor, partly belongs to Marwar. A marsh (*jheel*) in the Sachor district covers 50 m. in the rainy season. Salt is obtained at Sambhar and smaller deposits, and at Pachpadra is crystallised for wells. Zinc used to be worked at Sojat. Marble abounds at Makrana, 120 m. N.E. of Jodhpoor, and near Ghanerao on S.E. border, also limestone and red sandstone. The Rajpootana-Malwa Railway skirts E. border at Sojat Road station, 541 m. N.E. of Bombay, with branch to Sambhar; a metalled road runs for 100 m. from Ajmer to

Ahmedabad. **Jodhpoor**, the capital, named from Rao Jodha, the founder in 1549, on S. slope of sandstone hills, with fort (800 ft.) containing the large palace. The city is surrounded by 6 m. of walls with 70 gates, and contains many fine residences of the wealthy nobles. Three m. N. is **Mandor**, ruined capital of the Purihar predecessors of the Rahtors, with tombs rudely carved. **Nagor** (30,000), walled city, and old capital of N. portion of Marwar, with fort and palace of former rulers; scene of conflicts with Rao Chanda (1400 A.D.); captured by Akbar in 1561, and restored by him on marriage with chief's sister; now a place of trade. **Pali**, commercial capital, 45 m. S.E. of Jodhpoor on road between Ajmer and Ahmedabad; the principal trade is that of dyeing woollen cloths; the source of the Indian plague (*maha mari*) of 1836, like the Levantine plague. **Deedwana** (20,000), walled town with salt manufactures. **Nadolai**, old capital of Godwar province, ancient seat of Jains, with fine temple of Mahavira. **Phalodi** (12,000), with fort in N.W., near Jaisalmeer border. To S.W. is Pokaran fort, appanage of premier baron of Jodhpoor. **Jalor**, on S. border of the sandy plain of Marwar, with famous old fort built by Pramára dynasty early in the Christian era, and still in good preservation. Peepar, 39 m. N. of Jalor, old Pramára city, beside Sampu lake. Merta, near which De Boigne disastrously defeated the Rahtors in 1754, thus laying Rajpootana at the feet of the Marathas. The battle was on the embankment of the Dangolai tank, at Dangarwas, 2 m. from Merta.

Mallani, vassal state between Marwar proper and Sind, 18,000 sq. m. in area, with the high hill Nagar of Jasol near the right bank of the Loni. The chief towns are **Barmer**, Jasol, Sindari, Gura, and Nagar.

§ 14. *JAISALMEER STATE is bounded E. by Marwar and Bikaner, N. by Bahawalpoor, W. by Sind, and S. by Marwar. Area, 16,447 sq. m. of sandy desert, save at the capital and for 40 m. round, which is stony; the wells go down to a depth of 490 ft. in some cases, as at Choria, 32 m. S.E. of capital. Population, 72,000 yielding £10,000 annual revenue to the Maharawal, Yadu Bhatti, Rajpoot of the Somavansa or Lunar race. The Kakni and Lathika are the only small rivers, created by each rainy season. **Jaisalmeer** (8000), the capital, founded by Rao Jaisal in 1156 on rocky ridge capped by fort (250 ft.) and palace, remarkable for beautiful stone carving. Lodorva, in the neighbourhood, is the old Bhatti capital, now in ruins. The other towns and forts are Tanot, Kishaugarh, Ghotaroo, Nachna, Bikampoor, and Birsilpoor.

§ 15. *BIKANER STATE is bounded E. by Jaipoor and Hissar district of Panjab, N. by Sirsa district and Bahawalpoor, W. by Jaisalmeer, and S. by Marwar. Area, 22,340 sq. m. of waste sandhills, save at Gajner lakelet 20 m. from the capital. After rain the brushwood tract S. of the capital becomes green pasture-land. **Chapar** lake in S.E. corner is the principal source of salt. The population, 300,000, yield £105,000 annual revenue to the Maharaja, who is of the Rahtor clan of Rajpoots. **Bikaner** (36,000), founded by Bika 1488 on a stony elevation, where its walls, 3½ m. round, and temples present an imposing appearance, with the fort and palace above, and Bika's old fort still higher. Three m. E. is Devi Koond, the cremation place of the chief and, till 1825, of their Suttee widows, with the sepulchres of 12 Maharajas. **Soojangarh** (10,000), with British Residency, on S.E. border beside Marwar and Jaipoor. **Ratangarh** (10,000), near Soojangarh, a prosperous place. **Chooroo** (10,000), trade centre in E., near Panjab border. **Bhatnér Fort**, on left bank of dried-up Goghar, on direct route of invaders from Central Asia to India, captured at various times by Mahmood Ghaznavi, Taimoor, and Kamran, Hoomayoon's son; also by George Thomas in 1800.

§ 16. *JAIPOOR STATE is bounded E. by Karauli, Bhartpoor, and Alwar; N. by the Delhi State and Bikaner; W. by Marwar and Kishangarh; and S. by Mewar, Tonk, Boondee, and Gwalior. Area, 15,250 sq. m. Population, 1,250,000, yielding £750,000 annually to the Maharaja, who is of the Kachwáha clan of Rajpoots, one of the 36 royal races of India, and claims descent from Rama. The State, at its centre, is an elevated plateau (1400 to 1600 ft.), with slope to S.E., down which the **Banas** and the **Banganga**, fed by tributaries, carry the drainage to the Jumna. The **Sabi**, rising 24 m. due N. of the capital, flows N. past Alwar into the Nabha State, Panjab. The **Kaotli** flows N.W. through the Shaikawati division to the Bikaner desert, where it is lost. The **Sambhar Salt Lake**, leased to the British Government by Jaipoor and Marwar, lies E. of Aravalis and 40 m. N.W. of Ajmer in 26° 50′ N. lat. and 75° 5′ E. long.; its E. shore is 36 m. from Jaipoor, its W. shore 130 m. from Jodhpoor; it is the terminus of a branch railway 5½ m. from the Rajpootana-Malwa Railway at Phalera. In the rains the water extends 20 m. E. and W., with a breadth of 3 to 10 m., and 1 to 4 ft. deep; in the dry season "the treasury" or wet saline portion is 1 by ½ m. opposite the rocky promontory, Mata-ka-devi, when the lake looks like a great sheet of snow, dotted by pools and narrow paths. The salt pervades the black muddy bed in minute crystals, and is held in solution in the water. The lake yields 40,000 tons a year at a cost of 3 farthings for 82 lbs. **Jaipoor** (140,000), greatest modern Hindoo city in Rajpootana (or in India), founded in 1728 by Jai Singh II., the famous astronomer whose tables of stars (*Tij Muhammad Shahi*) corrected those of De la Hire, and one of whose 5 Observatories is still here. Railway station 699 m. from Bombay, 149 from Agra, and 191 from Delhi, seat of a Hindoo college, of United Presbyterian Mission, and of many educational and philanthropic institutions established by the late Maharaja. A beautiful walled city built largely of marble in an amphitheatre of hills, commanded on N.W. by the Nahargarh (tiger fort). To this the capital was transferred from **Amber**, now deserted, 4 m. N.E., exquisitely placed on a lake at mouth of a mountain gorge, with palace second only to Gwalior as specimen of Rajpoot architecture, and still the State treasury. **Bandikooi**, 56 m. E. of Jaipoor, is the railway junction for Delhi, Alwar, and Agra by Bhartpoor. **Sanganeer**, 7 m. S.W. of Jaipoor, a flourishing mart, 3 m. from railway station, with ancient temples. **Dosa**, railway station between Jaipoor and Bandikooi, where a battle was fought in 1857 and Tatia Topi was captured. Other towns of local importance are—Chatsu, 24 m. S.E. of Jaipoor; Chomu, residence of first noble of the State; Dooni, populous place, 70 m. S. of Jaipoor; Hindaun, large mart on Agra and Mhow road; Kotpootli, 74 m. N.E. of Jaipoor, captured by Lake from Marathas; Lakshmangarh, large fortified town; Narayana, old town, headquarters of Dadoo Panthee sect of theists.

Shaikhawati, vassal federation under Jaipoor, in N., 5400 sq. m. in area, with valuable copper mines at **Khetri**. Other towns are Bassan, 120 m. N.W. of Jaipoor; Fatehpoor, a fortified place; Seekar, Naolgarh, Uniara, and Ramgarh.

§ 17. *KISHANGARH STATE, an offshoot of Marwar, is hedged in between Jaipoor on E., Marwar on N., and Ajmer on W. With area of 724 sq. m. and population of 105,000, it yields £30,000 to the Maharaja. **Kishangarh**, the capital, is a station on Rajpootana-Malwa Railway, 18 m. E. of Ajmer and 21 N.E. of Naseerabad. Other towns are Roopnagar in N., and Borara.

§ 18. *ALWAR STATE is bounded E. by Bhartpoor and Goorgaon district, N. by Goorgaon and Nabha State, W. by Patiala and Jaipoor, and S. by Jaipoor. Area 3024 sq. m. Population, 800,000. Revenue, £230,000. The Maharao is a Rajpoot of the Narooka branch of the Jaipoor house, whose fathers gradually built up the State from Machéry, the district by which it was known in early East India Company's days. The State covers a large portion of Mewat, the famous hills and forts of the Meo brigands. It lies E. of the extended axis of the Aravali range; its hills rise to 2400 ft., or 1600 above the plain. The **Sabi** river forms the W. boundary for 16 m. The **Roopārel** or Barah and **Choohar Sidh** drain the hills W. and S. of Alwar city. There are 2 lakelets—Siliserh, 9 m. S.W. of Alwar, which it supplies with water; and Deoti, on S. border. **Alwar** (53,000) (*Alpur* = "strong city" or *Arbal* = Aravali hills), central capital of Mewat, walled with 5 gates, with fort (1000 ft.) on hill above the town and palace at its base, from which is fine view of cenotaph and tanks; the Banni Bilas palace is a mile distant. **Rajgarh** (12,500), in S., former capital of chiefs; Machéry is 3 m. distant. **Ramgarh** (5500), with pass through the hills to Delhi, 13 m. E. of Alwar. Eight m. S.E. is **Laswaree** (Naswari) village, the scene of Lake's sanguinary victory of 1st November 1803 over Sindia, which finally broke the Maratha power. Tijara (7500), 30 m. N.E. of Alwar, old capital of Mewat, visited by Baber, commanding the hill (1350 ft.) passes to Firozpoor in Goorgaon. **Jhirri**, in S.W., yields the finest white statuary marble, from quarries nowhere deep like those of Makrana in Marwar; Dosa is its railway station.

§ 19. *Bhartpoor State is bounded E. by Muttra and Agra; N. by Goorgaon; W. by Alwar; and S. by Jaipoor, Karauli, and Dholpoor. Area, 1974 sq. m. Population, 800,000 yielding £330,000 to the Jat Maharaja, descendant of one of the Jat hordes which molested successive Musalman invaders of India, from Mahmood to Baber. Popularly the land is known as Brij, or Krishna's, and the patois is Brijbhasha. It is part of the alluvial basin of the Jumna and Ganges, with ranges of low hills geologically known as Vindhyans and quartzites. The Upper Bhanrer sandstone to S. of the capital has supplied the finest dark-red and yellowish-white sandstones for the Mughul architecture of Agra, Fatehpoor Sikri, and Delhi, from the quarries of **Bansi**, **Paharpoor**, and **Roopbas**. The rivers are small—the Banganga or Utangan from Jaipoor, W. to E., the Roopārel from Alwar, the Gambheer from Jaipoor, and the Kakand from Karauli. **Bhartpoor** (62,000), named from the legendary Bharat, capital and famous fortress besieged by Lake in 1805 when Holkar held it and it surrendered; and by Combermere in 1827, who took it by assault. Bhartpoor is a railway station 35 m. W. of Agra and

112 E. of Jaipoor. **Deeg**, to N., on a marsh fed by the Manas Nai stream, captured from Holkar and the Jats by General Fraser in 1804, and dismantled after Combermere's siege of Bhartpoor. Still famous for the *Bhanwans* or marble palaces built by Sooraj Mal. **Kaman**, on N.E. frontier, sacred as a residence of Krishna, with curious temple of 84 pillars. **Kumbher**, 9 m. from Bhartpoor on road to Deeg, with large palace. **Wair**, with fort and palace, S. of Bhartpoor. **Bayana**, old capital of the Jadoos, where so many Musalmans fell at its capture by Mahmood's nephew (1004) that it is a second Mecca; here is a high monolith with inscription not yet deciphered. At Roopbas, on E. border, are colossal Pandava images and monoliths.

§ 20. *DHOLPOOR STATE is bounded E. and N. by Agra from which the Banganga divides it, W. by Bhartpoor and Karauli, and S. by Gwalior from which it is separated by the Chambal. Area 1174 sq. m. Population, 500,000 yielding £110,000 to the Jat Maharaj Rana. A ridge of fine red sandstone (560 to 1074 ft.) crosses the country for 60 m. from E. to W., rising into an isolated hill at Pahari, 12 m. S.E. of the capital. This is a grain-producing State. Besides the Chambal and Banganga, the streams are the Parbati from Karauli, an affluent of the latter, and the Merka and Merki which fall into the Parbati. **Dholpoor** (15,000), capital and railway station 3 m. N. of the Chambal, 34 m. S. of Agra, founded by Raja Dholan Deo of the Delhi Tuars in 11th century. **Rajakhera** ("Raja's village") (7500), 24 m. N.E. of Dholpoor. **Bari** ("staked enclosure") (9500), 22 m. S.W. of Dholpoor.

§ 21. *KARAULI STATE is bounded E. by Dholpoor, N. by Bhartpoor and Jaipoor, W. by Jaipoor and Boondee, and S. by Gwalior from which the Chambal divides it. Area 1870 sq. m. Population, 125,000 yielding £50,000 to the Maharaja, who is head of the Jadoos claiming descent from Krishna, or Yaduvansi, the Lunar race. The State is hilly, especially on N., the old centre of Jadoo rule, and above the Chambal. The Panchna, or five rivulets, unite 2 m. from the capital and flows N. to Banganga. **Karauli** (28,000), the capital, named from Kalianji temple, founded in 1348 among sandstone ravines 70 m. equidistant from Agra and Jaipoor, Muttra and Gwalior; with fine palace. Twelve m. S. is the Kaila Devi temple, where the State maintains a daily dole to the pilgrims. Machilpoor town lies N.E. of Karauli. Mandrayal, a prehistoric Jadoo fort, Taungarh, Narauli, and Utgeer forts are places of interest.

§ 22. *BOONDEE STATE is bounded S. and E. by Kotah

with the Chambal between, N. by Jaipoor and Tonk, W. by Mewar. Area, 2218 sq. m. Population, 225,000 yielding £80,000 to the Maharao Raja, of the Hara sept of the Chauhan clan of Rajpoots, which gives its name to the tract called **Haraoti**, embracing Kotah also. In 1804 the chief gave friendly aid to Colonel Monson against Holkar. From S.W. to N.E. the State is traversed by the central **Boondee Hills** (1793 ft.), a double range. In the centre is Boondee pass, commanded by the capital, through which runs the high road from the S. to Ajmer and Jaipoor; the other passes are on the Tonk road between the capital and Jainwas, and where the Mej river has cut a passage between Ramgarh and Katgarh. On a plain between the Awan and the Rajmahal and Todah ranges stands **Deolee** cantonment (1122 ft.). There is much fine limestone, of which the capital is built. The Chambal river washes the S.E. border of the State for 80 m. The **Mej**, the only drainage channel, falls into the Chambal just below Pali; it rises at 1700 ft. in Mewar, flows N. into Boondee and through the State for 92 m. E.; its chief tributaries are the Bajawas and Kural. **Boondee**, the capital, the most picturesque city in Rajpootana next to Oodaipoor, covers 2 sq. m. of the steep side of the pass of the same name (1500 ft.) on which the city rises in pinnacled terraces crowned by the palace. To S. is the Ser-bagh or Mahasatti, or cremation-place of the chiefs, with 13 mausolea, marking also the sacrifice of 237 widows in all. The arsenal is overhung by Taragarh fort. Ajitgarh fort stands on an isolated hill in a wild country, visited for the first time by a British officer in 1871. **Keshorai Patan** (4000), old town on N. bank of Chambal, 12 m. below Kotah, with large Hindoo temples. **Mainwah**, 30 m. N.E. of Boondee, between two artificial lakes, and strongly fortified. Indargarh, in N.E., and Dublana are the only other places of importance.

§ 23. *KOTAH STATE is bounded E. by Gwalior, N. and N.W. by Boondee with the Chambal between, W. by Mewar, and S. by Jhalawar and the Mokandara hills. Area, 3797 sq. m. Population, 450,000 yielding £200,000 to the Maharao, head of a younger branch of the Boondee house. Sloping gently from the Malwa plateau to S., Kotah is drained by the Chambal and its tributaries. The **Mokandara Range** (1200 to 1671 ft.) runs from S.E. to N.W. between Kotah and Jhalawar. The **Mokandara Pass**, below the highest peak (1671 ft.), is a picturesque defile from N. India to the Dekhan, famous for the disastrous retreat of Colonel Monson in 1804. The **Kali Sind** from S., with its feeder the Parwan, is the chief tributary of the Chambal, which it joins near Pipurda. The State is known for its parrots and "golden" lions. **Kotah**, the capital, is strongly placed on the right bank of the Chambal, on the route from Naseerabad to Sagar, a large place with the Kishor Sagar artificial lake to E. Other towns are Barod, Nahargarh, Rajgarh, Sangod, and Sultanpoor. This State supplies the contingent known as the Deolee Irregular Force.

§ 24. *JHALAWAR STATE, cut off from Kotah in 1838 to provide for the family of its Minister, Zalim Singh, consists of two detached tracts, one to S. of Kotah between the Parwan and Aoo rivers, and the other, with the capital, on the E. bank of the Parwan. Area, 2500 sq. m. Population, 226,000 yielding £160,000 to the Maharaj Rana. Opium and wheat are the chief crops. **Jhalra Patan** ("city of bells" or "city of springs") is the capital at the foot of hills on lake of same name, near the Chandrabagh affluent of the Kali Sind. Four m. distant is **Chaoni**, the permanent cantonment, with palace 2½ m. from Gagron fort. Other towns are Shahabad and Kailwara.

§ 25. *TONK STATE, in the six districts of Tonk, Rampoora, Nimbhera, Pirawa, Chapra, and Sironji, scattered tracts in S. and E. Rajpootana, seized by Ameer Khan, or granted to him by Holkar in 1798-1806, and confirmed to him by Lord Hastings in the Pindaree campaign of 1817. This is the only Musalman State in Rajpootana, held by a Nawab, a Pathan of the Bonér tribe. Area, 1800 sq. m. Population, 320,000 yielding £110,000 revenue. **Tonk**, capital, E. of Ajmer, a few miles N.E. of Deolee cantonment, on right bank of Banas. Lawa, Nimbhera, and Rampoora are the other towns.

Central India States.

§ 26. CENTRAL INDIA AGENCY.—From the Chutia Nagpoor hills of Bengal on E. to Baroda State and Goojarat on W., and between the N.W. Province and Rajpootana on N. and the Central Province on S., there stretch nine groups of Feudatory States, forming the **Central India Agency**, and controlled by the Governor-General's Agent from **Indore**, the capital of the largest, of which **Mhow** is the great British cantonment. These groups are, politically, from W. to E.: **Indore**, **Gwalior**, **Bhopal**, **Boondelkhand**, and **Baghelkhand**, the **Western Malwa**, **Bheel**, **Deputy Bheel**, and **Goona**. Geographically and historically they form the two great divisions of **Malwa** on the W., the alternate jungle and poppy-field out of which

Sindia and Holkar, the military chiefs of the Marathas, carved their present kingdoms, and **Boondelkhand** on E., a rugged land of hills, passes, and lakes, separated from Malwa by the narrow strip of the Jhansi and Lalitpoor districts of the N.W. Province, where these run into the Sagar district of the Central Province. The whole territory has an area of at least 89,098 sq. m., or one-third less than that of Italy, with a population of 9,200,881, or nearly that of the Empire of Brazil. Long the most backward portions of India, ravaged on the W. by the Marathas and on the E. isolated, if not inaccessible, from want of communication, the Central India States have during the last ten years been opened up by railways, roads, schools, and the enlightened administration of their chiefs under British influence. The Malwa division of the Rajpootana - Malwa Railway opens up the country from Khandwa on the Great Indian Peninsula line to Ajmer for Delhi and Agra. Farther E. the Bhopal Railway from Itarsi on the same line is to be continued to Sindia's line at Gwalior, passing through Lalitpoor and Jhansi, and branching N.E. from Jhansi to Cawnpoor.

§ 27. MALWA, or the W. and larger division of the Central India Agency, has an area of 61,700 sq. m. It is a tableland elevated above 2000 ft., sloping from the **Vindhyas** on S. to the Ganges on N., fertile and well cultivated, enclosed within the great rivers Ganges, Son, Chambal, and Narbada, and surrounded E. by Boondelkhand, N. by Hindustan proper, W. by Rajpootana, and S. by the Dekhan. Sir John Malcolm, who knew it best, states that there is a rise towards Malwa from all quarters except the N.W. To S. it is elevated 1700 ft. above the Narbada valley or Nimar. There is an equally well-marked ascent over the branches of the Vindhyas, which on the E. pass Bhopal and on the W. divide Malwa from Goojarat. To N.W. there is an ascent to Mewar at the Chittor range. From the Vindhyas the **Chambal**, with its tributaries the **Kali Sind**, lesser and greater, and the **Parbati** and **Betwa**, flow north to the Jumna and Ganges; the **Mahi**, from a small place 5 m. W. of Amjhera, flows N. and W. through Goojarat to the Gulf of Kambay. The rich black soil of Malwa produces especially fine wheat and opium. The latter gives the chief value to the land. Wheat and other cereals pay from 18d. to 6s. per *beegah;* opium yields £1 to £4 and even £6 for the same measure. Sindia and Holkar are the chief gainers locally; the latter has increased his rent-roll 40 per cent in ten years. Malwa opium yielded for export from Bombay 405,094 chests, representing

£24,578,272 duty to the British Government in the decade ending March 1879, or an increase of 63,682 chests and £4,467,822 over the previous ten years. Before the Musalman invasion, which, in 1387, placed Diláwar Khan Ghori on the throne at **Mandu**, Malwa was governed from **Oojain**, the capital of Vikramaditya, whose accession has made, 57 B.C., the *Samvat* era of the Hindoos. Akbar made it a Soobah or viceroy's province after his conquest of Goojarat in 1570; it was overrun by the Marathas on the decay of the Mughul empire, and practically divided between Sindia on N. and Holkar on S., while the Bheels held the hills. The Pindarees found an asylum there, which ended in their extirpation in the 4th Maratha war under Lord Hastings, and the civilisation that followed the rule of Malcolm after the Treaty of Mundisor in 1818. The principal States are six: Gwalior, Indore, Dhar, and Dewass are Maratha, and Bhopal and Jaora are Musalman. There are many mediatised chiefs of petty States, held under the immediate guarantee of the British Government, but having feudal relations with one or other of these larger States.

§ 28. BOONDELKHAND AND BAGHELKHAND, the E. corner of the triangular plateau of Central India, have an area of 24,400 sq. m. To W. the **Betwa**, and its tributary the **Dhasan**, and in the centre the **Ken**, flow N. to the Jumna; to E. the **Son** flows to the Ganges at the foot of the **Kaimor** the continuation of the Vindhya mountains. Between these and **Panna** range is the **S. Tons**, flowing N. to the Ganges. The country is more remarkable for its mineral than for its agricultural wealth; diamonds and iron have been worked fitfully. The early Gond possessors were supplanted by the Chandel Rajpoots, with their noble irrigation and fortification works, till in 1183 Parmal Deo, twentieth in succession from Chandra Varma, the founder, was defeated by Prithvi Raja of Delhi. After Musalman invasion had added to the anarchy, the Boondelas, of the Garuha tribe of Rajpoots, seized the country at the close of the 14th century, and ruled it from **Mahoni**. Under the treaty of Bassein, the British Government obtained Boondela territory (N.W. Province) and supremacy in 1818. Of 31 States in Boondelkhand, Oorcha or Tehree, Duttia, and Sumpthur alone have formal treaties with the British Government; the others are bound by deeds of fealty and obedience. Baghelkhand comprises Rewah, Nagode, Maihar, Sohawal, and Kotee, of which the first only is held under treaty. Surveys for a system of railway lines, chiefly as preventives of famine, are being made in Boondelkhand.

The British districts of Hameerpoor, Jalaun, Jhansi, Lalitpoor, and Banda, which, with these States, comprise Boondelkhand, have been described in detail under *North-Western Province.* The whole formed Ptolemy's kingdom of Prasiaké, lying to S. of the Jumna, with Kanagora or Kalinjar as chief town.

§ 29. *INDORE STATE, or Holkar's, is bounded E. by Nimar district, Dhar and Dewass States; N. by Gwalior; W. by Dhar and Burwani; S. by Khandesh district. Two other detached portions lie to N. around Rampoora and Mehidpoor, and one to W. around Dhie. Area of whole, 8075 sq. m. Population, 700,000 yielding £500,000 to the Maharaja Holkar ("inhabitant of Hol," ancestral village on Neera in Dekhan), a Maratha of the goat-herd tribe. The S. portion lies between the Satpoora and Vindhya ranges, forming a section of the Narbada valley. The N. is watered by the Chambal. The centre is the valley of Mandlésar. The Holkar (Malwa) railway runs from Khandwa on Great Indian Peninsula line N. for 86 m. to the capital, whence it proceeds N. through Neemach to Naseerabad and Ajmer. **Indore** (15,000), capital and residence of Governor-General's Agent for all Central India States, founded in 1770 by Ahalya Bai, the able queen, in place of Kampail, former capital, 18 m. S.E. of Indore, on left bank of the Katki or Kan river (1998 ft.), with spacious palace, British Residency and barracks, opium establishment, cotton mills, Rajkoomar college for Malwa chiefs and Mission of Presbyterian Church of Canada. **Mhow**, large cantonment and railway station on Gambri river (2019 ft.), 13 miles S. of Indore. **Mandlésar**, on right bank of Narbada, on route 30 m. S. of Mhow to Aseergarh. **Mehidpoor**, on right bank of Seepra; on the opposite bank Sir Thomas Hislop defeated Holkar in 1817. **Rampoora** (1360 ft.), below Chittor mountains, residence of Holkar till 1820, on N. bank of Taloyee. **Barwai**, railway station on the Narbada, with English school. Other towns are Khargaon, Mahésar, and Kanod.

§ 30. *DEWASS AND BAGLI STATES, N.E. of Indore. **Dewass** is divided between the senior branch with area of 1378 sq. m., pop. 63,000, and rev. £28,000, and the junior, with area of 1198 sq. m., pop. 59,000, and rev. £32,500. Both the Baba Sahib and Dada Sahib are Tuar Rajpoots of the same stock as the Dhar chief; they live in the capital of same name (6000), on high road from Indore to Gwalior and Agra. **Bagli**, with capital of same name, E. of Mhow, near Kali Sind river. Area, 300 sq. m. Population, 18,000 yielding £6500 to the Thakoor, a Champawat Rajpoot.

§ 31. *GWALIOR STATE, or Sindia's, is in detached districts, of which Gwalior, the principal, is bounded E. by Sagar district and Boondelkhand; N.E. by Agra and Etawah with the Chambal between; N.W. by the Chambal separating it from Karauli and Dholpoor; W. by Rajgarh, Kotah, and Jhalawar States; and S. by Bhopal and Dhar. Area, 33,119 sq. m. Population, 2,300,000 yielding £1,200,000 to Maharaja Sindia, fourth descendant of Ranojee, slipper-bearer of Balajee Peshwa, and a most loyal feudatory of the Empress, as seen in his whole career since 1843. His titles are "Master of the country, great in power, high in prestige, exalted in majesty, the great man of the age, pillar of the nobles, the great Raja, Raja of Rajas, the high of place, Maharaja Jayaji Rao Sindia Bahadoor, the victorious of the period, vassal of Her Majesty the honoured and exalted Queen of England," 1863. Comprising the greater part of Malwa the State is a plateau sloping gently from the **Mandu Range** of the Vindhyas N. or N.E. to the Chambal. **Shaizgarh** in that range rises to 2628 ft.; the high place of **Gwalior Rock** is one of the isolated hills on N.E. Between the Narbada on S. and Chambal on N. the Sind, Kuwari, Asar, and Sankh, are smaller streams. In the S.W. opium, cotton, and grain are largely produced. **New Gwalior** or **Lashkar** ("the camp") (100,000), opulent city, sprung up recently round S.E. skirt of Gwalior Rock on site of Daulat Rao's first encampment, 67 m. S. of Agra, now railway terminus of Sindia's broad gauge line to Agra; close by are the new palaces, Jai Indar Bhawan, and a smaller pleasure house in the Phoolbagh, or flower park, watered by the Sourékha, of which the Italian Sir Michael Filose is architect. **Old Gwalior** (25,000), town at N. angle of the base of the rock, famous for its singers in Akbar's time, with ruins. **Gwalior Fortress** is the fortified summit of a sandstone hill (1010 ft.), 2 m. in length, with area of 2000 acres, over which Sindia's orange serpent-flag flies, but garrisoned by British troops since 1857, when the sepoy contingent and local troops mutinied, and Sindia and his great Minister, Dinkar Rao, fled to Agra on the approach of Tatia Topi. The fort contains Jain temples, caves with colossal figures, and the Hindoo palace of Man Singh; these are all that is left of buildings which excited Baber's admiration. **Morar** (Umra), large British cantonment and village on river of same name, 4 m. E. of the Rock, with residences of Brigadier-General and civil and political staff, and fine barracks. **Pauniar**, 12 m. to S.W., and Maharajpoor, 15 m. to N.W. of Gwalior, where, on the same day, 29th December 1843, battles were fought by the British, the former under General Grey, the latter under

Sir Hugh Gough; Lord Ellenborough made of the captured guns a monument at Calcutta to commemorate the victories, which delivered the present Maharaja when a child from his nobles. **Oojain**, ancient capital of Malwa, one of the 7 sacred Hindoo cities and first meridian of their geographers, on right bank of Seepra, to which there is now a branch railway from Fatehabad on the Indore and Neemach section of the Malwa railway; Sindia's capital till he removed N. to Gwalior. **Chandéri**, 105 m. S. of Gwalior, with hill fort, a great city under the Delhi emperors. **Neemach**, British cantonment near Mewar boundary (1476 ft.), station on railway from Indore to Ajmer. **Mandesor**, 80 m. N. of Oojain, where treaty of same name was made in 1818, closing the Pindaree war.

§ 32. *BHOPAL STATE is bounded E. by Sagar district, N. by Sindia's and Dhar States, W. by Sindia's and Holkar's States, and S. by the Narbada separating it from the Central Province district of Hoshangabad. Area, 8200 sq. m. Population, 775,000 yielding £270,000 to Shah Jahan Begam, descendant of an Afghan who was in Aurangzeb's service, and whose house has always been actively loyal. The Begam, like her mother, encourages female education, and has a State railway from Hoshangabad, and Itarsi on Great Indian Peninsula line, to her capital, **Bhopal**, with waterworks, hospital, and schools; outside the walls is the palace in Fatehgarh fort, near a large artificial lake. Shahjahanabad is a new suburb, with street Kaisarganj, named after the Empress, or Kaisar-i-Hind. **Sehore**, on the Saven, 22 m. S.W. of Bhopal. **Bhilsa**, town 26 m. N.E. of Bhopal, on a rock with fort, remarkable as the centre of 6 groups of Boodhist topes or monuments marking sacred spots, of which **Sanchi** *stupa* is the greatest. At Sonari, 8 m. distant from Sanchi, are 8 topes, and at Bhojpoor 37, of which the largest is 66 ft. in diameter—all of the age between 250 B.C. and the first Christian century. **Raiseen**, hill fort in E., 50 m. N. of Hoshangabad on Sagar road, capitulated to Sher Shah in 1543.

§ 33. *EIGHT BHOPAL AGENCY STATES.—The Bhopal Political Agent controls also **Rajgarh**, to N.W.; area, 642 sq. m.; pop. 76,000 yielding £35,000 to the Nawab, a Rajpoot who became Muhammadan, though claiming descent from Vikramaditya; capital of same name **Narsingarh**, on W. border of Bhopal, with capital of same name; area, 720 sq. m.; pop. 88,000 yielding £40,000 to the Raja, an Omat Rajpoot. **Koorwai**, with capital of same name, N. of Bhopal; area, 126 sq. m.; pop. 17,000 yielding £10,000 to the Nawab. **Maksoodangarh**, on right bank of Parbati, with capital of same name, held from Sindia, who granted it to Colonel Jean Baptiste; area, 81 sq. m.; pop. 10,000 paying £3100 to the Rajpoot chief. **Kilchipoor**, W. of Rajgarh; area, 204 sq. m.; pop. 31,000 paying £17,500 to the Rao, a Khichi Rajpoot. **Basoda**, N.E. of Bhopal; area, 68 sq. m.; pop. 5500 paying £1000 to Nawab. **Mahomedgarh**, from which the former is an offshoot, N. of Bhilsa; area, 80 sq. m.; pop. 3000 paying £700 to the Nawab. **Pathari**, adjoining Sagar district; area, 22 sq. m.; pop. 4500 paying £1200 to the Nawab.

§ 34. *JAORA, RATLAM, SAILANA, AND SEETAMAU STATES form the Western Malwa Agency, with six small chiefships. **Jaora**, on W. border of Malwa, marching with the Partabgarh State of Rajpootana, has an area of 872 sq. m. and pop. of 86,000 yielding £80,000 to the Nawab, of an Afghan family secured in possession of the State after the Pindaree war. Jaora contains the best poppy-growing lands in Malwa, opened up by railway from Indore N. to Neemach and Ajmer. The capital is a railway station, 180 m. from Khandwa, on Great Indian Peninsula line. **Ratlam**, the capital of which is a chief opium mart and contains a central college (1577 ft.), 159 m. from Khandwa, has an area of 1200 sq. m. and pop. of 100,000 yielding £130,000 to the Raja, who is of the Jodhpoor Rajpoot family. Rattan Singh, the founder, obtained the State from the Emperor Shah Jahan, and gave it his own name. **Sailana**, once part of Ratlam, has an area of 500 sq. m. and pop. of 27,000 yielding £12,140 to the Raja, a Rahtor Rajpoot. **Seetamau**, also an offshoot of Ratlam, has an area of 350 sq. m. and pop. 30,000 yielding £15,000 to the Raja, a Rahtor Rajpoot.

§ 35. *BHEEL AGENCY STATES, in S.W. corner of Malwa, adjoining Goojarat on W. and Khandesh on S., and traversed by the Narbada. **Dhar**, with capital a few m. W. of Mhow, has an area of 2500 sq. m. and pop. of 150,000 paying £80,000 to the Raja, a Tuar Rajpoot. **Jhabooa** has an area of 15,000 sq. m. and pop. 56,000, chiefly Bheels (Billa = a bow), paying £22,500 to the Raja of the Jodhpoor house. There are schools in the capital, and at Thandla, Ramchapoor, and Ranapoor. **Barwanee**, wild and malarious tract on left bank of Narbada, with area of 2000 sq. m. and pop. 35,000 paying £8770 to the Rana, a Sesodia Rajpoot. **Ali Rajpoor**, whose Rana is of the same stock, has an area of 800 sq. m., pop. 30,000, and revenue of £1000; capital, Rajpoor. **Jobat**, a wild hilly tract, held by a Rana of the Jodhpoor stock, with area of 200 sq.

m., pop. 8000, and revenue of £1700. Ghora village is larger than Jobat, the capital. Other petty States are Mathwar, Chikalda, Pitláwad, Ratanmal, Kathiwara, and **Amjhera**. The last is 584 sq. m. in extent, and contains the town of **Bagh**, 25 m. S.W. of Dhar, near which are Boodhist caves (viharas) of the 6th century, "the homes of Hindoo mendicants, whose occupancy of them is shared by panthers, which appear to come and go without attempting to molest their fellow-lodgers."

The Deputy Bheel Agency, from the British district of **Manpoor**, controls Barwanee (above) Jumnia, of which Kimjrod is headquarters, Bharoodpoora, Kothide, Chiktiabar, Rajgarh, and Garhi.

§ 36. *RAGHOOGARH AND PARON STATES, with smaller chiefships, are controlled from **Goona**, station of the Central India Horse, on high road from Indore to Gwalior, and midway between the two. These States are small in area; the first is under a Chouhan Rajpoot Raja, who has £2400 a year. The Raja of Paron has £1200; he rebelled in 1857, but afterwards gave up Tatia Topi.

§ 37. *BOONDELKHAND STATES (Boondelas = Gaharwar Rajpoots, from *boond*, a drop of blood shed by their ancestor Pancham; or Bandelas, from *bandi*, a slave-girl) are controlled by a British Political Agent from the cantonment of **Nowgong**, on N. between Hameerpoor district and Chatarpoor State, where also is the Rajkoomar college, established by the chiefs in memory of Lord Mayo. **Tehree** or **Orcha**, a jungly and thinly-peopled State, the asylum of brigands (dacoits), lies to S. of Jhansi district, with which it is intermixed; area, 2000 sq. m., and pop. 200,000 paying £90,000 to the Maharaja, the oldest of the Boondela houses, which never acknowledged a superior till 1817, when fealty was pledged to the Governor-General, Lord Hastings. **Tehri**, in S.W. corner, with Tikamgarh fort, is the present capital; 40 m. N. and 142 m. S.E. of Agra is the old capital. **Orcha**, on the Betwa, with fort and palace built for Jahangeer. **Datia**, ceded by the Peshwa with other States under Bassein treaty in 1802, is bounded E. by Jhansi, and on other sides by Gwalior State. Area, 820 sq. m.; pop. 185,000 paying £10,000 to the Maharaja. The capital, of same name (40,000), stands on rocky site, on Agra and Sagar road, 125 m. S. of former; 4 m. off is a curious cluster of Jain temples. **Samthar**, surrounded by Jalaun and Jhansi districts on E. and S., and by Gwalior on N. and W., has an area of 174 sq. m. and pop. 110,000 paying

£45,000 to the Raja; capital of same name. **Panna**, the famous diamond State, on the tableland above the Vindhyan Ghats, lies S. of Banda, and N. of Dumoh and Jabalpoor districts. Area, 2555 sq. m.; pop. 185,000 paying £50,000 to the Maharaja, the senior representative of the great Chatar Sal. The capital (1300 ft.) is on the route from Jabalpoor to Banda, 169 m. N. of former, and 173 S.W. of Allahabad; it is now in ruins, but has a spacious palace and many temples, one of which contains idols of Krishna and Lakshman, whose eyes are said to be diamonds of great value. On N.E. of town are the "Panna mines," but the most important adamantiferous tract extends from 12 to 20 m. N.E., and is worked at Kamariya, Brijpoor, Bargari, Maira, and Etwa. The diamond bed proper is a conglomerate belonging geologically to a group at the base of the Lower Rewahs, distinguished as the Panna shales. The rock diggings, twenty minutes' walk from the town, cover a surface of only 20 acres on a low flat rising ground at the base of the slope from the Kaimor scarp; there are five or six pits worked. Colourless diamonds, of the first water, are rare. The revenue, raised by a tax of above 25 per cent on the produce, is estimated at £12,000 a year. It is shared by **Charkhari**, a grain-producing State within the Hameerpoor district, and on the Dhasān which separates it from Orcha. Area, 275 sq. m.; pop. 125,000 paying £50,000 to the Maharaja. The capital is picturesquely situated at base of a lofty hill, with fort above and lake below, on the route from Gwalior to Banda, 41 m. W. of the latter. **Bijawar**, at foot of an advanced ridge of the Vindhyas, a land poor and hilly, lies N. of the Dumoh district. Area, 920 sq. m.; pop. 105,000 paying £25,000 to Raja. The capital is 70 m. N.E. of Sagar, and 23 S. of **Chatarpoor**, which State lies S. of Hameerpoor and N. of Dumoh district, between the Dhasān and the Ken, in a hilly country with several lakes. Area, 1240 sq. m.; pop. 175,000 yielding £25,000 to Raja, a Tuar Rajpoot. The capital, of same name, is on the Banda-Sagar route, 10 m. N.E. of the latter, with ruins of the palace and tomb of Chatar Sal, after whom the town is named. Rajnagar was the former capital. The State used to be famed for its swords. **Ajaigarh**, S. of Banda district and Charkhari State, and E. of Chatarpoor, has an area of 340 sq. m. and pop. of 55,000 yielding £22,500 to the Raja, who lives at Naushahr at N. base of the granite and sandstone rock on which is the famous **Ajaigarh Fort** (1344 ft.) ("unconquerable fort" or "Aja's fort"), fronted by Bihouta hill, which commands it. Ajaigarh Fort is 16 m. from Kalinjar, and, like that, is as old as the 9th century. The plateau is covered with exquisitely carved remains of Jain temples, some of them obscene and now inhabited by snakes and baboons. In 1809 a British force took Raghauli heights, 8 m. N.W., Bihouta and Ajaigarh from the marauder Lakshman Dawa, and restored it to the Boondela Raja, whose house remained faithful in 1857. **Baonee** (Bawain = "52 villages"), a poor land overrun by bindweed, and the only Muhammadan State in Boondelkhand, lies near Kalpee in the doab between the Jumna and Betwa, surrounded by British districts except on S. Area, 127 sq. m.; pop. 25,000 paying £10,000 to the Nawab, who resides at Kadaura. **Baronda** (or Beergarh, or Páthar Kachar, from former capitals), S. and E. of Banda district, with capital in a difficult pass on the Banda-Rewah route, 35 m. S.E. of former. The State is partly below, but chiefly above the Ghats. Area, 230 sq. m.; pop. 15,000 yielding £2800 to the Raja, a Rajbansi Rajpoot. **Sareela**, in Hameerpoor district, with capital 42 m. from Hameerpoor town, and 25 m. S. of Kalpee, has an area of 35 sq. m. and pop. 7000 paying £3000 to the Raja. **Alipoora**, between Hameerpoor N. and E., and Jhansi W., has an area of 85 sq. m. and yields £5000 to Rao. **Kanyadhana**, a wild tract W. of the Betwa and S.W. of Orcha; area, 84 sq. m.; pop. 16,000 paying £2000 to the Raja. **Hashtbya Jageers**, originally, as the name signifies, eight appanages, to S. of Jhansi, into which the Orcha chief divided Baragaon, for his sons; four of these remain. **Dhoorwai**, 18 sq. m.; pop. 8000 paying £1200 to the Dewan. **Bijner**, 40 m. E. of Jhansi, 27 sq. m.; pop. and rev. as above. **Tori Fathipoor**, 36 sq. m.; pop. 10,000; rev. £3000. **Pahari Banka**, 4 sq. m.; pop. 5000 paying £500. The **Kalinjar Chaubés** are the petty States assigned in 1812 to the members of the family of Chaubé Kam Kishn, Chatar Sal's governor of Kalinjar Fort, who seized it for himself after resisting the Maratha ten years' siege by Ali Bahadoor. The estates lie to E. of the fort, and are **Paldeo, Tiraon, Bhaisaunda, Kamta Rajola**; Kamta is a famous centre of Hindoo pilgrims as an abode of Rama, in the Chitrakot tract, where the sacred streams Paisani and Mandagni meet; **Naigoa, Rebai, Jignee, Jassoo, Lughassi, Pahra.** Other petty States are **Behut, Behri, Gaurihar,** and **Girauli.**

§ 38. *BAGHELKHAND STATES, five in number, are divided from those of Boondelkhand on the E. roughly by the line of East India Railway from Allahabad to Jabalpoor. They lie between Chutia Nagpoor on E., Mirzapoor and Allahabad districts on N., Boondelkhand and Jabalpoor on W., and Bilaspoor and Mandla districts of Central Province on S. The Baghel Rajpoots are so named from Bheelagar or Beeag Deo, who left Goojarat in 580 and conquered the country from Kalpee to Chandalgarh, to which his son added Rewah, calling the whole Baghelkhand.

Rewah (with Sohagpoor), the most E. and important State, rises from the Ganges valley in three plateaux resting on the Bundachal, Panna, and Kaimor hills, drained by the **S. Tons**, Beher, and Biland. The **Son**, receiving the Mahanadi, flows from the S. through the State N.E. into Mirzapoor district; its basin is as yet unexplored. The State is rich in minerals and forests; coal of the Palamau field is found at Umaria, 34 m. from Kutnee railway station Area, 13,000 sq. m.; pop. 2,100,000 yielding £250,000 to the Maharaja. The capital, of same name, and fort founded in 1618, is 131 m. S.W. of Allahabad; residence of Political Agent. The chief resides at Govindgarh palace to S. Sutna is the principal railway station, nearly midway between Allahabad and Jabalpoor, 118 m. N.E. of latter. From Sutna a road 22½ m. to Bela joins the great Dekhan road leading to Rewah. E. near Son river is Chandrehi village with mounds, ruins of palace and fine Saivic temple. In the Kaimor range the most important passes, beginning from that pierced by the Jabalpoor Railway, are Sunai Ghat and Badanpoor Pass, from which old roads branch S. and S.E. towards the Central Province and Orissa, lined in some places, as at Gurgi, by ancient remains.

Nagodh, on E. border of Rewah and W. of Panna. Area, 450 sq. m.; pop. 80,000 paying £15,000 to the Raja. The capital, W. of Sutna railway station, is also a British cantonment on the route by Rewah from Sagar to Allahabad, 110 m. N.W. of Jabalpoor. The Raja's fort (1099 ft.) is on the Amran tributary of the S. Tons. The State is traversed by the East India Railway. **Maihar**, N. of Jabalpoor district. Area, 600 sq. m.; pop. 75,000 paying £7420 to the Raja. The capital is a railway station (Maihar), 97 m. N.E. of Jabalpoor on the route by Rewah to Allahabad. **Suhawal**, N. of Nagodh. Area, 300 sq. m.; pop. 55,000 paying £7000 to the Rais. The capital, with ruined fort, is on the Satni river (1059 ft.), 168 m. S.W. of Allahabad. **Kothi**, the capital of which is 66 m. S.E. of Banda on the route to Rewah, has an area of 100 sq. m.; pop. 35,000 paying £5000 to the Rais.

CHAPTER XVIII.

THE CENTRAL PROVINCE.

§ 1. Size. § 2. Position, Physical Divisions, Mountains, Rivers, and Lakes. § 3. Products, Trade, and Railways. § 4. Land Tenures and Taxation. § 5. The People and Districts.

Eighteen Districts.

§ 6. Nagpoor. § 7. Bhandara. § 8. Chanda. § 9. Wardha. § 10. Balaghat. § 11. Raipoor. § 12. Bilaspoor. § 13. Sambalpoor. § 14. Mandla. § 15. Seoni. § 16. Jabalpoor. § 17. Damoh. § 18. Sagar. § 19. Narsingpoor. § 20. Chindwara. § 21. Hoshangabad. § 22. Betool. § 23. Nimar.

**Fifteen States.*

§ 24. *Bastar. § 25. *Karond and Makrai. § 26. *Twelve Chatteesgarh States.

§ 1. Size.—The Central Provinces were formed into one Province under a Chief Commissioner by Lord Canning in 1861, out of the Sagar and Narbada districts of the N.W. Province, of the Nagpoor country on the disappearance of the Bhonsla Maratha kingdom, and of territories on the fringe of Orissa, Madras, Telingana, and Bombay. The new Province is larger than Italy, with somewhat less than half its population, having a total area of 113,042 sq. m. and population of 11,505,149. Its capital, Nagpoor city, is almost equidistant from Calcutta, Bombay, and Madras, and is on the direct line of railway, gradually being completed, between the two first. Along with Berar to the W. the Central Province will one day be administratively united with Bombay, to which, geographically, it is most allied. The home to which the non-Aryan tribes, Kolarian and Dravidian, were driven by Aryan invaders, is Gondwana, the Satpoora plateau. It is the varied meeting-place of languages and civilisations; Maratha prevails in S.W., Hindee in N., Ooriya in E., and Tamil in S. Long devastated by the Marathas, and exposed to famine and over-assessment of the land-tax even under British rule, the 18 districts of the Central Province and the 15 Feudatory States have had a scanty population. But since the establishment of a detailed and vigorous local administration in 1861 the population has grown nearly one-half, and cultivation, mining, trade, and education, have rapidly extended.

§ 2. POSITION AND PHYSICAL DIVISIONS.—The **Central Province**, the old Gondwána, is bounded S.E. by N. Madras and Orissa; N.E. by Chutia Nagpoor, Baghelkhand, and Boondelkhand States and districts; N.W. by Malwa States; and S.W. by Khandesh, Berar, and Haidarabad State. Of a total boundary of 2700 m., only 160 march with ordinary British districts at Khandesh. The Province lies between 17° 50′ and 24° 27′ N. lat., and 76° and 85° 15′ E. long., with an extreme breadth N. to S. of 500 m., and length E. to W. of 600 m. Of the total area, 84,208 sq. m. is occupied by British districts, having a population of 9,805,149; and 29,112 sq. m., or one-fourth, by Feudatory States, with a population of about 1,700,000. Roughly, the Province may be said to form a series of 3 terraced plateaux between the Ganges and Godavari valleys. Proceeding from the N. there is first the **Vindhyan Plateau**, on which the Sagar and Dumoh districts lie parallel. Then comes the **Narbada Valley**, in which are the districts of Jabalpoor, Narsingpoor, Hoshangabad, and part of Nimar; the other part lies in the Tapti valley. Then follows the main tableland, the **Satpoora Plateau** rising to 2000 ft., on which are Mandla, Balaghat, Seoni, Chindwara, and Betool districts. To the S. of all is the great **Nagpoor Plain**, formed by the Wardha and Waenganga valleys, in which are the districts of Nagpoor, Wardha, Bhandara, and Chanda, ending in a mass of hill and forest probably the wildest and the least known part of the Peninsula, in which chiefly are the Feudatory States. Eastward, and below the Ghats, is the **Chatteesgarh Plain** ("thirty-six forts"), a low plateau of red soil, containing Raipoor and Bilaspoor districts, the "land of threshing floors" (*khalanti*) to the Banjara traders, whose pack cattle carry off its surplus grain till superseded by the advancing railway. Farther E., Sambalpoor district, on the Mahanadi, pierces into Bengal, from which it was formerly administered. Running E. to W. 600 m., the Satpoora plateau forms the true barrier between Northern or Aryan, and Southern or Dravidian India; between Hindustan on N. and Maharashtra and the Dekhan on the S.W. and S. The range extends W. to the W. coast, from Amarkantak. That lofty plateau gives birth to the **Narbada**, which for 200 m. winds among the **Mandla hills**, passes through the rocky gorge known as the marble rocks of Jabalpoor, and thence flows W. in its own valley between the Vindhyan and Satpoora ranges to the Gulf of Kambay. The **Mahanadi** flows from the **Bastar hills**, which close in Chatteesgarh plain to S.; receives its first great affluent, the Seonath, a little above Seorinarain, and flows past Sambalpoor town to Sonpoor, Cuttak, and the Bay of Bengal. The **Waenganga**, from the Seoni plateau, drains the S. slopes of the Satpooras into the Wardha, which it joins 50 m. below Chanda town; in its course of 350 m. it receives the Thanwar E. of Keolari; turning S. it passes through a gorge into the Nagpoor plain, and flows through Balaghat, Bhandara, and Chanda districts. The **Wardha**, rising in the Satpooras 70 m. N.W. of Nagpoor city, separates the Province from Berar and Haidarabad; near Chanda town, 190 m. from its source, it receives the Paenganga, which drains E. and S. Berar; 64 m. lower it is joined by the Waenganga, and the united stream, named **Pranheeta**, flows on for 60 m. to the **Godavari** at Sironcha. Of the 900 m. course of the Godavari from Bombay Nasik to the Madras seaport of Coconada, it borders the Central Province to S.W. for 150 m.; from the Wardha falls, near Hinghanghat cotton mart, its course is compared by Sir R. Temple to that of the Rhine, especially where it breaks through the **Eastern Ghats** (2500 ft.) from its junction with the Sabari, its breadth of from 1 to 2½ m. being contracted into a narrow and very deep channel for a course of 20 m. In the E. and S., in Bhandara and Chanda, are fine lakes; the largest, **Nawagaon**, is 17 m. in circumference, with a depth of 90 ft. in some places.

§ 3. PRODUCTS, TRADE, AND RAILWAYS.—The Central Province possesses eight separate coal-fields—at Bandar, **Wardha**, **Warora** or **Chanda**, Kainaram, and Singareni in the Godavari valley; at Shahpoor in the Betool district; and at **Mohpani**, Tawa, and Pench in the Satpoora region. The Wardha field is the N. extremity of a vast tract of Gondwana rocks extending for 285 m. from N.W. to S.E. in the valleys of the Wardha, Pranheeta, and Godavari basins, containing 2525 million tons, of which 1714 million are available, as estimated by the Geological Survey. The Warora coal is deficient in fixed carbon and combustible volatile gases. Government has spent a very large sum in exploring and testing the Warora field, from which a branch railway conveys the coal 45 m. to Wardha on the Great Indian Peninsula line.

The out-turn in 1879-80 was 32,100 tons, but it is expected to be 10,000 tons a month. The Great Indian Peninsula Company have contracted for 50,000 tons a year at Rs. 5 (10s.) a ton at the pit's mouth. At Mohpani, 95 m. S.W. of Jabalpoor, the "Nerbudda Coal and Iron Company" raised 13,500 tons, and is worked with success; the fuel is sold to the Great Indian Peninsula Railway at Rs. 10 per ton, or considerably above the price of Raneeganj and Karharbari coals, and of English coal landed at Bombay, because of the cost of carriage. The State Forests cover 12½ millions of acres, or 19,666 sq. m., of which 2535 are first, and 16,850 second class reserves. In the N. the Province has been almost denuded of forests; in the S., especially in the hill States, which look down on the Nagpoor and Chatteesgarh plains, the population is scanty, and the destruction of trees has been stopped. The Nagpoor plain is a great rice field, with 4 millions of acres under that crop; the Narbada country, a wheat field covering 3½ millions of acres. Other food grains are raised on 6 millions of acres, oil-seeds on 1¼ millions, and cotton on less than 1 million. Thirteen millions of acres, or 85 per cent of the whole cultivated area, are under food grains. The annual rainfall is 45 inches. There are no canals. At Nagpoor city there is a model farm. There are manufactures of cotton in mills at Nagpoor, and of silk, cotton, and wool privately throughout the Province, also of iron, brass, pottery, and leather. The value of the exports from the Province, of cotton, grain, and cloth, is registered at about 3½ million pounds annually, and of the imports at 4⅛, in salt, sugar, and English piece goods, chiefly from and to Bombay and the N.W. Province. The great granary of the Chatteesgarh plain is being opened up by a State railway from Nagpoor, 95 m. E., to Amgaon, with branch to Toomsar from Dowhali junction, Nandgaon, and Dongarghar (126 m.), Bilaspoor (256 m.), and ultimately on the 5-6 gauge to the East Indian line at Barakar or Seetarampoor for Calcutta. The imports into the Province in 1880-81 were valued at £3,887,520 and the exports at a little less.

§ 4. Land Tenures and Taxation.—Almost every form of tenure which exists in India is to be found in this central meeting-place of its races and languages. (1) The feudal system prevails in the case of the chiefs who hold their estates on the two conditions of loyalty and good administration. The authority which they exercise is of a somewhat absolute character, sentences of death alone requiring the sanction of the Chief Commissioner. The succession to these chiefships follows ordinarily the law of primogeniture, but in each case the succession requires the approval of Government. (2) Among ordinary landed proprietors, non-feudatory chiefs, known locally as Zameendars, occupy the most prominent position. The estates are held by single proprietors who have usually been in possession for many generations, and succession is governed by the law of primogeniture. The junior branches of the family are entitled to maintenance, the nature and extent of which is ruled by custom, but they are not entitled to any share in the estate, as the Hindoo law of inheritance does not apply. The absolute proprietary right of the chief proprietor called "Zameendar" is only so far limited, that in individual villages an inferior proprietary right may have been acquired by a hereditary farmer and an absolute occupancy title by a hereditary tenant. Such cases are exceptional. The Talookdaree estates, called also in this Province Tahutdaree, are held by single proprietors, and succession usually follows the law of primogeniture. In comparison with Zameendaree tenures they are generally of recent origin, and therefore the villages included in the estates are often held by inferior proprietors on permanent tenure, who are perfectly protected from interference, so long as they make the prescribed annual payment to the superior proprietor. This payment is a certain percentage over the fixed Government assessment. Cultivators hold on the same conditions absolutely as in ordinary Malgoozaree villages. (3) Most of the estates in the Province are held on what is known as the "Malgoozaree" tenure. The estate, whether the property of one or many owners, is always managed by a single proprietor, and the land is held chiefly by cultivators whose rents are thrown into a common stock. The profits are divided or the losses made up with reference to the respective shares of the different proprietors. The ancient proprietary land in cultivation by the owners themselves, and known as "Seer," is either held and cultivated by the proprietors according to their shares or is cultivated in common. If any proprietor takes up extra land he pays regular rent thereon, which is thrown into the same stock with his cultivator's rents. When disputes occur a regular division takes place, and the whole lands of the village come to be divided and held in severalty according to shares, the tenure becoming Putteedaree. When, however, a body of proprietors has gone so far, the tendency in the Province is to separate altogether, and by complete partition to constitute the several portions separate estates. The estates which are held from Government revenue-free and at a quit-rent are usually on the Malgoozaree tenure and require no separate description. (4) The case of purchasers of waste lands is exceptional. Their proprietary title is absolute, and they are subject to no future revenue assessment. In the districts 53,068 sq. m. are settled for 30 years or upwards, and the leases will expire in June 1897; while 6843 sq. m. are settled for 10 years and under 30, the leases expiring in June 1888. The land revenue amounted to £623,491 in 1880-81, and the gross revenue to £1,503,034.

VARIETIES OF TENURE HELD DIRECT FROM GOVERNMENT.

NATURE OF TENURE.	Number of Estates.	Number of Villages.	Number of Holders and Shareholders.	Gross Area in Acres.	Average Area of each Estate.	Average Assessment of each Estate.
Large Zameendarees paying more than Rs. 5000 revenue—						
Under law of primogeniture . .	5	1,999	5	2,012,160	402,432	Rs. 22,800
Under ordinary law .	31	1,570	46	1,617,579	52,180	22,303
Small Zameendarees other than those of cultivating communities .	14,828	22,012	39,013	29,407,396	1,983	332
Proprietary cultivating communities paying in common	2,492	629	2,842	344,974	143	32
Proprietary cultivators paying separately, including all estates paying less than Rs. 100 .	28,013	8,195	34,603	6,273,477	224	19
Holders of revenue-free tenures—						
In perpetuity . .	3,331	1,210	3,699	620,542	186	...
For life . . .	4,374	655	5,682	295,741	67	...
Holders of quit-rent tenures—						
In perpetuity . .	899	940	1,124	882,162	981	...
For life . . .	784	664	906	546,737	697	...
Under Kham management	15	15	...	14,264	951	134
Landholders who have redeemed the revenue	1	1	1	1,090	1,090	...
Purchasers of waste lands	175	150	187	202,117	1,155	...
Total . .	54,858	38,040	88,108	42,218,239	...	...

VARIETIES OF TENURE NOT HELD DIRECT FROM GOVERNMENT.

NATURE OF TENURE.	Number of Holdings.	Average Area of each Holding.			Average Rent of each Holding.			Average Rent-rate per Acre.		
		A.	R.	P.	R.	A.	P.	R.	A.	P.
Intermediate holders between Zameendars and Ryots—										
On permanent tenure .	9,961	134	2	32	32	8	11	0	3	10
On farming leases .	8,203	488	3	33	117	8	7	0	3	10
Ryots holding at fixed rates	180,067	17	1	1	13	4	10	0	12	3
Ryots with right of occupancy at variable rates .	181,537	14	0	19	11	6	1	0	12	9
Cultivating tenants with no permanent rights .	502,033	13	0	2	8	14	8	0	10	8
Holders of service grants .	54,313	5	3	1	1	11	10	0	4	9

§ 5. THE PEOPLE AND DISTRICTS.—Gondwana was left quietly to the E. by successive invaders of the Dekhan, who followed the Narbada valley through the Nimar pass, commanded by Aseergarh fort. The Central Province had no history till the Bhonslas, one of the four great Maratha dynasties, of which Sindia, Holkar, and the Gaekwar of Baroda represent the other three, made Nagpoor their capital in 1743. Before that time the legendary Rama traversed the forest of Dandaka, from the Jumna to the Godavari, to a hermit at Ramtek, near Nagpoor. The lunar race of Rajpoots, called Haihayas, held Jabalpoor, while the Pramáras of Malwa ruled Nagpoor. After the Gauli shepherd kings had reigned from Deogarh, the Gond dynasty became powerful and great from the 16th century till the Maratha wave swept away the feudal civilisation, which had flourished subject only to the distant supremacy of the Delhi emperors, and ruined the peaceful peasantry. In 1818, on the deposition of Apa Sahib, the British annexed the Sagar and Narbada territories, and managed the Bhonsla Nagpoor till 1830, during the minority of Raghoji III. On his death in 1853 after refusing to adopt a successor, the State became British, and remained quiet, though restless, during 1857.

The census of 1881 shows an increase since 1872 from 8,173,824 to about 9,800,000 in the Districts, and from 1,049,710 to about 1,700,000 in the States. The total increase is about 2,300,000, or 25 per cent, consisting of nearly 20 per cent increase in the Districts, and nearly 60 per cent in the States. Abnormal increase indicates incomplete enumeration at the census of 1872 :—

	1872.	1881.
Raipoor	1,093,405	about 1,400,000
Bilaspoor	715,398	1,000,000
Sambalpoor	523,034	690,000
Jabalpoor	528,859	680,000
Bhandara	564,813	680,000
Bastar State . . .	78,856	190,000
Sambalpoor States .	529,500	950,000

The chief executive authority in the Central Province is the Chief Commissioner and Agent to the Governor-General since 1861. The Chief Commissioner is assisted by a Secretary with an Assistant, a Judicial Commissioner, a Sanitary Commissioner and Deputy Surgeon-General, a Commissioner of Customs, and four Commissioners of Revenue and Circuit, an Inspector-General of Police and Prisons, an Inspector-General of Education, a Conservator of Forests, and an Inspector-General of Registration, who is also Commissioner of Excise and Stamps.

AREA, POPULATION, AND REVENUE OF THE DISTRICTS.

Divisions.	Districts.	Judicial and Revenue Sub-divisions.	Area in square miles.	Population, 1872.	Number of Villages.	Total cost of officials and Police of all kinds.	Revenue.	
							Land.	Gross.
						Rs.	Rs.	Rs.
Nagpoor.	Nagpoor . .	5	3,786	631,109	2,170	2,03,365	8,29,160	14,20,531
	Bhandara . .	2	3,922	*680,000	1,772	1,20,002	4,04,030	6,84,700
	Chanda . .	5	10,785	558,856	2,793	1,52,374	2,79,817	5,73,065
	Wardha . .	3	2,401	354,720	1,372	1,29,527	5,14,136	8,13,586
	Balaghat . .	2	3,141	302,482	1,028	68,666	1,61,205	3,04,442
	Jabalpoor . .	4	3,918	*680,000	2,527	1,00,140	5,80,185	8,39,337
	Sagar . .	5	4,005	527,725	2,107	59,286	4,41,758	6,19,050
	Damoh . .	2	2,799	269,642	1,337	1,05,628	2,66,586	3,56,427
	Seoni . .	2	3,252	299,856	1,434	25,592	1,50,527	3,04,105
Narbada.	Mandla . .	2	4,719	213,018	1,614	69,780	98,172	2,83,437
	Hoshangabad .	4	4,376	449,977	1,396	1,60,905	4,40,664	7,23,873
	Narsingpoor .	2	1,916	339,395	1,084	1,06,441	4,25,555	5,79,391
	Betool . .	2	3,905	274,264	1,200	1,18,685	1,97,276	3,65,294
	Chindwara . .	2	3,853	316,095	1,818	87,297	2,21,596	3,53,696
	Nimar . .	2	3,340	211,176	684	1,26,847	1,81,243	4,18,804
Chatteesgarh.	Raipoor . .	4	11,885	*1,400,000	4,653	1,43,016	6,49,255	9,07,833
	Bilaspoor . .	3	7,798	*1,000,000	6,874	1,16,148	2,80,661	3,98,676
	Sambalpoor .	2	4,407	*690,000	2,252	92,165	1,16,454	2,25,076
	Total . .	53	84,208		32,115	19,95,864	62,38,230	1,01,21,322
						Revenue of reserved Forests		1,70,575
						Grand Total .		1,02,91,897

* Population in 1881.

CENTRAL PROVIN

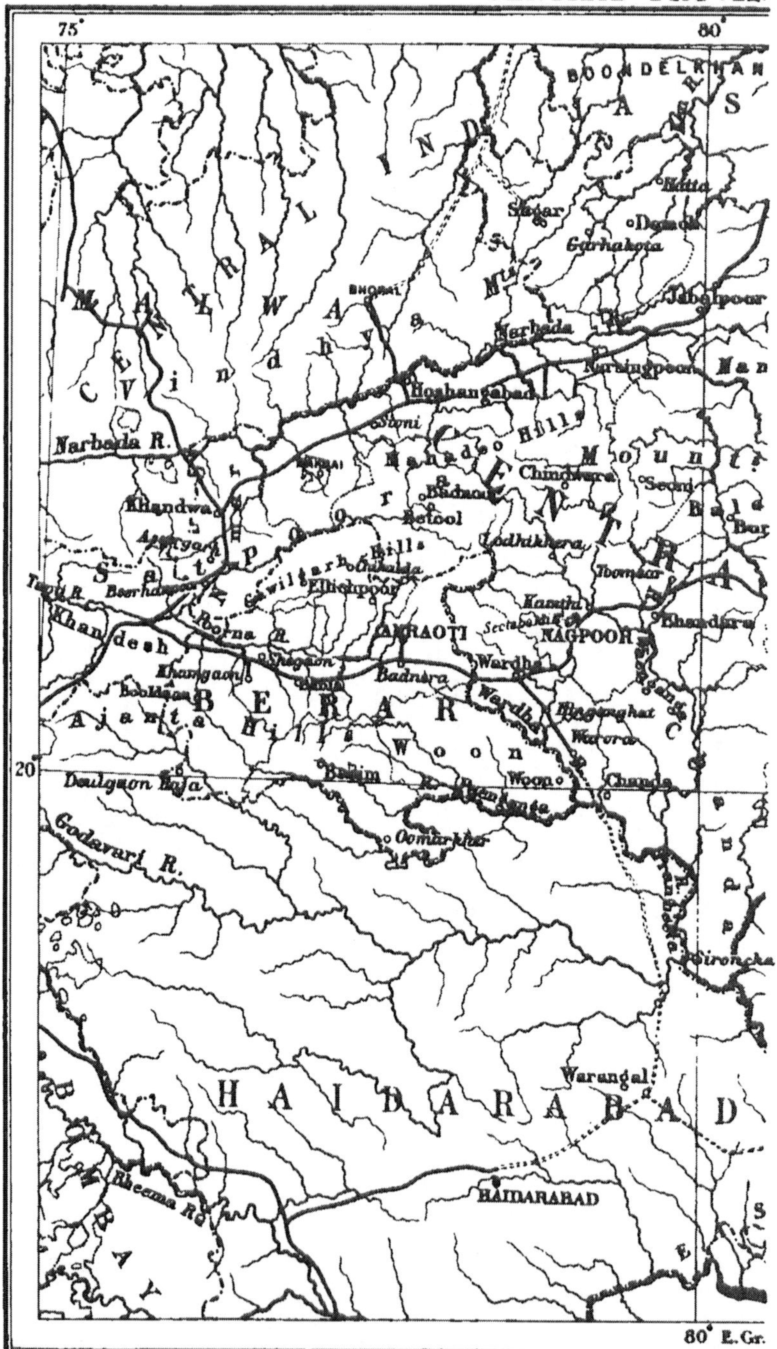

CE AND BERAR.

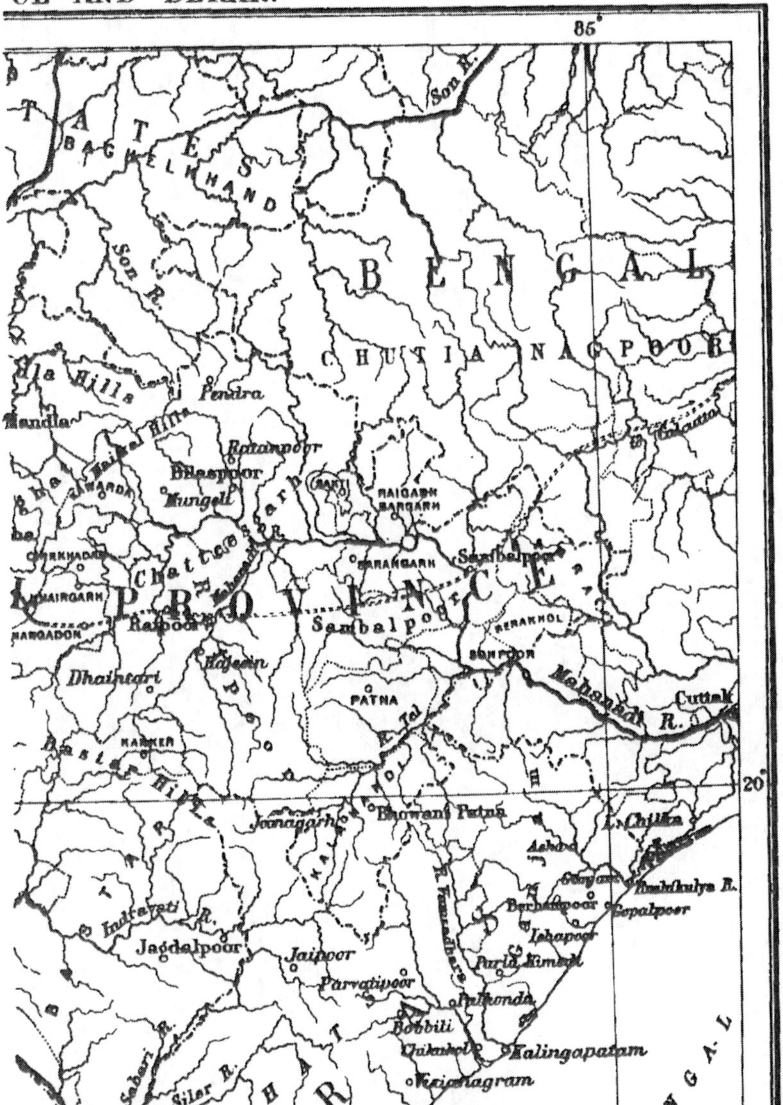

Stanford's Geog^l. Estab^t.

§ 6. NAGPOOR DISTRICT (the name of this country, as well as of Chutia Nagpoor to E., testifying to the serpent-worship of the Gonds with their Nagbansi or serpent-descended chiefs) is bounded E. by Bhandara, N. by Chindwara and Seoni, W. by Berar, and S.W. by Wardha. It is an irregular triangle, with the base resting on Bhandara and apex on Berar Area, 3786 sq. m. Population (1872), 631,109. Three hill ranges occur, spurs of the Satpooras; one chain forms the N. border; a second, the S.W., rises to **Kharki** hill (2000 ft.), and the third runs between the two from N. to S., culminating in **Pilkapar** (1899 ft.), and dividing the district into two unequal plains. The W. plain slopes to the Wardha river, which separates it from E. Berar, and is watered by its affluents the **Jam** and **Madár.** The larger E. plain slopes to the Waenganga, which receives the **Kanhán,** swollen by its tributaries the Pench, Kolar, Wana, Soor, and Bor; to S.E. are the isolated **Haldolee hills** (1300 ft.), and N.E. **Seetapahar** (1433 ft.), in Ramtek, with fort and temples curving round a lake and groves. The district belonged to the Gond kingdom of Deogarh, whose greatest sovereign, Bakht Buland, founded its capital (A.D. 1700), and the widow of whose son called in Raghoji Bhonsla from Berar, who gradually reduced all Deogarh. After Assye and Argaon Raghoji II. received a British Resident; the orientalist, H. T. Colebrooke, had previously resided two years at Nagpoor on a political mission. Under Apa Sahib, his usurping nephew, the Resident was besieged on Seetabaldi hill in 1817; Apa Sahib fled, and the country was administered till 1830 when Raghoji III. came of age. It lapsed to the paramount power in 1853. In June 1857 the mutiny of the irregular cavalry was prevented by timely intelligence given through Rev. S. Hislop, Free Church Missionary. **Nagpoor** (90,000), on the Nag stream, capital of the Central Province, 520 m. N.E. of Bombay. On N. and W. is the suburb and civil station of **Seetabaldi,** with Takli, prettily wooded and surrounded by gardens and tanks; in the centre is the hill with fort. The old Residency, where the Chief Commissioner lives, is in extensive grounds. Headquarters of Scottish Free Church Mission in civil station, and native city; also at Kamthi and Bhandara. The Nakarkhana gate marks the site of the Bhonsla palace, burned down in 1864, with its fine black basalt, profusely ornamented with wood-carving. The cruciform tomb of the great Raghoji, and those of the other Bhonslas, and also the Gonds, are in the Sukrawari quarter to S. of city. **Kamthi** (52,000), cantonment and town, 9 m. N.E. of Nagpoor, on right bank of Kanhan river, below its junction with the Pench and Kolar, covering 7 sq. m.; a first-class brigade command under Madras, and a prosperous mart since its establishment by General Adams in 1821. **Umrer** (12,000), 28 m. S.E. of Nagpoor, sloping to the Amb stream, noted for its manufactures of very fine cotton cloth with silk embroidery. **Khapa** (8500), on right bank of Kanhan, 20 m. N. of Nagpoor, a wealthy mart. **Narkher** (7200), agricultural town among groves, 25 m. from Nagpoor on Betool road. **Ramtek** (7500), 24 m. N. of Nagpoor, with famous shrine of Rama on hill and town at base. **Mohpa** (5700), garden town, 20 m. from Nagpoor, on left bank of Chandrabagh. **Saoner** (5500), 24 m. N.W. of Nagpoor, on the Kolar, old and still prosperous town belonging to the present Gond Raja. **Bela** (5200), on the Wana, 3 m. from Wardha border, with cloth manufactures. **Kalmeswar** (5000), 14 m. W. of Nagpoor, a flourishing town.

§ 7. BHANDARA DISTRICT is bounded E. by Raipoor, N. by Balaghat and Seoni, W. by Nagpoor, and S. by Chanda. Area, 3922 sq. m. Population, 680,000. This district is an open plain, stretching from the Waenganga on W. to the hills which shut it in on N. and E. Small forest-clad ranges run S. from the Satpoora chain. The **Ambagarh** or Sendurjhari hills (400 ft.) skirt S. of Chandpoor. Isolated granite rocks are the Balahi, Kanheri, and Nawegaon hills. The Bawanthari, Bagh, Kanhan, and Chulban streams fall into the Waenganga. This is the lake region of the Province; Nawegaon, Seoni, and Soregaon are the chief of 3648 tanks and sheets of water dammed off in hollows across the slopes, and used for irrigation. The inhabitants are noted for discourtesy and loose morality. Phallic worship is universal; near Murmari village the tomb of an English lady is venerated. **Bhandara** (12,500), chief town and railway station, on the Waenganga, close to the great eastern road, 39 m. E. of Nagpoor, with brass manufactures; seat of Scottish Free Church Mission. **Toomsar** (7500), railway station, 53 m. E. of Nagpoor, on an affluent of the Waenganga, grain entrepôt in fine mango groves. **Pauni** (9000), enclosed town, 32 m. S. of Bhandara, old and decaying place, known for its cloth. **Mohari** (6000), on the Sur, 10 m. N. of Bhandara, with cloth manufactures.

§ 8. CHANDA DISTRICT is bounded E. by Godavari district and Jaipoor State of Madras Province; N. by Bhandara, Nagpoor, and Wardha; W. by Wardha and the Pranheeta dividing it from Berar and Haidarabad State; and S. by the Godavari dividing it from Haidarabad. Area, 10,785 sq. m. Population (1872), 558,856. The district rises from low lands on the Wardha in

W. into hills isolated over ranges running S., and into a broad tableland (2000 ft.) E. of the Waenganga. Farther to S.E., in what was at one time the Upper Godavari district, the hills rise into **Gadulgatta range** (3285 ft.) of the **Eastern Ghats**, locally known as the **Marmedee hills** (4048), which form the Madras boundary. The Sironcha hills (1822 ft.), 18 m. from town of same name, were at one time tried as a sanitarium. The most noticeable ranges in the broad tableland of Chanda proper are those of Virgaon, Ambagarh, Panabáras, Kotgal, Koracha, Muramgaon, Dhanora, Aundhi, Khutgaon, Jarondi, Bhamragarh, Chimoor, and Mool; and the hills Tepagarh, Surjagarh, Perzagarh, and Dewalmaree. From N. to S. the district is rich in iron ores; gold is found in the sand of hill streams, and diamonds and rubies were once obtained in mines near Wairagarh. The coal deposits have been described (p. 323). Fine teak forests cover the hills, and rise to a great height on E. frontier. Lakes abound, made by closing the outlets of small valleys; 37 can be seen from Perzagarh heights. Cave temples are found at Bhandak, Winjbasani, Dewala, and Ghrigoos; in the Wardha bed is a rock-temple, below Ballapoor. The principal rivers flowing S.E. to the Godavari are the Waenganga and Wardha, forming at Seoni the Pranheeta, the Indravati and Talper, the Sabari and Seleru. The Mahanadi carries off the drainage of the eastern regions to Orissa. The Gond dynasty did much to civilise the people till Nilkaut Shah, the last, outraged them, and the Maratha Raghoji Bhonsla, in 1749, seized the country. In 1818 a British army took Chanda from the treacherous Apa Sahib, and prosperity was restored for a time. In 1858 two petty chiefs revolted and slew two telegraph officials. The chief town **Chanda** (18,000), with walls 5½ m. in circumference, is beautifully situated between the Jharpat and Virai, amid charming scenery, and is remarkable for the walls, waterworks, citadel, monoliths, and tombs of the Gond kings. The civil station is N. of the city, with the cantonment to W. Here is a Propagation Society's Mission. **Armori** (5500), on left bank of Waenganga, 80 m. N.E. of Chanda, a weaving and forest mart. **Warora**, 32 m. N.W. of Chanda and 12 N. of Woon in Berar, the chief colliery centre and terminus of the Wardha Coal State Railway, 45 m. from Wardha. **Sironcha** (1300), pleasantly placed on the left bank of the Pranheeta, 2 m. above its confluence with the Godavari, created since 1860; with fine oranges and fruits.

§ 9. WARDHA DISTRICT is bounded E. by Nagpoor, N. and W. by the Wardha river separating it from Berar, and S. by

Chanda. Area, 2401 sq. m. Population (1872), 354,720. The N. is hilly from a spur of the Satpooras; the S. is an undulating plain, broken by isolated hills. The central cluster of hills includes the survey stations of **Malegaon** (1726 ft.), **Nandgaon** (1874 ft.), and **Garamsoor** (2086 ft.), forming the watershed. The passes from Berar to Nagpoor are Talegaon, Chicholi, Dhamkoond, and Thanegaon. The district is named from its only great river, the **Wardha**, of which the **Wana** and **Bakli** are tributaries. The country is famous for trotting bullocks, and for a fine breed of buffaloes. It produces the best cotton next to the acclimatised New Orleans of the S. Maratha country. The Great Indian Peninsula Railway crosses the district, and sends off a coal branch to Warora in Chanda from the chief town **Wardha** (3800), built since 1866, 49 m. W. of Nagpoor. **Hinganghat** (10,000), chief cotton mart in Central India, centre of the Wardha valley cotton, and that of Edalabad in Paenganga valley, a railway station 21 m. S.E. of Wardha. **Arvi** (8000), mart, 34 m. N.W. of Wardha. **Deoli** (6000), large cotton mart, 11 m. S.W. of Wardha, held by the representative of the Bhonslas. Sindi (4500), railway station, 20 m. E. of Wardha. Ashti (4500), 52 m. N.W. of Wardha, with two fine mausolea of Afghan nobles.

§ 10. BALAGHAT DISTRICT is bounded E. by the Kawarda and Khairagarh States, N. by Mandla, W. by Seoni and Bhandara, S. by Raipoor. Area, 3141 sq. m., chiefly waste. Population (1872), 302,482. A highland plateau, shut against progress till 1866, when the peasantry of the Waenganga valley were encouraged to bring its wastes under the plough. Above Lanji the peaks rise to 2500 and 3000 ft.; the **Tepagarh** hill and **Bainsaghat Range** are the chief. The Waenganga's tributaries are the Bagh, Nahara, and Uskal; the Narbada's are the Banjar, Halon, and Jamoonia. The forests of teak, sal, and bamboo are extensive; especially the great sal reserve of **Topla** in N.E. corner. Iron and mica are worked by the Gonds. There are five principal passes. The administrative headquarters is **Burha**, a mile from the Waenganga and 10 m. N. of **Hatta** (3000), centre of cultivated plain of same name, with Gond fort 80 m. N.E. of Bhandara. **Lanji** (2500), 40 m. E. of Burha, named from a shrine of the goddess Kali.

§ 11. RAIPOOR DISTRICT, principal portion of the S.E. or Chatteesgarh division and largest district of the Central Province, is bounded E. by Sambalpoor, N. by Bilaspoor, W. by Balaghat and Chanda, S. by Bastar State. Area, 11,885 sq. m. Population, 1,400,000. This is the basin of the Upper

Mahanadi, surrounded by ranges branching from the Vindhyan chain. The **Mahanadi**, or stream so called in Raipoor, rises from "an insignificant puddle in a rice field" in S.E. near Seháwa town, flows W. for 30 m., then N.E. and N. till its junction in N.E. corner with the much larger **Seonath** from the hills of Panabaras in Chanda, which receives on the right bank in Raipoor the Gurnaria, Am, Soori, Garaghat, Ghogwa, and Hamp, and on the left, the Karkara, Tendoola, Karoon, and Khorsi. Before its junction the Mahanadi receives the Pairi and its Sundar affluent, the Kesho, Korar, and Naini. The chief town is **Raipoor** (19,500), on a plateau (950 ft.) 180 m. E. of Nagpoor on the advancing line of railway by Sambalpoor to Calcutta, with old fort and many tanks, centre of grain trade, military station, and seat of a Christian Mission among the casteless Satnami reformers of Hindooism. **Dhaintari** (6500), 36 m. S. of Raipoor, centre of rich grain and cotton tracts and of the lac trade. **Rajeein** (3000), 24 m. S.E. of Raipoor on right bank of Mahanadi at its junction with the Pairi, a pretty little town named from a temple which attracts thousands of pilgrims in April.

§ 12. BILASPOOR DISTRICT is bounded E. by Sambalpoor and Oodaipoor estate of Chutia Nagpoor, N. by Koria and Sirgooja chiefships of Chutia Nagpoor and by Sohagpoor portion of Rewah State, W. by Mandla and Balaghat highlands, and S. by the plain of Raipoor. Area, 7798 sq. m. Population, 1,000,000. This district is surrounded on all sides save to S. by branches of the sandstone range of the Vindhyas. The W. branch, or **Maikal Range**, runs S.W. from Amarkantak, just outside the district in Rewah State, to the Saletekri range in Bhandara. On E. the **Korba Hills** run S. into Sambalpoor, and after the break of the Mahanadi are continued by the **Sonakhan Hills**. From the isolated **Dahla Hill** (2600 ft.), 15 m. E. of Bilaspoor town, the expanse of plain in an amphitheatre of hills is best seen. The Mahanadi flows through the S.E. extremity for 25 m. The **Son** rises in a marshy hollow in Pendra. The Narbada rushes picturesquely over rocky heights from Amarkantak. Minor streams are the Sakri, Hamp, Teswá, Agar, Maniári, Arpa, Kharod, Leelagar, Jonk, and Barei. Waste lands abound. Hathibari is the State teak-reserve. In the N., especially in Mateen and Uprora estates and on the wooded slopes of the Hasdoo stream, wild elephants roam over the Vindhyan forests. Tanks are scattered near every village, more than 7000 in number. Bilaspoor was the centre of the 36 forts which give Chatteesgarh its name, till 750 A.D., when the country was divided into two kingdoms under the Haihai Bansi kings, of which the capitals were Ratanpoor and Raipoor. **Bilaspoor** (5000), chief town, pleasantly placed on S. bank of the Arpa, named from Bilasa, its fisher founder. **Ratanpoor** (5500), 12 m. N. of Bilaspoor, old Haihai capital, whence the Hindoos spread, covering 15 sq. m. of tanks and groves, temples and tombs, in a hollow at the base of the Kenda offshoots of the Vindhyas. **Mungeli** (4500), on the Agar, 36 m. W. of Bilaspoor on the Jabalpoor road.

§ 13. SAMBALPOOR DISTRICT is bounded on S. and E. by Cuttak, N. by Chutia Nagpoor, and W. by Bilaspoor and Raipoor. Area, 4407 sq. m. Population, 690,000. Sambalpoor district lies along the Mahanadi, and is surrounded by Feudatory States; it is an undulating plain surrounded by rugged hill ranges, of which the **Bara Pahar** (2267 ft. at Debreegarh) in N. is the largest, as its name signifies, covering 350 sq. m.; here the rebel Soorendra Sa escaped for some years after the Mutiny. At **Singhora Ghat**, through which the Raipoor and Sambalpoor road winds, Gonds, Marathas, and British have often fought. **Jarghati Range** (1693) crosses the Chutia Nagpoor road 20 m. N. of Sambalpoor. Of the S. ranges parallel with the Mahanadi, the heights are **Mandhar** (1563 ft.) and Bodapali (2331 ft.). The principal isolated hills are Sunari, Chela, and Rosora. The Mahanadi flows E. and S.E. through the district for 90 m.; its tributaries are the Ib, Keloo, and Jheera. Gold dust and diamonds have been found near Heerakhuda, or diamond island, at the junction of the Ib and Mahanadi. In 1849 Sambalpoor lapsed to the British; excessive land-tax led to Soorendra Sa's rebellion from 1857 to 1864. **Sambalpoor** (11,000) is the only town with above 5000, on N. bank of Mahanadi, with ruined fort to N.W.; on the Jagannath pilgrim route, by which trade is chiefly with Orissa.

§ 14. MANDLA DISTRICT is bounded N.E. by Rewah, S.E. by Bilaspoor, S.W. by Balaghat, and W. by Seoni and Jabalpoor. Area, 4719 sq. m. Population (1872), 213,018, largely of aboriginal Baigas and Gonds, in the two classes of Raj-Gonds and Rawan Bansis, subdivided into 42 castes. From W. to E. the district is a series of steppes rising to the **Maikal Hills** on S.E. border. These culminate in **Chauradadar** (3450 ft.), hill and plateau of 6 sq. m., 12 m. W. of the similar but prettier Amarkantak bluff in Rewah. The Shahpoor section of the Maikal range, N. of the Narbada and overlooking the **Johila** affluent of the **Son**, forms part of the watershed of

E. and W. India; the Johila flows E., receiving the Ganjar and Ganjari, after falls of 60 ft., near vast caves of unknown extent, and other streams flow W. to the Narbada, of which the Banjar and Halon are chief. **Mandla** (5000) (1770 ft.), 59 m. S.E. of Jabalpoor, surrounded on three sides by the Narbada, old capital of Garha-Mandla line of Gond Rajas, taken from the Marathas in 1818 by General Marshall. Has manufactures of bell-metal from zinc and copper. Bahmani (2000), a village on the Seoni road. Shahpoora village, 50 m. E. of Jabalpoor, in Ramgarh subdivision.

§ 15. SEONI DISTRICT is bounded E. by Mandla and Balaghat, N. by Mandla and Jabalpoor, W. by Narsingpoor and Chindwara, and S. by Nagpoor and Bhandara. Area, 3252 sq. m. Population (1872), 299,850. One of the most beautiful, temperate, and fertile districts in the Satpoora range, consisting of (1) plateau of **Lakhnadon** in N., between the **Sher** and **Banganga**; (2) plateau of Seoni in W., between the **Pench** and **Ganga**; (3) E. watershed of the Banganga and its affluents, the Nahra and Uskal; (4) **Dongartal**, rocky pasture-ground on S.W., running E. into Katangi valley, which supports a dense population. The fertile soil is fed by a rainfall of 61 inches a year. It was a portion of the Garha-Mandla kingdom of the Gonds, whose forts and ruined towns are found, especially at Ghansor, 20 m. N.E. of **Seoni** (10,000), chief town, half-way on the road between Nagpoor and Jabalpoor, with public gardens, market-place, and tank; seat of Mission of Scottish Original Secession Church. Chapára, 22 m. N.E. of Seoni, formerly chief town, now decaying.

§ 16. JABALPOOR DISTRICT is bounded E. by Rewah; N. by Maiheer and Panna; W. by Damoh; and S. by Narsingpoor, Seoni, and Mandla. Area, 3918 sq. m. Population, 680,000. A long plain of rich soil surrounded by Satpoora spurs on S., by **Bhanrér** and **Kaimor** hills on N. and W., and by the **Bhitreegarh** hills on E., and watered by the Narbada, Paret, and Heeran. Travellers from Jabalpoor N.W. to Mirzapoor cross the greatest watershed between the Gulf of Kambay and Bay of Bengal. The **Mandla-Mahanadi** (not the greater river of Chatteesgarh-Orissa) flows hence to the Son. The Narbada flows through the district E. to W. for 70 m. Coal and iron are found, and are workable at Lameta. The district was part of the Garha-Mandla kingdom of the Gonds. **Jabalpoor** (56,000), chief town and cantonment (1458 ft.), named Javalipattana in old inscriptions, junction of Great Indian Peninsula and East Indian Railway systems, 221 m. S.W. of Allahabad,

616 from Bombay, and 165 N.E. of Nagpoor; prettily laid out, surrounded by lakes and gardens, with high school, Thug and Dacoit school of industry famous for tents and carpets, and mission of Church Missionary Society. Nine m. S.W. down the Narbada at **Bheraghat** is the Dhuan-dhar ("misty shoot") or **Marble Rocks**, where the Narbada, confined to 100 yards, falls 30 ft. and flows for nearly 2 m. through beautiful saccharine white limestone, on each side of which marble bluffs rise for 120 ft. **Garha** (3000), old Gond capital, with ancient keep, the Madan Mahal, crowning the low granite range above, 200 m. S.W. of Allahabad. **Panagar** (3000), centre of iron manufacture, 9 m. from Jabalpoor on N. road. **Murwara** (3000), 57 m. N.E. of Jabalpoor on road to Mirzapoor. **Katangi** (3000), old village at foot of Bhanrer hills, 22 m. N.W. of Jabalpoor. **Sihora** (4500), grain mart, 27 m. from Jabalpoor on road to Mirzapoor. **Sleemanabad**, railway station, 40 m. N.E. of Jabalpoor, founded by Sir W. Sleeman. **Balihri**, 15 m. N. of Sleemanabad, old town, now in ruins but still famous for the pan-leaf cultivation, which gives it its name.

§ 17. Damoh District, forming with Sagar the Vindhyan plateau in N.W. corner of the Central Province, is bounded E. by Panna and Jabalpoor, N. by Panna and Chatrapoor, W. by Panna and Sagar, and S. by Narsingpoor and Jabalpoor. Area, 2799 sq. m. Population (1872), 269,642. On E. the low **Bhondla** hills pass into the **Bhanrer**. On W. the **Vindhyachal** hills form a picturesque country. The rivers flow N. to the Jumna: the **Sonar** and **Bairma** traverse the whole length of the district, receiving the Bias, Kopra, Guvaya, and other streams; the united rivers, after receiving the Ken from Boondelkhand, reach the Jumna. The country was successively under the Chandel Rajpoots of Mahoba in Boondelkhand, who administered it from Balihri in Jabalpoor, the Gonds, Mughuls, Chattersal and Marathas till 1818. **Damoh** (8500), chief town nearly midway on Jabalpoor and Sagar road, 45 m. E. of the latter. **Hatta** (6700), former headquarters, on right bank of Sunar, 24 m. N. of Damoh, with fort and manufactures of red cloth. **Hindoria** (3500), 9 m. N.E. of Damoh; in 1857 the villagers burned the public offices and records of Damoh. Raneh (2700), 21 m. N.E. of Damoh, with cotton manufactures.

§ 18. Sagar District is bounded E. by Damoh and Panna, N. by Lalitpoor and Boondela States, W. by Gwalior and Bhopal, and S. by Bhopal and Narsingpoor. Area, 4005 sq. m. Population (1872), 527,725. From the Bhanrer scarp, above the Narbada, the district slopes N.E. to the Vindhyas. The

Sonar, Bias, Dhupan, and **Bina** are the chief streams, all of which flow N. to the Jumna. The **Ramna** teak forest preserve in N. is the largest. Iron is found near Heerapoor village in N.E. The district has been held by the Mandla Gonds, the shepherd Baladeos with Rehli as their centre, the Boondela Chatar Sal, and the Marathas till 1818. In 1857 the Europeans were shut up by mutinous sepoys and rebel Rajas in Sagar fort for 8 months till relieved by Sir Hugh Rose's Central India Field Force. **Sagar** (46,000), chief town, fort, and cantonment, named from fine oval lake, 4 m. in circumference, on N.W. border of which it stands (1940 ft.), a large mart, well built, with high school and Swedish mission, said to be the Sageda of Ptolemy; 109 m. N.W. of Jabalpoor; Kareli is the railway station. **Garhakota** (9000), 27 m. E. of Sagar on angle formed by the Sonar and Gadhairi, with fort held by Baptiste for Sindia; breached by Sir Hugh Rose in 1858; the trade is in Hirdenagar suburb on E. bank of the Sonar; 2 m. N. are the ruins of summer palace and also a residence built by Sir Herbert Maddock, beside the Ramna forest. **Rehli** (4500), 28 m. S.E. of Sagar, for which it is a sanitarium (1350 ft.), with fort; a sugar mart and old centre of Gond, Baladeo, and Boondela rule. **Kurai** (5000), 32 m. N.W. of Sagar, well built; great cattle and meat market for British cantonments. **Deori** (2700), 37 m. S. of Sagar on Narsingpoor road, an agricultural centre.

§ 19. NARSINGPOOR DISTRICT is bounded E. by Seoni; N. by Jabalpoor, Damoh, Sagar, and Bhopal; W. by Hoshangabad; and S. by Chindwara and Seoni. Area, 1916 sq. m. Population (1872), 339,395. This district forms the upper half of the Narbada valley; an alluvial basin, originally a lake, opening out just below the Marble Rocks, and extending 225 m. to Handia in Hoshangabad, overlooked by the low Satpoora range on S. and the abrupt scarp of the Vindhyas on N. The **Sher** and **Shakar** are the affluents of the Narbada from the Satpooras on S. The Doodhi separates Narsingpoor from Hoshangabad; the Baroo-Rewa and Soner are other minor streams. The Garha-Mandla Gond Rajas ruled the land from the vast **Chauragarh** fort, on the outer range of the Satpooras. After the Maratha rule from Sagar, the fort was evacuated in 1817 by Apa Sahib's troops on the approach of General Wilson's left division. Here Sir W. Sleeman did good work. The iron and coal deposits are extensive and valuable. **Narsingpoor** (12,500), with Kandeli, chief town on W. bank of Singri, named from the Narsingha descent of Vishnoo, railway station

564 m. from Bombay, grain and cotton mart, seat of Swedish mission. **Gadarwara** (6000), on left bank of the Shakar, mart and railway station, 28 m. S.W. of Narsingpoor at junction of roads to Jabalpoor and Sagar. Singpoor (3000), 6 m. S. of Narsingpoor ; Kauria (3000), 2 m. from Gadarwara ; Tendukhera (3000), 22 m. N.W. of Narsingpoor, local marts. **Mohpani**, 11 m. from Gadarwara station, to which there is a railway, and 95 S.W. of Jabalpoor ; coal successfully worked by Nerbudda Coal and Iron Company ; output in 1879 = 13,491 tons.

§ 20. CHINDWARA DISTRICT is bounded E. by Seoni, N. and N.W. by Narsingpoor and Hoshangabad, W. by Betool, S.W. by Berar, and S. by Nagpoor. Area, 3853 sq. m. Population (1872), 316,095. The highland or N. region on the Satpoora range is named Balaghat, and descends by terraces through the Silawani pass to the Zeraghat or lowlands of the Nagpoor plain. The S. slopes of the Satpooras are covered with fine forests. The **Kanhan** is the largest of the streams, along which are strips of verdure and villages in mango groves. At Barkoi in 1852 the Rev. S. Hislop first discovered coal ; there are many seams in the bed of the Pench. At Mahaljheer, on E. of **Mahadeo hills**, is a hot spring. This is largely a Gond district ; its elevation above 2000 ft. causes it to be frequented by the European residents in the lowlands in the hot season. **Chindwara** (9200), chief town (2200 ft.), on the Bodri affluent of the Kolbeera, which falls into the Pench 76 m. N. of Nagpoor, with public garden and Scottish Free Church mission. **Lodhikhera** (5500), on the Jam, 38 m. S. of Chindwara, a rich mart. **Pandhurna** (5500), agricultural centre, 58 m. S.W. of Chindwara. **Mohgaon** (5500), municipal town on tributary of the Jam, 38 m. S. of Chindwara. **Deogarh**, now a village in the hills 24 m. S.W. of Chindwara, the picturesque old capital of the midland Gond kingdom, with fine limestone ruins.

§ 21. HOSHANGABAD DISTRICT is divided on E. from Narsingpoor by the Doodhi ; on N. from the Bhopal, Sindia's, and Holkar's States by the Narbada ; on W. from Nimar by its Tawa affluent and the Gulee tributary of the Tapti ; and S. by Berar, Betool, and Chindwara. The district is a long valley on the left bank of the Narbada for 150 m., and running up S. into the Satpooras at four places, the **Mahadeo hills** and the Malini, Rajaborari, and Kalibheet *talooks*. West of Handia the Vindhyas throw out the **Bairi hills**, which the Satpooras almost touch. Area, 4376 sq. m. Population (1872), 449,977. The Denwa and Bori are the finest forest reserves, and teak is common. Besides the great boundary streams, the Narbada and Tapti, the chief rivers are the Anjan, Tawá, Hathir, Denwa, Ganjal, Moran, and Doodhi. The **Pachmarhi plateau** (3538 ft.), guarded by the Chauradeo, Jata, and Dhoopgarh hills, of the Mahadeo group, with a rainfall of 82 inches, is "one of the greenest, softest, and most lovely of sanitaria that exist in India;" Piparia is the railway station. **Hoshangabad** (12,000), chief town, on S. side of Narbada, founded by Hoshang Shah, second of the Ghori kings of Malwa (1405 A.D.), conquered by Bhopal in 1720. Military station (1009 ft.), with railway to Itarsi and Bhopal. **Harda** (9000), which has supplanted old Handia 12 m. off, Sir John Malcolm's headquarters in 1817; railway station. **Sioni** (8000), chief cotton and grain mart and railway station in Narbada valley. **Sohagpoor** (7500), old Muhammadan town and railway station, 30 m. E. of Hoshangabad.

§ 22. BETOOL DISTRICT, W. section of great Satpoora plateau, is bounded E. by Chindwara, N. by Hoshangabad, W. by Berar, and S. by Berar and Nagpoor. Area, 3905 sq. m. Population (1872), 274,264. Save on the W., where is the deep valley of the **Tapti**, abrupt lines of stony hills shut in a level basin of rich soil, watered by the **Machna** and **Sampna**, and with the chief town in its centre. To S. is a rolling plateau of basalt, with the sacred town of **Multai** (3500) and the springs of the Tapti at its highest point. In S.W. corner is the high-level plateau on **Khamba hill** (3700 ft.), forming part of a range which adjoins the Chikalda and Gawilgarh hills in Berar, almost above the hot winds. **Betool** (4700), on the Sampna, with manufactures of pottery; from this the headquarters were removed to **Badnoor** (3000), on the Machna; not far off is Kherla, old capital of the Gond Rajas, with fort in ruins.

§ 23. NIMAR DISTRICT, most W. of the Central Province, is bounded E. by Hoshangabad, N. and W. by Holkar's and Dhar States, S. by Khandesh and Berar. Area, 3340 sq. m. Population (1872), 211,176. On N. it was the W. portion of the old Hindoo subdivision, Prant Nimar; on S. it belonged to the Hindoo Talner or Muhammadan Khandesh. It consists of two river valleys divided by a central range, on the crest of which (2300) stands the border fort of **Aseergarh**, 29½ m. S.W. of Khandwa, the chief highway between Upper India and the Dekhan. The **Hattees** (3000 ft.) watershed, a continuation of the Gawilgarh hills of Berar, marks the S. boundary. In N. the Sukta, Abna, Wana, Bham, Baldi, and Phiprar unite in the **Chota Tawa**, which falls into the Narbada; the other affluents are the Ajnal,

Kavari, and Bakoor. Iron and limestone abound. The history centres round Aseergarh, held by Chauhan Rajpoots after the Haihai kings of Maheswar and Brahmans of Mandhata. The Malwa Muhammadans succeeded (1387), then the Farukhi dynasty of Khandesh, till Akbar's conquest (1600). Maratha devastation was stopped by the British peace in 1818, and here the last of the Peshwas surrendered to Malcolm; here previously the Pindaree leader Cheetoo had been killed by a tiger. In 1858 Tatia Topi plundered the district, but the people remained quiet. **Khandwa** (14,500), district capital and railway junction for Indore and Ajmer, named from its 4 *kunds* or water reservoirs, with fine Jain ruins. **Boorhanpoor** (29,000), on N. bank of Tapti, 40 m. S.W. of Khandwa, named from a famous sheikh of Daulatabad by its founder in 1400, the first Farukhi king. Capital of Dekhan princes of the Mughul empire, described by Sir T. Roe (in 1614), who visited Jahangeer's son, the Governor, and by Tavernier (in 1641); taken by Wellington in 1803, now a decaying place, surrounded by brick walls 5½ m., with only one tomb worth a visit, that of Shah Nawaz Khan, whose daughter Shah Jahan married. Next to Surat, a chief place of the Bohora Musalman traders of Goojarat. **Mandhata Island**, on the Narbada, a central shrine of Shiva under the form of Omkar (Om), to which the local Brahmans expect the sanctity of the Ganges will be transferred at the beginning of the 20th century.

Fifteen States.

§ 24. *BASTAR STATE is the largest and (with Makrai) most isolated of the 15 Feudatory States of the Central Province, all of which are "protected" and controlled by the Chief Commissioner, to whose confirmation the orders of the chiefs are subject in matters of life and death. The other 13 States are in the division of Chatteesgarh. Bastar, controlled from Chanda, is bounded E. by the Jaipoor State of Madras, N. by Raipoor, W. by the S. parts of Chanda from which it is separated by the Indrawati. Area, 13,062 sq. m. Population, 190,000, chiefly Gonds. The Raja's house claims to be purely Rajpoot, driven from Warangal, capital of Telingana kingdom, in the Dekhan. His gross revenue is £9213, and he pays £305 tribute. The E. is an elevated plateau (2000 ft.), yielding rich crops. In N.W. a lofty range divides Bastar from Sironcha. In the centre is the **Bela Deela** range, named from a peak resembling a bullock's hump; a third range runs N. and S. near Narainpoor; the **Tangri Dongri** runs E. and W., and the **Toolsi Dongri** parallel to that and S. A small range runs N. and S. from Kutru on the Indravati to Doomagoodiem on the Godavari, where it forms the first river barrier. The Indravati, Sabari, and Tal flow into the Godavari. The State yields rice, oil-seeds, silk cocoons, and forest products; it has some iron; it sends teak timber to the E. coast. **Jagdalpoor**, only town with more than 1000, and Raja's residence on left bank of Indravati, 180 m. E. of Sironcha, and 40 from Jaipoor in Madras, subject to Vizagapatam. **Dantiwara**, shrine of Kali, under the name of Danteswari or Mauli, at confluence of the Sankani and Dankani, where Meriah or human sacrifices used to be offered.

§ 25. *KALAHANDI, OR KAROND, AND MAKRAI STATES.—Kalahandi is attached to Sambalpoor, between which and Patna State on N., Jaipoor on E. and S., and Bastar on W., it lies. Area, 3745 sq. m. Population, 100,000. Lying near the foot of the main line of the **Eastern Ghats**, and sharing the watersheds of both the Mahanadi and Indravati, it is well watered. **Nyangiri**, near Lanjigarh, is the highest point. The Hatti river feeds the Tel, which falls into the Narbada. The Raja is a Rajpoot, with £8000 gross revenue. His capital is **Bhowani Patna**, a flourishing plaçe, with extensive gardens. The former capital and chief town is **Joonagarh**, on the Hatti, 210 m. S.E. of Raipoor. Bhundesar is 20 m. N.E. of that, and Dadpoor 30 m. N.E. Other towns are Asurgarh, on a tributary of the Tel; Lanjigarh, at base of the Nyangiri hills in S.E.; and Kasipoor, in extreme S.

Makrai, in the Harda subdivision of Hoshangabad, has an area of 215 sq. m., with 92 villages, under a Gond Raja, who lives in an insignificant fort and village of the same name.

§ 26. *TWELVE CHATTEESGARH STATES.—**Patna**, under Sambalpoor (area, 2399 sq. m.), N. of Karond, watered by the Tel, Ong, Suktel, and Sundar, formerly head of the 18 Garjhat States. The Raja is a Rajpoot; the capital of same name is near the centre of the State. **Sarangarh**, on S. bank of Mahanadi, cut off from Sambalpoor on E. and S. by hills, under a Raj-Gond family of long pedigree. Area, 540 sq. m. **Raigarh Bargarh**, under Sambalpoor, between which and Chutia Nagpoor it lies. Area, 1486 sq. m.; under a Gond Raja. At Raigarh there is a school. **Sonpoor**, through which an important trade route passes from Raipoor and Sambalpoor at Sohela to the E. coast, on right bank of Mahanadi. Area, 906 sq. m.; under a Rajpoot family. **Rerakhol**, through which S. road passes from Sambalpoor to Cuttak *viâ* Angool. Area, 833 sq. m.; under a Rajpoot family. **Bamra**, N. of the above, with old road to Calcutta from W. to

E. Area, 1988 sq. m.; under a Rajpoot family. The Brahmani drains the State to False Point. Iron abounds. **Sakti**, under Bilaspoor district, skirting the base of the Gunji hills. Area, 115 sq. m.; under a Gond Raja. **Kawarda**, also under Bilaspoor, consists of Chilpi hills on W. Area, 912 sq. m.; under a Gond Raja. **Chinkhadan** or Kondka, under Raipoor district, N. of Kairagarh, at foot of Salétekri hill. Area, 174 sq. m.; under a chief of the Bairagi sect allowed to marry. **Kanker**, S. of Raipoor, in Upper Mahanadi valley. Area, 639 sq. m.; under an old Rajpoot family. **Nandgaon**, chief village of which is on great eastern road, 42 m. W. of Raipoor, stretching S. from the Salétekri hill. Area, 905 sq. m.; under a Bairagi or religious devotee, who adopts his successor.

CHAPTER XIX.

BERAR PROVINCE.

§ 1. Size and Position. § 2. Mountains, Rivers, and Resources. § 3. Land Tenures and Taxation. § 4. The People and Districts.

East Berar.

§ 5. Amraoti. § 6. Ellichpoor. § 7. Woon.

West Berar.

§ 8. Akola. § 9. Booldana. § 10. Basim.

§ 1. Size.—**Berar**, or Warar, is so named as the country separated by the Wardha from Nagpoor or the Central Province to the W. It consists of East and West Berar in six districts assigned by the previously insolvent Nizam of Haidarabad in 1853 and again in 1860 to the British Government, to yield £320,000 for the maintenance of a contingent or auxiliary force kept up for the use of His Highness, and to relieve him from the unlimited obligation of service in time of war. British administration has so increased the revenue of these Assigned Districts, that a surplus has since been paid to the Nizam of upwards of a million sterling. The Province is administered by the Government of India in a way similar to its management of Ajmer-Merwara, by a Commissioner who reports to the Resident at Haidarabad, as Chief Commissioner, or "Local Government, without any reference to His Highness the Nizam at all." The virtually British Province of Berar lies between 19° 26′ and 21° 46′ N. lat., and between 75° 58′ 45″ and 79° 11′ 13″ E. long. It is bounded by the Central Province on E. and N., by Bombay on W., and by Haidarabad State on S. It has an area of 17,728 sq. m. and a population of 2,672,673, an increase of 20 per cent in the fourteen years ending 1880. Berar is thus larger than Switzerland, and is the size of Greece before

1864, with nearly twice the population. In the thirty years since Brigadier Colin Mackenzie, C.B., took over the districts "without losing a rupee of revenue, or spilling a drop of blood," as Lord Dalhousie wrote, orderly administration has doubled their population, revenue; and prosperity. A department of public instruction has opened many schools, connected with the University of Bombay, and the Scottish Free Church has a native mission at the principal capitals.

§ 2. MOUNTAINS, RIVERS, AND RESOURCES.—Berar, officially described as "the very home of the cotton plant, and heart of the cotton trade in India," is a wide undulating valley of black soil running up eastward between the **Gawilgarh hills** (4200 ft.) of the sevenfold Satpoora chain on N., with a deep indent made by the **Mel-Ghat** tract, and the **Ajanta ridge** on S. It varies in breadth from 40 to 50 m., and is broader toward the E. end than at the mouth. The valley is locally known as *Paenghat* or lowlands; the Ajanta country above the passes, the extreme N. limit of the Dekhan plateau, as the *Balaghat* or uplands, which gradually fall S. to Haidarabad. On its most S. plateau, in Booldana district, is the salt lake of **Lonár**, like an enormous crater, with a circumference of 5 m. and depth of 510 ft., worked by Akbar for saltpetre; it is 4 m. N. of the boundary, and is the only crater in the great basaltic district of Central India. The only forest reserves cover 500 sq. m. in the Mel-Ghat tract, and are inhabited by Gond and Koorkoo aborigines. Berar valley is drained by the **Poorna**, into which the outer Gawilgarh hills send down their copious rainfall, and the Ajanta hills send the Kata Poorna; but the inner Gawilgarh highlands drain into the Tapti, of which the Poorna is an affluent. The Tapti forms the N. for a short section, and the Wardha the E. boundary, where also the Aran and Poos are considerable streams. The Paenganga or Pranheeta is the largest river of S. Berar. The staple cereal is Jowar, which occupies 37 per cent of the cultivated area, while cotton covers 29; there is a model farm at Akola. The Province imports 2 millions, and exports 2½ millions sterling worth of produce annually. The Wardha coal-field extends over Woon district, five-sixths of the whole, to the estimated bulk of 2400 millions of tons, of which 1655 millions are available, lying on the west or Berar side of the river at comparatively easy working depth. South of Yeotmahal, in the same district, there is iron ore of great value. The Great Indian Peninsula Railway to Nagpoor opens up the valley from beyond Nargaon station, 295 m. from Bombay, to beyond Poolgaon, 453 m., and has twenty stations in the Province. The Khamgaon State Railway runs S. for 8 m. through the cotton country from Jalamb station, 333 m. from Bombay, to Khamgaon. The Amraoti State Railway runs N. for 6 m. from Badnera, 413 m. from Bombay, to Amraoti.

§ 3. LAND TENURES AND TAXATION.—The Bombay system of survey and settlement according to fields has been adopted in Berar. The whole country is being surveyed, marked off into plots and assessed at rates which hold good for 30 years. The assessment of an entire district or village may be raised or lowered as may seem expedient, but the impost may not be altered to the detriment of any occupant on account of his own improvements. Of the restrictions on this principle some are intended to guard the rights of Government, and to check the tendency to excessive subdivision of land—the chief defect of a peasant proprietary system—and the rest to protect the rights of persons other than the occupant who may have an interest in the holding. First, if an occupant wishes to do anything which will destroy the value of his land, as to quarry in it, he must apply for permission to do so, and pay a fine to compensate Government for the prospective loss of assessment. Secondly, not less than the entire assessment of each field is to be levied. If, consequently, one share of a field is resigned, and the other sharers will not take it up themselves, nor get some one else to do so, the whole field must be resigned. Thirdly, a shared field once resigned must be taken up again as a whole, and no further subdivision of shares, after the settlement is once made, is permitted. An occupant may always resign his holding (or any portion of it, being an entire field or distinct share in one) by simply giving a written notice of his intention before a certain date, which frees him of all liabilities from the current year. When the registered holder alienates his estate, he does it by surrender and admittance, like an English copyholder. Indeed, the Berar occupancy tenure has many features resembling the copyhold estate in the reservations of manorial rights. The occupancy tenures of Berar are thus classified. Land is held—(1) By proprietors who manage each his own plot in his own family. (2) By proprietors working together on the joint-stock or co-operative system. (3) By the *Metairie*—halving the gross produce. (4) By the *Metairie*—halving the net produce. (5) By money rents. (6) By proprietors employing hired labour. Land is now very commonly held on the joint-stock principle. Certain persons agree to contribute shares of cultivating expenses, and to divide the profits in proportion to those shares, that proportion being usually determined by the number of plough-cattle employed by each partner. The gross revenue of Berar was £987,828 in 1880-81, and the surplus payable to the Nizam was £157,093, subject to adjustments. The proportion derived from the land was 64 per cent.

§ 4. THE PEOPLE AND DISTRICTS.—At first, doubtless, under the Chalookya Rajpoots who ruled from Kalyan near Goolbarga (to 1200 A.D.), and then under the Yadavas of Deogarh or Daulatabad, or the Rajpoots at Warangal, Berar had its own sovereigns, who governed from Ellichpoor, named after a Jain Raja Eel, in the brief interval before the Delhi Musalman invasion completed in 1319 by Mubarak Ghilzai. Akbar placed it under his son Danyal, as viceroy, and the Marathas ravaged it after Aurangzeb's death. The three victories of the Mughul viceroy of the Dekhan who became Nizam-ool-Moolk, at Boorhanpoor and Balapoor, and then at Fateh-Khelda in Booldana in 1724, made Berar subject nominally to Haidarabad, till the Nizam pledged it to the British for his debts and feudatory service. Since 1853 it has been virtually a British Province.

The chief executive authority in Berar is the Resident at Haidarabad. He is assisted by a Secretary, a Commissioner, a Judicial Commissioner, a Sanitary Commissioner and Inspector-General of Dispensaries, an Inspector-General of Police, Jails, and Registration, a Director of Public Instruction, and a Deputy-Conservator of Forests.

AREA, POPULATION, AND REVENUE OF THE DISTRICTS—1881.

DISTRICTS.	Judicial and Revenue Subdivisions.	Area in Square Miles.	Population, 1881.	Number of Villages	Total Cost of Officials and Police of all kinds.	REVENUE.	
						Land.	Gross.
					Rs.	Rs.	Rs.
Amraoti .	4	2,759	575,328	1,374	1,04,353	15,75,979	20,20,993
Akola . .	5	2,660	592,792	1,194	94,836	17,88,105	23,87,849
Ellichpoor .	3	2,623	313,805	1,461	51,135	9,18,301	12,25,149
Booldana .	3	2,804	439,763	1,010	74,616	9,47,979	11,51,940
Woon . .	4	3,907	392,102	1,565	74,151	5,13,095	7,87,712
Basim . .	3	2,958	358,883	950	65,956	5,93,563	7,12,832
Total .	22	17,711	2,672,673	7,554	4,65,047	63,37,022	82,86,475

The census of 1881 shows an increase since 1867 of from 30 per cent in Basim to 12½ in Ellichpoor district. Of the whole 2,672,673, the men numbered 899,125; the women, 822,790; male children under twelve, 481,367; female children, 469,391;—in all, 151 to the sq. m. As to creed, 1335 were Christians, of whom 214 were Europeans, 542 Eurasians, and 579 Natives; 2,426,179 were Hindoos; 187,555 were Muhammadans; 242 Parsees; 20,021 Boodhists and Jains; 3 Jews; and 37,338 Aborigines. As to occupation, 1,598,396 were returned as agriculturists, and 1,674,317 as non-agriculturists. Marathi is the prevailing language.

East Berar.

§ 5. AMRAOTI DISTRICT is bounded E. by Wardha, N. by Ellichpoor, W. by Ellichpoor and Akola, and S. by Basim and Woon. Area, 2759 sq. m. Population, 575,328. The plain (800 ft.) is broken by hills (500 ft.) between Amraoti and Chandoor to S.E. The Poorna flows W.; the smaller streams drain S. into the Wardha. **Amraoti** (23,000), named doubtfully from the Amba temple of Bhawani or Kali, is head-quarters of the Commissioner of the whole Province as well as of E. Berar, second to Khamgaon as a cotton mart, and terminus of State branch railway. So recently as 1842 cotton was sent on bullocks by Mirzapoor to Calcutta; now there are many cotton mills and presses under Europeans. **Badnera** (7000), railway junction and cotton mart; old residence of the Mughul officials. **Murtizapoor** (4000), 30 m. S.W. of Amraoti, cotton mart. **Karinja** (11,000), in S.W. corner, with fine carved woodwork in very ancient temples.

§ 6. ELLICHPOOR DISTRICT is bounded E. by Wardha, N. by Betool and Chindwara, W. by Nimar and Akola, and S. by Amraoti. Area, 2623 sq. m. Population, 313,805. The N. half consists of the **Mel-Ghat** tract of the Gawilgarh hills, culminating in **Bairat** (3987 ft.). The S. is drained by many small streams into the Wardha and Poorna. **Ellichpoor** (27,000), chief town, with **Paratwara**, civil station and cantonment (9500), 2 m. N. Old capital, still remarkable for Dalla Rahman's shrine, built by one of the Bahmani kings, and for the extensive palace and tombs of the Haidarabad governors. **Chikalda**, since 1839 sanitarium (3777 ft.), 20 m. N.W. of Ellichpoor in Mel-Ghat, a plateau 1 m. long and three-quarters broad, with beautiful scenery; the potato and tea-plant flourish. **Gawilgarh Fort** (3595 ft.) (from Gauli race), giving its name to the hills, 1½ m. from Chikalda, stormed and taken from the Marathas in 1803 by General Stevenson, whose march through the Damangon pass E. to Labáda Wellington described as a most difficult and successful operation; dismantled in 1853. **Narnala** (3161 ft.), hill fort near Chikalda, with ramparts running for several miles and enclosing fine ruins, Jain and Musalman, an advanced outwork 2 m. S. of main wall of Gawilgarh range. **Morsi** (5500), 40 m. E. of Ellichpoor, on the Narka. **Anjangaon** (8530), on the Shánur, 16 m. W. of Ellichpoor, where in 1803 the Duke of Wellington concluded treaty of Amraoti with Sindia's minister.

§ 7. Woon District is bounded E. by Chanda and Wardha, N. by Amraoti, W. by Basim, and S. by Haidarabad State. Area, 3907 sq. m. Population, 392,102. A wild country formed by three shoots of the Ajanta ridge, and watered by the Wardha and Paenganga; the latter carries off nearly all the drainage of the district, and is fed chiefly by the Aran, Waghari, and Kooni. The coal and iron deposits of the Wardha valley have been already described. **Woon** (5000), chief town in S.E. corner, on road from Nagpoor to Haidarabad, amid mango and tamarind groves and tanks. **Darwa** (4000), old town of the Bhonslas, in N.W. **Bham**, old town of yast stone ruins, on the Aran, once a centre of Raghoji Bhonsla, 16 m. S. of **Yeotmahal** (4500), in N. of district. **Digras**, 18 m. S. of Darwa, a cotton mart.

West Berar.

§ 8. Akola District is bounded E. by Amraoti and Ellichpoor, N. by Ellichpoor and Khandesh, W. by Khandesh and Booldana, and S. by Basim. Area, 2660 sq. m. Population, 592,792. The rich plain, drained by the Poorna and seven tributaries, is broken only by two conical hills. Salt wells extend on both sides of the Poorna for 50 m. **Akola** (17,614), chief town of district and of W. Berar, on the Morna, which divides the native city on W. from Tajnapet, the European quarter on E., a cotton mart. **Khamgaon** (12,400), chief cotton centre since 1820, and terminus of railway worked in the cotton season from December to July. **Shegaon** (11,079), 24 m. W. of Akola, Great Indian Peninsula line, rival of Khamgaon. **Akot** (16,200), 30 m. N. of Akola, cotton depot for despatch to Shegaon, with carpet manufactures. **Balapoor** (9363), 16 m. W. of Akola on the Mun, named from the goddess Bala; scene of one of the victories of the first Nizam over the Mughul army in 1721; its railway station is

Paras on the Great Indian Peninsula line. At **Patur** (7220), 20 m. S. of Akola, are two Brahmanical caves cut into the basalt; Nagarjoona, founder of the Mahayana or later Boodhist Vehicle 500 years after Boodha, was a native of Berar. **Jalgaon-Jambod** (10,400), near Satpoora pass leading to Aseergarh, with good springs, whence the name. Other towns are Barsi Takli (5377), Wadegaon (6100), and Hiwarkhad (7000).

§ 9. BOOLDANA DISTRICT is bounded E. by Basim and Akola, N. by Khandesh from which the Poorna divides it, W. by Khandesh, and W. and S. by Haidarabad State. Area, 2804 sq. m. Population, 439,763. The district rises from the Poorna valley in W. to the highlands in N. From its N.W. corner, 4 m. above Dewalghat, the **Paenganga** flows S.E. past Mekhar into Basim. The Nalganga, Viswaganga, and Ghan and lower into the Poorna. The Kata Poorna flows through the district into Haidarabad. The lake of **Lonar** is described above; its salts are now used for washing and dyeing chintzes. There, at Dewalghat on the Paenganga, at Mehkar S.E., and Pimpalgaon S., are Hemar Pantee temples of monoliths, believed by the natives to have been built in one night by demons, for whom Hemar Pant, the Cornelius Agrippa of the Dekhan, was forced to find work. The principal towns are **Deulgaon Raja** (7100), on the Amni, with cotton and silk weaving. **Deulghat** (4000), on the Paenganga, old town. **Pimpalgaon Raja** (15,000), on the Dainganga, in N.E. **Malkapoor** (8200), on the Nalganga, railway station, to which a Farukhi prince transferred the people of the neighbouring Patur; formerly a large cantonment of the Nizam. **Mehkar** (5000), in S.E., once a large place.

§ 10. BASIM DISTRICT (from Wach, a Rishi or sage) is bounded E. by Woon, N. by Amraoti and Akola, W. by Booldana, and S. by Haidarabad State. Area, 2958 sq. m. Population, 358,883. The W. part is a rich tableland (1000 ft.); the S.E., running into Haidarabad, is a succession of low waste hills (1150 ft.). The **Poos** and **Kata Poorna**, mountain streams, rise near each other at Kata N. of Basim town. **Basim** (11,500), chief town (1758 ft.), 50 m. S.E. of Akola, and 27 m. from Hingoli cantonment, with temple and tank. **Oomarkher** (6000), chief town of a subdivision. **Mangrool Peer** (6000), in N.E. corner, chiefly Musalman. **Risod** (5000), ("place of the Rishis"), local commercial centre. **Seerpoor** (4800), or Parasnath shrine, the Benares of Jains and Bhatias. **Poosád** (4000), on the Poos, 25 m. S.E. of Basim, a decaying place with two Hemar Pantee temples.

CHAPTER XX.

*HAIDARABAD STATE.

§ 1. Size, Position, and Resources. § 2. Rivers and Communications. § 3. Administration. § 4. Land Tenures and People. § 5. Districts. § 6. Haidarabad, Golkonda, and Warangal. § 7. Beedar, Goolbarga, and Raichoor. § 8. Aurangabad, Elura, and Ajanta.

§ 1. SIZE, POSITION, AND RESOURCES.—The **Nizam's or Haidarabad State** is the chief of the Musalman and, indeed, of all the tributary sovereignties of the Queen-Empress of India, although it is one of the most recently formed. It may be roughly described as nearly of the same size as the Island of Great Britain, with a third of the population, lying between the great Godavari river with its Paenganga affluent on the N., and the great Kistna river with its affluent the Toongabhadra on the S. It is a plateau (1250 ft. average), forming the greater part of the Dekhan, shut off from the Bay of Bengal on the E. by the Madras districts of Godavari and Masulipatam, and on the W. by the Bombay districts of Khandesh, Ahmednagar, Sholapoor, Belgaum, and Dharwar. On the N.E. the State is separated by the Godavari from the Chanda district of the Central Province, and by the Paenganga from Berar; on the S. by the Kistna from the Guntoor and Karnool, and by the Toongabhadra from the Bellary districts of Madras. The estimated area is 80,000 sq. m. with a population of 9,200,881, lying between N. latitudes 15° 10′ and 20° 10′, and E. longitudes 74° 40′ and 81° 32′. The western third consists of basalt, with the rich black soil which produces wheat and cotton. The eastern two-thirds is formed of granite, which has crops of rice chiefly. Ethnically the S.E. section surrounded by Madras is chiefly Telugoo, the S.W. chiefly Kanarese, and the N.W. and N. chiefly Maratha. In the sandstone near the junction of the Paenganga with the Godavari, in the geological groups known as Kamthi, Barakar, and Talcher rocks, there is coal. At Kamaram village, 40 m. N.E. of Warangal, are two seams of fair coal 9 and 6 ft. thick respectively. At Singareni, 30 m. S.E. of this, is a field which may prove to be of economic importance when brought within reach by the projected railway.

§ 2. Rivers and Communications.—The State is drained from W. to E. by the rivers which flow from Ajanta and the Sahyadri ranges into the Bay of Bengal. The **Godavari**, from near Nasik, after a course of 90 m. touches the State at Phooltamba, and forms its border to Mungi, whence it flows E. for 160 m. to Lasona, where it receives on the left the **Dudna** after that stream has been enlarged by the **Poorna**. On the right side, 85 m. lower down, it receives the **Manjeera**; 190 m. farther E. at Kulaisar it is joined on the left by the **Pranheeta**; turning S.E. it skirts the Bastar State for 155 m. to Kottoor, where it passes into the Godavari district of Madras. Of the 600 miles of its course in Haidarabad, the Godavari is navigable for 200 m. from June to February. The **Wardha**, from the Betool hills of the Central Province, enters Haidarabad at Gudra, flows S.E. 170 m. to Chanda, on the right receives the **Paenganga** from Berar, flows 60 m. till it is joined on the left by the Waenganga when it becomes the Pranheeta, which has a course of 80 m. to the Godavari at Kulaisar; it is navigable for 170 m. The **Kistna** from Mahableshwar, after a S.E. course of 320 m. borders Haidarabad for 10 m., enters it and flows N.E. for 75 m. to Kadlur, where, on the left, it receives the **Bheema**, and is spanned by the Great Indian Peninsula Railway. Thence, after a S.E. course of 80 m. it unites with the Toongabhadra from Mysore, which at Moodlapoor begins to form the S.E. border of Haidarabad for 200 m. to its confluence with the Kistna. There are many artificial lakes or tanks, of which the largest, at **Pakhal**, is 30 m. in circumference. The Nizam's State Railway starting from Wadi Junction on the Great Indian Peninsula line from Bombay to Raichoor and Madras, runs E. for 121 m. to Sikandarabad, 5 m. N. of Haidarabad, the thirteenth station; the currency is *Hali sicca* rupees, of which $116\frac{3}{4}$ = 100 Queen's rupees. It is proposed to continue this line to Warangal, and thence north to Chanda, and east to the Singareni coal-fields. The S.W. portion of the State is traversed by the main line from Gudar station on the Bombay to Toongabhadra station on the Madras line. There are three military roads through the State—N. to S. from Nagpoor through the capital to Bangalore; N.W. to S.E. from Bombay and Poona through the capital to Masulipatam and Madras; local from the capital N.W. to the old Dekhan capital, Aurangabad.

§ 3. ADMINISTRATION.—The Golkonda dynasty founded by Sultan Kooli Kutab established Haidarabad city as its new capital in 1589, and gave way to the Mughuls under Aurangzeb when he was his father's viceroy of the Dekhan. In 1713 the viceroy was the able soldier Asaf Jah, who was made Nizam-ool-Moolk, "regulator of the State." In the general scramble for power after that emperor's death Asaf Jah proclaimed his independence, and became the founder of the Asafia line, the ninth of which now rules as tributary sovereign, the family having been aided and aggrandised by its connection with the rising British power up to the close of the Mutiny of 1857. On Asaf Jah's death in 1748, disputes as to his successor were used by the French to threaten English ascendency, which ended in the third son of Asaf Jah, Salabat Jung, as Nizam, forming a treaty with the British in 1759. The Nizam's troops co-operated with the British under Wellington in the wars which ended in the fall of Tipoo, and gave Haidarabad a slice of Mysore. On the succession of the fourth Nizam in 1803, anarchy spread so that Metcalfe, when Resident, supervised the administration under British officers. On the discontinuance of that control under the sixth Nizam in 1829, the insolvency of the State seemed imminent, and Berar was assigned for the support of the Haidarabad Contingent. The Nizam's debt to the British of half a million sterling was cancelled, and new territory was granted to the State after the Mutiny of 1857.

The Nizam is locally known as the Bara Nawab, the term Nawab, which applies strictly to a ruler, being given in courtesy to all Musalmans of high position. He is, however, the only Chief, the Ameers or Umara being mere nobles. The State owes its very existence and its recent growth in good administration to an Arab, Meer Turab Ali, who is known as the Nawab Mookhtar-ool-Moolk ("governor of the State") Sir Salar Jung ("leader in battle") Bahadoor, G.C.S.I., with a salute of 17 guns, while the Nizam has 21. The Nizam is a Saiad, or of the same family as Muhammad. He has a gross revenue of about 3 millions sterling, including the Berar surplus. The State revenue amounts to £2,130,000 of this annually, derived from the land, excise, customs, octroi, and miscellaneous imposts. The value of the trade is stated at 4 millions sterling a year. The principal exports are cotton, oil-seeds, clarified butter, country cloth, and metal ware; the imports are salt and European piece goods and hardware. The Nizam maintains an irregular "army" of his own computed at

43,704 men, costing £940,000 annually, doing police duty, acting as feudal retainers, and garrisoning such forts as Golkonda, Daulatabad, Beedar, and Goolbarga. The Nizam's 5000 "Reformed Troops" consist of 2 batteries, 2 cavalry and 3 infantry corps under a European officer, disciplined after the model of the Haidarabad Contingent. Many Arabs and Rohillas are engaged as mercenaries, but the public peace has been maintained since 1857.

The State is controlled by the British Resident from outside Haidarabad city. The Haidarabad Subsidiary Force, for which districts now under Madras were ceded, has its headquarters at Sikandarabad. The Haidarabad Contingent, for which Berar is held, has its headquarters at Bolaram. The Resident has an escort at Haidarabad and Jalna; the British Government maintains two special bodies of police under British officers to suppress Thuggee and Dakoitee. There are 72 State schools in 55 of the larger towns; Persian is the official language; £9040 is annually spent on education.

§ 4. Land Tenures and People.—(1) In the Telugoo districts the ryotwar system prevails, with the addition of zameendar collectors entitled to dues, or farmers of the land-tax (surbustah). (2) In the Maratha districts the tenure is also ryotwar, but instead of zameendar middlemen the districts were often assigned to military chiefs and bankers, with the worst results to the people. Recently annual settlements have been made and cash payments fixed; in the districts of Dharaseo and Raichoor, which were settled and governed by British officers from 1854 to 1861, these summary settlements have been annually continued. A three years' settlement is now in progress. The land revenue has gradually risen from a million sterling in 1861. The strength of the agricultural population consists of the widespread Koonbee tribe. The educated class among the Hindoo people here, as in most parts of Central and Southern India, consists of Brahmans, who thereby secure a great preponderance in all situations depending on mental rather than physical labour; in this respect there is no class among the Dekhan Hindoos to compete with them. There are some Rajpoots, many of them representing ancient families or still possessing a feudal or other superior position. There are some Sikhs; their presence originally was attributed to events in the life of the founder, Gooroo Govind; their numbers have been since augmented owing to the fact of the man who was the Nizam's minister for nearly forty years belonging to their cult. The casteless orders, such as Ramoosees and

Dhêrs, often have exhibited nerve and courage stronger than that of their superiors. Among the banking and trading classes, the principal belong to that enterprising tribe whose members came, and still come, from Marwar in Rajpootana to spread over half the marts of India. The Muhammadans comprise representatives of most of the tribes of that section of the human family. There are the real Dekhanees, the Mughuls, the Pathans, and the Saiads, who have been connected with this part of India for centuries. The Mughul must be considered the governing race of modern days; and the Nizam's Dekhan is popularly known as the "Mughulai." There are also the Muhammadans whose advent to the Dekhan dates within the last century, such as the Arabs, the Rohillas, the Hubshees, and the Sindhees. The Parsees have several influential families. To the N.E. of the country, in the wilder parts, there are aboriginal tribes like those of the Central Province.

§ 5. Districts.—Large tracts of country are directly under the Nizam as his own lands (Surf-i-Khas) or for his bodyguard (Paegah), or under the chief ministers as fiefs (jageers around the capital) and private estates. But the rest of the State, excepting these isolated jurisdictions which are fatal to good government, has since 1865 had applied to it by Sir Salar Jung the Madras system of district administration. Each *Sirkar* is under a 1st, 2d, and 3d *talookdar*, corresponding to the district collector, sub-collector, and assistant collector of Madras; and two or three Sirkars are united to form a circle or division under a *saddar talookdar* or commissioner.

Division.	District.	Region.
I.	Nulgonda Kummum (Warangal)	Telingana.
II.	Indore Eelgundel Maidak	Godavari.
III.	Aurangabad Beer Parbhanee	North-West Dekhan.
IV.	Nandair Beedar Naldroog	Central Dekhan.
V.	East Raichoor West Raichoor Shorapoor	Kistna.

HAIDARABAD AND MYSORE STATES.

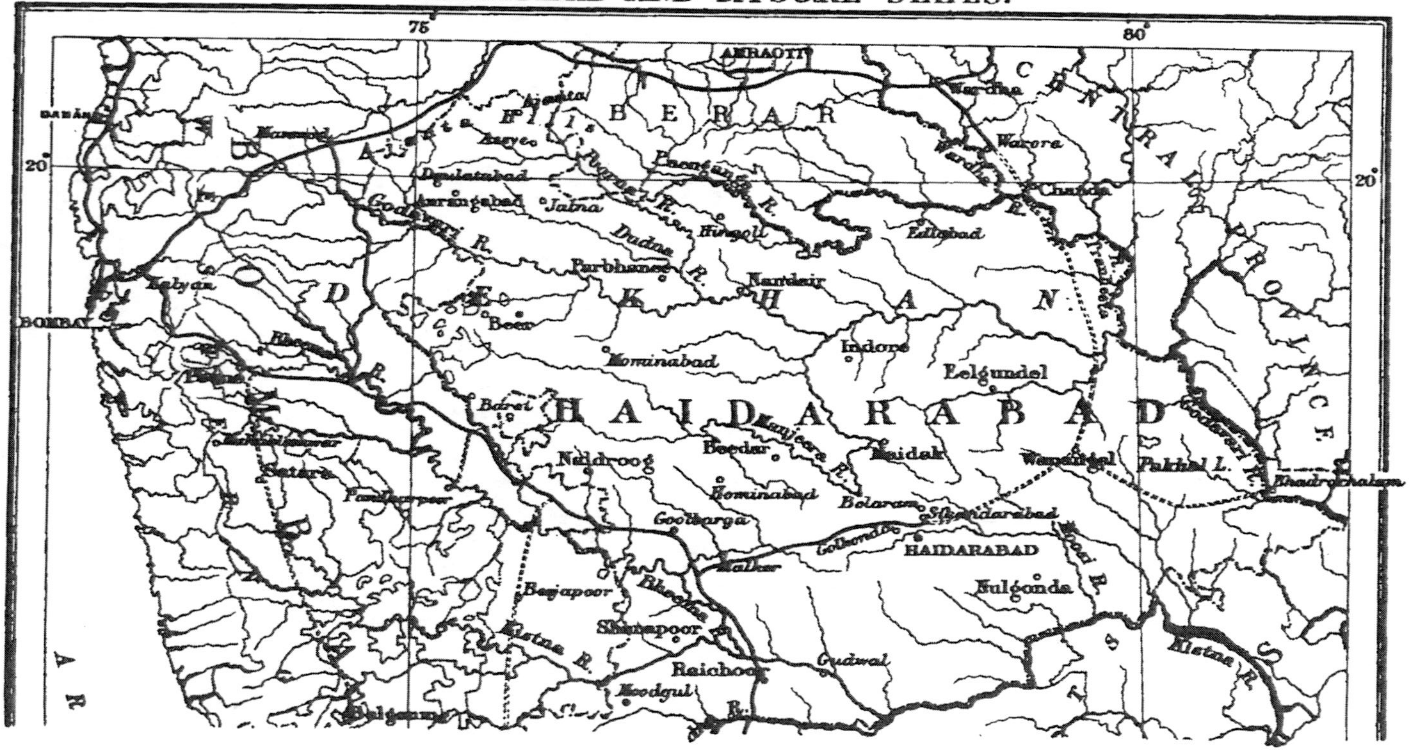

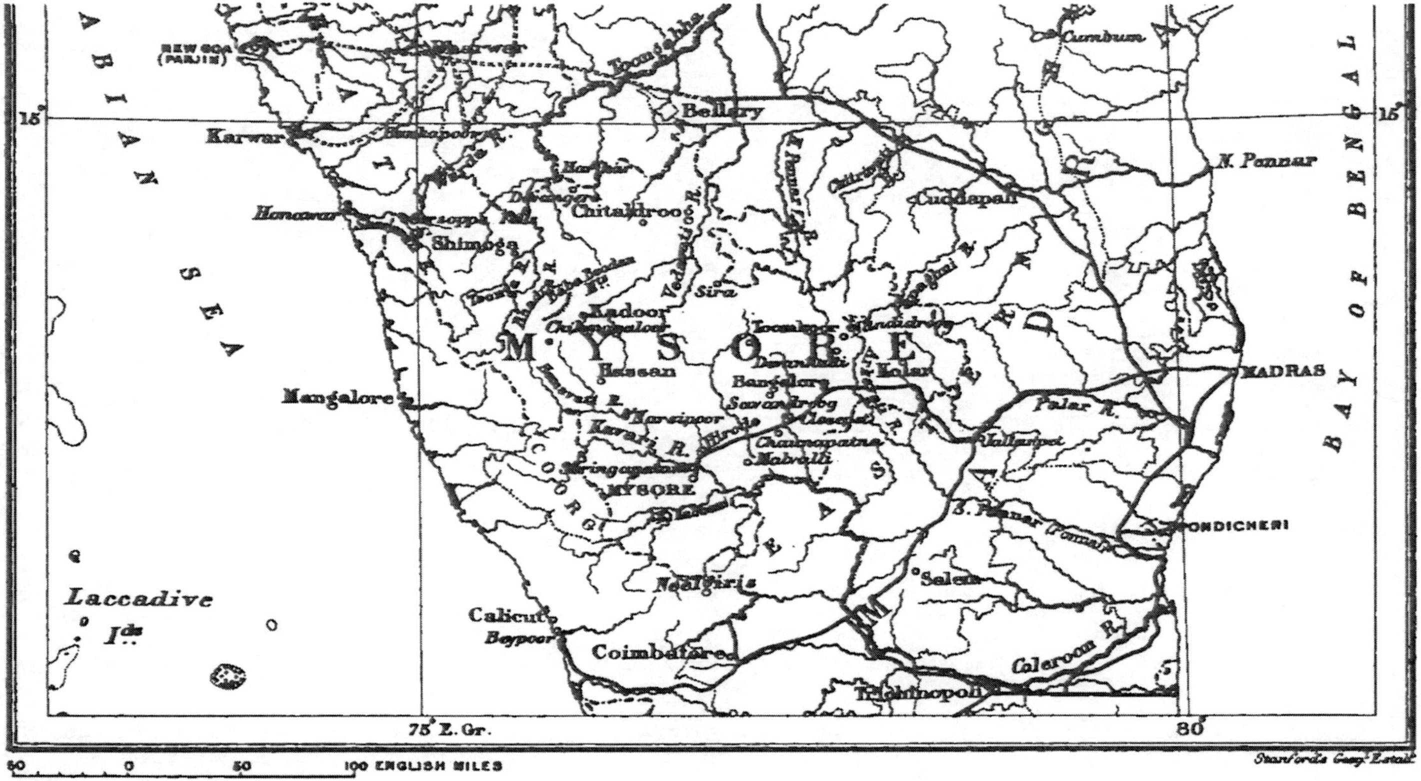
BAY OF BENGAL
MYSORE
NEW GOA (PANJIM)
Karwar
Honawar
Shimoga
Chitaldroog
Bellary
Cumbum
N. Pennar
Cuddapah
Sira
Kadoor
Hassan
Mangalore
Bangalore
Kolar
MADRAS
Palar R.
Kavari R.
COORG
MYSORE
Salem
Neilgiris
Calicut
Beypoor
Coimbatore
Trichinopoli
Caleroon R.
PONDICHERI
Laccadive Ids
15°
75° E. Gr.
80°
50 0 50 100 ENGLISH MILES
Stanford's Geogl. Estabt.

In these districts, chiefly towards the border, there are the following vassal Rajas:—Wunpurty, half-way between Haidarabad city and Karnool; Ummar Chunta, near Muktool; Goorgoonta, in Shorapoor; Gudwal, Jawalgiri, and Anagoondee, in Raichoor; Jutpól and Gopalpet, on S.E. border towards Masulipatam. These still represent the old Hindoo families prior to the Musalman invasion; the Raja of Anagoondee is of the Hindoo dynasty of Vijayanagar.

When he was the Resident, in 1868, Sir Richard Temple thus described the State.—Between the Paenganga and the Godavari there is the extreme upper valley of the Godavari. Its high cultivation, waving harvests, and general richness may be said to be the very flower of the Dekhan; it has many important places, such as Aurangabad, Tokub, Paitun, Patree, Gungakhair, Nandair (the Sikh colony), and Neermal. South of the Godavari is its affluent the Manjeera, which in a tortuous course embraces a tract often rugged and not very rich, but having several places fraught with martial tradition or strategic importance, such as Beer, Mominabad, Daroor, Oodjheer. But some parts of the Manjeera valley are fruitful, and Maidak in that circle is the old capital of a fine district. The great tract included between the Manjeera and the Bheema and Kistna on the other hand, is the most important in the Dekhan. Within it are situate at the western end Tooljapoor, Naldroog, Goolbarga (the capital of the first Muhammadan dynasty of the Dekhan), Hominabad, Kulleeanee; in the centre Beedar, the capital Haidarabad itself; to the E. Nulgonda, and Warangal the ancient capital of Telingana. The eastern portion is dotted all over with artificial lakes. Of these, the first by far is the Pakhal Lake, probably the largest sheet of water in India. No tract can be better calculated than this to raise our notions of the early Hindoo dynasties. It must have been in its original prime the finest scene of tank irrigation in all India. Between the Bheema and the Kistna there is a large tongue of land, which once formed the Hindoo State of Shorapoor, under the feudal suzerainty of the Nizam, but which, owing to the rebellion of its chief in 1857, has been brought under His Highness's direct administration. Lastly, on the extreme S., between the Kistna and Toongabhadra, is the Raichoor Doab, which is in parts fertile, and in which the principal places are Raichoor and Lingasagar, one of the stations of the Haidarabad Contingent.

§ 6. HAIDARABAD CITY (263,005 with suburbs), next in population to Calcutta, Bombay, and Madras, but only slightly above Lucknow, covers 2¼ sq. m. (10½ with suburbs) on the right bank of the Moosi, a generally fordable stream 500 ft. wide, 8 m. E. of the old fort and capital of Golkonda, 449 S.E. of Bombay and 389 N.W. of Madras. Its name is from Haidar, a son of the founder, Muhammad Kooli of the Kutub Shahi dynasty, who adorned the new capital with many buildings still perfect. The city stands on a stony plain, the barrenness of which was its safeguard against the Marathas, 2 m. N. of the Meeralam lake, 7 m. round, which supplies it with water. It is walled, with many gateways. From the W. Afzal or Delhi gate a broad street runs through the city, past the Barah-dari ("12 doors") or palace of Sir Salar Jung, who has governed the State for nearly 30 years; the rectangular Char Minar (four minarets, each 186 ft.), and Mecca mosque in which the Nizams are buried, to the Nizam's palace, finer than the Shah's at Tehran which it resembles, and that of Shams-ool-Umara from which a fine view is obtained, and so to the largest of the Nizam's palaces. One m. N.W. of the city, in the Chaddarghat suburb, approached by the Oliphant bridge over the Moosi, is the **Residency**, a fine building completed in 1808 in a park with noble trees, enclosed by a wall since an attack by a Rohilla mob in July 1857; in the little cemetery are the tombs of former Residents, and officials, Sydenham, Bushby, and Roberts, Sir William Rumbold, and other officers. The Residency school, hospital, medical school, and engineering college, are between this and the Afzal gate. The suburbs, consisting of gardens, palaces, mosques, and populous bazars, cover a larger area than the city. The melons and pine-apples of Haidarabad are famous. To N.W., over an area of 19 sq. m., are the largest cantonments in India, containing 8000 disciplined soldiers. (1) **Sikandarabad** (35,000) ("Alexander's city"), 5½ m. N.E. of the Residency, on the road to which are St. George's Church and the tomb and house of "King Palmer." Sikandarabad is headquarters of the Haidarabad Subsidiary Force; 2 m. S. are the lines of the Nizam's reformed troops. (2) Three m. N.E. of Sikandarabad are the entrenched camp of **Trimalgheri** with stores, and a military prison popularly called Windsor Castle from its appearance, the whole fortified as a centre for the Europeans in Sikandarabad; (3) **Bolaram**, 2 m. farther N., headquarters of the Haidarabad Contingent, and a sanitarium (1890 ft.). Here in 1855 General Colin Mackenzie, C.B., a hero of the 1st Afghan War, was cut down by the mutinous troops of the 3d Native ·lry, twenty months before the great Mutiny. In N.E. are ·at hills Mool Ali and Kadam Rusool, the latter named from a supposed impress of Muhammad's foot. On S.E. side of the city is the Saroor Nagar suburb, a famous hunting-ground, with tomb, on an eminence, of Raymond the gallant French soldier, who died in 1775. **Golkonda** city, ruined by pestilence, and fort on a granite ridge 7 m. W. of Haidarabad, capital of the Kutub Shahi kingdom which superseded the Bahmani and was destroyed by Aurangzeb; with a vast group of mausolea of the kings. The diamonds for which Golkonda was famous were merely cut there, being found at the village of Purtial near Kondapilli 150 m. S.E. on the Masulipatam road, bordering the Kistna. The fort has long been the Nizam's prison and treasury. **Warangal**, capital of the Hindoo kingdom of Telingana founded by the Narapati Andhras and finally in 1543 absorbed by the Golkonda kings, 112 m. N.E. of Haidarabad. Anamkonda and Mullungoor are fortresses to N. Ralkonda, Nirmal, and Edlabad are on the road N. from Haidarabad to Nagpoor; **Edlabad** is a centre of the culture of cotton which finds its way to Hinganghat.

§ 7. BEEDAR, old capital of the Bahmani kings, 75 m. N.W. of Haidarabad on the right bank of the Manjeera. A striking city, walled with 8 gates, and containing a citadel 2½ m. round, palaces inhabited by serpents and baboons, a once magnificent Madrasah with a minaret 190 ft. high, covered with encaustic tiles—blue, green, and yellow. N.E. are 12 tombs of the Bahmani kings, the largest being that of Ahmed Shah who moved the capital here from Goolbarga in 1432 and built the city wall. The town gives its name to the Bidri metal-ware, copper, lead, tin, and zinc worked into articles damascened in silver or gold. On the road from Haidarabad to Beedar are **Pattancheru**, a beautiful station and shooting centre, with gardens of Sir Salar Jung; **Kaulampet**, with ruined fort; **Sangam**, famous shooting spot near the Pakhol hills; **Sadashivapet**, straggling town with ruins of fortifications. **Malegaon**, 160 m. from Haidarabad and 200 from Poona, chief mart for Dekhan-bred horses. **Goolbarga** (35,000) a Great Indian Peninsula Railway station and fort, 353 m. from Bombay, the Bahmani capital of the Dekhan 1347-1435, with a unique Pathan mosque entirely roofed over and lighted from the side, covering 38,016 sq. ft.; also a unique arcaded bazar, a gigantic archway and grand old tombs with sloping walls, ⅓ m. to the S. The fort is 1½ m. S.W., and is stronger than that of Beedar. On a hill 3 m. N.E. is the shrine of Rukn-ood-deen, and 1 m. farther the ruins of old Goolbarga. **Malker**, near Goolbarga, seat of Rahtor dynasty which superseded the

Chalookyas for two centuries. **Raichoor**, railway junction of Bombay and Madras lines, 350½ m. N.W. of Madras and 443 S.E. of Bombay, the S. capital of Beejapoor, with old fort, from which there is a fine view. **Lingasagar**, W. of Raichoor 60 m., cantonment (1652 ft.) of Haidarabad Contingent. **Moodgul**, to S., old fort and Portuguese Catholic Mission. **Shorapoor**, chief town of former State of the same name in S.W. corner of Haidarabad, confiscated for rebellion in 1857-58, and presented to the Nizam; Captain Meadows Taylor administered the State for ten years with great success up to 1853; the town lies between two granite ranges, "a grim place to look at." **Gudwal**, chief town of feudatory Raja of the Nizam in the Raichoor Doab, between the Kistna and Toongabhadra. **Tooljapoor**, picturesque town E. of Seena affluent of the Bheema, near west border of Haidarabad, scene of Meadows Taylor's romance of *Tara*. At Chittapoor, a few miles distant, is a mission of Portuguese Catholics. **Hominabad**, central mart near Beedar on the Haidarabad and Sholapoor road. **Dundooty**, Awsa, and **Paraindah** are forts in this division. **Naldroog**, fortified town on the Bori or old frontier between Beejapoor and Ahmednagar, a few m. E. of Sholapoor. Between Awsa and Kalyana are the small Brahmanical and Jain caves of Karusá (500-700 A.D.) on a solitary hill near Hasagaon village.

§ 8. AURANGABAD (50,000) city, cantonment and old capital of the Dekhan, on the Doodhna tributary of the Godavari 270 m. N.W. of Haidarabad, 56 m. from Nandgaon station on Great Indian Peninsula Railway, and 175 N.W. of Bombay. Founded in 1610 by Malik Ambar of the Abyssinian faction in Ahmednagar State, now attractive for mausoleum built by Aurangzeb over the dust of his favourite daughter, Rabeea Dooranee; restored by the Nizam. Two m. to S.E. of cantonment is the ark or citadel built by Aurangzeb (now centre of the public offices), who held court in this Delhi of the south. One m. N. of city, in the precipitous S. scarp of hills (700 ft.), are 3 groups of Boodhist caves of the latest ornamented style (650 A.D.) of the Mahayana mythology, influenced by Christian teaching. **Daulatabad**, 10 m. N.W. of Aurangabad, the ancient Tagara, and the famous Deogarh or Deogiri stronghold of the Hindoo rulers of the Dekhan, to which Tughlak Shah's son, the mad emperor Muhammad, strove to transfer the capital from Delhi, giving the place its new name; this is an isolated conical rock of granite (500 ft.) scarped to from 80 to 120 ft. all round, and ascended only through a narrow pass hewn in the rock and leading to a vault from which a dark alley winds upwards. To S.E. is another hill **Pippal Ghat** with mosque, to N. of which is the emperor Aurangzeb's tomb, a simple marble and teak-wood screen. The country round is still famous for oranges and white and purple grapes introduced by the Portuguese Catholic Mission, when protected by the Beejapoor kings. Here also is **Rozah** tableland, a vast cemetery encircled by a stone wall, and containing many domed buildings, one of which is used as a rest-house.

From Rozah a road descends to the base of the scarp in which are the Boodhist, Jain, and Brahmanical caves of **Elura** (or Verula), 7 m. from Daulatabad and 13 from Aurangabad. At S. end are the Boodhist caves, at N. the Jain, 16 in all; and between are the Brahmanical, also 15 or 16. Chief of all is the Kailas or Ranga Mahal (725-800 A.D.), a great monolithic Dravidian temple of Shiva, nearly 100 ft. high, hewn out of the rock, highly sculptured outside and in; but "a temple in a pit," and therefore the last as well as greatest effort of the Brahmans to imitate and excel their Boodhist rivals. Visited by the missionary Dr. J. Wilson in 1832, to whom, when he preached in the Kailas, the natives declared that God Himself had made it. The temple stands in a court 154 by 276 ft., with a scarp of 107 ft. behind, all cut out of a detached boulder of trap. **Ajanta**, walled town, where Wellington's sick were received after Assye, and ravine with 29 famous cave temples, chiefly of the Mahayana or later sect of Boodhists, excavated between 500 and 650 A.D., at the head of one of the passes leading down from the Indhyadri or Ajanta range, which divides the Dekhan tableland from Khandesh in the Tapti valley. The caves are 4 m. N.W. of the village, in a wild glen best approached through Faidapoor village at foot of the Ghats, from Pachora station of Great Indian Peninsula Railway 34 m. distant, but also by horse *tonga* 56 m. from Aurangabad, a fatiguing route. The caves, infested by bees, form one of the most interesting spots in India; they are purely Boodhist, and cover the 8 centuries of Boodhist supremacy, 6 being of the earlier or Hinayana and 2 of the later or Mahayana forms; their fresco paintings are still tolerably complete. **Assye** (Asai) battlefield and village reached from Sirrod, 40 m. from Aurangabad, where, on 23d September 1803, Wellington with 4500 men of all arms defeated 50,800 of Sindia's and Bhonsla's Marathas, disciplined by Frenchmen, in a strong position between the Juah and Khelna rivers, and so broke the Maratha confederacy. **Jalna** (1652 ft.), British cantonment 38 m. E. of Aurangabad, and old town 2 m.

S.W., seat of Scottish Free Church Mission. **Bethel**, 3 m. S., on rising ground, a Christian town, the centre of a circle of out-stations the diameter of which is 30 m., founded by Rev. Narain Sheshadri. **Hingoli** (1495 ft.), E. of Jalna, on N. road from Haidarabad to Akola, 72 m. S. of latter and 190 N.W. of Sikandarabad. **Mominabad**, large cavalry station between Sikandarabad and Aurangabad. **Nandair**, originally a Sikh colony on the left bank of the Godavari, 145 m. N. of Haidarabad.

CHAPTER XXI.

MADRAS PROVINCE—GENERAL.

§ 1. Size and Position. § 2. Mountains and Rivers. § 3. Canals and Railways. § 4. Products and Trade. § 5. Land Tenures and Taxation. § 6. The People and Districts.

§ 1. SIZE AND POSITION.—**Madras**, as the Presidency of Fort St. George, is historically the oldest of the Twelve Provinces of British India, and that in which Christianity has made greatest progress under Apostolic missionaries of the 1st century, Jesuits of the 16th and 17th, Lutherans of the 18th, and Anglicans, Nonconformists, and Presbyterians of the 19th century. The total area of 150,248 sq. m. is not far short of that of Spain, and the population of 33,840,617 is more than double that of Spain; although the great famine of 1876-8 swept off at least 3 millions of the population of South India, besides Mysore, and has reduced its numbers 2 per cent in the ten years ending 1871, when the other eleven Provinces showed a large increase. Of the whole area, 9818 sq. m., and of the population 3,336,632 are in the five Native States of Travankor, Cochin, Poodookotta, Banaganapali, and Sandoor. The coast line extends for more than 1600 miles; but, from the absence of good natural harbours and great navigable rivers, the normal external trade does not exceed £17,000,000 a year. The country is well opened up by nearly a thousand miles of railway. The Province yielded a gross revenue of £9,840,000 in 1880-81. The central tableland of the S. Peninsula is occupied by the Central Province, Berar, Haidarabad, Mysore, and Coorg, but all S. and E. of these Provinces and States belongs to Madras, which has a busy coasting and labour traffic with the neighbouring crown colony of Ceylon. The army is 40,000 strong, under a local commander-in-chief. In its history, languages, and land tenures, Madras consists of three well-defined portions—(*a*) the Telugoo country of the north, from Orissa to and including Nellore; (*b*) the Tamil country of the south, or the Karnatic from Nellore to Tinnevelli; and (*c*) the Kanarese, Malayalam, and Tulu districts of the western Malabar coast to Cape Comorin. These five form the races and languages of **Dravida**, the non-Aryan or so-called Turanian land of the south, divided into the almost prehistoric kingdoms of Kalinga, between the Ganges and the Kistna, and Pandya, Chola, and Chera south of the Kistna. Here the Muhammadans, who first obtained a footing at the opening of the 14th century, made less impression than on the north; the Vijayanagar kingdom supplanted them till overborne by a federation of the four Dekhan principalities. The genius and energy of Clive foiled the plans of Dupleix, and by clinging to the British alliance the Delhi emperor's lieutenant, the Nizam of Haidarabad, consolidated his possessions against the Maratha anarchy and the Haidar-Tipoo ferocity. The close of the 18th century saw Madras settled very much as it now is, and Sir Thomas Munro lent all his influence to the peasant-proprietor tenure with increasing land-tax as against the large landlord tenure with a fixed rate.

§ 2. MOUNTAINS AND RIVERS.—Madras is bounded E. by the Bay of Bengal, extending for about 1000 m. of coast from Cape Comorin in lat. 8° 4′, to the S. of Orissa in lat. 20° 18′; on the W. it is bounded by the Arabian Sea for 540 m. to the W. extremity of Mysore State, in lat. 13° 50′, where the width across the peninsula is about 390 m. The irregular N. boundary almost tells the history of the Province. From Orissa it rises S.W. up the slopes of the Eastern Ghats, where it marches with the Central Province, and with the Dekhan, where it is overlooked by Haidarabad State, to the Western Ghats, where, arrested by Mysore, it runs round that State and drops down to the Arabian Sea, touching the Bombay border on either side of N. Mysore. The **Eastern Ghats**, springing from Balasor and the chaos of the Chutia Nagpoor hills of Bengal, run from S.W. nearly parallel with the E. coast of the Bay of Bengal, touch the coast at Vizagapatam, at a point 50 m. N. of Madras city sweep more to the W., and in the **Neelgiris** join the western hill system. Gallikonda (5346 ft.) and Galli Parvatam (4988 ft.) are the highest peaks. These hills have an average height of 1500 ft., are pierced by the great rivers from the west, and form a watershed only in the extreme north, where they have been but partially surveyed. The **Western Ghats**, already described under Bombay as the Sahyadris, reach their highest point in the **Dodabetta** peak (8640 ft.) of the Neelgiris. They form the other noble plateaux and subsidiary ranges which are known as the **Shivarai** in Salem, the **Anamalai** in Coimbatore, the **Palni** in Madura, and the **Travankor** or **Cardamom Hills** in Travankor, and end in the sacred peak of **Agastya** (6150 ft.) near Cape Comorin, having vast agricultural and mineral wealth, and an almost European climate. This great western range farther gives the Province its physical character by arresting the S.W. monsoon, which deluges the three west coast districts and two States, but is so kept from the twenty districts and States on the east as to expose them to frequent famine, when the normal rainfall of 40 inches a year fails. These are watered more bountifully by the N.E. monsoon, which begins in September, and by the great rivers with their canals and tributaries, the **Godavari**, **Kistna**, and **Kavari**, the two **Pennars**, **Palar**, **Vaiga**, **Vellar**, and **Tambraparni**. The only large lakes are those of **Kola** and **Pulikat** on E. coast. The latter is 33 m. long; it is really one of a series of backwaters or lagoons fed by rivers, but with outlets to the sea. The largest is **Cochin Backwater**, the centre of water communication practically from Cape Comorin up to S. Kanara. The east coast, for 166 m. N. of Cape Comorin, is rocky, and sends off to Ceylon the reefs, sandbeds, and islands which form **Adam's Bridge**, with two channels navigable by small steamers. The **Coromandel Coast** begins at Pont Kalymere to the N., passes the estuaries of the Kavari, and holds on for 297 m. farther N.E. to Gondegaon, where it is bounded by the Moosi river. There the **Golkonda Coast** commences, and crosses the estuaries of the Kistna and Godavari 270 m. to the S. of Vizagapatam district, whence the Orissa coast is reckoned to begin.

§ 3. CANALS AND RAILWAYS.—Besides the ordinary works of irrigation, which are 33,318 rain-fed reservoirs and 1212 channels supplied by them by means of dams watering 3½ millions of acres, there are 8 extraordinary works constructed from borrowed capital, and the projects of the Madras Irrigation and Canal Company. The sum of 1½ millions sterling has been expended on these eight works, which yield a net revenue of the third of a million—Godavari Delta, Kistna Delta, Pennar Anicut, Chembrambakam Tank, Palar Anicut, Pelandorai Anicut, Kavari Delta, Srivaikuntam Anicut. The Company's work completed by Government is the Toongabhadra Canal from Sunkesala, 15 m. above Karnool town, to the Kistnapatam estuary on the Nellore coast. There are 61 other irrigation and navigation works. The Madras Railway's South-West Line runs for 518 m. across the peninsula from the capital city to Beypoor port, with Neelgiri branch to Metapolliem; and North-West Line for 340 m. from Arkonam junction to Raichoor, where it connects with the Great Indian Peninsula line for Bombay, with branches to Mysore and Bellary. The narrow-gauge South Indian Railway runs S. from the capital city to Tuticorin port and Tinnevelli, with branches to Pondicheri, Negapatam port, and the Arkonam and Erode junctions of the S.W. line for 661 m. The projected line to Mormugao on W. coast will start from Hoobli and Bellary. Other lines under construction or survey are from Kullar to Coonoor on the Neelgiris, from Shoranoor to Cochin, from Madura to Kilakarai for Paumban, and from Tinnevelli to Trivandrum. Bimlipatam may be the port for the Madras terminus of the direct Bombay, Nagpoor, and Raipoor Railway, by the Raighar or Rayaghada route.

§ 4. PRODUCTS AND TRADE.—The gold of Madras is found in the quartz reefs which traverse the granites, gneisses, and other metamorphic rocks principally in the Wainad terrace, leading up from Malabar to the plateau of the Neelgiri hills. Mr. Brough Smyth, an Australian expert, has reported to Government on 200 outcrops in a tract of 500 sq. m., that the auriferous reefs are more numerous and proportionately wider and richer than in almost any part of Australia. Several companies are working the quartz with results the economic value of which has yet to be proved. The diamond-bearing strata appear to have of old been worked in Cuddapah, Karnool, Kistna, and Godavari districts, and in Banaganapali State. Coal of inferior quality is found in the carboniferous sandstones at Doomagoodiem on the Godavari; a shaft has been sunk at Bhadrāchalam. Excellent iron ore has been smelted by natives, and tried by the Porto Novo Company near Cuddalore, and at Beypoor; fine magnetic iron abounds in Salem. The forests within the Province cover an area of 5000 sq. m. In Ganjam are the Goomsoor and Soorada Reserves, of 583 sq. m.; in Cuddapah, Rullakunda; in N. Arcot, Mamandoor; in S. Arcot, Theumalai; in Malabar, Nelamboor. In Coimbatore, Karnool, and the Wainad, are extensive and rich timber tracts, yielding teak, ebony or blackwood, rose and red wood, and sandalwood. In ordinary years the ryotwar cultivation covers 16¾ millions of acres, exclusive of Malabar and S. Kanara. In the worst famine season that fell to 13 millions. Of the cereal cultivation 5½ millions are generally under rice, 3½ under cholam (*Sorghum vulgare*), 3 under cumbu (*Panicum spicatum*), 1¾ under varagu (*Panicum miliaceum*), and 1½ under ragi (*Eleusine corocana*). Cotton occupies 1½ millions of acres, and indigo one-fifth. Gingelly, or sesamum, is the most common oil-seed. Of the whole cultivation 80 per cent is "dry," or dependent on local rainfall. The coffee plant is covering the Shivarai, Palni, and Travankor hills, and partially the Neelgiris. There were 18,315 plantations in 1880, yielding 18½ million lbs. Tea is on a smaller scale; 84 gardens yielded 650,000 lbs. in 1880. The most remarkable success is that of the cinchona, introduced from Peru in 1860, fostered by the State on seven plantations, of which Nedivattam, Dodabetta, and Pykara are the chief, and now a commercial staple. Madras has few manufactures apart from the work of the village weavers, and the gold, silver, ivory, horn, and sandalwood products of Trichinopoli, Vizagapatam, and Kanara; the pearl fisheries of Tuticorin, under Government, and the tobacco industry.

§ 5. Land Tenures and Taxation.—As to land tenures no less than languages and history the Madras Province consists of three parts, the Telugoo country of the N., extending to and including Nellore; the Tamil country of the S., and the Kanarese and Malayalam districts of the W. or Malabar coast. The first division came most under the influence of the Muhammadans, and we find in it, as in Bengal, the zameendaree tenure of great landlords, acting as middlemen between the State and the actual cultivators. In 1802 the Regulations extended to this northern division the permanent settlement of Bengal, making it with the zameendars and not with the hereditary cultivators. In the southern division, where the Musalman influence had been very weak, the land was held by cultivating village communities who paid rent directly to the old Hindoo sovereigns. These original village shareholders, or Meerasidars, had tenants under them, and when the Musalmans obtained power and exercised their usual rapacity through farmers of the land revenue, the Meerasidars ceased to have any surplus income, and were practically reduced to the level of their own tenants who, though they cultivated, did not own the land. In the third or western division, the village or communal gives place to the individual right to land free of all rent to the State, known as *Jenm* or birthright. Not till Haidar Ali conquered Southern India from Mysore were Malabar and Kanara subjected to a land-tax. The landlords were bound to pay only one kind of service (military), and even then they received subsistence money. They had leasehold tenants without any right of occupancy from lapse of time. But the result of this was extravagance on the part of the landlords, and the growth of a class of mortgagees, chiefly Moplahs, who, under Haidar Ali, became the real owners. Thus, though the British succeeded to a heavy land-tax, they found Malabar owned chiefly by wealthy capitalists. South Kanara had been over-assessed. The cultivation of the Province, as to tenures, may be thus stated :—

Ryotwaree lands . . . 16¾ million acres (actual).
Inam (quit-rent) lands . . 4⅓ million acres (actual).
Zameendaree lands . . . 5⅓ million acres (estimated).
Malabar and S. Kanara . . 2¼ million acres (estimated).

In the Ryotwaree, or Government lands of other districts, the land-tax is fixed on each field in regard to its extent and quality, but in Malabar and Kanara the tax is upon the holding.

VARIETIES OF TENURE HELD DIRECT FROM GOVERNMENT, 1880-81.

Nature of Tenures.	Number of estates.	Number of villages.	Number of holders or share-holders.	Gross area in acres.	Average area of each estate.	Average assessment of each estate.
Great Zameendarees paying more than Rs. 50,000 Revenue—						
Held by individuals under the law of primogeniture .	15	9,636	16*	6,118,293	407,886	Rs. 1,84,309
Held by individuals and families under ordinary law . .	1	269	1	116,102	116,102	59,929
Large Zameendarees paying more than Rs. 5000 Revenue—						
Held under the law of primogeniture .	54	6,520	58*	9,543,405	176,730	14,848
Held under ordinary law	69	1,460	110	1,032,828	14,968	10,527
Small Zameendarees, Mootahs, etc., other than those of cultivating communities	602	3,023	881	2,378,282	3,950	1,389
Proprietary cultivating communities paying in common. . . .	1,060	672	12,112	22,655	21	65
Rented estates	422	333	1,510	88,564	209	481
Proprietary cultivators paying more than Rs. 100	44,749	9,690	83,843	3,052,704	68	184
Proprietary cultivators paying separately including all small estates paying less than Rs. 100	2,460,051	26,186	3,449,098	16,434,954	7	11
Holders of revenue-free tenures—						
In perpetuity . .	401,587	29,332	667,135	7,889,724	19	9
For life	1,841	932	2,345	30,905	16	10
Landholders who have redeemed the revenue .	430	162	556	3,003	7	...
Purchase of waste lands .	502	117	164	23,002	46	50

* The number of holders is more than the number of estates, as some of the Zameendarees are registered in the names of the widows of the deceased Zameendars.

MADRAS AND COORG PROVINCES.

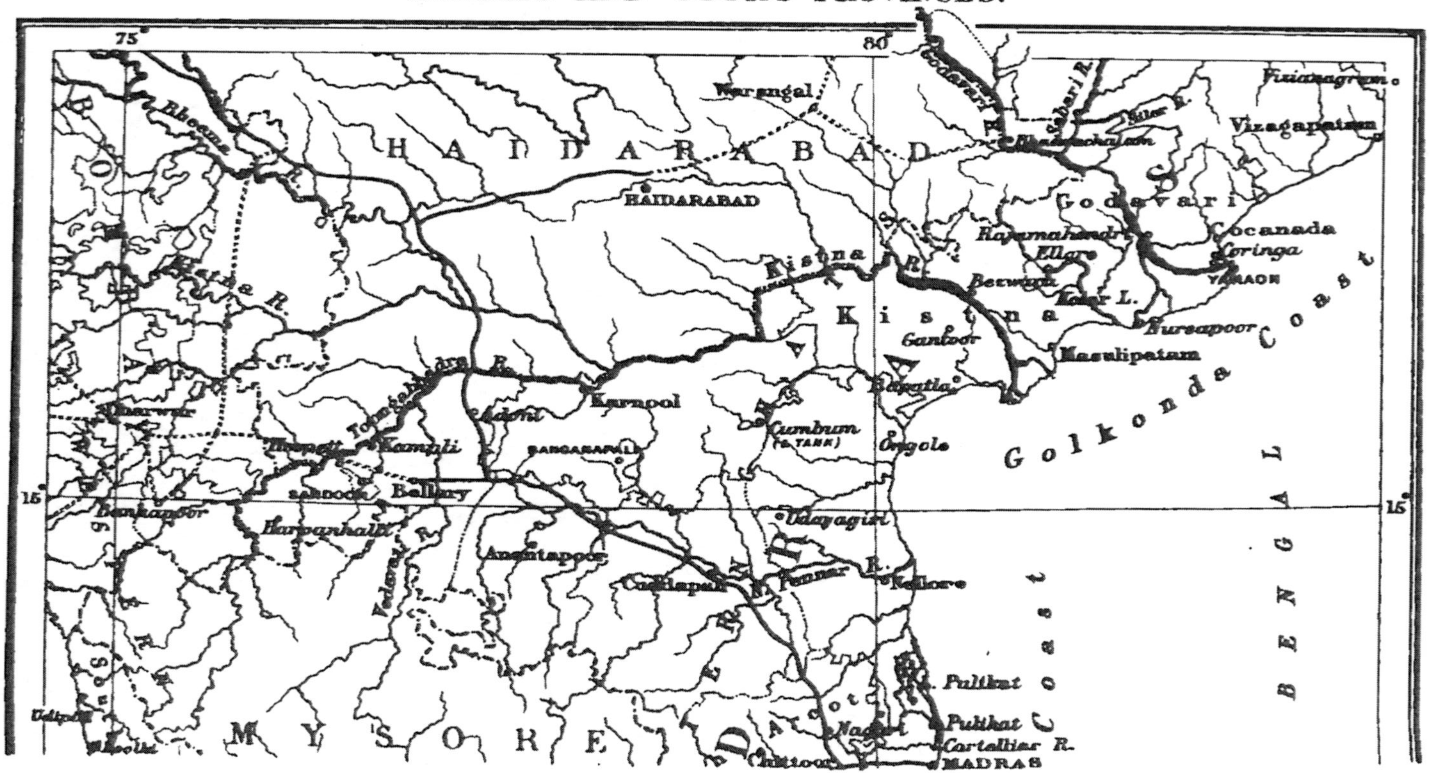

Mangalore
Bangalore
Saidapet
Chingalpat
R. Palar
Seringapatam
MYSORE
COORG
Cannanore
Tellicheri
MAHÉ
Calicut
Beypoor
Coimbatore
Ponani & R.
Palghat
Cochin
Alleppi
Quilon
Anjengo
Trivandrum
Kolachel
C. Comorin
Jawadi
Hills
Vellore
Arcot
Salem
Shivarai Hills
Vellar
R.
Cuddalore
Porto Novo
PONDICHERI
Chidambaram
Tranquebar
KARIKAL
Negapatam
Coleroon
Srirangam
Trichinopoli
Tanjore
POODOOKOTTA
Pt. Kalimere
PALK STRAIT
Pt. Pedro
Jaffna
Dindigul
Palni
Hills
Anamalai
Hills
Madura
Vaiga R.
Ramnad
Tuticorin
R. Tambraparni
Tinnevelli
GULF
OF MANAAR
Adam's Bridge
Trincomalee
CEYLON
COLOMBO
BAY OF
ARABIAN
SEA
Laccadive Islands
10°
75° E. Gr.
50
0
50
100 ENGLISH MILES

Of the gross revenue of £9,851,075 in 1880-81, the land-tax yielded £4,579,192, of which £613,862 was from permanently and favourably assessed lands, £3,547,826 from ryotwaree holdings, and £397,504 from miscellaneous sources.

§ 6. THE PEOPLE AND DISTRICTS.—Of the district population as revealed by the census of 1881 or 30,839,181, the number of males was 15,242,122, and of females 15,597,059. There was a diminution of 2·4 per cent on the 10 years since 1872, due to two or three years of famine. The figures in the districts relate to that earlier census when the district population was 31,597,872.

CIVIL DIVISIONS OF BRITISH TERRITORY, 1872.

DISTRICTS.	Area in square miles.	Population in 1872.	Number of villages.	Total cost of officials and Police of all kinds.	REVENUE.	
					Land.	Gross.
				Rs.	Rs.	Rs.
Ganjam . .	8,311	1,520,088	4,975	5,49,984	12,64,991	37,47,529
Vizagapatam .	17,380	2,296,351	12,304	6,87,981	13,82,681	24,70,675
Godavari .	7,345	1,620,634	2,462	10,61,819	41,19,268	59,32,563
Kistna . .	8,471	1,452,374	1,940	7,86,759	41,71,685	59,36,388
Nellore . .	8,739	1,376,811	2,132	4,59,366	24,60,607	41,02,193
Cuddapah .	8,745	1,351,194	1,313	3,65,536	19,06,932	22,74,307
Bellary . } Anantapoor }	10,871	1,653,010	2,565	8,65,782	23,25,162	29,28,106
Karnool . .	7,533	914,432	789	4,12,399	13,39,127	16,16,291
Madras . .	27	397,552	70	15,20,233	73,062	33,79,107
Chengalpat .	2,842	938,184	2,154	13,25,105	19,23,282	64,41,196
North Arcot .	7,256	2,015,278	5,305	7,33,303	28,18,024	33,73,437
South Arcot .	4,873	1,755,817	3,207	7,59,655	30,27,049	47,29,775
Tanjore . .	3,654	1,973,731	3,935	13,41,103	44,22,198	76,26,087
Trichinopoli .	3,383	1,200,408	1,634	9,42,301	13,39,678	16,67,550
Madura . .	9,502	2,266,615	5,463	8,36,598	25,07,812	35,13,560
Tinnevelli . .	5,381	1,693,959	1,633	3,83,424	27,89,699	51,21,098
Coimbatore .	7,842	1,763,274	1,562	9,44,359	26,41,315	30,64,016
Neelgiris .	957	74,719	18	2,07,020	52,413	2,67,341
Salem . .	7,653	1,966,995	4,688	5,35,409	21,21,643	25,82,624
South Kanara	3,902	918,362	1,289	4,48,866	12,24,369	19,89,473
Malabar . .	5,763	2,236,032	428	11,93,475	18,29,777	33,55,942
Total .	140,430	31,385,820	59,866	1,63,60,477	4,57,41,574	7,61,19,258

CHAPTER XXII.

MADRAS PROVINCE—DISTRICTS AND STATES.

East Central Districts.

§ 1. Madras City. § 2. Chengalpat. § 3. Nellore. § 4. South Arcot.

French Territory.

§ 5. Pondicheri.

North Central or Ceded Districts and States.

§ 6. North Arcot. § 7. Cuddapah. § 8. Bellary and Anantapoor. § 9. *Sandoor. § 10. Karnool. § 11. *Banaganapali.

Northern Districts.

§ 12. Kistna. § 13. Godavari. § 14. Vizagapatam. § 15. Ganjam.

West Central Districts.

§ 16. Salem. § 17. Coimbatore. § 18. Neelgiri Hills.

West Coast Districts.

§ 19. South Kanara. § 20. Malabar. § 21. Laccadive Islands.

Southern Districts and State.

§ 22. Tanjore. § 23. Trichinopoli. § 24. *Poodookotta. § 25. Madura. § 26. Tinnevelli.

**Cochin and Travankor States.*

§ 27. *Cochin. § 28. *Travankor.

§ 1. MADRAS CITY (406,112 in 1881), named probably from Madrasah = a Musalman college, capital of Madras Province, on the Coromandel or S.E. coast, 885 m. S.W. of Calcutta, and 794 S.E. of Bombay by railway. The Observatory, established in 1792, stands in N. lat. 13° 4′ 6″ and E. long. 80° 17′ 22″; from its meridian Indian railway time is taken. The municipality covers 27 sq. m., extending along the coast of the Bay of Bengal 7 m., and running inland 3½ m. The first piece of land secured in full possession by the English in India was 6 m. by 1 m., and was purchased for £600 a year from Sri Ranga Raja of Chandragiri, a fort 70 m. S.W., who represented the decaying Raj of Vijayanagar and governed the country around through Naiks or deputies. The title-deeds consisted of a plate of gold, in which the Raja stipulated that the new settlement should be called by his name; the plate was lost in 1746 at the French capture of the city. The local Naik of Chengalpat, or his father or brother, was named Chennappa, whence the native name of Madras is to this day Chenna-patnam. To this strip of coast Mr. Francis Day removed the East India Company's settlement at Armegaon, farther N. in the Nellore district, in March 1639, and here he constructed a factory, the nucleus of Fort St. George. The spot was close to the Portuguese city of St. Thomé, the scene of the martyrdom of the Apostle Thomas, as was believed; but its chief attraction was "the Island," as it is still called, formed on the land side by the river Kooum. This was soon walled round and named the White Town, none but Europeans being allowed to sleep there. The settlement of native weavers and others outside, to the N., became Black Town. The whole was under the East India Company's chief of the settlement at Bantam, in Java, till 1653, when Madras-patnam became the first and the chief Presidency in India. Soon the Golkonda dynasty became receivers of the annual rent, and its siege of St. Thomé first gave Madras city Portuguese inhabitants. In 1702, Aurangzeb's general, Daood Khan, followed by the Marathas in 1741, attempted to take the town, which was entirely surrounded by a wall, first of mud then of masonry; some of the bastions are still police stations. Labourdonnais first took Fort St. George in 1746, and the Company's officials returned to it in 1752. In 1758 Lally attacked the Fort from the Black Town, as described by Orme, but it was relieved by the British fleet. In 1749 the English had made St. Thomé, founded by the Portuguese in 1504, and held by the French for two years to 1674, a part of Madras city. The modern capital of S. India may now be divided thus, beginning at N.—(1) Rayapooram, centre of the railway workshops and goods warehouses, and emigration depot, with a Scottish Free Church medical mission, and many Eurasian mechanics; (2) Black Town, the mercantile and densely-inhabited square mile within the old walls, with High Court, offices of European bankers and merchants, and the Christian College and schools of the Free Church of Scotland, founded by Rev. John Anderson and now under Principal Miller, near the beach and stretching inland for 3 m. N. of the Kooum river; (3) the Fort, esplanade, island—now used as parade-ground—Government House, and other public buildings on a comparatively open space running S. for 2 m., the "lungs" of the city; (4) continuation of coast S. and W. through the crowded native quarters to St. Thomé; (5) the Eurasian quarter of Veperi and Pudupet, shading into the fine European suburbs of Egmore, Nungambakam, and Perambore, W. of Black Town; (6) the best European quarter to S.W. and S. of Adyar and Tanampet.

In this municipal area of 27 square miles are 23 villages, with 256 m. of roads. The drainage and purification of the Kooum have still to be cared for. The water supply is from two reservoirs drawn off the Cortelliar river and conveyed to the city in an open high-level channel 7 m. long. Fort St. George, begun by Francis Day in 1839, was improved during the three years' occupation by the French, and completed in 1787. It is not defensible against modern artillery. It contains the council chamber, civil and military secretariats, arsenal, barracks, and St. Mary's Church—the first Protestant Church in India—in which is the marble monument erected by the East India Company to the missionary Schwartz, whose tomb is at Tanjore where he died. The statue of Lord Cornwallis is in the Fort Square, and that of Sir Thomas Munro is on the Island, both by Chantrey; Colonel Neill's is near the Club, on the Mount Road, the principal thoroughfare since 1795 between the Fort and St Thomas's Mount, crossed by the Cathedral Road. The buildings most worth notice outside of the Fort are the Chepak Palace, the Presidency and Christian Colleges and Senate House, St. George's Cathedral, St. Andrew's Kirk, Patcheappah's Hall, the Central Railway Station, and Government House with the banqueting hall. Between the Observatory, 1 m. W. of the Central Museum, and Anderson's Bridge is the College containing the library of the Literary Society, the Mackenzie MSS., and a portrait of the Abbé Dubois in Hindoo dress. The Buckingham Canal connects the N. and S. systems. The People's Park, W. of the Central Railway Station, has a zoological collection. Triplicane quarter runs S. of the Fort from which the Kooum divides it, and parallel with the coast. In 1880 the municipality received Rs. 7,56,800, of which Rs. 6,71,988 was from taxation on houses and lands, trades, lighting, water and carriage rates, and tolls; it spent slightly more. On the basis of the census of 1872, when the population was 397,552 in 51,741 houses, the birth-rate in 1880 was 40·4, and the death-rate 37·4 per mille. The southern suburb of **Saint Thomé**, 2 m. S. of the Fort with an old Roman Catholic Church, is identified by Heber and by H. H. Wilson with the Mailapoor or Mihilapoor, where the Apostle Thomas is said to have been martyred on 21st December 58 A.D. The rocky knoll of the **Little Mount**, 5 m. S.W. of Fort, with church dedicated to St. Thomas, attracts crowds under the belief that the Apostle perished there. A cave in which he concealed himself, and a cell in which he worshipped are shown, but it has been proved that it is Thomas Aquinas whose name was given to this place. The model farm and race-course are in the neighbourhood. **Saint Thomas's Mount** (16,000) (220 ft.), railway station 8 m. S. of Madras, a knoll of greenstone and syenite, topped by an old Armenian Catholic church; at the base is the cantonment, the head-quarters of the Madras Artillery. The battle of the Mount, in 1759, in which Captain Calliaud forced Lally's troops to retreat, was one of the fiercest struggles in the Franco-British war. **Pallavaram** (4500), 11½ m. S. of Madras, the old presidency cantonment (450 ft.), now garrisoned by one regiment and European pensioners. **Poonamalai** (5000), 13 m. W. of Madras and 4 N. of St. Thomas's Mount, cantonment for European recruits and invalids, with old fort of some note in the Karnatic wars. **Guindy**, 6½ m. from Fort St. George, Governor's country house and extensive park.

§ 2. CHENGALPAT DISTRICT ("brick village") is bounded E. by Bay of Bengal, N. by Nellore, W. by N. Arcot, S. by S. Arcot. Area, 2842 sq. m. Population, 968,184.[1] This flat and dreary coast district rises from below sea-level near some of the backwaters to 300 ft. on the W. The **Nagalapooram** hills (2500 ft.), and a ridge of which Kambakam Droog is the highest peak (2548 ft.), are in the N.; through these run three principal passes to the plateau above. The **Palar** ("milk stream") from Mysore and N. Arcot is the chief river; having received the Poini it enters the district W. of Conjeveram, 8 m. E. of which it is joined by the Cheyar at Toruppakoodal, and flows for 30 m. farther to the sea 3 m. S. of Sadras. The **Cortelliar** from N. Arcot, fed by small streams and tapped by weirs for the Cholavaram and Red Hill reservoirs which supply Madras city, falls into the Ennore backwater N. of Madras. The **Cheyar**, flowing from the foot of the hills which divide N. Arcot from Salem, enters the district W. of Uttiranmeroor. The **Aramyanadi**, another alluvial stream, passes across the

[1] The population of districts and towns is according to the census of 1872. Details of the Madras census of 1881 have not yet been published (Nov. 1882).

N. to the sea near Pulikat under the name of the Naranavaram. The Kooum (Kuvam) is formed of the surplus of the tank of the same name in the Conjeveram portion of the district, and flows through Madras city to the sea at the Marine Villa. The Adyar becomes a respectable stream as it approaches the capital; it can be traced to Guduvanchéri village. Of the lagoons formed by ridges of blown sand into a network along the coast, the chief is the **Pulikat Lake**, 37 m. long, in the N. The high ground between some of them is cut by the **Cochrane** and **East Coast Canal**; the former runs N. from Black Town through the Pulikat Lake into Nellore; the latter runs S. from the Adyar to the mouths of the Palar: during the famine of 1876-8 the N. and S. Canals were united in Madras. Along the coast-line of 155 m. the surf wave breaks, from 3 ft. in fine weather to 12 or 14 ft. high in gales; it breaks at 300 ft. from shore in calm, and at 450 to 1000 feet in stormy weather. Pulikat shoal, 14 m. N. of Madras city, and Covelong reef, 25 m. S., are the only points of danger. Some 14,000 fishermen, chiefly Roman Catholic Christians, carry on the sea fisheries. The Nawab of Arcot granted the district to the East India Company in 1760, soon after which Haidar Ali swept it by the sword, and famine extended the desolation. **Saidapet** (4700), village on Mount Road, 5 m. S.W. of Fort St. George, headquarters of the Collector; the offices are in Homes' Gardens. **Chengalpat** (8000), 36 m. S.W. of Madras railway station, including Goontoor and Nattam, with Scottish Free Church and Roman Catholic missions: the old fort was the key of the British possessions during the Mysore wars; the hills and tank make Chengalpat a pretty place in the rains. **Sadras** (2000), with ruins of old Dutch fort and cemetery, on coast 35 m. S. of Madras. **Covelong** (Kovilam), a village 20 m. S. of Madras, formerly seat of Dutch and of Ostend East India Company traders; taken by the French by stratagem in 1750, and capitulated to Clive in 1752. Between Sadras and Covelong, near East Coast Canal, is **The Seven Pagodas** of Mahabalipooram ("city of the Mahamalla race," subdued by the Chalookyas), a marvellous series of five Dravidian monolithic temples, fourteen caves, and bas-reliefs cut on and in a ridge of granite boulders 1500 ft. long, on the open sea-beach, about 700 A.D. Two m. N. is the tiger cave of Saluvankuppum; "here not one but a dozen of tiger heads welcome the horite to his abode." **Madarantakam** (4000), 50 m. S. adras, with tank remarkable for its fine calingula or . Two m. N. is Karanguli (3000), the fort of which

Eyre Coote took from Lally's troops in 1759, after Wandewash, and again from Haidar Ali's force in 1781. **Conjeveram** (37,000) (Kanchi or Kanchipooram = the "shining" or "golden city"), the Benares of South Indian Hindooism, one of the seven sacred cities, 45 m. S.W. of Madras, on the junction railway between Arkonam and Chengalpat. Second in antiquity only to Surat, part of the *Arcati Regia Sorae* of Pliny, and long the Boodhist capital of Dravida. Three great pagodas and seven sacred tanks still remain; the oldest is of Shiva, and headquarters of the Adwaitam or non-dualistic doctrine; the richest is of Vishnoo, and centre of the Vasishtadwaita school of ethics, with a hundred-pillared *mantapam* or hall, and jewels of which Clive presented a gold necklace worth £368. Here the Scottish Free Church has a mission. Clive marched through Conjeveram on his way to Arcot in 1751, took it soon after, and it became the principal British cantonment in the Karnatic for a time. A few m. N.W. Baillie's detachment was cut to pieces by Haidar Ali, and Sir Hector Munro threw his guns and baggage into the temple tank during his retreat to Chengalpat. **Wallajahabad** (5000), on the Palar, 8 m. S. of Conjeveram, a British cantonment till 1860. **Tiruvalloor** (5000), railway station 26 m. W. of Madras, has temple with tower (Gopuram) of 156 ft. and hall of 688 pillars. Two m. W. is Tipassore, old station of East India Company's cadets, and now for European pensioners, in fort. Ennore (4500), 8 m. N. of Madras, on backwater into which the Cortelliar falls, with several European residences. **Pulikat** (Paliyaverkádu = "jungle of old mimosa trees") (5000), port at S. end of island dividing sea from the lake, site of first settlement of the Dutch in India, with interesting cemetery. N. is Coromandel (3000) or Kareimanal = "sand coast," once supposed to have given its name to the whole coast, which is really a corruption of Cholamandalam = land of the Cholas.

§ 3. NELLORE DISTRICT is bounded E. by Bay of Bengal, N. by Kistna district, W. by Karnool and Cuddapah with the Eastern Ghats between, and S. by N. Arcot and Chengalpat. Area, 8739 sq. m. Population, 1,376,811. This portion of the Telugoo-speaking north country of Madras is a sandy strip of coast 170 m. long and 70 broad between the sea and the **Eastern Ghats**, which run N.W. from the S. of Venkatagiri to the N. of Kanigiri, and rise to their highest point (3000 ft.) at Penchalakonda. Dense jungle and bamboos cover the slopes; there is sometimes large timber of little value. The **Udayagiri Droog** (3079 ft.) is an isolated stronghold held of old by a petty Musalman lord. The **Pennar** river, from the Nandidroog hills in Mysore, enters the district through the Somesila gorge of the Eastern Ghats, 285 m. from its source, and flows E. for 70 m. to the Bay of Bengal, which it reaches 18 m. below Nellore town, having received the small Bogeru and Biraperu in its course. It is tapped by anicuts or weirs for irrigation. The **Suvarnamookhi** flows from the Chittoor hills parallel to the Pennar, and after a course of 15 m. in the district falls into the Bay of Bengal 34 m. S. of that river. The **Gundlakamma** rises in the Cumbum tank in Karnool, and is fed by the drainage of the Nallamallai hills. The **East Coast Canal**, from Kistnapatam, is carried S. along the W. border of the island of **Sriharikota** for 20 m., a ridge of sand dividing Pulikat Cape from the sea. Next to Cuddapah Nellore produces most indigo on the Bengal system. Nellore, as part of old Telingana, between Orissa and the Tamil country, was successively under the Yadava, Chalookya, Kalyana, and Ganpatti dynasties. In 1628 the East India Company, after the Amboyna massacre by the Dutch, settled at **Armegaon**, S. of the village of Durgarayapatam, which Mr. Francis Day named after its headman, Armugam Modelliar, until in 1639 the same "factor" founded Madras. Armegaon is now only a lighthouse to warn ships off the shoal. **Nellore** (30,000), ("town of the Nelli tree"), the chief town, is on the right bank of the Pennar, 8 m. from its mouth, and 107 m. N. of Madras. Here, in the ruins of a Hindoo temple, a pot of Roman gold coins and medals of the 2d century was found. Tradition places this old site, under the name of Simbapooram = "lion town," in the forest wilderness known as *Dandaka Aranyam*, at the present European suburb of Doorgametta. The offices are in the old fort. There are Protestant Missions of the American Baptists, Scottish Free Church, and Hermansburg Lutherans, and a Roman Catholic mission. **Ongole** (6000), 11 m. N. of the Moosi and 189 N. of Madras, with iron ores, ruined fort, and American Baptist Mission. **Venkatigiri** (7500), seat of the oldest Hindoo family which assisted the English against Haidar Ali, and is head of the Vimala caste.

§ 4. SOUTH ARCOT DISTRICT (*Aru-kadu* = "six deserts") is bounded E. by the Bay of Bengal, N. by Chengalpat and N. Arcot, W. by Salem, and S. by Trichinopoli. Area, 4873 sq. m. Population, 1,755,817. On W. are the **Kalrayan Hills** (3500 ft.), connected with the Shivarai, and in the N.W. the **Jawadi** group; between the two the **Chengam Pass** leads into Salem. The isolated **Trinomalai Peak** (2668 ft.) is covered with jungle and accessible only on foot. There are 3 rivers navigable throughout the year for a short distance from their mouths. The **Coleroon** (Kolidam) flows for 36 m. along S.E. border and debouches into the sea 3 m. S. of Porto Novo. The **Vellar** has a course of 82 m. in the district, receives the Manimookta near Vidrachalam, and reaches the sea at Porto Novo. The **Gaddilam** (Garuda-nadi), issuing from the Yegal tank, is connected with the Ponniar by the Mallatar, and after a course of 59 m. passes by Fort St. David and falls into the sea a mile N. of Cuddalore. The **Ponniar** reaches the sea 2 m. farther N., having risen near Nandidroog on the Mysore plateau, and flowed 75 m. through the district from near Manikal. The **Gingee**, from the Naranamangalam tank, receives the Toudayar and Pombayar, and runs into the sea by two mouths. Historically S. Arcot is full of interest, from 1674 when the Khan of Gingee's invitation led the president of Fort St. George to open a trading settlement at Cuddalore, Conimeer, and Porto Novo; and in 1687 the East India Company purchased from the Marathas the site of Fort St. David. During the Franco-British wars of the latter half of the 18th century the most prominent place was the chief town **Cuddalore** new and old (40,500) (Goodaloor), railway stations 124-7 m. S. of Madras, on the backwater connecting the Gaddilam and Paravanar rivers; the old factory is now the jail; the Propagation Society holds the church taken from the Jesuits on their expulsion as French spies in 1749; Clive-street is a memorial of the great Clive who in 1747 received his first commission from the Court of Directors as Ensign, in these terms—"Mr. Robert Clive, writer in the service, being of martial disposition, and having acted as a volunteer in our late engagements, we have granted him an ensign's commission upon his application for the same." He was the last Governor of **Fort St. David**, a barrack-yard the wretched casemates and subterranean ways of which still exist 1½ m. from Cuddalore. The fort was destroyed in 1758, when Clive was in Bengal, by the French, who at the same time took and held Cuddalore for 2 years till Eyre Coote's advance. **Porto Novo** (71,000), railway station and fort at mouth of the Vellai, where the English succeeded the Portuguese in 1683, and in 1781 Eyre Coote fought Haidar Ali. For many years an iron company attempted here to work ore brought from Salem; the buildings have now reverted to Government. **Chedamburam** (*Chitt'ambalam* = "atmosphere of wisdom") (16,000), one of the five old seats of Shiva-worship, 26 m. S. of Cuddalore. Its pagoda, containing the *Akása* = "air" lingam, or "secret of Chedamburam" (represented by a curtain behind which the phallic emblem is invisible), covers 39 acres, and is constructed of granite brought from a great distance to form its 1100 carved pillars each a solid block, its 70 circular monoliths, its great gateways and long flights of steps to the very deep "golden" tank of green water used only for washing. In 1781 Haidar Ali's garrison beat off Sir Eyre Coote from the pagoda. **Srimushnam** (2000), 19 m. W. of Cuddalore, with great pagoda, one of the eight Vaishnava shrines. **Trinomalai** (9000), another of the five Shiva centres, with large pagoda at foot of the hill, 24 m. W. of **Gingee**, consisting of 3 strongly fortified hills, which, Orme says, 10 men could defend against 10,000; chief stronghold of the Gingee country under successive dynasties, till captured by the English in 1761. **Tindivanam** (*Tinthrani Vanam* = "the tamarind jungle") (6500), railway station, 75 m. S. of Madras. Six m. E. is the rock of Permacoil or Perumookal (= "great travail" of Seeta), often captured by the English and French. **Panruth** (7000), railway station 110 m. S. of Madras, is a large commercial centre. **Valavanoor** (7000) yields the largest revenue in the district. Villupooram (6000), junction of South Indian Railway for Pondicheri, 98 m. S. of Madras.

This District contains 32,000 Christians, chiefly Roman Catholics. Ziegenbalg, of the Danish Evangelical Lutheran Mission, opened a Tamil school at Cuddalore in 1716; there Sartorius died; there Kiernander taught before he went to Calcutta; and there Schwartz landed in 1750. The Leipzig Lutheran Mission is at Chedamburam, and also near Cuddalore. The Propagation Society is at Cuddalore. The American Reformed Church works in the N. about Trinomalai and Tindivanam. The 11 Roman Catholic Missions are under the Bishop of Flaviopolis at Pondicheri, an offshoot of Robert de Nobili's Madura Mission in 1606, chiefly in the Gingee country. Jean de Britto resided at Tattuvancheri, N. of the Coleroon.

French Territory.

§ 5. PONDICHERI (Puthuchéri), chief of the small French territories in India, also railway station and free port, surrounded by the Cuddalore subdivision of S. Arcot district, through whose Collector business with the British Government is negotiated by the French Governor. The port is 86 m. S. of Madras in lat. 11° 53′ N., and long. 79° 56′ E. The French settlement covers 113 sq. m., with a population of 156,094 in the three districts of Pondicheri, Villianoor, and Bahoor. The whole French possessions cover 178 sq. m., with a population of 280,381. Chandarnagar, in the Hoogli district of Bengal, with 3 sq. m., has been already described. Karikal (32 sq. m.), Mahé (5 sq. m.), and Yanaon (5 sq. m.), will be found in the Madras districts which enclose them. The five places yield an annual revenue of about 1¾ million francs, one-eighth of which is paid to France towards the cost of the civil and military establishments. The salt allowance of £44,066, paid by the British Government under the treaty of 1815, is the principal source of revenue, to prevent the interference of France with the salt monopoly. **Pondicheri Town** was founded by François Martin in 1674, captured by the Dutch in 1693, and held by them for 6 years, besieged four times by the English, and held by them for 34 years on three different occasions. A canal divides it into the white and black town. The white town, on the sea, is well built, containing Government House, two churches, bazar, clock tower, lighthouse, barracks, hospital, and town hall. It has a fine iron pier and water supply. It is the seat of a Roman Catholic Apostolic Prefecture, the headquarters of the French Mission in the Karnatic. There are spinning, weaving, dyeing, and tanning industries. There are betel and tobacco monopolies. Villupooram is the junction on the South India Railway 24 m. W. from Pondicheri.

North Central or Ceded Districts and States.

§ 6. NORTH ARCOT DISTRICT is bounded E. by Chengalpat, N. by Nellore and Cuddapah, W. by Mysore, and S. by Salem. Area, 7256 sq. m. Population, 2,015,278. The **Eastern Ghats** run from N.E. to S.W., throwing out spurs to S. The **Nagari Hills** run across the N. corner. The **Jawadi Range** (3000 ft.) touch the S.E. The **Palar**, entering the district in S.W., flows E. to the sea; it receives the **Cheyair** and **Poini**. The portion above the Ghats formed, with part of Salem district, the **Baramahal** ("twelve estates"), dominated by 12 forts. The Nizam ceded to the East India Company all the territories which its armies had secured to him by the Mysore treaties of 1792 and 1799, to pay his debt for the subsidiary force, to maintain it for the first time, and to protect him in the sovereignty of Haidarabad. These were the Ceded Districts, further remarkable for Sir Thomas Munro's settlement of them 1800-1807, and the people's gratitude to him whom they called "father." **Chittoor** ("little town") (6000), administrative headquarters, in the valley of the Poini, 18 m. N. of Vellore railway station and 100 from Madras; occupied by Eyre Coote in 1781: here the Moghili pass leads up to the Mysore plateau; 3½ m. N.E. are the cromlech-like sepulchres of Panduvaram Dewal. **Arcot** ("six forests") (12,000), on right bank of the Palar, 5 m. from railway station, old capital of Nawabs of Karnatic, and famous for the capture and defence by Clive, immortalised by Orme and Macaulay. Clive's room is shown in the dismantled walls at the Delhi gate. The European station is **Ranipet**, on left bank of Palar, 3 m. from railway, formerly a cantonment. **Vellore** (38,000), cantonment and railway station, 80 m. W. of Madras and 15 of Arcot, famous for fortress of Vijayanagar line, held by the English for two years against Haidar Ali; and for mutiny of the sepoys in 1806, put down by Colonel Gillespie, after which Tipoo's family were transferred as parole prisoners to the suburbs of Calcutta. In the fort is one of the finest and oldest *mantapam* or pagoda porches in S. India. **Walajapet** (12,000), named from princes of Arcot, from which it is 3 m. distant, a pleasant town and railway station on left bank of Palar, known for its carpets. **Goodiattam** (11,000), railway station, 15 m. W. of Vellore; with weaving industry and rice exports; the Symgunta pass leads hence to Mysore. **Tripalty** (Tirupati, the Tripetty of Orme) (10,500), railway station, 83 m. N.W. of Madras, near one of the most frequented hill (2500 ft.) pagodas of Vishnoo in S. India; here in 1772 occurred the first recorded outburst of cholera. On the seven-peaked hill are 16 waterfalls. Lower Tripalty, nearest to hill, is 6 m. from railway station. **Wandiwash** (4500), now chief town of a subdivision, its fort belonging to Arcot family, was the scene of sieges and a treaty in the Karnatic wars; here Coote took Bussy prisoner, and won the most important victory over the French in 1760. Lieutenant Flint held the fort for 3 years against Haidar Ali. Kalahasti (Calastri) (6700), on right bank of Sivarnamookhi, 16 m. N.E. of Tripalty; now known for its glass beads. Punganoor, in N. (2000 ft.), now produces hardware. The Scottish Established Church, the American Baptists, and Roman Catholics have missions in N. Arcot district.

§ 7. CUDDAPAH DISTRICT, between the W. slopes of the Eastern Ghats and the opposing face of the Mysore plateau, is bounded E. by Nellore, N. by Karnool, W. by Bellary and Mysore, S. by Mysore and North Arcot. Area, 8745 sq. m. Population, 1,351,194. From Tripalty hill in North Arcot the Eastern Ghats (3000 ft.) strike N. between Cuddapah and the Nellore littoral; and the **Palkonda Range** ("milk" or pasture), N.W. to Cuddapah town, which lies in the valley between it and its offshoots the **Sheshachalam Hills** (1500 ft.), dividing the district into two distinct climes. From opposite the end of the Palkondas the **Nallamalai** ("black hills") range runs N. parallel with the Eastern Ghats into Karnool. The rivers which drain the Mysore slopes are the **Chitravăti** (one of Shiva's wives), **Papagni** (sin-destroyer), and **Cheyair**, falling into the **N. Pennar**, which has worn the deep and picturesque gorge of Gandikota ("fort of the gorge"), and finds a final exit through the Sunkesala pass of the Eastern Ghats. The country has many extravagant traditions of Sir Thomas Munro, who tamed its poligars or feudal barons, and gave its peasants the ryotwaree settlement, so that they are prosperous farmers and famous producers of indigo, sugar, and cotton. Yet the district suffered greatly in 1877, as in its predecessors, from alternate famine and flood. A canal runs from **Proddatoor** (6709) ("sun-town") to Cuddapah, and the N.W. line of the Madras Railway traverses the E. and N. portions, with 10 stations. **Cuddapah** ("threshold" of the pass to Tripalty) (16,000), railway station, in a hot hollow, 161 m. from Madras, capital of a Nawab, from whom the Marathas and Haidar Ali wrested his lands, on N. bank of the Boogair river. Patha ("old") Cuddapah is a neighbouring hamlet. Chennoor, village near Cuddapah, where diamonds are found. **Sidhaut** ("hermit's banian tree"), on the Pennar, 10 m. E. of Cuddapah town, famed for its melons, and called the Southern Benares from its sanctity and resemblance to Benares. **Outimetta** ("solitary hill"), railway station, 8 m. from Sidhaut, with frequented pagoda; produces indigo and turmeric. **Badvail** (8500), in N.E., an indigo and mineral centre. Rayachoti ("Raja's abode") (5000), in central subdivision. **Kadiri** ("tree" under which the idol was found), in W., a bad pilgrim resort, where a tiger used to be let loose. **Madanapalli** ("hamlet of Madana" = Cupid) (7000), in S.W. The London Missionary Society, Americans, and Roman Catholics have missions here.

§ 8. BELLARY AND ANANTAPOOR DISTRICTS[1] (Valahari) are bounded E. by Cuddapah and Karnool, N. and N.W. by Haidarabad State from which it is separated by the Toongabhadra, S.W. by Dharwar, and S. by Mysore. Area, 10,871 sq. m. Population,

[1] As this passes through the press, the Madras Government has divided the old District of Bellary, nearly the size of Belgium, into two, or Bellary to the W. and Anantapoor to the E.

1,653,010. The district is a treeless plateau (1200 ft.) of black cotton and red soil, sloping from the Eastern Ghats towards the Sahyadri or Western Ghats. The principal hills are the **Sandoor** and **Kampli Ranges** to W., with dome-shaped granite clusters crowned with forts near Vijayanagar; and the **Lankamalai Range** on E. border. To S. are the isolated clusters of Palsamoodram and Pennakonda, and in the neighbourhood of Adoni. The **Copper Mountain** (3148 ft.), S.W. of Bellary, is so called because Haidar Ali worked the ore there. The **Toongabhadra, Pennar, Haggan,** and **Chitravăti** from Mysore, are the chief rivers. The Hindri, from the hills near Pattikonda, flows for 30 m. to Karnool, where it falls into the Toongabhadra. The district is the dividing line between the Kanarese and Telugoo-speaking peoples. The former or Kernata house fixed their capital at Vijayanagar in Bellary, as the Telingana Rajas did at Warangal in Haidarabad, in their combination against their Musalman conquerors. After the Golkonda, Maratha, Aurangzeb, Haidar Ali, and Nizam conquests, the territory came under Munro's civilising hands in 1800, and there the great Governor died. **Bellary** (52,000), chief town, cantonment, and terminus of branch railway, 305 m. N.W. of Madras from Goontakool junction extending W. to Goa and Karwar, built round a granite rock (450 ft.), defended by an upper and lower fort; S. is the native town, with fine military bazar, Cowle bazar (18,500), Bruce-pettah, and Mellor-pettah (19,000), named from officials. Seat of London Missionary Society and Roman Catholic missions. **Hospett** ("new town") (9500), near, and **Kampli** (9000), on the Toongabhadra. **Harpanhalli** (6000), 66 m. S.W. of Bellary, seat of powerful chief, who surrendered to General Harris in 1800. **Adoni** (23,000), railway station, 307 m. N.W. of Madras, a weaving town; its now ruined fort on five granite peaks (800 ft.), N.W., commanded the doab of the Kistna and Toongabhadra. **Gooti** (6700), railway station 275 m. N.W. of Madras, with fort, the stronghold of the Maratha Morari Rao, who assisted Clive after Arcot; here is the tomb of Sir T. Munro, who died of cholera on 6th June 1827 at Pattikonda, where is another memorial, a well; his remains now rest in St. Mary's Church, Fort St. George.

Anantapoor (the "eternal city") (5000), 50 m. S.E. of Bellary, former headquarters of Ceded Districts, and residence of Munro, between whose house (in ruins) and the town is a noble avenue of banian trees. **Hampi**, site of **Vijayanagar** capital on S. bank of Toongabhadra, 36 m. N.W. of Bellary; the ruins of the city described by Cæsar Frederick as 24 m. in circuit, now cover 9 sq. m., including Kamlapoor and the later capital of Anagoondi. The finest is the temple-group of Vittala, a form of Vishnoo; the main street parallel with the river is lined with temples and palaces; from the hill above a magnificent panorama is seen. **Tadpatri** (7800), railway station on right bank of Pennar, 227 m. N.W. of Madras. **Pennakonda** (5000), in hilly S. country, old fortress of Vijayanagar kings, still of architectural interest, with palace and mosque.

§ 9. *SANDOOR STATE, in Bellary District, a valley covering 140 sq. m., with a population of 10,530, isolated by hills of the same name, of which the chief is **Ramandroog** (3150 ft.) or **Ramanamalai**, 38 m. W. of Bellary, a convalescent depot for troops since 1846, like Bangalore in climate. Bheemagoondi is the N.E. pass; Ramanagoondi is the N. pass; and the W. pass is Oblagoondi, through which the stream flows that feeds the lake of Daroji. The jageerdar, a descendant of Moram Rao, the Maratha chief of Gooti, has a revenue of £4700. In the S. is the old pagoda of the Hindoo Mars, Komara or Kartika, frequented by pilgrims.

§ 10. KARNOOL DISTRICT is bounded E. by Nellore and the Kistna, N. by Haidarabad State from which it is divided by the Kistna and Toongabhadra rivers, W. by Bellary, S. by Bellary and Cuddapah. Area, 7533 sq. m. Population, 914,432. The **Mallamalai** and **Yellamalai Ranges**, running N. and S. parallel to the **Velikonda** or main edge of the Eastern Ghats, divide the district into three tracts. The E. is the Cumbum valley (600 ft.), in which is the magnificent **Cumbum Tank**, formed by a dam across the Gundlakamma river, and covering 15 sq. m. From this valley the Nandikamma ghat (2000 ft.) and Mantial pass lead across the Nallamalais to the central division, a flat cotton-soil valley, crossed by the watershed between the Pennar and Kistna, drained by the Bhavanasi and Kundair, and traversed by the Madras Irrigation Company's Canal. The W. division is a bare rocky track forming the N. edge of the Mysore plateau, 900 ft. at Karnool town, and drained by the Hindri, which falls into the Toongabhadra. An anicut or weir at **Sunkesala**, 18 m. above Karnool, sends off from the Toongabhadra that Company's irrigation and navigation canal for 189 m. to Cuddapah, of which 142 are in this district. Forests cover the three ranges of hills; the Nallamalai forests, 2000 sq. m. in extent, yield the finest teak in the Eastern Ghats. There are 14 diamond localities in Karnool, of which Ramulkota, 18 m. S.W. of Karnool, seems to be the Raolconda of Tavernier. **Karnool** (25,000), chief town at junction of Hindri and Toongabhadra, 80 m. N.E. of Gooti, nearest railway station, a hot place, with mausoleum of first Nawab. **Nandial** ("place of Shiva's bull") (9000), chief town of a subdivision and of Shiva-worship. **Cumbum** (7000), beside the great tank, with embankment 57 ft. high. **Goodoor** (6000), 19 m. N.W. of Karnool; former headquarters, with cotton and silk weaving. Meddikera (8500), Kodumoor (6000), and Paikali (5000) are other places of local trade and industry. The American Baptists and Roman Catholics have missions in this district.

§ 11. *BANAGANAPALI STATE, in S.W. corner of Karnool, comprises the W. half of the basin of the Kunder, and is watered by the Junver also. Area, 275 sq. m. Population, 30,667, in 63 towns and villages. The capital (8000) of the same name, 90 m. E. of Bellary and 250 N. of Madras, lies in a gorge watered by a stream, half a mile from the diamond workings, which are in a damp clayey conglomerate and breccia, and run westward for some miles. The Nawab was a jageer-dar of the Nizam, is a Saiad of the Sheea sect, and has a gross revenue of £25,000.

Northern Districts.

§ 12. KISTNA DISTRICT (Krishna) is bounded E. by Bay of Bengal, N. by Godavari, W. by Haidarabad and Karnool, S. by Nellore. Area, 8471 sq. m. Population, 1,452,734. This flat district, broken in the interior by low hills (1857 ft.), of which the chief are Bellamkonda, Kondavir, Kondapali, and Jamalavoidroog, is cut by the Kistna river into the Masulipatam and Gantoor divisions. The **Kistna** turns S. from the E. Ghats and falls into the sea by two mouths; its delta for the 80 intervening miles forms the district. Between the Kistna and the Godavari deltas, to N., is the **Kolar Lake**, where the land is formed more slowly, covering 100 sq. m. in the monsoon; the Metapolliem river is its outlet. **Masulipatam** ("fish town," or rather the Maisolia of the Greeks) (36,500), chief town and port, first factory established by East India Company on E. coast in 1611, under a "golden firman" from Golkonda king; succeeded by Armegaon and then Madras; had a rich trade with the Spice Islands. Colonel Forde, sent by Clive from Calcutta, retook the town from the French in 1759, and held it under the Delhi emperor's patent of 1765 granting the five N. Circars. On the public drive is "Eliza's tree," so called from Mrs. Draper, Sterne's correspondent. Church Missionary Society's centre of influence on the Telugoo country; here Fox and Noble lived and died for the people. **Gantoor** (18,000), on trunk road 46 m. from Masulipatam, headquarters of the Judge; has trade in cotton and grain. An American Lutheran Mission works here. **Bezwara** (8000), on the Kistna, at the gorge of the E. Ghats, 20 m. N.E. from Gantoor, at the junction of the Calcutta, Madras, and Haidarabad roads; this is the Dhanakaketa of Hwen T'hsang, with rock-cut temples, the most S. Boodhist remains. The weir, 1280 yards long, 305 ft. broad, and 21 ft. above low level, sends off one canal on left bank 39 m. to Ellore, and the other 49 m. to Masulipatam, branching also to Nizapatam and Comamoor, in all 254 m., irrigating a quarter of a million of acres, and producing £89,000 annual revenue. **Jaggayapet** (9000), on Masulipatam road, near Haidarabad border, a prosperous mart and weaving town. **Chirala** (9000), formerly in Nellore district, with cotton manufactures. **Bapatla** (10,500), head of a subdivision, 30 m. S. of Gantoor. **Vinukonda** (5000), town and hill fort ("hill of hearing") (600 ft.), at which Rama is said to have first heard of Seeta's abduction. In this district, on Sir Walter Elliott's report, the five large zameendarees, being in arrears of rent, were bought up by the State, so that, under the ryotwari assessment fixed in 1873 for 30 years, there are 137,880 holdings owned by 169,036 proprietors, each paying £2 : 4s. as land-tax. **Amravati**, on S. bank of Kistna, 20 m. N.W. of Gantoor, near site of ancient Dharamkota, famous for its Boodhist stupa or tope and ornamental rails.

§ 13. GODAVARI DISTRICT is bounded E. by the Bay of Bengal and Vizagapatam, N. by Vizagapatam and the Central Province, W. by Haidarabad, and S. by Kistna and the Bay of Bengal. Area, 7345 sq. m. Population, 1,620,634. One of the 5 N. Circars, Godavari is divided by the river from which it takes its name. At Dowlaishvaram, 30 m. inland, the **Godavari** separates into two main streams, which enclose the central subdivision; the French settlement of **Yanaon** (5 sq. m.) is at the mouth of the northern, the **Koringa** and **Nursapoor** (7000) at the mouth of the southern. The Godavari has seven mouths—the Tulyabhaga, the Atreya, the Gantami, the Vruddhagantami, the Bharadwajam, the Kausika, and the Vasishta; each is considered sacred, the river being one of the 12 at which the *Pushkaram* feast is observed. From **Dowlaishvaram** ("white Shiva") (7500) the river sends off, by a weir, 19 navigable canals to the coast. Four m. higher is **Rajamahendri** (20,000), old seat of the Orissa kings in S., and of the Vengi kings; from which the French were driven by Forde after the battle of Condore in 1758; former headquarters of a district. Innespet is the European suburb. Farther N. is the picturesque **Patapatteshim Island** and **Polaveram** timber mart. At **Papikonda** (4200 ft.) is the magnificent gorge of the E. Ghats, through which the river breaks. The chief town of the district since 1861 is **Cocanada** ("crow-country") (18,000), port with European trade on coast 315 m. N. of Madras and 545 S. of Calcutta, connected by navigable canal with Samalkotta and Dowlaishvaram. **Ellore** ("ruling town") (20,000), on the Tammaler river, 255 m. N. of Madras, with Church and Lutheran missions; old capital of the N. Circars, with ruins of fort built from Boodhist remains of Vengi. **Pithapooram** (9500), centre of subdivision and zameendaree near coast N. of Cocanada. **Peddapooram** (9000), the same, to west. Amalapooram ("sinless city") (7000), in Godavari central delta. **Samulkotta** (5500), 7 m. N. of Cocanada, formerly a cantonment. **Bhadrachalam** (2000), chief village of estate on upper Godavari, with old temple, 100 m. above Rajamahendri and 15 below **Dumagoodiem**, once headquarters of engineering operations to open up the navigation of upper Godavari, abandoned after an expenditure of £700,000. **Coringa** (ancient Kalinga, the "stag" of the *Ramayan*, the Kalingon of Pliny) (5700), port 8 m. S. of Cocanada, once the chief port on the coast, but now silted up; at Tallarevu, adjoining, are shipbuilding yards.

§ 14. VIZAGAPATAM DISTRICT is bounded E. by the Bay of Bengal and Ganjam, N. by Ganjam, W. by Chatteesgarh and Bastar State, S. by Godavari and the Bay. Area, 17,380 sq. m. Population, 2,296,351. In form an octagon, this picturesque hilly district, fertile on the coast, is largely occupied by the **Eastern Ghats**, running N.E. to S.W. (5000 ft.), and clothed with tall tree jungle, while the bamboo flourishes in the valleys. From this watershed the drainage on the E. is carried to the sea by numerous streams, and on the W. to the Godavari by the **Indravati** or the **Sabari** and **Siler**. Another watershed runs along the N. of the Jaipoor tract, separating the drainage between the Godavari and Mahanadi; in this are the sources of several tributaries of the Mahanadi, of which the chief is the **Tél**. The **Nimgiri Hills** (4972 ft.), in the extreme N., are separated from the E. Ghats by valleys of some 1200 ft. From these the principal rivers in the plain are the Nagavali, with its two feeders the Makkura and Saloor, which reaches the sea at Chikakol; the Gostani, at Konāda; the Bimlipatam; the Sharada and Varāha, which reach the sea at Wattāda 35 m.

S. of Vizagapatam town. First a portion of the old Kalinga, then of the eastern Chalookya kingdom, of which Vengi, near Ellore, was the capital, Vizagapatam afterwards came under the Gajapati Rajas of Orissa, then under the Kutub Shahi rulers of Delhi, and finally under Aurangzeb, whose viceroy ruled it from Chikakol. From the Nizam the tract was held in 1753 by the French, when Bussy took Bobbili. In 1759 Colonel Forde landed at Vizagapatam town and drove the French out of the N. Circars. In 1794 Colonel Prendergast defeated the Vizianagram Raja at Padmanabham, a village between his capital and Bimlipatam. In 1802 the land was permanently settled with that family and other 41 zameendars. The N. tracts are inhabited by the Saura and Khond tribes, the latter long guilty of the *meriah* or human sacrifice to the Earth goddess. **Vizagapatam** ("town of Vishaka" = Kartika or Mars) (32,500), chief town and port in a small bay between the Dolphin's Nose (1500 ft.) S. and **Waltair** N., the European station and cantonment. The East India Company early established a factory here. On the Europeans being murdered in 1689, the fort was built on a small river which separates the town from the Dolphin's Nose. Waltair is high and healthy, but relaxing; seat of London Missionary Society and Roman Catholic missions. Famous for art-work in silver, ivory, horn, and wood, and for honest cloth. **Vizianagram** ("city of Vijaya" = its founder) (23,000), British cantonment and palace-fort of an enlightened Maharaja, with public market and institutions commemorating visit of the Prince of Wales, 17 m. N.W. of **Bimlipatam** ("place of Bhima" = Pandu prince) (9000), port on river of same name, 18 m. N.E. of Vizagapatam, and 454 S.W. of Calcutta, with roadstead sheltered by Oopada and sugar-loaf headlands; here the Dutch early had a factory, made over to East India Company under treaty of 1824. Since 1846 there has been a considerable trade by English and French houses. **Palkonda** (8700), near Ganjam border, on Languliya river, seat of old and now prosperous zameendaree leased to Arbuthnot and Company of Madras. **Parvatipoor** (9000), centre of the Belgam zameendaree, and entrepot between hills and plains. **Bobbili** ("royal tiger") (14,500), centre of famous estate of same name, 70 m. N.W. of Vizagapatam; Bussy's siege of the fort (1753) is memorable in history and ballad for the Raja's desperate defence, so that neither man nor woman and only one child was found alive by the victor, and four fugitives assassinated the Raja's rival of Vizianagram. **Jaipoor** ("city of victory") (9500), centre of Jaipoor estate (11,526 sq. m.), on W. slope of E. Ghats, residence of the Raja and a sub-magistrate. The Assistant Agent's headquarters is **Korapat**; three vassal chiefs, Khonds, occupy the upper portion at Godavari, Bissemkatak, and Singapoor; Goonapoor and Rajagudda are also large villages, beyond which lies the Saura country. **Saloor** (10,700), centre of zameendaree long subject to Jaipoor. Ankapilli (13,500), centre of rich estate of same name, with fine garden.

§ 15. GANJAM DISTRICT ("a granary"), most N. of Madras, is bounded E. by Bay of Bengal, N. by Pooree district of Orissa, W. by Kalahandi, and Patna and Jaipoor estates, S. by Vizagapatam. Area, 8311 sq. m. Population, 1,520,088. The Eastern Ghats, locally named **Maliyas** (2000 ft.), nearly meet the coast, giving this district an hour-glass form, with swelling plains N. and S. covered with groves. The chief peaks are Mahendragiri (4923 ft.), Singharaj (4976 ft.), and Deodonga (4534 ft.). The Kalinga Ghat is the only pass for wheeled traffic. The **Rushikulya**, in N., falls into the sea near Ganjam town after a course of 100 m. The **Vamsadhara** ("bamboo river"), from the Jaipoor hills, flows for 145 m. and falls into the sea near Kalingapatam. The Languliya from Kalahandi State flows for 115 m. to the sea at Maphuz Bazar. Lakes, fresh or brackish, run along the coast, separated from the sea by sand-hills; pearl oysters are found in the Sonapoor backwater, and in the canal from the Chilka lake (see "Pooree" in "Bengal") to the Rushikulya. Like Vizagapatam, Ganjam, known as the Ichhapoor Province, was under successive masters till in 1768 the East India Company's Resident, Mr. E. Cotsford, founded a factory there. Disturbances in Parla Kimedi and Goomsoor led to campaigns in 1834-37, during which the English first came into contact with the Khonds, and put down their *meriah* rite. **Berhampoor** ("Brahma's town") (22,000), chief town and cantonment (Banpoor) on great N. road, 52 m. N.E. of Madras; **Gopalpoor** (3000) is its port, seat of sugar and silk trade; with German Baptist mission. **Ganjam** (4500), port, and former headquarters, at mouth of the Rushikulya. **Chikakol** ("Shiva's town") (16,000), on the Languliya, 4 m. from the sea, famed for fine muslins. **Kalingapatam** (5000), port 16 m. N. on the Vamsadhára, with ruins of capital of old Kalinga; the safest roadstead on the coast. **Ichapoor** ("city of desire") (13,000), 16 m. S.W. of Berhampoor, and former capital of Circar of same name; 6 m. to S.W. are the Boadagiri hills. **Aska** (4500), centre of zameendaree, and large sugar manufacture, on road from Berhampoor to **Russellkonda** (3000), named from Commissioner Russell in 1835, headquarters of the Assistant Agent for the Hill Tracts, 50 m. N.W. of Ganjam town. Six m. S.E. is **Goomsoor** (2500), centre of subdivision, and former seat of the Khond chief who rebelled in 1835, after which *meriah* was put down. **Parla Kimedi** (16,000), centre of largest zameendaree in Ganjam (993 sq. m.), whose family claim descent from the Gajapati sovereigns of Orissa. From 1768 frequent outbreaks disturbed the peace to 1835, since which the estate has been improved during minorities.

West Central Districts.

§ 16. SALEM DISTRICT (Chelam = "rocks") is bounded E. by Trichinopoli, N. and S. Arcot; N. by N. Arcot and Mysore; W. by Mysore and Coimbatore; S. by Coimbatore and Trichinopoli. Area, 7653 sq. m. Population, 1,966,995. The district, hilly except in S., consists of three tracts, from E. to W. the Talaghat ("below the E. Ghats") on the level of the Karnatic; the Baramahal, partly below and partly on the face of the Ghats; and the Balaghat ("above the Ghats") on the plateau occupied chiefly by Mysore. The chief range is the **Shivarai Hills** (*Seervarayar malai*), covering 100 sq. m., with a plateau (4500 ft.) of 20 sq. m., reached by two passes—on S. from Salem town 6 m. long, on N. from the Baramahal; Mallapooram is the railway station 8 m. from the base: the highest portion is the **Green Hills** (5410 ft.), with coffee gardens, all forming a sanitarium which has the flora of the Neelgiris; the chief European settlement is Yerkaud, on the plateau nearest to Salem. Other hills are the **Kalrayans** (4000 ft.), in Atoor subdivision, the home of the Malayális; the **Melagiris** (4580 ft.), in Osoor subdivision, also Malayáli, with Ponasiheta peak (4969 ft.); the **Kollamalais** (4663 ft., highest), in Ahtoor subdivision chiefly; **Pachamalais** ("green mountains") (2500 ft.), running S. into Trichinopoli district; **Yellagiris** (4437 ft. highest); also the Jevadi, Vatthalamalai, Erlvani, Valasaimalai, Bodamalai, Thalamalai, and Thopoor hills, all chiefly gneissic. The principal river is the **Kavari** from Coorg in the W. Ghats S.E. through Mysore; it irrigates the Tiruchengod and Namakal subdivision. The **Palar** touches the N. corner of the Tirupatoor subdivision. The **S. Pennar** from Mysore flows through Osoor and Krishnagiri subdivision to Uttankarai near S. Arcot, where it is joined by the Pambar and Vaniar. The Sanath-kumara, Vasishta, and Swetha fertilise much land before passing into S. Arcot. Forests of some value still clothe the Jevadi and Yellagiri hills. The district became British under the Mysore treaties of 1792 and 1799. After the failure of the permanent settlement with large landholders, the ryotwaree settlement was perfected in 1869-1874. **Salem** (50,000), chief town and railway station, 206 m. S.W. of Madras, on the Tirumanimuttar, in a pretty valley (900 ft.) 6 m. from the foot of the Shivarai hills; the European suburb is Hastanpet, 3½ m. from the railway suburb of Suramangalam, captured by Wood in 1768, now a busy weaving town and seat of London Society's Mission. **Tirupatoor** (13,000), 137 m. S.W. of Madras, centre of trade, with two Christian missions. **Shendamangalam** (12,000), with ironworks. **Jollarpet** (1500), 132 m. S.W. of Madras, railway junction for Bangalore and Mysore. **Atoor** ("village by the river") (8500), on Vashista river, and road from Salem to Cuddalore, with fort commanding the pass to Sankaridroog, of note in the wars with Haidar and Tipoo.

§ 17. COIMBATORE DISTRICT is bounded E. by Trichinopoli and Salem; N. by Mysore; W. by the Neelgiris, Malabar, and Cochin States; S. by Travankor State and Madura. Area, 7842 sq. m. Population, 1,763,274. The district slopes N.W. to E. from the Mysore plateau, from which it is divided by the **Balirangam Hills**, a double range (15,000 ft.) enclosing a valley (4000 ft.), the resort of wild elephants captured by the State. The Hassanoor and Burghoor passes lead thence to the plain, which undulates S. from Coimbatore town (1350 ft.) to Karoor (500 ft.). On S. the **Anamalai Hills** ("elephant"), spurs of the W. Ghats, run into Travankor State, in a higher (8000 ft.) and lower range, with teak forests of 80 sq. m., which long supplied the Bombay dockyards; on extreme W. **Anamoodi peak** (8850 ft.) is the highest in S. India. The timber centre is Anamalai (23,000), a cluster of villages on the Aliyar river, 23 m. S.E. of **Palghat Gap**, through which the S.W. monsoon cools and fertilises Coimbatore. The forest superintendent's centre is Tunakáchi, 15 m. distant. The **Kavari** flows rapidly along the N. border, and receives the **Bhavani**, **Noyil**, and **Amravati**; soon after leaving Mysore it forms the **Shivasamoodram** ("sea of Shiva") **Island** and noble **Waterfalls** (200 ft.). Coimbatore and the Salem plain formed part of the Dravidian Chera kingdom, with capital near Karoor, conquered in 9th century by the Chola dynasty, and afterwards merged in the Pandya dominions. Then it was part of the Madura kingdom in the 16th century, was long ravaged by Haidar and Tipoo, and its weak British garrisons were carried captive to Seringapatam. In 1799 it became British. There are missions of the London, Leipzig, and Lutheran Societies, and of the Jesuits. **Coimbatore** (35,500), chief town and railway station on Neelgiri branch, 305 m. S.W. of Madras and 50 from Ootakamand, on left bank of Noyil. Its fort used to command the Palghat approach to W. and the Gazalhatti pass to N. Peroor, with temple shrines, is 3 m. distant. **Metapolliem** (5000), terminus of Neelgiri branch railway, on the Bhavani. **Erode** (10,500), on the Kavari, 243 m. S.W. of Madras, junction for South Indian Railway to Trichinopoli, 90 m. **Arava-kurichi** (11,000), seat of Labhay traders, 19 m. S.W. of Karoor ("black town") (9500), on the Amravati near its junction with the Kavari, old capital of Chera kingdom, mentioned by Ptolemy, also called Vengi and Garbhapoori; long a frontier post of Mysore.

§ 18. NEELGIRI HILLS DISTRICT ("blue mountains") is bounded E. by Coimbatore, N. by Mysore, W. by Malabar, and S. by Malabar and Coimbatore. Area, 957 sq. m. Population, 74,719. The area consists of the **Neelgiri plateau**, of 704 sq. m., raised like a wall out of the plains to an average of 6000 ft., of 35 sq. m. in the **Ochterlony valley**, and of 236 in the **Wainad** on N., from which the hills are separated by the Moyar river descending by a fall at Neddiwattam in N.E. angle. Only a precipitous ridge of granite peaks, projecting from the base of the Yellamalai cone to the W. Ghats, prevents the complete isolation of the plateau. The peaks range from Dodabetta (8760 ft.) to Koonoor (5886 ft.), by which ghat is the principal approach, from the railway at Metapolliem, which is to be continued to Kailar and Koonoor, 12 m. on the Rigi system up the heavy gradients. The Segoor and Goodaloor ghats lead from Mysore and Wainad. The beautiful Koondah pass leads to the Kanara coast. The plateau consists of grassy undulating hills divided by valleys, each with a stream or swamp; *sholas* or small picturesque woods nestle in the hill-sides. There is one lake nearly 2 m. long at Ootakamand. The **Moyar** flows from the foot of Neelgiri peak into the Bhavani in Coimbatore, receiving the **Paikara**. The **Calicut** flows W. to the Indian Ocean at Beypoor, near Calicut town. The aboriginal Todas ("herdsmen"), Badagas ("northmen"), and Kotas ("cow-killers"), are peculiar to the range; the Kurumbas ("shepherds") and Iralas ("dark ones") also live in its forests; the whole number 24,000. Scytho-druidical stone monuments are everywhere found, attributed to the Pandyan kings. Three chiefs ruled the land a century before Haidar and Tipoo seized the three forts. In 1814 the Survey Department explored the hills, and in 1821 Mr. Sullivan built the first English house. Isolated as this plateau is at 6000 ft., between two seas, two monsoons, and two hill ranges, with a mean temperature of 58° F., it soon became the great sanitarium of S. India. Now plantations of coffee, tea, and cinchona are covering its expanse, on which thousands of Mysore coolies, directed by more than 150 European planters, turn out annually 4000 tons of coffee, 30,000 lbs. of tea, and cinchona bark from seven gardens with 600,000 trees. The chief town is **Ootakamand** (10,000) (7228 ft.), 32 m. from the railway by the new ghat, and 22 hours from Madras, seat of the Commissioner of the district, crowded by European visitors from March to June; with churches, banks, schools, etc. The Lawrence Military Asylum is at **Lovedale**, 5 m. from the post-office. The cinchona plantation is at Dodabetta, 1 m. The barracks are at **Wellington** or Jakatalla, 10½ m. The Basel Mission is at Keti, 5 m. S.E. **Koonoor** (3500) (6100 ft.), on the ascent from the railway, is 6° warmer than Ooty, from which it is 12 m. distant. The Katharu waterfall to N.E. is nearly half-way to **Kotagiri**, 14 m. from Ooty, centre of tea gardens, and preferred by many as the best climate on the hills. S.E., **Wainad** has become remarkable for the numerous auriferous quartz reefs traversing the metamorphic granites and gneisses, of which the Government Commissioner, Mr. Brough Smyth, reports that the quartz is richer than that of Australia (see Book II.).

West Coast Districts.

§ 19. **South Kanara District** is bounded E. by Mysore and Coorg, N. by the Bombay district of North Kanara, W. by the Indian Ocean, S. by Malabar. Area, 3902 sq. m. Population, 918,362. The **Sahyadri Range** (3000 to 6000 ft.) throws out spurs close to the coast, along which there runs a broken tableland of laterite, lying on granite, with a breadth of from 5 to 20 m. The Jemalabad rock and the hill, Asses' Ears, are landmarks. The passes connecting the plateau of Coorg and Mysore with the district and Mangalore are Sampaji, Agumbi, Charmádi, Hendar Ghur or Hasangadi, Manjarabad, and Koloor. The rivers dash down from the mountains to the Indian Ocean in the rainy season, and many are navigable for several miles from the coast. The chief are the **Netrávati**, **Gurpoor**, **Gongoli**, and **Chendragiri**. At Karakal there is a small lake, and at Kundapoor a freshwater lagoon. The clay and kaolin deposits are worked by many manufacturers. The forests and lands are chiefly private property, divided into *wargs* or estates, on each of which as a whole land-tax is paid. The people of this district are rather of Malabar, and speak Tulu and Malayálam than Kanarese, which is the tongue of Mysore, Coorg, and the Ceded Districts, and has given a name to the Karnatic below the E. Ghats. After the Vijayanagar power was overthrown at Talikot (1564), the kingdom of Bednoor included Kanara, and was overthrown by Haidar. Tipoo cruelly forced some of the Christians to apostatise. After many struggles, the East India Company became masters in 1791. There was a slight insurrection in 1837 after the fall of Coorg. The Christian population has steadily increased, and there are many Moplas or Muhammadans of Arab descent. **Mangalore** ("glad town") (30,000), chief town, port, and cantonment, separated from the Indian Ocean by a backwater formed by the Netrávati and the Gurpoor; hence the coffee of Coorg is shipped, and there is trade with Arabia and the Persian Gulf. Headquarters of the Basel Lutheran Mission, with noble industrial mission house and press. The Carmelites have large missions here. **Karakal** ("black stone") (3500), on road from Mangalore to Mysore by the Agoombi Pass, a Jain village with interesting remains. **Udipi** (4000), in N., with vast pagoda, most frequented of Kanarese shrines of Krishna; its suburb, Kalyanapoor, is believed to be the Kalliena of Cosmas Indicopleustes (545 A.D.). **Moolki**, seat of Basel Mission, 15 m. N. of Mangalore, on the Shambavati, where the New Testament was translated into Tulu. **Bantwel** (5000), entrepot on the Netrávati, 15 m. E. of Mangalore.

§ 20. MALABAR DISTRICT is bounded E. by Coimbatore, Neelgiris, and Coorg; N. by S. Kanara; W. by the Arabian Sea; S. by Cochin and Travankor States. Area, 5763 sq. m. Population, 2,336,032. This district, extending along the coast of the same name for 145 m., stretches back to the **Sahyadri Mountains** for from 25 m. on N. to 70 on S., broken by long spurs and valleys, with rivers discharging into backwaters. The Sahyadris are thrown back on either side for 24 m. to form the **Palghat Gap**, with the Neelgiris on N. and the Anamalais on S. Abreast of Calicut the Sahyadris recede E. and form with the **Wayut Hills** ("camel's hump") the **Ernad** valleys. The Atapadi valley (200 sq. m.), in which the Bhavani river rises, lies in the low range E. of the Koondas, which on the N. join the Sahyadris. The chief rivers are the **Beliapatam** from Coorg, the **Darmapatam** from Wainad; the **Kota**, navigable for 20 m. from the sea; the **Mahé**, the **Beypoor**, the **Kadelundi**, and the **Ponani**, which last floats down timber when in flood. Parallel to the coast is an almost continuous series of backwaters, of which the chief are — in N. the Kavai and Beliapatam; in middle, Payangadi, Quilandi, and Elatoor; in S., Chetwal and Kodungaloor. The **Trichoor** or **Yenamakal Lake**, dammed up from tidal influence, is in dry weather planted with rice, which produces splendid crops, reaped by the whole Nair population with difficulty from the floods of the S.W. monsoon. **Tanoor Lake** is a small sheet of fresh water.

Malabar or Malayálam ("mountain region") is the Arab form which in Cosmas Indicopleustes appears as "Malé, whence the pepper comes." With Travankor, Malabar, the ancient Kerala, formed part of the Chera kingdom, of which Cheruman Perumal was the last viceroy (4th to 7th century). From that time to the British ascendency in 1792, under the treaty of Seringapatam, Malabar was broken up under small Rajas, of whom the best known are the Zamorin (*samuri*) in S. and Kolastri or Cherakal in N. The Portuguese in 1498, the Dutch in 1656, and the French in 1720, were all supplemented by the English, who established themselves at Calicut in 1664, and took the French possessions in 1761. The ravages of Haidar and Tipoo ceased in 1792, after which there were outbreaks of the fanatic Moplas; in one the magistrate, Mr. H. V. Conolly, brother of the Bokhara hero, was assassinated, after which the crime was put down by a special Act. The Nazarani, or Syrian (Jacobite) Christians have long been settled in S., where the intolerance of the Portuguese Catholics vainly tried to extinguish them; the Carmelite order has still many stations. The Basel missionaries work in the principal towns as centres. The chief town is **Calicut** ("fort of goddess Kali") (48,000), port 6 m. N. of Beypoor railway terminus, in palm groves, said to have been founded by Cheruman Perumal, and granted to the Zamorin; here Covilham landed about 1486, and Vasco da Gama in 1498 (11th May), ten months and two days after his departure from Lisbon. The cotton cloth exported first from Calicut was called calico. **Cannanore** (10,500), N., port and cantonment captured by British in 1784, when its princess (*Beebee*) became tributary. **Tellicheri** (20,500), S. of Cannanore, picturesquely built on wooded hills running down to the sea; here the East India Company established a factory in 1683 for the pepper and cardamom trade. The old citadel and Residency are still used.

Mahé (1444 acres), the only French settlement left on W. coast, 4 m. S. **Beypoor** (6500), port near mouth of river of same name, 6 m. S. of Calicut, terminus of South-West Railway from Madras, whence coffee from E. Wainad is despatched. Adjoining are the site of Tipoo's projected capital, Ferokhi, and Chataparamba ("field of death"), with Scytho-druidical monuments. **Cochin** ("small" port) (14,000), on entrance to Travankor estuary, fronted by Vypin island, with Jewish settlement and Syrian Christians; visited by Ralph Fitch in 1585; here Vasco da Gama died (1524), and Xavier preached (1530). The Roman Catholic Church of St. Francis, with nave 142 ft. long by 41 broad, still stands, the oldest in India next to that of Calicut. **Palghat** (31,000), inland in the gap, 68 m. E. of Calicut, with fort thrice captured by British; railway station, 332 m. S.W. of Madras and 74 from Beypoor. **Manantadi** (11,000 in township), headquarters of the highlands and coffee plantations of the Malabar portion of the **Wainad Plateau** (3000 ft.), 60 m. by 30 in the Sahyadris, surrounded by Mysore E., Coorg N., Neelgiris S., and Malabar W.; it is a terrace between the lowlands of Malabar and the lofty plateau of the Neelgiris, to which the S.E. Wainad belongs. **Nelamboor** (11,500) is the centre of auriferous quartz and State teak reserves. **Anjengo** ("five cocoa-nut trees") (2500 Christians), surrounded by Travankor State, 78 m. N.W. of Cape Comorin, where the East India Company had a factory from 1684 to 1810, and Orme the historian was born. **Ponani** (11,500), Mopla port between Calicut and Cochin, headquarters of the Tangal or high-priest, with Musalman college. Here the English retired from Cochin in 1662, and Colonels Macleod and Humberstone repulsed Tipoo and Lally in 1782.

§ 21. Laccadive Islands ("the hundred thousand islands"), called also Amindivi, or Divi, from the principal island, is a group of 14 coral islands, 200 m. W. of the Malabar coast, of which 9 are inhabited by a Musalman population descended from Hindoos, 2 are uninhabited, and 3 are open reefs; lying between 10° and 14° N. lat. and 71° 40′ and 74° E. long. The population number 13,500 in 2450 houses, and speak Malayálam. They live by soaking coir, the fibre of the cocoa-nuts which is the only cultivation, and exporting it to the mainland. The trade is of the value of £17,000 a year. Five of the islands are administered by a sub-magistrate of S. Kanara—Amini or Amindivi, Chetlat, Kadarnat, Kiltan, and Botra, the last uninhabited. The southern group of six is administered by revenue Ameens of Malabar district from

Cannanore—Agathi, Kavarathi, Antrot, Kalpeni, Minikoi, and Suheli, the last uninhabited. Minikoi belongs rather to the 19 groups of **Maldives** ("islands of Mali" = king's island, the capital), which are subordinate to the Crown Colony of Ceylon. At Minikoi one mail steamer has been wrecked, and the low reefs, often swept by cyclones, are avoided, although containing safe and wide channels. The S. Kanara islands fell to the British Government in 1793 under the Beebee of Cannanore's agreement. The southern islands, held by her son Ali Raja, were attached for arrears of land-tax in 1875, since which time the people have been contented.

Southern Districts and States.

§ 22. TANJORE DISTRICT is bounded E. and S.E. by Bay of Bengal; N. by South Arcot and Trichinopoli from which it is separated by the Coleroon; W. by Trichinopoli, Madura, and Poodookotta State; and S.W. by Madura. Area, 3654 sq. m. Population, 1,973,731. This deltaic and coast tract is the garden of South India; although its soil is poor it is well watered, and highly cultivated by a dense population. The **Coleroon**, forming the N. boundary, is little utilised from its low level. The main **Kavari** enters the district 8 m. E. of Trichinopoli, and covers N. Tanjore with a network of fertilising channels, creating a vast rice-field. Where these two rivers approach, near the W. border, the Grand Anicut, 1080 ft. long, 40 broad, and 15 to 18 deep, was made by the Chola dynasty in the 3d century to prevent the Kavari waters being drawn off by the low-level Coleroon. Sir A. Cotton added the Upper Anicut, two dams, and the Lower Anicut, all irrigating an area of 800,000 acres, and yielding a land-tax of £443,350, four-fifths of which is due to irrigation. The surf beats along the coast of 170 m. Tanjore, under the Dravidian dynasties, became a land of temples; of these there are more than thirty groups, any one of which cost more to build than a cathedral. This is the first district in which Protestant Missions began, and now it is second only to Tinnevelli in the number of its Christian population. The Maratha Venkaji, Shivaji's brother, in 1678 founded the line of Tanjore Rajas, and held the State till 1779; in 1799 the Raja Sharabhoji, Schwartz's pupil, ceded it to the East India Company, and on the death of his son without an heir in 1855 the house became extinct. **Tanjore City** (43,000), 217 m. S.W. of Madras, and railway junction for Negapatam, its port, 48 m. E. Last capital of the Chola dynasty; captured by the British in 1773. Famous for the little fort containing the finest temple in India, the *Peria Kovil* or "great temple" of Shiva; the great fort containing the Raja's palace and noble library of 8000 Sanskrit MSS., of which the lamented Orientalist, Dr. Burnell, made a catalogue; Schwartz's house and church, with memorial group by Flaxman. Six m. W. is Vallam, the picturesque residence of the Collector. **Negapatam** (49,000), chief port and terminus of South India Railway, seat of Wesleyan and Jesuit missions; 3 m. N. is Nagar, with mosque whose 5 minarets are a sailors' landmark. Point Kalimere ("hill of the Euphorbya") is 31 m. S. The French **Karikal** ("fish pass"), with an area of 52 sq. m. and population of 93,000, is 12 m. N. of Negapatam; the port is on a mouth of the Kavari. Six m. N. of this is the old Danish capital of **Tranquebar** ("village on the wave") (14,000), which the first Danish ship reached in 1616, and the British purchased (with Serampoor in Bengal) in 1845. Here Ziegenbalg founded the first Protestant Mission in 1706, now under the Leipzig Evangelical Lutheran Society. Ziegenbalg's church has been swept away by the sea, but his "New Jerusalem" (1718), in which he and Gründler lie buried, and his house, stand. Europeans live in the old fort; the Danneluga citadel is the jail. **Combaconum** ("water-jar mouth") (47,000), centre of richest portion of Kavari delta, the Oxford of S. India, with many pagodas, 193 m. S.W. of Madras. **Mayaveram** ("peacock town") (21,500), 173 m. S.W. of Madras, on banks of the Kavari, with great pagoda (*butkadah* = idol temple). **Mannargoodi** (18,000), 24 m. S.E. of Tanjore, with cloth and metal trade; seat of a Wesleyan mission.

§ 23. TRICHINOPOLI DISTRICT (Tri-sira-palli = "place of the three-headed" giant) is bounded E. and S.E. by Tanjore, N. and N.E. by South Arcot, N.W. by Salem, W. by Coimbatore, S. by Madura and Poodookotta State. Area, 3383 sq. m. Population, 1,200,406. This hot and dry district has its flat surface broken by isolated masses of crystalline gneiss, like those at and near the chief town. The **Pachamalais** ("green hills") extend into Salem, separated by a narrow valley from the Kollimalais, which form the boundary between Trichinopoli and Salem. The **Vellar** river separates Trichinopoli and S. Arcot on the N. The chief rivers are the **Kavari** ("turmeric," from its muddy colour) and its branch the **Coleroon** ("place of slaughter"). At 11 m. W. of Trichinopoli town the Kavari sends off the Coleroon to the N.E. They rejoin 10 m. E. of the town in Tanjore, where they are separated by the Great Anicut. The land which they thus enclose is **Srirangam Island**, W. of which the river is called the Agunda or Broad Kavari. The Chola dynasty had its capital at one time at Uraiyoor ("city of habitation"), the Orthoura of Ptolemy, now a suburb of Trichinopoli town. By the close of the 16th century the country came under Vishwanatha, son of a Vijayanagar officer, who, at Madura in 1559, established the Nayakkam dynasty, of which Tirumala was the most famous. Tirumala's grandson made Trichinopoli his capital and built the Nawab's palace. The English and French wars described by Orme, and the Haidar and Tipoo wars, were fought around and in the place. To draw off its besiegers, Clive made his famous expedition to Arcot. Major Lawrence twice defeated the French, in the battles of the Golden Rock and the Sugar-loaf Rock. **Trichinopoli City** (76,500), chief town and cantonment with two railway stations, on right bank of Kavari, 56 m. from the Bay of Bengal, 248 S.W. from Madras, and 195 N.E. of Tinnevelli, from which to Tuticorin Fort it is the junction. The rectangular fort, with the Trichinopoli Rock (273 ft. above street) inside, the tank, and Clive's house, attract visitors; the Nawab's palace, restored under Lord Napier and Ettrick, to S., contains the public offices; the cantonment is to S. In St. John's Church lies the dust of Bishop Heber, who died here in 1826. The Propagation Society, Wesleyans, Lutherans, and Jesuits, have missions here. The city is known for its cheroots, made from Dindigal tobacco, and its gold filigree work. **Srirangam** ("celestial pleasure"), island, town (11,500), and pagoda of Vishnoo, 2 m. N. of Trichinopoli, the largest but most debased, in every sense, of idol shrines, from which Dr. Duff fled in 1849. The Shiva temple is at Jambukeshwar ("lord of India" = Shiva), 1¼ m. off. The other towns are Taraiyoor (6500), Mahadanapooram (6000), Udaiarpalaiyam (6000), Ariyaloor (6000), and Kurambaloor (5000). There are 96 large villages, with more than 2000 inhabitants.

§ 24. *POODOOKOTTA STATE, under the control of the Collector of Trichinopoli, between which, on the S.E. border, and Madura it lies, has an area of 1380 sq. m. and population of 315,000 paying a gross revenue of about £45,000 to the Raja, who is known as Tondaman ("ruler"). Having furnished the British troops with supplies during the siege of Trichinopoli by the French in 1752-3, and again in the Mysore wars, the Raja, who is of the Kallar or Colleries (Orme) caste, is exempt from tribute, save one elephant yearly for the fort and district of Killanelli, bestowed as a reward on the condition of not oppressing the people. The country is a flat plain, interspersed with fort-topped rocks, and well cultivated save in S. and W., where are jungly hills. It is irrigated from 3000 tanks, some of considerable size. The State is in 3 subdivisions—Kolattoor, Alangoodi, and Tirumayam, traversed by the Vellar from N.W. to S.E. In the second is the chief town, **Poodookotta** (14,000), unusually well built, clean and airy since 1820, when Sir W. Blackburne was Political Agent; there is a good school. There are 13,000 Native Christians in the State, and fewer Musalmans. The Sirkele, on Rs. 350 a month, is chief administrative officer under the Raja.

§ 25. MADURA DISTRICT is bounded E. by Palk's Strait; N. by Tanjore, Poodookotta, Trichinopli, and Coimbatore; W. by Travankor; S. by Tinnevelli and the Gulf of Manaar. Area, 9502 sq. m. Population, 2,266,615. This district is a plain sloping from three spurs of the Western Ghats—(1) the **Travankor Hills**, S.E. to the sea, and divided almost equally by the **Vaiga River**, which receives the Suruli from the S.W. and the Varáha ("pig") and Vattila-goondoo from the N.W., the last after a magnificent fall from (2) the **Palni Hills**, (3) the **Nagamalais** ("snake-hills"). The **Palnis** run N.E. for 54 m. with an average breadth of 15 m., and are of the same system as the Anamalais, in two groups—the higher or W. (7000 ft.), and the lower or E. (4000 ft.), being covered with coffee plantations. The **Seerumalais** (4000 ft.), farther E., are a confused mass, shunned from dread of fever. On the coast facing Ceylon the land runs out 15 m. to the foot-shaped **Pambam** ("a snake") or **Rameswaram Island**, between which and **Manaar Island** is the **Pambam Passage**, of sandstone rocks, deepened to 14 ft. at low spring tides for a length of 4232 ft. and width of 80 ft. The **Kilkarai Passage** to S., 2100 ft. long and 150 wide, is deepened to 12 ft. Upwards of 3000 coasting vessels use these passages annually. Manaar Island is separated from Ceylon by a very shallow strait. The whole forms Adam's Bridge; formerly a continuous isthmus, said to have been breached by a violent storm in 1480. The Pandya line ruled Madura from the 5th century B.C. to the 11th A.D., when the last, Soondara, yielded to a northern invader, probably Muhammadan. After being a province of Vijayanagar, in the 16th century Madura became the splendid capital of the Nayak kings, who ruled through 72 feudal *paligars*. Tirumala, the greatest king, fostered disunion among the Hindoo chiefs of S. India, which led to the Muhammadan and Maratha troubles that were closed by the British Peace in 1801, when Madura was ceded by the Nawab of the Karnatic to the East India Company. Under Tirumala the Jesuit Mission flourished, famous from the names of Robert de Nobilibus (1606), John de Britto, and Beschi. Besides this there are a Goa Mission and an American, which have done much for the people by medical and educational agencies. **Madura City** (52,000), on S. bank of the Vaiga, railway station, 344 m. S.W. of Madras and 98 N. of the Port of Tuticorin; famous for its pagoda and tank, Tirumala's palace restored by British Government, and the Vasanta *mantapam* or hall. **Dindigal** ("rock of Dindu," a demon) (13,000), railway station, 306 m. S.W. of Madras, with fort (1223 ft.) commanding the passes between Madura and Coimbatore. Twenty miles W. is **Kodaikanal** ("forest of creepers") (1000), sanitarium (7209 ft.) in the Palni hills, preferred by many to Ootakamand; 40 m. from the Ammayana-yakanoor railway station. **Palni** (13,000), 32 m. W. of Dindigal, gives its name to the hills. **Kilkarai** (11,500), port on Gulf of Manaar, the *Korkhoi* of the Periplus. **Ramnad** (15,500), seat of chief of the Maravar caste, who is Setupati or lord of the legendary (Adam's) bridge by which Rama invaded Ceylon; here are the Propagation Society's mission, and rest houses for pilgrims to **Rameswaram**, town on Pambam or Rameswaram Island (14,000), with massive temple, exhibiting at once all the beauties in detail and defects in design of the Dravidian style. **Shivaganga** (7500), centre of estate of same name, permanently settled like Ramnad, of which it is N., and long in the civil courts as a Hindoo succession case. Other towns of local importance are Tirumangalam, Paramagoodi, Periyakulam, and Aruppukottai.

§ 26. Tinnevelli District, which divides with Travankor State on W. the extreme point of the peninsula of India, is bounded S.E. and S. by the Gulf of Manaar, N.E. and N. by Madura, W. by the S. Ghats dividing it from Travankor. The coast-line extends for 95 m. from Vembar nearly to Cape Comorin; the greatest breadth is 74 m. Area, 5381 sq. m. Population, 1,693,959. The district is an epitome of the whole Madras Province; it is a well-cultivated plain, with an average elevation of 200 ft., sloping to E. from the lowest or **Southern Ghats** section (above 4000 ft.) of the Sahyadris, from which rivers and streams supply some 900 tanks and 40,000 acres of channel-fed lands. For from 10 to 20 m. at the base of the hills is a belt of red loam and sand, decomposed gneiss and quartz. Along the coast is a belt 3 to 15 m. wide, of light gray and red soil, with an excess of sand. Between these, N. of Tinnevelli town, are the broad black-soil plains which make this the fourth cotton-producing tract in the Province, in order. The **Tambraparni** ("copper-coloured") flows for 80 m. from the Agastya peak (6200 ft.) to the sea. S. of Tuticorin and beyond the ancient fort of **Kolkai**, it leaves the hills in the beautiful **Papanasam Fall**. Its affluents are the **Chittar** ("little"), Guttana, Rama, Manimoota, and Pacheyar. The Vaiga drains the N. of the Tambraparni basin into Madura; the Numbiar, and in the extreme S., the Hanama drain the S. portion of the range. The **Vaipar**, flowing parallel with the N. border, reaches the sea at the town of the same name.

Six centuries B.C. the Pandyan kingdom was established at Kolkai; Megasthenes mentions it B.C. 302. Dr. Caldwell shows that it was Pandian and not Porus who sent an embassy to Augustus, and that the Indian products mentioned in the Old Testament (1 Kings x. 22; 2 Chron. ix. 21) were from what Ptolemy called Kolkoi Emporium. As the line of coast became raised, that gave place to **Kayal**, between it and the sea, the Cail of Marco Polo, at which "all the ships touch that come from the West, as from Hormus and from Kis and from Aden and all Arabia, laden with horses, and with other things for sale." Tinnevelli followed the fortunes of the two previous districts till 1781, when the Nawab of Arcot assigned its revenues to the East India Company, and Colonel Fullarton reduced some of its Poligars. Since it became wholly British in 1801 its chief interest has been this, that it has become the most Christian district of all India, both Roman Catholic and Protestant. In 1532, Michael Vaz, afterwards Archbishop of Goa, assisted the Paravar fishermen against the Muhammadans, since which time they have been Roman Catholics. Ten years after, Xavier lived among them. Then the Jesuit fathers of the Madura Mission worked there, notably Beschi, whom Dr. Caldwell places in the first rank of Tamil poets of the second class because of his Epic, the *Tembavani*, and who died at **Manaparai** in 1746. In 1780 Schwartz baptized, at Palamkotta, the Brahman woman Clarinda, who erected there the first English church S. of Trichinopoli, which in 1784 was put under Satyanada, the first Hindoo-born minister of the Church of England. The Shanar drawers of *tadi*, the juice of the palmyra palm, and devil-worshippers, who form a fifth of the whole population, were first led to Evangelical Christianity in 1797 by Soondaram, one of themselves, who became a Christian at Tanjore, and was sent as a catechist to his own village of Kallanguddi, where in 1799 the 28 converts built Mudaloor ("first town") (1200). There are some 350,000 Protestant Christians in S. India, chiefly in Tinnevelli and surrounding Districts and States, in churches largely self-supporting, self-governing, and self-propagating, under Drs. Sargent and Caldwell, missionary bishops of the Church Missionary Society, which has three-fifths, and the Gospel Propagation Society, which has two-fifths of the jurisdiction, and under the London, Wesleyan, and American Societies.

Tinnevelli (22,000) is the chief town, 1½ m. from left bank of the Tambraparni, terminus of branch of South India Railway, 18 m. W. of Maniyachi junction, with double Shiva pagoda of architectural interest, and seat of a missionary bishopric. **Palamkotta** (18,500), 3½ m. E. of Tinnevelli, and 1 m. from the Tambraparni, is the administrative headquarters, with cantonment, dismantled fort, and Church Missionary Society's Institution; where Rev. J. Hough, chaplain in 1816, and historian of Christianity in India, revived the Protestant Mission. **Kuttalam** (Courtallum) (1500), 38 m. N.W., on the Chittar, with 3 waterfalls, a pretty sanitarium (700 ft.), cooled to 15° below the temperature of the arid plains by S.W. monsoon through gap in the W. Ghats. **Papanasham** ("sin-effacing") fall (80 ft.), and shrine, on the Tambraparni, 30 m. due W. of Tinnevelli. **Satoor** (7500), railway station, on the Vaipar, old centre of zameendaree. **Tuticorin** (11,000), chief port and railway terminus between the mouths of the Tambraparni and Vaipar, centre of the pearl and conch-shell fishery, with schooners to Ceylon; headquarters of the Paravar Roman Catholics. **Tiruchendoor** (7500), 18 m. S., with frequented temple built out into the sea. There are hundreds of Protestant villages developing into towns, and bearing Christian names, of which the most important are **Eydenkoody** ("shepherds' dwelling"), Bishop Caldwell's most S. town, where the palmyra palm culture gives place to the pastures which prevail around Cape Comorin. **Suvisessipooram** ("Gospel town"), first of Bishop Sargent's 800 stations. **Mengnanapooram** ("True Wisdom town"), where in 1837 Rev. John Thomas built the finest church in S. India, the spire of which is a landmark, and Bishop Cotton has described the worship; Kadachapooram ("Grace town"), Nalloor ("Good town"), Christianagram, etc. From Kudankulam Observatory, in extreme S., to Rhadapooram (5500) the Propagation Society's Station, the Cape Comorin base line of the Great Trigonometrical Survey is measured.

§ 27. *COCHIN STATE (Kuchi = "small") is bounded E. by Coimbatore, N. by Malabar, W. by the Arabian Sea, and S. by Travankor. Area, 1361 sq. m. Population, 601,114 in 1875. Along with Travankor, the State is controlled by a British Resident. The Raja, of the Kshatriya caste, claims to hold from Cheruman Perumal, Chola viceroy and afterwards ruler of Kerala in 9th century. He pays £20,000 tribute to Government, and has an annual revenue of about £130,000. A fourth of the whole population are Christian—Nazaranis, or descendants of the earliest converts made by Syrian missionaries before the visit of Pantænus of Alexandria in the 2d century; Roman Catholics under early Portuguese influence, and Protestants chiefly under the Church Missionary Society. The town which gives the State its name is a British port in Malabar district. From the Western Ghats, where the **Neliampatti Range** is attracting capital to coffee cultivation, the chief rivers are the **Ponani**, **Tattamangalam**, **Karuvanoor**, and **Shalakoodi**; also the Alwai or **Periyar** passes through part of the State. These feed the backwaters or series of shallow lakes which run from N. to S. for 120 m. beyond the State's boundaries, with a breadth of from 10 m. to a few yards. The sea is touched at Cochin town, Cranganore, and Chatwai. In N.E. the Irwari timber-tract has dense teak forests. **Ernakolam** (14,500), the capital, on a backwater 2 m. E. of and opposite to Cochin town, with Darbar palace and public offices. The Raja resides at Tripoontera (8500), 9 m. E. To S.E. is Udiampoor where the Portuguese Menezes held the infamous Synod of Diamper in 1599, which destroyed the independence of the Apostolical Syrian Church.

Native Cochin (14,000), on Travankor estuary, half a mile S. of British Cochin, former capital of State; gives its name to the form of elephantiasis known as the Cochin leg. Hence there is canal and backwater communication for 45 m. with **Trichoor** (11,000) (Tri-sova-per-oor = place named after sacred Shiva) in N., a very old town, a chief centre of Brahmanism, with palace, wealthy Sanskrit college, Shiva temple, and Church Mission. **Shoranoor**, railway station, 360 m. S.W. of Madras and 46 S.E. of Beypoor, at which the S.W. line touches Cochin State. Hence a line is projected to Cochin. **Kodangaloor** (Cranganore) (10,000), on the Chatwai opening of the Cochin breakwater, 18 m. N.W. of Cochin town, where in A.D. 52 St. Thomas is said to have begun his mission, and where Cheruman Perumal had his capital. Here the Black Jews were settled, in the 4th century at least, and the Portuguese drove many to Cochin; their present synagogue is two centuries old. At Ambalkota, inland, the Jesuits had a mission, and the first Malayalam book was printed in 1577. **Kunankulam**, in N., one of the largest Christian towns, with Syrian and Church Missionary Society establishments. **Narakal** (4500), port, 3 m. W. of Cochin city, protected from the sea by a mud bank, which shelters vessels in S.W. monsoon. Cochin is known for gold and silver work and wood and ivory carving.

§ 28. *TRAVANKOR STATE (Tiru-varung-kodu = "the sacred, prosperous kingdom") forms with Tinnevelli district, which bounds it on E., the extreme S. of the Indian Peninsula ending in **Cape Comorin** (Kumari = "the virgin," *i.e.* Doorga). The coast extends 174 m. N. to Pairankoo-kota, with a maximum breadth of 75 m. from Cochin city to Doodaval Peak and average breadth of 40 m. The area is 6730 sq. m., and population 2,401,158. The Maharaja is of Kshatriya caste, a master of English, Sanskrit, and many other languages, highly educated and enlightened. Nearly a fourth of the people are Christians of the Syrian Church, and London and Church Missionary Societies. The Namboori Brahmans form one of the most ancient landed aristocracies, liberally supported by the State, whence the name *Dharma Bhumi*. The petty chiefs after the death of Cheruman Perumal were gradually brought under the Travankor Raja, especially between 1758 and 1799, when he had an army drilled by a Flemish adventurer. In 1789 Tipoo made his famous attack on the lines which defended the country on its N. or Cochin frontier, and wasted the people. The British Government came to the rescue, and since the treaty of 1795 prosperity has prevailed. The Raja pays £81,000 tribute, and has a gross revenue of £550,000. This picturesque country, watered by fourteen rivers, lies on the W. Ghats (8000 ft.) as its E. border, where the **Travankor Hills** and **Anamalais** ("elephant hills") end in the S. **Peak of Agastya**. The highest peak S. of the Himalaya is here, **Anamoodi** (8837 ft.). South of that is the lower region of the **Cardamom Hills**. The whole hill region abounds in plateaux such as Erevimalai or Hamilton's valley, and Ashembu, only partially surveyed, covered with fine forests on which coffee and tea cultivation is fast encroaching. The chief river is the **Periyar**, which flows W. from the higher ranges for 140 m. to the backwater at Kodangaloor, and is navigable for 60 m. From the same lake which sends the E. Tambraparni through Tinnevelli to the Bay of Bengal flows the **Western Tambraparni**. Other rivers are the Pambar with its tributary the Achinkoil, the Kallada, and the Paralar and Kodai, on which the old Pandyan rulers made weirs for irrigation. The area of the Backwater Lakes is 158 sq. m. in Travankor, 54 in Cochin, and 16 in British territory. The largest is Vembanad, E. of Alleppi. **Trivandrum** (58,000), the capital, 2 m. from the sea near the Karumanai stream, with the British Residency, principal buildings, and country houses on laterite hills overlooking the fort, in which are the palaces and temple of the "lotus-naveled" Vishnoo under the name of Padmanábha. N. is the cantonment of the Nair brigade of 1400 men under British officers. Outside the town is a well-equipped Observatory (195 ft.), of which there is a branch on the top of Agastya. **Alleppi** (30,000), chief port, 33 m. S. of Cochin, protected by a mud bank, and connected by a canal with the great backwater to N.E.; station of the Church Missionary Society. **Quilon** (Kollam) (14,500), old port mentioned by Ptolemy, the re-foundation of which in 1019 A.D. gives Travankor its era. Early seat of Syrian Christians and of the Bishop of Columbum, and chief entrepot of pepper and ginger on the Malabar coast. To E. is Nair cantonment. A road leads over the Arian-kavu pass to Tinnevelli. A line of railway has been surveyed from the South Indian terminus at Tinnevelli, over the S. Ghats to Quilon and Trivandrum. **Shenkotta** (10,000), 65 m. E. of Quilon centre of coffee trade, on Tinnevelli road. **Sharretalai** (9500), a centre of Syro-Roman Christians, and chief town of a subdivision. **Kottayam** (6500), principal Church Missionary Society station, with college for Syrians, on a stream running into the Cochin backwater. **Nagarkoil** (6500), in S., chief station of London Missionary Society, famous for the lace-work of its Christian girls since 1817; a suburb of **Kottar** (7500), mentioned by Ptolemy, old capital and port of Travankor. **Kolachel** (5000), coffee port of S. Travankor, old factory of the Danes, and the Kolias of Strabo. **Attingah**, or Attungal, 5 m. E. of the old port of Anjengo, with fort and palace, the residence of the Ranees or Tumbrattees through whom, according to the polyandrous custom of the Nairs, is the line of succession to the throne. **Purávoor** (6700) is the largest mart in N. **Verapoli**, island 7 m. N.E. of Cochin, headquarters of the Carmelite Mission. **Mavalikara** (5000), 25 m. N. of Quilon, fort and a centre of the Church Missionary Society.

CHAPTER XXIII.

COORG PROVINCE.

§ 1. The Country. § 2. The People and their History. § 3. Land Tenures. § 4. Towns and Roads.

§ 1. The Country.—**Coorg** (Kodagu = "steep highlands") is the smallest Province of British India, under a Chief Commissioner, who was the Chief Commissioner of Mysore also, till that was made a Native State in 1881, of which he became the Resident. What Wales is to England Coorg is to Mysore, in miniature; a picturesque mountain region situated on its western side. Coorg covers 1583 sq. m. of the summits and E. declivities of the Western Ghats within from 20 to 30 m. from the Arabian Sea, and has a population of 178,302, which had increased in the decade ending 1881 by 6 per cent, the normal rate over all India. Coorg is bounded on E. by the tableland of Mysore into which it merges, the Kavari flowing between for some distance; N. by Mysore from which the rivers Kumaradhari and Hemavati partially separate it; N.W. by S. Kanara or the Tulu country; and S.W. by the wooded tracts of Wainad and N. Malabar. It lies between N. lat. 11° 55′ and 12° 50′, and between E. long. 75° 25′ and 76° 14′. From the top of the Brahma-giri, near the source of the Kavari, on a November morning the eye may take in the most widely beautiful view in all India, stretching from the Indian Ocean and Malabar coast intersected with broad rivers to the distant Neelgiri Hills. Coorg proper is the central portion of the country covered with forests, in which are seen the clearings of the coffee planter, patches of ragi, the food of the people, and park-like open glades. The cultivated area is 191 m., and only 100 more are culturable. The range of the **Western Ghats** runs for more than 60 m. from Subrahmanya in N.W. to the farthest point of the Brahma-giri in S., presenting an imposing line from the coast near Cannanore. The subdivisions are, the **Brahma-giri** or Marenad hills (4500 ft.) between Coorg and Wainad, of which Davasi-betta is the highest peak. The main chain, for 30 m. from the Perambadi pass near Virajpet to the Tadikana pass near the source of the Kavari, culminates in Tadiandamol peak (5729 ft.). This chain sends due E. the **Benga-nad** range, on which is the Merkara tableland (3809 ft.). The main drainage is E. towards the Bay of Bengal, but torrents fall down the steep western declivities, of which the Barápol is the most considerable. The **Kavari**, the chief river, which flows for 400 m. E. to the Bay, rises in the Brahma-giri at Tale Kavari, where the very verge of the W. Ghats forms a sharp angle with the Benga-nad range. There and at the neighbouring source of the Kanake which joins the Kavari at the foot of the hill, are much-frequented temples. In its tortuous and generally tranquil course, save when the monsoon rains make it a thundering torrent, the Kavari receives many streams with waterfalls of great beauty, of which the Jessy Fall near Merkara is best known. After leaving Coorg it is joined by the **Hemavati** from Mysore, the N. boundary of Coorg, and the **Lakshmantirtha** from the Davasi-betta plateau which, in its fall over an almost perpendicular mountain wall, forms a cataract visited by thousands of the superstitious because invested by the Brahmans with sin-cleansing virtue. The mean annual rainfall is 123 inches. Nowhere are the forests so beautiful, with evergreen trees and vast bamboo jungles, described by Basil Hall as "the clustered columns of some enormous and enchanted Gothic cathedral," but in a state of decay every 50 or 60 years during the periodical seeding. Rice is the staple product; the cultivation of the cardamom, which grows spontaneously in the evergreen forests, comes next in importance. There are few Europeans or natives not interested in the Coffee culture, which since 1854 has spread in Merkara, Sampaji Ghat, Perambadi Ghat, and the Christian settlement of Anandapoor ("place of joy"). There are now 4300 estates covering 110,000 acres, half of which is held by European planters. The cinchona is cultivated by Government near Merkara. The plantain, wild and cultivated, is the favourite fruit of Coorg. The gross revenue in 1880-1 was £74,476, of which £32,118 was from land.

§ 2. THE PEOPLE.—The census of 1881 showed a population of 178,302 in the 6 subdivisions, or 112·64 to the square mile, in 512 towns and villages with 22,357 inhabited and 3233 uninhabited houses. Of the whole, 162,489 were Hindoos, 12,541 Musalmans, 99 Jains, 21 Parsees, and 3152

Christians. The Basel Society and the Roman Catholics have each a mission. Of the Christians, 228 are Europeans, chiefly planters, 287 Eurasians, and 2637 Natives. The Coorg clan numbers 26,558, and their priestly or upper class, the Amma Coorgs (Mother's Coorgs, devoted to Mother Kavari), 475; they worship ancestors and demons, and avoid Brahmanical influences. They and their former predial slaves, the Holeyas, speak Kodagu, a dialect midway between old Kanarese and Tulu: their *pulamé*, or old chant and ballad literature, is full of interest. The Coorgs are a manly, patriotic, and, to the Queen-Empress since their conquest, a loyal clan of tall highlanders. They are said to be a division of the Nair tribe; from time immemorial they have been lords of the soil. They delighted Dr. Leyden in 1805; and are in many respects the finest race in India. The Kodageetees, or women, are fair, handsome, and industrious. Haidar Ali, after long effort, subdued Coorg only by taking advantage of a dispute between two brothers. The younger, Viraraja, escaped from him, cleared the country of invaders, and co-operated with the British against Tipoo. In 1799 he became a British feudatory, his annual tribute being one trained elephant. He, his brother and successor in 1809, and Virarajendra Wodyar, 1820-34, the last of the Coorg Rajas, were all so insanely cruel that the last was declared by Lord William Bentinck a public enemy, and sent to Benares after a short war. His daughter, Victoria Gauramna, became a ward of the Queen, married an English officer, and died. Since 1834 the country has increased in prosperity. The people so proved their active loyalty in 1857 that they were specially exempted from the Disarming Act.

§ 3. Land Tenures.—Besides the rent-free temple-lands, there are four tenures peculiar to Coorg. (1) *Jamma* is derived from the Sanskrit Jamma, a word conveying the meaning of hereditary by birth, and is the holding of the privileged class called jamma ryots, comprising Coorgs, Amma Coorgs, Higgada, Umbakala, Arris, Konoyas, Moplais, and Gaudas. The holders of these lands pay half assessment, or Rs. 5 per 100 bhattis (2 acres) of wet land, with its accompanying Bane and Narike, and are liable to be called out for military, police, or other duties when required. In these days opportunities for military service do not arise, but the jamma ryots are expected to furnish police and treasure guards. They are therefore allowed to carry arms, and embarrassment has sometimes resulted from the fact that a few Moplas, whose ancestors migrated to Coorg under the native dynasty, are found in their ranks. Jamma ryots are debarred from selling, mortgaging, or in any way alienating the land held on this tenure, except with the sanction of Government. (2) *Sagu* is derived from the Kanarese word "Sagu," meaning under "cultivation." It is the normal ryotwaree tenure, all others being exceptional. The rate of assessment is Rs. 10 for every 100 bhattis of land, and the holders are not bound to render any feudal or any other description of service to the State. The sagu ryots may claim remission of assessment for those fields of their farms which they are unable to cultivate. (3) The lands under the denomination of *Ambli*, which means service of any kind, were granted on account of services performed by certain ryots in the Raja's times, and are lightly assessed at rates varying from one to three rupees per 100 bhattis. (4) Certain lands which are taxed at the jamma rates come under the head of *Jódi*. The only distinction between these two tenures seems to be that jodi grants were made for a special purpose, or in consideration of a particular kind of service, while jamma ryots were bound to perform duties of a general nature. No remission of jodi can be claimed by the holders of Jamma, Ambli, and Jodi lands.

§ 4. TOWNS AND ROADS.—**Merkara** (Madhu-keri) (8146), the capital, founded in 1681 on a plateau (3809 ft.), 130 m. S.W. of Bangalore and 47 N.E. of Cannanore, consists of the native quarter of Mahadevapet, a fort, with palace and offices commanded by neighbouring hills, and cantonment. **Virarajendrapet** (3413), on main road, 20 m. S. of Merkara, founded by the hero of Coorg independence whose name it bears, where he met General Abercromby leading the Bombay column against Seringapatam; the chief mart of Coorg, prettily placed at the foot of the Maletambiram hill; Kukaluru (632) is its suburb. Fraserpet (2000), trading place on E. frontier, 20 m. S. of Merkara, on left bank of Kavari; named after the first Commissioner, but called by natives Kushálnagar ("joy town") since Haidar Ali here received news of Tipoo's birth. Kodlipet, near right bank of Hemavati, 45 m. N. of Merkara, an entrepot for trade with Mysore. Nalknad, in the W., the principal country palace of the Coorg Rajas, near the foot of the lofty mountain Todiandamol. Two trunk roads cross Coorg from Hoonsoor in Mysore to the W. coast. One passes by Periyapatna, Fraserpet, and Merkara, to Mangalore by the Sampaji Ghat; the other by Anechankur, and somewhat S. of Virarajendrapet, to Cannanore by the Penambadi Ghat.

CHAPTER XXIV.

*MYSORE STATE.

§ 1. The Country. § 2. Land Tenures. § 3. The People. § 4. Bangalore. § 5. Kolar. § 6. Toomkoor. § 7. Mysore. § 8. Hassan. § 9. Shimoga. § 10. Kadoor. § 11. Chitaldroog.

§ 1. The Country.—**Mysore** (Mahesh-asura = buffalo-headed monster destroyed by Kali, as Chamoondi, tutelary deity of the Maharaja's family) is the rocky triangle between the Eastern and Western Ghats before they unite in the Neelgiri Hills. It stretches from a point within 10 m. of the Arabian Sea E. to 120 m., and its S. frontier is 250 m. N. of Cape Comorin, between 11° 38′ and 15° 2′ N. lat., and between 74° 42′ and 78° 36′ E. long. With an area of at least 30,500 sq. m., and population reduced, by the famine of 1876-8, 17 per cent to 4,186,399 in 1881, the State is the size of Scotland, but has a larger population. Except on W., where the Bombay districts of Dharwar and N. Kanara on N.W. and Coorg on S.W. form the boundaries, Mysore is surrounded by the Province of Madras; on E. by Salem, N. Arcot, Cuddapah, and Bellary; on N. by Bellary; on S. by Wainad and Coimbatore. The undulating plateau rises from 2000 ft. along the N. and S. borders to 3000 ft. along the central water-parting which separates the basin of the Kistna from that of the Kavari. The magnificent country on the W. is the *Malnad* ("hill region"), and rests on the W. Ghats; the larger section, or all to the E. of a line from Shikarpoor to Periyapatna, is the *Maidán* ("plain") or open country. The two Ghat ranges have been compared to the antlers of a stag, the branching tynes being the parallel chains which start N. from the central watershed, and are connected by cross ridges along their S. extremities. Isolated massy rocks, droogs or doorgs (*door-ga* = difficult of access) rise frequently to a height of 4000 and 5000 ft., each with a supply of water, and of old crowned with forts deemed impregnable. The loftiest elevations are **Shivaganga** (4400 ft.), 30 m. from Bangalore. **Nandidroog** (4700 ft.), 36 m. from Bangalore, a bold cliff, which was the most trusted stronghold of Haidar, and his State prison; "Tipoo's Drop," from which European captives were hurled, is pointed out; apparently impregnable, Nandidroog was taken by escalade in 1791 by a portion of the army of Lord Cornwallis: here the Pennar rises. **Bilikalrangan Hills** (4800 ft.), in Ashtragam Division, clothed with jungle, and inhabited only by the rude Soligars. **Baba Boodan Range** (6317 ft.), or Chandradona, a horseshoe cluster of magnificent hills in Nagar Division, so named from a Musalman saint, whose tomb is on one of the peaks, the scene of extending coffee culture. **Kudurimookha** (6215 ft.), in Nagar, with the Balalrayan droog (4940 ft.). With the exception of streams in the N.W. which unite in the **Sharavati**, and hurl themselves down the Western Ghats in the great **Gersoppa Falls**, and some minor streams of Nagar and Manjarabad, which flow into the Gargita and Netravati, the drainage of Mysore finds its way E. to the Bay of Bengal in three river systems, the **Kistna** on N., **Kavari** on S., and the two **Pennars** and the Palar on E. A line drawn E. from Balalrayan droog to Nandidroog and S. to Anekal, with one from Devaray droog N. to Pavugada, indicates the watershed which separates the three main river basins thus:—

	Total Length.	Total Area of Basins.
KISTNA (with Toongabhadra and Hagari) .	611 m.	11,031 sq. m.
KAVARI (with Hemavati and other affluents)	646 „	9,486 „
N. PENNAR (with Chitravati and Papaghni)	167 „	2,280 „
S. PENNAR	32 „	1,541 „
PALAR	47 „	1,036 „
SHARAVATI	103 „	1,881 „

None are navigable, though Haidar vainly attempted to open up the Toonga; but timber floats are carried down the Toonga, Bhadra, and Kabbani at certain seasons. All, and especially the Kavari and its tributaries, feed a vast and ancient system of irrigation by chains of tanks numbering 37,682; the **Sulekere**, 40 m. in circumference, is the largest. Forests of teak and blackwood clothe the sides of the Western Ghats to the extent of 2870 sq. m. Sandalwood grows spontaneously, in the Mysore chiefly, and is a State monopoly; of the whole, 450 sq. m. are reserved. Besides timber, the chief exports are coffee, areca or betel-nut, and ragi, the staple food of the people. The Madras North-Western Railway runs from Jollarpet junction in Salem through Bangalore to Mysore town, and will be continued to Tripatoor and Hassan by light feeders. The principal passes through the Western Ghats to N. and S. Kanara are the Gersoppa, Koloor, Haidargarh, and Agumh Ghats in Shimoga; the Bund or Kodekal, on the border of Kadoor and Hassan; and the Manjarabad, just N. of Coorg.

§ 2. LAND TENURES.—State lands are held under the ryotwaree tenure either on kandayam, *i.e.* a fixed money assessment, or on batayi. This term signifies the temporary occupation of Government land by a ryot without paying money assessment, but sharing the produce with the Government. Except in the settled talooks, where the term of the settlement is fixed at thirty years, kandayam lands are held on annual leases, but the assessment is seldom altered and hardly ever raised. By far the larger portion of the land in the Province is held on this tenure. Under the batayi system the land is held direct from Government, but the share of Government is paid in grain. In Mysore the proportion generally claimed by Government is one-half, but it is probable that in reality only one-third is received, the remaining two-thirds being shared between the ryots and the village servants. The batayi tenure will wholly cease with the completion of the survey and the settlement in each talook. In the case of private estates, such as inam and kayamgutta villages and large farms of Government lands cultivated by payakaris or under-tenants, the land is held on the following tenures:—*Warum*, under which an equal division of produce is made between the landlord and the tenant, the former paying the assessment of the land to the Government; *Mukkuppe*, under which two-thirds of the produce go to the cultivator, and one-third to the landlord, who pays the assessment of the land; *Arakandaya* or *Chatarbhaga*, under which the landlord gets one-fourth of the produce and pays only a half of the Government revenue, the remaining half being discharged by the cultivator who enjoys as his share three-fourths of the produce; *Volakandaya*, in which the tenant pays a fixed money rate to the landlord. This may either be equal to or more than the assessment of the land. A hereditary right of occupation is attached to all kandayam lands. As long as the puttedar pays the Government dues he has no fear of displacement, and virtually possesses an absolute tenant right as distinct from that of proprietorship. *Kans* are large tracts of forest, extending in one case over eight miles in length, for which a cess is paid. The kans are preserved for the sake of the wild pepper vines, bagni palms, and certain gum trees. Inam, or rent-free tenures, are numerous. Grants of land for coffee cultivation are made out of the Government jungles chiefly in the Western Ghats forming the Nagar and Ashtagram Malnad. An excise of 4 annas (6d.) is exacted on each maund (28 lb.) of coffee produced; and in the case of cardamom cultivation, of Rs. 2 (4s.). Mysore is still the chief, as it was the first coffee country of India. Of the annual production of coffee in the world, which has doubled since 1859, rising to 1,300,000,000 lbs., Brazil supplies 560 millions; Netherlands, India, 150 millions; British India and Ceylon, 140 millions; and Venezuela about 100 millions.

§ 3. The PEOPLE AND DISTRICTS.—The population may be conveniently divided under Brahmans, Vaisayas, Soodras, Marathas, and Muhammadans. The Brahmans are Maratha, Karnataka, Telugoo, and Dravida, according to the reputed derivation of their ancestors. In respect of doctrine they are divided into three schools, viz. the Smarta, the Madhva, and the Srivaishnava. The Smarta is said to be the oldest sect of the three, and its distinctive doctrine is pantheism; while the essential tenet of the Madhvas is that the Creator and the creature are eternally different from each other. The Smartas use a horizontal, and the Madhvas a perpendicular, mark on their foreheads. The Madhvas also stamp themselves on their arms, head, and back daily after ablution, with sandalwood paste. The Srivaishnava school, while adopting the more rational doctrine of the two, that of the Madhvas, adds that after salvation the creature obtains the form of the Creator. This sect, which is subdivided into Vadagale and Tengale, is said to have been founded by Ramanuja Chariar, who being persecuted by the Chola kings, fled to Mysore and settled at Melkote. The Srivaishnavas are distinguished by a trident mark on the forehead. *Vaisayas* (commonly called Komatis) are exclusively employed on trade and monetary transactions. Like Brahmans, the Vaisayas are supposed to be strictly vegetarian and to abstain from the use of spirituous liquors. *Soodras* are very numerous. The principal sects are the Vakkaligars, who are agriculturists by profession; the Kurubars and Gollars, who are shepherds and herdsmen; the Beders, who are huntsmen; and the Lingayats, who are the worshippers of Isvara, and wear a silver box in which is their "Lingam," suspended by a thread round their neck; a large number of the Mysore ryots belong to this class. The *Marathas* and *Muhammadans* became naturalised in Mysore at a more recent date than any of these castes, and owe their introduction to foreign invaders. The Muhammadans of Mysore do not exhibit the energy which is possessed by the class in Northern India; since the days of Tipoo, continued depression and poverty have told greatly on their morale. The prevailing language of the Province is Kanarese; but Tamil, Telugoo, Hindustanee, and Maratha also are spoken. Musalmans ordinarily converse in Hindustanee.

In no part of South India was the famine so severe as in Mysore, so that the population in 1881 was only 4,186,399 against 5,055,412 ten years before. The following table gives the Districts, their area and population as in November 1871, but the Survey is showing the area to be larger, and the population is smaller at the present time.

Division.	District.	Square Miles.	Population 1871.
NANDIDROOG	Bangalore	2,914	828,354
	Kolar	2,577	618,954
	Toomkoor	3,606	632,239
ASHTAGRAM	Mysore	4,128	943,187
	Hassan	3,291	669,961
NAGAR	Shimoga	3,797	498,976
	Kadoor	2,294	332,381
	Chitaldroog	4,471	531,360
		27,078	5,055,412

In the Hindoo Epics, Mysore appears as the land of Sugriva, whose general, the monkey-god Hanooman, helped Rama in his expedition against Lanka or Ceylon. Boodhists and Jains were followed by the first historical dynasty of the Kadambas, who ruled the north from Banawasi, mentioned by Ptolemy, and by the Cheras who held the south from Karoor in Coimbatore, and then from Talkad on the Kavari, where the Cholas overturned their power in the 8th century. Then came the Kalachurias for a short time, and the Jain kings known as Háisala Ballála, who ruled from Dwarasamoodra till 1310, when the Delhi emperors sacked the place, now Halebeel, still remarkable for the Haisaleshwara temple. In 1336 the Vijayanagar sovereignty rose on the Toongabhadra. The present Maharaja's ancestors, two brothers, came to Mysore in 1399, and by marrying the daughter of a petty chief one of them laid the foundation of the Hindoo kingdom. The ninth chief took Seringapatam from the Vijayanagar dynasty. At the siege of Devanhalli, Haidar Ali, a volunteer trooper, showed such courage that he was promoted to command, which ended in his assuming the government for himself and his son Tipoo. In 1799 the British Government virtually created a new Hindoo sovereignty over so much of Mysore as the Partition Treaty assigned, and selected as ruler Kristna Raja Wodyar, a child of three, grandson of the prince deposed by Haidar forty years before. Lord Wellesley acted thus in opposition to the advice of Sir Thomas Munro, but declared at the time that the "nominal" kingdom "constituted substantially an integral portion of our own dominions." On coming of age, the Raja squandered the revenues accumulated by the able Brahman minister, Poornaya, and so outraged the people that he was deposed by Lord W. Bentinck in 1831. He remained generously pensioned at Mysore town; in 1865 he adopted, so far as his private property was concerned, a boy of three. On his coming of age on 25th March 1881, under the orders of a former Secretary of State, Mysore was made over to the present Maharaja Chamrajendra Wodyar of the Yadava clan akin to the Rajpoot caste, who had been carefully educated for the responsibility. His Highness has no jurisdiction over Bangalore cantonment or European British subjects; a British official will continue to administer the district most frequented by European coffee-planters. Of the revenue which under direct British rule more than doubled, rising to upwards of a million sterling, a fourth, and hereafter a third, is to be paid as tribute for military defence and political expenditure. This second creation of a Hindoo sovereignty as an act of grace is unique in India, and the experiment will be watched with interest alike by those who have always condemned it as a wrong to the subjects of the Queen, and by those who hope that lessons may be taught in the art of ruling natives.

§ 4. BANGALORE DISTRICT is bounded N.E. by Kolar, N.W. by Toomkoor, S.W. by Mysore district, S. for 10 m. by the Kavari which divides it from Coimbatore, and S.E. by Salem. Area, 2914 sq. m. Population, 828,354. The district is the valley of the **Arkavati** which flows N. to S. for 120 m. into the Kavari, from Brahma-giri hill to W. of Nandidroog; it receives the Kumadvati from W., and the Vrishabhavati from N.E. The east portion of the district includes the upper basin of the **S. Pennar**; the west, a small part of that of the Shimsha. The whole forms part of the tableland of Mysore, broken to the W. by rugged hills and deep valleys. **Bangalore City** and British cantonment (Bengalou = "beans" here supplied to the Ballala king, its founder, when hunting), (140,000) covers nearly 14 sq. m. 71 m. N.E. of Seringapatam, near centre of Mysore plateau (3000 ft.). One of the healthiest and coolest towns in India, consisting of (1) the cantonment with Government House, public offices in Cubbon Park, new palace, college, pleasure garden of the Lal Bagh, and (2) the old native Pét or town to S.W. The railway station is 84 m. W. of Jollarpet junction, and 216 W. of Madras city. Carpets and silks are the principal manufactures. **Dod-ballapoor** ("great" Ballapoor = place of good omen, where a cow used to drop a *balla* of her milk daily), on right bank of Arkávati, 27 m. N.W. of Bangalore, a cotton cloth mart. **Chaunapatna** ("handsome city") (7000), 37 m. S.W. of Bangalore, with manufactures of lacquered ware and toys. **Closepet** (5000), named from Sir Barry Close, Resident, on left bank of Arkávati, 30 m. S.W. of Bangalore. **Anekal** ("hailstone") (6500), 20 m. S.E. of Bangalore, a prosperous place. **Devanhalli** (5500), 23 m. N. of Bangalore, at siege of which Haidar Ali first came into notice, and where his son Tipoo was born; taken by army of Lord Cornwallis in 1791. **Savandroog** or Magadi, W. of Bangalore, a fort and hill of granite (4024 ft.), with two peaks, "white" and "black," well supplied with water, memorable for its capture by Colonel Stuart under the eye of Lord Cornwallis in 1791, as described by Wilks. Sivaganga is a conical peak (4559 ft.), with shrines N.W. of Bangalore, called by Hindoos the second Benares. Kankanhalli, town on right bank of Arkavati 36 m. S. of Bangalore, the Konkanapoora of the Chinese pilgrim Hwen T'hsang in the 7th century.

§ 5. KOLAR DISTRICT is bounded E. by Northern Arcot and Cuddapah, N. by Bellary, W. by Toomkoor and Bangalore, and S. by Salem. Area, 2577 sq. m. Population, 618,954. The border touches the **Eastern Ghats** on N.E. and S.; the chief watershed lies in N.W. around **Nandidroog** (4810 ft.), from which the principal mountain chain runs N. into Bellary. Parallel with this, 30 m. to E., is a range separating the Chitrávati and Papaghni valleys, and known as the **Dongala**. Seven rivers radiate from Nandidroog—the **Arkavati** to S., the **N. Pennar** to N., the **Chitrávati** and **Papaghni** to N.E., the **Palar** to E., and the **S. Pennar** to S. From all a succession of 5497 tanks intercepts the water for irrigation; the largest is the Ramsagar from the Palar. At **Ooregaum**, 6 m. from Kolar road station at Bowringpet, the metamorphic quartz is worked for gold. The Madras South-Western Railway ascends the Ghats at Koopam pass, and runs through the district into Bangalore. **Kolar** (9500), chief town, 10 m. N. of railway at Bowringpet, with tomb of the father of Haidar Ali, who was born at Budikot, at the foot of **Nandidroog Fort**, 31 m. N. of Bangalore, captured by Lord Cornwallis's army in 1791, and a favourite retreat of Sir Mark Cubbon and Europeans in the hot season. **Chikballapoor** (9500), 36 m. N.W. of Kolar, stronghold of the Gauda family, captured by Haidar Ali in 1761. **Sidlaghata** (7000), 30 m. N.W. of Kolar, centre of Gauda conquests, now a municipality. **Hosoor** (5500), in N.W., a large mart. Maloor (3000), railway station and municipality, 18 m. S.W. of Kolar. Avani hill, S.E. of Kolar, was a residence of the poet Valmiki, author of the *Ramayan*, and one of the ten places of greatest Hindoo sanctity. The chief manufacture of the district is sugar.

§ 6. TOOMKOOR DISTRICT is bounded E. by Bangalore and Kolar, N. by Bellary, W. by Chitaldroog and Hassan, and S. by Mysore district. Area, 3606 sq. m. Population, 632,239. The hill range, which in W. Bangalore is represented by Shivaganga and Savandroog, runs S. and N. through E. Toomkoor, and forms the E. boundary of the Kistna river-system. The prominent peaks are Madgiri-droog (3935 ft.), Channarayandroog, Koratagiri, and Devaray-droog (3940 ft.), Nijagal, Hutaridroog, and Haliyoor-droog (3086 ft.). The principal streams, all small, are the Jayamangali, from Devaray N.E. into the N. Pennar, which touches the district for 2 m. at N.E.; and the Shimsha, S. of the same hills, which flows S. to the Kavari. The Kumadvati or Kundar flows from a detached group of hills around Mahakali-droog (3610 ft.), between Toomkoor and Bangalore, into the N. Pennar. On the Devaray hills is a State forest of 18 sq. m. In S.W. the quarry of Karekalgudda yields the fine "black stone" from which it takes the name, an amorphous hornblende, out of which the great *basava* or bull at **Taruvekeri** has been cut and polished. **Toomkoor** (11,000) ("a tabret," the town having been granted to the herald of the Raja), chief town at S.W. base of Devaray hills, 43 m. N.W. of Bangalore, prettily placed amid groves, with Wesleyan Mission. **Sira** (4000), 33 m. N.W. of Toomkoor, once a great place, from which Tipoo transported 12,000 families to his new town on Seringapatam island. **Madgiri** ("honey hill") (4000), 24 m. N. of Toomkoor, at the N. base of Madhu-giri hill, one of Tipoo's capitals. **Kumgal** (Shiva's "dancing stone") (3500), 22 m. S. of Toomkoor, horse-breeding centre for the Mysore Siladars. **Chiknayakanhali** (4500), 40 m. N.W. of Toomkoor, a prosperous mart in groves of palms. **Gubbi** (3700), 13 m. W. of Toomkoor, seat of principal annual fair and entrepot of areca-nut trade with North Arcot.

§ 7. Mysore District, most S. of the State, is bounded E. by Coimbatore and Bangalore, N. by Toomkoor and Hassan, W. by Coorg, and S. by Malabar and Neelgiri districts. Area, 4128 sq. m. Population, 943,187. Lofty ranges, the home of the wild elephant, shut in the district on W., S., and E., save where the Kavari hurls itself (300 ft.) down the **Falls** of Gagana Chukki and Bar Chukki (200 ft.) at **Shivasamoodram** ("sea of Shiva") **Island**, into Coimbatore, after being swollen by the Kabbani, so as to have a maximum flood discharge at Bannoor of 239,000 cubic ft. a second; a fine stone bridge, constructed by a native landholder, spans the stream. **Talkad**, 12 m. S.W., is the Chera capital, nearly buried in sand, the scene of the threefold curse of Talkad. **Bilgirirangan Hills** (5500 ft.) form the chief range. The isolated **Gopalswami Hills** (4500 ft.) are in S., and **Bettadpoor** (4350 ft.) in N.W. The **Chamoondi Hill** (3489 ft.) is S. of Mysore, and the **French Rocks** (2882 ft.) N. of Seringapatam. Besides the Kavari the chief streams are the Lakshmantirtha and Kabbani, Shimsha, Nugu, Suvarnavati, and Gundal, from anicuts on which 497 m. of channels irrigate the land, yielding a revenue of £27,500 a year. Asbestos abounds, and is used by physicians as an antiphlogistic. The State forests cover 180 m. **Mysore Town** (57,000), a terminus of Madras Railway, 10 m. S.W. of Seringapatam at base of Chamoondi hill, covering 3 sq. m., with fort containing Maharaja's palace, in which are a fig-wood throne overlaid with ivory, said to have been given by Aurangzeb to Chikka Deva Raja in 1699, and the stall in which was the cow worshipped by the late Maharaja. The Residency in the English quarter is E., with pertico built by Colonel Wilks and great-room by Malcolm, now the Ashtagram Commissioner's residence. The magistrate's court was built and occupied by the Duke of Wellington. A mile E. is Nazarabad ("visited by the eye of the Almighty"), a fort to which Tipoo removed the ancient residence of the Hindoo Rajas, but the stones and palace were restored to Mysore town.

Seringapatam (Sri-ranga-patna = Vishnoo's place), a municipal town (10,000) at W. or upper end of an island, on the Kavari, 3 m. long and 1 broad; the end is occupied by the prosperous suburb of Ganjam. The town is on the Bangalore-Mysore high road, 77 m. S.W. of former, by rail, and 10 N.E. of latter. On the Vaishnava sectary Ramanujachari converting the Balala king from Jainism he received the tract around Seringapatam, still known as Ashtagrama ("eight townships"), and now one of the three administrative divisions of Mysore. From 1610 to 1799 Seringapatam was the capital of the Hindoo rulers, of Haidar and Tipoo. About 60 yards S.E. of the bastion, on the W. angle, General Harris delivered the famous assault on 4th May 1799, since which the island has been British property, leased to Mysore. The spot where Tipoo fell is on the N. face. Mud walls mark the old palace, and two tall minarets in front of the Mysore gate are conspicuous from a distance. Outside the fort is Tipoo's favourite Dariya Daulat Bagh ("garden of the wealth of the sea"), the caricature pictures on the walls of which, representing Baillie's defeat at Conjeveram in 1780, etc., and defaced by Tipoo before the siege, have been twice restored, by the Duke of Wellington and the Marquis of Dalhousie. At the lower end of the island is the mausoleum of Haidar Ali, built by his son, with double doors inlaid with ivory, given by Lord Dalhousie. The inscription on Tipoo's tomb represents him as a "martyr for the faith of Muhammad." The British Government maintains the establishment; crimson palls cover both tombs. The whole place is unhealthy; its Ganjam suburb is the commercial quarter. Four m. N. is **Hirode** or **French Rocks**, still a cantonment where the French in Haidar's and Tipoo's service were stationed. **Malvalli** (5000), 28 m. N.E. of Mysore, with ruined fort and garden of Tipoo; 2 m. off is the battlefield where he encountered General Harris during the march on Seringapatam. **Hoonsoor** (4000), 28 m. W. of Mysore, headquarters of a cattle-breeding establishment, and coffee works where the berry is prepared for shipment.

§ 8. HASSAN DISTRICT is bounded E. by Toomkoor, N. by Kadoor, W. by South Kanara, S. by Coorg and Mysore district. Area, 3291 sq. m. Population, 669,961. This, the most beautiful and the principal coffee district, is the basin of the **Hemavati** ("golden"), which flows S.E. from Kottigehara in Manjarabad to the Kavari, receiving the Yagachi ("jujube-tree"). The Western Ghats extend from the pass at the Bisale Ghat N. to the Boondh Ghat, including within the grand panorama the towering height of **Subrahmanya** (5583 ft.), on S.W. border, Banagiri, Moorkan-gudda ("hill of the three-eyed one" = Shiva), the columnar peak of Siskal-betta, Malebid-gudda, Deven-betta, and the superb Jenkal-betta ("honey-rock hill"), all in the Manjarabad side of the district, which rests on the brow of the W. Ghats and drains to the N. Shetravati in S. Kanara. In E. border of district a chain of lower hills begins at Kannambadi, on the Kavari, contains the sacred height of Melukote, and runs N. into the Chitaldroog hills. The isolated **Indra-betta** (3309 ft.), at Sravan Belgola, is crowned by a colossal Jain statue.

Where the Malnad or W. highlands touch Coorg there is the richest park scenery like that of England. The district is watered through 215 m. of channels. The temperature is that of Bangalore, or 76° mean; in the coffee districts it is lower from the moisture that causes malaria, to which the European settlers become more quickly acclimatised than the natives. The rainfall varies from 36 inches at Hassan town to 100 at Bisale Ghat. The rich red loam of the primeval forests of the Manjarabad highlands is favourable to the coffee plant, first introduced in 1843. Now every peasant has a few trees in his garden. **Hassan** (6500), chief town, called after Hasin-amma, the "smiling goddess," who directed its Ballala founder to the site, 114 m. W. of Bangalore. **Narsipoor** (5000), on right bank of Hemavati, 21 m. S.E. of Hassan, a cloth mart. **Sakleshpoor** ("the fragmentary Ishwara") (1100), 23 m. W. of Hassan, chief place of the subdivision of Manjarabad (457 sq. m.), in which are 155 British coffee estates, covering 21,000 acres, and 9500 native holdings, on the Ghat road from Hassan to Mangalore. Sathalli (658) is a village 10 m. S.W. of Hassan, a centre of caste Christians, the fruit of the work of Abbé Dubois.

§ 9. SHIMOGA DISTRICT is bounded E. by Chitaldroog, N. by Dharwar, W. by North Kanara, S. by Kadoor. Area, 3797 sq. m. Population, 498,976. The district consists chiefly of the W. slopes of the upper Toongabhadra valley. The west side rests on the W. Ghats, the highest point of which here is the Kodachadri peak (4446 ft.), 10 m. N.W. of Nagar. Govardhangiri in Sagar and Chandragutti (2836 ft.) in Sorab are conspicuous hills. The streams to S.E. and N. of this central watershed flow to the Toongabhadra, those on W. to the Sharavati, those on S.W. to the Gargita. The **Toongabhadra** is formed at Kudali by the union of the Toonga and Bhadra, and flows N. to the border, which it follows N.E. beyond Harihar. The **Sharávati**, or "arrow-born" as rising in the Ambu-tirtha formed by a stroke of Rama's arrow, flows N.W., receives the Haridravati on right and Yenne Hole on left, and on arriving at the Bombay frontier bends to the west before it precipitates its waters down the **Falls of Gersoppa**, or Geru-sappe, a village really 18 m. distant, called by the natives the *Jog* ("a moist place"). The Falls are situated in 14° 14′ N. lat. and 74° 50′ E. long., between Mysore and Kanara, 60 m. from Shimoga and 30 from the port of Honore. Flowing over a rocky bed 250 yards wide, the river reaches a tremendous chasm of gneiss 960 ft. deep, over which it leaps in four torrents—(1) the Raja Fall, an unbroken column of 830 ft., which, half-way down, is met by (2) the Roarer Fall, which precipitates itself into a vast cup, and then, at an angle of 45 degrees, dashes violently into the Raja; (3) the Rocket Fall shoots down in a series of jets; (4) the Dame Blanche glides quietly over the precipice in a sheet of foam. The best view is obtained in the cold season from the Mysore side, at Watkins' platform. The falls are excelled in height only by the Cerasoli and Evanson cascades in the Alps, and those of the Arve in Savoy, but surpass these in volume; at Niagara a river, contracted from 2 m. to less than half, is hurled over a precipice of 164 ft. in two vast torrents. The Gersoppa Falls are "perhaps unique as a scene of natural beauty in India free from all signs of idolatry" (*Official Mysore Gazetteer*). **Shimoga** ("face of Shiva") (11,000), chief town of division and district on left bank of Toonga, 171 m. N.W. of Bangalore, on Gersoppa road. **Nagar** or **Bednoor** (1300), above Haidarghar Ghat, the old Keladi capital, with walls eight miles round and ten gates, captured by Haidar Ali, who took out of it booty valued at 12 millions sterling, and called it Haidar-nagar; it is now a village. Other sites of old cities in this district are—Ikkeri and Keladi, associated with the same Lingayat barons; Basvapatna, with the Tarikere chiefs; Humcha ("golden bit") with Jainism, and Banavasi with Boodhism. Sagar, on the left bank of the Varada; and Chennagiri, 25 m. N.E. of Shimoga, are rising modern towns.

§ 10. KADOOR DISTRICT is bounded E. by Chitaldroog, N. by Shimoga, W. by South Kanara, S. by Hassan. Area, 2294 sq. m. Population, 332,281. The most mountainous tract in South India, the scene of *Ramayan* legends, and the source of the sacred Toongabhadra, this district is also the first home of the coffee culture in India. The W. Ghats range themselves into the central N. and S. ridge, the east of which is the **Baba Boodan** mountains, which form a gigantic outwork of the alpine wall, rising in **Mulaina** to 6317 ft., and in the navigator's landmark of the **Kudure-mookh** ("horse-face") to 6215 ft. On the W. of the main ridge is the valley in which stands **Sringeri** (Rishya-sringa-giri), where was born, without a natural mother, the sage of that name, who performed the horse-sacrifice of the Epic, which resulted in the birth of Rama himself; here also lived Sankaracharya, the Shivaite reformer of the 8th century, and this is still the headquarters of the high priest of the Smarta Brahmans. The main ridge separates the basin of the **Toonga** from that of the **Bhadra**, twin streams which rise at Gangamoola in the Varáha hill. The **Hemavati** rises at Javali and passes quickly into Hassan district. The twin Gauri-halla and Avati spring from the E. of the Baba Boodans; the former expands into the **Ayan-kere Lake**, an artificial sheet dotted with islands and 7 m. in circumference; the latter forms the **Madaga-kere.** The State forests cover 78 sq. m. Coffee cultivation was introduced by the Muhammadan pilgrim Baba Boodan two centuries ago, who brought a few berries in his wallet, and now covers 65,000 acres owned by 22 Europeans and 4760 natives. **Chikmagaloor** ("younger daughter's town") (2000), chief town on the Hassan-Shimoga road, 130 m. N.W. of Bangalore, in a fertile valley of the Baba Boodan hills. **Tarikeer** (5000), 30 m. S., on the Bangalore-Shimoga road, the chief of which rebelled in 1830-4. **Kadoor** ("elk-town") (2700), chief town of the district till 1865, on the Bangalore-Shimoga road; an old Jain settlement.

§ 11. CHITALDROOG DISTRICT is bounded N.E. and N. by Bellary, S.E. and S. by Toomkoor, W. by Shimoga and Kadoor, and N.W. by Dharwar. Area, 4471 sq. m. Population, 531,360. The belt of low **Chitaldroog Hills**, 20 m. broad, runs N.W. to S.E., rising to Jogi Maradi (3803 ft.) S. of Chitaldroog town; all the rest is an open pasture plain needing only water to fertilise it; the average rainfall is 24 inches. The whole is included in the valley of the **Vedavati** or **Hagari**; the Toongabhadra touches the N.W. border. **Chitaldroog** ("picturesque" or "umbrella rock") (5700), chief town and stone fort 126 m. N.W. of Bangalore, on the road to Harihar, held by old poligars from 1508, on the weakness of the Vijayanagar sovereigns, till seized by Haidar Ali. Outside are the public offices, and the residence of the chief priest of the Lingayats. Two m. S. the Jogi Math (3803 ft.), surrounded with hills, is a sanitarium in the hot season. **Devangere** (6500), 40 m. N.W. of Chitaldroog, is the most populous mart. **Harihar** (6400), on the right bank of the Toongabhadra on the Dharwar border, is an old town with neighbouring cantonment now given up, and a fine bridge across the river.

CHAPTER XXV.

COLONIES AND COUNTRIES WITHIN THE POLITICAL SYSTEM OF INDIA.

§ 1. Ceylon. § 2. Mauritius and Réunion. § 3. Hong-Kong and Macao. § 4. Straits Settlements and Malay States. § 5. The Three Borneo Settlements—Labuan, Sarawak, and Sabah. § 6. Siam. § 7. Upper Burma. § 8. Tibet and Eastern Toorkestan. § 9. Afghanistan. § 10. Persian N. Frontier. § 11. Turkish Arabia and the Persian Gulf. § 12. Abyssinia. § 13. Muscat and Zanzibar.

§ 1. Ceylon (Singhala = "lion-land," the Taprobanê of the Greeks from the Tambraparni river opposite, the Lankā of the *Ramayan* Epic) is geographically part of India, and was politically under Madras till "an injudicious attempt to introduce the Madras fiscal system, which nearly resulted in a general revolt," led to its becoming a Crown Colony in 1798. In 1664 the British Government of India sent an unsuccessful embassy to the King of Kandy for the release of captive English sailors. In 1763 its embassy of friendship also led to nothing. In 1782 the Madras Government followed up the conquest of the Dutch settlements on the Coromandel coast by sending a force to Ceylon, but not till 1795 did it reduce the coast districts of the island and form its first treaty with the King of Kandy, which he afterwards refused to ratify. In 1815 the king, put on the throne by British influence, was deported to Vellore, where he died in 1832, and the chiefs vested the sovereignty in the British Crown. Since 1831-3 the colony has been under a Governor, with an Executive Council of five, and a Legislative Council of fifteen.

Lying like a pear south of the Tinnevelli and Madura districts of Madras, between N. lat. 5° 56′ and 9° 56′, and E. long. 80° and 82′, Ceylon is 266 m. long from Points Palmyra and Pedro N. to Dondra Head, and 140½ wide from Colombo W. to Sangemankande S., with an area of 24,702 sq. m. and population of 2,638,540, or equal to two districts of India. Of these, 1½ million are Boodhists; half a million are Hindoos, chiefly Shivaites; one-sixth million are Musalmans, and the rest are Christians. Of the last, 182,613 were Roman Catholics, 24,756 Protestants, 6071 Wesleyans, 3101 Presbyterians, and 1478 Baptists, by the former census of 1871. The revenue of the colony is 1½ million sterling and the sea-borne trade 10 millions, equally divided between imports and exports. The coffee export is valued at 2½ millions, and that of cinnamon at £100,000. There are 176 m. of railway. The island is 40 m. from the mainland of India, with which it is partially connected by a chain of islands separating **Palk's Strait** from the **Gulf of Manaar**. This is the Rama-setu ("pier") of the Hindoos, or line of rocks and sandbanks which the monkey hosts carried from the Himalayas to assist Rama in his invasion of Lankā; and the Adam's Bridge of the Muhammadans by which Adam was expelled from the paradise island. It consists of (1) **Manaar Island** (see p. 397), 18 m. long and 2½ broad; (2) **Adam's Bridge**, sand ridge, 30 m. long, with 3 or 4 ft. of water above it at high tide; and (3) **Rameswaram Island**, or "pillar" of the Eastern Herakles, with Cyclopean temple ascribed to Rama himself, whose idol is daily washed with Ganges water, and attracts thousands of pilgrims. The view is wide. The **Pambam** passage is between this and the Madura town of the same name. The Maldive Islands are attached to Ceylon, raising the total area to 25,742 sq. m. The island rises from the coast into the healthy coffee districts, which culminate in **Pedrotallagalla** (8280 ft.), **Totapella** (7720 ft.), and **Adam's Peak** (7420 ft.). The central hills send off a spur from N., which forms the watershed between the Gulf of Manaar and Bay of Bengal. The **Mahawila Ganga**, from its S. slopes, flows N.E. for 200 m. into the Bay of Trincomálee.

The colony is divided into 7 provinces—Central, North Central, West, North-West, South, East, and North, each under a Government Agent, with a civil and judicial service costing £370,000 a year. The Singhalese proper occupy the centre; the Tamils from the coast of India, fixed and floating, are chiefly in the N. and E.; the Vadda aborigines are in the mountains and forests. There are about 6000 British and 14,000 other whites of European descent. **Colombo** (Corumbu = "harbour") (100,240), the capital and chief port on W. coast connected by railway (75 m.) with the old capital, **Kandy** ("hill"), chief town of the Central Province and coffee culture; 4 m. off is **Peradeniya** Botanic Garden. **Newara Ellia** (6210 ft.), on S. side of central highland, the sanitarium. **Point de Galle** (47,000), on S.W., long a central port of call for ocean steamers for Australia, China, Madras, and Calcutta. **Trincomálee**, on N.E., naval station with fine harbour. **Jaffna** (35,000), chief town in peninsula on N. coast, and centre of coolie trade with India; old Dutch settlement. Other W. coast towns are Aripo, a centre of the pearl fishery in Condatchy Bay, 3 m. off; Calpenteen, Negombo, and Caltura, all taken from the Dutch. Matura, S., where Sir Henry Lawrence was born 1806; celebrated for its stones, which led his mother to say of him, "There's *my* Matura diamond." Batticaloa, port on small island on E. coast, 68 m. S. of Trincomálee.

§ 2. MAURITIUS AND RÉUNION, British and French Colonies E. of Madagascar, and called the Mascarenhas Isles, receive nearly their whole labouring population from India, the latter under a convention made in 1860 by Lord Russell with the last Emperor of the French, of the nature of an Asiento Treaty, and more than once suspended because of the ill-treatment of the coolies. **Mauritius**, between S. lat. 20° 27′ and 19° 53′, and E. long. 57° 16′ and 57° 35′, 400 m. W. of Madagascar, has an area of 676 sq. m. and population of 360,000, of whom 250,000 are from India. Discovered by the Portuguese, who named it Cerne; settled by the Dutch, who called it after Prince Maurice; occupied in 1721 by the French, who named it Ile de France, and whose Governor, De Labourdonnais, made it of importance; a centre of pirates and privateers till 1810, when it capitulated to Lord Minto's expedition. The capital is Port Louis (67,000), on N.W. coast; centre of the sugar trade, and of a mission to the coolies, who settle here on the expiry of their five years' indentures. Mahebourg, or Grand Port, is the other town. The 29 **Seychelles**, with a refuge for liberated Africans; Rodriguez (360 m. E. of Mauritius), and Diego Garcia, from 300 to 900 m. distant, are dependent islands of Mauritius. The Cargados group, or St. Brandon Bank, produce only salt fish. The Colony is under a Governor and Executive Council of five, and Legislative Council of twenty. The revenue is three-quarters of a million sterling; the whole trade is 5½ millions in value, of which two-thirds are exports, the sugar alone being valued at £138,000. Two railways (92 m.) connect Port Louis with Grand River and Savanne. Mahé is the largest of the Seychelles; its town is Port Victoria (6000).

Réunion, formerly named Bourbon, an oval island S.W of Mauritius, 38 m. long by 28 broad, with an active volcano,

Pitou de la Fournaise (7218 ft.). St. Denis is the capital on N. The whole population is 180,000, of whom 2000 are French. The French first settled here in 1665, and were temporarily ousted by the British in 1810.

§ 3. HONG-KONG AND MACAO.—The East India Company had trading and quasi-political factories in China, at Canton chiefly, from 1685 to 1833, when it ceased to trade directly, but the Government of India has always shipped the bulk of its opium to the treaty ports. In 1841-43, under the treaty of Nanking, the Chinese ceded to Great Britain the **Island of Hong-Kong**, so named either from the Kong-hong or company of Chinese merchants through whom the East India Company had traded, or from Hiang-Kiang ("sweet waters"). It lies 75 m. S.E. of Canton and 40 E. of Macao, at the mouth of the Chu-Kiang, a broken ridge (1800 ft.) with an area of 29 sq. m. and population of 140,000, of whom only 40,000 are females. The half-mile strait, Ly-ee-moon pass, separates it from the mainland, where the opposite peninsula of Koo-loon has formed part of the colony since the cession of 1861. **Victoria City**, the capital, is on the N. side, with a fine harbour. The island is the financial and steamer centre of the China and Japan trade. It is under a Governor, with Executive Council of three, and Legislative Council of nine. It has a revenue of £200,000 and trade of 5 millions sterling. **Macao**, on a peninsula of the island of Heong-shan, at the entrance of Canton river, in N. lat. 22° 10′, and E. long. 113° 32′, was given to the Portuguese in 1586, and was the only settlement possessed by Europeans till the British obtained Hong-Kong. Till their expulsion from Japan and decadence, the Portuguese had no richer settlement than Macao. It is an extensive stone city; the East India Company's factory was near the Governor's house, opposite the landing-place. Of late Macao has been the seat of an inhuman trade in coolies. It was long administratively subject to Goa. Here Camoens wrote the *Lusiad*, and Dr. Morrison translated the Bible into Chinese. Area, 28 sq. m. Population, 70,000.

§ 4. THE STRAITS SETTLEMENTS AND MALAY STATES.—The **Malay Peninsula**, from the Pakchan boundary of British Burma to the island of Singapore at its S. extremity, is divided between the British on the W. slope and the Siamese on the E. The **Straits of Malacca**, between the Peninsula and Sumatra, connecting the Indian Ocean and China Sea, are 700 m. long and from 60 to 250 broad. The three settlements of Singapore, Malacca, and Penang, with Province Wellesley on the Straits of Malacca, were part of the British Indian

Empire till 1867, when they were transferred to the Colonial Office, and have since been a Crown Colony like Ceylon. They have an area of 1350 sq. m. and a population of 320,000, of Malays, Chinese, and white settlers, with a sex-proportion of one female to two males. The general policy of the Indian and now the British Government in the Eastern Seas is regulated by the treaty of 1824, under which the Dutch connection with the Peninsula of Malacca was severed; and by the treaty of 1871, by which the British Government withdrew the right granted by the former treaty to stop the extension of the Netherlands dominion in the adjoining island of Sumatra, where the East India Company once had trading settlements. **Singapore** ("lion city") (82,000), the capital, is a free port on S.E. coast of island, 77 m. N. of Equator, with adjoining small islands (223 sq. m.), separated from the Johore State of the Malay peninsula by "the old Straits of Singapore," a narrow passage. The settlement was founded in 1819 by Sir Stamford Raffles. Singapore is the entrepot, and lies on the highway of the rich trade between India, China, Batavia, and Australia, which passes through Singapore Strait, and touches at the free port. **Malacca**, taken from the Dutch in 1795, after it had been long held by the Portuguese since 1511, lies on W. coast of the peninsula, between 2° and 2° 30′ N. lat., and 102° and 102° 45′ E. long. Its area is 640 sq. m., and its population 75,000. The chief town and port of same name (25,000) is near the mouth of the Malacca river. **Penang**, or Prince of Wales's Island, is 2 m. off W. coast of peninsula, in 5° N. lat., with an area of 106 sq. m., a sanitarium (2922 ft.), and population of 62,000. George Town is the chief place. The island was purchased from the Rajah of Kĕdah in 1786 to put down piracy; also **Province Wellesley**, on the mainland, with an area of 236 sq. m. and population of 72,000; the land is held chiefly by sugar planters, and, like a great part of the peninsula, is mined for tin by the Chinese.

The **Malay States**, recently surveyed, are **Kĕdah** (Quedah), N. of Province Wellesley; **Pérăk**, S.; **Patani**, E. of Kedah, sloping to the China Sea; **Ligor**, **Kĕlantam**, **Tringánu**, and **Pahang**, S. of Patani, and similarly sloping; **Sĕlángor**, between Perak and Malacca, famed for limestone caves at Batu; **Sungie Ujong**, **Rambow**, **Johole**, and **Sree Menanti**, confederate States between Selangor and Malacca; **Johore**, chief State of the peninsula between Malacca and Singapore, from the Tumongong of which Singapore was purchased. The whole peninsula has an area of 33,000 sq. m., sparsely occupied by Chinese, and by Malays who migrated from Sumatra in recent times. In the British Settlements there is a population of 330 to the square mile; in the badly governed States, especially under Siam, there are only 5 or 6, and only 1 acre in 300 is cultivated.

§ 5. THE THREE BORNEO SETTLEMENTS.—**Labuan** ("anchorage"), Crown Colony, 15 m. N.E. of estuary of the river of Borneo or Brunai (300,000 sq. m.) whose Sultan ceded it in 1846, to complete the abolition of piracy commenced by Sir Harry Keppel, Sir Thomas Cochrane, and Sir G. Rodney Mundy. Area, 45 sq. m. Population, 5000; chiefly Chinese. Revenue, £7000. Has rich coal deposits, hitherto imperfectly worked. Chief town and port, Victoria, residence of the Governor. The suppression of piracy was due above all to the Bengal civilian Sir James Brooke, to whom, as Raja in 1843, the Sultan of Brunai transferred **Saráwak** (28,000 sq. m.; population, 22,000), with capital, Kuching ("the cat"), on Saráwak river, 17 m. from W. coast, seat of a consul since 1864. Another English settlement in Borneo received a charter from the British Government in 1882 for the occupation of **Sabah** (20,000 sq. m.), purchased from the Sultans of Brunai and Sulu, and consisting of the N. and N.E. of Borneo, or the portion not occupied by Sarawak on the N.W., and by the Dutch in S., whose boundary is the Atlas river, in 3° N. lat. on S., and the Kumanis on W. Sabah contains the great bay of Maruda on its N. extremity, which commands the fairway of British trade with China and Japan, Australia and India, and is midway between Hong-Kong and Singapore. Sandakan, on the E. coast, is described as the finest harbour in the world; Gaya and Ambong, on the W. coast of the new Settlement, are hardly inferior to these. Here the East India Company had treaty rights after the capture of Manilla in 1762, and here it traded in 1601.

§ 6. SIAM, visited unsuccessfully by the Mission of Mr. John Crawfurd in 1821, Captain Burney in 1826, and Sir James Brooke in 1850, formed treaties with the Queen in 1855, and with the Viceroy and Governor-General of India in 1874, the King having visited Calcutta in 1872. Under these the boundaries have been marked out, and the country to Bangkok partly surveyed. Called Thaï ("free") by its people, Siam, or the valley of the Me-nam ("mother of waters"), with its feudatories Malay, Laos, and Shan, claims an area of 309,000 sq. m. in the centre of the Malay Peninsula, between N. lat. 4° and 21°, and E. long. 98° and 107° 20′, and a population of 6 millions, Muhammadan and Boodhist, who speak a monosyllabic language of the Tai group. The country is in 41 administrative divisions. The Salween separates W. Siam, occupied by the Chiangmai or Zimmay Shans, from E. Karengnee. Under the treaty of 1874, which has given peace to the British and Siamese feudatory tracts of the Upper Salween, the British Superintendent of the Yoonzaleen district of British Burma exercises political and magisterial powers. The watershed of the Tenasserim Roma range, called by the Siamese Taneri Toung-ghyee ("big mountain"), continues the W. boundary to S., where the Pakchan river and Isthmus of Kra were defined by the Convention of 1868. **Bangkok** (500,000), the capital, on left bank of the Me-nam, near its mouth, is called "the Venice of the East," because of its floating population; Paknam is at the mouth of the river, "the Cronstadt of Siam." Ayuthia is the former capital to N. on the Me-nam, where the East India Company had a factory, withdrawn in 1623. Korat is a great mart on the To Kron, 150 m. N.E. of Ayuthia. **Phra Pratom**, 30 m. W. of Bangkok, with the largest pagoda (and fair) in the country, covering with enclosure 3251 ft., cloistered and terraced, on successive plateaux, from the centre of which the bell-shaped spire springs to 347 ft. above the general level. The Indian Trigonometrical Survey mapped 8033 sq. m. in 1880, and fixed the position of these towns, besides the capital—Pechaburi, Thacheen, Paknam, Meklong, Kanburi, and Ratburi, also the route from Phra Pratom *viâ* Kanburi to the **Natyadoung Pass** on the Tenasserim frontier, 55 m. higher up than the **Amya Pass** above Mergui. **Laos** and **Kambodia** to E., between the Me-nam and Me-khong, assert independence, but are claimed, the former by Burma, and the latter by the French of Cochin China, who secured its independence of Siam by the treaty of 1863. Kambodia is remarkable for its old Brahmanical civilisation, as seen by the magnificent ruins of temples and palaces of the Khmer Kings at Angkor-Wat and Nakhoor-Wat, recently explored anew, and also for possessing the greatest fresh-water lake in South Asia, the **Tale Sap Lake**. The capital is Phnom-Penh, at the confluence of the Me-khong with the lake. Udong is on the lake, and Kampot is a port on the S.E.

§ 7. UPPER BURMA, since Lord Dalhousie's enforced conquest of Pegu in 1852, has had an area of 192,000 sq. m., with a population of 3½ millions, yielding a diminishing revenue of a million sterling, of which one-fourth is in produce and labour. In spite of treaties from 1826 to 1867, and an embassy to the Viceroy and Governor-General in 1882, the barbarous Burman sovereign has, since his accession in 1878, continued to set humanity, honour, and the good of the people at defiance. **Mandalay** (65,000), the wooden capital for the last 22 years only, on the Nawadi, is a square of 1 m. every way, surrounded by a brick wall with 12 gates, and encloses in the centre the palace, stockaded with birch and teak. The former capitals Amarapoora and Ava were lower down the river, all on the left bank. **Bhamo**, on the upper course of the Irawadi, a stockaded town through which British expeditions and missionaries passed to and from China so long as the British Political Agent resided there under the treaty of 1867. The Shan, Kareng, Singpho, Kachin, and other feudatories around the upper valley of the Irawadi have long refused practically to acknowledge the suzerainty of the now impotent dynasty of Aloung bhoora (Alompra). Its timber and mineral wealth, and the industrial and artistic skill of its people, are arrested or directed into other channels, until British treaty rights shall be respected, and the old influence of the British Political Agent be restored.

§ 8. TIBET (Bod-land) and **East Toorkestan**, the vast Western Provinces of the Chinese Empire, march with the whole extent of the N. border of British India, from Assam in the E. to Kashmeer and Afghanistan in the W., save where there are independent savage tribes, as at Assam, or the Protected States of Bhootan and Nepal. Notwithstanding repeated efforts since 1774, when Warren Hastings, the first Governor-General, sent George Bogle of the Bengal Civil Service on an apparently successful mission to the Teshu Lama at Teshu Lumbo; and treaties with the Emperor of China, under which passports are given which secure safety to travellers in China proper at least, no British or Russian envoys or travellers have yet been able to cross Tibet in any direction. Native surveyors alone, disguised, have been sent from India periodically as far as Lhasa. E. Toorkestan or Kashgaria was open to travellers like Johnson and Shaw, and to the Forsyth embassy from the Viceroy and Governor-General, which surveyed up to the Thian Shan and Great Pamir, only when the short-lived rule (1864-77) of Ameer Yakoob Khan prevailed against the Chinese power. **Tibet** has an estimated area of 650,000 sq. m., being 1500 m. from E. to W., and 600 and 700 from S. to N. It seems to be divided administratively with Eastern Tibet, of which **Lhasa** is the capital and residence of the chief or Dalai

Lama; and Western Tibet, of which **Teshu Lumbo** is the principal town and the residence of the second or Teshu Lama. Another division is that into the 4 provinces of **Kam**, on the E. bordering the Sechuen province of China proper; **Ari**, on the W. of the Mariam-la or pass, claiming to include the Ladak district of Kashmeer; **U** and **Tsang** or **Utsang**, which form Great or Central Tibet and the north valley of the Brahmapootra.

East Toorkestan, Kashgaria or **Djetishahr** ("country of the seven cities"), is the most westerly Province of the Chinese Empire, between the Karakoram portion of the Himalaya and the Thian Shan range, up to which Russia has advanced from N., and the Gobi desert on the E. to the Pamir slopes. It is best known under the three sections, with capitals of the same name, of **Khotan, Yarkand**, and **Kashgar**, the last the chief capital, at which the Muhammadan ruler who expelled the Chinese for 14 years, Yakoob Khan, received more than one envoy from the Viceroy of India, sent at his request. East Toorkestan has an area of 244,000 sq. m., and a population of upwards of 1 million. The chiefly commercial treaty of 1874 with the enlightened Muhammadan power is of course in abeyance, and the growing trade from Amritsar *viâ* Leh to Yarkand and Kashgar has ceased.

§ 9. AFGHANISTAN (Vilayat), since the rectification of the British frontier by the treaty of Gandamak in May 1879 has been departed from, may be regarded as consisting of the territory, neutral as between Russia and Great Britain, defined by the two Governments in 1872, or **Kabul, Jalalabad, Ghazni, Kandahar, Herat**, and **Balkh** or **Afghan Toorkestan.** The whole forms a square 600 miles long and broad, with an average elevation of 4000 ft. rising to 7000 in the heights of the over-estimated Hindu Koosh, and with a population of 2½ millions. The **Hindu Koosh** stretches 200 miles west from Pushtkhar, where it meets the Himalaya, to Bamian, and is continued in the **Koh-i-Baba** down to Herat, whence there runs the offshoot of the Caucasus, which bounds Persia to the north. This range is crossed by the following passes, going from east to west:—(1) Chitral, (2) Ishtirak, (3) Kagram, (4) Nuksan, (5) Kharteza, (6) Dara, from Chitral to Badakshan; of those from Kafiristan to Badakshan, used only by Siaposh, nothing is known. From Deh Poorian, in the Panjshēr valley, a pass leads by (1) Anjaman to Badakshan; the others are (2) Thal, (3) Khawk, (4) Bazārak, (5) Shatpal, (6) Parwan, (7) Saralang, (8) Kaoshan, (9) Gwalian, (10) Gwazgar, (11) Chardar,

(12) Gholalaj, (13) Farinjal, (14) Ghorband. The Khawk and Saralang passes have been traversed by artillery. The great military route is that of Khoolm and Bamian, improved during the first Kabul war. The tribes on the immediate border of the Panjab are practically independent of the Ameer. The Toorkestan States which acknowledge the suzerainty of the Ameer in proportion as he is weak or strong, are the Hazaras of the Hindu Koosh, **Maemana, Andkhoi, Shibargan, Saripool, Balkh, Khoolm** or Tashkoorgan, **Koondooz, Badakshan**, and **Wakhan**, all on the left side of the Oxus save Wakhan, which is on both sides of its uppermost course. The northern boundary, approved of by the British and the Russian Governments in 1872, is described by General Walker, R.E., as trending E.N.E., in a nearly straight line, from the point where the Hari Rood river crosses the parallel of 36° to Khoja Salih ferry on the Oxus. It is carried thence up the course of the Oxus and the principal branch of that river, the Panja, to Wood's Victoria Lake. The W. boundary runs S. from Sarakhs along the Hari Rood, till that river turns E. towards Herat, when the line continues S. to the E. shore of Seistan Lake and Baloochistan at 30° N. lat. In 1871-72, commissioners representing the Government of India and the various countries fixed the boundaries between Afghanistan and Persia, giving Seistan Lake chiefly to the latter, and between Persia and Baloochistan.

Kabul (50,000) (6396 ft.), the capital, is near the junction of the Kabul and Logar rivers, 190 m. from Peshawar, 103 from Jalalabad, 318 from Kandahar, 88 from Ghazni, 687 from Herat by Kandahar and 500 direct through the Hazara country, and 357 from Balkh. The city, 3 m. in circumference, is at the W. extremity of a spacious plain, in an angle formed by the two inferior ridges, Koh Takht Shah and Koh Khoja Safar; with the exception of a suburb the city lies on the right bank of the Kabul river. To E. and S.E. is the Bala Hissar citadel. **Kandahar** (50,000) (3484 ft.), between the Argandab and Tarnak rivers, 144 m. N.W. of Quetta, 343 N.W. of Jacobabad, and 360 W. of Dera Ismail Khan, on a level plain covered with cultivation. The city is an irregular oblong, having a circuit of 3¾ miles, with hard mud walls and six gates. The citadel is to N. The place commands the route to India from Herat, and is described by Sir Henry Durand as the centre of the mountain frontier of India, offering a choice of several passes by which to descend to the Indus, to which the Sibi Railway has now brought it near.

§ 10. PERSIAN N. FRONTIER.—At Gombroon, now Bandar Abbas, the visit of the two Sherleys at the beginning of the 17th century led Shah Abbas the Great, of the Suffavean dynasty, to encourage the erection of English, French, and Dutch factories. After the disappearance of a short-lived Afghan dynasty, the murder of Nadir Shah in 1747, and half a century of confusion, the able Aga Mahomed Khan founded the present or Kajar dynasty in 1795. Under his nephew and successor, Fath Ali Khan, the British connection with Persia became politically close, from the fear of an Afghan invasion of India, and French and Russian designs. Hence Malcolm's treaties of 1801 and 1809, and that of 1814. In 1823 the pacification of Europe and a change of policy in England led to the transfer of the British relations with Persia from a plenipotentiary of the Crown to an envoy of the Governor-General. This continued for nearly forty years till the resignation of Sir Henry Rawlinson, when the direct control of the embassy at the court of Tehran was again transferred to the Foreign Office in London. The Government of India, however, continue to pay a large proportion of the cost of the embassy and to receive information from the British minister at Tehran. The southward progress of Russia throughout the century was hastened by the Treaty of Toorkomanchai in 1828. After the brief campaign the Treaty of Paris, concluded in 1857, defined the British political relations with Persia, and revived only an earlier convention for the suppression of slavery in the Persian Gulf. More recent conventions regulate the Indo-European lines of telegraph through Persia. General Goldsmid's commissioners in 1871-72 laid down the Afghan and Balooch borders of Persia as already described. British intervention has frequently assisted in settling disputes in the border districts of Persia and Turkey; and in 1876 these two Governments agreed to a convention for regulating the position of their subjects there. The **Northern boundary**, where it marches with the recent acquisitions of Russia from its Caspian base, is thus described by General Walker, R.E. It runs along the entire course of the **Atrek** from the point where that river enters the Caspian Sea to the point where its principal source is supposed to originate. Thence it is drawn E. for about 100 m., and then S.E. in a nearly straight line to the point where the Hari Rood crosses the parallel of 36°, where it meets the N. boundary of Afghanistan.

§ 11. TURKISH ARABIA AND THE PERSIAN GULF.—In 1639 there was an English factory at **Basrah** subordinate to that of Gombroon. But it was not till 1798 that an officer was appointed East India Company's Resident at **Baghdad**, the capital of Turkish Arabia, chiefly to watch the proceedings of Napoleon's emissaries, and to transmit intelligence overland. In 1812 the official became Political Agent, as now, with the duty of checking the slave-trade. In 1864 a treaty was concluded between Great Britain and Turkey for establishing telegraphic communication between the Ottoman territory and India by a submarine cable from Bushire to the mouth of the Shat-el-Arab, there to join the Ottoman land line, which is connected with the Persian line at Khanakain.

The N. shore of the Persian Gulf from Cape Jask to Mohammerah is under Persian **Lingah**, where there is a Native Agent. **Bandar Abbas, Bahrein Island**, centre of the pearl fishery, and the 6 "Trucial Chiefs" of the maritime tribes from El Kutr, beyond Bahrein, along the coast E. to Ras-ool-Kheimah, are, under treaties, controlled by the British Resident in the Persian Gulf, who keeps the maritime peace, and prevents piracy and the slave traffic. A Native Agent is stationed at Shargah.

§ 12. ABYSSINIA (the Habsh = "confusion" of races, of the Arabs, Abassinos of the Portuguese, and Itiopia or Ethiopia of the people themselves) was always more or less closely connected with India till May 1868, when the victorious British and Indian army left the country after the capture of Magdala. Prince Kassai of Tigré province, having assisted Lord Napier's expedition, was presented with arms, ammunition, and stores, made himself master of the whole country, and in 1872 was crowned at Axam, the ancient capital, as Negoos or King Johannes. Since that time he has been successful in conflicts with the late Khedive of Egypt. The country is a quadrilateral territory of 158,400 square miles, with a population of about 4 millions, having Nubia N. and N.W., the Blue Nile W., the Gallas S., and the Danakils E. The last, inhabiting the arid and unhealthy flat coast of the Red Sea, which broadens from a few miles at Massowah in the N. to 300 m. at Tajoora in the S., are hostile tribes claimed by the Khedive of Egypt. The probability that this earliest of Christian peoples will succeed in again holding the coast, and recent events in Egypt, make it desirable that the political connection of India with Abyssinia should be resumed. The three chief upland Provinces are **Tigré** in the N., with Adowa, its capital; **Amhara** in the centre, with Gondar (7000), the capital; and **Shoa** in the S., with Ankóbar, its capital. Tigré lies between Gondar and

Massowah. Shoa is nearly separated from Amhara by the Muhammadan tribe of Wolla Gallas. The Government of Bombay in 1841 sent Major W. C. Harris on a mission to Sahela Selassie, the hereditary king of Shoa, at Ankóbar ("gate of Anko," a Galla queen), 370 m. W. of Tajoora. A commercial treaty was concluded at Angollala, the western or Galla capital. Friendly intercourse has since been maintained with Menilek, the present king, by letters and presents.

§ 13. MUSCAT AND ZANZIBAR.—The Muscat Arabs drove the Persians from Oman two centuries ago, and on the death of Nadir Shah they made Ahmed bin Saeed, then Governor of **Sohar**, Imam of **Muscat**, opposite Baloochistan. A British alliance with his successors, chiefly to put down the slave trade, supported Muscat against the aggression of the Wahabees of Nejd, to the N. In 1856, on the death of the Imam of that day, who had left Muscat and Zanzibar to his two sons generally, Lord Canning, as arbiter, decided that Zanzibar should be independent, even feudally, of Muscat, while Muscat remains under the Government of India's Foreign Office. The Sultan of Zanzibar, who has visited England, in 1873 made a treaty with the Queen for the suppression of the slave-trade. His apparently honest endeavour, under the guidance of Sir John Kirk, has driven the traffic farther north to Egypt and the Red Sea.

Zanzibar ("coast of the blacks") **Island** has an area of 600 sq. m. and 380,000 inhabitants, of whom 80,000 are in the capital; many of these are British Indian subjects. It is 30 m. from the mainland of Africa. The Zanzibar dominions extend from Toonger, frontier of Portuguese territory S. of Cape Delgado, about 700 m. N. along the coast, and as far inland as the Sultan can exercise his influence. Zanzibar (Ungooja = native name), the capital, is on W. shore of island. Other islands are Pemba (227 sq. m.) and Mafia (200 sq. m.). The chief trading towns on the mainland are Bagomoyo, opposite Zanzibar, the starting-point for Lakes Tanganyika and Nyanza; Dar es Salaam, the Sultan's occasional residence, 20 m. S. of Zanzibar, from which a road runs towards the head of Lake Nyassa; Rovuma, Kilwa, Mombasa, Usambara, Malindi, and Lamo. The trade is in the hands of British Indian subjects from the Bombay coast. Three English and two Scottish Missions have, since Dr. Livingstone's death, extended their operations from the E. coast and from the Zambesi on the S., westward to the three great Lakes, rediscovered by him and by the Indian officers, Burton, Speke, and Augustus Grant.

BOOK II.

PHYSIOGRAPHY.

CHAPTER I.

GEOLOGY OF PENINSULAR INDIA.

§ 1. The Geological Survey. § 2. Peculiarities of Indian Geology. § 3. Divisions. § 4. Classified List of Peninsular Formations. § 5. Metamorphic or Gneissic. § 6. Mineralogical Character. § 7. Auriferous Gneissoid Rocks. § 8. Transition or Sub-Metamorphic. § 9. Vindhyan. § 10. Diamond-bearing Conglomerates. § 11. Gondwana System. § 12. Coal-Measures. § 13. Jurassic Marine. § 14. Cretaceous Marine. § 15. Dekhan Trap. § 16. Tertiary and Laterite.

§ 1. THE GEOLOGICAL SURVEY.—In 1818, when the Science of Geology was in its infancy, **Dr. Voysey** joined the Trigonometrical Survey of India as its geologist and surgeon. He explored many parts of the peninsula, from Agra south through the Dekhan to the Kistna, including the valleys of the Tapti and the Godavari and the diamond mines. The Survey officers, and many of the officers of Indian Engineers and Artillery not on the staff of the Survey, reported on the rocks, their minerals and fossils, in many Districts and Provinces. Of non-official explorers and observers the most able were the French naturalist **Jacquemont**, especially in Rewah State, where valuable coal has just been discovered; **Stephen Hislop**, missionary of the Free Church of Scotland, especially in Nagpoor and the rich coal strata since worked there; and **Dr. Buist**, the Bombay editor and *savant*, whose premature death, like that of Hislop, Jacquemont, and Voysey, was a loss to science. In 1833 **Mr. James Calder** published, in the eighteenth volume of the *Asiatic Researches*, the first brief summary of Indian Geology. Its special value lies in the correct indication, at that period, of the general distribution of the overlying trap in Central and Western India, and of the prevalence of granitic and gneissic formations not only in the peninsula but throughout the Himalaya. **Captain Newbold**, from Karnool where he was Assistant Resident, personally investigated much of the geology of Southern India, of which, from 1844 to 1850, he published a summary, still of much value as acknowledged by the professional reporters of the Geological Survey. With the one exception of associating the rocks of the Gondwana system with the ancient "diamond sandstone" of transition or Vindhyan age, his observations correctly described and classed the metamorphic rocks; the diamond sandstone and limestone; the cretaceous (fossiliferous) limestone of Pondicheri; the freshwater limestones and cherts intercalated with the Dekhan traps; the laterite, with which the Cuddalore sandstone and marine sandstone of Ramnad and Cape Comorin are associated; the older alluvium, including regur or black cotton soil, and kankar or nodular limestone; the modern alluvium and sand dunes; such plutonic rocks as granite and greenstone, and the newer or overlying trap. In 1854-57 **Dr. Carter** published a more extensive but less valuable summary and reprint of papers on the geology of the whole of Peninsular India, and **Mr. Greenough** exhibited to the British Association the first Geological Map of India.

The growing importance of the carboniferous formation in the Damodar Valley, where coal was first worked in 1777, led to the appointment by the East India Company in 1845 of Mr. D. H. Williams as Geological Surveyor, succeeded by Dr. M'Clelland. In March 1851 **Dr. Oldham**, Professor of Geology at Trinity College, Dublin, first organised the regular Geological Survey, under Lord Dalhousie, then Governor-General. But it was not till 1856 that his preliminary inquiries led Lord Canning to order a systematic survey, by an increased staff, in districts of which the Revenue and Topographical Surveys had completed the maps, and which promised the most valuable results, economic and scientific. Notwithstanding delays due to the want of maps, to a frequently insufficient staff thinned by disease and death from exposure in a tropical country and malarious districts at all seasons, the results, both scientific and practical, have been most satisfactory. These are published periodically in the valuable illustrated series of *Memoirs* and *Records*, and in the magnificent *Palæontologia Indica*, in which there are figured and described by authorities like Professor Huxley the Cephalopoda and Gasteropoda of the cretaceous rocks of S. India, the flora of the Rajmahal, and the vertebrate fossils of the Panchet rocks, previously met with only in South Africa. To the general reader, as well as to the geologist not familiar with India, the most important result of the thirty years' survey is the *Manual of the Geology of India, chiefly compiled from the Observations of the Geological Survey*, by Mr. H. B. Medlicott, its present superintendent, Mr. W. T. Blanford, the deputy-superintendent, and Professor V. Ball, long one of the surveyors, in four volumes (1879-81), of which one forms a map on the scale of 64 miles to the inch. The Survey possesses a Museum, Library, and Mining Record Office in Calcutta. In 1880 the first native of India, a Bengalee graduate of the London University, was appointed to the graded staff.

§ 2. PECULIARITIES OF INDIAN GEOLOGY.—The geology of the peninsular portion of India differs from that of Europe, or of any other region in the world which has supplied the data for the classification familiar to ordinary students of the science. (1) Several of the Indian peninsular formations extend over hundreds of thousands of square miles. (2) The fossils that are found point to the conclusion that the peninsula formed at one time a portion of a vast continent stretching from South Africa to Malaysia, and separated from India by the breadth, at least, of what is now the Indo-Gangetic Plain. (3) There is a remarkable absence of any evidence of that disturbance in late geological times which marks the rest of Asia. The principal mountain chains of the Indian Peninsula are, with the exception of the Aravali range, not coincident with axes of disturbance or elevation. They are merely plateaux, or portions of plateaux, which have escaped denudation. The peninsula is a tableland worn away by subaërial denudation; and, perhaps, to a minor extent on its margins by the sea. The low valleys of Central India are denudation hollows cut by rain and rivers out of the original plateau. The exceptions, where the strike and dip of the rocks appear to have affected the contour of the country, are among the metamorphic and transition formations. (4) Unlike the rest of Asia and Europe, there is in the peninsular area a remarkable absence of marine representatives of the palæozoic and lower mesozoic formations. Over the whole vast area there is no known marine deposit of older date than the Cretaceous epoch, except the Jurassic beds of Kach and Jaisalmeer in the north-west, and a few outcrops of similar age along the east coast, near Madras, Ongole, and Ellore. This absence of marine fossils is not due to alteration of the strata nor to the deficiency of rocks suited for the preservation of organic remains. As the Grauwacke of Europe was long supposed to be unfossiliferous, the transition, and especially the Upper Vindhyan rocks of India, may yet be found to yield fossils. But the European Silurian and Cambrian beds revealed organic remains on the first systematic search, and the ancient Indian formations have been explored in vain by the most experienced geologists. It is not, therefore, expected that in them any conspicuous marine organisms such as mollusca, corals, or crustacea, will be detected.

§ 3. Divisions of Indian Geology.—In considering the whole geographical extent of the British Indian Empire we found it to consist of the Himalaya, the Indo-Gangetic Plain, and the Peninsula, which are really the geological divisions. Reversing the order, that the most ancient formations may be taken first, we proceed to follow the official *Manual of Geology* in its detailed treatment of—

I. **Peninsular India.**
II. **Indo-Gangetic Plain.**
III. **Himalaya**, or Extra-Peninsular Region.

The peculiarities of the geology of the peninsular area render it difficult to correlate the strata with the series found elsewhere. The great European divisions of the geological sequence, as palæozoic, mesozoic, and cænozoic or tertiary, are ill adapted for the classification of these Indian beds. The correlation of the Extra-Peninsular formations is even more imperfect; but only because our knowledge of these is still so scanty, the different tracts being separated from each other by countries like Nepal and Afghanistan, which are shut to the surveyor. Peninsular rocks are found in three localities in Extra-Peninsular India—in Sind there is a thin representative of the Dekhan trap; in Sikkim and Bhootan, at the base of the Himalaya, fossiliferous Damodar or Lower Gondwana beds occur; in the Khasi and Garo hills of Assam are representatives of the metamorphic and cretaceous (marine) rocks of the peninsula, and probably of the transition beds and Rajmahal traps.

§ 4. Classified List of Peninsular Formations.—The following is the Survey's list of formations in Peninsular India, including Kathiawar and Kach. The lower are classed simply as azoic. The subdivisions are not always strictly consecutive; some of the marine cretaceous rocks being of the same age as the Dekhan traps, and the marine jurassic beds being contemporaneous with the Upper Gondwanas.

Classified List of Formations in Peninsular India.

Era	Group	Division	Formations	Approximate maximum thickness.
	Recent and post-tertiary.		Blown sand. Soils, including black soil or regur. Modern alluvial deposits of rivers, estuaries, and the sea coast. *Kadar* of Indo-Gangetic Plain, etc. Raised shell beds of coast. Low-level laterite. Older alluvial deposits of Ganges, Narbada, Godavari, etc. Cave deposits.	Unknown; 700 feet deepest boring.
Cænozoic.	Tertiary.		Miliolite of Kathiawar. Pliocene, miocene, and eocene (nummulitic) beds of Kach and Goojarat. Sandstones, clays, and lignites of the west coast, Travankor and Ratnagiri. Cuddalore sandstones. High-level laterite.	2,700
Cænozoic. / Mesozoic.	Dekhan trap series.		Upper traps and intertrappeans of Bombay. Middle traps. Lower traps and intertrappeans of Central India, Rajamahendri, etc. Lameta or infra-trappean group. Infra-trappeans of Rajamahendri.	6,000
Mesozoic.	Marine cretaceous rocks.		Arialoor, Trichinopoli, and Utatoor groups. Bagh beds. Neocomian of Kach.	3,000
Mesozoic.	Marine jurassic rocks.		Umia, Katrol, Chari, and Pachham groups of Kach. Jaisalmeer limestones. Trippeti and Ragavapooram beds of east coast.	6,000
Mesozoic.	Gondwana system.	*Upper*	Kach and Jabalpoor. Rajmahal and Mahadeva.	11,000
Palæ.?	Gondwana system.	*Lower*	Panchet. Damodar: — Raneeganj or Kamthi, ironstone shales, and Barakar. Karharbari and Talcher.	13,000
Azoic.	Vindhyan series.	*Upper*	Bhanrer (Bundair). Rewah. Kaimoor.	12,000
Azoic.	Vindhyan series.	*Lower*	Karnool. Bheema. Son. Semri . . .	2,000 ?
Azoic.	Transition or sub-metamorphic rocks.	*Upper*	Gwalior, Cuddapah, and Kaladgi series . .	20,000
Azoic.	Transition or sub-metamorphic rocks.	*Lower*	Bijawars. Champaner beds. Aravali. Malani beds. Transition rocks of Behar and Shillong (the last Extra-Peninsular).	
Azoic.	Metamorphic or gneissic.		Gneiss, granitoid and schistose rocks, etc.	?

The following is the succession of the more important fossiliferous peninsular rocks, the marine beds being omitted from the sequence, but classed as equivalent to their supposed representatives amongst the formations without marine fossils :—

		Peninsular Rocks.	Supposed Marine Equivalents. Indian.	European.
CÆNOZOIC		High-level laterite	Nummulitic	Middle eocene.
	Dekhan traps.	Upper Dekhan traps	?	Lower eocene.
MESOZOIC	Dekhan traps.	Middle traps	Arialoor	Upper chalk.
		Lower traps	Trichinopoli	Lower chalk.
		Infra-trappeans or Lameta	Bagh beds, Utatoor	Upper green-sand.
	Gondwana.	Jabalpoor and Kach	Umia and Katrol	Jurassic.
		Mahadeva and Rajmahal	Chari and Pachham	
		Panchet . .	. .	Triassic.
PALÆOZOIC		Damodar . .	. .	Upper palæozoic ?
		Talcher . .		

The geological horizon of the upper mesozoic and tertiary beds is ascertained with a fair amount of precision ; but the determination of the position in the series to be assigned to the Lower Gondwana formations is far more doubtful, and nothing is known of the age of the Vindhyan and older rocks.

Azoic Rocks.

§ 5. Metamorphic or Gneissic.—The peninsular gneissic and transition series are ancient sedimentary beds, although no fossils have yet been found in them. Whether they were deposited in the sea or in rivers and lakes, it is impossible to tell. The rocks may have been the scene of organic life, but its traces have been obliterated by the alteration which they have undergone. We have to pass through many upward stages of transition rocks, and to cross a great gap in the ascending sequence of formations, before we meet with the first trace of life in Peninsular India. An indigenous school of geology would probably have held very strict doctrines upon an absolute abrupt commencement of life upon the globe. There are three gneissic regions which exceed in area that of all other groups together. (1) The **Boondelkhand Gneiss**, the oldest known rock of India, is a compact semicircular area to the north of the Vindhyan plateau, which for 200 miles on its north-north-east face is gradually overspread by the Gangetic alluvium, and on its convex southern margin is bounded by a scarp of Vindhyan sandstones. The Boondelkhand Gneiss was altered before the deposition of the Bijawar transition rocks, and was probably metamorphosed after Bijawar times. (2) The **Main or Eastern Gneiss**, with a mean breadth of 350 miles, extends up the peninsula in a straight line for 1400 miles, from Cape Comorin to Colgong on the Ganges, with the exception of a narrow strip of overlying strata in the Godavari basin, connecting the eastern seaboard with the spread of the Dekhan trap. After a gap of 150 miles, through which the Ganges and Brahmapootra find their way to the sea, we come to the northmost outlier of the same natural group, to which the later mountain systems of the Himalaya and Burma have been added, the gneissic rocks which form the bases of the Shillong plateau and Lower Assam. The varied surface configuration of this vast formation is due to denudation, such as the uplands of Hazaribagh and Chutia Nagpoor; the high-level gneissic mass beneath the Dekhan trap on the Mandla plateau, extending east to Sirgooja, and west through Chindwara and Betool; the highlands of the east Jaipoor watershed between the Mahanadi and Godavari; the gneissic plateau of Haidarabad, and the loftier masses of Mysore; the Neelgiris culminating in Dodabetta (8760 feet), which are separated from the Palnais and Anamalais of Travankor by the Palghat gap. In the northern area the dome-gneiss is so called from its weathering into such ellipsoidal masses as the Kalapahar and Bhanrer hills on the north of Hazaribagh, and the Mandar hill of Bhagalpoor. Compared with the Boondelkhand Gneiss, trap-dikes are rare in the Eastern Gneiss. A small auriferous tract occurs in the Dambal or Kappatgudd hills immediately south of the Southern Maratha country, in a broad band of chloritic, hornblendic, argillaceous, and hæmatitic schists, between two strong bands of granitoid gneiss; the most productive reefs have a north-north-west strike, and the sources of the streams said to be auriferous are within a tract of pseudo-diorite. The most extensive gold-bearing tract is that of the South-East Wainad, or the uplands of Mysore, at the north-west base of the Neelgiris. (3) The **Aravali Gneiss** extends from Delhi through Rajpootana into Goojarat. The crystalline region is separated from the Boondelkhand area by 70 miles of Vindhyan rocks, which extend to near Agra, and less distinctly by 50 miles of covering Dekhan trap, from the Main Eastern Gneiss. Its relative age is uncertain.

§ 6. MINERALOGICAL CHARACTER OF THE GNEISS.—The ordinary peninsular gneiss is pink, the prevailing felspars being orthoclase (monoclinic in crystallising) and oligoclase (triclinic), while there is more hornblende than mica. The older Himalayan gneiss is usually white or gray, the common felspars being orthoclase and albite; it contains more mica than hornblende, and is more uniform in character than the peninsular. Thus early, in the oldest known rocks, does the contrast begin between the Peninsular and Himalayan regions.

§ 7. AURIFEROUS GNEISSOID ROCKS.—In India gold is ultimately derived chiefly from the quartz veins of metamorphosed rocks. The subaërial degradation and erosion of the surface by rain and rivers break up and sift auriferous masses, and so afford a scanty subsistence to the poorest classes of the natives of India from gold-washing. Of late the success of gold mining from the quartz veins of the almost unaltered lower Silurian rocks of Australia, has led to the formation of many companies to work the gneissoid rocks of the Main or Eastern Gneissic Region, stretching from Mysore and the Neelgiris south to Travankor. In South Wainad there are four belts of gneiss: the quartzo-hornblendic gneiss of the north face of the Neelgiris, and north of it (below) the Devalla band of highly felspathic gneiss, with two minor belts of chloritic gneiss; north of this is the quartzose and ferruginous band of the Marpanmoodi range. The auriferous quartz reefs are most developed in the Devalla band. Their lie is peculiar; the strike is north-north-west, corresponding with that of the gneiss in the country to the north, and at right angles to that of the rocks in which they occur, yet they generally have a low dip, from 10° to 30°, always easterly. One small trap-dike occurs in the Devalla band; it runs east by north, nearly in the strike of the gneiss.

In October 1879 Mr. R. Brough Smyth, a mining engineer of Australian experience, submitted to the Madras Government a careful report of 100 folio pages on *The Gold Mines of the South-Eastern Portion of the Wainad and the Carcoor Ghat.* After surveying the country and coffee and cinchona estates over an area of 500 square miles of this region, Mr. Brough Smyth reported these conclusions, scientific and practical:—

General Character of the Auriferous Quartz Veins.

"The quartz veins of the Wainad differ in some respects from those intersecting the almost unaltered lower Silurian rocks of Australia, but they are usually as thick, or thicker, and quite as persistent. The auriferous veins, those which have yielded well both on the large scale and by tests in the laboratory, are laminated and more or less pyritous, and those which up to the present time are regarded as less auriferous are composed of saccharoid, often snow-white opaque quartz with transparent particles of quartz impacted, and have generally an obscurely granular appearance—more indeed like quartzite than vein-quartz, and in many places they exhibit a tendency to become granitic, large plates of muscovite and apparently a hydrated muscovite in smaller plates, with here and there a little felspar giving them a character which separates them at once from the well-known rich pyritous veins near Devalla. Some of the massive quartz near Moopenaad and Vellirymulla micacised and in structure simulating granite, or partaking of the character of the country rock, might well be supposed to be bedded and not vein-quartz, and contemporaneous with the gneissoid rocks with which it is associated. There was no true quartzite seen in these places, but it may be conjectured that the induration and alterations of composition and structure, which have resulted in the formation of the foliated gneissoid rocks, would not be without influence on purely silicious granular interbedded masses.

"From the larger (true) veins 'leaders' are thrown off, most commonly to the westward. The leaders usually dip at a low angle, but in some places they are so large and of such a form as almost to give the character of 'saddle' reefs to the masses of quartz.

"The ordinary 'casing' of the reefs is a talcose schist (easily separable into thin laminæ) with oxide of iron and the minerals ordinarily therewith associated; and gold in small flat particles, visible to the eye, is not rare in the casing. The casing of many of the larger auriferous reefs is quartzose and ferruginous rudely laminated, and with scales of ripidolite and talc scattered through the mass.

"The average thickness of the true quartz veins is about five feet. Some are less than two feet in thickness, and others again exceed fourteen feet. The greater number, however, vary from four to seven feet. The direction of the veins is usually N. 30° W.—S. 30° E., and some are nearly due north and south; and the dip, though nearly always easterly, is irregular. On the summits of the steep hills the veins are commonly almost flat, or with a very slight dip to the eastward, but at a little depth from the surface the dip is, as might be expected, very different. It is not seldom as much as 30°, 40°, and 60°.

"These sudden variations may be due partly to the changes produced on the surface by the heavy rains which fall yearly. Much decomposed and almost solid rock is moved in masses, and 'the action of gravitation on substances loosened by weathering, or the 'weight of the hill' as it has been called,' would account for the difference of dip as measured near the surface and at some depth from the surface.

"The direction or strike of the quartz veins is, in a district like the Wainad, broken up, as it is, into rounded hills of varying height not easy to trace, unless regard be had to the elevation of each point where an outcrop of quartz is seen. An outcrop on a hill is thrown to the westward, and the same reef outcropping in a valley is necessarily eastward of the line which would appear if the ground were of the mean level.

"It is not yet possible to say what number of separate veins of quartz there are in the area which has been examined, but there are at least two hundred outcrops—not necessarily distinct reefs. From Moopenaad to Cherambadi, a distance of 11½ miles by the road, twenty-three outcrops were observed, many of them indicating reefs of great thickness; from Cherambadi to near Nadukani in a straight line south-easterly, twelve miles, there are at least eighteen separate veins; and east and south-easterly of Devalla the reefs are from 5, 5½, 7, 10, 16, and 23 chains apart. Between Moopenaad and Cherambadi the rocks are in places arenaceous.

Distribution of Gold.

"Gold is almost universally distributed throughout the soils and quartz veins of the Wainad. It occurs also in the sands and soils both on the east, west, north, and south. In South-East Wainad, on washing a few dishes of the surface soil anywhere, a few specks of very fine gold will be found; in the vicinity of the reefs rather heavy gold is often got by sluicing; and if a suitable spot be selected the native miners will obtain, even by their methods, sufficient gold to remunerate them for their labour. The character of the rocks, the nature of the climate, and the formation of the country, have all contributed to prevent the accumulation of drifts such as are found in California and Australia. There are here no gullies having in their beds shallow deposits with a well-defined auriferous stratum, no 'deep *leads*' covered and protected by layers of volcanic rock; there are only, as a rule, in the district now under consideration 'surfacing' and 'quartz mining.'

"On the Seeputtee river there is an accumulation of well-rounded boulders of quartz and gneissoid rock embedded in hard clay and sandy soil which may be regarded almost as a 'cement.' It is no more than the old bed of the river, which owing to the 'cutting back' action of the water has lowered its level and left this drift on its banks. It is probable that, as in other similar cases, the 'cement' will be found in patches on both sides of the river, in places which were formerly bends of the old stream. The bed-rock on which the gravel, clay, and boulders lie is at no great height above the level of the existing watercourse; and the part of the drift which has been worked is about thirty feet in thickness.

"This drift, and those which are to be found in the beds of the swamps, may be said to represent the alluvial deposits of the Wainad. Some of these are probably rich in gold, but it is only under favourable conditions that they could remunerate the miner.

"It would be extremely difficult and costly, and in many cases almost impracticable, to drain the swamps by artificial channels, and the expense of pumping the water from a shaft would be very great. Still, if the lowest stratum should prove to be highly auriferous, it might be found remunerative to resort even to pumping, care being taken to carry off the surface water from the swamps by constructing races. Below the Wainad plateau and bordering on the tertiaries there are in the beds of the streams rather deep deposits of drift. At Karambaut the water-worn gravels and rounded blocks of country rock and quartz are of considerable thickness. Below Eddacurra the bed-rock is covered with quite recent deposits and tertiary strata (laterite). It is not known whether the stratum immediately overlying the bed-rock is generally auriferous; but wherever the latter is intersected by quartz veins, more or less gold will be found in the disintegrated rocks.

Conclusion.

"Gold has been found on the south near Eddacurra and on the north near Nellacottah, on the west near Vyteri, and on the east as far as Bolingbroke, that is to say, over an area of 500 square miles. The reefs are very numerous, and they are more than of the average thickness of those found in other countries; they are of great longitudinal extent, some being traceable by their outcrops for several miles; they are strong and persistent and highly auriferous at an elevation of less than 500 feet above the sea, and they can be traced thence upwards to a height of nearly 8000 feet; near them gold can be washed out of almost every dish of earth that is dug; the proportion of gold in some of the soils and reefs in the neighbourhood of Devalla is large; and, the country presenting the greatest facilities for prosecuting mining operations at the smallest cost, it must be apparent to all who have given attention to this question that sooner or later gold mining will be established as an important industry in Southern India. The retardation of this event will be caused, not by the meagreness of the resources—they are large—but probably by the mistaken notion that wherever there is gold all the care, all the forethought that would be deemed requisite in other pursuits may be disregarded in conducting mining operations."

Out of 137 samples of auriferous quartz assayed, the average yield was 2 oz. 13 dwts. 2 grs. per ton; or, if one exceptional sample which yielded 204½ oz. and another which gave 25½ oz. be left out, the average yield was 102·8 dwts. 22 grs. per ton. In a paper read before the British Association at its 1881 meeting, Mr. W. King, of the Survey, said the Wainad reefs would not yield more gold than seven pennyweight to the ton. While he was hopeful of the moderate paying quality of the field, he was decidedly of opinion that the results obtained so far did not warrant the wild expectations which had prevailed in England and India, nor did they justify the enormous prices which had been paid there for land and "concessions." The Wainad reefs are developed over a very large area of country, but their auriferousness is displayed only over a portion, mainly in the south-east of the district, and in the adjacent low country of Malabar in a general east and west belt. Outside this belt the reefs are fewer, and only locally auriferous. The leaders or offshoots of the reefs are numerously developed, and, with the "casings," are rich in gold. It is these adjuncts, and not the reefs themselves, which were so extensively worked by the ancient miners. On the other hand the reefs, as far as is known, do not as yet show any continual steadiness in auriferousness, but they may be said to be capriciously permeated with the precious metal. The gold of the reef is pale-coloured, and of about the "touch" of standard gold; that of the leaders and casings is yellow, and of superior quality. In the outcrop of the quartz of Travankor only mere traces of gold have been found, and there are no traces of gold workings in that district.

§ 8. TRANSITION OR SUB-METAMORPHIC.—This second of the peninsular formations, in ascending series, covers a great area, and has very great thickness. Of its two subdivisions the Lower or older shows a close connection with the gneissic strata by partial metamorphism, conformable sequence or granitic intrusion, from which the Upper is free. The transition beds were deposited before the last great disturbances which affected the strata of the peninsula. Although the great mountain systems are due to the action of denudation, except the Aravali, many of the minor ranges and of the smaller river valleys coincide in direction with the foliation of the gneiss or the stratification of the older transition rocks. These, indeed, are probably the remnants of great ranges formed before the dawn of geological history. (1) Of the Lower subdivision the earliest is the **Bijawar** band, so named from the Boondela State, in which are its northern outcrops. This principal band of transition rocks stretches for about 700 miles in a west-south-west to east-north-east direction, obliquely across the peninsula from Bengal to the Narbada valley in Nimar. Its commonest bottom-rock in Boondelkhand is a quartzite, resting horizontally or with a slight dip on a denuded surface of the gneiss; with these are intimately associated a hornstone-breccia and a lime-stone. As in the case of the gneissic formation, the Shillong Transition Series in Lower Assam are more allied to the Peninsular than to the Himalayan beds. The Aravali region supplies the largest area of transition rocks in India; but it has still to be explored in detail. In the south-western quarter of that region is the **Champaner** basin of transition rocks, between the gneissic upland and alluvial tracts at the head of the Gulf of Kambay, and locally named from the old town, which was the Musalman capital of Goojarat. The **Aravali** proper, in its central area north of Aboo, is a transition watershed strongly metamorphic. The "flexible sandstone" of Kariana, much quarried for quern stones, is a locally decomposed condition of a band of gneissoze quartzite, 60 miles west of Delhi. The **Malani** beds, in the south-west quarter of the Aravali, are very ancient eruptive rocks ranking with the Lower Transition Series. (2) The Upper Transition rocks form three widely separated basins. That of **Gwalior**, the smallest, is named from the city which stands upon it, surrounding the scarped outlier of Vindhyan sandstone on which the Fort is built. Its base is the Par sandstone or semi-quartzite, on the top of which is a calcareo-silicious bed, the peculiar coralloid forms of which have been thought to be of organic origin. Iron ore is largely mixed in the Gwalior formation, as thin flakes of hæmatite and clay different from the massive concretionary hæmatite of the Bijawars. The **Cuddapah** basin is in these four groups—Kistna, Nallamalai, Cheyair, and Papagni—of enormous thickness, covering 13,500 square miles. Its eastern edge forms a segment of the Eastern Ghats known locally as the Yellakonda ridge. The two **Kaladgi** basins, Kaladgi and Bheema, in the Southern Maratha country, are 8 miles apart at the Kistna, where the gneiss passes between them. The Vingorla and other small islands off the coast consist of the very hard rocks belonging to this quartzite series, on the southern border of the great area occupied by the Dekhan trap.

§ 9. VINDHYAN.—This term was first applied to the quartzite sandstones, shales, and limestones in the great rock basin which stretches east and west for 600 miles from Sasseram to Neemach, and north and south for 300 miles from Agra to Hoshangabad. The break between the uppermost Transition beds and the Lower Vindhyans was not great; but the Upper Vindhyans have a far more recent aspect, due to a smaller amount of disturbance and of alteration. In face of the great probability that the earliest forms of organised being existed long before the appearance of Brachiopoda and Crustacea in the Cambrian formation, and even of Foraminifera in the Laurentian, the likelihood of the Vindhyans dating from a time when the world was devoid of life appears small. It is probable that marine life existed before the fresh waters and the land were inhabited, and the tropical lands and fresh waters may have been too hot for life after the sea teemed with living beings. But mathematicians have not yet decided whether the direction of the earth's axis has been constant, and there are indications that a low temperature prevailed in the Indian area at very ancient epochs. Meanwhile, the Vindhyans must be considered the latest azoic rocks of the peninsula. It is probable that India was then a land area, or part of a land area. The Salt Range of the Panjab may mark a portion of the limit of the ancient peninsular land.

(1) The Lower Vindhyans appear earliest in the **Karnool** formation of limestone, with subordinate bands of sandstone and shale, in the four groups of Khundair, Paneum, Jamalmadgu, and Banaganapali. In the last, a sandstone, diamonds are worked for by sinking shallow pits for 15 feet and driving short galleries in the diamond layer close to the bottom bed. The **Bheema** series is limestone mainly, with a width of 25 miles where the Bheema river crosses the outcrop nearly at its middle. The basement pebble bed at Bachimali, the extreme east point of the southern expansion of this basin, resembles the diamond layers of the lower Kistna valley, and seems to have been searched for diamonds. The diamond-washings of the Mahanadi a little above Sambalpoor are exclusively

from alluvial diggings; but the fact that they occur just outside and below the great Lower Vindhyan basin has suggested the conjecture that the gems are derived from those rocks, on the ground that these are the equivalents of the diamond-bearing beds of Southern India. The Lower Vindhyans are seen in their original boundary in the Son valley. From Sasseram they are continuous at the base of the Kaimoor scarp for 240 miles, and they disappear at the Son-Narbada watershed, where the Upper Vindhyans sweep across into contact with the submetamorphic rocks. The Semri rocks under the Kaimoor scarp in South-Eastern Boondelkhand are the same, but are more irregular due to this being the original edge of the deposits.

(2) The Upper Vindhyan formation ranks third in superficial extent within the rock-area of the peninsula, occupying in a single basin a larger surface than the combined areas of any other formation except the gneiss and the Dekhan trap. The form of the basin is peculiar: there is a great area, 250 miles long, between Chittorgarh on the west and Sagar on the east, and 225 miles broad from Indargarh on the north to Barwai (or Mortaka) on the south, all presumably occupied by Upper Vindhyans, although a very large part of it is covered by the trap of the Malwa plateau. From Sagar a long arm, with a maximum width of 50 miles, stretches eastwards for 340 miles to Sasseram in Behar. Another broader tract extends northwards from Sagar, and passes under the Gangetic alluvium between Agra and Gwalior. The gneissic mass of Boondelkhand lies between these prolongations. The exposed surface of the Upper Vindhyan deposits is about 40,000 square miles, and with the area beneath the trap the basin would occupy about 65,000. This upper division is in the main a sandstone formation, with distinct bands of shales, mostly coarse and flaggy. The only limestone is a subordinate band occurring pretty constantly throughout the area in the Bhanrer group, but the lower Rewah shales (Panna) are locally calcareous.

	NORTHERN INDIA. Vindhyan Formation.		MADRAS. Karnool Formation.
Upper .	Bhanrer Group Rewah ,, (*diamonds*) Kaimoor ,,		Absent.
Lower .	Tirhowan limestones Palkoa shales	=	Khundair shales and limestones.
	Dalchipoor sandstones	=	Paneum quartzites.
	Semri shales and limestone	=	Jamalmadgu shales and limestone.
	Semri sandstone	=	Banaganapali sandstone (*diamonds*).

§ 10. DIAMOND-BEARING CONGLOMERATES.—It is doubtful whether a diamond has yet been found in India in its original matrix. The lowest diamond-bearing stratum, at the base of the Karnool series, is itself a detrital conglomerate, and the diamonds may, like the other ingredients, have been derived from some older metamorphosed rocks. In the main Vindhyan basin, diamonds are known to occur only in the Upper Vindhyans. Here, as everywhere, the great majority of the diggings are alluvial; but the principal workings, upon which most labour is spent, are in a bed at the very base of the Rewah shales. Notwithstanding the immense range of this group, it is known to be productive only within a small area of the Panna State, on the borders of the Boondelkhand Gneiss; and the surface-diggings are confined to the same neighbourhood. The search for diamonds in Panna is not, however, confined to positions in which the gems could be derived from any existing outcrop of the Rewah shales. There are numerous pits, all apparently surface-diggings, in the gorges and on the slope of the Upper Rewah sandstone south of Panna, and at a much higher elevation than any present outcrop of the bottom shales or of the Lower Vindhyans.

Mr. Griesbach, of the Geological Survey of India, has recently published some interesting remarks upon the correlation of the Vindhyan rocks of India with certain series occurring in South Africa, to one of which the sandstones of the Table Mountain belong. There is a possibility of the Cape diamonds, therefore, belonging to a period or horizon directly comparable with that which includes the Indian diamonds. A comparison of the geology of Borneo also with that of India may prove productive of interesting results in this respect.

Palæozoic Rocks.

§ 11. GONDWANA SYSTEM.—Organic remains now appear for the first time in the peninsula. The coast line now begins to assume its present form. In many places along the east coast, from near Cuttak to Trichinopoli, small patches of Upper Gondwana rocks are found, in several cases interstratified with marine beds, but yet distinctly, in part, shown to be either of fluviatile, deltaic, or littoral origin, from the coarseness of the materials and the abundance of remains of land plants. In some places, too, as near Ellore, these Upper Gondwana beds of east coast rest upon a denuded slope partly of gneissic and partly of Lower Gondwana rocks, having the appearance of a plane of marine denudation. Gondwana beds occur near the east coast farther still to the north, close to Cuttak, but no marine beds are associated; and to the north and north-east no marine jurassic rocks are known to exist. The marine older and middle mesozoic, and probably the upper palæozoic formations of other countries, are represented in the peninsula of India by this great system of beds, chiefly composed of sandstones and shales, which appear, with the exception of the rocks just noticed along the east coast, to have been deposited by rivers. Remains of animals are very rare in these rocks, and the few which have hitherto been found belong chiefly to the lower vertebrate classes of reptiles, amphibians, and fishes. Plant remains are more common, and evidence of several successive floras has been detected. The subdivisions of this great plant-bearing series have been described under a number of local names, of which the oldest and best known are Talcher, Damodar, Mahadeva, and Rajmahal, but the Geological Survey has now adopted the term Gondwana for the whole series. This term is derived from the old name for the countries south of the Narbada valley, which were formerly Gond kingdoms, and now form the Jabalpoor, Nagpoor, and Chatteesgarh divisions of the Central Province. In this region of Gondwana the most complete sequence of the formations constituting the present rock system is to be found. The area occupied by the beds of the Gondwana system, although very extensive, is mainly confined to the country between the Narbada and Son to the north and the Kistna to the south; and a very large portion of this region to the westward is occupied by newer beds. The only outliers in the peninsula beyond the limits named are near the east coast, and to the westward in Kathiawar, Kach, and Jaisalmeer, and consist of Upper Gondwana beds alone; but Lower Gondwanas have been traced for some distance along the base of the Eastern Himalaya. The Gondwana beds are distributed in large basins, some of which show a remarkable coincidence with the existing river valleys.

We can form some slight conception of the physical geography of India in the Upper Gondwana period. The sea then, as now, occupied the Bay of Bengal, and a portion, at all events, of the Arabian Sea; and large rivers traversed the land then, as now, though not in precisely the same courses. The general form of the southern part of the peninsula may have agreed more nearly with the present contour than the northern; for the sea occupied the Indian desert and portions of the Panjab and Himalaya. There is not the same clue to the form of the land in the Lower Gondwana period; and all that can be said with certainty is, that the northern part of the peninsula was a terrestrial area, traversed by great rivers. To the north-east the occurrence of Damodar beds at the base of the Himalayas, in Sikkim and Bhootan, may intimate an extension of land in that direction, and a possible connection with the Chinese area, in which plants allied to those of the Damodar are known to have been found.

(1) Of the Lower Gondwanas the Talcher group almost always forms the base, named from the Orissa State where it was first clearly distinguished. It consists of fine silty shales and soft sandstone of lacustrine or river valley origin. Rolled boulders and pebbles occur, believed to have been transported to their final position by ground ice, as in the similar beds in South Africa, and the breccias of the highest Permian rocks which are of the same age, all suggesting the probability that the globe passed through a period of low temperature at the close of the palæozoic epoch. The Talcher fossils yet found are very few. Of animal remains only the wing of a neuropterous insect and some annelide tracks have been discovered, whilst the plant remains consist of three ferns, Gangamopteris cyclopteroides, G. angustifolia, and a form of Glossopteris, represented by a single fragment, some equisetaceous stems, and a plant, hitherto not distinctly identified, resembling Noeggerathia hislopi. The only evidence of vegetable life hitherto found has been in the higher beds of the group, and there is a remarkable absence of plants in the lower shales, which are admirably suited for preserving vegetable impressions. The **Karharbari** group supplies coal superior to that of the Talcher and Damodar series, and contains fossils like theirs, but of other very remarkable species. The rocks of the Karharbari group consist almost solely of sandstones, grits, and conglomerate, with seams of coal. Very little shale occurs. The coal of Karharbari is rather dull-coloured and tolerably homogeneous in structure, the layers of very bright jetty coal, which are so conspicuous in the Damodar seams in general, being few and ill marked. So far as mining has hitherto proceeded, the coal-seams appear to be somewhat variable in thickness, but to undergo very little change in composition throughout the small field in which they are found. The whole thickness is probably about 500 feet. The only fossils yet found in this group consist of plants, Equisetaceæ, Filices, Cycadeaceæ, and Coniferæ, which have well-marked relations to the lower Triassic or Bunter

flora of Europe, and, in one case, to the palæozoic coal measures of New South Wales.

The **Damodar** Series is of the highest economical importance, as containing a quantity of valuable minerals, greater than that known to occur in all the other rock groups of India together. Its middle division yields an oxide of iron or hæmatite. Named from the river in West Bengal, on the banks of which are some of the richest coal-fields, the Damodar series in Bengal consists of three subdivisions. These are, in ascending order—Barakar beds, Ironstone shales, and Raneeganj beds. The first and lowest is also found in the Son, Mahanadi, Narbada, and Godavari valleys, the upper subdivisions being represented by groups differing in mineral character from the Bengal beds. In the Satpoora area the Damodar subdivisions are known as the Barakar, Motoor, and Bijori groups; and in the Godavari valley, above the Barakar group—there, as in the Satpoora basin, the only coal-bearing formation—a single member of the upper Damodar beds occurs, and is known as the Kamthi group. A similar arrangement prevails in the Mahanadi and Brahmini area, only two Damodar subdivisions being found, which appear to correspond to those of the Godavari region. All consist of sandstones and shales with more or less ferruginous bands, and some contain coal. Slight unconformity between the different groups has been noticed in places, and the Barakar beds are frequently unconformable to the Talchers. The whole thickness of the Damodar series is 8400 feet in the Raneeganj field, and about 10,000 feet in the Satpoora basin. It thus constitutes the most important portion of the Gondwana system. The only animal fossils found are of Crustacea, the Estheria mangaliensis; and of Vertebrata, the Labyrinthodont amphibians, Archegosaurus, and Brachyops laticeps from the Bijori beds of the Satpoora basin.

The chief peculiarity of the Damodar flora is the abundance of ferns with simple undivided fronds, and especially of the forms with veins forming a network. To this last group belong Glossopteris, Gangamopteris, Sagenopteris, and Belemnopteris, comprising altogether thirteen species out of the twenty-two ferns, and thirty species of plants altogether. When to these thirteen forms are added the three species of Tæniopteris and one of Palæovittaria, having simple fronds and parallel venation, the ferns with undivided leaves will be found to compose more than half the known flora. Nor is this all, for the genus Glossopteris especially is remarkable for the abundance of individuals as well as of species, so that it is the characteristic fern-genus of the formation. The simple-leaved ferns are certainly more abundant in mesozoic than in palæozoic rocks in Europe, but still they never prevail to the same extent as in the Damodar series. The only plants, besides ferns, which are of common occurrence, are Equisetaceæ, stems of which, supposed to belong to Phyllotheca and Schizoneura, are met with in great abundance, whilst Vertebraria, which is probably the root of an equisetaceous plant, is as common and characteristic as Glossopteris. Cycads and conifers are scarce.

There is a wide diversity between the composition of the Damodar flora and that found in any European formation. In Australia, however, there is a series of plant-bearing beds which appear closely to resemble those of India in two points, the paucity of marine animal remains throughout the greater portion of the series, and the prevalence in particular beds of the genus Glossopteris, associated, as in India, with Vertebraria and equisetaceous stems closely resembling some of those found in the Indian coal-fields and referred to the genus Phyllotheca. Gangamopteris is also met with. The remarkable point is, that some of the commonest plant fossils of the Indian coal-fields, Glossopteris, Phyllotheca, and Vertebraria, are also those most abundantly represented in Australia, and that neither Glossopteris, Gangamopteris, nor Vertebraria has hitherto been found in mesozoic or palæozoic European rocks, whilst Phyllotheca is rare, being known in Europe only from the oolites of Italy. Some of the peculiar genera of plant fossils of the Indian coal-fields have also been found in China on the one hand and South Africa on the other, in the Uitenhage formation (jurassic) and Karoo series of the latter. The **Panchet** group in the Raneeganj field, the base of the Panchet hill, is distinguished from the typical Damodars by the presence of red clay and the absence of carbonaceous shales, and, as a rule, by the sandstone being much more micaceous. It is of the same triassic age as the Beaufort beds in South Africa.

Mesozoic Rocks.

(2) The Upper Gondwana groups are most fully represented in the Satpoora basin. The **Mahadeva** Series, first applied to the sandstone of the Pachmari hills in the Satpoora which bear that name, comprise also all the upper beds of coarse sandstone, grit, and conglomerate in the Satpoora basin above the Damodars of the upper Denwa valley, except the Jabalpoors.

The **Rajmahal** group consists of a succession of basaltic lava-flows or traps with interstratifications of shale and sandstone on the east coast of the peninsula, in outcrops scattered from Cuttak to Trichinopoli. The many fossil plants of this group have been obtained from two bands of fine-grained whitish shales separated by a lava-flow. The **Kota-Maleri** group, near the junction of the Waenganga with the Godavari, has yielded many fossil fish and reptilian bones; the rocks are like those of the Panchets of Bengal. The **Jabalpoor** group consists of clays, shales, and earthy sandstones, with some thin beds of jet-coal. **Kach** supplies the highest jurassic group, named Umia, from a village 50 miles north-west of Bhooj. It contains at the base a marine fauna with several species of mollusca common to the Portland zone of the European oolites.

§ 12. COAL-MEASURES.—The following table of the areas of the Indian coal-measures, and associated younger rocks which may conceal coal-measures, was drawn up by Mr. Hughes of the Survey for its *Records*:—

Godavari and affluents . . .	11,000 square miles.
Son	8,000 ,,
Sirgooja and Orissa, etc. . .	4,500 ,,
Assam	3,000 ,,
Narbada and affluents . . .	3,500 ,,
Damodar	2,000 ,,
Rajmahal area	300 ,,
Unsurveyed, etc.	2,700 ,,
	35,000

For the sake of comparison other countries with greater areas are enumerated:—

United States	500,000 square miles.
China	400,000 ,,
Australia	240,000 ,,

India comes next, or fourth on the list.

LIST OF SEPARATE COAL-FIELDS.

Bengal.

1. Rajmahal Hills . .	North of Damodar River.
2. Beerbhoom . . .	
3. Deogarh	
4. KARHARBARI . . .	
5. RANEEGANJ . . .	Damodar Valley.
6. Jeriah	
7. Bokaro	
8. Raingarh	
9. Karanpoora, N. . .	
10. Karanpoora, S. . .	

Bengal (continued).

11.	Chopé	West of Damodar Valley.
12.	Itkoori	
13.	Aurunga	
14.	Hutar	
15.	DALTONGANJ	
16.	Tattapani	Son and Mahanadi Valleys.
17.	S. Rewah and Sohagpoor	
18.	Jhilmilli	
19.	Bisrampoor	
20.	Lukanpoor	
21.	Rampoor	
22.	Raigarh and Hingir	
23.	Oodaipoor and Korba	
	Orissa.	
24.	Talcher	

Central Province.

25.	MOHPANI	Satpoora Region.
26.	Tawa	
27.	Pench	
28.	Bandar	Godavari Valley.
29.	WARDHA or CHANDA	
30.	Kamaram	
31.	Singareni	

Sikkim.

32. Sikkim.

Assam.

33.	Makoom	Valley of the Brahmapootra.
34.	Jaipoor	
35.	Naziaa	
36.	Jangi	
37.	Desai	

In the above list, localities, situated chiefly in the North-Western Province, Assam, and Burma, where tertiary coal occurs, but not in sufficient quantity to constitute workable coal-fields, have not been included. Of the thirty-seven separate coal-fields only five are at present worked with regularity. These are Raneeganj, Karharbari, and Daltonganj, in Bengal, and Mohpani and Wardha in the Central Province.

The coal of Peninsular India is a laminated bituminous fuel, in which dull and bright layers alternate. Much of it does not cake freely; a considerable proportion will not do so at all. The proportion of fixed carbon in the Raneeganj coal is under 55 per cent; in the Karharbari field it is 10 per cent higher. The total consumption of coal in India in 1879-80 was 1,455,873 tons. Of this 587,634 was imported, 469,699 was Raneeganj, 362,844 Karharbari, 25,078 Wardha, and 10,618 Mohpani. The price of Indian coal at the pit's mouth is Rs. 2½ to 3 at Raneeganj, and Rs. 10 at Mohpani; to this Rs. 2·5 per ton per 100 miles must be added for the cost of carriage. The average value of European coal at the Indian ports is Rs. 18·2, or, allowing for exchange, £1 : 10s. per ton.

§ 13. Jurassic Marine.—In the intermediate belt between the Indian Peninsula and the rest of Asia several European series are admirably represented in the Jurassic formations, of which there are four groups. The jurassics of Kach, already noticed in association with some of the Upper Gondwanas, occupy a number of post-tertiary islands now connected by alluvial flats. The largest, 120 miles long and 40 broad, forms the west and central portion of Kach; to the north-east is Wagher, 50 by 25 miles; farther north are the so-called islands in the Rann, of Pachham, Kareer, Bela, and Chorar. The beds are in four groups. The lowest is the **Pachham**, of light gray limestones and marls, yellow sandstones and limestones, corresponding to the Bath or lower oolite of the Middle Jurassic. The **Chari** group, named from a village 32 miles north-west of Bhooj, represents the Kelloway and Oxford middle oolites. The **Katrol** group, resting on the upper subdivision of the Chari beds, is equivalent to the Upper Oxford and Kimmeridge of the Upper Jurassic. The **Umia** group contains at the base a marine fauna, with several species of mollusca common to the Portland zone of the European oolites, and some forms, such as two Trigoniæ, characteristic of certain very high jurassic beds in South Africa. The correspondence, not only with the European jurassic rocks as a whole, but with the different groups into which they are divided, is remarkable, and greater than is known in any other Indian formations, the only other series of Indian rocks of which the fauna has been sufficiently examined to justify the comparison—the cretaceous series of Southern India—showing much less close agreement in the distribution of the fauna, and especially of the Cephalopoda, with the corresponding groups in Europe. The only remarkable instance in which the Cephalopoda of the Kach jurassics differ from their representatives in the jurassic rocks of Europe, is in the prevalence in the Indian area of the macrocephali ammonites (Stephanoceras) at a higher horizon than in Europe. The Balmeer and Jaisalmeer sandstones complete this formation.

§ 14. Cretaceous Marine.—Besides Neocomian beds of ferruginous oolitic rock seven miles south-east of Lakhpat in North-Western Kach, there are but two areas, widely separated from each other, in which marine cretaceous rocks have hitherto been described as occurring in the Indian Peninsula. The more important of these is in the neighbourhood of Pondicheri and Trichinopoli in Southern India; the other is in the Narbada valley between Mandlesir and Broach. (1) The South India series is in three groups. The lowest, **Utatoor**, named from a village 20 miles north-north-east of Trichinopoli, resembles the coral-reef limestone of the present day, and corresponds to the chalk marl and upper greensand of England. The **Trichinopoli**, or middle group, differs from that in the occurrence of granite pebbles; it yields the shell-limestone of Garoodamangalam, which is well known as Trichinopoli marble. The highest or **Arialoor** group, named from a town 34 miles north-east of Trichinopoli, is more sandy than these two, and is the richest in fossils. The South Indian cretaceous deposits yield a grand total of nearly 800 species of animals; of the whole Invertebrata 16½ per cent consist of European forms. Similar fossils are not found elsewhere in India; but in South Africa there is again, as in the Gondwana and marine jurassic beds, a singularly close connection with the rocks of Southern India. In some marine cretaceous strata of Natal, the majority of the fossils found are identical with those of the Trichinopoli formations. As the fossils are chiefly shallow-water and littoral forms, it appears a probable conclusion, that a line of coast extended in cretaceous times from India to South Africa. This coast may have been the south shore of a land barrier separating the seas of Europe, Arabia, and Western India from those in which the deposits of the Assam hills, Trichinopoli, and Natal were accumulated. There was thus very probably in cretaceous times the same union with Africa, as already indicated, in the later palæozoic and older mesozoic period, and the same coast-line along the eastern shore of the Indian Peninsula as in the jurassic epoch, but perhaps extending much farther to the north-east. In cretaceous times, as in earlier mesozoic periods, there is no indication of any deposits having taken place in the Ganges valley; and the absence of any mesozoic beds between the tertiaries of the Sub-Himalaya and the ancient rocks of the mountains is rather opposed to any large accumulation of strata, either subaërial or aqueous, having been formed, in the intervening epochs, within the area of the Gangetic plain.

(2) The cretaceous beds of the Narbada valley named **Bagh**, from a town 35 miles west-south-west of Dhar, were first discovered from the circumstance that blocks of their fossil limestone were found in the ruins of the old capital of

Mandoo, 15 miles off. In strange contrast with the wide difference between the known fauna of the Bagh beds and that of the South Indian deposits is the similarity between the fossil remains of the Narbada valley and those found in two localities, Ras Fartak and Ras Sharwen on the south-east coast of Arabia. The cretaceous beds of the Lower Narbada valley are about 750 miles distant from those of Southern India, and twice as far from the Arabian localities. The marked contrast between the fossil fauna in the one case and the similarity in the other tend to suggest the probability that a land barrier interposed in middle cretaceous times between Southern India with Assam and Arakan on the one side, and the Western Narbada region with the south coast of Arabia on the other. We have thus another argument in favour of the Indian Peninsula being the portion of an ancient land area; and taking into consideration the marked connection between the faunas of the South Indian and South African cretaceous deposits and the circumstance that both appear to be of littoral origin, it is probable that this land area extended to Africa.

§ 15. DEKHAN TRAP.—Whilst the upper cretaceous beds were being deposited on the south-eastern coast of India, the volcanic outbursts of the Dekhan traps must in all probability have commenced. These rocks form one of the grandest masses of bedded traps to be found in the world, and present several very interesting problems. The Dekhan traps consist of a great series of basaltic lava flows, for the most part assuming the form of basalt; all either nearly horizontal, or presenting the appearance of having been so originally. They possess a vertical thickness of between 4000 and 5000 feet in some of the Sahyadri scarps, and probably where thickest amount to 6000 feet at least. They cover an area roughly estimated at 200,000 square miles, and in all probability originally very much greater. These basalts thin out towards the extremity of the area, but they are traced from Sind to Chutia Nagpoor, and from Belgaum to north of Goona, or throughout 16 degrees of longitude and 9½ of latitude. The railway from Bombay to Nagpoor, 519 miles long, never leaves the volcanic rocks until it is close to the Nagpoor station, and the traps extend without a break from the sea coast at Bombay to Amarkantak at the head of the Narbada, and from near Belgaum to north of Goona. Outliers are found east of Amarkantak as far as Jumera Pat in Sirgooja (longitude 84° east), and to the south-east a small outcrop occurs close to Rajamahendri, whilst to the westward the series is well developed in Kathiawar and Kach, and it has even been found represented, though by two very thin bands, west of Kotri in Sind.

This series gives a character to the scenery and vegetation of Western and Central India. Great undulating plains, divided from each other by flat-topped ranges of hills, occupy the greater portion of the country; and the hill-sides are marked by conspicuous terraces, which may often be traced for great distances, and are due to the outcrop of the harder basaltic strata, or of those beds which resist best the disintegrating influences of exposure. In some parts of the area great scarps are found, some of those in the Sahyadri range being 4000 feet in height, all conspicuously banded with horizontal terraces. From the prevalence of long grass, the paucity of large trees, and the deciduous nature of all bushes and trees except near the sea, the whole uncultivated country presents during the cold season, from November till March, a uniform straw-coloured surface, with but few spots of green to break the monotony; whilst from March, when the grass is burnt, until the commencement of the rains in June, the black soil, black rocks, and blackened tree stems present a most remarkable aspect of desolation. During the rainy season, however, the country is covered with verdure, and in many parts it is very beautiful, the contrast afforded by the black rocks only serving to bring into relief the bright green tints of the foliage. The prevailing rock is some form of dolerite or basalt. Almost throughout their range, the Dekhan traps may be recognised by the occurrence of the amygdaloidal basalts with green earth, or of the porphyry with crystals of glassy felspar. Of the secondary minerals found in the trap, apophyllite is the finest. Its colour is usually white, more rarely pink or green; some crystals are perfectly transparent, and one of the most magnificent associations of minerals to be found anywhere is seen when, as occasionally happens, perfectly clear vitreous crystals of apophyllite, of large size, are inserted on a mass of orange stilbite. Some apophyllite crystals are as much as three and four inches across.

One of the most remarkable characters of the Dekhan traps is their persistent flatness or near approach to horizontality throughout the greater portion of their area. The separate lava flows do not exceed 15 feet in thickness. Sedimentary bands, frequently fossiliferous, have been found in several places interstratified with the lava flows, and have become widely known and described as intertrappean beds. At the base of the whole series also there is found, in many places, a small group of limestones, sandstones, and clays, known as the **Lameta** group, from its occurrence at Lameta Ghat, on the Narbada, near Jabalpoor. The principal fossils which have been found in it consist of some bones of a large dinosaurian reptile, Titanosaurus Indicus, allied to Pelorosaurus of the Wealden and Cetiosaurus of the Bath oolite. The next group of intertrappean beds of **Nagpoor** and the **Narbada Valley** comprises freshwater beds containing an abundance of freshwater and terrestrial animals. The **Rajamahendri** marine beds associated with trap, 210 miles distant from the nearest point of the great Dekhan area north-west of Sironcha, are both infratrappean and intertrappean. The **Bombay** and **Salsette** upper intertrappean beds have an inclination of from 5° to 10° to the westward, from Kalyan and Thana, whilst farther east from Kalyan to the Sahyadri range the traps are horizontal. From 1200 to 1500 feet of rock are exposed in Bombay Island, so that it is evident that the lowest beds seen on the island are higher in the series than the highest flows seen on the Sahyadri mountains to the eastward, even although some of the higher portions of the range are 4000 feet above the sea. The most important bed is that which underlies the basalt of Malabar Hill and Worlee Hill, forming the broken ridge along the western or sea face of the island; consequently this stratum is immediately beneath the highest lava flow known to occur anywhere throughout the trap area. Its fossils represent the life of a shallow marsh. The frogs occur in large numbers, and their bodies have evidently been deposited near the spot where they died, as the whole skeleton is found perfect; in some cases, the skeleton has been dragged along the surface of the shale in which it is embedded, probably by wind. The tortoise is a marsh or river form, the nearest living ally being a genus found in fresh water in South America.

As to their origin, the evidence clearly shows that the traps were in a great part of subaërial formation, but their horizontality has not yet been thoroughly explained, because no such process is now going on. Nor have all the sources of the great volcanic series of Western India been ever approximately determined. It is probable that the traps flowed from vents without the formation of volcanic cones, as no traces of the inclined beds of such cones have been found; and the distinction may have been due to the greater fluidity and larger mass of ejected lava, and to its consequently increased power of transporting all the materials brought to the surface by igneous agency to a much greater distance from the point of emission.

Mr. W. T. Blanford thus recapitulates the whole evidence:—

"We find that a great area of the Indian Peninsula, in times subsequent to middle cretaceous, formed part of a land surface, very uneven and broken in parts, but apparently chiefly composed to the eastward of extensive plains, which, by some slight changes of level preceding the volcanic period, were converted into lakes. There is much probability that springs charged with silica were common either at this epoch or shortly after. The lakes had apparently been drained, and the deposits, which had accumulated in them, had locally been subject to denudation before the first outbursts of lava took place; these occurred at considerable intervals, small and very shallow lakes or marshes being formed in the meantime by the interruptions to the drainage produced by lava flows, or by changes of level accompanying the volcanic eruptions. In these lakes a rich fauna of fish, mollusca, entomostracous crustacea and water plants existed, whilst a varied and probably a rich vegetation occupied the surrounding country. There is evidence of the existence of insects and of reptiles (whether terrestrial or aquatic has not been determined), but hitherto no remains of mammals or birds have been found—a circumstance which by no means proves that they did not exist. Fresh flows of lava filled up the first lakes, and covered over the sedimentary deposits which had accumulated in the waters; but these very flows, by damming up other lines of drainage, produced fresh lakes, so that several alternations of lava and sedimentary beds were produced in places. Gradually the lakes seem to have disappeared; whether the lava flows succeeded each other so rapidly that there was no time for the accumulation of sediment in the interval, or whether, as is more probable, the surface had been converted into a uniform plain of basalt by the enormous lava streams which had been poured out, it is difficult to say, but no further traces of life have hitherto been found until towards the close of the volcanic epoch. It is possible that at the end, as at the commencement of the period, the intervals between eruptions became longer, and the animal and vegetable life which may have been seriously diminished, or altogether driven out of the country, during the rule of igneous conditions, resumed its old position, but a great change had taken place in the long interval, the old lacustrine fauna had died out, and the animals and plants which now appeared in the country seem to have differed from those which had formerly occupied it. Lastly, in the north-western portion of the area, parts of the volcanic country were depressed beneath the sea, and marine tertiary deposits began to be formed from the detritus of the extinct volcanoes and their products. A great tract of the volcanic region, however, appears to have remained almost undisturbed to the present day, affected by subaërial erosion alone, and although probably for a time at a lower elevation than at present, depressed beneath the sea-level."

Cænozoic Rocks.

§ 16. TERTIARY AND LATERITE.—The close of the volcanic outbursts left all the surface of Western India a huge plain of basaltic rock, which later denudation has carved into the hills and valleys of the peninsula. The only formation superposed upon the basalt throughout the greater part of the area, with the exception of gravels and clays of late tertiary or sub-recent date, is the high-level laterite, or iron clay, a ferruginous and argillaceous rock, from 30 or 40 to 200 feet thick, capping the summit of many of the highest trap plateaux, and also occurring on other rocks, beyond the limits of the trap area, in such a manner as to show that the caps now remaining are merely isolated fragments of a bed once far more extensive. This bed probably covered a large portion of the trap area and the neighbouring regions, and perhaps extended throughout the greater portion of Peninsular India. Nor is this all. In the nummulitic beds of Goojarat, Kach, Sind, and the Salt Range of the Panjab, and in the Subathoo beds of the Sub-Himalaya, all of middle eocene age, there are found one or more beds of ferruginous rocks absolutely undistinguishable from laterite, and probably, from their wide extent, of contemporaneous origin. In many places the laterite bed passes into the uppermost traps, and hence it has been very naturally inferred that laterite is merely an altered form of the basaltic rock itself. But it appears most probable that decomposed basalt, when iron peroxide is added, forms laterite, and that consequently passage from the one into the other is natural; but that the high-level laterite bed is really throughout of detrital origin, as it is proved to be in places by containing pebbles and sand. It probably consists of altered volcanic detritus, perhaps of scoriæ and lapilli; the excess of iron being either due to the ferruginous nature of the volcanic outbursts, or to a process of washing by which the lighter, less ferruginous matters were carried farther away from the original source of the materials, and formed deposits less easily consolidated, and, in consequence, more easily destroyed by denuding agencies. Other laterite formations, deposited after much denudation of the traps had taken place, and found at low levels in various parts of India, may have been derived, in some cases at least, from materials provided by the denudation of the high-level form.

There are five tertiary regions of India, all small and on the outskirts of the peninsular area. All in which marine fossils have been detected are either along the west coast or on the border of the Indus valley. It is probable that the peninsular area was land during tertiary, as it was for the most part during mesozoic and probably in palæozoic times. The tertiary outcrops on the margin of Peninsular India may be thus classed: —(1) East coast of the peninsula (Cuddalore sandstones); (2) West coast of the peninsula, Travankor (and Ratnagiri ?); (3) Goojarat (Surat, Broach, Perim Island off Kathiawar); (4)

Kach; (5) Jaisalmeer. Only three of these—the Cuddalore sandstones, the tertiary beds of Goojarat, and those of Kach—are sufficiently developed or sufficiently known to be of importance. Mr. Blanford thinks it may reasonably be inferred that during part of the early tertiary period India was united to Africa, and the union may have been continuous from the cretaceous period to miocene times. The course of the old continent may perhaps be traced by the Maldive and Chagos archipelagoes, and by the banks between the Mascarenhas Islands and the Seychelles. That portions of the old land remained, broken up into islands, long after the connection had been severed, is probable from some peculiarities amongst the birds of the Seychelles and Mascarenhas islands; thus the genus Hypsipetes, a characteristically Oriental form, is represented in Madagascar, Bourbon, Mauritius, and the Seychelles; and Copsychus, an equally typical Eastern genus, occurs also in Madagascar and the Seychelles. It is easily conceivable that birds should fly, or be blown, from island to island long after the distance was too great to be traversed by mammals. The circumstance that the mammalian fauna of the Oriental region shows less affinity with Madagascar than with that of the African continent, is perhaps due to Madagascar having been separated before the submergence of the land connecting Africa and India.

The southern portion of the Indian Peninsula with Ceylon may have been united to the Malay countries in tertiary times, perhaps later than with Africa. This, however, is not clear: despite some remarkable points of affinity to the Malay fauna, there are very remarkable differences; and when representative forms are found in Southern India or Ceylon and in the Malay countries, such forms are frequently, perhaps most frequently, generically distinct. One of the most singular cases of generic alliance is the occurrence of a species of Draco, a Malay genus of lizard, in Malabar; but this is exceptional. Most of the genera of Ceylonese and South Indian lizards and snakes are peculiar; and one family of snakes is confined to the sub-region, and to some hill-tops in Southern India. So far as the sea bottom between Ceylon and the Malay archipelago is known, there is nothing to indicate a former continuity of land in this direction; and the similarity of the fauna may have another explanation.

CHAPTER II.

GEOLOGY OF THE INDO-GANGETIC PLAIN.

§ 1. POST-TERTIARY AND RECENT FORMATIONS.—The post-pliocene or quaternary and recent formations of India occupy one-fourth of its whole area, but their geological importance is small, and that centres in the wide plains of the Indus, Ganges, and Brahmapootra, from the outer margin of which the Himalaya ranges rise. In Europe the glacial epoch marks the post-tertiary from the tertiary formations, but in India there is no evidence of a cold period, although it must be remembered that the general refrigeration which would produce an Arctic climate in Central Europe would not diminish the temperature of the Indian Peninsula below that of the temperate zone. There is no such proof of the former existence of glaciers on the hills of Southern India as those of the Himalaya. But the fossils and the present higher elevation of the southern hills show that a lower temperature existed at a comparatively recent geological period. Himalayan plants and animals occur in the higher ranges of Southern India, due to the retreat of these species to the equator, and then to higher altitudes as the temperature increased.

All known post-tertiary deposits, except near the sea coast, are of freshwater origin, including the unconsolidated and undisturbed deposits of the river valleys. In the older valley deposits, as in the post-pliocene rocks of Europe, bones of extinct mammals are found together with recent forms of freshwater and terrestrial mollusca, whilst the newer gravels, sand, and clay contain only the remains of mammalian species identical with those now inhabiting the country. The works of man have now been found in two instances in Indian post-pliocene beds, but no human remains have hitherto been detected in older formations. In Burma, however, tertiary mammals are found in the beds of the river valleys. As to **level**, whilst throughout the rock area of the Indian Peninsula there are numerous proofs of an elevation of land during late geological epochs, the evidence of depression is equally marked in the delta of the Ganges, and probably in that of the Indus. It must not be forgotten that the great belt of **volcanoes** which extends throughout the Malay Islands, Java, Sumatra, etc., terminates in the eastern portion of the Bay of Bengal, at a considerable distance from the coast of the Indian Peninsula, at Narkondam. **Lonar Lake**, 40 miles east by north of Jalna, must be due to volcanic explosion, but it is isolated, is unaccompanied by the eruption of melted rock, and is long posterior to the epoch of the Dekhan trap. It is a nearly circular hollow, a mile in diameter, and from 300 to 400 feet deep, containing shallow salt water, without an outlet. The only mammaliferous **cave deposit** yet found in the peninsula is at Billa Soorgam, north of Banaganapali, in the Karnool district. **Kankar** ("gravel"), or ghootin, the concretionary carbonate of lime in irregular nodules, occurs in river-beds and alluvial deposits, and is valued as a flux for iron-smelting as well as for building purposes.

§ 2. AREA OF INDO-GANGETIC ALLUVIUM.—The richest and most populous part of India is the alluvial plain of the Ganges, Indus, and Brahmapootra rivers which, varying in width from 90 to 300 miles, covers 380,000 square miles, including the greater part of the Provinces of Assam, Bengal, North-Western and Oudh, Panjab and Sind. Its highest level is 924 feet, on the road from Saharanpoor to Lodiana, which is the lowest part of the watershed between the Indus and the Ganges. The prevailing formation is some form of clay, more or less sandy. The older deposits generally contain kankar. In the Indus valley the alluvial deposits are much more sandy than in the Ganges valley, and the surface of the ground is paler in colour, except where marshy conditions prevail. The deposits of the Brahmapootra valley in Assam are also sandy. In both these valleys nearly the whole area is occupied by the newer alluvial deposits, whilst the greater portion of the Ganges plain, except towards the delta, is composed of an older alluvial formation. Of the whole thickness attained by the alluvial deposits of the great Indian rivers, not the faintest idea can be formed. It must be very great, or rock would be more exposed. The only information is derived from three borings: one, 481 feet deep, at Fort William, Calcutta, within the delta and close to a tidal river; the second at Amballa, 701 feet deep, at nearly the highest level of the plain away from the slope of detritus along the margin; the third, carried to 464 feet at Sabsal-ka-kot on the right (west) bank of the Indus, about 21 miles east by north of Rajanpoor and about 400 feet above sea-level. All these boreholes were made for the purpose of obtaining water.

§ 3. THE PARTICULAR KINDS OF SURFACE OF THE INDO-GANGETIC PLAIN are described by Hindee terms. *Bhabar* is the gravel slope along the Himalaya base, which is insignificant compared with the deposits in the dry regions of Central Asia, nowhere in India exceeding 1000 feet. *Tarai* (*Morang* in Nepal) is the marshy forest at the base of the slope in which the water of Himalayan rivers reappears after it has percolated through the gravel. *Bhangar* is the high land, the flat of older alluvium, especially in the North-Western Province, and *Khadar* ("strath") is the low land, annually flooded, which constitutes the plain itself. *Bhoor* is the raised bank of rivers in the Upper Provinces, caused by blown sand. *Reh* or *Kalar* is the salt efflorescence, consisting chiefly of sulphate of soda, which is due to a want of water circulation in the subsoil, throughout many generations, in the drier tracts of Upper India, and which is increased by canals not at a considerable depth below the surface, so that the land becomes *Oosar* or "barren," although sweet water is obtainable at from 60 to 80 feet down. In no part of the great plain have more important changes taken place since the dawn of history than in the neighbourhood of the watershed between the Indus and Ganges. The traditions of the Hindoos point to a time when a great and sacred river, the **Saraswati**, ran in the extreme east of the present Panjab, between the Satlej and the Jumna. The modern Sarsooti or Saraswati is an unimportant stream, fed by small tributaries from the outer Himalayan ranges, deriving none of its water from snows, becoming nearly dry in the hot season, and losing itself in the Rajpootana desert. It seems to have formerly formed the Satlej, which pursued an independent course to the sea, under such names as Hakra, Sotra, and Wahind, by (1) the line of what is still the Eastern Nara in Sind; (2) the desert south-east of Bahawalpoor, where there are numerous remains of an earlier civilisation. Mr. James Fergusson's theory is accepted by Mr. Blanford as correct, that the Saraswati raised its channel while the Jumna has cut down its *khadar*, whence the water—doubtless demolished by the destruction of forests—which supplied the former river now runs into the latter.

§ 4. THE RANN OF KACH is an old marine gulf, now silted up, stretching for 200 miles from east to west, and 100 from north to south. The Nal, the brackish alluvial tract which divides Ahmedabad from Kathiawar, connects the Rann with the head of the Gulf of Kambay. The great earthquake of 1819 caused the depression of an area of 2000 square miles around the fort of Sindri in the western part, and the elevation of a tract said to be 50 miles in length and in places 16 miles across. This has now been again silted up. A depression of not more than 50 feet would now convert Kathiawar into an island. Kach is now an island during the south-west monsoon, when the sea, raised by the wind, dams back the water brought into the Rann by the various rivers which drain into the flat from Rajpootana, Goojarat, and Kach, in the same manner as the level of the creeks is raised in the Indus delta. At this time portions of the Rann are 7 feet under water, but the average depth does not exceed 5 feet. The inundation lasts from July to the end of November.

§ 5. COAST ALLUVIUM.—Along the east coast from the delta of the Ganges to near Cape Comorin there is a broad belt of alluvial deposits, nowhere exceeding 50 miles, due chiefly to the detritus brought down by the rivers. It consists of clays, with kankar, and, near the hills, pisolitic nodules of iron peroxide, the latter being in places sufficiently abundant to render the deposit a kind of laterite gravel. Gravels and sand also occur, frequently more or less mixed with ferruginous concretions, and there is in many localities an apparent passage between the ferruginous gravel of the alluvium and the low-level form of laterite. At **Madras** and Pondicheri estuarine shells of recent species have been found in wells and beds of clay at from 5 to 20 feet down, or considerably above the present sea-level. They are so numerous at Madras as to be collected for burning into the fine lime (chunam) of that city. Along the western shore of the peninsula there is no such continuous plain of alluvium as on the east coast; the ground between the Sahyadri range and the sea, where not hilly, consists generally of a gentle slope towards the coast, composed of rock, covered in many places by laterite. Alluvial plains, of comparatively recent formation, connect the hills of **Bombay** and Salsette Island, a few creeks alone remaining to show the position of the marine channels which formerly existed. Farther north these plains gradually increase in extent, until they merge in the alluvial flat of Goojarat. Mr. W. T. Blanford declares it to be evident that Bombay harbour is the last remaining inlet out of many which formerly indented the Bombay coast, and that this harbour is gradually silting up and being converted into dry land. The process, however, is slow, and it may be ages before its progress is such as to affect the trade of Bombay; but, unless depression takes place in the area, or means are devised for checking the deposition of mud, there can be no question of the ultimate result. The **Goojarat Plain**, 30 miles broad near Surat, and 60 miles near Baroda, from Daman in the south to the Rann of Kach in the north, resembles the alluvium of the east coast.

§ 6. SOILS AND AGRICULTURE.—Soils are of two classes: upland, resulting from the decomposition of rock *in situ;* and alluvial, due to the surface alteration of river and flood deposits. Mr. W. T. Blanford thus classifies the agricultural soils:—

The Indian Peninsula is so vast, and the variations in climate in different portions so great, that the ingredients of the soil are only one amongst many factors determining the agricultural products of the country. The other principal elements are temperature and rainfall. Very roughly India might be divided into three agricultural regions:—

1. Extra-tropical India; the wheat region. This consists of the great plains of Northern India in which the rainfall is moderate or small, and the winter temperature comparatively low. The region almost corresponds with that lying north of the January isotherm of 65°. The principal grains are wheat and barley.
2. The damper portions of tropical India; the rice country. This comprises all Bengal proper, and all the region north of the Kistna from the Bay of Bengal to the edge of the trap country in the Dekhan, together with the coasts and delta lands of Southern India. The principal grain is rice.
3. The drier parts of tropical India and all the black soil country; the millet region. Besides the whole Dekhan trap area, with the exception of the western coast, this comprises all the black soil tracts of Southern India, and a very large portion of the undulating red soil country. The principal grains are jawari or cholam (Holcus sorghum) and bajri or cumbu (Holcus spica).

Of course, these divisions are not clearly separated from each other. The important point in connection with the geology is the fact that nowhere in the black soil regions, nor on any of the soils derived from the Dekhan traps, except in a small strip of country, with a heavy rainfall, near the western coast, is rice the staple grain of the country. In the Central Province, especially in the neighbourhood of Nagpoor, the difference between the agriculture of the trap country, with fields of millet, pulses of several kinds, cotton, linseed, etc., produced without irrigation, and the cultivated area of the sandstone and metamorphic rocks, where little is seen growing, except rice and sugar irrigated from large tanks, is as marked as the distinction between the rocks themselves. The wild vegetation of the two formations is as different as the cultivated grains. The whole distinction is of course due to the difference in the soils derived from different rocks.

The two most remarkable surface formations of India are the

Red Soil, a sandy clay coloured red by iron peroxide, and common on the metamorphic rocks; and the **Black Soil** or **Cotton Soil** or **Regur** (Telugoo, *regada*). The latter is a fine dark soil, highly argillaceous, somewhat calcareous, and very adhesive, resulting, as first suggested by Hislop, from the impregnation of certain argillaceous formations with organic matter, and probably covered at one time with luxuriant forest. The fertility of this soil is so great, that some of the black soil plains are said to have produced crops for 2000 years without manure, without having been left fallow, and without irrigation. On the other hand, some varieties of black soil, occurring near the coast of Southern India, are comparatively infertile. It retains water, requires less irrigation than sandy soils, and in Central India and the Western Dekhan is not irrigated at all.

AREA of each Province, with the proportions of Cultivated, Culturable, and Unculturable Areas, so far as can be ascertained.

PROVINCE.	Total Area.	Area Cultivated.	WASTE LANDS. Area Culturable.	WASTE LANDS. Area Unculturable.
	Sq. miles.	Sq. miles.	Sq. miles.	Sq. miles.
Bengal . .	No information for this Province.			
Assam . .	*a*32,826	*a*7,531	*a*18,823	*a*6,472
British Burma	87,220	4,978	37,479	45,013
North-Western Province	81,748	*b*38,070	13,837	29,868
Oudh . . .	24,213	*b*12,930	6,302	4,024
Panjab . .	107,010	36,656	36,706	33,648
Central Province . .	84,208	22,840	26,755	34,613
Berar . . .	17,728	*c*11,162	2,273	4,276
Bombay . .	*f*73,609	*bc*35,053	4,022	34,534
Sind . . .	46,599	4,183	No information.	
Madras . .	*d*86,439	31,056	30,764	*e*24,619
*Mysore . .	30,500	*c*7,903	5,108	16,622
Total .	672,100	212,362	182,069	233,689

REMARKS.

a. Exclusive of the Garo and Naga hills.

b. Includes assessed lands only.

c. Includes fallow, pasture, and meadow lands.

d. Exclusive of the Madras district, and of the area of the Zameendarees or permanently settled lands, comprising 53,498 square miles.

e. Includes culturable and pasture lands in Malabar which cannot be separately stated.

f. Excluding the district of Kanara, and the Collectorate of Bombay.

§ 7. DESERT TRACTS.—Sand dunes, drifted by the wind, are found along the sea coast, where they form backwaters, and on the banks of rivers (*bhoor*). The most important accumulation of blown sand is the **Great Indian Desert**, between Sind and Rajpootana, consisting partly of a grazing region thinly inhabited, and partly of absolutely barren tracts of sand dunes like the **Thar**, which extends along the edge of the Indus alluvium from the neighbourhood of the Rann of Kach to north-east of Rohri, and towards Bahawalpoor. This tract is about 60 miles across near Umarkot, and 50 miles east of Rohri. The sand-hills are arranged in regular parallel ridges running north-east and south-west near Umarkot, whilst to the north their direction is from south-south-west to north-north-east. Farther south than Umarkot and near the Rann, the general direction of the sand ridges is said to be nearly east and west, and they are much higher than they are elsewhere, some having an elevation of as much as 400 or 500 feet. Another tract to the east extends from the Rann along the west side of the Loni river towards Bikaner, and is 40 miles broad between Jodhpoor and Pokaran. The enormous quantity of sand in the desert region is derived from the south-west, and it has been transported by the strong winds of the hot season. It is probable that the central portion of the desert was land, whilst the Indus valley, the Rann, and the Loni valley were occupied by sea. Besides the occasional sand-hills of the Indus valley in Sind, there are some much larger tracts in the Panjab, repeating, on a smaller scale, the phenomena of the Thar and the Rajpootana desert. The most important of these is in the Sind Sagar Doab between the Indus and Jhelam, but there is a barren tract in the Rechna Doab between the Chenab and Ravi, and sand-hills occur in places also in the Bari Doab between the Ravi and the Satlej.

§ 8. RELATION OF THE INDO-GANGETIC DEPRESSION TO THE ELEVATION OF THE HIMALAYA.—Mr. W. T. Blanford arrives at the conclusion that the Indo-Gangetic depression is of contemporaneous origin with the disturbance and contortion of the Himalaya and the other extra-peninsular ranges, and that the physical features of the two areas are closely connected. The coincidence in general outline, the parallelism in fact between the great area of depression and the ranges north, east, and west of it, tend to confirm this view. The plain of the Ganges and Brahmapootra continues along the foot of the Himalaya throughout; the Indus plain turning southward where the ranges in the Western Panjab and Sind run north and south, and the estuaries of the Ganges and Brahmapootra being similarly deflected in front of the north and south hills of Tipura and Chittagong. It is not unreasonable to believe that the crust movements, to which the elevation of the Himalaya, and of the Panjab, Sind, and Burmese ranges are due, have also produced the depression of the Indo-Gangetic Plain, and that the two movements have gone on *pari passu*. The depression of the deltaic area of the Ganges and the disturbing forces affecting the Himalaya are still in action. Independently of the circumstance that the lateral movement appears to have come from the north, neither the elevation nor the folding of the Himalaya is due to the depression of the Gangetic plain alone. The formation of the Indo-Gangetic depression and of the Himalaya and other mountain chains is probably due to the same forces, without the one being in any way the cause or effect of the other.

CHAPTER III.

GEOLOGY OF THE HIMALAYA REGION.

§ 1. Classified List of Extra-Peninsular Formations. § 2. Sind and Baloochistan. § 3. Panjab Hills west of the Jhelam. § 4. Sub-Himalaya Tertiary Rocks. § 5. Outer or Lower Himalaya Metamorphics. § 6. Main or Central Himalaya Gneiss. § 7. Assam Range and Coal-Measures. § 8. Burma and its Minerals. § 9. The Andaman and Nicobar Islands.

§ 1. Classified List of Extra-Peninsular Formations.—Our acquaintance with the geological structure of the Himalaya region, including Sind, Assam, and Burma, is as yet more fragmentary than our knowledge of the geology of the peninsula. This is due to political difficulties in States like Afghanistan, Nepal, and Bhootan; to the physical impediments caused by altitude, climate, forests, and want of roads and population everywhere; and to the disturbance and metamorphism which the rocks have undergone in many places. Hence it is not practicable to describe each formation by itself through the whole region. The Survey *Manual* enumerates the representatives of different geological horizons in the five separate tracts of—I. Sind; II. Panjab hills west of the Jhelam; III. Himalaya; IV. Assam, Sylhet, Chittagong, etc.; V. Burma. An asterisk shows that a formation is unfossiliferous, and a note of interrogation that the position is doubtful.

Classified List of Formations in Extra-Peninsular Territories belonging to India.

Recent and Post-Tertiary	Alluvial and lake deposits. Sub-Himalayan high-level gravels.*
Pliocene . .	Upper Manchars of Sind. Upper and Middle Siwaliks of Sub-Himalaya, Panjab, etc. Mammaliferous deposits of Western Tibet. Dehing group* of Assam. Fossil-wood deposits of Pegu.
Miocene . .	Lower Manchars and Gaj of Sind. Marree beds* (in part). Nahan.* Tipam group of Assam?* Pegu group of Burma.

EOCENE	*Upper*	Nari group of Sind. Kasauli and Dagshai* group of Sub-Himalaya.
	Middle	Nummulitic limestone of Sind, Panjab, Assam, Burma, etc. Khirthar of Sind. Subathoo of Sub-Himalaya. Indus or Shingo beds of Western Tibet. Coal-measures of Assam ?
	Lower	Ranikot beds of Sind. Lower nummulitics of Salt Range.
CRETACEOUS	*Upper*	Dekhan trap.* Carditi beaumonti beds and cretaceous sandstones of Sind. Olive group of Panjab Salt Range. Disang group* of Assam ? Upper cretaceous of Khasi Hills. Negrais beds of Burma ? (*N.B.*—It is not certain that some of these formations may not be, in part at least, eocene.)
	Middle	Hippuritic limestone of Sind. Cretaceous beds of Mount Sirban in Hazara and of Kohat. Chikkim beds of North-Western Himalaya. Cretaceous beds of Assam (in part). Mai-ee group of Burma.
	Lower or *Neocomian.*	Beds in Chichali Pass, Salt Range.
JURASSIC	*Upper*	Salt Range. Gieumal and Spiti beds of Northern Panjab and North-Western Himalaya.
	Middle	Variegated group of Salt Range. Part of Spiti shales in North-Western Himalaya ?
	Lower or *Lias.*	Upper Tagling limestone of North-Western Himalaya. Sylhet trap ? *
TRIAS	*Upper including Rhætic.*	Lower Tagling limestone of North-Western Himalaya. Nerinæa beds of Mount Sirban, Hazara. Para limestone of North-Western Himalaya. Beds with Megalodon and Dicerocardium at Mount Sirban, Hazara.
	Middle	Salt Range ? Lilang series of North-Western Himalaya and Kashmeer. Axial group of Burma ?
	Lower	Ceratite beds of Salt Range. Infra-triassic* of Hazara, in part ?

PERMIAN AND CARBONIFEROUS	Salt Range carboniferous limestone. Damodars of Sikkim and Bhootan? Infra-triassic* of Hazara? Krol limestone* of Peer Panjal? Krol* limestone and Infra-Krol* of Western Himalaya? Kuling series of North-Western Himalaya and Kashmeer. Maulmein group of Burma.
SILURIAN	Obolus beds of Salt Range. Atak slates* of Upper Panjab? Slates* and traps* of Peer Panjal and Kashmeer? Muth and Bhabeh series of North-Western Himalaya. Blaini* and Infra-Blaini* of Simla area?
INFRA-SILURIAN	Salt marl* of Salt Range? Gneiss* of Peer Panjal and Ladak. Upper gneiss of Zanskar range. Shillong series* of Assam hills? Mergui group?* Lower or central gneiss* of Himalaya. Gneiss* of Assam and Burma.

The thickness of the different formations has been determined in only a few instances. The amounts are very great, the tertiary rocks alone attaining a vertical development in places, as in Sind, of nearly 30,000 feet.

§ 2. SIND AND BALOOCHISTAN.—The ranges of hills in Sind are simple anticlinals, with parallel axes running nearly north and south, changing to the westward in Baloochistan and to the northward in the Panjab. They are composed principally of tertiary rocks. Exclusive of the alluvium there are seven groups of rock formations in Sind, beginning from below. (1) **Cretaceous** beds are found in the Laki range; the lowest member is exposed at the base of Barrah hill, 10 miles south-west of Amri, on the Indus. A hippurite found there shows that the white limestone may be a representative of the hippuritic limestone extensively developed in Persia, from Tehran to east of Karinan in long. 58°, ten degrees west of Laki. (2) An interstratified band of **Dekhan trap** rests on the above, over an area of 22 miles from Jakhmari, 19 miles south of Sehwan to (3) **Ranikot**, the lowest tertiary subdivision, named from a hill-fort of the Ameer's in the Laki range. It consists of lower eocene soft sandstones, shales, and clays, with a small bed of coal or lignite 6 feet thick, too poor to be of value. (4) The **Khirthar Group**, lower and upper, comprises the most conspicuous rock, the massive nummulitic limestone of which all the higher ranges in Sind consist. The characteristic nummulites and alveolina in extraordinary abundance, and the foraminifera especially, are eocene. Around Khelat, to the northward, this band appears to be extensively exposed, but to the westward, near Gwadar, the rocks supposed to represent the older tertiary beds consist of an immense thickness of shales, shaly sandstones, and unfossiliferous calcareous bands, resembling the lower Khirthars of the Gaj, and the beds of the Habb valley. (5) The **Nari Group**, lower and upper, named from a stream in the lower portion of the Khirthar range, is well developed in the hills on the Upper Sind frontier. It is a yellow or brown limestone, with dark shales and sandstone. (6) The **Gaj Group**, named from the only stream which cuts its way through the Khirthar range, forms a conspicuous ridge on its eastern flanks in Upper Sind. The hard dark-brown limestone bands near the base of the formation resist the action of denudation far more than the soft sandstones of the Nari beds, and rise into peaks of 1000 and 1500 feet, escarped to the westward and sloping to the east; Amru, the highest summit of the Gaj ridge, being 2700 feet above the sea. Still the greater part of the group consists of sandy shales, clays with gypsum, and, towards the base, sandstones. There is a very large area of Gaj beds north and north-east of Karachi; they form the low hills which extended south-west, past the hot spring at Magar or Mangah Peer, to the end of Cape Monze, and furnish the materials of which the houses in Karachi are mostly built. A small island called Churna, in the sea, west of Cape Monze, also consists of Gaj rocks. (7) The **Manchar Group**, the highest subdivision of the Sind tertiary series, has been named from a large lake, a few miles west of Sehwan. The group, doubtless, represents generally the far better known Siwaliks of Northern India, and it is probable that the upper and lower limits of the two may be the same, but the fossiliferous bands are at different horizons. This group, lower and upper, consists of clays, sandstones, and conglomerates, and attains in places a thickness of but little, if at all, less than 10,000 feet on the flanks of the Khirthar range. The Manchar beds extend along the edge of the alluvium, and form a broad fringe to the Khirthar range, throughout Upper Sind, from west of Shikarpoor to the Manchar Lake, but the breadth of the outcrop varies greatly, being as much as 14 miles where broadest west of Larkana, and diminishing both to the north and south. The marine **Makran Group** of hard marls which form the headlands of Ras Malan, Ormara, and Gwadar, probably represent the freshwater Manchars and Siwaliks on the edge of the Indo-Gangetic Plain. There is evidence of great post-pliocene disturbance in Western Sind since the Upper Manchar beds were deposited, forming an abrupt and startling change from the peninsular phenomena.

§ 3. PANJAB HILLS WEST OF THE JHELAM.—Just beyond 32° N. latitude a series of curved hill ranges, of which the most important, between the Indus and Jhelam, is known as the **Salt Range**, crosses the Province from Shaik Budeen, a little north of Dera Ismail Khan, to Jhelam, and to the northward of these ranges, which cross the Indus at Kalabagh, a tract of more or less hilly country extends to the foot of the Himalaya, and of the great mountain ranges between the Himalaya of Western Kashmeer and the Hindu Koosh. But this tract may again be subdivided into three high level plains, more or less broken up by ravines, and separated from each other by ranges of hills. The south-eastern plain extends from the Salt Range to beyond Rawal Pindi, and closely approximates in dimensions with the basin of the river Soan, a tributary joining the Indus a little above Kalabagh. This plain is sometimes known as the **Potwar or Rawal Pindi plateau**; it extends from the Indus nearly to the Jhelam; it has a superficial area of about 7000 square miles, and a general elevation of about 1000 feet above the Indo-Gangetic Plain to the south of the Salt Range. The surface is greatly cut up by deep ravines in the soft Siwalik beds, of which almost the whole area is composed. North of this southern plain there is a series of hill ranges known as Margalla, Chitapahar, Cherat, etc., which have a general east and west direction, and connect the Marree and Hazara with the Afreedee mountains. These hill ranges traverse the Northern Panjab south of Atak, and repeat, on a diminished scale, the remarkable curves of the Salt Range and Chichali or Shingarh hills. North of the Cherat and Afreedee hills is the alluvial **Peshawar Plain**, and this again is bounded on the north by the hills of Swat and Yusufzai, the geology of which is unknown. A third plain, more to the westward, of smaller extent than either of the former, exists in the neighbourhood of Bannoo. The **Bannoo Plain** (1200 feet) comprises 1500 square miles, and is drained by the Kooram. The Marree and Bhoogtee hills and the Sulaiman range are principally, like the Khirthar and other hills of Sind, composed of tertiary beds, amongst which nummulitic limestone and the conglomerates, sandstones, and clays of the upper tertiaries (Manchar or Siwalik) are the most conspicuous rocks. In the northern part of the Sulaiman hills, however, older formations appear, some of them metamorphic. The Shaik Budeen and Shingarh hills, west of the Indus, are a continuation of the Salt Range, and contain to a great extent the same rocks.

In the Salt Range there is a remarkable series of formations, from older palæozoic to later tertiary, many of them fossiliferous, the oldest rocks being found along the southern base of the range, and all the beds, despite much irregular disturbance, having a general northerly dip. At the base of all the Salt Range section is a great thickness, at least 1500 feet, of red **Salt Marl**, containing thick bands of rock salt and gypsum, and a few layers of dolomite. In one spot in the Khewra gorge, near Pind Dadan Khan, is a small quantity of bituminous shale. Mr. W. T. Blanford thus describes the rock salt which forms so important a source of supply to North-Western India :—

"The beds of rock salt to which the group owes its name are very rich, some separate bands being as much as 100 feet in thickness, and there being frequently several thick beds at one locality. Thus at the Mayo Mines of Khewra there are altogether no less than 550 feet of pure and impure salt in the upper 1000 feet of the salt marl: of this thickness, 275 feet, or one-half, consists of nearly pure salt; the other half, known as *kalar*, being too earthy and impure to be of marketable value without refining. The salt of the Panjab is transported and sold in the market as it is dug from the mine, without being refined. The beds of salt, so far as they are known, are most abundant in the upper portion of the group, and the principal bands of gypsum overlie the salt beds. The salt bands do not appear to be continuous over a large area, but owing to the manner in which the outcrops are usually dissolved by rain, and then covered up by the marl, it is impossible to trace the beds. The salt itself is white, gray, or reddish, and is frequently composed of alternating white and reddish layers, differing in translucency as well as in colour. Some bands are almost pure, others contain small quantities of sulphate of lime and chlorides of calcium and magnesium. At the Mayo Mines one band has been found, 6 feet thick, composed of a mixture of sylvine (chloride of potassium) and kieserite (sulphate of magnesia, with only one equivalent of water), and the latter salt prevails throughout about 7 feet beneath the sylvine band. Epsom salts (sulphate of magnesia, with seven equivalents of water) are produced when water from the atmosphere is absorbed by the kieserite, and they frequently weather out on the surface, showing that the magnesian salt is of common occurrence in the rock. Glauberite (anhydrous sulphate of soda and lime) has also been found by Dr. Warth, to whom the discovery of most of the salts mentioned is due."

The **Hazara and North Panjab Rock Groups** near Atak and Peshawar differ to a very great extent from the Salt Range beds. Although the formations are, in many cases, of similar age, marine eocene, cretaceous, jurassic, and triassic rocks being found in both areas, there is a marked distinction, both in mineral character and in fossils, between the mesozoic rocks in Hazara and those in the Salt Range, and no connection has been traced between any of the palæozoic groups. The nummulitic limestone also exhibits differences in the two regions. The mesozoic rocks of the Northern Panjab are more closely connected, both by mineral character and fossils, with the comparatively distant Trans-Himalaya beds of Zanskar, Roopshu, and Spiti, than with the strata of the Salt Range. The total thickness of the Panjab tertiary series comprises 25,000 feet of strata, all of which is destitute of marine remains except the lower 2000 or 3000 feet. The upper tertiary or Siwalik formation (15,000 feet thick) differs little from the typical Siwalik series of the Sub-Himalaya. **Erratic Blocks**, some measuring 50 feet in girth and more, and attributed to ice flotation from the Himalaya, are abundant along the Indus, even at 20 miles away from its banks, as far up as Amb, on the left bank of the river, in the gorge of the Sirun and for some miles below Atak, around Jhand about 20 miles farther south, and farther still to the southward near the village of Trap, on the lower course of the Soan. **Indus floods**, due to a portion of the upper valley being blocked by landslips or by glaciers, and to the sudden destruction of the barriers thus formed, occurred in 1841 and 1858, and have doubtless taken place in past ages. In 1841 the waters of the Kabul river were forced backwards for 20 miles by the rise of the Indus. Drew has shown that the lake in Gilgeet formed by the landslip in 1840-41 must have been 35 miles long, and upwards of 300 feet deep. Enormous quantities of detritus must be carried down by the violent floods, and if the low temperature of the glacial epoch was felt in India, such lakes at an elevation of 5000 or 6000 feet above the sea would have been deeply frozen in winter, and large blocks from the river bed and dam might easily have been embedded in the ice; glaciers also in the North-Western Himalaya must have been more extensive than they now are, and the formation of lakes dammed up by glaciers was probably of common occurrence. Shaw has called attention to the occurrence of heaps of stone and gravel of all sizes brought 80 miles down the Shayok tributary of the Upper Indus in Ladak, by blocks of ice; and a similar action on a larger scale on the Indus may easily have supplied the erratics of the Upper Panjab. If the Potwar was a lake, the dispersion of the erratic blocks is easily understood; if not, the area over which the masses of rock are found may be due to variation in the course of the Indus, and to the reversed flow of its tributaries in great floods.

§ 4. SUB-HIMALAYA TERTIARY ROCKS.—The Himalaya, with more regularity of structure than the Alps, may be considered, geologically as geographically (page 19), in three natural zones: (1) Sub-Himalaya, of tertiary rocks; (2) Outer or Lower Himalaya, of crystalline metamorphic rocks; and (3) Main or Central Himalaya, of several parallel axes of gneissic rocks and intervening synclinal basins of little-altered fossiliferous formations.

(1) Except at two places on the Bhootan frontier, where the marginal slopes of the plains reach to the Lower Himalaya base, the **Sub-Himalaya** fringe of tertiary rocks is continuous for 1500 miles from the Jhelam to the Brahmapootra. West of the Satlej a repetition of low ridges and intervening "doons" makes up an equivalent increase in the width of this zone.

SUB-HIMALAYA SYSTEM	Siwalik series	Upper.
		Middle.
		Lower (Nahan).
	Sirmoor series	Upper (Kasauli).
		Middle (Dagshai).
		Lower (Subathoo: nummulitic).

The striking agreement in character between the Sub-Himalaya rocks and the actual deposits now in progress of formation from Himalaya debris, at once suggests that the mountain border must have been to some extent defined, and the Himalaya area undergoing denudation, from early tertiary times. The distribution of the Siwalik conglomerates shows that during the later tertiary times the configuration of the mountains must have been very similar to what it is now. The original type area of the Sirmoor series is around **Simla**, on the watershed between the Satlej and the Jumna, where a remnant of the lower tertiary formations has been elevated on the margin of the Lower Himalaya. The **Siwalik Series**, named by Sir P. Cautley from Shib-wala, the native name of the range which separates Dehra Doon from the plains, have become classical. Here that officer, Sir Henry Durand, Baker, and Falconer, first revealed the tertiary vertebrata of India. The Survey now reports a complete list of all species hitherto identified in the miocene, pliocene, and post-pliocene deposits of British India and its dependencies, showing a fauna of 45 genera represented by 84 specific forms. Of the genera 24 comprising 53 species still exist, whilst 21 with 30 species are extinct. Of the extinct genera these ten are peculiar to the Indian tertiaries:—CARNIVORA — Enhydriodon; UNGULATA ARTIODACTYLA — Hippopotamodon, Tetraconodon, Hippohyus, Merycopotamus, Sivatherium, Hydaspitherium, Peribos, Amphibos, Hemibos. Of the remaining eleven genera, four—Pseudælurus, Amphicyon, Listriodon, and Dorcatherium—are known in Europe only from miocene beds, Pseudælurus being also found in pliocene rocks in America; whilst Machærodus, Hyænarctus, Ictitherium, Mastodon, Acerotherium, Chalicotherium, and Hipparion, are both miocene and pliocene; the first and fourth ranging into post-pliocene beds also; the former in Europe, the latter in America. Of the other extinct forms, two, Hippohyus and Merycopotamus, belong to the less specialised types characteristic in general of the older and middle tertiaries. Several others, such as Tetraconodon, with its enormously developed premolar teeth, and the huge four-horned Sivatherium, differ widely from anything now existing; but, being highly specialised forms, there is nothing in their organisation to indicate that they are of earlier age than newer tertiary. The collection of extinct mammalia discovered at Pikermi in Attica singularly resembles that of the Siwalik beds; both are of pliocene age. Of 30 genera of mammals found in the beds of Greece, besides Helladotherium, scarcely distinguishable from the female of Sivatherium, 13 are found in the Siwaliks of India. Moreover, the fauna bears the same similarity to that of Africa now which the Siwalik mammals bear to their living Indian representatives. Mr. W. T. Blanford thus compares Siwalik and recent faunas:—

"The Siwalik genera not now living in Northern India, but still existing elsewhere, are Meles and Camelus, now confined in the wild state to the palæarctic region, and Hippopotamus and Camelopardalis, both surviving in Africa. All the other living forms are common to India and Africa south of the Sahara, except Semnopithecus, Macacus, Ursus, Cervus, Ovis, and Rhizomys, whilst Hyæna, Canis, Mellivora, Equus, Antilope, and Ovis, are unknown in the Malay regions. The genera common to the Siwalik fauna and Malayasia, but not found in Africa, are Semnopithecus, Macacus, Ursus, Cervus, and Rhizomys. The first two and the last of these are, however, represented by allied forms in Africa, whilst no such near Malayan representatives of any of the Siwalik-African forms, except Canis (replaced by Cuon), can be mentioned. It may be added that of the twelve genera of living Indian Carnivora unrepresented in the Siwaliks, the majority are Malayan forms inhabiting the Himalaya. It is clear that the Siwalik fauna resembles that now inhabiting Southern Africa more than it does the assemblage of living Mammalia now found in Malayasia, and it is probable that this resemblance is due to both the pliocene Siwaliks and the recent Ethiopian faunas, together with a very large proportion of the animals now inhabiting the plains of India, being descended partly or wholly from the same ancestors, and perhaps from their ancestors having originally migrated southward from the miocene lands of Central Europe and Asia. We know nothing of the miocene mammals of Southern Africa, but such information as we possess of the upper miocene fauna of Northern India renders it probable that most of the Siwalik mammals emigrated about the close of the miocene epoch, and a portion of the descendants of the Siwalik immigrants may have inhabited the country ever since. Many forms have, however, died out, and it is probable that in comparatively recent times some of these extinct forms have been replaced by Malayan types, either introduced from the eastward, or spreading northward from the singularly isolated Malayan faunas now inhabiting the Malabar coast and the South Indian hills. Many, however, of the forms which at first sight appear to have distinctly Malayan affinities, such as Cervus (Rucervus) duvaucelli and Bos gaurus, despite their close alliance with living Malay forms, and the want of related species in Africa, are probably descended from Siwalik ancestors, and are not Malayan immigrants. Again, in a few cases, as in that of the Indian gazelle, some of the species which, judging by their range and their close connection with forms inhabiting other countries, are amongst the most recent additions to the Indian fauna, come from the west and not from the eastward.

§ 5. OUTER OR LOWER HIMALAYA METAMORPHICS.—(2) Except in the north-west, where the ridges of the Main or Central Himalaya, the Dhauladar, and Peer Panjal overhang the Sub-Himalaya zone, the **Lower Himalaya** occupy the area 50 miles wide between the plains and the gneissic axis of the great snowy range. The terminal area of the Lower Himalaya in 77° E. longitude, near Símla and at Spiti, contains a series of unfossiliferous schists, quartzites, sandstones, shales, and limestones, termed, in ascending order, Infra-Blaini, Blaini, Infra-Krol, and Krol; of these the Blaini are considered to be silurian and the Krol to be triassic. The **Chor** mountain (11,982 feet), between the Giri and Tons rivers, 25 miles south-east of Simla, represents the gneissose schists of this area; the entire crest is formed of most massive granitoid gneiss, at least 5000 feet thick, surrounded by the slate and limestone series. The Chor must have been already a mountain in palæozoic times. From the confluence of the Palar with the Giri the limestone crosses to the north, and spreads over a large area east of the Chor, to the Deoban mountain (9347 feet) in Jaunsar. Along the ridge at **Mussooree** the Krol limestone occurs frequently, as on the Abbey and Camel's-back summits. On the top of **Landhaur** it is mixed with sandstones, and appears again by itself on the Tapuban point. The Blaini limestone and conglomerate are well seen on the flanks of the Sirkanda summit, and again in the Ganges at its confluence with the Hinnalgar. In Kumaun and Garhwal districts the earliest geological survey work was done by Captain Herbert in 1825, followed by General R. Strachey twenty-five years after. The ridge at **Naini Tal** is a great synclinal range, with many local fractures and contortions, like its type the Krol range. The great limestone that forms many of the summits to the south of the lake is very like the Krol limestone. The same appears on the **Kathmandoo** section of Nepal, 250 miles east. The Sikkim area, 250 miles farther east, is more like that of the Simla region, and has rocks containing fossil plants of the Damodar formation. Here are three series of the **Darjeeling Gneiss**, forming the whole of the mountain masses above 2000 to 3000 feet; the Daling series extending along the outer border, up the gorge of the Teesta, and into the valleys of the Rangeet and Rangchu, and the Damodar coal-measures. On the Bhootan border there is the Buxa series, in which dolomites are present in force. More than 250 miles to the east of Buxa, in the Dikrang valley, inhabited by the Daphla tribes, Colonel Godwin-Austen has described, immediately inside the tertiary zone, a belt, about 1000 feet in thickness, of dark hard sandstones with carbonaceous shales and seams of crushed flaky coal, probably Damodar. Should the relation of the Simla and Sikkim series be established throughout the range, a connection will have been made out between this peculiar Lower Himalaya region and a primitive gneissic mass, forming a fundamental nucleus for the whole series of Himalaya formations.

§ 6. MAIN OR CENTRAL HIMALAYA GNEISS.—(3) All the great peaks are said to be formed of granite or massive gneiss, but our detailed knowledge is confined to the north-western subterminal portion, where the main geological axes of the Himalaya seem to be continuous with those of the Hindu Koosh. Dr. F. Stoliczka, whose palæontological researches applied the key to the geology of this region, lies buried at Leh, "in the very centre of the field of his achievements." Considering the immense range of formations—metamorphic, palæozoic, and mesozoic—represented in the sections of the North-Western Himalaya, the general uniformity of distribution and symmetry of arrangement, so far observed, give much promise that, ultimately, a very complete history of the region can be made out. From end to end of the partially known ground, about 500 miles, two gneissic axes are more or less continuous. (*a*) The southern of these is the **Himalaya range proper**, of which, in Sikkim and again west of Nepal for 300 miles, gneiss is the predominant rock, many of the highest and most massive peaks being formed of it; while the slates on the north sometimes run up to an equal altitude, and the passes, through the continuous line of greatest elevation (the watershed), are generally to the north even of these slates. North of the Simla region, corresponding with the termination of the Lower Himalaya area, this main gneissic range divides into three, two of which come to an end well within the Himalaya limits; the third probably does so too. (*b*) The **Ladak axis**, the second, runs parallel to the first at a distance of from 50 to 80 miles, forming a steady range of moderate elevation which separates the Indus from its Shayok tributary of the Pangkong Lake. To the north-west this gneiss would run up to the crest of the Mustagh range in Baltestan; to the south-east it passes on both sides of the Indus through Roopshu into Tibet. Between these two axes is the long fossiliferous basin (200 miles) termed the **Hundes** and **Zanskar Synclinal**. North of the Ladak axis is the broad **Karakoram Synclinal** basin, stretching to the third gneissic axis which forms the core of the Kuenlun range. South of the Zanskar basin is the minor **Kashmeer Synclinal**. The **Pamir** is mainly formed of a pale fine-grained mica-gneiss, which Dr. Stoliczka considered to be the same as the central gneiss of the Himalaya. In a summary of this section Mr. H. B. Medlicott pronounces it quite clear that the special Himalaya contortion had been practically completed, and the mountains had very approximately assumed their present sculpture, when the undisturbed strata of the Hundes basin were deposited. If those deposits are Siwalik, it would be plain that the very considerable contortion of the latest Siwaliks of the Sub-Himalaya zone took place long after the principal contortion of the mountains as a whole, and after they had approximately assumed their present contours. There remains, however, the very important question of elevation, as distinguished from form and structure; it is strongly objected, that the rhinoceros could not have lived at the present elevation of the Hundes deposits. When the possibilities of this condition are fixed, we may be able to record another, and perhaps the latest, event in the physical history of the mountains—a great continental elevation of the area, without sensible contortion of the rocks, and after the sculpturing of the mountains to very nearly their present shape had been accomplished. Any clear evidence of simple and extensive upheaval, distinct from, and long subsequent to the chief special plication so characteristic of the mountain region, would be an interesting contribution to the theory of mountain-formation.

§ 7. THE ASSAM RANGE AND COAL-MEASURES.—The post-tertiary deposits of the Brahmapootra *khadar* or strath, 420 miles from the Brahmakoond to Dhoobri, show that this alluvial plain is not only of later date than the Gangetic, but is newer than many parts of the Ganges delta. We have to do here with the residual area of the hills which bound the valley continuously on the south. A system of deep longitudinal valleys separates these hills on the south-east from the Barail ridge; so that, instead of naming these sections according to the tribes—

Garo, Khasi, Jaintia, Meekir, and Naga—the term **Assam Range** should be applied to the whole. The gneissic mass of this range, as distinguished from the adjoining Shillong plateau, is affiliated to that of Peninsular India. The newer portions, studied at the two areas of Cherrapoonjee and the Khasi section and in the coal-fields of the Naga section, are in ascending order—Jurassic, or the stratified Sylhet trap; Cretaceous, or sandstones and shales with local coal basins; and Tertiary, or an immense thickness of soft sandstones and clays, based upon a nummulitic group in which limestone is locally in force and coal also occurs. The cretaceous coal is found in little primitive basins on the Cherra plateau, such as that at Maubilarkar, between Surarim and Moflong, which used to supply Shillong station. The mineral is less of a true coal than that of the overlying nummulitic group; the abundance of pyrites in it is a serious defect. Cretaceous coal of serviceable quality and thickness occurs in the Habiang Garo hills, at the very edge of the plains, within easy reach of water carriage. The coal basins of Rongreng and Darang, on the Upper Sumesari, north of the Tura range, have undergone some special depression in tertiary times. The seams are valueless. Along the foot of the plateau in the Khasi and Jaintia areas the disturbed upper tertiary rocks have been almost entirely removed by denudation. East of Jaintiapoor they appear again in force, and expand rapidly into the Barail range, which is made up of them, rising steeply from the alluvial valley of Cachar, drained by the Soorma or Barak. On the south this valley is very undefined, long lateral valleys running up from it to the south, between the low meridional ridges of the Tipura and Lushai hills, formed of the same soft upper tertiary rocks, some of which ridges strike up to within ten miles of the east and west Barail range. The Cachar valley seems to be excavated out of what must be the very broken ground where these two conflicting strikes meet. As the Barail curves to the north-east into the strike of the Patkai, north of Manipoor, the confluence with the ridges from the south takes place more easily. It is only in the north-east, in the Patkai, that the range forms the main watershed. The northern drainage of the Barail passes through that range, by the deep gorge of the Jatinga, into Cachar. From the edge of the plateau, immediately over the Jatinga valley, the drainage flows to Assam. This great accumulation of late tertiary strata may be largely formed of early Himalaya debris, from the discharge of the great eastern torrents, the Dihong-Dibong, the Brahmapootra, and others; the diversion of these through Assam into Bengal was the result of the crushing together of those deposits in the lines of the Burmese mountain system.

The **Assam Coal-Fields** occur isolated inside the great fault, which is traced from end to end of the area as basins of dislocation, save in the **Jaipoor field** on the Dehing and the Disang. There the measures crop up with a high dip along a narrow band at the north base of the Tipam range for about 20 miles, when they are covered over in both directions by the alluvium. East of the gorge of the Dehing at Jaipoor, the Tipam range comes to an end, and the alluvium passes behind it up to the edge of the **Mákoom field**, along the main fault. This is the most extensive of the Assam coal-fields: to the south-west its exact limit is not known, but it is certainly cut out before reaching the Disang; to the north-east it extends beyond the limits of exploration, into the Singpho country. The **Nazira field** occurs along the great fault, on the Dikhu and Saffrai rivers, for a length of about 16 miles. This coal differs from that of the peninsular fields in having a homogeneous structure and no lamination; the assay indicates a higher quality of fuel also. The deposits are of vast importance for the opening up of the Province by steamer and railway.

§ 8. BURMA.—Recent alluvium, post-tertiary alluvium, and a pliocene fossil-wood group constitute the greater portion of the Irawadi valley; the Pegu Roma consists entirely of the miocene Pegu group; and the Arakan Roma, and the spurs to the eastward and westward of the main range, are chiefly composed of nummulitic, cretaceous, and triassic beds. The carboniferous limestone and its associated beds, together with the Mergui group, are, in British Burma, nearly confined to the Tenasserim provinces; the former extending northward into Martaban, whilst the main area of metamorphic rocks lies to the east of all the other formations. At Mai-ee, in the north part of the Sandoway district, there is a cretaceous group. In the extreme south of Tenasserim, on the Lenya river, there is a **Cretaceous** bed of **coal** of very laminar structure, and containing numerous small nodules of a resinous mineral like amber. This peculiar association of mineral resin is characteristic of the cretaceous coals in the Assam hills, and it is highly probable that the Tenasserim mineral is of the same age. The tertiary formations of Tenasserim consist of conglomerates, sandstones, soft shales, and beds of coal. The most important **tertiary coal** localities known are Thatay-khyoung and Heinlap on the great Tenasserim river, about six miles apart. At the former locality there is a workable coal-seam, seven feet in thickness, including small partings of shale and clay; at the latter the seam is between 17½ and 18 feet thick. The quality of the coal is fair, the proportion of volatile matter being large, but the percentage of ash is small. At Kaumapying, three-quarters of a mile north of Heinlap, there is a seam of about eight feet in thickness, but containing much iron pyrites. Some coal also occurs on the Little Tenasserim river; but the only known seam is not more than three feet thick.

The most important **petroleum wells** in Burma are at Ye-nan-khyoung, 60 miles north of the British frontier. The rocks contain marine fossils, and probably belong to the Pegu group. The wells are situated on an anticlinal; all the rocks are very soft—too much so for any fissures to remain open in them—and the mineral oil is apparently derived from a porous stratum. About 50 miles north-north-east of Ye-nan-khyoung, and 25 to 30 miles east-south-east of Pagán, both large towns on the Irawadi, the extinct **volcano of Puppa** rises to a height of about 3000 feet above the undulating country, composed of pliocene sands and gravels. The best known vents of "mud volcanoes" are those of Memboo on the Irawadi, 42 miles north of the British frontier, and those of the islands of Ramree and Cheduba on the Arakan coast. The dozen or more Ramree vents are subject to paroxysmal eruptions of great violence. But the action is in no sense volcanic; it differs from an ordinary emission of marsh gas or light carburetted hydrogen only in this, that the gas traverses a bed capable of being easily mixed with water so as to form mud, and this, with water and petroleum, is carried to the surface with the gas.

§ 9. THE ANDAMAN AND NICOBAR ISLANDS.—The Andamans, and probably the Nicobars, are a continuation of the Arakan Roma, the islands of Preparis and the Cocos being parts of the same line of elevation, and serving to connect the northernmost of the Andaman group with Cape Negrais. To the southward, the same line of elevation may be continued in Sumatra and Java, as the rocks of all these islands present some points of similarity. But no trace of the volcanic band, so conspicuously developed in Java and Sumatra, is known to exist in the Nicobars or Andamans; and the northern extremity of the great series of igneous vents which traverses the Malay Peninsula may probably be found in Barren Island and Narkondam, and perhaps still farther north, in the extinct volcanoes of Upper Burma and Yunnan. The formations of Middle and South Andaman are extremely similar in appearance to the rocks of the Arakan Roma, and in all probability belong to the same group. The prevailing rock is sandstone, fine-grained, gray or greenish in colour, and often containing shales intercalated. Traces of coal occur, chiefly in nests, no true seam having been detected.

The Nicobar rocks comprise recent coral reef formations; marine deposits, consisting of sandstone, shales, and clay; and serpentine and gabbro (intrusive). The whitish clays of Camorta and Nankowri contain Polycistina in great abundance, no fewer than 300 species having been identified from Camorta alone. The species are nearly the same as those composing similar clays in Barbadoes in the West Indies, and are considered as probably of miocene age. The upraised coral reefs found on the coasts of all the Nicobar Islands in places, form a raised flat fringe, a few feet above the sea, and are covered by a forest of cocoa-nut palms. On Car Nicobar, Bompoka, and several other islands, these coral banks are of great thickness, and are raised 30 or 40 feet above the sea. The formation is clearly the same as the "littoral concrete" of Arakan and Western India, but richer in corals. Barren Island certainly, and Narkondam probably, are recent volcanoes.

CHAPTER IV.

METEOROLOGY OF INDIA.

§ 1. Meteorological Observations in India. § 2. Advantages of Indian Meteorology. § 3. Meteorological Influence of the Surface of India. § 4. Of Ceylon. § 5. The Monsoons. § 6. Temperature. § 7. Sun-Spots. § 8. Atmospheric Pressure and Winds. § 9. Cloud and Rainfall. § 10. Land-Storms and Sea-Storms. § 11. Annual Mean Elevation, Pressure, Temperature, Vapour Tension, Cloud Proportion, and Rainfall of 56 Stations.

§ 1. METEOROLOGICAL OBSERVATIONS IN INDIA, on a regular plan, were first suggested by Sir John Herschel, who, when at the Cape, sent a circular recommending that "term observations" should be taken, or hourly observations for 24 hours together at the time of the equinoxes and solstices on the 21st of March, June, September, and December. Since 1829 a regular series of daily and, since 1856, hourly observations has been kept at the Calcutta Survey Office, and monthly and yearly abstracts of these have been published. Since 1796 the successive Astronomers of the Madras Observatory, from Goldingham to Pogson, have registered a complete series; the local Revenue Board has published rain returns from 350 stations since 1852; for the 12 years ending 1858 observations were taken on the summit of Dodabetta peak (8640 ft.); those taken at the Trivandrum Observatory from 1837 to 1865 and the Agastya peak commanding the whole south of the Peninsula from Adam's Bridge to Cochin, and reduced by Mr. Brown, are of great value. The Bombay Observatory at Kolaba, formed in 1823 for magnetic, tidal, and meteorological observations, added much to the early knowledge of the climate of Western India under Buist, Sykes, and Chambers. The cyclone of 1864 led to the appointment of Meteorological Reporters by the three Provincial Governments of Bengal, the North-West, and the Panjab. The Sanitary Commissioners, imperial and provincial, under the same Governor-General, Lord Lawrence, began systematic observations to show the effect of climate on diseases, especially on epidemics like cholera, regarding which the late Dr. Brydone arrived at striking statistical results. In 1875, as Meteorological Reporter to the Government of India, Mr. Henry F. Blanford, F.R.S., issued the first report on the meteorology of the whole Indian Empire. He has continued to report, with elaborate tables from no fewer than 365 stations, on these eight heads of the meteorology of each year—Temperature of solar radiation; Temperature of nocturnal radiation; Air temperature; Atmospheric pressure; Anemometry; Hygrometry; Cloud proportion; and Rainfall. Full registers of the six stations—Calcutta, Lucknow, Lahore, Nagpoor, Bombay, and Madras—are separately published. Mr. Blanford has farther done a signal service to science by the publication, in two volumes, of *The Indian Meteorologist's Vade Mecum*, the second part of which, on the Meteorology of India, he has permitted us to condense.

§ 2. ADVANTAGES OF INDIAN METEOROLOGY.—The practical object of Meteorology, as of all Science, is to enable us to make quantitative predictions of phenomena; to foretell not only their occurrence, but their time and exact measure. Here a great part of the field is inaccessible, and very much more is imperfectly accessible. An isolated tract under a wide range of latitude, girdled round by a giant mountain chain completely shutting in millions of square miles of the atmosphere, and resting on a surface as varied as that of the earth, watched from balloons and fixed observatories well distributed at different heights, so that each section should be under a meteorological blockade, is the ideal of the meteorologist. India offers the nearest approach to such a region. It is an epitome of atmospheric physics as England is of stratigraphic geology. It is a secluded and independent area, while it presents within itself the most varied conditions of form and surface, and, together with its seas, the great primary contrast of continent and ocean, ranging through nearly 30 degrees of latitude, and during five months of the year bathed in the intense radiation of a vertical sun. On the north the Himalaya, shutting in the lower half of the atmosphere, constitutes the natural limit of the monsoons. On the south, an only less defined meteorological frontier exists in the zone of all but unvarying barometric pressure of the equatorial belt. For although the monsoons do, at certain seasons of the year, blow across this belt, between Australia on the one hand and India on the other, it is a kind of neutral axis, the fulcrum on which the plane of equal pressure turns, inclining alternately to north and south; and the meteorological conditions on its opposite sides bear a very simple relation of reciprocity. Order and regularity are as prominent characteristics of the atmospheric phenomena of India as are apparent caprice and uncertainty those of their European counterparts.

§ 3. METEOROLOGICAL INFLUENCE OF THE SURFACE OF INDIA.—The average elevation of the **Himalaya** (19,000 feet) is equal to the height of the lower half of the atmosphere. Across this barrier there is a constant flow of air northwards to the arid plateau of Tibet. It is probable that this is more active in the daytime than at night, since the observed diurnal variation of the barometric pressure on the lower plains and at hill stations, as well as that of the winds on the high plains and passes, seems to indicate that the transfer of the portion of the higher atmosphere from over the low plains to the mountains, and even to the lower hills and tablelands of the peninsula, takes place as a secondary effect of the diurnal heating of the land. Unless in the loftiest regions of the atmosphere beyond the range of observation no transfer of air takes place across the Himalaya in a southerly direction; but from the southern slopes a nocturnal flow of cooled air is felt as a strong wind where the rivers debouch on the plains, especially in the early morning. The **Eastern Himalaya** is clothed with a dense forest; Sikkim and Bhootan receive an abnormally copious rainfall discharged full on the face of the range. As the chain recedes to the drier north-west, the greater is the distance to be traversed by the vapour-bearing winds in reaching it, and the more easterly is their direction; since, whether coming from the Bay of Bengal, or from the Arabian Sea, on reaching the Gangetic valley they turn and blow more or less parallel to its axis and that of the mountain range. Farther west the **Sulaiman** and **Khirthar** ranges, at right angles to the Himalaya, are still more arid, being subject to dry winds from the desert tracts of Persia and Baloochistan, and dependent on the winter snows or rare showers from the eastward for the scanty cultivation beyond the influence of the Indus and the larger local streams. The west of the Indo-Gangetic plain, from the desert of Rajpootana to the saline swamps of Kach, rarely sees the rain, which is more frequent twice a year in the **North Panjab**, where it feeds the belt of wheat 100 miles wide. The vigorous planting of trees and construction of canals since the British occupation of the Panjab has so ameliorated the climate already, that dust-storms are far less frequent than before.

Up or down the **Gangetic Plain** the monsoon winds

sweep at right angles to their nominal course, discharging as snow or rain on the Western Himalaya the vapour from the Bay of Bengal. The rainfall diminishes from 100 inches at the south-east corner of the Gangetic delta to less than 30 inches at Agra and Delhi, and there is an average difference of from 15 to 25 inches between the northern and southern borders of the plain. At Sirsa and Mooltan, the average annual rainfall does not exceed 6 inches. On the east the climate of the **Brahmapootra** and **Soorma Valleys** is damp and equable; the rainfall is prolonged and heavy, especially on the southern slopes of the hills. A meteorological peculiarity of some interest has been noticed, more especially at the stations of Seebsagar and Silchar, viz. the great range of the diurnal variation of barometric pressure during the afternoon hours; which is the more striking, since at Roorkee, Lahore, and other stations near the foot of the Himalaya, this range is less than out in the open plains. A similarly exaggerated range is, however, exhibited by Leh in the Indus valley. It would seem that the daily fall is exaggerated in narrow deep valleys, but reduced at stations situated on the margin of a broad plain immediately below a lofty hill mass. These facts, and the well-known peculiarity of the oscillation on elevated mountain peaks and ridges, together with the oft-described phenomenon of the strong afternoon winds which blow up through the high passes and across the elevated plains of Roopshu and Ladak, have led Mr. Henry F. Blanford to the conclusion that the effect of the diurnal solar heating of the atmosphere is to cause a transfer of air from the plains and deep valleys to the hills during the hotter hours similar to that which takes place between land and sea.

The **Peninsular Watershed of the Satpoora** does not, indeed, form the boundary between the easterly summer monsoon of the Gangetic plain and the westerly monsoon of the peninsula proper, which crosses the plateau of Malwa and Baghelkhand to the north of the range; but, together with the two parallel valleys of the Narbada and Tapti, which drain the flanks of its western half, it gives, at opposite seasons of the year, a decided easterly and westerly direction to the winds of this part of India, and condenses a tolerably copious rainfall during the south-west monsoon. The **Northern Plateau of Malwa and Baghelkhand**, which terminates against the Aravali range on the west, exerts an important influence on the direction of the wind, and also on the rainfall. At **Ajmer**—an old-established meteorological station at the eastern foot of the range—the wind is predominantly south-west; there and at Mount Aboo the south-west monsoon rains are a regularly recurrent phenomenon, which can hardly be said of the region of scanty and uncertain rainfall extending from the western foot of the range, and merging in the Bikaner desert. The **Southern Plateau of the Dekhan and Mysore**, south of the Satpoora, is swept by the south-western monsoon, but not until that has surmounted the western barriers of the Sahyadri Ghats from which the plateau slopes to the Bay of Bengal. Hence the rainfall is light at Poona and places similarly situated under the lee of the range, and moderate over the more easterly parts of the plateau. The rains, however, are prolonged three or four weeks later than in India to the north of the Satpoora, since they are brought by the easterly winds which blow from the Bay of Bengal in October and the early part of November; when the recurved southerly wind ceases to blow up the Gangetic valley, and sets towards the Carnatic. This was formerly thought to be the north-east monsoon; but the rainy wind is really a diversion of the south-west monsoon.

The cantonment of **Wellington** (6200 feet) is now the meteorological station of the Neelgiri hills where the Eastern join the Western Ghats. The Palghat gap (1500 feet), 25 miles wide, which separates the Neelgiris from the Anamalai, Palnai, and Travankor hills, ending in Agastya peak above Cape Comorin, affords a passage to the winds, which elsewhere are barred by the hills of the Ghat chain. The country to the east of the gap receives the rainfall of the south-west monsoon; and during the north-east monsoon, ships passing Beypoor meet with a stronger wind from the land than is felt elsewhere on the Malabar coast. **Coimbatore** is the meteorological station, situated near the eastern entrance of the Palghat gap, under the lee of the last outlying ridges of the Neelgiris. The rainfall of the **Konkan and Malabar coasts**, from above Bombay to Cape Comorin, is heavy, the climate is damp and warm, and the vegetation is dense and tropical. The backwaters, which extend for 350 miles, are enclosed by the sandspits, which are formed between the action of the rivers and of the rain, 9 million tons of which fall annually on every square mile of the Malabar coast, and the surf and wind which beat back the silt and sand thus carried from the western face of the Ghats seawards. The corresponding **Eastern fringing plain** is much broader. It forms the modern section of the Carnatic up to Madras city, occupying from one-third to one-half of the width of the peninsula. It extends up the Kavari to the foot of the Neelgiri hills (2000 feet), forming the rich section of Tanjore made and irrigated by that river, with the town of Salem nestling at the mouth of one of the gorges of the hill groups which stand out in advance of the Eastern Ghats, and Trichinopoli, 20 miles from their south-east corner. North of Madras the coast plain of the Paen-Ghat is narrowed to 30 or 40 miles, and runs along the foot of the Nallamalai hills to the delta of the Kistna and Godavari. From Vizagapatam the coast is formed by a rocky ridge which runs parallel to the line of the Ghats; but, in general, the whole of this coast line, from Cape Comorin to the mouth of the Hoogli, is a low alluvial flat, bordered by a strip of sand.

In **Burma** the western face of the Arakan Roma range, like the Sahyadri farther west, receives a heavy rainfall from the full force of the south-west monsoon, amounting at Sandoway to 250 inches, and even at Chittagong in Bengal to 100. The Pegu Roma is lower in the south, but to the east of Mandalay and Bhamo, in the Kachin hills which border China, the range reaches from 5000 to 6000 feet, running north-east and south-west with a breadth of 25 miles. The Irawadi valley lies between. Throughout the year there is a steady upper current of clouds from the south-west, such as has been already noticed over the Himalaya. The rainfall in the lower part of the Irawadi valley—the delta and the neighbouring part of Pegu—is very heavy, and the climate is very mild and equable at all seasons; but higher up, and especially north of the Pegu frontier, the country is drier, and is characterised by a less luxuriant vegetation and a retarded and more scanty rainfall. There are two observatories for the Andaman and Nicobar Islands at Port Blair and Nankowri.

§ 4. CEYLON is, in meteorological as in other physical respects, inseparably connected with India. Mr. H. F. Blanford thus describes it:—

"The north of the island, as well as a part of the mainland opposite, is formed of upraised coral reef; indeed, the whole of Ceylon affords indications of a recent elevation of the land. The northern half of the island is a plain of the older crystalline rocks, still much covered with forest, while the central part of the southern half is occupied by a tableland of similar geological structure, with lofty hills which rise to more than 7000 feet, and, on their western face, are clad with dense forest, except where cleared for the coffee cultivation. The eastern part of the plateau, under the lee of the loftier hills, like the corresponding part of the Neelgiris, consists, however, of open, rolling, grassy downs, with forest in the hollows and valleys. To the south and west of the hills the country is rugged and hilly down to the coast. The rainfall is here frequent and heavy; and the temperature being high and equable, the vegetation is dense and very luxuriant, such as is characteristic of islands in tropical seas, and also of the coast of Travankor. The plains on the east coast are drier, and both in climate and vegetation bear much resemblance to those of the Carnatic. When the south-west monsoon is blowing in May and June, discharging torrents of rain on the forest-clad spurs and slopes that face to windward, the contrast presented by the eastward face of the same hills is very striking, and the two phases of climate are sharply demarcated. Newara Eliya, at 6200 feet, day after day, and even week after week, lies under a dense canopy of cloud, which shrouds all the higher peaks, and pours down almost incessant rain. But let the traveller leave the station by the Badulla road, and, crossing the *col* of the main range, at the distance of two or three miles from Newara Eliya, begin the descent towards Wilson's bungalow, and he emerges on a panorama of the grassy downs of the lower hills, bathed in dazzling sunshine; while, on the ridge above, he sees the cloud masses ever rolling across from the westward and dissolving away in the drier air to leeward. Hence, the east and west coasts of the island are as strongly contrasted in climate as those of the southern extremity of the peninsula of India."

§ 5. THE MONSOONS.—The predominating feature of Indian Meteorology is the semi-annual reversal of the wind system. In the causes which bring about this reversal, and in the associated phenomena, we have a field of study second in interest to none in the whole range of meteorological science. The Asiatic monsoons consist not of one current flowing alternately to and from Central Asia, but of several currents, each having its own land centre. The centre which, at opposite seasons of the year, is alternately the source and goal of the Indian monsoons lies to the south of the Himalaya. At two seasons of the year, viz. in the months of March, April, and May, and again in the months of October and November—that is to say, at the change of the monsoons—the interchange of air currents between land and sea is, in a great measure, restricted to India and its two seas, and has but little concern with the region south of the equator. But a few weeks before the solstices, and two or three months afterwards, these currents are continuous across the equinoctial line, connecting the Indian wind system with those of the Sunda Islands and of Australia, and, at one season, with the trade winds of the South Indian ocean. These are the monsoons, as known to sailors. In India itself, the period of transition between the north-easterly or winter monsoon and the south-westerly or summer monsoon is much longer than that of the opposite change, and presents marked characteristics of its own, which justify its being distinguished as a third, viz. the hot season. In extra-tropical India, the transition from the south-west monsoon or the rains to the cold season is tolerably abrupt; and only in Southern India and Ceylon is it marked by peculiar features, being the chief rainy season of the Carnatic.

§ 6. TEMPERATURE.—The variation of the quantity of solar heat received by the land surface of India, according as the sun is in north or south declination, is the primary cause of this annual reversal of the wind system. The general law of the quantity of the sun's heat incident at any given moment on a given area, say a square foot of level surface, is that it is inversely as the square of the earth's distance from the sun, and, disregarding the atmospheric absorption, directly as the sine of the sun's altitude. Heat falling on a water surface is largely used up in evaporating the water; and, owing to the high specific heat of water, its temperature is raised but little as compared with that of a land surface. Hence a water surface changes its temperature but slowly. The primary cause of the summer monsoon lies in the fact that the most northern part of India is included in that zone of the earth's surface which, during the summer months, receives the greatest proportion of the sun's heat, and which, being at the same time a land surface, acquires therefore a proportionally high temperature. The northward progression of the region of highest temperature, as the sun ascends in declination from March to June, is unfailingly regular. In March the hottest part of India is the central and eastern part of the peninsula south of the Satpoora, which is included within the isotherm of 80°, but is below 85°. In April and May the temperature rises more rapidly in Rajpootana and the Panjab; and in the second of these months the greater part of Rajpootana, with Indore, Bhopal, Berar, and the western part of Nagpoor, is surrounded by the isotherm of 95°. Finally, in June, the seat of maximum heat is transferred to the Panjab, where, allowing for elevation, the average temperature of the day is little below 100°. The **Isotherms**, or lines of equal temperature, in May are concentric curves following almost exactly the contours of the peninsula and of the mountain belt; the highest temperature prevailing in the latitude of 24° or 26°.

The setting in of the rains, in June and July, reduces the temperature, save when the fall is scanty in the Panjab and Sind, in which there is the highest temperature till the sun has retreated to the south of the equator, when, about the end of September, it becomes lowest. Meanwhile the Carnatic has received little rain, and has the sun vertical during August, so as then to have a higher temperature than any other part of India in November and December. Hence the south-west monsoon is deflected to its coast and to Eastern Ceylon, and the autumn rains of the Carnatic are the result. In the cold weather months, as the temperature depends chiefly on the obliquity with which the sun's rays fall on the earth's surface, the course of the isothermal lines is more or less parallel to the

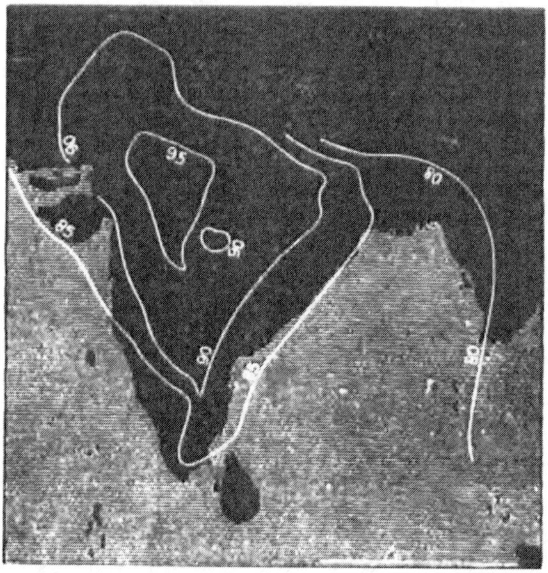

Isothermal Chart of India in May.

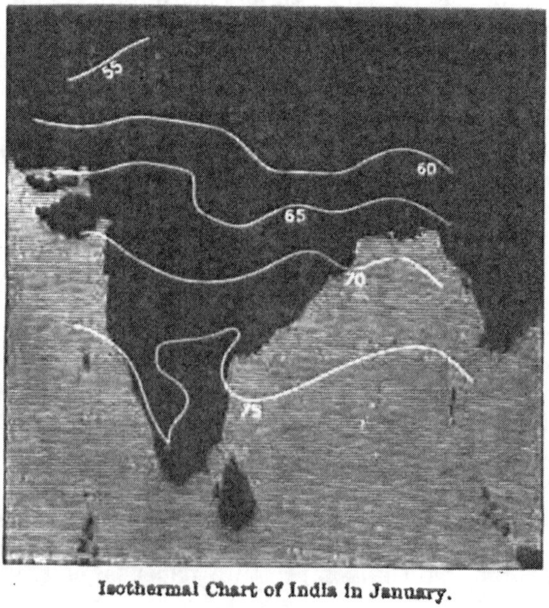

Isothermal Chart of India in January.

lines of latitude, but less so in the peninsula than in Northern India, since the peninsular temperature is affected unequally by cooler currents from the north, and by differences of radiation.

The hills of the peninsula afford, for equal elevations, a greater reduction of temperature than do the Himalaya stations; and the advantage thus gained varies less with the season of the year. The summer temperature of the Himalaya stations, at about the same elevation, is apparently the higher the farther the station lies to the north-west; but the winter temperature is very nearly the same in all parts of the chain. The range of temperature, both in the annual and diurnal period, varies very greatly in different parts of India. The Panjab is the seat of the greatest variation; and Ceylon and the Andaman and Nicobar Islands that of the least range. The absolute annual range at such stations as Dera Ismail Khan, Mooltan, Rawal Pindi, Sialkot, Lahore, and Lodiana is between 90° and 100°; on the other hand, at Galle, on the south-west coast of Ceylon, the difference between the highest and lowest temperatures in 1875 was only 16·2°, and that at Nankowri 20·9°. The average diurnal range at these Panjab stations is about 30° on the mean of the year, and in April 40°; in the Central Province, between 20° and 25° on the mean of the year, and in March from 30° to 35°; while at Galle the annual average is only 6½°, and the greatest monthly average not 9°.

§ 7. SUN-SPOTS.—Solar radiation, the source of all atmospheric energy, is subject to variation affecting the activity of the meteorological changes of our atmosphere. At the beginning of the century Sir W. Herschel held that "years of remarkably abundant or deficient spots have been also remarked for their high or low general temperature, and especially for abundant and deficient harvests." The recurrence of drought, and especially the great famine of 1877-8 in the peninsula proper, led Mr. Pogson to revive the opinion. A certain periodicity, corresponding to that of the abundance of sun-spots, has been traced in several kinds of meteorological phenomena. Mr. H. F. Blanford writes thus on the subject:—

"It is now well known, from the researches of Hofrath Schwabe of Dessau, Professor Wolf of Berne, and more recently of Carrington, Balfour Stewart and Loewy, that the abundance of the spots on the sun's face undergoes a periodical increase and decrease in a cycle of about 11·11 years. In addition to, and superimposed on this, the Wolfian period, are other variations of longer period; but the law of these is less accurately known. Sun-spots, as we know now from the observations of Chacornac and Lockyer, are not, as was at one time supposed, cooled solid masses or even clouds floating on the solar

2 K

surface, but rather gaseous maelströms in the luminous envelope, the photosphere, caused by the descent of streams of the external cooled atmosphere into the body of the sun. They indicate, therefore, increased activity in the movements of the solar atmosphere and a withdrawal of a portion of the cooled and absorbing envelope; and, as might be anticipated, the recent discussion of observations of radiation temperatures by Mr. Baxendall of Manchester, and also, in India, by the writer, have gone to confirm the original idea of Sir W. Herschel, and to show that the solar radiation is greatest in years of abundant sun-spots and *vice versâ*. What is the amount of its variation is not yet known, and can be ascertained only by long-continued observations with the actinometer. The results of 11 stations, in different parts of India, showed an increase of at least 6° in the mean equilibrium temperature of solar radiation at the earth's surface, between 1868 and 1871 (the last following a year of maximum sun-spots); and this, I am inclined to think, is in defect of the truth. The variation is thus by no means inconsiderable. These facts afford evidence that, to a certain small extent, our sun must take rank among the variable stars. It is true that, viewed from the distance of even the nearest of the (so-called) fixed stars, such small variations as have been recorded during the last two centuries would be absolutely inappreciable. But greater degrees of obscuration are recorded in past times, as, *e.g.*, in the year A.D. 536, when the sun is said to have suffered a great diminution of light, which continued fourteen months; and in those remote epochs which geology deals with, there are evidences of such vicissitudes of climate as seem inexplicable on any other hypothesis than that of a great variation of the solar heat. Such, for instance, is the occurrence of remains of a warm temperate flora of the Miocene epoch in the now ice-bound rocks of Greenland; and, on the other hand, the abundant evidence of glaciers down to low levels in the Himalaya and the Patkoi Hills of Assam, in times which are certainly prehistoric, but not, perhaps, anterior to the existence of man. Such cases as these, and of extensive accumulations of ice-borne boulders in latter palæozoic times in South Africa and in India, far down in the tropical zone, can hardly be explained by the ingenious theory of Mr. Croll; and seem to point to an amount of variation in the solar heat, both in excess and defect of its present intensity, that would entitle our sun to a place among the more variable of the stars."

§ 8. ATMOSPHERIC PRESSURE AND WINDS.—Any difference of pressures in the same horizontal plane of the atmosphere tends to produce an air-current from the seat of higher to that of lower pressure. **Isobaric Planes** are planes of equal pressure more or less undulating or inclined. As their several parts are variously inclined to a horizontal or water-level surface, the slope is the **Baric Gradient.** Thus in the south-west monsoon the mean barometric gradient over the Bay of Bengal is one-tenth of an inch in 400 miles, or 0·25 inch in 100 miles; and in cyclones, the gradients near the centre of the storm sometimes amount to 1 inch in 50 miles, or 2 inches in 100 miles. **Isobars** are the lines along which the successive isobaric planes intersect one and the same horizontal plane.

They are, therefore, lines of equal pressure on a horizontal plane. As laid down on charts, they generally show the pressures at the sea-level; or the hypothetical equivalent, at that level, of the pressures actually observed. The term Cyclone is not restricted to violent revolving storms, to be afterwards considered, but is applied to cases where the winds circulate around an area of relatively low pressure without attaining to any very high velocity. On the other hand, around a region of relatively high pressure, the winds blow spirally outwards, constituting an anti-cyclone. In a cyclone, or around a region of low pressure in the Northern Hemisphere, the direction of the circular motion is left-handed, or opposite to that of the clock hands, and right-handed in an anti-cyclone around a region of high pressure. In the Southern Hemisphere the direction of the circulation is reversed, cyclones being all right-handed spirals, and anti-cyclones left-handed.

This deviation of the winds from the radial direction is a consequence of the earth's rotation (Ferrel's law) which causes railway trains, steamers, rivers, marine currents, and winds, to deviate to the right in the Northern, and to the left in the Southern Hemisphere. The law of the wind's rotation, or the tendency of a wind to "veer," so that in the Northern Hemisphere a north-west wind tends to become easterly, and in the Southern to follow an opposite course, was recorded as a fact of observation by Lord Bacon. This tendency to veer is less striking in India than in higher latitudes. The annual oscillation of pressure at the hill stations, in all parts of India, is different from that on the plains. With very few exceptions, the highest pressure occurs in December everywhere on the plains of India; that of January being nearly as high; and the lowest in June or July. But, on the hills, the pressure in December is almost universally below that of November; and the further fall in January and February becomes more and more decided as we ascend to greater heights. At Leh (11,500 feet above the sea) the pressure of February is the absolute minimum of the year. At stations of 6000 feet elevation and upwards (frequently at lower altitudes), the pressure rises again after February to a second maximum in March or April; but this maximum is, in all cases, subordinate to that of November. The chief feature of the difference consists in the barometric depression of the winter season, which is felt above elevations of 5000 or 6000 feet; and, in the North-Western Himalaya, sets in in November, and attains its minimum in February. In October and November the winds and movements of the high clouds over the mountains appear to be chiefly from the north-west; and this is the case so long as the sky and mountain-tops remain unclouded. But in December, or sometimes a little later, the hill stations become clouded, snow falls, and the current is then from the south-west or some other southerly quarter. This current is the **anti-monsoon**, the upper return current, corresponding to the anti-trade, which, in Western Europe, prevails during the winter months, and while it raises the temperature and lowers the pressure in virtue of its diminished density, brings also the snow and rain, which then fall more copiously than at any other time of year. The anti-monsoon probably takes its rise in the belt which, in the winter months, intervenes between the south-west trade of the South Indian Ocean and the north-east monsoon of the Indian seas. The average distribution of pressure in January and August is represented in the Isobaric Charts on the opposite page.

(1) The north-east or, more correctly, **Winter Monsoon** (Arabic moussin = "a season") radiates out with a certain anti-cyclonic curvature from the region of high pressure in the Panjab in November and December. Its winds then form a steady outflow of cooled air, true convection currents. But in January and February, with the rising temperature, the general southerly set of the surface currents ceases, except in the south of the Bay, where this monsoon blows with more steadiness than in either November or December. In the following interval of three or four months (2) the **hot land winds** prevail from the west and north-west in Northern and Central India. The well-known hot winds of April and May spring up about 9 or 10 in the morning, and blow with considerable force till 4 or 5 in the evening, and occasionally far into the night. These winds are doubtless of similar origin to those of South Australia and other dry desert tracts. In Lower Bengal the sea-breeze prevails for some distance inland from the coast. On the Madras coast the land and sea winds blow alternately with much regularity, and on the Mysore plateau hot diurnal winds prevail from the east till the setting in of the south-west monsoon. (3) Then the east and south-east sea winds of Bengal become more persistent and changed, with a copious rush of saturated air, the hot winds of Upper India and the Dekhan give way to westerly winds all across the peninsula; on the Madras coast the long shore winds blow from the south-west, all ushering in the longed-for south-west or **Summer Monsoon**. It is in two branches, from the Arabian Sea and the Bay of Bengal. The former, with the higher velocity,

blows right across the peninsula over the plateaux on both sides of the Satpooras, even to Orissa and the confines of the Gangetic

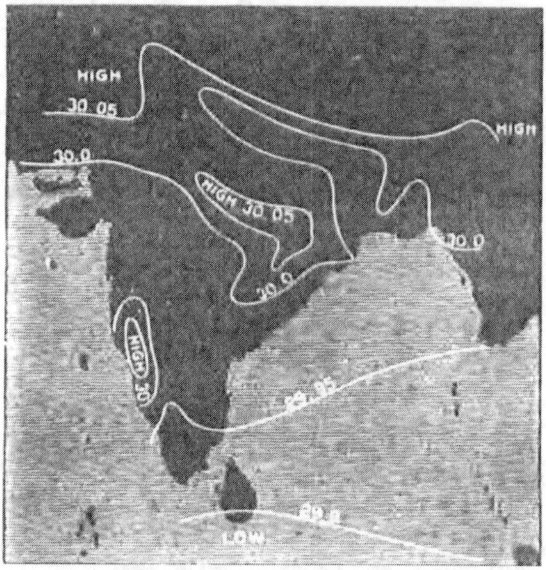

Isobaric Chart of India in January.

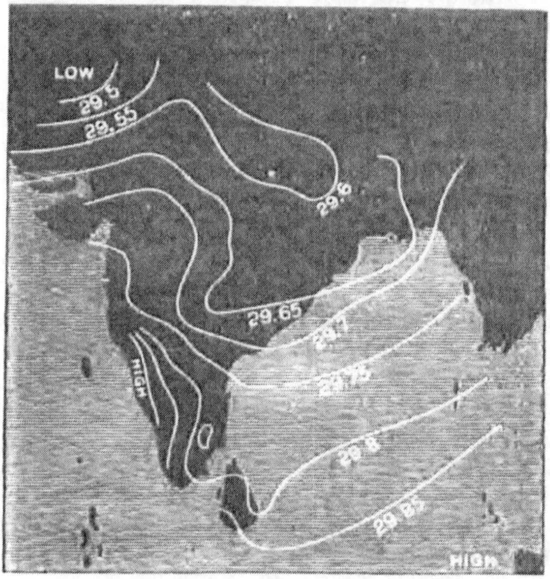

Isobaric Chart of India in August.

plain. The latter prevails in Burma and Arakan, in Eastern Bengal and Assam, the Gangetic delta and the Gangetic plain; but in the last area not exclusively; for much of the rain of this season, and indeed some of the heaviest falls, come with a south-west wind. In the upper Gangetic valley and the Panjab the two currents seem to coalesce; and around the plain of the five rivers the tendency of the winds is distinctly cyclonic. During the height of this summer monsoon the tract between the equator and 9° N. latitude, from Ceylon to Sokotra, known as "the soft place in the monsoon," is taken advantage of by navigators, especially by steamers, going westward towards the entrance of the Red Sea. It is expected that the discussion of the official logs collected by the London Meteorological Office will explain this phenomenon.

The irregular or **Non-Periodic Variations of Pressure** in India and other tropical lands are so small that observers, whose experience of the barometer as a weather-glass has been gained in extra-tropical countries, are apt to conclude that its indications are altogether fallacious in India. This, however, is far from being the case. Although small, rarely exceeding 0·2 or 0·3 in the course of a month (after deducting the diurnal oscillation), they have an important meaning, and only require to be carefully interpreted and considered in their geographical relations—that is to say, as affecting different parts of the country in different degrees—to afford very important information relative to the weather changes in progress. But the study of weather changes in India, except in connection with the cyclones of the Bay of Bengal, is at present almost a virgin field. Year after year each season is characterised by a certain scheme of pressure distribution, which determines the course of the winds at that season. But the distribution is not *exactly* the same in successive years. Now that the Panjab, Rajpootana, and other parts of India are equally available for comparison, Mr. H. F. Blanford expects that the study of these protracted variations will throw much light on the causes of drought and floods, and may even render it possible, to some extent, to forecast the seasons.

§ 9. CLOUD AND RAINFALL.—From the seas around India Mr. H. F. Blanford assumes $\frac{1}{10}$ inch daily as the **average evaporation**, or 232,320 cubic feet per square statute mile of sea surface. Since at the temperature of 80° one cubic foot of pure water weighs 62·3074 lbs. avoirdupois, the weight of water evaporated from each square mile daily will be, in round figures, 14,475,000 lbs., requiring at 80° Fahr. the absorption of 7,975,725,000 units of heat. When we consider that each unit of heat thus locked up is potentially equal to lifting a pound weight of the atmosphere through 772 feet, against gravity, we may form some vague conception of the enormous quantity of energy which thus passes into the atmosphere and may become kinetic on the condensation of the vapour. The Andaman and Nicobar Islands and the west coast of Travankor and Ceylon are the most persistently humid regions, being near the seat of the highest mean yearly temperature, and sea coasts where the prevailing winds are those from the sea. On the other hand—Mooltan and Dera Ismail Khan have a uniformly dry climate; Calcutta and Berhampoor, one in which the change from drought to dampness is gradual; and Nagpoor and Roorkee, one where it is sudden and strongly contrasted.

Clouds at any elevation indicate that the atmosphere is there in a state of saturation; and the lower the cloud, the more humid (relatively) is the atmosphere. The forms of the clouds may give information as to the changes of temperature and the cause of these changes. Their movements show what winds are blowing high up in the atmosphere, and even the rate of the movement. If indeed the height of the clouds is measured, they serve both as a wind-vane and anemometer, whose precision leaves little to desire. Poëy thus classifies clouds—(1) Cirrus, (2) Cirro-stratus, (3) Cirro-cumulus, (4) Pallium, (5) Pallio-cirrus, (6) Pallio-cumulus, (7) Cumulus, (8) Fracto-cumulus. Of these, the first three and fifth are the higher clouds. The last three are the clouds of the lower atmosphere. The cirrus is the most lofty of all clouds, appearing still at a great elevation, even when seen from the greatest heights of the Himalaya, and probably never lower than six miles. It consists of minute snow crystals forming feathery groups or brushes, parallel, diverging or curled, very thin, and always more or less fibrous in appearance. The cirro-stratus is also a lofty cloud, but lower, denser, and more sheet-like than cirrus. It is at such a height that it also consists of snow crystals, but is sometimes of such thickness as to dim the sun's disc, and even almost completely obscure it. In the winter season, after the interval of fine clear weather which prevails when the rains have ceased, the appearance of cirrus wisps at very great elevations is the first harbinger of the anti-monsoon. This is followed by a sheet of cirro-stratus at a much lower level, and eventually by pallio-cumulus, but the height of the rain-cloud appears to be much greater at this season than during the hot weather and rains. In Northern India there are two annual periods of minimum and two of maximum cloudiness; the latter corresponding to the summer monsoon and the winter anti-monsoon respectively. In Southern India there is but one well-marked minimum, viz. in February or March. In all parts of India, with the exception of the drier tracts of the Panjab, the most cloudy season is the beginning of the summer monsoon, either in June or July. Only at Mooltan and Lahore is the cloudiness of January slightly the greater.

While **Rainfall** follows the same general laws as the variation of the relative humidity of the air and of cloud, it is influenced by such local conditions as the form of the ground and the volume of vapour-loaded air which reaches a place, condenses, and precipitates its vapour and passes on. At **Cherrapoonjee** (4588 feet), on the south face of the Khasi hills of the Assam Range, the conditions favouring rain are combined, and hence it has the highest recorded fall in the world. From the *jheels* of Sylhet these hills rise abruptly to 4000 feet and arrest the summer monsoon from the Bay of Bengal. Besides this, the station stands on a little plateau of thick-bedded sandstones, bounded on two sides by precipices of 2000 feet sheer descent, which close in gorges, debouching southwards on the plains. The south-west wind blows up these as well as on the southern face of the general scarp, and, having reached the heads of the gorges, ascends vertically. Thus the spot is surrounded, or nearly so, by vertically ascending currents of saturated air, the dynamic cooling of which is the cause of the enormous precipitation which has made this place famous, or 368½ inches in each of the three years ending 1876, and 805 inches in 1861. The **Sahyadri Ghats**, **Arakan**, and the outer slopes of Sikkim and Bhootan, come next in abundant rainfall. At Sandoway it is 230 inches; at Akyab, 205; at Mahableshwar and Uttrai Malai in Travankor, 260 inches. **Bombay** has 72 inches, Goa 83, and Colombo 75. On the lee or **Dekhan** side of the Sahyadri the rainfall is moderate and the increase beyond is gradual. Poona has only 32 inches, Satara 39, Sholapoor 28, and Dharwar 37. But Belgaum, which is opposite the low parts of the Ghats about Vingorla, has as much as 47 inches annually. Bangalore has about 34, and Bellary 17·5 inches. All through the Maratha country, and as far as Nagpoor, the annual distribution of rain is the same as at Bombay, *i.e.* practically restricted to the season of the summer monsoon. But from Nagpoor eastwards, spring storms are not unfrequent which augment the total annual fall, so that at Nagpoor the average is 45 inches, at Raipoor and Sambalpoor about 50 inches, and at Chanda 48 inches. South of the Godavari and Kistna the summer monsoon rains are not much felt on the east coast. At **Madras** the average fall from January to the end of May is $4\frac{1}{2}$ inches, from June to September inclusive 15 inches; and it is in October and

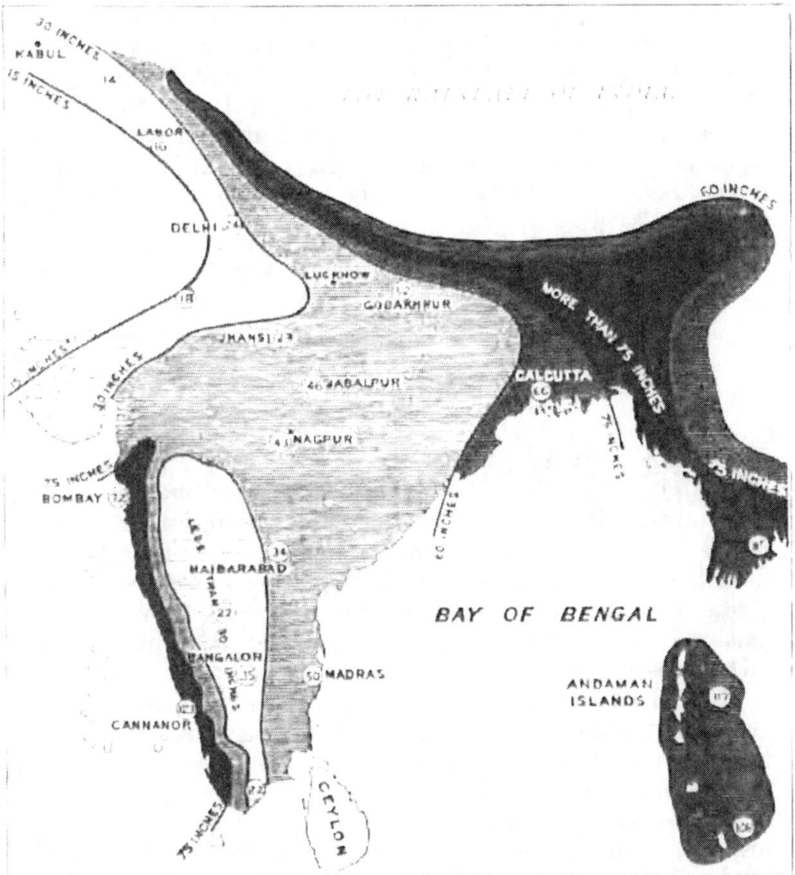

Lines of equal Rainfall ~ *Local Annual Rainfall in inches* (66)

November, more especially when the southerly monsoon has ceased to blow in Northern India, but recurves towards the region of low pressure in the Carnatic, that that part of India receives its chief rainfall. The average of these two months is not less than 24 inches, and about 5 inches fall in December. In **Bengal** and the **Gangetic Plain**, November, December, and January are comparatively rainless. From December, the most rainless month at **Calcutta**, onwards to May, the average fall is 10½ inches, and 18½ at Dacca. This spring rainfall is much more frequent and copious in Assam, the districts of which it fits for the cultivation of tea. In Lower Bengal the summer monsoon usually sets in about the middle of June, and at slightly later dates up to July as we proceed north-east. Along the river lines we have for the total annual rainfall of Calcutta 66 inches, for Berhampoor 53·5 inches, for Bhagalpoor 47 inches, for Patna 38½ inches, for Benares about the same, for Allahabad 42 inches, and for Agra 30 inches. Again, taking series of stations at successively greater distances from the mountains, we have the following:—

Station	Rainfall	Station	Rainfall
Sylhet	154 inches.	Gorakhpoor	50 inches.
Maimansingh	95 ,,	Benares	39 ,,
Dacca	71 ,,		
		Dehra	89 ,,
Jalpaigori	127 ,,	Roorkee	42 ,,
Dinajpoor	79 ,,	Meerut	29 ,,
Malda	53 ,,	Agra	30 ,,

The farther west we proceed the scantier is the summer rainfall. **Ajmer** receives 21 inches in the four months ending September. In the **Panjab** the winter or anti-monsoon rainfall is more important, as in the temperate zone. At Dera Ismail Khan the average rainfall from June to September does not exceed 4·7 inches, while from December to March it amounts to 2·7 inches; and at Peshawar the former is 5·6 inches, the latter 4·6 inches.

§ 10. LAND-STORMS AND SEA-STORMS.—(1) **Land-storms** are caused immediately by the high temperature imparted to that stratum of the atmosphere which rests on the ground by the diurnal heating of the sun, and by the increased production of vapour which reduces the density of the stratum and furnishes a store of energy for action when the vapour becomes condensed as a cumulus cloud. In Upper India and Sind **Dust-storms** are often violent, and the friction of their solid particles generates copious electricity. The **Simoom**, or "poison-wind" of the desert, is free from dust, thunder, and lightning, is attended by a well-marked sulphurous colour, kills animal and vegetable life in its straight track like the blast of a furnace, and occurs in the hot months. Dr. H. Cook of Bombay, who, when in Khelat, reported its ravages, suggests that the fatal effects of this blast may be due to its being charged with ozone.

The **North-Westers** of Bengal, akin to the summer storms of Europe, occur from March to May, when the sea wind is met by the hot west wind, which blows them seawards above the stratum of the cumulus clouds. **Hail-storms** occur in all parts of India, especially between February and May, generated by the meeting of a very dry wind with a damp wind. The most remarkable occurred at Naini Tal on 11th May 1855, when some of the stones weighed 6, 8, and 10, and one or two more than 24 ounces, with circumferences varying from 9 to 13 inches. **Tornados**, or whirlwinds, are circular storms of small dimensions, but of great violence; they are sometimes as much as a mile in diameter, but generally much less; and are very destructive wherever they pass. They occur generally in the earlier months of the year; and not unfrequently originate as **Waterspouts**. The formation of both Mr. H. F. Blanford believes to be identical with that of dust-storms and "devils," viz. a sudden disturbance of the vertical equilibrium of the atmosphere, whereby an upward rush of air is generated, which rapidly becomes spiral. A waterspout measured by Captain Sherwill at Dum Dum with a theodolite, on the 7th October 1859, was found to be 1500 feet high.

(2) Of sea-storms the most important around India is the **Cyclone**, which differs from a tornado chiefly by its greater size and duration. Meteorologically a cyclone is a spiral circulation of the winds around a region of low barometric pressure in contradistinction to Galton's term anti-cyclone. But originally it was designed by Mr. Piddington as a specific name for those violent storms which are peculiar to certain tropical seas; and the gyration of which was established by the labours of Redfield and Reid in the West Indies, and those of Thom and Piddington himself in the case of Indian seas. Both cyclone and tornado consist of an atmospheric vortex, a whirlpool of air pouring upwards. The winds of the lower atmosphere blow from all quarters, more or less obliquely towards it; and, in the vortex itself, become more tangential, and at the same time more violent; the greatest strength of the storm being near its centre. But, in the centre, there is an absolute calm; or, at the utmost, light variable winds. This calm region, which is circular or nearly so in form, is sometimes as much as 15 or 20 miles in diameter, at other times not half that extent; and, on its opposite borders, the wind directions are from directly opposite quarters. The lowest authentic pressure recorded at sea was 27·58 inches on the pilot brig *Coleroon*, in the central calm of the Midnapoor and Bardwan cyclone of 15th October 1874.

The lowest at any land station was in the Calcutta cyclone of 5th October 1864, the centre of which passed over Contai to the south where an aneroid showed a pressure of 28·083, while it was 29·34 at Calcutta. As the distance between the two in a direct line is 70 miles, this represents an average gradient of 1·8 inch in 100 statute miles, or one inch in 48 nautical miles.

Dr. Buist's catalogue, enlarged by Mr. H. F. Blanford, shows 115 cyclones in the Bay of Bengal since 1737, the majority of which occurred at the change of monsoons, and especially at the close of the summer monsoon. Against 21 in May and 10 in June there have been 31 in October and 18 in November. None are recorded as having occurred in February, which is the month of their greatest frequency in the South Indian Ocean. In the China seas, where the sea is not limited to latitudes below 22°, the whole season of the summer monsoon is characterised by frequent cyclones, and the month of their greatest frequency appears to be September. Strictly speaking, the whole of the summer monsoon is equally a cyclone season in India; but the cyclones, being chiefly formed on land, do not attain to any degree of violence. They never occur within 6° or 7° of the equator in either hemisphere. The Andaman and Nicobar Islands, as the region of lowest pressure circumscribed by higher pressures, is the cradle of some of the most destructive storms that have ravaged the coasts of India. That which was formed in the neighbourhood of the Andamans, about the 22d October 1842, travelled thence to Pondicheri, crossed the Peninsula, passed out at the Palghat Gap, and was afterwards traced to east longitude 60° on the 1st November, having completed a course of 2000 miles and lasted nine days.

Mr. H. F. Blanford comes to these conclusions as to the origin and signs of cyclones in the Bay of Bengal :—

(1) The primary cause of cyclone formation is the production and ascent of a large quantity of vapour, which is condensed with the liberation of its latent heat over the place of its production, instead of being carried away to some distant region, and the consequent local lowering of the atmospheric pressure, causing or tending to cause an indraught of air towards the place of minimum pressure.

(2) However strongly the winds may blow on the shores of Bengal and in Orissa, *if they are from the south, with any westing in them, there is no fear of a cyclone.*

The **Storm-wave** which probably accompanies every cyclone is often far more destructive, especially when it is piled up on a low coast with shelving foreshore, and arrives there at the time of flood during the height of the spring-tides ; still worse, where a broad shallow river estuary, like the Hoogli and the Megna, stretches up into the land to the right of the storm track. The reduction of atmospheric pressure at the centre of the storm, amounting sometimes to two barometric inches, would of necessity cause a rise of the mean level of the sea, amounting to about 13 inches for each barometric inch of diminished pressure; and, in addition to this, the winds, in virtue of their friction on the sea surface, and the spiral incurvature of their course, must tend to pile up a head of water in the central part of the vortex. Its full effects are most felt on the right of the central track of the cyclone, for the direction of the wind there coincides with the advance of the wave ; whereas, on the left of the track, the wind generally opposes its advance. The cumulative effects of such cyclonic waves have caused the greatest national catastrophes on record. On 7th October 1737 a wave of 40 feet is said to have thus swept away 300,000 souls in the Hoogli basin. In May 1787, at Coringa, near the mouth of the Godavari, a storm-wave is said to have swept away 20,000 souls. The loss of life in the Calcutta cyclone of 1864 was 48,000 human beings and 100,000 head of cattle, when the wave rose 16·48 feet only above the level of high spring-tides at Cowcolly lighthouse, and 11·9 feet at the junction of the Roopnarain and the Hoogli. The most terrible of all, as tested by scientific inquiry by Mr. Elliott, was the storm-wave of 31st October and 1st November 1876, which, following the tidal bore and rising to 45 feet in the hours from midnight to dawn, swept obliquely across the mouth of the Megna, its islands and Bakirganj, and destroyed 115,000 of a busy fisher and peasant population, with their villages, cattle, and crops, till the land and the rivers stank and pestilence ensued as under the worst of the Plagues of Egypt.

§ 11. ANNUAL MEAN ELEVATION, PRESSURE, TEMPERATURE, VAPOUR TENSION, CLOUD PROPORTION, AND RAINFALL OF 56 STATIONS.—The following table is compiled from those of the Meteorological Reporter to the Government of India, which show the monthly as well as annual mean based on the observations of a series of years ranging from 2, as at Leh, to 10 as at Calcutta :—

STATIONS.	Elevations.	Pressures.	Temperatures.	Vapour Tensions.	Cloud Proportions.	Rainfall.
Leh	11,538	19·652	38·7	0·191	5·17	31·74
Lahore . . .	732	29·029	75·1	·493	2·60	18·87
Delhi . . .	718	·034	76·4	·564	3·17	25·90
Dera Ismail Khan .	573	·201	73·6	·456	1·98	8·32
Mooltan . . .	420	·357	76·2	·480	1·75	6·21
Ajmer . . .	1,632	28·178	77·9	·512	3·33	23·70
Chakrata . . .	7,052	23·289	56·4	·337	4·46	58·39
Dehra . . .	2,232	27·559	70·4	·532	3·86	81·85
Roorkee . . .	887	28·890	74·9	·519	3·05	42·11
Ranikhet . . .	6,069	24·050	60·7	·336	4·38	48·35
Bareilly . . .	568	29·195	75·9	·560	3·07	42·01
Agra . . .	555	29·214	77·9	·533	2·36	29·30
Lucknow . . .	369	·417	78·0	·574	3·66	43·35
Jhansi . . .	860	28·939	78·7	·489	1·60	34·94
Benares . . .	268	29·530	78·0	·601	3·32	38·22
Patna . . .	179	·615	77·8	·624	4·08	38·52
Gaya . . .	347	·416	79·3	·619	3·37	42·73
Hazaribagh . .	2,010	27·788	74·3	·491	4·27	50·83
Berhampoor . .	64	29·723	78·6	·717	4·93	54·03
Bardwan . . .	99	·697	78·6	·735	3·81	58·58
Dacca . . .	35	·778	78·4	·782	4·39	71·45
Silchar . . .	87	·758	75·8	·738	4·71	120·13
Seebsagar . .	332	·512	72·0	·690	7·68	94·75
Goalpara . . .	386	·417	74·8	·692	4·68	95·81
Darjeeling . .	6,912	23·367	54·7	·370	6·40	120·61
Chittagong . .	90	29·742	77·4	·774	3·90	104·64
Calcutta . . .	18	·788	79·8	·786	..	65·81
Sagar Island . .	6	·794	79·5	·843	4·61	74·55
Cuttak . . .	80	29·744	80·4	·751	3·69	56·62
Jabalpoor . .	1,351	28·446	75·2	·503	4·07	52·57
Pachmari . .	3,504	26·406	68·5	·407	3·79	85·53
Seoni . . .	2,030	27·776	74·8	·360	4·62	48·44
Hoshangabad . .	1,020	28·796	78·1	·492	3·52	47·62
Nagpoor . . .	1,025	·756	78·7	·479	4·45	42·35
Akola . . .	923	·872	78·0	·539	3·58	24·60
Karachi . . .	49	29·773	77·0	·632	3·93	7·03
Deesa . . .	474	·345	78·9	·520	3·25	24·57
Bombay . . .	37	·809	78·8	·776	4·39	70·10
Poona . . .	1,992	27·845	76·9	·551	4·88	31·68
Belgaum . . .	2,550	27·348	73·6	·581	4·30	47·39
Vizagapatam . .	81	29·789	82·6	·776	3·77	42·21
Sikandarabad . .	1,787	28·043	78·3	..	2·59	29·98
Bellary . . .	1,457	28·380	80·8	·472	5·18	17·62
Bangalore . .	2,989	26·921	73·2	·518	4·65	34·42
Madras . . .	22	29·852	80·8	·785	4·77	48·51
Salem . . .	940	28·943	81·1	·639	5·11	34·73
Wellington . .	6,200	24·208	61·1	..	5·48	42·96
Coimbatore . .	1,348	28·509	77·2	·618	5·29	21·06
Negapatam . .	15	29·848	81·8	·749	4·90	35·29
Trichinopoli . .	275	·557	82·7	·652	5·74	29·53
Madura . . .	448	·388	81·8	·658	4·66	36·08
Cochin . . .	11	·897	79·7	·814	4·61	107·66
Akyab . . .	20	·833	78·5	·806	4·46	201·19
Port Blair . .	61	·796	80·5	·880	4·63	116·40
Nankowri . .	78	·783	79·8	·836	5·86	107·72
Colombo . . .	42	·840	81·3	·868	5·95	79·73

APPENDIX.

BIBLIOGRAPHY.

B.C.

43-288. The Mahawanso, translated, etc., by Turnour. 1837.

408. Herodoti Historiæ.

384. Ctesiæ Quæ Supersunt. Gottingæ.

300. Megasthenis Indica. Fragmenta Collegit E. A. Schwanbeck.

55. Diodori Siculi Bibliotheca Historica.

54. Strabonis Geographia.

A.D.

45. Pomponii Melæ de Situ Orbis Libri Tres.

70. Q. Curtii Rufi. De Gestis Alexandri Magni.

77. C. Plini Secundi. Naturalis Historia.

88-90. Periplus of the Erythræan Sea.

130. Aeliani Varia Historia.

150. Arriani Anabasis Alexandri; Indica; Periplus Ponti Euxini.

150. Claudii Ptolemæi Geographia.

250. Flavii Philostrati Quæ Supersunt.

—— The Two First Books concerning the Life of Apollonius Tyaneus, by Charles Blount. London, 1680.

—— The Life of Apollonius Tyanæus, by John Henry Newman.

329-413. Fa Hian's Pilgrimage, from the French Edition of the Foe Koue Ki of MM. Remusat, Klaproth, and Landresse, with additional notes and illustrations. Calcutta, 1848. Rev. S. Beal's Translation is best.

374. S. Ambrosii (?) Tractatus in quo Loca, Doctrinam ac Mores Brachmanorum describit.

400. Palladius De Gentibus Indiæ et Bragmanibus.

420. Nonni Dionysiaca.

545. Cosmas Indicopleustes; Topographia Christiana.

629-645. Hwen T'hsang. Mémoires translated by M. Stanislas Julien.

851-867. Ancient Accounts of India and China by Two Mohammedan Travellers. From the Arabic by Renaudot. 1733.

863. Photii Bibliotheca.

A.D.

To 333. BUNBURY's History of Ancient Geography. 2 vols. 1879.
GEOGRAPHI GRÆCI MINORES. Carolus Mullerus. III. vol.
GEOGRAPHIÆ VETERIS SCRIPTORES GRÆCI MINORES, cum annot. Jo. Hudson. IV. vol. Oxoniæ.
VINCENT. The Voyage of Nearchus from the Indus to the Euphrates. 1797.
—— Dissertation on Arrian's Periplus and the Trade to the East Indies by means of the Euxine Sea. Oxford, 1805.
Dr. W. SMITH's Dictionary of Greek and Roman Geography. 2 vols.

1160-1173. BENJAMIN OF TUDELA. Travels from Spain to China.

1253. WILLIAM DE RUBRUQUIS. Travels into different parts of the East.

1298. MARCO POLO. Ye Book of Ser Marco Polo, ye Venetian, concerning ye Kingdoms of ye East. Newly done into English by Henry Yule, C.B. In 2 vols. Second Edition Revised, 1875.

1300-1600. GUBERNATIS Storia dei Viaggiatori Italiani nelle Indie Orientali. 1875.

1316-1330. ODORICUS. Itinerarium.

1325. Sir JOHN MANDEVILLE, Kt. Voiage and Travail. 1684.

1330-50. IBN BATUTA. Travels of, translated by Rev. S. Lee. London, 1829.

1360. JOHN OF IYPRES. Chronicle; Livre des Merveilles

1400-1500. India in the 15th Century, a Collection of Narratives of Voyages. Edited by R. H. Major for the Hakluyt Society, 1859.

1403-6. CLAVIJO. Narrative of the Embassy of Ruy Gonzalez de Clavijo to the Court of Timour at Samarcand. Translated, etc., by Clements R. Markham, F.R.G.S. Hakluyt Society, 1859.

1418-1530. MAJOR's Discoveries of Prince Henry the Navigator. 1877.

1430. NICHOLAS CONTI. Travels from Damascus to India.

1497-1813. MILBURN, W. Oriental Commerce. 2 vols.

To 1500. CATHAY and the Way Thither. 2 vols. By Colonel H. Yule, C.B. Hakluyt Society, 1866.

1503-8. LUDOVICO DI VARTHEMA. Travels, translated by John Winter Jones, Esq., F.S.A., and edited by George Percy Badger. Hakluyt Society, 1863.

1516. DUARTE BARBOSA. The Coasts of E. Africa and Malabar. Hakluyt Society, 1865.

1520-30. BABER's Memoirs, translated by Leyden and Erskine. 1826.

1541. XAVIER, FRANCIS. Life and Letters, by Henry James Coleridge. 3d edition, 1876.
—— Missionary Life and Labours, by Henry Venn, B.D. 1862.

A.D.

1541. Xavier, Francois Hieronymus (the Nephew), as in Hayus, *infra.*

1552. Barros y Couto. Decadas da Asia.

1563-81. Cæsar Frederick. Travels.

1579. Gaspar Balbi, as in Purchas.

1579. Hayus. De Rebus Japonicis, Indicis et Peruvianis, Epistolæ Recentiores a Joanne Hayo Scoto, Societatis Jesu in librum unum coacervatæ. Antverpiæ, 1605.

1579. Thomas Stephens. Letter from Goa in Hakluyt's Voyages.

1583. Ralph Fitch, as in Purchas.

1583. Van Linschoten. Voyages to the East Indies.

1590. Abul Fazl. Ain I Akbari, translated by H. Blochmann, M.A. Vol. I.

1590. Maffeii. Historiarum Indicarum, Libri XVI.

1600. The Sherleys. Relation of Travels into Persia.

1601. Pyrard de Laval. Voyage à Goa.

1602. Benedict Goez, as in Murray's "Historical Account."

1611-16. Thomas Coryate's Crudities and Letters. Reprinted, 1776.

1612-1708. Philip Anderson. The English in Western India, being the Early History of the Factory at Surat, of Bombay, and the Subordinate Factories on the Western Coast. 1854.

1615. Jarrici Thesaurus.

1615. Sir Thomas Roe. Journals and Letters to the East India Company.

1616. Terry's Voyage to the East Indies. 1655.

1616. Van den Broeck. Voyage (Surat).

1618. Jahangeer's Memoirs, by Price. 1829.

1625. Purchas, his Pilgrimes. London, 1625.

1626. Andrada, A. Voyage du Thibet.

1627. Olearius. Voyages, etc., of the Ambassadors. 1669.

1630. Lord. A Display of Two Forraigne Sects in the East Indies, viz. the Banians and Persees.

1631. De Laet. De Imperio Magni Mogolis, Sive India Vera. Lug. Bat. Ex Officina Elzeviriana.

1631. Guido Pancirollus. Rerum Memorabilium Sive Deperditarum, Pars Prior et Posterior. The same in English, 1715.

1635. Sir Thomas Herbert's Travels into divers parts of Africa and Asia the Great.

1638-40. Mandelslo's Remarks and Observations in his passage through several countries of the Indies. London, 1669.

1650. Pietro della Valle. Travels (Rome).

1550-1653. Pinto (F. M.). Voyages and Adventures, done into English.

1655-9. Thevenot. Les Voyages aux Indes Orientales.

1655-66. Baldæus. Description of the Coasts of Malabar and Coromandel.

1657. Bernier. Travels in the Mogul Empire.

A.D.

1658. CATROU's History of the Moghul Dynasty, founded on Manouchi.

1661. GRUEBER. Literae (Travels from Peking to Agra, as in Ogilby's translation, 1669).

1663. GODINHO. Journey from Goa overland to Lisbon; as in Murray's Historical Account.

1666-75. FARIA Y SOUSA. Asia Portuguesa, Lisboa.
—— John Stevens' Translation. London, 1695.

1670. DELLON. Relation de l'Inquisition de Goa. 1719.

1670. TAVERNIER. Les Six Voyages. A Utrecht.
—— Made English by J. P. London, 1678.

1671. Sir JOHN CHARDIN. Travels into Persia and the East Indies.

1672. OLOF FOREEN's Voyage to Surat.

1673-81. JOHN FRYER's New Account of E. India and Persia.

1689. OVINGTON. A Voyage to Suratt in the year 1689.

1712. DESIDERI, as in Les Lettres Édifiantes.

1724-6. VALENTIJN. Dutch Collection of Voyages to the East Indies, etc. 5 vols., fol.

1727. HAMILTON's New Account of the East Indies. Edinburgh.

1738. DU HALDE. Description of China, Chinese Tartary, and Tibet, with maps. In 2 vols. London.

1740. SEEUR-OOL-MOOTAKHEREEN, or View of Modern Times, from the Persian of Ghoolam Hossein Khan. Calcutta, 1789.

1741. HORACE DELLA PENNA, as in "Journal Asiatique."

1743. VAN DE PUTTE, as in "Journal Asiatique."

1744-6. CHURCHILL's Collection of Voyages and Travels. 6 vols.

1744. HARRIS. A Complete Collection of Voyages and Travels. 2 vols. London.

1753. HANWAY's Travels and Works. 4 vols.

1757. Historical and Ecclesiastical Sketches of Bengal from the Earlier Settlement until the Virtual Conquest in 1757.

1757. STEWART's History of Bengal to 1757, published in 1813.

1763-78. ORME's History of Indostan from 1745 to 1758. In 3 vols.
—— Historical Fragments, etc., from 1759.

1765-82. FORBES (J.). Oriental Memoirs (Bombay). 1834.
—— (A. K.). Ras Mala (Goojarat).

1766. HOLWELL's Interesting Historical Events relative to the Provinces of Bengal.

To 1767. BROOME. History of the Rise and Progress of the Bengal Army.

1771. STAVORINUS. Voyages to the East Indies. Translated from the Dutch by Wilcocke. In 3 vols.

1772. BOLTS. Considerations on India Affairs, with map chiefly from actual surveys.

1772. VERELST's View of the Rise, Progress, and Present State of the English Government in Bengal in reply to the above.

1774. HOLWELL's India Tracts. (Third edition.)

A.D.
1774. HAMILTON. History of the Rohillas.
1774. Commentaries of the Great Afonso Dalboquerque. Hakluyt Society, 1875.
1774-81. SONNERAT. Voyage aux Indes Orientales. 1782.
1775. D'ANVILLE. Antiquité Géographique de l'Inde et de plusieurs autres contrées de la Haute Asie. A Paris.
1775. TRIAL OF MAHA RAJAH NUNDOCOMAR, Bahader, for Forgery. London, 1776 (T. Cadell).
1776-89. BARTOLOMEO. Voyage to the East Indies. Translated from the German by William Johnston.
N. D. CARRACIOLI's Life of Robert, Lord Clive, Baron Plassey.
1776. NIEBUHR's (Carsten) Voyage. English translation published in Edinburgh, 1792.
1776. TIEFFENTHALER, ANQUETIL DU PERRON, JAQUES RENNELL, JEAN BERNOUILLI } Description Historique et Geographique de l'Inde en trois volumes enrichis de 64 cartes et autres planches. A Berlin.
1780. HODGES. Travels in India.
1780. DE BORGNE's Mémoires. 1829.
1780. FERISHTA's History of Dekkan, and of Bengal, to 1780. By Jonathan Scott. 1794.
1788-1839. Asiatic Researches. 21 vols.
1790. FORSTER's Journey from Bengal to England. 2 vols. 1798.
1790. BARTOLEMEO. Grammatica Samscrdaamica.
1791. ROUSE on the Landed Property of Bengal.
1792. CHARLES GRANT. Observations on the State of Society among the Asiatic Subjects of Great Britain. Printed by House of Commons, 1813.
1793. RENNELL. Memoir of a Map of Hindoostan or the Mogul Empire. (Third edition.)
1793-1801. GEORGE THOMAS, Military Memoirs of, by Francklin.
1795. SYMES. Embassy to the Kingdom of Ava.
1800. TURNER. Account of an Embassy to Tibet.
To 1801. MACPHERSON, D. Annals of Commerce. 4 vols.
1807-22. BUCHANAN-HAMILTON's Journey through Mysore, Canara, and Malabar. 3 vols.
—— Account of the Kingdom of Nepal.
—— Account of the Fishes of the Ganges.
—— Thirty Folios of MSS., Statistical Survey of Bengal, in India Office Library.
—— Description of Dinajpoor. 1833.
1810. BRUCE's Annals of the East India Company.
1810. MALTE-BRUN Précis de la Geographie Universelle.
1810-17. WILKS' Mysore. 3 vols.
1811. KIRKPATRICK. Account of the Kingdom of Nepaul.
1814. BUCHANAN (CLAUDIUS). Christian Researches in Asia.

A.D.

1817. ABBÉ DUBOIS. Description of the People of India.
—— Letters, in which the Conversion of the Hindoos is considered impracticable.

1818. WARD. View of the History, Literature, and Mythology of the Hindoos. (Second edition.)

1820. FRASER (J. B.). Tour through part of the Snowy Range of the Himala Mountains.

1820. MOORCROFT and TREBECK'S Travels in the Himalaya Provinces. 2 vols.

1820. HUGH MURRAY. Historical Account of Discoveries and Travels in Asia. 3 vols.

1826. GRANT DUFF. History of the Marathas. 3 vols. 1826. Reprinted in Bombay.

1828. HAMILTON (Walter). East India Gazeetter. 2 vols.

1829. TOD'S Annals and Antiquities of Rajast'han.
—— Travels in Western India.

1830. EVEREST. An Account of the Measurement of an Arc of the Meridian between the parallels of 18° 3′ and 24° 7′, being a continuation of the Grand Meridional Arc of India, as detailed by the late Lieutenant-Colonel Lambton in the volumes of the Asiatic Society of Calcutta.

HEBER, Life of.

1824-25. —— Narrative of a Journey through India.

1830. JOSEPH WOLFF'S Travels and Adventures. 1861.

1830-31. COTTINEAU. Historical Sketch of Goa. Madras.

To 1831. HOUGH'S History of Christianity in India. 5 vols. 1839-60.

1832-1882. Journal of the Asiatic Society of Bengal, with "Proceed- "ings" from 1865.

1835. HÜGEL'S Travels in Kashmir and the Panjab. Translated, with Notes, by Major T. B. Jervis, F.R.S.

1836-9. Transactions of the Bombay Geographical Society.

1844. DUKE OF WELLINGTON'S Dispatches during his various campaigns in India, etc. Vol. I.

1845. LAWRENCE, Sir H. Adventures of an Officer in the Service of Runjeet Singh.

1847-62. LASSEN (Chr.). Indische Alterthumskunde. 5 vols.

1855. YULE (Col.). Mission to the Court of Ava.

To 1875. GERMANN Die Kirche der Thomaschristen. Gütersloh, 1877.

VICTOR JACQUEMONT'S Letters from India. In 2 vols. (Second edition.) London, 1833.

Dr. THOMAS THOMSON, F.L.S. Western Himalaya and Tibet. 1847-8.

Dr. GEORGE BUIST. Papers on India.

Captain JAMES ABBOTT. Some account of the Camps and Battlefield of Alexander and Porus (now occupied [Jan. 1849] by the mutinous Sikh Army under the Raja Sher Singh). 1849.

MASON. Burmah: its People, etc. 1860.

FORBES, Captain. British Burmah and its People. 1878.
THE BURMAN: His Life and Notions. 1882.
CLEGHORN, Dr. H. Forests and Gardens of South India. 1861.
CUNNINGHAM, Major-General. The Ancient Geography of India. I.—The Buddhist Period. 1871.
—— Ladak. 1854.
FERGUSSON (JAMES). History of Indian and Eastern Architecture. 1876.
FERGUSSON and BURGESS. The Cave Temples of India. London, 1880.
JOHN CRAWFURD, F.R.S. Descriptive Dictionary of the Indian Islands and Adjacent Countries. 1856.
HARRIS, Major. The Highlands of Æthiopia. 3 vols. 1844.
WRIGHT, T. Early Christianity in Arabia. 1855.
Sir WILLIAM MUIR. Life of Mahomet. First Edition (Vol. I.), 1861.
—— The Apology of Al Kindy. 1882.
Dr. JOHN MUIR. Original Sanskrit Texts on the Origin and History of the People of India. (Second edition.) 5 vols. 1872.
MONIER WILLIAMS. Indian Wisdom, with a brief history of the chief departments of Sanskrit Literature. 1875.
—— Modern India and the Indians. 1878.
MAX MULLER. History of Ancient Sanskrit Literature. (Second edition.) 1860.
—— Lectures on the Science of Language. 1861.
DREW. Jummoo and Kashmir Territories: a Geographical Account.
BELLEW. Kashmir and Kashgar. 1875.
—— General Report on the Yusufzais. 1864.
ROBERT SHAW. Visits to High Tartary, Yarkand, and Kashgar, and Return Journey over the Karakoram Pass. 1871.
MARKHAM. Narratives of the Mission of George Bogle to Tibet, and of the Journey of Thomas Manning to Lhasa. 1876.
—— Memoir on the Indian Surveys. 1871.
TEMPLE, Sir R. Panjab Administration Reports. Report on the North-West Frontier to 1864.
—— India in 1880.
—— Asia, by A. H. Keane. 1882.
O'DONOVAN. The Merv Oasis. 1882.
REYNELL G. TAYLOR's Memorandum on Dera Ismail Khan.
HUGH R. JAMES's Report on Peshawur District. 1865.
DALTON. Descriptive Ethnology of Bengal. Illustrated by portraits from photographs. 1872.
BLOCHMANN. Contributions to the Geography of Bengal.
Dr. RAJENDRALALA MITRA, C.I.E., Buddha Gaya. 1878.
—— The Antiquities of Orissa. 2 vols. 1880.
Dr. D. B. SMITH. Report on Pilgrimage to Juggernauth in 1868.
EGERTON (P. H.). Journal of a Tour through Spiti to the frontier of Chinese Tibet. 1864.

Dr. D. Wright. History of Nepal from the *Parbatiya*. 1877.
Dr. John Wilson's Papers on the Population of Bombay, and Memoirs on Cave Temples.
—— Indian Caste, in 2 vols. 1877.
George Smith. Life of Dr. John Wilson. 1878.
—— Life of Dr. Alexander Duff. 1879.
—— Fifty Years of Foreign Missions. 1879.
Sherring. Hindu Tribes and Castes. 2 vols. 1879.
—— Benares.
—— History of Protestant Missions in India. 1875. With map.
Strickland and Marshall. Catholic Missions in Southern India to 1865.
Dixon. Sketch of Mairwara. 1850.
Oldham. On the Geological Structure of the Khasi Hills. 1854.
Malcolm. Memoir on Central India. 2 vols. (Second edition.) 1824.
—— History of Persia. 1815.
Jenkins. Report on the Territories of the Rajah of Nagpoor. 1827; reprinted 1866.
Hislop (Rev. S.). Papers relating to the Aboriginal Tribes of the Central Provinces. Edited by Sir R. Temple. 1866.
Gill. River of Golden Sand, with Essay by Colonel Yule. 1880.
Ince (Dr.). Kashmir Hand-Book. 1872.
Day (Dr.). Cochin, or Land of the Permauls. 1863.
Mateer. "The Land of Charity," a descriptive account of Travancore. 1871.
Birdwood (Sir George). Industrial Arts of India. 1880.
—— Catalogue of the Vegetable Productions of Bombay. 1865.
Baden Powell. Manufactures and Arts of the Panjab. 2 vols. Lahore, 1872.
Digby. Famine Campaign in South India. 1876-78.
Prejevalsky. Mongolia, with Essay by Colonel Yule. 1876.
—— From Kulja across the Tian Shan. 1879.
Gordon. The Roof of the World. 1876.
Floyer. Unexplored Baluchistan. 1882.
Aitchison, Dr. Handbook of the Trade Products of Leh. 1874.
Report of the Punjab Missionary Conference. 1862-63.
—— The General Missionary Conference held at Allahabad. 1872-73. With map.
—— The Missionary Conference, South India and Ceylon. 1879. With map.
Downes. Kafiristan as a Suitable Field for Missionary Labour. 1873.
Murray's Hand-Books (by E. B. Eastwick) of Bengal, Bombay, and Madras. 1879-1882.
Encyclopædia Britannica. (Ninth edition.) Articles by Colonel Yule, and by General R. Strachey on the Himalaya.
Friend of India, Weekly Newspaper, as edited successively at Seram-

pore from 1835 to 1875 by John Clark Marshman, C.S.I.; Meredith Townsend, and George Smith. 41 vols.

ANNALS OF INDIAN ADMINISTRATION, as edited successively from 1858 to 1875 by Meredith Townsend and George Smith. 19 vols.

CALCUTTA REVIEW, from May 1844, edited successively by Sir John Kaye, Dr. Duff, Dr. W. S. Mackay, Dr. T. Smith, M. Townsend, Dr. G. Smith, and Sir R. Temple, to 1860.

PROCEEDINGS OF THE ROYAL GEOGRAPHICAL SOCIETY and Monthly Record of Geography to November 1882.

OFFICIAL.

CHARTERS granted to the East India Company from 1601 and Treaties to 1772.

AITCHISON'S Collection of Treaties, Engagements, and Sunnuds relating to India and Neighbouring Countries. 7 vols. (Second edition.) 1876.

CORRESPONDENCE regarding the Comparative Merits of British and Native Administration. 1867.

LEPEL H. GRIFFIN. The Panjab Chiefs. 1865.

—— The Law of Inheritance to Sikh Chiefships. 1869.

TRUMPP. The Adi Granth, with Introductory Essays. 1877.

AUBER. Analysis of the Constitution of the East India Company. 2 vols. 1826.

—— China, an Outline . . . of Intercourse with that Empire. 1834.

FIFTH REPORT from the Select Committee on the Affairs of the East India Company. 1812.

BENGAL AND ASSAM. A Statistical Account, by W. W. Hunter, B.A., LL.D. 22 vols.

INDIA. The Imperial Gazetteer, by the same. 9 vols. 1880.

BRITISH BURMA Gazetteer. In 2 vols. Compiled by H. R. Spearman. 1880.

ANDAMAN AND NICOBAR ISLANDS. Lieutenant Blair's Survey in 1793. Home Department Selections No. XXV. 1859, and No. LXXVII. 1870.

NORTH-WESTERN PROVINCE Gazetteer. A Statistical, Descriptive, and Historical Account. Edited by Edwin T. Atkinson, B.A. Six volumes published to October 1882.

OUDH Gazetteer. In 3 vols. Introduction by W. C. Bennett, Assistant Commissioner.

PANJAB, Land Settlement Reports.

Sir R. H. DAVIES. On the Trade and Resources of the Countries on the N.W. Boundary of British India. 1862. With maps.

SIND Gazetteer. By A. W. Hughes, F.S.S. (Second edition.)

BOMBAY Gazetteer. Vols. 2, 3, 4, 5, 6, 10, and 12, published to October 1882. Edited by James M. Campbell.

ADEN. Account compiled by Captain F. M. Hunter, F.R.G.S. 1877.
—— Playfair's History of Arabia Felix or Yemen. 1859.
AJMER AND RÁJPOOTANA STATES Gazetteer. By various Political Officers. 1877-9.
BARODA, CENTRAL INDIA, AND NATIVE STATES generally. Memoranda prepared for His Royal Highness the Prince of Wales. In 5 vols.
CENTRAL PROVINCE Gazetteer. Edited by Charles Grant, Esq. (Second edition.)
—— Land Settlement Report of each District.
BERAR Gazetteer. Edited by Sir A. C. Lyall.
HAIDARABAD STATE. Report on the Administration of the Government of His Highness the Nizam. By Sir Richard Temple. 1868.
MADRAS. Manual of each of the Districts—S. Arcot, Chengalpat, Tinnevelli, Madura, Trichinopoli, Cuddapah, Bellary, Vizagapatam, Nellore, and Godavari—published up to October 1882.
—— Land Settlement and Survey Reports.
COORG AND MYSORE Gazetteer. In 3 vols. By Lewis Rice.
ADMINISTRATION REPORTS OF THE TWELVE PROVINCES for the three years ending 30th March 1881.
REPORTS OF THE NATIVE STATES, Travankor, Cochin, Baroda, and so far as not contained in the Administration Reports.
SELECTIONS from the Records of Travankor. 1860.
REPORTS OF THE SURVEY OF INDIA to 30th September 1881.
MEMOIRS OF THE GEOLOGICAL SURVEY OF INDIA. 18 vols.
RECORDS of the same. 14 vols.
MANUAL OF THE GEOLOGY OF INDIA. By Medlicott, Blanford, and Ball. In 4 vols. With map.
Dr. A. GEIKIE'S Text-Book of Geology. 1882.
INDIAN METEOROLOGIST'S VADE MECUM. By H. F. Blanford, F.R.S. In 2 vols.
REPORTS AND MEMOIRS ON THE METEOROLOGY OF INDIA to 1880.
REPORT ON THE MARINE SURVEY OF INDIA in 1880-81.
REPORTS ON THE 1881 CENSUS OF THE PROVINCES OF INDIA, so far as issued up to October 1882.
REPORT ON RAILWAYS IN INDIA for 1881-82.
STATISTICAL ABSTRACTS RELATING TO BRITISH INDIA, from 1870-1 to 1879-80.
ARCHÆOLOGICAL SURVEY—Of N. India, Reports by General Cunningham, 14 vols.; of W. India, by Dr. Burgess.
MONTGOMERIE'S Routes in the Western Himalayas, Kashmir, etc., with Polymetrical Tables. Dehra Doon, 1872.
GAZETTEERS OF THE COUNTRIES OF CENTRAL ASIA AND OF KASHMIR. Compiled for military and political reference by Officers of the Quartermaster-General's Department. Calcutta, 1871-4.
LUMSDEN'S MISSION TO KANDAHAR IN 1858. Calcutta, 1860.

EDWARDES' Memorandum on the Same. 1858.

BELLEW'S RECORD OF POLLOCK'S MISSION TO SEISTAN. Foreign Department Records, No. CIV.

MEMORANDUM ON AFGHAN-TURKESTAN. By J. Talboys Wheeler. 1869.

SUMMARY OF FOREIGN AFFAIRS, 1864-69. By the same. 1868.

MINUTES OF LORD LAWRENCE and others on Afghanistan. 1867-1873.

MAPS.

INDIA 1752. M. D'Anville's Carte de l' Inde.

INDIA 1788. Rennell's Map of Hindoostan, or the Mogul Empire. From the latest authorities.

INDIA 1881. (Preliminary edition.) Scale, 1 inch = 32 miles. Published under the direction of Lieutenant-General J. T. Walker, C.B., R.E., F.R.S., Surveyor-General of India. 1882.

TURKESTAN AND THE COUNTRIES BETWEEN THE BRITISH AND THE RUSSIAN DOMINIONS IN ASIA. Scale, 1 inch = 32 miles, or $\frac{1}{2027520}$, mapped on the Basis of the Surveys made by British and Russian Officers up to 1881. Compiled under the orders of Lieutenant-General Walker, and photo-zincographed at the office of the Trigonometrical Branch Survey of India. Dehra Doon. September 1881.

—— GENERAL WALKER'S Notes on ditto. Edition of 1873.

ALLGEMEINER MISSIONS-ATLAS. *Nach Originalquellen.* Von Dr. R. Grundemann. 1867-1871, Gotha: Justus Perthes.

INDEX.

ABBREVIATIONS.—*b.*, bay; *c.*, cape; *can.*, canal; *des.*, desert; *dis.*, district; *div.*, division; *est.*, estuary; *f.*, fort, fortress; *for.*, forest; *g.*, gulf; *i.*, island; *l.*, lake; *m.*, mountain; *p.*, pass; *pen.*, peninsula; *pl.*, plain; *plat.*, plateau; *prov.*, province; *r.*, river; *ry.*, railway; *st.*, state; *str.*, strait; *v.*, valley.

Printed by R. & R. Clark, *Edinburgh.*

MR. MURRAY'S LIST OF SCHOOL BOOKS.

MURRAY'S STUDENT'S MANUALS.

A Series of Class-books for advanced Scholars.

Forming a Chain of History from the Earliest Ages down to Modern Times.

"We are glad of an opportunity of directing the attention of teachers to these admirable schoolbooks."—THE MUSEUM.

English History and Literature.

THE STUDENT'S HUME: A History of England, from the Earliest Times to the Revolution in 1688. By DAVID HUME. Incorporating the Researches of recent Historians. New Edition, revised, corrected, and continued to the Treaty of Berlin in 1878, by J. S. BREWER, M.A. With Notes, Illustrations, and 7 Coloured Maps and Woodcuts. (830 pp. Post 8vo. *7s. 6d.*

*** *Questions on the "Student's Hume."* 12*mo.* 2*s.*

THE STUDENT'S CONSTITUTIONAL HISTORY OF ENGLAND. From the Accession of Henry VII. to the Death of George II. By HENRY HALLAM, LL.D. (680 pp.) Post 8vo. *7s. 6d.*

THE STUDENT'S MANUAL OF THE ENGLISH LANGUAGE. By GEORGE P. MARSH. (538 pp.) Post 8vo. *7s. 6d.*

THE STUDENT'S MANUAL OF ENGLISH LITERATURE. By T. B. SHAW, M.A. (510 pp.) Post 8vo. *7s. 6d.*

THE STUDENT'S SPECIMENS OF ENGLISH LITERATURE. Selected from the Best Writers, and arranged Chronologically. By THOS. B. SHAW, M.A. (560 pp.) Post 8vo. *7s. 6d.*

Scripture and Church History.

THE STUDENT'S OLD TESTAMENT HISTORY. FROM THE CREATION OF THE WORLD TO THE RETURN OF THE JEWS FROM CAPTIVITY. With an Introduction to the Books of the Old Testament. By PHILIP SMITH, B.A. With 40 Maps and Woodcuts. (630 pp.) Post 8vo. *7s. 6d.*

THE STUDENT'S NEW TESTAMENT HISTORY. WITH AN INTRODUCTION, CONTAINING THE CONNECTION OF THE OLD AND NEW TESTAMENTS. By PHILIP SMITH, B.A. With 30 Maps and Woodcuts. (680 pp.) Post 8vo. *7s. 6d.*

THE STUDENT'S MANUAL OF ECCLESIASTICAL HISTORY. By PHILIP SMITH, B.A.

PART I.—From the TIMES OF THE APOSTLES to the FULL ESTABLISHMENT OF THE HOLY ROMAN EMPIRE AND THE PAPAL POWER (A.D. 30—1003). (654 pp.) With Woodcuts. Post 8vo. *7s. 6d.*

PART II.—The MIDDLE AGES AND THE REFORMATION (A.D. 1003—1598). Woodcuts. Post 8vo. *7s. 6d.*

THE STUDENT'S MANUAL OF ENGLISH CHURCH HISTORY. By G. G. PERRY, M.A., Canon of Lincoln.

1st Period. From the Planting of the Church in Britain to the Accession of Henry VIII. (A.D. 596—1509). (576 pp.) Post 8vo. *7s. 6d.*

2nd Period. From the ACCESSION OF HENRY VIII. to the Silencing of Convocation in the EIGHTEENTH CENTURY (A.D. 1509—1717). (635 pp.) Post 8vo. *7s. 6d.*

Ancient History.

THE STUDENT'S ANCIENT HISTORY OF THE EAST. From the Earliest Times to the Conquests of Alexander the Great, including Egypt, Assyria, Babylonia, Media, Persia, Asia Minor, and Phœnicia. By PHILIP SMITH, B.A. With 70 Woodcuts. (608 pp.) Post 8vo. *7s. 6d.*

THE STUDENT'S HISTORY OF GREECE. FROM THE EARLIEST TIMES TO THE ROMAN CONQUEST. With Chapters on the History of Literature and Art. By WM. SMITH, D.C.L. With Coloured Maps and Woodcuts. (640 pp.) Post 8vo. *7s. 6d.*

*** *Questions on the "Student's Greece." 12mo. 2s.*

THE STUDENT'S HISTORY OF ROME. FROM THE EARLIEST TIMES TO THE ESTABLISHMENT OF THE EMPIRE. With Chapters on the History of Literature and Art. By DEAN LIDDELL. With Coloured Map and Woodcuts. (686 pp.) Post 8vo. *7s. 6d.*

THE STUDENT'S GIBBON: AN EPITOME OF THE HISTORY OF THE DECLINE AND FALL OF THE ROMAN EMPIRE. By EDWARD GIBBON. Incorporating the Researches of recent Historians. With 100 Woodcuts. (700 pp.) Post 8vo. *7s. 6d.*

Europe.

THE STUDENT'S HISTORY OF EUROPE DURING THE MIDDLE AGES. By HENRY HALLAM, LL.D. (650 pp.) Post 8vo. *7s. 6d.*

THE STUDENT'S HISTORY OF MODERN EUROPE. FROM THE END OF THE MIDDLE AGES TO THE TREATY OF BERLIN, 1878. Post 8vo. [*In Preparation.*

France.

THE STUDENT'S HISTORY OF FRANCE. FROM THE EARLIEST TIMES TO THE ESTABLISHMENT OF THE SECOND EMPIRE, 1852. With Notes and Illustrations on the Institutions of the Country. By W. H. JERVIS, M.A. With Woodcuts. (724 pp.) Post 8vo. *7s. 6d.*

Geography and Geology.

THE STUDENT'S MANUAL OF ANCIENT GEOGRAPHY. By CANON BEVAN, M.A. With 150 Woodcuts. (710 pp.) Post 8vo. *7s. 6d.*

THE STUDENT'S MANUAL OF MODERN GEOGRAPHY, MATHEMATICAL, PHYSICAL, AND DESCRIPTIVE. By CANON BEVAN, M.A. With 120 Woodcuts. (684 pp.) Post 8vo. *7s. 6d.*

THE STUDENT'S MANUAL OF THE GEOGRAPHY OF BRITISH INDIA. By GEORGE SMITH, LL.D. With Maps. Post 8vo. *7s. 6d.*

THE STUDENT'S ELEMENTS OF GEOLOGY. By SIR CHARLES LYELL, F.R.S. With 600 Woodcuts. (602 pp.) Post 8vo. *9s.*

Law and Philosophy.

THE STUDENT'S MANUAL OF MORAL PHILOSOPHY. With Quotations and References. By WILLIAM FLEMING, D.D. (440 pp.) Post 8vo. *7s. 6d.*

THE STUDENT'S BLACKSTONE. AN ABRIDGMENT OF THE ENTIRE COMMENTARIES. By R. MALCOLM KERR, LL.D. (670 pp.) Post 8vo. *7s. 6d.*

THE STUDENT'S EDITION OF AUSTIN'S JURISPRUDENCE. Compiled from the larger work. By ROBERT CAMPBELL. (544 pp.) Post 8vo. *12s.*

AN ANALYSIS OF AUSTIN'S LECTURES ON JURISPRUDENCE. By GORDON CAMPBELL. (214 pp.) Post 8vo. *6s.*

HORTENSIUS: AN HISTORICAL ESSAY ON THE OFFICE AND DUTIES OF AN ADVOCATE. By WILLIAM FORSYTH, Q.C. Adapted for School Prizes. Woodcuts. 8vo. *7s. 6d.*

Dr. Wm. Smith's Smaller Histories.

These Works have been drawn up for the Lower Forms, at the request of several teachers, who require more elementary books than the STUDENT'S HISTORICAL MANUALS.

A SMALLER SCRIPTURE HISTORY OF THE OLD AND THE NEW TESTAMENT. In Three Parts:—I. Old Testament History. II. Connection of Old and New Testaments. III. New Testament History to A.D. 70. Edited by WM. SMITH, D.C.L. With 40 Illustrations. (370 pp.) 16mo. 3*s*. 6*d*.

This book is intended to be used with, and not in the place of, the Bible. The object has been to supply a condensed manual of Scripture history, comprehensive, but at the same time concise, for Junior Classes.

"Students well know the value of Dr. Wm. Smith's larger Scripture History. This abridgment omits nothing of importance, and is presented in such a handy form that it cannot fail to become a valuable aid to the less learned Bible Student."—*People's Magazine*.

A SMALLER ANCIENT HISTORY OF THE EAST. From the Earliest Times to the Conquest of Alexander the Great By PHILIP SMITH, B.A. With 70 Woodcuts. (310 pp.) 16mo. 3*s*. 6*d*.

"This book is designed to aid the study of the Scriptures, by placing in their true historical relations those allusions to Egypt, Assyria, Babylonia, Phœnicia, and the Medo-Persian Empire, which form the background of the history of Israel from Abraham to Nehemiah. The present work is an indispensable adjunct of the 'Smaller Scripture History;' and the two have been written expressly to be used together."

A SMALLER HISTORY OF GREECE. From the Earliest Times to the Roman Conquest. By WM. SMITH, D.C.L. With Coloured Maps and 74 Woodcuts. (268 pp.) 16mo. 3*s*. 6*d*.

This history has been drawn up at the request of several teachers, for the use of lower forms, elementary pupils. The table of contents presents a full analysis of the work, and has been so arranged, that the teacher can frame from it QUESTIONS FOR THE EXAMINATION OF HIS CLASS, the answers to which will be found in the corresponding pages of the volume.

A SMALLER HISTORY OF ROME. From the Earliest Times to the Establishment of the Empire. By WM. SMITH, D.C.L. With Coloured Map and 70 Woodcuts. (324 pp.) 16mo. 3*s*. 6*d*.

The "Smaller History of Rome" has been written and arranged on the same plan, and with the same object, as the "Smaller History of Greece." Like that work it comprises separate chapters on the institutions and literature of the countries with which it deals.

A SMALLER CLASSICAL MYTHOLOGY. With Translations from the Ancient Poets, and Questions on the Work. By H. R. LOCKWOOD. With 90 Woodcuts. (300 pp.) 16mo. 3*s*. 6*d*.

This work has been prepared by a lady for the use of schools and young persons of both sexes. In common with many other teachers, she has long felt the want of a consecutive account of the heathen deities, which might safely be placed in the hands of the young, and yet contain all that is generally necessary to enable them to understand the classical allusions they may meet with in prose or poetry, and to appreciate the meanings of works of art.

A carefully prepared set of QUESTIONS is appended, the answers to which will be found in the corresponding pages of the volume.

A SMALLER MANUAL OF ANCIENT GEOGRAPHY.

By CANON BEVAN, M.A. (240 pp.) With Woodcuts. 16mo. 3*s*. 6*d*.

"This work has been drawn up chiefly for the lower forms in schools, at the request of several teachers who require for their pupils a more elementary work than the 'Student's Manual of Ancient Geography.' The arrangement of the two works is substantially the same. The more important towns alone are mentioned; the historical notices are curtailed; modern names are introduced only in special cases, either for the purpose of identification or where any noticeable change has occurred; and the quotations from classical works are confined for the most part to such expressions as are illustrative of local peculiarities. A very ample Index is supplied, so that the work may supply the place of a dictionary for occasional reference."

A SMALLER MANUAL OF MODERN GEOGRAPHY,

PHYSICAL AND POLITICAL. By JOHN RICHARDSON, M.A. 16mo. (290 pp.) 2*s*. 6*d*.

"Great pains appear to have been spent on the verification of facts, and the arrangement is a model of good method. Throughout the book there are unmistakable indications of solid, conscientious work, sound judgment, and practical acquaintance with teaching."—*School Guardian.*

This "Smaller Manual" has been compiled for pupils who are acquiring for the first time the chief facts of General Geography, and no pains have been spared to render the learner's task as easy and as pleasant as the nature of the subject admits of. Accuracy as to details has been striven after, in order that the young student may have a solid and safe foundation for his future studies in the advanced branches of the Sciences.

A SMALLER HISTORY OF ENGLAND. FROM THE EARLIEST TIMES TO THE PRESENT DAY.

By PHILIP SMITH, B.A. With Coloured Maps and 60 Woodcuts. (400 pp.) 16mo. 3*s*. 6*d*.

"The most recent authorities have been consulted, and it is confidently believed that the Work will be found to present a careful and trustworthy account of English History for the lower forms in schools, for whose use it is chiefly intended."—*Preface.*

"This little volume is so pregnant with valuable information, that it will enable anyone who reads it attentively to answer such questions as are set forth in the English History Papers in the Indian Civil Service Examinations."—*Reader.*

A SMALLER HISTORY OF ENGLISH LITERATURE:

Giving a sketch of the lives of our chief writers. By JAMES ROWLEY. (276 pp.) 16mo. 3*s*. 6*d*.

The important position which the study of English literature is now taking in education has led to the publication of this work, and of the accompanying volume of specimens. Both books have been undertaken at the request of many eminent teachers, and no pains have been spared to adapt them to the purpose for which they are designed—as elementary works to be used in schools.

SHORT SPECIMENS OF ENGLISH LITERATURE.

Selected from the chief authors and arranged chronologically. By JAMES ROWLEY. With Notes. (368 pp.) 16mo. 3*s*. 6*d*.

While the "Smaller History of English Literature" supplies a rapid but trustworthy sketch of the lives of our chief writers, and of the successive influences which imparted to their writings their peculiar character, the present work supplies choice examples of the works themselves, accompanied by all the explanations required for their perfect explanation. The two works are thus especially designed to be used together.

Dr. Wm. Smith's Biblical Dictionaries.

FOR DIVINES AND SCHOLARS.

A DICTIONARY OF THE BIBLE: COMPRISING ITS ANTIQUITIES, BIOGRAPHY, GEOGRAPHY, AND NATURAL HISTORY. By Various Writers. Edited by WM. SMITH, D.C.L. and LL.D. With Illustrations. 3 vols. (3158 pp.) Medium 8vo. 5*l.* 5*s.*

"Dr. Smith's Bible Dictionary could not fail to take a very high place in English literature; for no similar work in our own or in any other language is for a moment to be compared with it."—*Quarterly Review.*

"Our Churches could scarcely make a better investment than by adding this work of unsurpassed excellence to their pastor's library."—*Baptist Magazine.*

"A book of reference alike for scholar and student. The most complete, learned, and trustworthy work of the kind hitherto produced."—*Athenæum.*

A CONCISE DICTIONARY OF THE BIBLE. Condensed from the larger Work. For Families and Students. With Maps and 300 Illustrations. (1039 pp.) 8vo. 21*s.*

A Dictionary of the Bible, in some form or another, is indispensable for every family. The Divine, the Scholar, and all who seek to investigate thoroughly the various subjects connected with the Bible, and to master those controversies which are now exciting such deep and general interest, must still have recourse to the Larger Dictionary; but to students in the Universities, and in the Upper Forms at Schools, to private families, and to that numerous class of persons who desire to arrive at *results* simply, this CONCISE DICTIONARY will, it is believed, supply all that is necessary for the elucidation and explanation of the Bible.

A SMALLER DICTIONARY OF THE BIBLE. Abridged from the larger Work. For Schools and Young Persons. With Maps and Illustrations. (620 pp.) Crown 8vo. 7*s.* 6*d.*

A smaller and more elementary work than the preceding Dictionaries is needed for the use of schools, Sunday School Teachers, and young persons in general. This "Smaller Dictionary" contains such an account of Biblical antiquities, biography, geography, and natural history as a young person is likely to require in the study of the Bible. In addition to the woodcuts inserted in the text, several maps are added to illustrate the articles relating to geography and history.

"An invaluable service has been rendered to students in the condensation of Dr. Wm. Smith's Bible Dictionary. The work has been done as only a careful and intelligent scholar could do it, which preserves to us the essential scholarship and value of each article."—*British Quarterly Review.*

Dr. Wm. Smith's Ancient Atlas.

AN ATLAS OF ANCIENT GEOGRAPHY. BIBLICAL AND CLASSICAL. Intended to illustrate the "Dictionary of the Bible," and the "Classical Dictionaries." Compiled under the superintendence of WM. SMITH, D.C.L., and GEORGE GROVE, LL.D. With Descriptive Text, Indices, &c. With 43 Maps. Folio, half-bound. Price Six Guineas.

"The students of Dr. Smith's admirable Dictionaries must have felt themselves in want of an Atlas constructed on the same scale of precise and minute information with the article they were reading. This want has at length been supplied by the superb work before us. The indices are full, the engraving is exquisite, and the delineation of the natural features very minute and beautiful. It may safely be pronounced—and higher praise can scarcely be bestowed—to be a worthy companion of the volumes which it is intended to illustrate."—*Guardian.*

Dr. Wm. Smith's Latin Dictionaries.

"I consider Dr. Wm. Smith's Dictionaries to have conferred a great and lasting service on the cause of classical learning in this country."—DEAN LIDDELL.

"I have found Dr. Wm. Smith's Latin Dictionary a great convenience to me. I think that he has been very judicious in what he has omitted, as well as what he has inserted."—DR. SCOTT.

A COMPLETE LATIN-ENGLISH DICTIONARY. BASED ON THE WORKS OF FORCELLINI AND FREUND. With Tables of the Roman Calendar, Measures, Weights, and Money. By WM. SMITH, D.C.L. and LL.D. (1200 pp.) Medium 8vo. 21*s.*

This work holds an intermediate place between the Thesaurus of Forcellini and the ordinary School Dictionaries. It makes no attempt to supersede Forcellini, which would require a dictionary equally large; but it aims at performing the same service for the Latin language as Liddell and Scott's Lexicon has done for the Greek. Great attention has been paid to Etymology, in which department especially this work is admitted to maintain a superiority over all existing Latin Dictionaries.

"Dr. Wm. Smith's 'Latin-English Dictionary' is lifted, by its independent merit, far above comparison with any school or college dictionary commonly in use."—*Examiner.*

A SMALLER LATIN-ENGLISH DICTIONARY, WITH A SEPARATE DICTIONARY OF PROPER NAMES, TABLES OF ROMAN MONEYS, &c. Abridged from the above Work, for the Use of Junior Classes. (672 pp.) Square 12mo. 7*s.* 6*d.*

"This abridgment retains all the characteristic excellences of the larger work—its clearness and correctness of explanation, simplicity of arrangement, sufficiency of illustration, exhibition of etymological affinities and modern derivatives."—*Athenæum.*

A COPIOUS AND CRITICAL ENGLISH-LATIN DICTIONARY. Compiled from Original Sources. By WM. SMITH, D.C.L. and LL.D., and THEOPHILUS D. HALL, M.A. (970 pp.) Medium 8vo. 21*s.*

It has been the object of the Authors of this work to produce a more complete and more perfect ENGLISH-LATIN DICTIONARY than yet exists, and every article has been the result of original and independent research.

Great pains have been taken in classifying the different senses of the *English words,* so as to enable the Student readily to find what he wants.

Each meaning is illustrated by examples from the classical writers; and those phrases are as a general rule given in both English and Latin.

"This work is the result of a clear insight into the faults of its predecessors as to plan, classification, and examples. In previous dictionaries the various senses of English words are commonly set down hap-hazard. This has been avoided in the present instance by the classification of the senses of the English words according to the order of the student's need. Not less noteworthy is the copiousness of the examples from the Latin, with which every English word is illustrated; and, last not least, the exceptional accuracy of the references by which these examples are to be verified."—*Saturday Review.*

A SMALLER ENGLISH-LATIN DICTIONARY. Abridged from the above Work, for the use of Junior Classes. (730 pp.) Square 12mo. 7*s.* 6*d.*

"An English-Latin Dictionary worthy of the scholarship of our age and country. It will take absolutely the first rank and be the standard English-Latin Dictionary as long as either tongue endures. Even a general examination of the pages will serve to reveal the minute pains taken to ensure its fulness and philological value, and the 'work is to a large extent a dictionary of the English language, as well as an English-Latin Dictionary.'"—*English Churchman.*

Dr. Wm. Smith's Educational Series.

"The general excellence of the books included in Mr. Murray's educational series is so universally acknowledged as to give in a great degree the stamp of merit to the works of which it consists."—SCHOOLMASTER.

INTRODUCTION TO THE LATIN COURSE.

THE YOUNG BEGINNER'S FIRST LATIN BOOK: Containing the Rudiments of Grammar, Easy Grammatical Questions and Exercises, with Vocabularies. Being a Stepping Stone to Principia Latina, Part I., for Young Children. (112 pp.) 12mo. 2*s.*

THE YOUNG BEGINNER'S SECOND LATIN BOOK: Containing an easy Latin Reading Book, with an Analysis of the Sentences, Notes, and a Dictionary. Being a Stepping Stone to Principia Latina, Part II., for Young Children. (98 pp.) 12mo. 2*s.*

Latin Course.

PRINCIPIA LATINA, Part I. FIRST LATIN COURSE. A Grammar, Delectus, and Exercise Book with Vocabularies. (200 pp.) 12mo. 3*s.* 6*d.*

The main object of this work is to enable a Beginner to fix the Declensions and Conjugations thoroughly in his memory, to learn their usage by constructing simple sentences as soon as he commences the study of the language, and to accumulate gradually a stock of useful words. It presents in one book all that the pupil will require for some time in his study of the language.

The Cases of the Nouns, Adjectives, and Pronouns are arranged both AS IN THE ORDINARY GRAMMARS AND AS IN THE PUBLIC SCHOOL PRIMER, together with the corresponding Exercises. In this way the work can be used with equal advantage by those who prefer either the old or the modern arrangement.

APPENDIX TO PRINCIPIA LATINA, Part I. Containing Additional Exercises, with Examination Papers. (125 pp.) 12mo. 2*s.* 6*d.*

PRINCIPIA LATINA, Part II. READING BOOK. An Introduction to Ancient Mythology, Geography, Roman Antiquities, and History. With Notes and a Dictionary. (268 pp.) 12mo. 3*s.* 6*d.*

PRINCIPIA LATINA, Part III. POETRY. 1. Easy Hexameters and Pentameters. 2. Eclogæ Ovidianæ. 3. Prosody and Metre. 4. First Latin Verse Book. (160 pp.) 12mo. 3*s.* 6*d.*

PRINCIPIA LATINA, Part IV. PROSE COMPOSITION. Rules of Syntax, with Examples, Explanations of Synonyms, and Exercises on the Syntax. (194 pp.) 12mo. 3*s.* 6*d.*

PRINCIPIA LATINA, Part V. SHORT TALES AND ANECDOTES FROM ANCIENT HISTORY, FOR TRANSLATION INTO LATIN PROSE. (102 pp.) 12mo. 3*s.*

LATIN-ENGLISH VOCABULARY. Arranged according to Subjects and Etymology; with a Latin-English Dictionary to Phædrus, Cornelius Nepos, and Cæsar's "Gallic War." (190 pp.) 12mo. 3*s.* 6*d.*

THE STUDENT'S LATIN GRAMMAR. FOR THE HIGHER FORMS. (406 pp.) Post 8vo. 6*s.*

SMALLER LATIN GRAMMAR. FOR THE MIDDLE AND LOWER FORMS. Abridged from the above. (220 pp.) 12mo. 3*s.* 6*d.*

TACITUS. GERMANIA, AGRICOLA, AND FIRST BOOK OF THE ANNALS. With English Notes. (378 pp.) 12mo. 3*s.* 6*d.*

*** *Keys may be had by* AUTHENTICATED TEACHERS *on application.*

Greek Course.

INITIA GRÆCA, Part I. A FIRST GREEK COURSE, containing Grammar, Delectus, Exercise Book, and Vocabularies. 12mo. (284 pp.) 3*s*. 6*d*.

**** The present Edition has been very thoroughly revised, and many additions and improvements have been introduced.*

The great object of this work, as of the "Principia Latina," is to make the study of the language as easy and simple as possible, by giving the grammatical forms only as they are wanted, and by enabling the pupil to translate from Greek into English and from English into Greek as soon as he has learnt the Greek characters and the First Declension. For the convenience of teachers the cases of the nouns, &c. are given according to the ordinary grammars as well as according to the arrangement of the Public Schools Latin Primer.

APPENDIX TO INITIA GRÆCA, Part I. Containing Additional Exercises, with Examination Papers and Easy Reading Lessons with the Sentences Analysed, serving as an Introduction to INITIA GRÆCA, Part II. (110 pp.) 12mo. 2*s*. 6*d*.

INITIA GRÆCA, Part II. A READING BOOK. Containing short Tales, Anecdotes, Fables, Mythology, and Grecian History. With a Lexicon. 12mo. (220 pp.) 3*s*. 6*d*.

INITIA GRÆCA, Part III. PROSE COMPOSITION. Containing the Rules of Syntax, with copious Examples and Exercises. 12mo. (202 pp.) 3*s*. 6*d*.

THE STUDENT'S GREEK GRAMMAR. FOR THE HIGHER FORMS. By PROFESSOR CURTIUS. Edited by WM. SMITH, D.C.L. Post 8vo. (386 pp.) 6*s*.

The Greek Grammar of Dr. Curtius is acknowledged by the most competent scholars to be the best representative of the present advanced state of Greek scholarship. It is, indeed, almost the only Grammar which exhibits the inflexions of the language in a really scientific form; while its extensive use in schools, and the high commendations it has received from practical teachers, are a sufficient proof of its excellence as a school-book. It is surprising to find that many of the public and private schools in this country continue to use Grammars which ignore all the improvements and discoveries of modern philology.

A SMALLER GREEK GRAMMAR. FOR THE MIDDLE AND LOWER FORMS. Abridged from the above Work. 12mo. (220 pp.) 3*s*. 6*d*.

THE GREEK ACCIDENCE. Extracted from the above Work. 12mo. (125 pp.) 2*s*. 6*d*.

PLATO: THE APOLOGY OF SOCRATES, THE CRITO, AND PART OF THE PHÆDO; with Notes in English from STALLBAUM. SCHLEIERMACHER'S Introductions. 12mo. (242 pp.) 3*s*. 6*d*.

**** Keys may be had by* AUTHENTICATED TEACHERS *on application.*

French Course.

FRENCH PRINCIPIA, Part I. A FIRST FRENCH COURSE. Containing Grammar, Delectus and Exercises, with Vocabularies and Materials for French Conversation. 12mo. (202 pp.) 3*s.* 6*d.*

This work has been compiled at the repeated request of numerous teachers who, finding the "Principia Latina" and "Initia Græca" *the easiest books for learning Latin and Greek*, are anxious to obtain equally elementary French books on the same plan. There is an obvious gain in studying a new language on the plan with which the learner is already familiar. The main object is to enable a beginner to acquire an accurate knowledge of the chief grammatical forms, to learn their usage by constructing simple sentences as soon as he commences the study of the language, and to accumulate gradually a stock of words useful in conversation as well as in reading.

APPENDIX TO FRENCH PRINCIPIA, Part I. Containing Additional Exercises and Examination Papers. (110 pp.) 12mo. 2*s.* 6*d.*

FRENCH PRINCIPIA, Part II. A READING BOOK. Containing Fables, Stories, and Anecdotes, Natural History, and Scenes from the History of France. With Grammatical Questions, Notes, and copious Etymological Dictionary. 12mo. (376 pp.) 4*s.* 6*d.*

FRENCH PRINCIPIA, Part III. PROSE COMPOSITION. Containing a Systematic Course of Exercises on the Syntax, with the Principal Rules of Syntax. 12mo. [*In preparation.*

THE STUDENT'S FRENCH GRAMMAR: PRACTICAL AND HISTORICAL. FOR THE HIGHER FORMS. By C. HERON-WALL. With INTRODUCTION by M. LITTRÉ. Post 8vo. (490 pp.) 7*s.* 6*d.*

This grammar is the work of a practical teacher of twenty years' experience in teaching English boys. It has been his special aim to produce a book which would work well in schools where Latin and Greek form the principal subjects of study.

"This book as a whole is quite a monument of French Grammar, and cannot fail to become a standard work in high class teaching."—*School Board Chronicle.*

"It would be difficult to point more clearly to the value of Mr. Wall's work, which is intended for the use of Colleges and Upper Forms in schools, than by quoting what M. Littré says of it in an introductory letter:—'I have carefully tested the principal parts of your work, and have been completely satisfied with the accuracy and correctness which I found there.'"—*Saturday Review.*

A SMALLER FRENCH GRAMMAR. FOR THE MIDDLE AND LOWER FORMS. Abridged from the above Work. 12mo. (230 pp.) 3*s.* 6*d.*

*** *Keys may be had by* AUTHENTICATED TEACHERS *on application.*

German Course.

GERMAN PRINCIPIA, Part I. A First German Course. Containing a Grammar, Delectus and Exercise Book, with Vocabularies and materials for German Conversation. 12mo. (244 pp.) 3s. 6d.

*** *The present edition has undergone a very careful revision, and various improvements and additions have been introduced.*

This work is on the same plan as the "French Principia," and therefore requires no further description, except in one point. Differing from the ordinary grammars, all German words are printed in Roman, and not in the old German characters. The latter add to the difficulty of a learner, and as the Roman letters are not only used by many modern German writers, but also in Grimm's great Dictionary and Grammar, there seems no reason why the beginner, especially the native of a foreign country, who has learnt his own language in the Roman letters, should be any longer debarred from the advantage of this innovation. It is believed that this alteration will facilitate, more than at first might be supposed, the acquisition of the language. But at the same time, as many German books continue to be printed in the German characters, the exercises are printed in both German and Roman letters.

GERMAN PRINCIPIA, Part II. A Reading Book. Containing Fables, Stories, and Anecdotes, Natural History, and Scenes from the History of Germany. With Grammatical Questions, Notes, and Dictionary. 12mo. (272 pp.) 3s. 6d.

PRACTICAL GERMAN GRAMMAR. With a Sketch of the Historical Development of the Language and its Principal Dialects. Post 8vo. (240 pp.) 3s. 6d.

*** *Keys may be had by* Authenticated Teachers *on application.*

Italian Course.

ITALIAN PRINCIPIA, Part I. A First Italian Course. Containing a Grammar, Delectus, Exercise Book, with Vocabularies, and Materials for Italian Conversation. By SIGNOR RICCI, Professor of Italian at the City of London School. (288 pp.) 12mo. 3s. 6d.

ITALIAN PRINCIPIA, Part II. A First Italian Reading-Book, containing Fables, Anecdotes, History, and Passages from the best Italian Authors, with Grammatical Questions, Notes, and a Copious Etymological Dictionary. By SIGNOR RICCI. 12mo. 3s. 6d. [*Nearly Ready.*

*** *Keys may be had by* Authenticated Teachers *on application.*

English Course.

A PRIMARY ENGLISH GRAMMAR for Elementary Schools. With 134 Exercises and Questions. By T. D. HALL, M.A. (120 pp.) 16mo. 1*s.*

This Work aims at the very clearest and simplest statement possible of the first principles of English Grammar. It is designed for the use of children of all classes from about eight to twelve years of age.

"We doubt whether any grammar of equal size could give an introduction to the English language more clear, concise, and full than this."—*Watchman.*

*** *Keys may be had by* AUTHENTICATED TEACHERS *on application.*

A SCHOOL MANUAL OF ENGLISH GRAMMAR. With 194 Exercises. By WM. SMITH, D.C.L., and T. D. HALL, M.A. With Appendices. (256 pp.) Post 8vo. 3*s.* 6*d.*

This Work has been prepared with a special view to the requirements of Schools in which English, *as a living language*, is systematically taught, and differs from most modern grammars in its thoroughly practical character. A distinguishing feature of the book is the constant appeal for every usage to the authority of Standard English Authors.

"Dr. Smith and Mr. Hall have succeeded in producing an admirable English Grammar. We cannot give it higher praise than to say that as a school grammar it is the best in this country. The writers have throughout aimed at making a serviceable working school-book. There is a more complete and systematic treatment of Syntax than in any other works of the kind. It is a work thoroughly well done."—*English Churchman.*

A MANUAL OF ENGLISH COMPOSITION. With Copious Illustrations and Practical Exercises. Suited equally for Schools and for Private Students of English. By T. D. HALL, M.A. (210 pp.) 12mo. 3*s.* 6*d.*

"Mr. Hall's 'Manual' is certainly the most sensible and practical book upon English composition that we have lately seen. The great variety of subjects which it suggests as themes for exercising the imagination as well as the literary powers of young students will be found a great assistance to teachers, who must often be sorely puzzled to hit upon subjects sufficiently diversified without being ridiculously beyond the scope of youthful experience."—*Saturday Review.*

A PRIMARY HISTORY OF BRITAIN. Edited by WM. SMITH, D.C.L. and LL.D. (368 pp.) 12mo. 2*s.* 6*d.*

This book is a Primary History in no narrow sense. It is an honest attempt to exhibit the leading facts and events of our history, free from political and sectarian bias, and therefore will, it is hoped, be found suitable for schools in which children of various denominations are taught.

"This Primary History admirably fulfils the design of the work. Its style is good, its matter is well arranged, and the pupil must be very stupid who fails to gather from its lively pages an intelligent account of the history of our united nation. It cannot fail to be a standard book."—*John Bull.*

A SCHOOL MANUAL OF MODERN GEOGRAPHY, PHYSICAL AND POLITICAL. By JOHN RICHARDSON, M.A. (400 pp.) Post 8vo. 5*s.*

This work has been drawn up for Middle Forms in Public Schools, Ladies' Colleges, Training Colleges, Assistant and Pupil Teachers, Middle Class and Commercial Schools, and Civil Service Examinations.

"It fully sustains the high reputation of Mr. Murray's series of school manuals, and we venture to predict for it a wide popularity. Bearing in mind its high character, it is a model of cheapness."—*School Guardian.*

A SMALLER MANUAL OF MODERN GEOGRAPHY. FOR SCHOOLS AND YOUNG PERSONS. By JOHN RICHARDSON, M.A. (200 pp.) 16mo. 2*s.* 6*d.*

"Great pains appear to have been spent on the verification of facts, and the arrangement is a model of good method. Throughout the book there are unmistakable indications of solid, conscientious work, sound judgment, and practical acquaintance with teaching."—*School Guardian.*

Standard School Books.

A CHILD'S FIRST LATIN BOOK. COMPRISING NOUNS, PRONOUNS, AND ADJECTIVES, WITH THE ACTIVE VERBS. With ample and varied Practice of the easiest kind. Both old and new order of Cases given. By THEOPHILUS D. HALL, M.A. 16mo. (124 pp.) 2*s*.

The speciality of this book lies in its presenting a great variety of *vivâ voce* work for class-room practice, designed to render the young beginner thoroughly familiar with the use of the Grammatical forms.

This edition has been thoroughly re-cast and considerably enlarged; the plan of the work has been extended so as to comprise the Active Verbs; and all Paradigms of Nouns, Adjectives, and Pronouns are given a second time at the end of the book, WITH THE CASES ARRANGED AS IN THE OLDER GRAMMARS.

"This work answers thoroughly to its title. The explanations are very clear and very full, indeed AN INEXPERIENCED TEACHER WILL FIND HERE A METHOD SUPERIOR TO ANYTHING OF THE KIND WE HAVE SEEN."—*Watchman.*

KING EDWARD VI.'s LATIN GRAMMAR; or, An Introduction to the Latin Tongue. (324 pp.) 12mo. 3*s*. 6*d*.

KING EDWARD VI.'s FIRST LATIN BOOK. THE LATIN ACCIDENCE. Syntax and Prosody, with an ENGLISH TRANSLATION. (220 pp.) 12mo. 2*s*. 6*d*.

OXENHAM'S ENGLISH NOTES FOR LATIN ELEGIACS, designed for early proficients in the art of Latin Versification. (156 pp.) 12mo. 3*s*. 6*d*.

HUTTON'S PRINCIPIA GRÆCA. AN INTRODUCTION TO THE STUDY OF GREEK. A Grammar, Delectus and Exercise Book, with Vocabularies. (154 pp.) 12mo. 3*s*. 6*d*.

MATTHIÆ'S GREEK GRAMMAR. Abridged by BLOMFIELD. Revised by E. S. CROOKE, B.A. (412 pp.) Post 8vo.

LEATHES' HEBREW GRAMMAR. With the Hebrew text of Genesis i.—vi., and Psalms i.—vi. Grammatical Analysis and Vocabulary. (252 pp.) Post 8vo. 7*s*. 6*d*.

Natural Philosophy and Science.

THE FIRST BOOK OF NATURAL PHILOSOPHY; an Introduction to the Study of Statics, Dynamics, Hydrostatics, Light, Heat, and Sound, with numerous Examples. By SAMUEL NEWTH, M.A., D.D., Fellow of University College, London. (200 pp.) Small 8vo. 3*s*. 6*d*.

*** This work embraces all the subjects in Natural Philosophy required at the Matriculation Examination of the University of London.

ELEMENTS OF MECHANICS, INCLUDING HYDROSTATICS. With numerous Examples. By SAMUEL NEWTH, M.A., D.D., Principal of New College, London, and Fellow of University College, London. (362 pp.) Crown 8vo. 8*s*. 6*d*.

This Edition (the Sixth) has been carefully revised throughout, and with especial reference to changes recently made in the Regulations of the University of London.

MATHEMATICAL EXAMPLES. A Graduated Series of Elementary Examples in Arithmetic, Algebra, Logarithms, Trigonometry, and Mechanics. (378 pp.) Small 8vo. 8*s*. 6*d*.

THE STUDENT'S ELEMENTS OF GEOLOGY. By SIR CHARLES LYELL. Third Edition, thoroughly revised. With 600 Woodcuts. Post 8vo. 9*s*.

"The work before us may be regarded as an almost perfect introduction to the sciences of geology and palæontology. Sir Charles Lyell has admirably abridged some portions of his larger work, and has adverted briefly to some of the more important recent discoveries. He has entirely succeeded in his attempt to unite brevity with the copiousness of illustration, which is almost a necessity in a volume intended for beginners."—*Examiner.*

THE CONNECTION OF THE PHYSICAL SCIENCES. By MARY SOMERVILLE. Revised by A. B. Buckley. Portrait and Woodcuts. (468 pp.) Post 8vo. 9s.

"Mrs. Somerville's delightful volume. The style of this astonishing production is so clear and unaffected, and conveys, with so much simplicity, so great a mass of profound knowledge, that it should be placed in the hands of every youth, the moment he has mastered the general rudiments of education."—*Quarterly Review.*

PHYSICAL GEOGRAPHY. By MARY SOMERVILLE. Revised by John Richardson, M.A. Portrait. (548 pp.) Post 8vo. 9*s*.

"Mrs. Somerville's 'Physical Geography' is the work she is most generally known by, and notwithstanding the numerous works on the same subject that have since appeared, it still holds its place as a first authority."—*Nature.*

Mrs. Markham's Histories.

"Mrs. Markham's Histories are constructed on a plan which is novel and we think well chosen, and we are glad to find that they are deservedly popular, for they cannot be too strongly recommended."—JOURNAL OF EDUCATION.

HISTORY OF ENGLAND, FROM THE FIRST INVASION BY THE ROMANS. *New and revised edition.* Continued down to 1880. With Conversations at the end of each Chapter. With 100 Woodcuts. (528 pp.) 12mo. 3*s.* 6*d.*

"Mrs. Markham's 'History of England is the best history for the young that ever appeared, and is far superior to many works of much higher pretensions. It is well written, well informed, and marked by sound judgment and good sense, and is moreover extremely interesting. I know of no history used in any of our public schools at all comparable to it."—QQ in *Notes and Queries.*

HISTORY OF FRANCE, FROM THE CONQUEST OF GAUL BY JULIUS CÆSAR. *New and revised edition.* Continued down to 1878. With Conversations at the end of each Chapter. With 70 Woodcuts. (550 pp.) 12mo. 3*s.* 6*d.*

"Mrs. Markham's Histories are well known to all those engaged in the instruction of youth. Her Histories of England and France are deservedly very popular; and we have been given to understand, in proof of this assertion, that of her Histories *many thousand copies* have been sold."—*Bell's Messenger.*

HISTORY OF GERMANY, FROM ITS INVASION BY MARIUS. *New and revised edition.* Continued down to the completion of Cologne Cathedral in 1880. With 50 Woodcuts. (460 pp.) 12mo. 3*s.* 6*d.*

"A very valuable compendium of all that is most important in German History. The facts have been accurately and laboriously collected from authentic sources, and they are lucidly arranged so as to invest them with the interest which naturally pertains to them."—*Evangelical Magazine.*

LITTLE ARTHUR'S HISTORY OF ENGLAND. By LADY CALLCOTT. *New and revised edition.* Continued down to 1878. 430*th thousand.* With 36 Woodcuts. (286 pp.) 16mo. 1*s.* 6*d.*

"I never met with a history so well adapted to the capacities of children or their entertainment, so philosophical, and written with such simplicity."—MRS. MARCETT.

ÆSOP'S FABLES. A NEW VERSION. Chiefly from the Original Sources. By REV. THOMAS JAMES. With 100 Woodcuts. (168 pp.) Post 8vo. 2*s.* 6*d.*

"Of ÆSOP'S FABLES there ought to be in every school many copies, full of pictures."—*Fraser's Magazine.*

"This work is remarkable for the clearness and conciseness with which each tale is narrated; and the book has been relieved of those tedious and unprofitable appendages called 'morals,' which used to obscure and disfigure the ancient editions of this work."—*The Examiner.*

THE BIBLE IN THE HOLY LAND. BEING EXTRACTS FROM DEAN STANLEY'S SINAI AND PALESTINE. With Woodcuts. (210 pp.) 16mo. 2*s.* 6*d.*

JOHN MURRAY, ALBEMARLE STREET.

Bradbury, Agnew, & Co.] [Printers, Whitefriars.